Seventh Edition

Theories of Personality

Jess Feist
McNeese State University

Gregory J. Feist
San Jose State University

 **Higher Education**

Boston   Burr Ridge, IL   Dubuque, IA   New York   San Francisco   St. Louis
Bangkok   Bogotá   Caracas   Kuala Lumpur   Lisbon   London   Madrid   Mexico City
Milan   Montreal   New Delhi   Santiago   Seoul   Singapore   Sydney   Taipei   Toronto

Mc
Graw
Hill **Higher Education**

Published by McGraw-Hill, an imprint of The McGraw-Hill Companies, Inc., 1221 Avenue of the Americas, New York, NY 10020. Copyright © 2009, 2006, 2002, 1998. All rights reserved. No part of this publication may be reproduced or distributed in any form or by any means, or stored in a database or retrieval system, without the prior written consent of The McGraw-Hill Companies, Inc., including, but not limited to, in any network or other electronic storage or transmission, or broadcast for distance learning.

1 2 3 4 5 6 7 8 9 0 FGR/FGR 0 9 8

ISBN: 978-0-07-338270-8
MHID: 0-07-338270-1

Editor in Chief: *Michael Ryan*
Publisher: *Beth Mejia*
Sponsoring Editor: *Mike Sugarman*
Marketing Manager: *James Headley*
Developmental Editor: *Meghan Campbell*
Editorial Coordinator: *Jillian Allison*
Senior Production Editor: *Carey Eisner*
Manuscript Editor: *Margaret Moore*
Design Manager and Cover Designer: *Allister Fein*
Senior Photo Research Coordinator: *Nora Agbayani*
Freelance Photo Researcher: *PoYee Oster*
Production Supervisor: *Richard DeVitto*
Composition: *10/12 Times New Roman by Aptara, Inc.*
Printing: *45# New Era Matte Plus, Quebecor World*

Cover: © Rosemary Calvert/Getty Images

Library of Congress Cataloging-in-Publication Data

Feist, Gregory J.
   Theories of personality/Gregory Feist, Jess Feist. — 7th ed.
      p. cm.
   Includes bibliographical references and index.
   ISBN-13: 978-0-07-338270-8 (alk. paper)
   ISBN-10: 0-07-338270-1 (alk. paper)
  1. Personality—Textbooks.   I. Fiest, Jess.   II. Title.
   BF698.F365 2009
   155.2—dc22

                                    2008024664

About the Authors

Jess Feist is Professor Emeritus from the psychology department at McNeese State University, Lake Charles, Louisiana. Besides coauthoring *Theories of Personality,* seventh edition, he has coauthored with Linda Brannon, *Health Psychology: An Introduction to Behavior and Health,* fifth edition. He has an undergraduate degree from St. Mary of the Plains and graduate degrees from Wichita State University and the University of Kansas. His research interest is in early childhood recollections.

Gregory J. Feist is Associate Professor of Psychology in the Department of Psychology at San Jose State University. He has also taught at the College of William & Mary and University of California, Davis. He received his PhD in personality psychology in 1991 from the University of California at Berkeley and his undergraduate degree in 1985 from the University of Massachusetts–Amherst. He is widely published in the psychology of creativity, the psychology of science, and the development of scientific talent. His recent book, *The Psychology of Science and the Origins of the Scientific Mind,* was awarded the William James Book Award from the American Psychological Association (APA). He is founding president of the International Society for the Psychology of Science & Technology and founding editor-in-chief of the *Journal of Psychology of Science & Technology.* His research in creativity has been recognized by an Early Career Award from the Division for Psychology of Aesthetics, Creativity and the Arts (Division 10) of APA, and he is former president of Division 10.

Contents

Preface

What makes people behave as they do? Are people ordinarily aware of what they are doing, or are their behaviors the result of hidden, unconscious motives? Are some people naturally good and others basically evil? Or do all people have potential to be either good or evil? Is human conduct largely a product of nature, or is it shaped mostly by environmental influences? Can people freely choose to mold their personality, or are their lives determined by forces beyond their control? Are people best described by their similarities, or is uniqueness the dominant characteristic of humans? What causes some people to develop disordered personalities whereas others seem to grow toward psychological health?

These questions have been asked and debated by philosophers, scholars, and religious thinkers for several thousand years; but most of these discussions were based on personal opinions that were colored by political, economic, religious, and social considerations. Then, near the end of the 19th century, some progress was made in humanity's ability to organize, explain, and predict its own actions. The emergence of psychology as the scientific study of human behavior marked the beginning of a more systematic approach to the study of human personality.

Early personality theorists, such as Sigmund Freud, Alfred Adler, and Carl Jung, relied mostly on clinical observations to construct models of human behavior. Although their data were more systematic and reliable than those of earlier observers, these theorists continued to rely on their own individualized way of looking at things, and thus they arrived at different conceptions of the nature of humanity.

Later personality theorists tended to use more empirical studies to learn about human behavior. These theorists developed tentative models, tested hypotheses, and then reformulated their models. In other words, they applied the tools of scientific inquiry and scientific theory to the area of human personality. Science, of course, is not divorced from speculation, imagination, and creativity, all of which are needed to formulate theories. Each of the personality theorists discussed in this book has evolved a theory based both on empirical observations and on imaginative speculation. Moreover, each theory is a reflection of the personality of its creator.

Thus, the different theories discussed in these pages are a reflection of the unique cultural background, family experiences, and professional training of their originators. The usefulness of each theory, however, is not evaluated on the personality of its author but on its ability to (1) generate research, (2) offer itself to falsification, (3) integrate existing empirical knowledge, and (4) suggest practical answers to everyday problems. Therefore, we evaluate each of the theories discussed in this book on the basis of these four criteria as well as on (5) its internal consistency and (6) its simplicity. In addition, some personality theories have fertilized other fields, such as sociology, education, psychotherapy, advertising, management, mythology, counseling, art, literature, and religion.

✖ The Seventh Edition

The seventh edition of *Theories of Personality* continues to emphasize the strong and unique features of earlier editions, namely the overviews near the beginning of each chapter, a lively writing style, the thought-provoking concepts of humanity as seen by each theorist, and the structured evaluations of each theory. Annotated suggested readings are available online on the book's website at *www.mhhe.com/feist7* to facilitate online research. As were the previous editions, the seventh edition is based on original sources and the most recent formulation of each theory. Early concepts and models are included only if they retained their importance in the later theory or if they provided vital groundwork for understanding the final theory.

For select chapters, we have developed a Web-enhanced feature titled Beyond Biography, which is directly linked to additional information on the book's website at *www.mhhe.com/feist7*.

The seventh edition of *Theories of Personality* uses clear, concise, and comprehensible language as well as an informal writing style. The book is designed for undergraduate students and should be understood by those with a minimum background in psychology. However, we have tried not to oversimplify or violate the theorist's original meaning. We have made ample comparisons between and among theorists where appropriate and have included many examples to illustrate how the different theories can be applied to ordinary day-to-day situations. A glossary at the end of the book contains definitions of technical terms. These same terms also appear in boldface within the text.

The present edition continues to provide comprehensive coverage of the most influential theorists of personality. It emphasizes normal personality, although we have also included brief discussions on abnormality, as well as methods of psychotherapy, when appropriate. Because each theory is an expression of its builder's unique view of the world and of humanity, we include ample biographical information of each theorist so that readers will have an opportunity to become acquainted with both the theory and the theorist.

What's New?

As in the sixth edition, we have reorganized *Theories of Personality* to conform more to the historical and conceptual nature of the theories. After the introductory Chapter 1, we present the psychodynamic theories of Sigmund Freud, Alfred Adler, Carl Jung, Melanie Klein, Karen Horney, Erich Fromm, Harry Stack Sullivan, and Erik Erikson. These theories are now followed by the humanistic/existential theories of Abraham Maslow, Carl Rogers, and Rollo May. Next are the dispositional theories of Gordon Allport, Hans Eysenck, and Robert McCrae and Paul Costa, Jr. The final group of chapters include the behavioral and social learning theories of B. F. Skinner, Albert Bandura, Julian Rotter, Walter Mischel, and George Kelly, although Kelly's theory nearly defies categorization. This new organization gives the reader a better view of the chronology and development of personality theories.

In addition to this reorganization, we made changes that more accurately reflect the theory's meaning or update the research testing the scientific status of the theory. For example, in the chapter on Klein and object relations we changed "fantasies" to "phantasies" because Klein was clear she wanted to use the term in a unique way. Moreover, we made several changes that maintain the challenging and informative yet reader-friendly nature of this text. Most noticeably, we have added half a chapter of new material on the Big Five trait theory of Robert McCrae and Paul Costa, Jr. This five-trait approach has recently evolved from a taxonomy to a full-fledged theory.

The primary changes in the seventh edition involve updating the related research that examines each of the major theories. For example, for Fromm's theory we have added new research that examines the burden of freedom and political persuasions; for Maslow we added current research on positive psychology and personality development, growth, and goals; for Skinner we now include research on reinforcement and the brain; for McCrae and Costa we summarize the most current research on the Big Five dimensions and emotions; and for Bandura we have updated the related research section with new findings on self-efficacy and terrorism and on self-efficacy and diabetes.

⚔ Supplementary Materials

For Instructors

Instructor's Manual and Test Bank

The Instructor's Manual accompanying this book includes learning objectives, a lecture outline, teaching suggestions, essay questions, and a test bank of multiple-choice items. The learning objectives are designed to provide instructors with concepts that should be important to the student. The lecture outline is intended to help busy instructors organize lecture notes and grasp quickly the major ideas of each chapter. With some general familiarity with a particular theory, instructors should be able to lecture directly from the lecture outline. Teaching suggestions reflect class activities and paper topics that the authors have used successfully with their students. The Instructor's Manual is available on the password-protected side of the book's website (www.mhhe.com/feist7).

In the Test Bank, we have included three or four essay questions and answers from each chapter for instructors who prefer this type of student evaluation. For those who prefer multiple-choice questions, we have provided a test bank with nearly 1,500 items, each marked with the correct answer. The test items are available in Word files and in computerized format on the password-protected side of the book's website (www.mhhe.com/feist7).

For Instructors and Students

Online Learning Center

This extensive website, designed specifically to accompany Feist and Feist's *Theories of Personality,* seventh edition, offers an array of resources for both instructors and students. For students, the Online Learning Center (OLC) contains multiple-choice, essay, and true-false questions for each chapter, a Beyond Biography section that further explores the backgrounds of the many theorists presented in the text, suggested readings for each chapter, and many other helpful learning tools. The OLC also includes the Study Guide. For instructors, there is a password-protected website that provides access to the Instructor's Manual. Please go to *www.mhhe.com/feist7* to access the Online Learning Center.

For Students

Study Guide
By Jess Feist

Students who wish to organize their study methods and enhance their chances of achieving their best scores on class quizzes may access the free study guide for the seventh edition of *Theories of Personality* online at *www.mhhe.com/feist7*. This study guide includes learning objectives and chapter summaries. In addition, it contains a variety of test items, including fill-in-the-blanks, true-false, multiple-choice, and short-answer questions.

⚔ Acknowledgments

Finally, we wish to acknowledge our gratitude to the many people who have contributed to the completion of this book. First of all, we want to acknowledge and thank Chad Burton, who helped in summarizing and writing the new material for all updated related research sections. We are also grateful for the valuable help given by those people who reviewed earlier editions of *Theories of Personality*. Their evaluations and suggestions helped greatly in the preparation of this new edition. These reviewers include the following: Robert J. Drummond, University of North Florida; Lena K. Ericksen, Western Washington University; Charles S. Johnson, William Rainey Harper College; Alan Lipman, George Washington University; John Phelan, Eric Rettinger, Elizabeth Rellinger, Evert Community College; Linda Sayers, Richard Stockton College of New Jersey; Mark E. Sibicky, Marietta College; Connie Veldink, Illinois College; Dennis Wanamaker; Kevin Simpson, Concordia University; Lisa Lockhart, Texas A&M University–Kingsville; Natalie Denburg, University of Iowa Hospitals and Clinics; Kristine Anthis, Southern Connecticut State University; Eros DeSouza, Illinois State University; Yozan D. Mosig, University of Nebraska–Kearney.

In addition, we are also grateful to the following reviewers whose feedback helped to shape the seventh edition: Angie Fournier, Virginia Wesleyan College; Atara Mcnamara, Boise State University; Randi Smith, Metro State College of Denver; and Myra Spindel, Florida International University–Miami.

We appreciate the strong support we have had from our publisher. We would like to express our special thanks to Beth Mejia, publisher; Mike Sugarman, executive editor; Dawn Groundwater, director of development; Meghan Campbell, managing editor; and Jillian Allison, editorial coordinator.

We are also indebted to Albert Bandura for his helpful comments on the chapter dealing with social cognitive theory. We also wish to thank these other personality theorists for taking time to discuss appropriate sections of earlier editions of this book: Albert Bandura, Hans J. Eysenck (deceased), Robert McCrae, Paul T. Costa, Jr., Carl R. Rogers (deceased), Julian B. Rotter, and B. F. Skinner (deceased).

Finally, we thank Mary Jo Feist, Linda Brannon, and Erika Rosenberg for their emotional support and other important contributions.

As always, we welcome and appreciate comments from readers, which help us continue to improve *Theories of Personality*.

Jess Feist
Lake Charles, LA

Gregory J. Feist
Oakland, CA

PART ONE

Introduction

Introduction to Personality Theory

Why do people behave as they do? Do people have some choice in shaping their own personality? What accounts for similarities and differences among people? What makes people act in predictable ways? Why are they unpredictable? Do hidden, unconscious forces control people's behavior? What causes mental disturbances? Is human behavior shaped more by heredity or by environment?

For centuries, philosophers, theologians, and other thinkers have asked these questions as they pondered the nature of human nature—or even wondered whether humans have a basic nature. Until relatively recent times, great thinkers made little progress in finding satisfactory answers to these questions. A little more than 100 years ago, however, Sigmund Freud began to combine philosophical speculations with a primitive scientific method. As a neurologist trained in science, Freud began to listen to his patients to find out what hidden conflicts lay behind their assortment of symptoms. "Listening became, for Freud, more than an art; it became a method, a privileged road to knowledge that his patients mapped out for him" (Gay, 1988, p. 70).

Freud's method gradually became more scientific as he formulated hypotheses and checked their plausibility against his clinical experiences. From this combination of speculation and clinical evidence, Freud evolved the first modern theory of personality. Later, a number of other men and women developed theories of personality—some were based largely on philosophical speculation; others, mainly on empirical evidence, but all used some combination of the two. Indeed, this chapter shows that a useful theory should be founded on *both* scientific evidence and controlled, imaginative speculation.

What Is Personality?

Psychologists differ among themselves as to the meaning of personality. Most agree that the word "personality" originated from the Latin **persona,** which referred to a theatrical mask worn by Roman actors in Greek dramas. These ancient Roman actors wore a mask (persona) to project a role or false appearance. This surface view of personality, of course, is not an acceptable definition. When psychologists use the term "personality," they are referring to something more than the role people play.

However, personality theorists have not agreed on a single definition of personality. Indeed, they evolved unique and vital theories because they lacked agreement as to the nature of humanity, and because each saw personality from an individual reference point. The personality theorists discussed in this book have had a variety of backgrounds. Some were born in Europe and lived their entire lives there; others were born in Europe, but migrated to other parts of the world, especially the United States; still others were born in North America and remained there. Many were influenced by early religious experiences; others were not. Most, but not all, have been trained in either psychiatry or psychology. Many have drawn on their experiences as psychotherapists; others have relied more on empirical research to gather data on human personality. Although they have all dealt in some way with what we call personality, each has approached this global concept from a different perspective. Some have tried to construct a comprehensive theory; others have been less ambitious and have dealt with only a few aspects of personality. Few personality theorists have formally defined personality, but all have had their own view of it.

No two people, not even identical twins, have exactly the same personalities.

Although no single definition is acceptable to all personality theorists, we can say that **personality** is a pattern of relatively permanent traits and unique characteristics that give both consistency and individuality to a person's behavior. **Traits** contribute to individual differences in behavior, consistency of behavior over time, and stability of behavior across situations. Traits may be unique, common to some group, or shared by the entire species, but their *pattern* is different for each individual. Thus each person, though like others in some ways, has a unique personality. **Characteristics** are unique qualities of an individual that include such attributes as temperament, physique, and intelligence.

What Is a Theory?

The word "theory" has the dubious distinction of being one of the most misused and misunderstood words in the English language. Some people contrast theory to truth or fact, but such an antithesis demonstrates a fundamental lack of understanding of all three terms. In science, theories are tools used to generate research and organize observations, but neither "truth" nor "fact" has a place in a scientific terminology.

Theory Defined

A scientific **theory** is *a set of related assumptions that allows scientists to use logical deductive reasoning to formulate testable hypotheses.* This definition needs further explanation. First, a theory is *a set* of assumptions. A single assumption can never fill all the requirements of an adequate theory. A single assumption, for example, could not serve to integrate several observations, something a useful theory should do.

Second, a theory is a set of *related* assumptions. Isolated assumptions can neither generate meaningful hypotheses nor possess internal consistency—two criteria of a useful theory.

A third key word in the definition is *assumptions*. The components of a theory are not proven facts in the sense that their validity has been absolutely established. They are, however, accepted *as if* they were true. This is a practical step, taken so that scientists can conduct useful research, the results of which continue to build and reshape the original theory.

Fourth, *logical deductive reasoning* is used by the researcher to formulate hypotheses. The tenets of a theory must be stated with sufficient precision and logical consistency to permit scientists to deduce clearly stated hypotheses. The hypotheses are not components of the theory, but flow from it. It is the job of an imaginative scientist to begin with the general theory and, through deductive reasoning, arrive at a particular hypothesis that can be tested. If the general theoretical propositions are illogical, they remain sterile and incapable of generating hypotheses. Moreover, if a researcher uses faulty logic in deducing hypotheses, the resulting research will be meaningless and will make no contribution to the ongoing process of theory construction.

The final part of the definition includes the qualifier *testable*. Unless a hypothesis can be tested in some way, it is worthless. The hypothesis need not be tested immediately, but it must suggest the possibility that scientists in the future might develop the necessary means to test it.

Theory and Its Relatives

People sometimes confuse theory with philosophy, or speculation, or hypothesis, or taxonomy. Although theory is related to each of these concepts, it is not the same as any of them.

Philosophy

First, theory is related to philosophy, but it is a much narrower term. Philosophy means love of wisdom, and philosophers are people who pursue wisdom through thinking and reasoning. Philosophers are not scientists; they do not ordinarily conduct controlled studies in their pursuit of wisdom. Philosophy encompasses several branches, one of which is **epistemology,** or the nature of knowledge. Theory relates most closely to this branch of philosophy, because it is a tool used by scientists in their pursuit of knowledge.

Theories do not deal with "oughts" and "shoulds." Therefore, a set of principles about how one should live one's life cannot be a theory. Such principles involve values and are the proper concern of philosophy. Although theories are not free of values, they are built on scientific evidence that has been obtained in a relatively unbiased fashion. Thus, there are no theories on why society should help homeless people or on what constitutes great art.

Philosophy deals with what ought to be or what should be; theory does not. Theory deals with broad sets of *if-then* statements, but the goodness or badness of the outcomes of these statements is beyond the realm of theory. For example, a theory might tell us that if children are brought up in isolation, completely separated from human contact, *then* they will not develop human language, exhibit parenting behavior, and so on. But this statement says nothing about the morality of such a method of child rearing.

Speculation

Second, theories rely on speculation, but they are much more than mere armchair speculation. They do not flow forth from the mind of a great thinker isolated from empirical observations. They are closely tied to empirically gathered data and to science.

What is the relationship between theory and science? **Science** is the branch of study concerned with observation and classification of data and with the verification of general laws through the testing of hypotheses. Theories are useful tools employed by scientists to give meaning and organization to observations. In addition, theories provide fertile ground for producing testable hypotheses. Without some kind of theory to hold observations together and to point to directions of possible research, science would be greatly handicapped.

Theories are not useless fantasies fabricated by impractical scholars fearful of soiling their hands in the machinery of scientific investigation. In fact, theories themselves are quite practical and are essential to the advancement of any science. Speculation and empirical observation are the two essential cornerstones of theory building, but speculation must not run rampantly in advance of controlled observation.

Hypothesis

Although theory is a narrower concept than philosophy, it is a broader term than hypothesis. A good theory is capable of generating many hypotheses. A **hypothesis** is an educated guess or prediction specific enough for its validity to be tested through the use of the scientific method. A theory is too general to lend itself to direct verification, but a single comprehensive theory is capable of generating thousands of hypotheses. Hypotheses, then, are more specific than the theories that give them birth. The offspring, however, should not be confused with the parent.

Of course, a close relationship exists between a theory and a hypothesis. Using *deductive reasoning* (going from the general to the specific), a scientific investigator can derive testable hypotheses from a useful theory and then test these hypotheses. The results of these tests—whether they support or contradict the hypotheses—feed back into the theory. Using *inductive reasoning* (going from the specific to the general), the investigator then alters the theory to reflect these results. As the theory grows and changes, other hypotheses can be drawn from it, and when tested they in turn reshape the theory.

Taxonomy

A **taxonomy** is a classification of things according to their natural relationships. Taxonomies are essential to the development of a science because without classification of data science could not grow. Mere classification, however, does not constitute a theory. However, taxonomies can evolve into theories when they begin to generate testable hypotheses and to explain research findings. For example, Robert McCrae and Paul Costa began their research by classifying people into five stable personality traits. Eventually, this research on the Big Five taxonomy led to more than a mere classification; it became a theory, capable of suggesting hypotheses and offering explanations for research results.

Why Different Theories?

If theories of personality are truly scientific, why do we have so many different ones? Alternate theories exist because the very nature of a theory allows the theorist to make speculations from a particular point of view. Theorists must be as objective as possible when gathering data, but their decisions as to what data are collected and how these data are interpreted are personal ones. Theories are not immutable laws; they are built, not on proven facts, but on assumptions that are subject to individual interpretation.

All theories are a reflection of their authors' personal backgrounds, childhood experiences, philosophy of life, interpersonal relationships, and unique manner of looking at the world. Because observations are colored by the individual observer's frame of reference, it follows that there may be many diverse theories. Nevertheless, divergent theories can be useful. The usefulness of a theory does not depend on its commonsense value or on its agreement with other theories; rather, it depends on its ability to generate research and to explain research data and other observations.

Theorists' Personalities and Their Theories of Personality

Because personality theories grow from theorists' own personalities, a study of those personalities is appropriate. In recent years a subdiscipline of psychology called **psychology of science** has begun to look at personal traits of scientists. The psychology of science studies both science and the behavior of scientists; that is, it investigates the impact of an individual scientist's psychological processes and personal characteristics on the development of her or his scientific theories and research (Feist, 1993, 1994, 2006; Feist & Gorman, 1998; Gholson, Shadish, Neimeyer, & Houts, 1989). In other words, the psychology of science examines how scientists' personalities, cognitive processes, developmental histories, and social experience affect the kind of science they conduct and the theories they create. Indeed, a number of investigators (Hart, 1982; Johnson, Germer, Efran, & Overton, 1988; Simonton, 2000; Zachar & Leong, 1992) have demonstrated that personality differences influence one's theoretical orientation as well as one's inclination to lean toward the "hard" or "soft" side of a discipline.

An understanding of theories of personality rests on information regarding the historical, social, and psychological worlds of each theorist at the time of his or her theorizing. Because we believe that personality theories reflect the theorist's personality, we have included a substantial amount of biographical information on each major theorist. Indeed, personality differences among theorists account for fundamental disagreements between those who lean toward the quantitative side of psychology (behaviorists, social learning theorists, and trait theorists) and those inclined toward the clinical and qualitative side of psychology (psychoanalysts, humanists, and existentialists).

Although a theorist's personality partially shapes his or her theory, it should not be the sole determinant of that theory. Likewise, your acceptance of one or another theory should not rest only on your personal values and predilections. When evaluating and choosing a theory, you should acknowledge the impact of the theorist's personal history on the theory, but you should ultimately evaluate it on the basis of scientific criteria that are independent of that personal history. Some observers (Feist, 2006; Feist & Gorman, 1998) have distinguished between *science as process* and *science as product.* The scientific process may be influenced by the personal characteristics of the scientist, but the ultimate usefulness of the scientific product is and must be evaluated independently of the process. Thus, your evaluation of each of the theories presented in this book should rest more on objective criteria than on your subjective likes and dislikes.

What Makes a Theory Useful?

A useful theory has a mutual and dynamic interaction with research data. First, a theory generates a number of hypotheses that can be investigated through research, thus yielding research data. These data flow back into the theory and restructure it. From this newly contoured theory, scientists can extract other hypotheses, leading to more research and additional data, which in turn reshape and enlarge the theory even more. This cyclic relationship continues for as long as the theory proves useful.

Second, a useful theory organizes research data into a meaningful structure and provides an explanation for the results of scientific research. This relationship between theory and research data is shown in Figure 1.1. When a theory is no longer able to generate additional research or to explain related research data, it loses its usefulness and is set aside in favor of a more useful one.

In addition to sparking research and explaining research data, a useful theory must lend itself to confirmation or disconfirmation, provide the practitioner with a guide to action, be consistent with itself, and be as simple as possible. Therefore, we have evaluated each of the theories presented in this book on the basis of six criteria: A useful theory (1) generates research, (2) is falsifiable, (3) organizes data, (4) guides action, (5) is internally consistent, and (6) is parsimonious.

Generates Research

The most important criterion of a useful theory is its ability to stimulate and guide further research. Without an adequate theory to point the way, many of science's present empirical findings would have remained undiscovered. In astronomy, for example, the planet Neptune was discovered because the theory of motion generated the hypothesis that the irregularity in the path of Uranus must be caused by the presence of another planet. Useful theory provided astronomers with a road map that guided their search for and discovery of the new planet.

A useful theory will generate two different kinds of research: descriptive research and hypothesis testing. *Descriptive research,* which can expand an existing theory, is concerned with the measurement, labeling, and categorization of the units employed in theory building. Descriptive research has a symbiotic relationship with

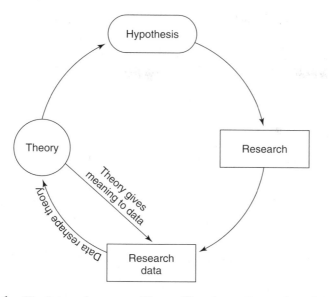

FIGURE 1.1 *The Interaction among Theory, Hypotheses, Research, and Research Data.*

theory. On one hand, it provides the building blocks for the theory, and on the other, it receives its impetus from the dynamic, expanding theory. The more useful the theory, the more research generated by it; the greater the amount of descriptive research, the more complete the theory.

The second kind of research generated by a useful theory, *hypothesis testing,* leads to an indirect verification of the usefulness of the theory. As we have noted, a useful theory will generate many hypotheses that, when tested, add to a database that may reshape and enlarge the theory. (Refer again to Figure 1.1.)

Is Falsifiable

A theory must also be evaluated on its ability to be confirmed or disconfirmed; that is, it must be **falsifiable.** To be falsifiable, a theory must be precise enough to suggest research that may either support or fail to support its major tenets. If a theory is so vague and nebulous that both positive and negative research results can be interpreted as support, then that theory is not falsifiable and ceases to be useful. Falsifiability, however, is not the same as false; it simply means that negative research results will refute the theory and force the theorist to either discard it or modify it.

A falsifiable theory is accountable to experimental results. Figure 1.1 depicts a circular and mutually reinforcing connection between theory and research; each forms a basis for the other. Science is distinguished from nonscience by its ability to reject ideas that are not supported empirically even though they seem logical and rational. For example, Aristotle used logic to argue that lighter bodies fall at slower rates than heavier bodies. Although his argument may have agreed with "common sense," it had one problem: It was empirically wrong.

Theories that rely heavily on unobservable transformations in the unconscious are exceedingly difficult to either verify or falsify. For example, Freud's theory suggests that many of our emotions and behaviors are motivated by unconscious tendencies that are directly opposite the ones we express. For instance, unconscious hate might be expressed as conscious love, or unconscious fear of one's own homosexual feelings might take the form of exaggerated hostility toward homosexual individuals. Because Freud's theory allows for such transformations within the unconscious, it is nearly impossible to either verify or falsify. A theory that can explain everything explains nothing.

Organizes Data

A useful theory should also be able to organize those research data that are not incompatible with each other. Without some organization or classification, research findings would remain isolated and meaningless. Unless data are organized into some intelligible framework, scientists are left with no clear direction to follow in the pursuit of further knowledge. They cannot ask intelligent questions without a theoretical framework that organizes their information. Without intelligent questions, further research is severely curtailed.

A useful theory of personality must be capable of integrating what is currently known about human behavior and personality development. It must be able to shape as many bits of information as possible into a meaningful arrangement. If a personality theory does not offer a reasonable explanation of at least some kinds of behavior, it ceases to be useful.

Guides Action

A fourth criterion of a useful theory is its ability to guide the practitioner over the rough course of day-to-day problems. For example, parents, teachers, business managers, and psychotherapists are confronted continually with an avalanche of questions for which they try to find workable answers. Good theory provides a structure for finding many of those answers. Without a useful theory, practitioners would stumble in the darkness of trial and error techniques; with a sound theoretical orientation, they can discern a suitable course of action.

For the Freudian psychoanalyst and the Rogerian counselor, answers to the same question would be very different. To the question "How can I best treat this patient?" the psychoanalytic therapist might answer along these lines: *If* psychoneuroses are caused by childhood sexual conflicts that have become unconscious, *then* I can help this patient best by delving into these repressions and allowing the patient to relive the experiences in the absence of conflict. To the same question, the Rogerian therapist might answer: *If,* in order to grow psychologically, people need empathy, unconditional positive regard, and a relationship with a congruent therapist, *then* I can best help this client by providing an accepting, nonthreatening atmosphere. Notice that both therapists constructed their answers in an *if-then* framework, even though the two answers call for very different courses of action.

Also included in this criterion is the extent to which the theory stimulates thought and action in other disciplines, such as art, literature (including movies and television dramas), law, sociology, philosophy, religion, education, business administration, and psychotherapy. Most of the theories discussed in this book have had some influence in areas beyond psychology. For example, Freud's theory has prompted research on recovered memories, a topic very important to the legal profession. Also, Carl Jung's theory is of great interest to many theologians and has captured the imagination of popular writers such as Joseph Campbell and others. Similarly, the ideas of Alfred Adler, Erik Erikson, B. F. Skinner, Abraham Maslow, Carl Rogers, Rollo May, and other personality theorists have sparked interest and action in a broad range of scholarly fields.

Is Internally Consistent

A useful theory need not be consistent with other theories, but it must be consistent with itself. An internally consistent theory is one whose components are logically compatible. Its limitations of scope are carefully defined and it does not offer explanations that lie beyond that scope. Also, an internally consistent theory uses language in a consistent manner; that is, it does not use the same term to mean two different things, nor does it use two separate terms to refer to the same concept.

A good theory will use concepts and terms that have been clearly and operationally defined. An **operational definition** is one that defines units in terms of observable events or behaviors that can be measured. For example, an extravert can be operationally defined as any person who attains a predetermined score on a particular personality inventory.

Is Parsimonious

When two theories are equal in their ability to generate research, be falsified, give meaning to data, guide the practitioner, and be self-consistent, the simpler one is preferred. This is the law of **parsimony.** In fact, of course, two theories are never exactly equal in these other abilities, but in general, simple, straightforward theories are more useful than ones that bog down under the weight of complicated concepts and esoteric language.

In building a theory of personality, psychologists should begin on a limited scale and avoid sweeping generalizations that attempt to explain all of human behavior. That course of action was followed by most of the theorists discussed in this book. For example, Freud began with a theory based largely on hysterical neuroses and, over a period of years, gradually expanded it to include more and more of the total personality.

Dimensions for a Concept of Humanity

Personality theories differ on basic issues concerning the nature of humanity. Each personality theory reflects its author's assumptions about humanity. These assumptions rest on several broad dimensions that separate the various personality theorists. We use six of these dimensions as a framework for viewing each theorist's concept of humanity.

The first dimension is *determinism versus free choice.* Are people's behaviors determined by forces over which they have no control, or can people choose to be what they wish to be? Can behavior be partially free and partially determined at the same time? Although the dimension of determinism versus free will is more philosophical than scientific, the position theorists take on this issue shapes their way of looking at people and colors their concept of humanity.

A second issue is one of *pessimism versus optimism.* Are people doomed to live miserable, conflicted, and troubled lives, or can they change and grow into psychologically healthy, happy, fully functioning human beings? In general, personality theorists who believe in determinism tend to be pessimistic (Skinner was a notable exception), whereas those who believe in free choice are usually optimistic.

A third dimension for viewing a theorist's concept of humanity is *causality versus teleology.* Briefly, **causality** holds that behavior is a function of past experiences, whereas **teleology** is an explanation of behavior in terms of future goals or purposes. Do people act as they do because of what has happened to them in the past, or do they act as they do because they have certain expectations of what will happen in the future?

A fourth consideration that divides personality theorists is their attitude toward *conscious versus unconscious determinants of behavior.* Are people ordinarily aware of what they are doing and why they are doing it, or do unconscious forces impinge on them and drive them to act without awareness of these underlying forces?

The fifth question is one of *biological versus social influences on personality.* Are people mostly creatures of biology, or are their personalities shaped largely by their social relationships? A more specific element of this issue is heredity versus environment; that is, are personal characteristics more the result of heredity, or are they environmentally determined?

A sixth issue is *uniqueness versus similarities.* Is the salient feature of people their individuality, or is it their common characteristics? Should the study of personality concentrate on those traits that make people alike, or should it look at those traits that make people different?

These and other basic issues that separate personality theorists have resulted in truly different personality theories, not merely differences in terminology. We could not erase the differences among personality theories by adopting a common language. The differences are philosophical and deep-seated. Each personality theory reflects the individual personality of its creator, and each creator has a unique philosophical orientation, shaped in part by early childhood experiences, birth order, gender, training, education, and pattern of interpersonal relationships. These differences help determine whether a theorist will be deterministic or a believer in free choice, will be pessimistic or optimistic, will adopt a causal explanation or a teleological one. They also help determine whether the theorist emphasizes consciousness or unconsciousness, biological or social factors, uniqueness or similarities of people. These differences do not, however, negate the possibility that two theorists with opposing views of humanity can be equally scientific in their data gathering and theory building.

Research in Personality Theory

As we pointed out earlier, the primary criterion for a useful theory is its ability to generate research. We also noted that theories and research data have a cyclic relationship: Theory gives meaning to data, and data result from experimental research designed to test hypotheses generated by the theory. Not all data, however, flow from experimental research. Much of it comes from observations that each of us make every day. To observe simply means to notice something, to pay attention.

You have been observing human personalities for nearly as long as you have been alive. You notice that some people are talkative and outgoing; others are quiet and reserved. You may have even labeled such people as extraverts and introverts. Are these labels accurate? Is one extraverted person like another? Does an extravert always act in a talkative, outgoing manner? Can all people be classified as either introverts or extraverts?

In making observations and asking questions, you are doing some of the same things psychologists do, that is, observing human behaviors and trying to make sense of these observations. However, psychologists, like other scientists, try to be *systematic* so that their *predictions* will be consistent and accurate.

To improve their ability to predict, personality psychologists have developed a number of assessment techniques, including personality inventories. Much of the research reported in the remaining chapters of this book has relied on various assessment procedures, which purport to measure different dimensions of personality. For these instruments to be useful they must be both reliable and valid. The **reliability** of a measuring instrument is the extent to which it yields consistent results.

Personality inventories may be reliable and yet lack validity or accuracy. **Validity** is the degree to which an instrument measures what it is supposed to measure. Personality psychologists are primarily concerned with two types of validity—construct validity and predictive validity. *Construct validity* is the extent to which an instrument measures some hypothetical construct. Constructs such as extraversion, aggressiveness, intelligence, and emotional stability have no physical existence; they are hypothetical constructs that should relate to observable behavior. Three important types of construct validity are *convergent validity, divergent validity,* and *discriminant validity.* A measuring instrument has convergent construct validity to the extent that scores on that instrument correlate highly (converge) with scores on a variety of valid measures of that same construct. For example, a personality inventory that attempts to measure extraversion should correlate with other measures of extraversion or other factors such as sociability and assertiveness that are known to cluster together with extraversion. An inventory has divergent construct validity if it has low or insignificant correlations with other inventories that do *not* measure that construct. For example, an inventory purporting to measure extraversion should not be highly correlated with social desirability, emotional stability, honesty, or self-esteem. Finally, an inventory has discriminant validity if it discriminates between two groups of people known to be different. For example, a personality inventory measuring extraversion should yield higher scores for people known to be extraverted than for people known to be introverted.

A second dimension of validity is *predictive validity,* or the extent that a test predicts some future behavior. For example, a test of extraversion has predictive validity if it correlates with future behaviors, such as smoking cigarettes, performing well on scholastic achievement tests, taking risks, or any other independent criterion. The ultimate value of any measuring instrument is the degree to which it can predict some future behavior or condition.

Most of the early personality theorists did not use standardized assessment inventories. Although Freud, Adler, and Jung all developed some form of projective tool, none of them used the technique with sufficient precision to establish its reliability and validity. However, the theories of Freud, Adler, and Jung have spawned a number of standardized personality inventories as researchers and clinicians have sought to measure units of personality proposed by those theorists. Later personality theorists, especially Julian Rotter, Hans Eysenck, and the Five-Factor Theorists have developed and used a number of personality measures and have relied heavily on them in constructing their theoretical models.

Key Terms and Concepts

- The term "personality" comes from the Latin *persona,* or the mask that people present to the outside world, but psychologists see personality as much more than outward appearances.
- *Personality* includes all those relatively permanent traits or characteristics that render some consistency to a person's behavior.
- A *theory* is a set of related assumptions that allows scientists to formulate testable hypotheses.
- Theory should not be confused with *philosophy, speculation, hypothesis,* or *taxonomy,* although it is related to each of these terms.
- Six criteria determine the usefulness of a scientific theory: (1) Does the theory *generate research?* (2) Is it *falsifiable?* (3) Does it *organize and explain knowledge?* (4) Does it *suggest practical solutions to everyday problems?* (5) Is it *internally consistent?* and (6) Is it simple or *parsimonious?*
- Each personality theorist has had either an implicit or explicit *concept of humanity.*
- Concepts of human nature can be discussed from six perspectives: (1) *determinism versus free choice,* (2) *pessimism versus optimism,* (3) *causality versus teleology,* (4) *conscious versus unconscious* determinants, (5) *biological versus social* factors, and (6) *uniqueness versus similarities* in people.

PART TWO

Psychodynamic Theories

Freud: Psychoanalysis

Freud

From ancient history to the present time, people have searched for some magic panacea or potion to lessen pain or to enhance performance. One such search was conducted by a young, ambitious physician who came to believe that he had discovered a drug that had all sorts of wonderful properties. Hearing that the drug had been used successfully to energize soldiers suffering from near exhaustion, this physician decided to try it on patients, colleagues, and friends. If the drug worked as well as he expected, he might gain the fame to which he aspired.

After learning of the drug's successful use in heart disease, nervous exhaustion, addiction to alcohol and morphine, and several other psychological and physiological problems, the doctor decided to try the drug on himself. He was quite pleased with the results. To him, the drug had a pleasant aroma and an unusual effect on the lips and mouth. More importantly, however, was the drug's therapeutic effect on his serious depression. In a letter to his fiancée whom he had not seen in a year, he reported that during his last severe depression, he had taken small quantities of the drug with marvelous results. He wrote that the next time he saw her he would be like a wild man, feeling the effects of the drug. He also told his fiancée that he would give her small amounts of the drug, ostensibly to make her strong and to help her gain weight.

The young doctor wrote a pamphlet extolling the benefits of the drug, but he had not yet completed the necessary experiments on the drug's value as an analgesic. Impatient to be near his fiancée, he delayed completion of his experiments and went off to see her. During that visit, a colleague—and not he—completed the experiments, published the results, and gained the recognition the young doctor had hoped for himself.

These events took place in 1884; the drug was cocaine; the young doctor was Sigmund Freud.

Overview of Psychoanalytic Theory

Freud, of course, was fortunate that his name did not become indelibly tied to cocaine. Instead, his name has become associated with **psychoanalysis,** the most famous of all personality theories.

What makes Freud's theory so interesting? First, the twin cornerstones of psychoanalysis, sex and aggression, are two subjects of continuing popularity. Second, the theory was spread beyond its Viennese origins by an ardent and dedicated group of followers, many of whom romanticized Freud as a nearly mythological and lonely hero. Third, Freud's brilliant command of language enabled him to present his theories in a stimulating and exciting manner.

Freud's understanding of human personality was based on his experiences with patients, his analysis of his own dreams, and his vast readings in the various sciences and humanities. These experiences provided the basic data for the evolution of his theories. To him, theory followed observation, and his concept of personality underwent constant revisions during the last 50 years of his life. Evolutionary though it was, Freud insisted that psychoanalysis could not be subjected to eclecticism, and disciples who deviated from his basic ideas soon found themselves personally and professionally ostracized by Freud.

Although Freud regarded himself primarily as a scientist, his definition of science would be somewhat different from that held by most psychologists today. Freud relied more on deductive reasoning than on rigorous research methods, and he made observations subjectively and on a relatively small sample of patients, most of whom were from the upper-middle and upper classes. He did not quantify his data, nor did he make observations under controlled conditions. He utilized the case study approach almost exclusively, typically formulating hypotheses after the facts of the case were known.

Biography of Sigmund Freud

Sigismund (Sigmund) Freud was born either on March 6 or May 6, 1856, in Freiberg, Moravia, which is now part of the Czech Republic. (Scholars disagree on his birth date—the first date was but 8 months after the marriage of his parents.) Freud was the firstborn child of Jacob and Amalie Nathanson Freud, although his father had two grown sons, Emanuel and Philipp, from a previous marriage. Jacob and Amalie Freud had seven other children within 10 years, but Sigmund remained the favorite of his young, indulgent mother, which may have partially contributed to his lifelong self-confidence (E. Jones, 1953). A scholarly, serious-minded youth, Freud did not have a close friendship with any of his younger siblings. He did, however, enjoy a warm, indulgent relationship with his mother, leading him in later years to observe that the mother/son relationship was the most perfect, the most free from ambivalence of all human relationships (Freud, 1933/1964).

When Sigmund was three, the two Freud families left Freiberg. Emanuel's family and Philipp moved to England, and the Jacob Freud family moved first to Leipzig and then to Vienna. The Austrian capital remained Sigmund Freud's home for nearly 80 years, until 1938 when the Nazi invasion forced him to emigrate to London, where he died on September 23, 1939.

When Freud was about a year and a half old, his mother gave birth to a second son, Julius, an event that was to have a significant impact on Freud's psychic development. Sigmund was filled with hostility toward his younger brother and harbored an unconscious wish for his death. When Julius died at 6 months of age, Sigmund was left with feelings of guilt at having caused his brother's death. When Freud reached middle age, he began to understand that his wish did not actually cause his brother's death and that children often have a death wish for a younger sibling. This discovery purged Freud of the guilt he had carried into adulthood and, by his own analysis, contributed to his later psychic development (Freud, 1900/1953).

Freud was drawn into medicine, not because he loved medical practice, but because he was intensely curious about human nature (Ellenberger, 1970). He entered the University of Vienna Medical School with no intention of practicing medicine. Instead, he preferred teaching and doing research in physiology, which he continued even after he graduated from the university's Physiological Institute.

Freud might have continued this work indefinitely had it not been for two factors. First, he believed (probably with some justification) that, as a Jew, his opportunities for academic advancement would be limited. Second, his father, who helped finance his medical school expense, became less able to provide monetary aid. Reluctantly, Freud turned from his laboratory to the practice of medicine. He worked for 3 years in the General Hospital of Vienna, becoming familiar with the practice of various branches of medicine, including psychiatry and nervous diseases (Freud, 1925/1959).

In 1885, he received a traveling grant from the University of Vienna and decided to study in Paris with the famous French neurologist Jean-Martin Charcot. He spent 4 months with Charcot, from whom he learned the hypnotic technique for treating **hysteria,** a disorder typically characterized by paralysis or the improper functioning of certain parts of the body. Through hypnosis, Freud became convinced of a psychogenic and sexual origin of hysterical symptoms.

While still a medical student, Freud developed a close professional association and a personal friendship with Josef Breuer, a well-known Viennese physician 14 years older than Freud and a man of considerable scientific reputation (Ferris, 1997). Breuer taught Freud about **catharsis,** the process of removing hysterical symptoms through "talking them out." While using catharsis, Freud gradually and laboriously discovered the *free association* technique, which soon replaced hypnosis as his principal therapeutic technique.

From as early as adolescence, Freud literally dreamed of making a monumental discovery and achieving fame (Newton, 1995). On several occasions during the 1880s and 1890s he believed he was on the verge of such a discovery. His first opportunity to gain recognition came in 1884–1885 and involved his experiments with cocaine, which we discussed in the opening vignette.

Freud's second opportunity for achieving some measure of fame came in 1886 after he returned from Paris, where he had learned about *male* hysteria from Charcot. He assumed that this knowledge would gain him respect and recognition from the Imperial Society of Physicians of Vienna, whom he mistakenly believed would be impressed by the young Dr. Freud's knowledge of male hysteria. Early physicians

Sigmund Freud with his daughter, Anna, who was a psychoanalyst in her own right.

had believed that hysteria was strictly a female disorder because the very word had the same origins as uterus and was the result of a "wandering womb," with the uterus traveling throughout women's bodies and causing various parts to malfunction. However, by 1886, when Freud presented a paper on male hysteria to the Society, most physicians present were already familiar with the illness and knew that it could also be a male disorder. Because originality was expected and because Freud's paper was a rehash of what was already known, the Viennese physicians did not respond well to the presentation. Also, Freud's constant praise of Charcot, a Frenchman, cooled the Viennese physicians to his talk. Unfortunately, in his autobiographical study, Freud (1925/1959) told a very different story, claiming that his lecture was not well received because members of the learned society could not fathom the concept of male hysteria. Freud's account of this incident, now known to be in error, was nevertheless perpetuated for years, and as Sulloway (1992) argued, it is but one of many fictions created by Freud and his followers to mythologize psychoanalysis and to make a lonely hero of its founder.

Disappointed in his attempts to gain fame and afflicted with feelings (both justified and otherwise) of professional opposition due to his defense of cocaine and his belief in the sexual origins of neuroses, Freud felt the need to join with a more respected colleague. He turned to Breuer, with whom he had worked while still a medical student and with whom he enjoyed a continuing personal and professional relationship. Breuer had discussed in detail with Freud the case of Anna O, a young woman Freud had never met, but whom Breuer had spent many hours treating for hysteria several years earlier. Because of his rebuff by the Imperial Society of Physicians and his desire to establish a reputation for himself, Freud urged Breuer to collaborate with him in publishing an account of Anna O and several other cases of hysteria. Breuer, however, was not as eager as the younger and more revolutionary Freud to publish a full treatise on hysteria built on only a few case studies. He also could not accept Freud's notion that childhood sexual experiences were the source of adult hysteria. Finally, and with some reluctance, Breuer agreed to publish with Freud *Studies on Hysteria* (Breuer & Freud, 1895/1955). In this book, Freud introduced the term "psychical analysis," and during the following year, he began calling his approach "psycho-analysis."

At about the time *Studies on Hysteria* was published, Freud and Breuer had a professional disagreement and became estranged personally. Freud then turned to his friend Wilhelm Fliess, a Berlin physician who served as a sounding board for Freud's newly developing ideas. Freud's letters to Fliess (Freud, 1985) constitute a firsthand account of the beginnings of psychoanalysis and reveal the embryonic stage of Freudian theory. Freud and Fliess had become friends in 1887, but their relationship became more intimate following Freud's break with Breuer.

During the late 1890s, Freud suffered both professional isolation and personal crises. He had begun to analyze his own dreams, and after the death of his father in 1896, he initiated the practice of analyzing himself daily. Although his self-analysis was a lifetime labor, it was especially difficult for him during the late 1890s. During this period, Freud regarded himself as his own best patient. In August of 1897, he wrote to Fliess, "the chief patient I am preoccupied with is myself. . . . The analysis is more difficult than any other. It is, in fact what paralyzes my psychic strength" (Freud, 1985, p. 261).

A second personal crisis was his realization that he was now middle-aged and had yet to achieve the fame he so passionately desired. During this time he had suffered yet another disappointment in his attempt to make a major scientific contribution. Again he believed himself to be on the brink of an important breakthrough with his "discovery" that neuroses have their etiology in a child's seduction by a parent. Freud likened this finding to the discovery of the source of the Nile. However, in 1897 he abandoned the seduction theory and once again had to postpone the discovery that would propel him to greatness.

Why did Freud abandon his once-treasured seduction theory? In a letter dated September 21, 1897, to Wilhelm Fliess, he gave four reasons why he could no longer believe in his seduction theory. First, he said, the seduction theory had not enabled him to successfully treat even a single patient. Second, a great number of fathers, including his own, would have to be accused of sexual perversion because hysteria was quite common even among Freud's siblings. Third, Freud believed that the unconscious mind could probably not distinguish reality from fiction, a belief that later evolved into the Oedipus complex. And fourth, he found that the unconscious memories of advanced psychotic patients almost never revealed early childhood sexual experiences (Freud, 1985). After abandoning his seduction theory and with no Oedipus complex to replace it, Freud sank even more deeply into his midlife crisis.

Freud's official biographer, Ernest Jones (1953, 1955, 1957), believed that Freud suffered from a severe psychoneurosis during the late 1890s, although Max Schur (1972), Freud's personal physician during the final decade of his life, contended that his illness was due to a cardiac lesion, aggravated by addiction to nicotine. Peter Gay (1988) suggested that during the time immediately after his father's death, Freud "relived his oedipal conflicts with peculiar ferocity" (p. 141). But Henri Ellenberger (1970) described this period in Freud's life as a time of "creative illness," a condition characterized by depression, **neurosis,** psychosomatic ailments, and an intense preoccupation with some form of creative activity. In any event, at midlife, Freud was suffering from self-doubts, depression, and an **obsession** with his own death.

Despite these difficulties, Freud completed his greatest work, *Interpretation of Dreams* (1900/1953), during this period. This book, finished in 1899, was an outgrowth of his self-analysis, much of which he had revealed to his friend Wilhelm Fliess. The book contained many of Freud's own dreams, some disguised behind fictitious names.

Almost immediately after the publication of *Interpretation of Dreams,* his friendship with Fliess began to cool, eventually to rupture in 1903. This breakup paralleled Freud's earlier estrangement from Breuer, which took place almost immediately after they had published *Studies on Hysteria* together. It was also a harbinger of his breaks with Alfred Adler, Carl Jung, and several other close associates. Why did Freud have difficulties with so many former friends? Freud himself answered this question, stating that "it is not the scientific differences that are so important; it is usually some other kind of animosity, jealousy or revenge, that gives the impulse to enmity. The scientific differences come later" (Wortis, 1954, p. 163).

Although *Interpretation of Dreams* did not create the instant international stir Freud had hoped, it eventually gained for him the fame and recognition he had sought. In the 5-year period following its publication, Freud, now filled with renewed self-confidence, wrote several important works that helped solidify the foundation of psychoanalysis, including *On Dreams* (1901/1953), written because *Interpretation of Dreams* had failed to capture much interest; *Psychopathology of Everyday Life* (1901/1960), which introduced the world to Freudian slips; *Three Essays on the Theory of Sexuality* (1905/1953b), which established sex as the cornerstone of psychoanalysis; and *Jokes and Their Relation to the Unconscious* (1905/1960), which proposed that jokes, like dreams and Freudian slips, have an unconscious meaning. These publications helped Freud attain some local prominence in scientific and medical circles.

In 1902, Freud invited a small group of somewhat younger Viennese physicians to meet in his home to discuss psychological issues. Then, in the fall of that year, these five men—Freud, Alfred Adler, Wilhelm Stekel, Max Kahane, and Rudolf Reitler—formed the Wednesday Psychological Society, with Freud as discussion leader. In 1908, this organization adopted a more formal name—the Vienna Psychoanalytic Society.

In 1910, Freud and his followers founded the International Psychoanalytic Association with Carl Jung of Zürich as president. Freud was attracted to Jung because of his keen intellect and also because he was neither Jewish nor Viennese. Between 1902 and 1906, all 17 of Freud's disciples had been Jewish (Kurzweil, 1989), and Freud was interested in giving psychoanalysis a more cosmopolitan flavor. Although Jung was a welcome addition to the Freudian circle and had been designated as the "Crown Prince" and "the man of the future," he, like Adler and Stekel before him, eventually quarreled bitterly with Freud and left the psychoanalytic movement. The seeds of disagreement between Jung and Freud were probably sown when the two men, along with Sandor Ferenczi, traveled to the United States in 1909 to deliver a series of lectures at Clark University near Boston. To pass the time during their travels, Freud and Jung interpreted each other's dreams, a potentially explosive practice that eventually led to the end of their relationship in 1913 (McGuire, 1974).

The years of World War I were difficult for Freud. He was cut off from communication with his faithful followers, his psychoanalytic practice dwindled, his home was sometimes without heat, and he and his family had little food. After the war, despite advancing years and pain suffered from 33 operations for cancer of the mouth, he made important revisions in his theory. The most significant of these were the elevation of *aggression* to a level equal to that of the sexual drive, the inclusion of repression as one of the defenses of the ego; and his attempt to clarify the female Oedipus complex, which he was never able to completely accomplish.

What personal qualities did Freud possess? A more complete insight into his personality can be found in Breger (2000), Clark (1980), Ellenberger (1970), Ferris (1997), Gay (1988), Handlbauer (1998), Isbister (1985), E. Jones (1953, 1955, 1957), Newton (1995), Noland (1999), Roazen (1993, 1995, 2001), Silverstein (2003), Sulloway (1992), Vitz (1988), and dozens of other books on Freud's life. Above all, Freud was a sensitive, passionate person who had the capacity for intimate, almost secretive friendships. Most of these deeply emotional relationships came to an unhappy end, and Freud often felt persecuted by his former friends and regarded them as enemies. He seemed to have needed both types of relationship. In *Interpretation of Dreams,* Freud both explained and predicted this succession of interpersonal ruptures: "My emotional life has always insisted that I should have an intimate friend and a hated enemy. I have always been able to provide myself afresh with both" (Freud, 1900/1953, p. 483). Until he was well past 50, all these relationships were with men. Interestingly, Freud, the man who seemed to be constantly thinking of sex, had a very infrequent sex life himself. After Anna, his youngest child was born in 1895, Freud, not yet 40 years old, had no sexual intercourse for several years. Much of his sparse sexual life stemmed from his belief that use of a condom, coitus interruptus, as well as masturbation were unhealthy sexual practices. Because Freud wanted no more children after Anna was born, sexual abstinence was his only alternative (Breger, 2000; Freud, 1985).

In addition to balancing his emotional life between an intimate friend and a hated enemy, Freud possessed an outstanding talent as a writer, a gift that helped him become a leading contributor to 20th-century thought. He was a master of the German tongue and knew several other languages. Although he never won the coveted Nobel prize for science, he was awarded the Goethe prize for literature in 1930.

Freud also possessed intense intellectual curiosity; unusual moral courage (demonstrated by his daily self-analysis); extremely ambivalent feelings toward his father and other father figures; a tendency to hold grudges disproportionate to the alleged offense; a burning ambition, especially during his earlier years; strong feelings of isolation even while surrounded by many followers; and an intense and somewhat irrational dislike of America and Americans, an attitude that became more intense after his trip to the United States in 1909.

Why did Freud have such a disdain for Americans? Perhaps the most important reason is that he rightly believed Americans would trivialize psychoanalysis by trying to make it popular. In addition, he had several experiences during his trip to the United States that were foreign to a proper bourgeois Viennese gentleman. Even before he embarked on the *George Washington,* he saw his name misspelled as "Freund" on the passenger list (Ferris, 1997). A number of other events—some of which seem almost humorous—made Freud's visit more unpleasant than it might have been. First, Freud experienced chronic indigestion and diarrhea throughout his visit, probably because the drinking water did not agree with him. In addition, he found it both peculiar and problematic that American cities did not provide public restrooms on street corners, and with his chronic indigestion he was frequently in search of a public lavatory. Also, several Americans addressed him as Doc or Sigmund while challenging him to defend his theories, and one person tried—unsuccessfully, of course—to prevent him from smoking a cigar in a nonsmoking area. Moreover, when Freud, Ferenczi, and Jung went to a private camp in western Massachusetts, they were greeted by a barrage of flags of Imperial Germany, despite the fact that none of them was German and each had reasons to dislike Germany. Also at camp, Freud, along with the others, sat on the ground while the host grilled steaks over charcoal, a custom Freud deemed to be both savage and uncouth (Roazen, 1993).

Levels of Mental Life

Freud's greatest contribution to personality theory is his exploration of the unconscious and his insistence that people are motivated primarily by drives of which they have little or no awareness. To Freud, mental life is divided into two levels, the **unconscious** and the **conscious.** The unconscious, in turn, has two different levels, the unconscious proper and the **preconscious.** In Freudian psychology the three levels of mental life are used to designate both a process and a location. The existence as a specific location, of course, is merely hypothetical and has no real existence within the body. Yet, Freud spoke of *the* unconscious as well as unconscious processes.

Unconscious

The unconscious contains all those drives, urges, or instincts that are beyond our awareness but that nevertheless motivate most of our words, feelings, and actions. Although we may be conscious of our overt behaviors, we often are not aware of the mental processes that lie behind them. For example, a man may know that he is attracted to a woman but may not fully understand all the reasons for the attraction, some of which may even seem irrational.

Because the unconscious is not available to the conscious mind, how can one know if it really exists? Freud felt that its existence could be proved only indirectly. To him the unconscious is the explanation for the meaning behind dreams, slips of the tongue, and certain kinds of forgetting, called *repression.* Dreams serve as a particularly rich source of unconscious material. For example, Freud believed that childhood experiences can appear in adult dreams even though the dreamer has no conscious recollection of these experiences.

Unconscious processes often enter into consciousness but only after being disguised or distorted enough to elude censorship. Freud (1917/1963) used the analogy of a guardian or censor blocking the passage between the unconscious and preconscious and preventing undesirable anxiety-producing memories from entering awareness. To enter the conscious level of the mind, these unconscious images first must be sufficiently disguised to slip past the *primary censor,* and then they must elude a *final censor* that watches the passageway between the preconscious and the conscious. By the time these memories enter our conscious mind, we no longer recognize them for what they are; instead, we see them as relatively pleasant, nonthreatening experiences. In most cases, these images have strong sexual or aggressive motifs, because childhood sexual and aggressive behaviors are frequently punished or suppressed. Punishment and **suppression** often create feelings of anxiety, and the anxiety in turn stimulates **repression,** that is, the forcing of unwanted, anxiety-ridden experiences into the unconscious as a defense against the pain of that anxiety.

Not all unconscious processes, however, spring from repression of childhood events. Freud believed that a portion of our unconscious originates from the experiences of our early ancestors that have been passed on to us through hundreds of generations of repetition. He called these inherited unconscious images our **phylogenetic endowment** (Freud, 1917/1963, 1933/1964). Freud's notion of phylogenetic endowment is quite similar to Carl Jung's idea of a collective unconscious (see Chapter 4). However, one important difference exists between the two concepts. Whereas Jung placed primary emphasis on the collective unconscious, Freud relied on the notion of inherited dispositions only as a last resort. That is, when explanations built on individual experiences were not adequate, Freud would turn to the idea of collectively inherited experiences to fill in the gaps left by individual experiences. Later we will see that Freud used the concept of phylogenetic endowment to explain several important concepts, such as the Oedipus complex and castration anxiety.

Unconscious drives may appear in consciousness, but only after undergoing certain transformations. A person may express either erotic or hostile urges, for example, by teasing or joking with another person. The original drive (sex or aggression) is thus disguised and hidden from the conscious minds of both persons. The unconscious of the first person, however, has directly influenced the unconscious of the second. Both people gain some satisfaction of either sexual or aggressive urges, but neither is conscious of the underlying motive behind the teasing or joking. Thus the unconscious mind of one person can communicate with the unconscious of another without either person being aware of the process.

Unconscious, of course, does not mean inactive or dormant. Forces in the unconscious constantly strive to become conscious, and many of them succeed, although they may no longer appear in their original form. Unconscious ideas can and do motivate people. For example, a son's hostility toward his father may masquerade itself in the form of ostentatious affection. In an undisguised form, the hostility would create too much anxiety for the son. His unconscious mind, therefore, motivates him to express hostility indirectly through an exaggerated show of love and flattery. Because the disguise must successfully deceive the person, it often takes an opposite form from the original feelings, but it is almost always overblown and ostentatious. (This mechanism, called a *reaction formation,* is discussed later in the section titled Defense Mechanisms.)

Preconscious

The preconscious level of the mind contains all those elements that are not conscious but can become conscious either quite readily or with some difficulty (Freud, 1933/1964).

The contents of the preconscious come from two sources, the first of which is conscious perception. What a person perceives is conscious for only a transitory period; it quickly passes into the preconscious when the focus of attention shifts to another idea. These ideas that alternate easily between being conscious and preconscious are largely free from anxiety and in reality are much more similar to the conscious images than to unconscious urges.

The second source of preconscious images is the unconscious. Freud believed that ideas can slip past the vigilant censor and enter into the preconscious in a disguised form. Some of these images never become conscious because if we recognized them as derivatives of the unconscious, we would experience increased levels of anxiety, which would activate the final censor to repress these anxiety-loaded images, forcing them back into the unconscious. Other images from the unconscious do gain admission to consciousness, but only because their true nature is cleverly disguised through the dream process, a slip of the tongue, or an elaborate defensive measure.

Conscious

Consciousness, which plays a relatively minor role in psychoanalytic theory, can be defined as those mental elements in awareness at any given point in time. It is the only level of mental life directly available to us. Ideas can reach consciousness from two different directions. The first is from the **perceptual conscious** system, which is turned toward the outer world and acts as a medium for the perception of external stimuli. In other words, what we perceive through our sense organs, if not too threatening, enters into consciousness (Freud, 1933/1964).

The second source of conscious elements is from within the mental structure and includes nonthreatening ideas from the preconscious as well as menacing but well-disguised images from the unconscious. As we have seen, these latter images escaped into the preconscious by cloaking themselves as harmless elements and evading the primary censor. Once in the preconscious, they avoid a final censor and come under the eye of consciousness. By the time they reach the conscious system, these images are greatly distorted and camouflaged, often taking the form of defensive behaviors or dream elements.

In summary, Freud (1917/1963, pp. 295–296) compared the unconscious to a large entrance hall in which many diverse, energetic, and disreputable people are milling about, crowding one another, and striving incessantly to escape to a smaller adjoining reception room. However, a watchful guard protects the threshold between

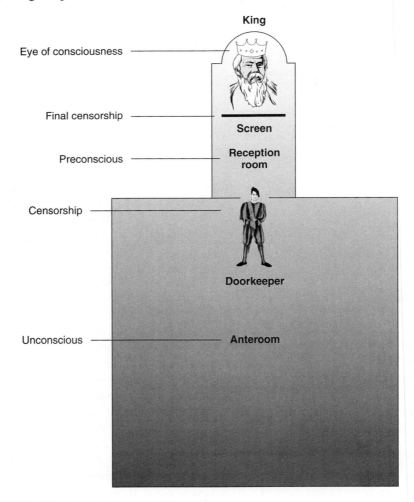

FIGURE 2.1 *Levels of Mental Life.*

the large entrance hall and the small reception room. This guard has two methods of preventing undesirables from escaping from the entrance hall—either turn them back at the door or throw out those people who earlier had clandestinely slipped into the reception room. The effect in either case is the same; the menacing, disorderly people are prevented from coming into view of an important guest who is seated at the far end of the reception room behind a screen. The meaning of the analogy is obvious. The people in the entrance hall represent unconscious images. The small reception room is the preconscious and its inhabitants represent preconscious ideas. People in the reception room (preconscious) may or may not come into view of the important guest who, of course, represents the eye of consciousness. The doorkeeper who guards the threshold between the two rooms is the primary censor that prevents unconscious images from becoming preconscious and renders preconscious images unconscious by throwing them back. The screen that guards the important guest is the final censor, and it prevents many, but not all, preconscious elements from reaching consciousness. The analogy is presented graphically in Figure 2.1.

Provinces of the Mind

For nearly 2 decades, Freud's only model of the mind was the topographic one we have just outlined, and his only portrayal of psychic strife was the conflict between conscious and unconscious forces. Then, during the 1920s, Freud (1923/1961a) introduced a three-part structural model. This division of the mind into three provinces did not supplant the topographic model, but it helped Freud explain mental images according to their functions or purposes.

To Freud, the most primitive part of the mind was *das Es,* or the "it," which is almost always translated into English as **id;** a second division was *das Ich*, or the "I," translated as **ego;** and a final province was *das Uber-Ich,* or the "over-I," which is rendered into English as **superego.** These provinces or regions have no territorial existence, of course, but are merely hypothetical constructs. They interact with the three levels of mental life so that the ego cuts across the various topographic levels and has conscious, preconscious, and unconscious components, whereas the superego is both preconscious and unconscious and the id is completely unconscious. Figure 2.2 shows the relationship between the provinces of the mind and the levels of mental life.

The Id

At the core of personality and completely unconscious is the psychical region called the id, a term derived from the impersonal pronoun meaning "the it," or the not-yet-owned component of personality. The id has no contact with reality, yet it strives constantly to reduce tension by satisfying basic desires. Because its sole function is to seek pleasure, we say that the id serves the **pleasure principle.**

A newborn infant is the personification of an id unencumbered by restrictions of ego and superego. The infant seeks gratification of needs without regard for what is possible (that is, demands of the ego) or what is proper (that is, restraints of the superego). Instead, it sucks when the nipple is either present or absent and gains pleasure in either situation. Although the infant receives life-sustaining food only by

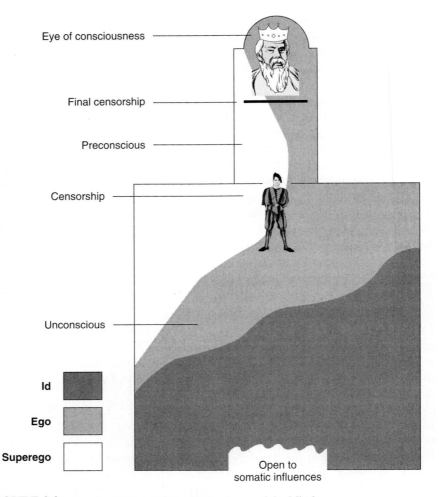

Eye of consciousness ———

Final censorship ———

Preconscious ———

Censorship ———

Unconscious ———

Id

Ego

Superego

Open to
somatic influences

FIGURE 2.2   *Levels of Mental Life and Provinces of the Mind.*

sucking a nurturing nipple, it continues to suck because its id is not in contact with reality. The infant fails to realize that thumb-sucking behavior cannot sustain life. Because the id has no direct contact with reality, it is not altered by the passage of time or by the experiences of the person. Childhood wish impulses remain unchanged in the id for decades (Freud, 1933/1964).

Besides being unrealistic and pleasure seeking, the id is illogical and can simultaneously entertain incompatible ideas. For example, a woman may show conscious love for her mother while unconsciously wishing to destroy her. These opposing desires are possible because the id has no morality; that is, it cannot make value judgments or distinguish between good and evil. However, the id is not immoral, merely amoral. All of the id's energy is spent for one purpose—to seek pleasure without regard for what is proper or just (Freud, 1923/1961a, 1933/1964).

In review, the id is primitive, chaotic, inaccessible to consciousness, unchangeable, amoral, illogical, unorganized, and filled with energy received from basic drives and discharged for the satisfaction of the pleasure principle.

As the region that houses basic drives (primary motivates), the id operates through the **primary process.** Because it blindly seeks to satisfy the pleasure principle, its survival is dependent on the development of a **secondary process** to bring it into contact with the external world. This secondary process functions through the ego.

The Ego

The ego, or I, is the only region of the mind in contact with reality. It grows out of the id during infancy and becomes a person's sole source of communication with the external world. It is governed by the **reality principle,** which it tries to substitute for the pleasure principle of the id. As the sole region of the mind in contact with the external world, the ego becomes the decision-making or executive branch of personality. However, because it is partly conscious, partly preconscious, and partly unconscious, the ego can make decisions on each of these three levels. For instance, a woman's ego may *consciously* motivate her to choose excessively neat, well-tailored clothes because she feels comfortable when well dressed. At the same time, she may be only dimly (i.e., *preconsciously*) aware of previous experiences of being rewarded for choosing nice clothes. In addition, she may be *unconsciously* motivated to be excessively neat and orderly due to early childhood experiences of toilet training. Thus, her decision to wear neat clothes can take place in all three levels of mental life.

When performing its cognitive and intellectual functions, the ego must take into consideration the incompatible but equally unrealistic demands of the id and the superego. In addition to these two tyrants, the ego must serve a third master—the external world. Thus, the ego constantly tries to reconcile the blind, irrational claims of the id and the superego with the realistic demands of the external world. Finding itself surrounded on three sides by divergent and hostile forces, the ego reacts in a predictable manner—it becomes anxious. It then uses repression and other *defense mechanisms* to defend itself against this anxiety (Freud, 1926/1959a).

According to Freud (1933/1964), the ego becomes differentiated from the id when infants learn to distinguish themselves from the outer world. While the id remains unchanged, the ego continues to develop strategies for handling the id's unrealistic and unrelenting demands for pleasure. At times the ego can control the powerful, pleasure-seeking id, but at other times it loses control. In comparing the ego to the id, Freud used the analogy of a person on horseback. The rider checks and inhibits the greater strength of the horse but is ultimately at the mercy of the animal. Similarly, the ego must check and inhibit id impulses, but it is more or less constantly at the mercy of the stronger but more poorly organized id. The ego has no strength of its own but borrows energy from the id. In spite of this dependence on the id, the ego sometimes comes close to gaining complete control, for instance, during the prime of life of a psychologically mature person.

As children begin to experience parental rewards and punishments, they learn what to do in order to gain pleasure and avoid pain. At this young age, pleasure and pain are ego functions because children have not yet developed a conscience and ego-ideal: that is, a superego. As children reach the age of 5 or 6 years, they identify with their parents and begin to learn what they should and should not do. This is the origin of the superego.

The Superego

In Freudian psychology, the superego, or above-I, represents the moral and ideal aspects of personality and is guided by the **moralistic** and **idealistic principles** as opposed to the pleasure principle of the id and the realistic principle of the ego. The superego grows out of the ego, and like the ego, it has no energy of its own. However, the superego differs from the ego in one important respect—it has no contact with the outside world and therefore is unrealistic in its demands for perfection (Freud, 1923/1961a).

The superego has two subsystems, the **conscience** and the **ego-ideal.** Freud did not clearly distinguish between these two functions, but, in general, the conscience results from experiences with punishments for improper behavior and tells us what we *should not do,* whereas the ego-ideal develops from experiences with rewards for proper behavior and tells us what we *should do.* A primitive conscience comes into existence when a child conforms to parental standards out of fear of loss of love or approval. Later, during the Oedipal phase of development, these ideals are internalized through identification with the mother and father. (We discuss the Oedipus complex in a later section titled Stages of Development.)

A well-developed superego acts to control sexual and aggressive impulses through the process of *repression.* It cannot produce repressions by itself, but it can order the ego to do so. The superego watches closely over the ego, judging its actions and intentions. Guilt is the result when the ego acts—or even intends to act—contrary to the moral standards of the superego. Feelings of inferiority arise when the ego is unable to meet the superego's standards of perfection. Guilt, then, is a function of the conscience, whereas inferiority feelings stem from the ego-ideal (Freud, 1933/1964).

The superego is not concerned with the happiness of the ego. It strives blindly and unrealistically toward perfection. It is unrealistic in the sense that it does not take

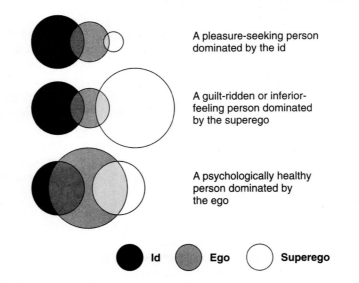

FIGURE 2.3   *The Relationship among Id, Ego, and Superego in Three Hypothetical Persons.*

into consideration the difficulties or impossibilities faced by the ego in carrying out its orders. Not all its demands, of course, are impossible to fulfill, just as not all demands of parents and other authority figures are impossible to fulfill. The superego, however, is like the id in that it is completely ignorant of, and unconcerned with, the practicability of its requirements.

Freud (1933/1964) pointed out that the divisions among the different regions of the mind are not sharp and well defined. The development of the three divisions varies widely in different individuals. For some people, the superego does not grow after childhood; for others, the superego may dominate the personality at the cost of guilt and inferiority feelings. For yet others, the ego and superego may take turns controlling personality, which results in extreme fluctuations of mood and alternating cycles of self-confidence and self-deprecation. In the healthy individual, the id and superego are integrated into a smooth functioning ego and operate in harmony and with a minimum of conflict. Figure 2.3 shows the relationships among id, ego, and superego in three hypothetical persons. For the first person, the id dominates a weak ego and a feeble superego, preventing the ego from counterbalancing its incessant demands of the id and leaving the person nearly constantly striving for pleasure regardless of what is possible or proper. The second person, with strong feelings of either guilt or inferiority and a weak ego, will experience many conflicts because the ego cannot arbitrate the strong but opposing demands of the superego and the id. The third person, with a strong ego that has incorporated many of the demands of both the id and the superego, is psychologically healthy and in control of both the pleasure principle and the moralistic principle.

Dynamics of Personality

Levels of mental life and provinces of the mind refer to the *structure* or composition of personality; but personalities also *do* something. Thus, Freud postulated a *dynamic,* or motivational principle, to explain the driving forces behind people's actions. To Freud, people are motivated to seek pleasure and to reduce tension and anxiety. This motivation is derived from psychical and physical energy that springs from their basic drives.

Drives

Freud used the German word *Trieb* to refer to a drive or a stimulus within the person. Freud's official translators rendered this term as *instinct,* but more accurately the word should be "drive" or "impulse." Drives operate as a constant motivational force. As an internal stimulus, drives differ from external stimuli in that they cannot be avoided through flight.

According to Freud (1933/1964), the various drives can all be grouped under two major headings: sex or Eros and aggression, distraction, or Thanatos. These drives originate in the id, but they come under the control of the ego. Each drive has its own form of psychic energy: Freud used the word **libido** for the sex drive, but energy from the aggressive drive remains nameless.

Every basic drive is characterized by an impetus, a source, an aim, and an object. A drive's *impetus* is the amount of force it exerts; its *source* is the region of the body in a state of excitation or tension; its *aim* is to seek pleasure by removing that excitation or reducing the tension; and its *object* is the person or thing that serves as the means through which the aim is satisfied (Freud, 1915/1957a).

Sex

The aim of the sexual drive is pleasure, but this pleasure is not limited to genital satisfaction. Freud believed that the entire body is invested with libido. Besides the genitals, the mouth and anus are especially capable of producing sexual pleasure and are called **erogenous** zones. The ultimate aim of the sexual drive (reduction of sexual tension) cannot be changed, but the path by which the aim is reached can be varied. It can take either an active or a passive form, or it can be temporarily or permanently inhibited (Freud, 1915/1957a). Because the path is flexible and because sexual pleasure stems from organs other than the genitals, much behavior originally motivated by Eros is difficult to recognize as sexual behavior. To Freud, however, all pleasurable activity is traceable to the sexual drive.

The flexibility of the sexual *object* or person can bring about a further disguise of Eros. The erotic object can easily be transformed or displaced. Libido can be withdrawn from one person and placed in a state of free-floating tension, or it can be reinvested in another person, including the self. For example, an infant prematurely forced to give up the nipple as a sexual object may substitute the thumb as an object of oral pleasure.

Sex can take many forms, including narcissism, love, sadism, and masochism. The latter two also possess generous components of the aggressive drive.

Infants are primarily self-centered, with their libido invested almost exclusively on their own ego. This condition, which is universal, is known as **primary narcissism.** As the ego develops, children usually give up much of their primary narcissism and develop a greater interest in other people. In Freud's language, narcissistic libido is then transformed into object libido. During puberty, however, adolescents often redirect their libido back to the ego and become preoccupied with personal appearance and other self-interests. This pronounced **secondary narcissism** is not universal, but a moderate degree of self-love is common to nearly everyone (Freud, 1914/1957).

A second manifestation of Eros is love, which develops when people invest their libido on an object or person other than themselves. Children's first sexual interest is the person who cares for them, generally the mother. During infancy children of either sex experience sexual love for the mother. Overt sexual love for members of one's family, however, ordinarily is repressed, which brings a second type of love into existence. Freud called this second kind of love aim-inhibited because the original aim of reducing sexual tension is inhibited or repressed. The kind of love people feel for their siblings or parents is generally aim-inhibited.

Obviously, love and narcissism are closely interrelated. Narcissism involves love of self, whereas love is often accompanied by narcissistic tendencies, as when people love someone who serves as an ideal or model of what they would like to be.

Two other drives that are also intertwined are sadism and masochism. **Sadism** is the need for sexual pleasure by inflicting pain or humiliation on another person. Carried to an extreme, it is considered a sexual perversion, but in moderation, sadism is a common need and exists to some extent in all sexual relationships. It is perverted when the sexual aim of erotic pleasure becomes secondary to the destructive aim (Freud, 1933/1964).

Masochism, like sadism, is a common need, but it becomes a perversion when Eros becomes subservient to the destructive drive. Masochists experience sexual pleasure from suffering pain and humiliation inflicted either by themselves or by others. Because masochists can provide self-inflicted pain, they do not depend on another person for the satisfaction of masochistic needs. In contrast, sadists must seek and find another person on whom to inflict pain or humiliation. In this respect, they are more dependent than masochists on other people.

Aggression

Partially as a result of his unhappy experiences during World War I and partially as a consequence of the death of his beloved daughter Sophie, Freud (1920/1955a) wrote *Beyond the Pleasure Principle,* a book that elevated **aggression** to the level of the sexual drive. As he did with many of his other concepts, Freud set forth his ideas tentatively and with some caution. With time, however, aggression, like several other tentatively proposed concepts, became dogma.

The aim of the destructive drive, according to Freud, is to return the organism to an inorganic state. Because the ultimate inorganic condition is death, the final aim of the aggressive drive is self-destruction. As with the sexual drive, aggression is flexible and can take a number of forms, such as teasing, gossip, sarcasm, humiliation. humor, and the enjoyment of other people's suffering. The aggressive tendency is present in everyone and is the explanation for wars, atrocities, and religious persecution.

The aggressive drive also explains the need for the barriers that people have erected to check aggression. For example, commandments such as "Love thy neighbor as thyself" are necessary, Freud believed, to inhibit the strong, though usually unconscious, drive to inflict injury on others. These precepts are actually *reaction formations.* They involve the repression of strong hostile impulses and the overt and obvious expression of the opposite tendency.

Throughout our lifetime, life and death impulses constantly struggle against one another for ascendancy, but at the same time, both must bow to the reality principle, which represents the claims of the outer world. These demands of the real world prevent a direct, covert, and unopposed fulfillment of either sex or aggression. They frequently create anxiety, which relegates many sexual and aggressive desires to the realm of the unconscious.

Anxiety

Sex and aggression share the center of Freudian dynamic theory with the concept of **anxiety.** In defining anxiety, Freud (1933/1964) emphasized that it is a felt, affective, unpleasant state accompanied by a physical sensation that warns the person against impending danger. The unpleasantness is often vague and hard to pinpoint, but the anxiety itself is always felt.

Only the ego can produce or feel anxiety, but the id, superego, and external world each are involved in one of three kinds of anxiety—neurotic, moral, and realistic. The ego's dependence on the id results in neurotic anxiety; its dependence on the superego produces moral anxiety; and its dependence on the outer world leads to realistic anxiety.

Neurotic anxiety is defined as apprehension about an unknown danger. The feeling itself exists in the ego, but it originates from id impulses. People may experience neurotic anxiety in the presence of a teacher, employer, or some other authority figure because they previously experienced unconscious feelings of destruction against one or both parents. During childhood, these feelings of hostility are often accompanied by fear of punishment, and this fear becomes generalized into unconscious neurotic anxiety.

A second type of anxiety, **moral anxiety,** stems from the conflict between the ego and the superego. After children establish a superego—usually by the age of 5 or 6—they may experience anxiety as an outgrowth of the conflict between realistic needs and the dictates of their superego. Moral anxiety, for example, would result from sexual temptations if a child believes that yielding to the temptation would be morally wrong. It may also result from the failure to behave consistently with what they regard as morally right, for example, failing to care for aging parents.

A third category of anxiety, **realistic anxiety,** is closely related to fear. It is defined as an unpleasant, nonspecific feeling involving a possible danger. For example, we may experience realistic anxiety while driving in heavy, fast-moving traffic in an unfamiliar city, a situation fraught with real, objective danger. However, realistic anxiety is different from fear in that it does not involve a specific fearful object. We would experience fear, for example, if our motor vehicle suddenly began sliding out of control on an icy highway.

These three types of anxiety are seldom clear-cut or easily separated. They often exist in combination, as when fear of water, a real danger, becomes disproportionate to the situation and hence precipitates neurotic anxiety as well as realistic anxiety. This situation indicates that an unknown danger is connected with the external one.

Anxiety serves as an ego-preserving mechanism because it signals us that some danger is at hand (Freud, 1933/1964). For example, an anxiety dream signals our censor of an impending danger, which allows us to better disguise the dream images. Anxiety allows the constantly vigilant ego to be alert for signs of threat and danger. The signal of impending danger stimulates us to mobilize for either flight or defense.

Anxiety is also self-regulating because it precipitates repression, which in turn reduces the pain of anxiety (Freud, 1933/1964). If the ego had no recourse to defensive behavior, the anxiety would become intolerable. Defensive behaviors, therefore, serve a useful function by protecting the ego against the pain of anxiety.

Defense Mechanisms

Freud first elaborated on the idea of **defense mechanisms** in 1926 (Freud, 1926/1959a), and his daughter Anna further refined and organized the concept (A. Freud, 1946). Although defense mechanisms are normal and universally used, when carried to an extreme they lead to compulsive, repetitive, and neurotic behavior. Because we must expend psychic energy to establish and maintain defense mechanisms, the more defensive we are, the less psychic energy we have left to satisfy id impulses. This, of course, is precisely the ego's purpose in establishing defense mechanisms—to avoid dealing directly with sexual and aggressive implosives and to defend itself against the anxiety that accompanies them (Freud, 1926/1959a).

The principal defense mechanisms identified by Freud include repression, reaction formation, displacement, fixation, regression, projection, introjection, and sublimation.

Repression

The most basic defense mechanism, because it is involved in each of the others, is *repression.* Whenever the ego is threatened by undesirable id impulses, it protects itself by repressing those impulses; that is, it forces threatening feelings into the unconscious (Freud, 1926/1959a). In many cases the repression is then perpetuated for a lifetime. For example, a young girl may permanently repress her hostility for a younger sister because her hateful feelings create too much anxiety.

No society permits a complete and uninhibited expression of sex and aggression. When children have their hostile or sexual behaviors punished or otherwise suppressed, they learn to be anxious whenever they experience these impulses. Although this anxiety seldom leads to a complete repression of aggressive and sexual drives, it often results in their partial repression.

What happens to these impulses after they have become unconscious? Freud (1933/1964) believed that several possibilities exist. First, the impulses may remain unchanged in the unconscious. Second, they could force their way into consciousness in an unaltered form, in which case they would create more anxiety than the person could handle, and the person would be overwhelmed with anxiety. A third and much more common fate of repressed drives is that they are expressed in displaced or disguised forms. The disguise, of course, must be clever enough to deceive the ego. Repressed drives may be disguised as physical symptoms, for example, sexual impotency in a man troubled by sexual guilt. The impotency prevents the man from having to deal with the guilt and anxiety that would result from normal enjoyable sexual activity. Repressed drives may also find an outlet in dreams, slips of the tongue, or one of the other defense mechanisms.

Reaction Formation

One of the ways in which a repressed impulse may become conscious is through adopting a disguise that is directly opposite its original form. This defense mechanism is called a **reaction formation.** Reactive behavior can be identified by its exaggerated character and by its obsessive and compulsive form (Freud, 1926/1959a). An example of a reaction formation can be seen in a young woman who deeply resents and hates her mother. Because she knows that society demands affection toward parents, such conscious hatred for her mother would produce too much anxiety. To avoid painful anxiety, the young woman concentrates on the opposite impulse—love. Her "love" for her mother, however, is not genuine. It is showy, exaggerated, and overdone. Other people may easily see the true nature of this love, but the woman must deceive herself and cling to her reaction formation, which helps conceal the anxiety-arousing truth that she unconsciously hates her mother.

Displacement

Freud (1926/1959a) believed that reaction formations are limited to a single object; for example, people with reactive love shower affection only on the person toward whom they feel unconscious hatred. In **displacement,** however, people can redirect their unacceptable urges onto a variety of people or objects so that the original impulse is disguised or concealed. For example, a woman who is angry at her roommate may displace her anger onto her employees, her pet cat, or a stuffed animal. She remains friendly to her roommate, but unlike the workings of a reaction formation, she does not exaggerate or overdo her friendliness.

Throughout his writings, Freud used the term "displacement" in several ways. In our discussion of the sexual drive, for example, we saw that the sexual object can be displaced or transformed onto a variety of other objects, including one's self. Freud (1926/1959a) also used displacement to refer to the replacement of one neurotic symptom for another; for example, a compulsive urge to masturbate may be replaced by compulsive hand washing. Displacement also is involved in dream formation, as when the dreamer's destructive urges toward a parent are placed onto a dog or wolf. In this event, a dream about a dog being hit by a car might reflect the dreamer's unconscious wish to see the parent destroyed. (We discuss dream formation more completely in the section on dream analysis.)

Fixation

Psychical growth normally proceeds in a somewhat continuous fashion through the various stages of development. The process of psychologically growing up, however, is not without stressful and anxious moments. When the prospect of taking the next step becomes too anxiety provoking, the ego may resort to the strategy of remaining at the present, more comfortable psychological stage. Such a defense is called **fixation.** Technically, fixation is the permanent attachment of the libido onto an earlier, more primitive stage of development (Freud, 1917/1963). Like other defense mechanisms, fixations are universal. People who continually derive pleasure from eating, smoking, or talking may have an oral fixation, whereas those who are obsessed with neatness and orderliness may possess an anal fixation.

Regression

Once the libido has passed a developmental stage, it may, during times of stress and anxiety, revert back to that earlier stage. Such a reversion is known as **regression** (Freud, 1917/1963). Regressions are quite common and are readily visible in children. For example, a completely weaned child may regress to demanding a bottle or nipple when a baby brother or sister is born. The attention given to the new baby poses a threat to the older child. Regressions are also frequent in older children and in adults. A common way for adults to react to anxiety-producing situations is to revert to earlier, safer, more secure patterns of behavior and to invest their libido onto more primitive and familiar objects. Under extreme stress one adult may adopt the fetal position, another may return home to mother, and still another may react by remaining all day in bed, well covered from the cold and threatening world. Regressive behavior is similar to fixated behavior in that it is rigid and infantile. Regressions, however, are usually temporary, whereas fixations demand a more or less permanent expenditure of psychic energy.

Projection

When an internal impulse provokes too much anxiety, the ego may reduce that anxiety by attributing the unwanted impulse to an external object, usually another person. This is the defense mechanism of **projection,** which can be defined as seeing in others unacceptable feelings or tendencies that actually reside in one's own unconscious (Freud, 1915/1957b). For example, a man may consistently interpret the actions of older women as attempted seductions. Consciously, the thought of sexual intercourse with older women may be intensely repugnant to him, but buried in his unconscious is a strong erotic attraction to these women. In this example, the young man deludes himself into believing that he has no sexual feelings for older women. Although this projection erases most of his anxiety and guilt, it permits him to maintain a sexual interest in women who remind him of his mother.

An extreme type of projection is **paranoia,** a mental disorder characterized by powerful delusions of jealousy and persecution. Paranoia is not an inevitable outcome of projection but simply a severe variety of it. According to Freud (1922/1955), a crucial distinction between projection and paranoia is that paranoia is always characterized by repressed homosexual feelings toward the persecutor. Freud believed that the persecutor is inevitably a former friend of the same sex, although sometimes people may transfer their delusions onto a person of the opposite sex. When homosexual impulses become too powerful, persecuted paranoiacs defend themselves by *reversing* these feelings and then projecting them onto their original object. For men, the transformation proceeds as follows. Instead of saying, "I love him," the paranoid person says, "I hate him." Because this also produces too much anxiety, he says, "He hates me." At this point, the person has disclaimed all responsibility and can say, "I like him fine, but he's got it in for me." The central mechanism in all paranoia is projection with accompanying delusions of jealousy and persecution.

Introjection

Whereas projection involves placing an unwanted impulse onto an external object, **introjection** is a defense mechanism whereby people incorporate positive qualities of another person into their own ego. For example, an adolescent may introject or adopt the mannerisms, values, or lifestyle of a movie star. Such an introjection gives the adolescent an inflated sense of self-worth and keeps feelings of inferiority to a minimum. People introject characteristics that they see as valuable and that will permit them to feel better about themselves.

Freud (1926/1959a) saw the resolution of the Oedipus complex as the prototype of introjection. During the Oedipal period, the young child introjects the authority and values of one or both parents—an introjection that sets into motion the beginning of the superego. When children introject what they perceive to be their parents' values, they are relieved from the work of evaluating and choosing their own beliefs and standards of conduct. As children advance through the latency period of development (approximately ages 6 to 12), their superego becomes more personalized;

that is, it moves away from a rigid identification with parents. Nevertheless, people of any age can reduce the anxiety associated with feelings of inadequacy by adopting or introjecting the values, beliefs, and mannerisms of other people.

Sublimation

Each of these defense mechanisms serves the individual by protecting the ego from anxiety, but each is of dubious value from society's viewpoint. According to Freud (1917/1963), one mechanism—sublimation—helps both the individual and the social group. **Sublimation** is the repression of the genital aim of Eros by substituting a cultural or social aim. The sublimated aim is expressed most obviously in creative cultural accomplishments such as art, music, and literature, but more subtly, it is part of all human relationships and all social pursuits. Freud (1914/1953) believed that the art of Michelangelo, who found an indirect outlet for his libido in painting and sculpting, was an excellent example of sublimation. In most people, sublimations combine with direct expression of Eros and result in a kind of balance between social accomplishments and personal pleasures. Most of us are capable of sublimating a part of our libido in the service of higher cultural values, while at the same time retaining sufficient amounts of the sexual drive to pursue individual erotic pleasure.

In summary, all defense mechanisms protect the ego against anxiety. They are universal in that everyone engages in defensive behavior to some degree. Each defense mechanism combines with repression, and each can be carried to the point of psychopathology. Normally, however, defense mechanisms are beneficial to the individual and harmless to society. In addition, one defense mechanism—sublimation—usually benefits both the individual and society.

Stages of Development

Although Freud had little firsthand experience with children (including his own), his developmental theory is almost exclusively a discussion of early childhood. To Freud, the first 4 or 5 years of life, or the **infantile stage,** are the most crucial for personality formation. This stage is followed by a 6- or 7-year period of **latency** during which time little or no sexual growth takes place. Then at puberty, a renaissance of sexual life occurs, and the **genital stage** is ushered in. Psychosexual development eventually culminates in **maturity.**

Infantile Period

One of Freud's (1905/1953b, 1923/1961b) most important assumptions is that infants possess a sexual life and go through a period of pregenital sexual development during the first 4 or 5 years after birth. At the time Freud originally wrote about infantile sexuality, the concept, though not new, was met with some resistance. Today, however, nearly all close observers accept the idea that children show an interest in the genitals, delight in sexual pleasure, and manifest sexual excitement. Childhood sexuality differs from adult sexuality in that it is not capable of reproduction and is exclusively autoerotic. With both children and adults, however, the sexual impulses can be satisfied through organs other than the genitals. The mouth and anus are particularly sensitive to erogenous stimulation (Freud, 1933/1964).

Freud (1917/1963) divided the infantile stage into three phases according to which of the three primary erogenous zones is undergoing the most salient development. The oral phase begins first and is followed in order by the anal phase and the phallic phase. The three infantile stages overlap, with one another and each continues after the onset of later stages.

Oral Phase

Because the mouth is the first organ to provide an infant with pleasure, Freud's first infantile stage of development is the **oral phase.** Infants obtain life-sustaining nourishment through the oral cavity, but beyond that, they also gain pleasure through the act of sucking.

The sexual aim of *early oral* activity is to incorporate or receive into one's body the object-choice, that is, the nipple. During this *oral-receptive* phase, infants feel no ambivalence toward the pleasurable object and their needs are usually satisfied with a minimum of frustration and anxiety. As they grow older, however, they are more likely to experience feelings of frustration and anxiety as a result of scheduled feedings, increased time lapses between feedings, and eventual *weaning.* These anxieties are generally accompanied by feelings of ambivalence toward their love object (mother), and by the increased ability of their budding ego to defend itself against the environment and against anxiety (Freud, 1933/1964).

Infants' defense against the environment is greatly aided by the emergence of teeth. At this point, they pass into a second oral phase, which Freud (1933/1964) called the *oral-sadistic* period. During this phase, infants respond to others through

Infants satisfy oral needs one way or another.

biting, cooing, closing their mouth, smiling, and crying. Their first autoerotic experience is thumb sucking, a defense against anxiety that satisfies their sexual but not their nutritional needs.

As children grow older, the mouth continues to be an erogenous zone, and by the time they become adults, they are capable of gratifying their oral needs in a variety of ways, including sucking candy, chewing gum, biting pencils, overeating, smoking cigarettes, pipes and cigars, and making biting, sarcastic remarks.

Anal Phase

The aggressive drive, which during the first year of life takes the form of oral sadism, reaches fuller development during the second year when the anus emerges as a sexually pleasurable zone. Because this period is characterized by satisfaction gained through aggressive behavior and through the excretory function, Freud (1933/1964) called it the *sadistic-anal phase* or, more briefly, the **anal phase** of development. This phase is divided into two subphases, the early anal and the late anal.

During the *early anal period,* children receive satisfaction by destroying or losing objects. At this time, the destructive nature of the sadistic drive is stronger than the erotic one, and children often behave aggressively toward their parents for frustrating them with *toilet training.*

Then, when children enter the *late anal period,* they sometimes take a friendly interest toward their feces, an interest that stems from the erotic pleasure of defecating. Frequently, children will present their feces to the parents as a valued prize (Freud, 1933/1964). If their behavior is accepted and praised by their parents, then children are likely to grow into generous and magnanimous adults. However, if their "gift" is rejected in a punitive fashion, children may adopt another method of obtaining anal pleasure—withholding the feces until the pressure becomes both painful and erotically stimulating. This mode of narcissistic and masochistic pleasure lays the foundation for the **anal character**—people who continue to receive erotic satisfaction by keeping and possessing objects and by arranging them in an excessively neat and orderly fashion. Freud (1933/1964) hypothesized that people who grow into anal characters were, as children, overly resistant to toilet training, often holding back their feces and prolonging the time of training beyond that usually required. This anal eroticism becomes transformed into the **anal triad** of *orderliness, stinginess,* and *obstinacy* that typifies the adult anal character.

Freud (1933/1964) believed that, for girls, anal eroticism is carried over into penis envy during the phallic stage and can eventually be expressed by giving birth to a baby. He also believed that in the unconscious the concepts of penis and baby—because both are referred to as a "little one"—mean the same thing. Also, feces, because of its elongated shape and because it has been removed from the body, is indistinguishable from baby, and all three concepts—penis, baby, and feces—are represented by the same symbols in dreams.

During the oral and anal stages, no basic distinction exists between male and female psychosexual growth. Children of either gender can develop an active or a passive orientation. The active attitude often is characterized by what Freud (1933/1964) considered the masculine qualities of dominance and sadism, whereas the passive orientation is usually marked by the feminine qualities of voyeurism and masochism. However, either orientation, or any combination of the two, can develop in both girls and boys.

Phallic Phase

At approximately 3 or 4 years of age, children begin a third stage of infantile development—the **phallic phase,** a time when the genital area becomes the leading erogenous zone. This stage is marked for the first time by a dichotomy between male and female development, a distinction that Freud (1925/1961) believed to be due to the anatomical differences between the sexes. Freud (1924/1961, p. 178) took Napoleon's remark that "History is destiny" and changed it to "Anatomy is destiny." This dictum underlies Freud's belief that physical differences between males and females account for many important psychological differences.

Masturbation, which originated during the oral stage, now enters a second, more crucial phase. During the phallic stage, masturbation is nearly universal, but because parents generally suppress these activities, children usually repress their conscious desire to masturbate by the time their phallic period comes to an end. Just as children's earlier experiences with weaning and toilet training helped shape the foundation of their psychosexual development, so too does their experience with the *suppression of masturbation* (Freud, 1933/1964). However, their experience with the Oedipus complex plays an even more crucial role in their personality development.

Male Oedipus Complex   Freud (1925/1961) believed that preceding the phallic stage an infant boy forms an *identification* with his father; that is, he wants to be his father. Later he develops a sexual desire for his mother; that is, he wants to *have* his mother. These two wishes do not appear mutually contradictory to the underdeveloped ego, so they are able to exist side by side for a time. When the boy finally recognizes their inconsistency, he gives up his identification with his father and retains the stronger feeling—the desire to have his mother. The boy now sees his father as a rival for the mother's love. He desires to do away with his father and possess his mother in a sexual relationship. This condition of rivalry toward the father and incestuous feelings toward the mother is known as the simple male **Oedipus complex.** The term is taken from the Greek tragedy by Sophocles in which Oedipus, King of Thebes, is destined by fate to kill his father and marry his mother.

Freud (1923/1961a) believed that the bisexual nature of the child (of either gender) complicates this picture. Before a young boy enters the Oedipus stage, he develops some amount of a feminine disposition. During the Oedipal period, therefore, his feminine nature may lead him to display *affection toward his father* and express *hostility toward his mother,* while at the same time his masculine tendency disposes him toward hostility for father and lust for mother. During this ambivalent condition, known as the *complete Oedipus complex,* affection and hostility coexist because one or both feelings may be unconscious. Freud believed that these feelings of ambivalence in a boy play a role in the evolution of the **castration complex,** which for boys takes the form of **castration anxiety** or the fear of losing the penis.

To Freud (1905/1953b, 1917/1963, 1923/1961b), the castration complex begins after a young boy (who has assumed that all other people, including girls, have genitals like his own) becomes aware of the absence of a penis on girls. This awareness becomes the greatest emotional shock of his life. After a period of mental struggle and attempts at denial, the young boy is forced to conclude that the girl has had her penis cut off. This belief may be reinforced by parental threats to punish the boy for his sexual behaviors. The boy is then forced to conclude that the little girl has been punished by having her penis removed because she masturbated or because she seduced her mother. For the boy, the threat of castration now becomes a dreaded possibility. Because this castration anxiety cannot long be tolerated, the boy represses his impulses toward sexual activity, including his fantasies of carrying out a seduction of his mother.

Prior to his sudden experience of castration anxiety, the little boy may have "seen" the genital area of little girls or his mother, but this sight does not automatically instigate the castration complex. Castration anxiety bursts forth only when the boy's ego is mature enough to comprehend the connection between sexual desires and the removal of the penis.

Freud believed that castration anxiety was present in all boys, even those not personally threatened with the removal of their penis or the stunting of its growth. According to Freud (1933/1964), a boy does not need to receive a clear threat of castration. Any mention of injury or shrinkage in connection with the penis is sufficient to activate the child's phylogenetic endowment. *Phylogenetic endowment* is capable of filling the gaps of our individual experiences with the inherited experiences of our ancestors. Ancient man's fear of castration supports the individual child's experiences and results in universal castration anxiety. Freud stated: "It is not a question of whether castration is really carried out; what is decisive is that the danger threatens from the outside and that the child believes in it." He went on to say that

> hints at . . . punishment must regularly find a phylogenetic reinforcement in him. It is our suspicion that during the human family's primaeval period castration used actually to be carried out by a jealous and cruel father upon growing boys, and that circumcision, which so frequently plays a part in puberty rites among primitive peoples, is a clearly recognizable relic of it. (pp. 86–87)

Once his Oedipus complex is dissolved or repressed, the boy surrenders his incestuous desires, changes them into feelings of tender love, and begins to develop a primitive superego. He may identify with either the father or the mother, depending on the strength of his feminine disposition. Normally identification is with the father, but it is not the same as pre-Oedipal identification. The boy no longer wants to be his father; instead, he uses his father as a model for determining right and wrong behavior. He introjects or incorporates his father's authority into his own ego, thereby sowing the seeds of a mature superego. The budding superego takes over his father's prohibitions against incest and ensures the continued repression of the Oedipus complex (Freud, 1933/1964).

Female Oedipus Complex   The phallic phase takes a more complicated path for girls than for boys, and these differences are due to anatomical differences between the sexes (Freud, 1925/1961). Like boys, pre-Oedipal girls assume that all other children have genitals similar to their own. Soon they discover that boys not only possess different genital equipment, but apparently something extra. Girls then become envious of this appendage, feel cheated, and desire to have a penis. This experience of **penis envy** is a powerful force in the formation of girls' personality. Unlike castration anxiety in boys, which is quickly repressed, penis envy may last for years in one form or another. Freud (1933/1964) believed that penis envy is often expressed as a wish to be a boy or a desire to have a man. Almost universally, it is carried over into a wish to have a baby, and eventually it may find expression in the act of giving birth to a baby, especially a boy.

Preceding the castration complex, a girl establishes an identification with her mother similar to that developed by a boy; that is, she fantasizes being seduced by her mother. These incestuous feelings, according to Freud (1933/1964), are later turned into hostility when the girl holds her mother responsible for bringing her into the world without a penis. Her libido is then turned toward her father, who can satisfy her wish for a penis by giving her a baby, an object that to her has become a substitute for the phallus. The desire for sexual intercourse with the father and accompanying feelings of hostility for the mother are known as the *simple female Oedipus complex.* Incidentally, Freud (1920/1955b, 1931/1961) objected to the term *Electra complex,* sometimes used by others when referring to the female Oedipus complex, because it suggests a direct parallel between male and female development during the phallic stage. Freud believed that no such parallel exists and that differences in anatomy determine different courses in male and female sexual development after the phallic stage.

Not all girls, however, transfer their sexual interest onto their father and develop hostility toward their mother. Freud (1931/1961, 1933/1964) suggested that when pre-Oedipal girls acknowledge their castration and recognize their inferiority to boys, they will rebel in one of three ways. First, they may give up their sexuality— both the feminine and the masculine dispositions—and develop an intense hostility toward their mother; second, they may cling defiantly to their masculinity, hoping for a penis and fantasizing being a man; and third, they may develop normally: that is, they may take their father as a sexual choice and undergo the simple Oedipus complex. A girl's choice is influenced in part by her inherent bisexuality and the degree of masculinity she developed during the pre-Oedipal period.

The simple female Oedipus complex is resolved when a girl gives up masturbatory activity, surrenders her sexual desire for her father, and identifies once again with her mother. However, the female Oedipus complex is usually broken up more slowly and less completely than is the male's. Because the superego is built from the relics of the shattered Oedipus complex, Freud (1924/1961, 1933/1964) believed that the girl's superego is usually weaker, more flexible, and less severe than the boy's. The reason the girl's superego is not as strict as the boy's is traceable to the difference between the sexes during their Oedipal histories. For boys, castration anxiety follows the Oedipus complex, breaks it up nearly completely, and renders unnecessary the continued expenditure of psychic energy on its remnants. Once the Oedipus complex is shattered, energy used to maintain it is free to establish a superego. For girls, however, the Oedipus complex *follows* the castration complex (penis envy), and because girls do not experience a threat of castration, they experience no traumatic sudden shock. The female Oedipus complex is only incompletely resolved by the girl's gradual realization that she may lose the love of her mother and that sexual intercourse with her father is not forthcoming. Her libido thus remains partially expended to maintain the castration complex and its relics, thereby blocking some psychic energy that might otherwise be used to build a strong superego (Freud, (1931/1961).

In summary, the female and male phallic stages take quite different routes. First, the castration complex for girls takes the form of penis envy—not castration anxiety. Second, penis envy *precedes* the female Oedipus complex, whereas for boys the opposite is true; that is, the castration anxiety *follows* the male Oedipus complex. Third, because penis envy takes place prior to the female Oedipus complex, little girls do not experience a traumatic event comparable to boys' castration anxiety. Fourth, because girls do not experience this traumatic event, the female Oedipus complex is more slowly and less completely dissolved than the male Oedipus complex.

The simple male and female Oedipus complexes are summarized in Table 2.1.

Freud presented his views on the female Oedipus complex more tentatively than he did his ideas regarding the male phallic stage. Although he framed these views on femininity in a tentative and provisional manner, he soon began to vigorously defend them. When some of his followers objected to his harsh view of women, Freud became even more adamant in his position and insisted that psychological differences between men and women could not be erased by culture because they were the inevitable consequences of anatomical differences between the sexes (Freud, 1925/1961). This rigid public stance on feminine development has led some writers (Brannon, 2005; Breger, 2000; Chodorow, 1989, 1991, 1994; Irigaray, 1986; Krausz, 1994) to criticize him as being sexist and uncomplimentary to women.

Despite his steadfast public position, Freud privately was uncertain that his views on women represented a final answer. One year after his pronouncement that "anatomy is destiny," he expressed some doubts, admitting that his understanding of girls and women was incomplete. "We know less about the sexual life of little girls than of boys. But we need not feel ashamed of this distinction; after all, the sexual life of adult women is a 'dark continent' for psychology" (Freud 1926/1959b, p. 212).

TABLE 2.1

Parallel Paths of the Simple Male and Female Phallic Phases

Male Phallic Phase	Female Phallic Phase
1. *Oedipus complex* (sexual desires for the mother/hostility for the father)	1. *Castration complex* in the form of *penis envy*
2. *Castration complex* in the form of *castration anxiety* shatters the Oedipus complex	2. *Oedipus complex* develops as an attempt to obtain a penis (sexual desires for the father; hostility for the mother)
3. *Identification* with the father	3. Gradual realization that the Oedipal desires are self-defeating
4. Strong *superego* replaces the nearly completely dissolved Oedipus complex	4. *Identification* with the mother
	5. Weak *superego* replaces the partially dissolved Oedipus complex

Throughout his career, Freud often proposed theories without much clinical or experimental evidence to support them. He would later come to see most of these theories as established facts, even though he possessed no intervening substantiating evidence. For as long as he lived, however, he remained doubtful of the absolute validity of his theories on women. Freud once admitted to his friend Marie Bonaparte that he did not understand women: "The great question that has never been answered and which I have not yet been able to answer, despite my thirty years of research into the feminine soul is 'What does a woman want?'" (E. Jones, 1955, p. 421). Such a question posed after many years of theorizing suggests that Freud regarded women not only as quite different from men, but as enigmas, not comprehensible to the male gender.

 Beyond Biography   **Did Freud misunderstand women? For information on Freud's lifelong struggle to understand women, see our website at** *www.mhhe.com/feist7*

Latency Period

Freud believed that, from the 4th or 5th year until puberty, both boys and girls usually, but not always, go through a period of dormant psychosexual development. This *latency stage* is brought about partly by parents' attempts to punish or discourage sexual activity in their young children. If parental suppression is successful, children will repress their sexual drive and direct their psychic energy toward school, friendships, hobbies, and other nonsexual activities.

However, the latency stage may also have roots in our phylogenetic endowment. Freud (1913/1953, 1926/1951b) suggested that the Oedipus complex and the subsequent period of sexual latency might be explained by the following hypothesis. Early in human development, people lived in families headed by a powerful father who reserved all sexual relationships to himself and who killed or drove away his sons, whom he saw as a threat to his authority. Then one day the sons joined together, overwhelmed, killed, and devoured (ate) their father. However, the brothers were individually too weak to take over their father's heritage, so they banded together in a clan or totem and established prohibitions against what they had just done; that is, they outlawed both killing one's father and having sexual relations with female members of one's family. Later, when they became fathers, they suppressed sexual activity in their own children whenever it became noticeable, probably around 3 or 4 years of age. When suppression became complete, it led to a period of sexual latency. After this experience was repeated over a period of many generations, it became an active though unconscious force in an individual's psychosexual development. Thus, the prohibition of sexual activity is part of our phylogenetic endowment and needs no personal experiences of punishment for sexual activities to repress the sexual drive. Freud (1926/1951b) merely suggested this hypothesis as one possible explanation for the latency period, and he was careful to point out that it was unsupported by anthropological data.

Continued latency is reinforced through constant suppression by parents and teachers and by internal feelings of shame, guilt, and morality. The sexual drive, of course, still exists during latency, but its aim has been inhibited. The sublimated libido now shows itself in social and cultural accomplishments. During this time children form groups or cliques, an impossibility during the infantile period when the sexual drive was completely autoerotic.

Genital Period

Puberty signals a reawakening of the sexual aim and the beginning of the *genital period*. During puberty, the diphasic sexual life of a person enters a second stage, which has basic differences from the infantile period (Freud, 1923/1961b). First, adolescents give up autoeroticism and direct their sexual energy toward another person instead of toward themselves. Second, reproduction is now possible. Third, although penis envy may continue to linger in girls, the vagina finally obtains the same status for them that the penis had for them during infancy. Parallel to this, boys now see the female organ as a sought-after object rather than a source of trauma. Fourth, the entire sexual drive takes on a more complete organization, and the component drives that had operated somewhat independently during the early infantile period gain a kind of synthesis during adolescence; thus, the mouth, anus, and other pleasure-producing areas take an auxiliary position to the genitals, which now attain supremacy as an erogenous zone.

This synthesis of Eros, the elevated status of the vagina, the reproductive capacity of the sexual drive, and ability of people to direct their libido outward rather than onto the self represent the major distinctions between infantile and adult sexuality. In several other ways, however, Eros remains unchanged. It may continue to be repressed, sublimated; or expressed in masturbation or other sexual acts. The subordinated erogenous zones also continue as vehicles of erotic pleasure. The mouth, for example, retains many of its infantile activities; a person may discontinue thumb sucking but may add smoking or prolonged kissing.

Maturity

The genital period begins at puberty and continues throughout the individual's lifetime. It is a stage attained by everyone who reaches physical maturity. In addition to the genital stage, Freud alluded to but never fully conceptualized a period of *psychological maturity,* a stage attained after a person has passed through the earlier developmental periods in an ideal manner. Unfortunately, psychological maturity seldom happens, because people have too many opportunities to develop pathological disorders or neurotic predispositions.

Although Freud never fully conceptualized the notion of psychological maturity, we can draw a sketch of psychoanalytically mature individuals. Such people would have a balance among the structures of the mind, with their ego controlling their id and superego but at the same time allowing for reasonable desires and demands (see Figure 2.3). Therefore, their id impulses would be expressed honestly and consciously with no traces of shame or guilt, and their superego would move beyond parental identification and control with no remnants of antagonism or incest. Their ego-ideal would be realistic and congruent with their ego, and in fact, the boundary between their superego and their ego would become nearly imperceptible.

Consciousness would play a more important role in the behavior of mature people, who would have only a minimal need to repress sexual and aggressive urges.

Indeed, most of the repressions of psychologically healthy individuals would emerge in the form of sublimations rather than neurotic symptoms. Because the Oedipus complex of mature people is completely or nearly completely dissolved, their libido, which formerly was directed toward parents, would be released to search for both tender and sensual love. In short, psychologically mature people would come through the experiences of childhood and adolescence in control of their psychic energy and with their ego functioning in the center of an ever-expanding world of consciousness.

Applications of Psychoanalytic Theory

Freud was an innovative speculator, probably more concerned with theory building than with treating sick people. He spent much of his time conducting therapy not only to help patients but to gain the insight into human personality necessary to expound psychoanalytic theory. This section looks at Freud's early therapeutic technique, his later technique, and his views on dreams and unconscious slips.

Freud's Early Therapeutic Technique

Prior to his use of the rather passive psychotherapeutic technique of free association, Freud had relied on a much more active approach. In *Studies on Hysteria* (Breuer & Freud, 1895/1955), Freud described his technique of extracting repressed childhood memories:

> I placed my hand on the patient's forehead or took her head between my hands and said: "You will think of it under the pressure of my hand. At the moment at which I relax my pressure you will see something in front of you or something will come into your head. Catch hold of it. It will be what we are looking for.— Well, what have you seen or what has occurred to you?"
>
> On the first occasions on which I made use of this procedure . . . I myself was surprised to find that it yielded me the precise results that I needed. (pp. 110–111)

Indeed, such a highly suggestive procedure was very likely to yield the precise results Freud needed, namely, the confession of a childhood seduction. Moreover, while using both dream interpretation and hypnosis, Freud told his patients to expect that scenes of childhood sexual experiences would come forth (Freud, 1896/1962).

In his autobiography written nearly 30 years after he abandoned his seduction theory, Freud (1925/1959) stated that under the pressure technique, a majority of his patients reproduced childhood scenes in which they were sexually seduced by some adult. When he was obliged to recognize that "these scenes of seduction had never taken place, and that they were only phantasies which my patients had made up or which *I myself had perhaps forced upon them* [italics added], I was for some time completely at a loss" (p. 34). He was at a loss, however, for a very short time. Within days after his September 21, 1897, letter to Fliess, he concluded that "the neurotic symptoms were not related directly to actual events but to phantasies. . . . I had in fact stumbled for the first time upon the *Oedipus complex*" (Freud, 1925/1959, p. 34).

Freud's consulting room.

In time, Freud came to realize that his highly suggestive and even coercive tactics may have elicited memories of seduction from his patients and that he lacked clear evidence that these memories were real. Freud became increasingly convinced that neurotic symptoms were related to childhood *fantasies* rather than to material reality, and he gradually adopted a more passive psychotherapeutic technique.

Freud's Later Therapeutic Technique

The primary goal of Freud's later psychoanalytic therapy was to uncover repressed memories through free association and dream analysis. "Our therapy works by transforming what is unconscious into what is conscious, and it works only in so far as it is in a position to effect that transformation" (Freud, 1917/1963, p. 280). More specifically, the purpose of psychoanalysis is "to strengthen the ego, to make it more independent of the superego, to widen its field of perception and enlarge its organization, so that it can appropriate fresh portions of the id. Where id was, there ego shall be" (Freud, 1933/1964, p. 80).

With **free association,** patients are required to verbalize every thought that comes to their mind, no matter how irrelevant or repugnant it may appear. The purpose of free association is to arrive at the unconscious by starting with a present conscious idea and following it through a train of associations to wherever it leads. The process is not easy and some patients never master it. For this reason, *dream analysis* remained a favorite therapeutic technique with Freud. (We discuss dream analysis in the next section.)

In order for analytic treatment to be successful, libido previously expended on the neurotic symptom must be freed to work in the service of the ego. This takes place in a two-phase procedure. "In the first, all the libido is forced from the symptoms into the transference and concentrated there; in the second, the struggle is waged around this new object and the libido is liberated from it" (Freud, 1917/1963, p. 455).

The transference situation is vital to psychoanalysis. **Transference** refers to the strong sexual or aggressive feelings, positive or negative, that patients develop toward their analyst during the course of treatment. Transference feelings are unearned by the therapist and are merely transferred to her or him from patients' earlier experiences, usually with their parents. In other words, patients feel toward the analyst the same way they previously felt toward one or both parents. As long as these feelings manifest themselves as interest or love, transference does not interfere with the process of treatment but is a powerful ally to the therapeutic progress. Positive transference permits patients to more or less relive childhood experiences within the nonthreatening climate of the analytic treatment. However, **negative transference** in the form of hostility must be recognized by the therapist and explained to patients so that they can overcome any **resistance** to treatment (Freud, 1905/1953a, 1917/1963). Resistance, which refers to a variety of unconscious responses used by patients to block their own progress in therapy, can be a positive sign because it indicates that therapy has advanced beyond superficial material.

Freud (1933/1964) noted several limitations of psychoanalytic treatment. First, not all old memories can or should be brought into consciousness. Second, treatment is not as effective with **psychoses** or with constitutional illnesses as it is with phobias, hysterias, and obsessions. A third limitation, by no means peculiar to psychoanalysis, is that a patient, once cured, may later develop another psychic problem. Recognizing these limitations, Freud felt that psychoanalysis could be used in conjunction with other therapies. However, he repeatedly insisted that it could not be shortened or modified in any essential way.

Ideally, when analytic treatment is successful, patients no longer suffer from debilitating symptoms, they use their psychic energy to perform ego functions, and they have an expanded ego that includes previously repressed experiences. They do not experience a major personality change, but they do become what they might have been under the most favorable conditions.

Dream Analysis

Freud used **dream analysis** to transform the manifest content of dreams to the more important latent content. The **manifest content** of a dream is the surface meaning or the conscious description given by the dreamer, whereas the **latent content** refers to its unconscious material.

The basic assumption of Freud's dream analysis is that nearly all dreams are *wish fulfillments*. Some wishes are obvious and are expressed through the manifest content, as when a person goes to sleep hungry and dreams of eating large quantities of delicious food. Most wish fulfillments, however, are expressed in the latent content and only dream interpretation can uncover that wish. An exception to the rule that dreams are wish fulfillments is found in patients suffering from a traumatic experience. Dreams of these people follow the principle of **repetition compulsion** rather than wish fulfillment. These dreams are frequently found in people with

posttraumatic stress disorder who repeatedly dream of frightening or traumatic experiences (Freud, 1920/1955a, 1933/1964).

Freud believed that dreams are formed in the unconscious but try to work their way into the conscious. To become conscious, dreams must slip past both the primary and the final censors (refer again to Figure 2.1). Even during sleep these guardians maintain their vigil, forcing unconscious psychic material to adopt a disguised form. The disguise can operate in two basic ways—condensation and displacement.

Condensation refers to the fact that the manifest dream content is not as extensive as the latent level, indicating that the unconscious material has been abbreviated or condensed before appearing on the manifest level. *Displacement* means that the dream image is replaced by some other idea only remotely related to it (Freud, 1900/1953). Condensation and displacement of content both take place through the use of symbols. Certain images are almost universally represented by seemingly innocuous figures. For example, the phallus may be symbolized by elongated objects such as sticks, snakes, or knives; the vagina often appears as any small box, chest, or oven; parents appear in the form of the president, a teacher, or one's boss; and castration anxiety can be expressed in dreams of growing bald, losing teeth, or any act of cutting (Freud, 1900/1953, 1901/1953, 1917/1963).

Dreams can also deceive the dreamer by inhibiting or reversing the dreamer's affect. For example, a man with homicidal feelings for his father may dream that his father has died, but in the manifest dream content, he feels neither joy nor sorrow; that is, his affect is inhibited. Unpleasant feelings can also be reversed at the manifest dream level. For example, a woman who unconsciously hates her mother and would unconsciously welcome her extinction may dream of her mother's death, but the unconscious joy and hatred she feels is expressed as sorrow and love during the manifest level of the dream. Thus, she is fooled into believing that hate is love and that joy is sorrow (Freud, 1900/1953, 1901/1953, 1915/1957a).

After the dream's latent (unconscious) content has been distorted and its affect inhibited or reversed, it appears in a manifest form that can be recalled by the dreamer. The manifest content, which nearly always relates to conscious or preconscious experience of the previous day, has little or no psychoanalytic significance; only the latent content has meaning (Freud, 1900/1953).

In interpreting dreams, Freud (1917/1963) ordinarily followed one of two methods. The first was to ask patients to relate their dream and all their associations to it, no matter how unrelated or illogical these associations seemed. Freud believed that such associations revealed the unconscious wish behind the dream. If the dreamer was unable to relate association material, Freud used a second method— dream symbols—to discover the unconscious elements underlying the manifest content. The purpose of both methods (associations and symbols) was to trace the dream formation backward until the latent content was reached. Freud (1900/1953, p. 608) believed that dream interpretation was the most reliable approach to the study of unconscious processes and referred to it as the "royal road" to knowledge of the unconscious.

Anxiety dreams offer no contradiction to the rule that dreams are wish fulfillments. The explanation is that anxiety belongs to the preconscious system, whereas the wish belongs to the unconscious. Freud (1900/1953) reported three typical anxiety dreams: the embarrassment dream of nakedness, dreams of the death of a beloved person, and dreams of failing an examination.

In the embarrassment dream of nakedness, the dreamer feels shame or embarrassment at being naked or improperly dressed in the presence of strangers. The spectators usually appear quite indifferent, although the dreamer is very much embarrassed. The origin of this dream is the early childhood experience of being naked in the presence of adults. In the original experience, the child feels no embarrassment but the adults often register disapproval. Freud believed that wish fulfillment is served in two ways by this dream. First, the indifference of the spectators fulfills the infantile wish that the witnessing adults refrain from scolding. Second, the fact of nakedness fulfills the wish to exhibit oneself, a desire usually repressed in adults but present in young children.

Dreams of the death of a beloved person also originate in childhood and are wish fulfillments. If a person dreams of the death of a younger person, the unconscious may be expressing the wish for the destruction of a younger brother or sister who was a hated rival during the infantile period. When the deceased is an older person, the dreamer is fulfilling the Oedipal wish for the death of a parent. If the dreamer feels anxiety and sorrow during the dream, it is because the affect has been reversed. Dreams of the death of a parent are typical in adults, but they do not mean that the dreamer has a present wish for the death of that parent. These dreams were interpreted by Freud as meaning that, as a child, the dreamer longed for the death of the parent, but the wish was too threatening to find its way into consciousness. Even during adulthood the death wish ordinarily does not appear in dreams unless the affect has been changed to sorrow.

A third typical anxiety dream is failing an examination in school. According to Freud (1900/1953), the dreamer always dreams of failing an examination that has already been successfully passed, never one that was failed. These dreams usually occur when the dreamer is anticipating a difficult task. By dreaming of failing an examination already passed, the ego can reason, "I passed the earlier test that I was worried about. Now I'm worried about another task, but I'll pass it too. Therefore, I need not be anxious over tomorrow's test." The wish to be free from worry over a difficult task is thus fulfilled.

With each of these three typical dreams, Freud had to search for the wish behind the manifest level of the dream. Finding the wish fulfillment required great creativity. For example, one clever woman told Freud that she had dreamed that her mother-in-law was coming for a visit. In her waking life, she despised her mother-in-law and dreaded spending any amount of time with her. To challenge Freud's notion that dreams are wish fulfillments, she asked him, "Where was the wish?" Freud's (1900/1953) explanation was that this woman was aware of Freud's belief that a wish lies behind every nontraumatic dream. Thus, by dreaming of spending time with a hated mother-in-law, the woman fulfilled her wish to spite Freud and to disprove his wish fulfillment hypothesis!

In summary, Freud believed that dreams are motivated by wish fulfillments. The latent content of dreams is formed in the unconscious and usually goes back to childhood experiences, whereas the manifest content often stems from experiences of the previous day. The interpretation of dreams serves as the "royal road" to knowledge of the unconscious, but dreams should not be interpreted without the dreamer's associations to the dream. Latent material is transformed into manifest content through the dream work. The dream work achieves its goal by the processes of condensation, displacement, and inhibition of affect. The manifest dream may have little resemblance to the latent material, but Freud believed that an accurate interpretation will reveal the hidden connection by tracing the dream work backward until the unconscious images are revealed.

Freudian Slips

Freud believed that many everyday slips of the tongue or pen, misreading, incorrect hearing, misplacing objects, and temporarily forgetting names or intentions are not chance accidents but reveal a person's unconscious intentions. In writing of these faulty acts, Freud (1901/1960) used the German *Fehlleistung,* or "faulty function," but James Strachey, one of Freud's translators, invented the term **parapraxes** to refer to what many people now simply call "Freudian slips."

Parapraxes or unconscious slips are so common that we usually pay little attention to them and deny that they have any underlying significance. Freud, however, insisted that these faulty acts have meaning; they reveal the unconscious intention of the person: "They are not chance events but serious mental acts; they have a sense; they arise from the concurrent actions—or perhaps rather, the mutually opposing action—of two different intentions" (Freud, 1917/1963, p. 44). One opposing action emanates from the unconscious; the other, from the preconscious. Unconscious slips, therefore, are similar to dreams in that they are a product of both the unconscious and the preconscious, with the unconscious intention being dominant and interfering with and replacing the preconscious one.

The fact that most people strongly deny any meaning behind their parapraxes was seen by Freud as evidence that the slip, indeed, had relevance to unconscious images that must remain hidden from consciousness. A young man once walked into a convenience store, became immediately attracted to the young female clerk, and asked for a "sex-pack of beer." When the clerk accused him of improper behavior, the young man vehemently protested his innocence. Examples such as this can be extended almost indefinitely. Freud provided many in his book *Psychopathology of Everyday Life* (1901/1960), and many of them involved his own faulty acts. One day after worrying about monetary matters, Freud strolled the tobacco store that he visited every day. On this particular day, he picked up his usual supply of cigars and left the store without paying for them. Freud attributed his neglect to earlier thoughts about budgetary issues. In all Freudian slips, the intentions of the unconscious supplant the weaker intentions of the preconscious, thereby revealing a person's true purpose.

Related Research

The scientific status of Freud's theory is one of the more hotly contested and disputed questions in all Freudian theory. Was it science or mere armchair speculation? Did Freud propose testable hypotheses? Are his ideas experimentally verifiable, testable, or falsifiable?

Karl Popper, the philosopher of science who proposed the criterion of falsifiability, contrasted Freud's theory with Einstein's and concluded that the former was not falsifiable and therefore not science. It would be fair to say that for much of the 20th century, most academic psychologists dismissed Freudian ideas as fanciful speculations that may have contained insights into human nature but were not science.

During the last 5 to 10 years, the scientific status of Freudian theory has begun to change, at least among certain circles of cognitive psychologists and neuroscientists. Neuroscience is currently experiencing an explosive growth through its investigations of brain activity during a variety of cognitive and emotional tasks. Much of this growth has been due to brain imaging technology afforded by functional magnetic resonance imaging (MRI) that maps regions of the brain that are active during particular tasks. At about the same time, certain groups of cognitive psychologists began doing research on the importance of nonconscious processing of information and memory, or what they called "implicit" cognition. John Bargh, one of the leaders in the field of social-cognitive psychology, reviewed the literature on the "automaticity of being" and concluded that roughly 95% of our behaviors are unconsciously determined (Bargh & Chartrand, 1999). This conclusion is completely consistent with Freud's metaphor that consciousness is merely the "tip of the iceberg."

By the late 1990s, the findings from neuroscience and cognitive psychology began to converge on many cognitive and affective processes that were very consistent with basic Freudian theory. These commonalties have become the foundation for a movement started by some cognitive psychologists, neuroscientists, and psychiatrists who are convinced that Freud's theory is one of the more compelling integrative theories—one that could explain many of these findings. In 1999, a group of scientists began a society called Neuro-Psychoanalysis and a scientific journal by the same name. For the first time, some eminent cognitive and neuroscience psychologists such as Nobel laureate for physiology, Eric Kandel, along with Joseph LeDoux, Antonio Damasio, Daniel Schacter, and Vilayanur Ramachandran, were publicly declaring the value of Freud's theory and contending that "psychoanalysis is still the most coherent and intellectually satisfying view of the mind" (as cited in Solms, 2004, p. 84). Neuroscientist Antonio Damasio wrote: "I believe we can say that Freud's insights on the nature of consciousness are consonant with the most advanced contemporary neuroscience views" (as cited in Solms & Turnbull, 2002, p. 93). Twenty years ago, such pronouncements from neuroscientists would have been nearly unthinkable.

Mark Solms is probably the most active person involved in integrating psychoanalytic theory and neuroscientific research (Solms 2000, 2004; Solms & Turnbull, 2002). He argued, for instance, that the following Freudian concepts have support from modern neuroscience: unconscious motivation, repression, the pleasure principle, primitive drives, and dreams (Solms, 2004). Similarly, Kandel (1999) argued that psychoanalysis and neuroscience together could make useful contributions in these eight domains: the nature of unconscious mental processes; the nature of psychological causality; psychological causality and psychopathology; early experience and the predisposition to mental illness; the preconscious, the unconscious, and the prefrontal cortex; sexual orientation; psychotherapy and structural changes in the brain; and psychopharmacology as an adjunct to psychoanalysis.

Although there are some gaps in the evidence (Hobson, 2004), the overlap between Freud's theory and neuroscience is sufficient to make at least a suggestive, if not compelling, case for their integration. We have reviewed some of the empirical evidence for unconscious mental processing, the id and the pleasure principle and the ego and the reality principle, repression and defense mechanisms, and dreams.

Unconscious Mental Processing

Many scientists and philosophers have recognized two different forms of consciousness. First is the state of not being aware or awake, and second is the state of being aware. The former is referred to as "core consciousness," whereas the latter is referred to as "extended consciousness." The brain stem, and the ascending activating system in particular, is the part of the brain most directly associated with core consciousness, or unconsciousness in the sense of not being awake. For instance, comas come from damage to this region of the brain stem and render a person unconscious. In contrast, being aware and able to reflect on one's knowledge and self is more a function of activity in the prefrontal cortex (the dorsal frontal cortex) (Solms, 2004; Solms & Turnbull, 2002).

Moreover, a major theme of cognitive psychology over the last 20 years has been the phenomenon of nonconscious mental processing, or what is referred to as "implicit," "nonconscious," or "automatic" thought and memory (Bargh & Chartrand, 1999; Schacter, 1987). By this, cognitive psychologists are referring to mental processes that are neither in awareness nor under intentional control, and thereby come close to Freud's definition of unconscious. Of course, Freud's concept of the unconscious was more dynamic, repressive, and inhibiting, but—as we see next—cognitive neuroscience is uncovering a similar kind of unconscious.

Pleasure and the Id: Inhibition and the Ego

Findings from many different neuroscientific programs of research have established that the pleasure-seeking drives have their neurological origins in two brain structures, namely the brain stem and the limbic system (Solms, 2004; Solms & Turnbull, 2002). Moreover, the neurotransmitter dopamine is most centrally involved in most pleasure-seeking behaviors. In Freud's language, these are the drives and instincts of the id.

In 1923, when Freud modified his view of how the mind works and proposed the structural view of id, ego, and superego, the ego became a structure that was mostly unconscious, but whose main function was to inhibit drives. If the part of the brain that functions to inhibit impulses and drives is damaged, we should see an increase in the id-based pleasure-seeking impulses. That is precisely what happens when the frontal-limbic system is damaged. Many case studies and more systematic brain-imaging research have demonstrated the connection between the frontal-limbic system and impulse regulation (Chow & Cummings, 1999; Pincus, 2001; Raine, Buchsbaum, & LaCasse, 1997). The first reported and best-known case of this was the 19th-century railroad worker Phineas Gage. While working on the railroad, an explosion caused a metal rod to shoot upward and through the bottom of his jaw up and out the top of his forehead, damaging his frontal lobes. Amazingly, perhaps because the speed of the rod cauterized brain tissue, Gage never lost consciousness and survived. Physically (except for loss of brain tissue) he was relatively fine, but his personality changed. By all accounts, this rather mild-mannered, responsible, and reliable worker became, in the words of his doctor, "fitful, irreverent, indulging at times in the grossest profanity (which was not previously his custom), manifesting but little deference for his fellows, impatient of restraint or advice when it conflicts with his desires, at times pertinaciously obstinate, yet capricious and vacillating" (as cited in Solms & Turnbull, 2002, p. 3). In other words, he became hostile, impulsive, and not at all concerned with social norms and appropriateness. In Freudian lingo, his ego no longer could inhibit basic drives and instincts and he became very id-driven.

According to Solms, the underlying theme in the frontal lobe-injured patients is their inability to stay "reality-bound" (ego) and their propensity to interpret events much more through "wishes" (id); that is, they create the reality they wanted or wished for. All of this, according to Solms, provides support for Freud's ideas concerning the pleasure principle of the id and the reality principle of the ego.

Repression, Inhibition, and Defense Mechanisms

Another core component of Freud's theory involved the defense mechanisms, especially repression. The unconscious actively (dynamically) keeps ideas, feelings, and unpleasant or threatening impulses out of consciousness. The area of defense mechanisms remains an active area of study for personality researchers. Some of this research has focused on the use of projection and identification in childhood and adolescence (Cramer, 2007), whereas other work has investigated who is more likely to be a target of projection (Govorun, Fuegen, & Payne, 2006).

From the neuropsychological perspective, Solms (2004) reports cases that explore the areas of the brain that may be implicated in the use and perseverance of defense mechanisms. Specifically, Solms (2004) describes cases demonstrating repression of unpalatable information when damage occurs to the right hemisphere and, if this damaged region becomes artificially stimulated, the repression goes away; that is, awareness returns. Additionally, these patients frequently rationalize away unwelcome facts by fabricating stories. In other words, they employ Freudian wish-fulfilling defense mechanisms. For instance, one patient, when asked about the scar on his head, confabulated a story about its being a result of dental surgery or a coronary bypass, both of which he had had years before. Furthermore, when the doctor asked this patient who he was, the patient would variously respond that he (the doctor) was either a colleague, a drinking partner, or a teammate from college. All of these interpretations were more wish than reality.

A study by Howard Shevrin and colleagues (Shevrin, Ghannam, & Libet, 2002) examined the neurophysiological underpinnings of repression. More specifically, they addressed the question of whether people with repressive personality styles actually require longer periods of stimulation for a brief stimulus to be consciously perceived. Prior research had established that people in general vary from 200 ms to 800 ms in how long a stimulus needs to be present before being consciously perceived. The study by Shevrin et al. included six clinical participants between the ages of 51 and 70, all of whom years prior had undergone surgical treatment for motoric problems (mainly parkinsonism). During these surgeries, a procedure had been performed in which electrodes stimulated parts of the motor cortex, and the length of time it took for the stimulus to be consciously perceived was recorded. The results of this procedure showed that these six participants also ranged from 200 ms to 800 ms in how long they took to consciously perceive the stimulus. For this, four psychological tests were administered at the patients' homes and then scored on their degree of repressive tendencies. These tests were the Rorschach Inkblot Test, the Early Memories Test, the Vocabulary Test of the WAIS (an IQ test), and the Hysteroid-Obsessoid Questionnaire. The first three tests were rated by three "blind" clinical judges on their degree of repression, and the fourth test was scored objectively for its degree of repression.

The results showed that the combined ratings from the three judges were significantly and positively associated with the time it took for a stimulus to be consciously perceived. Moreover, the objectively scored Hysteroid-Obsessoid Questionnaire confirmed the result. In other words, the more repressive style people have, the longer it takes them to consciously perceive a stimulus. Neither age nor IQ is related to the length of time it takes for the stimulus to be perceived. As the authors acknowledge, this finding is but a first step in demonstrating how repression might operate to keep things out of conscious awareness, but it is the first study to report the neurophysiological underpinnings of repression.

Research on Dreams

In the 1950s, when the phenomenon of rapid eye movement (REM) sleep was first discovered and found to be strongly associated with dreaming, many scientists began to discount Freud's theory of dreams, which was based on the idea that dreams have meaning and are attempts at fulfilling unconscious wishes. Moreover, the REM research showed that only brain-stem regions and not higher cortical regions were involved with REM states. If these cortical structures were not involved in REM sleep and yet they were where higher level thinking took place, then dreams are simply random mental activity and could not have any inherent meaning. From the perspective of this so-called activation-synthesis theory, meaning is what the waking mind gives to these more or less random brain activities, but meaning is not inherent in the dream.

Solms's primary research area is dreams and, based on current dream research, including his own, he takes issue with each of the assumptions of the activation-synthesis theory of dreams (Solms, 2000, 2004). Most importantly, Solms argued that dreaming and REM are not one and the same. First, in about 5% to 30% of the wakings during REM sleep, patients report no dreams, and during about 5% to 10% of non-REM wakings patients do report dreaming. So there is no one-to-one correspondence between REM and dreaming. Second, lesions (due to injury or surgery) to the brain stem do not completely eliminate dreaming, whereas lesions to the forebrain regions (in the frontal lobes and parietal-temporal-occipital juncture) have eliminated dreaming and yet preserved REM sleep.

In addition, dreams appear not to be random in content. Daniel Wegner and colleagues (2004) tested one aspect of Freud's theory of dreams. As Freud wrote in *Interpretation of Dreams,* "wishes suppressed during the day assert themselves in dreams" (1900/1953, p. 590). Wegner and colleagues examined whether this was so in a group of more than 300 college students. First, participants were instructed right before bed (they opened the instructions only directly before going to sleep) to think of two people, one whom they had had a "crush" on and one whom they were "fond of" but did not have a crush on.

Next, participants were assigned to one of three conditions: suppression, expression, and mention. In the suppression condition, students were instructed not to think about a target person (either the "crush" or the "fond of" person) for 5 minutes; in the expression condition, different participants were instructed to think about the target person during this 5-minute period; and in the mention condition, other participants were instructed to think about anything at all after noting (mentioning) the target person's initials. Moreover, during the 5-minute period when they were either to think or not think about the target person, they wrote a "stream-of-consciousness" report and put a check mark on the side of the report every time they thought of the target person. This was a validity check to establish whether the suppression manipulation technique worked. It did. When they awoke the next morning, participants reported whether they dreamed, and if so, how much they dreamed and how much they dreamed of the target and nontarget people (self-rated dreaming). Lastly, they wrote a report describing the dream (dream report). The stream-of-consciousness and dream reports were coded by a rater blind to conditions on frequency of target and nontarget appearances.

Results showed that students dreamed more about the suppressed targets than nonsuppressed ones; they also dreamed more about the suppressed targets than the suppressed nontargets. In other words, students were more likely to dream about people they spend some time thinking about (target), but especially those targets they actively try not to think about (suppression). Suppressed thoughts, the authors concluded, are likely to "rebound" and appear in dreams. This finding is quite consistent with Freud's theory and not consistent with the activation-synthesis theory that REM sleep provides random activation of brain activity that is devoid of meaning. In the words of Wegner et al. (2004), "although there remains much to be learned about how dreams are formed, the finding that suppressed thoughts rebound in dreams provides a bridge linking an early insight of psychoanalysis to the discoveries of cognitive neuroscience" (p. 236).

However, the current trends in neuropsychoanalytic research neither confirm nor even mention Freud's psychosexual stage theory, especially its more controversial elements of Oedipal conflicts, castration anxiety, and penis envy. Instead, neuropsychoanalytic research has focused on those parts of Freud's theory that appear to be empirically standing the test of time. The neglect of Freud's psychosexual stage theory is somewhat consistent with much post-Freudian and neo-Freudian theorizing that has either downplayed or abandoned this part of Freud's theory. So, while many of Freud's major ideas—unconscious, pleasure seeking, repression, id, ego, and dreams—might be garnering neuroscientific support, not all are, and still others are in need of modification.

One area that has recently received attention is the work of the dream censor (Boag, 2006). The dream censor, according to Freud (1917/1963), is the mechanism that converts the latent content of dreams into the more palatable and less frightening manifest content. Boag (2006) articulates how one conceptualization of the dream sensor is to think of it as a mechanism that engages in repression and/or inhibition. This conceptualization is helpful if one is interested in empirically testing Freud's notions regarding dreams because there is a large amount of neuroscience research on inhibition (Aron & Poldrack, 2005; Praamstra & Seiss, 2005). Specifically, Boag (2006) proposes that the basal ganglia and amygdala may be key brain structures responsible for dreams including the conversion of latent content into manifest content. Arguments such as Boag's (2006) and those of other scholars in the neuropsychoanalysis field make an out-of-hand dismissal of Freud from a scientific perspective more and more difficult as findings from cognitive psychology and neuroscience accumulate that support basic assumptions of Freud's theory.

Critique of Freud

In criticizing Freud, we must first ask two questions: (1) Did Freud understand women? (2) Was Freud a scientist?

Did Freud Understand Women?

A frequent criticism of Freud is that he did not understand women and that his theory of personality was strongly oriented toward men. There is a large measure of truth to this criticism, and Freud acknowledged that he lacked a complete understanding of the female psyche.

Why didn't Freud have a better understanding of the feminine psyche? One answer is that he was a product of his times, and society was dominated by men during those times. In 19th-century Austria, women were second-class citizens, with few rights or privileges. They had little opportunity to enter a profession or to be a member of a professional organization—such as Freud's Wednesday Psychological Society.

Thus, during the first quarter century of psychoanalysis, the movement was an all-men's club. After World War I, women gradually became attracted to psychoanalysis and some of these women, such as Marie Bonaparte, Ruth Mack Brunswick, Helene Deutsch, Melanie Klein, Lou Andreas-Salomé, and Anna Freud, were able to exercise some influence on Freud. However, they were never able to convince him that similarities between the genders outweighed differences.

Freud himself was a proper bourgeois Viennese gentleman whose sexual attitudes were fashioned during a time when women were expected to nurture their husbands, manage the household, care for the children, and stay out of their husband's business or profession. Freud's wife, Martha, was no exception to this rule (Gay, 1988).

Freud, as the oldest and most favored child, ruled over his sisters, advising them on books to read and lecturing to them about the world in general. An incident with a piano reveals further evidence of Freud's favored position within his family. Freud's sisters enjoyed music and found pleasure in playing a piano. When music from their piano annoyed Freud, he complained to his parents that he couldn't concentrate on his books. The parents immediately removed the piano from the house, leaving Freud to understand that the wishes of five girls did not equal the preference of one boy.

Like many other men of his day, Freud regarded women as the "tender sex," suitable for caring for the household and nurturing children but not equal to men in scientific and scholarly affairs. His love letters to his future wife Martha Bernays are filled with references to her as "my little girl," "my little woman," or "my princess" (Freud, 1960). Freud undoubtedly would have been surprised to learn that 130 years later these terms of endearment are seen by many as disparaging to women.

Freud continually grappled with trying to understand women, and his views on femininity changed several times during his lifetime. As a young student, he exclaimed to a friend, "How wise our educators that they pester the beautiful sex so little with scientific knowledge" (quoted in Gay, 1988, p. 522).

During the early years of his career, Freud viewed male and female psychosexual growth as mirror images of each other, with different but parallel lines of development. However, he later proposed the notion that little girls are failed boys and that adult women are akin to castrated men. Freud originally proposed these ideas tentatively, but as time passed, he defended them adamantly and refused to compromise his views. When people criticized his notion of femininity, Freud responded by adopting an increasingly more rigid stance. By the 1920s, he was insisting that psychological differences between men and women were due to anatomical differences and could not be explained by different socialization experiences (Freud, 1924/1961). Nevertheless, he always recognized that he did not understand women as well as he did men. He called them the "dark continent for psychology" (Freud, 1926/1959b, p. 212). In his final statement on the matter, Freud (1933/1964) suggested that "if you want to know more about femininity, enquire from your own experiences of life or turn to the poets" (p. 135).

Although some of Freud's close associates inhabited the "dark continent" of womanhood, his most intimate friends were men. Moreover, women such as Marie Bonaparte, Lou Andreas-Salomé, and Minna Bernays (his sister-in-law), who did exert some influence on Freud, were mostly cut from a similar pattern. Ernest Jones (1955) referred to them as intellectual women with a "masculine cast" (p. 421). These women were quite apart from Freud's mother and wife, both of whom were proper Viennese wives and mothers whose primary concerns were for their husbands and children. Freud's female colleagues and disciples were selected for their intelligence, emotional strength, and loyalty—the same qualities Freud found attractive in men. But none of these women could substitute for an intimate male friend. In August of 1901, Freud (1985) wrote to his friend Wilhelm Fliess, "In my life, as you know, woman has never replaced the comrade, the friend" (p. 447).

Why was Freud unable to understand women? Given his upbringing during the middle of the 19th century, parental acceptance of his domination of his sisters, a tendency to exaggerate differences between women and men, and his belief that women inhabited the "dark continent" of humanity, it seems unlikely that Freud possessed the necessary experiences to understand women. Toward the end of his life, he still had to ask, "What does a woman want?" (E. Jones, 1955, p. 421). The question itself reveals Freud's gender bias because it assumes that women all want the same things and that their wants are somehow different from those of men.

Was Freud a Scientist?

A second area of criticism of Freud centers around his status as a scientist. Although he repeatedly insisted that he was primarily a scientist and that psychoanalysis was a science, Freud's definition of science needs some explanation. When he called psychoanalysis a science, he was attempting to separate it from a philosophy or an ideology. He was not claiming that it was a natural science. The German language and culture of Freud's day made a distinction between a natural science (*Naturwissenschaften*) and a human science (*Geisteswissenschaften*). Unfortunately, James Strachey's translations in the *Standard Edition* make Freud seem to be a natural scientist. However, other scholars (Federn, 1988; Holder, 1988) believe that Freud clearly saw himself as a human scientist, that is, a humanist or scholar and not a natural scientist. In order to render Freud's works more accurate and more humanistic, a group of language scholars are currently producing an updated translation of Freud. (See, for example, Freud, 1905/2002.)

Bruno Bettelheim (1982, 1983) was also critical of Strachey's translations. He contended that the *Standard Edition* used precise medical concepts and misleading Greek and Latin terms instead of the ordinary, often ambiguous, German words that Freud had chosen. Such precision tended to render Freud more scientific and less humanistic than he appears to the German reader. For example, Bettelheim, whose introduction to Freud was in German, believed that Freud saw psychoanalytic therapy as a spiritual journey into the depths of the soul (translated by Strachey as "mind") and not a mechanistic analysis of the mental apparatus.

As a result of Freud's 19th-century German view of science, many contemporary writers regard his theory-building methods as untenable and rather unscientific (Breger, 2000; Crews, 1995, 1996; Sulloway, 1992; Webster, 1995). His theories were not based on experimental investigation but rather on subjective observations that Freud made of himself and his clinical patients. These patients were not representative of people in general but came mostly from the middle and upper classes.

Apart from this widespread popular and professional interest, the question remains: Was Freud scientific? Freud's (1915/1957a) own description of science permits much room for subjective interpretations and indefinite definitions:

> We have often heard it maintained that sciences should be built up on clear and sharply defined basic concepts. In actual fact no science, not even the most exact, begins with such definitions. The true beginning of scientific activity consists rather in describing phenomena and then in proceeding to group, classify and correlate them. Even at the stage of description it is not possible to avoid applying certain abstract ideas to the material in hand, ideas derived from somewhere or other but certainly not from the new observations alone. (p. 117)

Perhaps Freud himself left us with the best description of how he built his theories. In 1900, shortly after the publication of *Interpretation of Dreams,* he wrote to his friend Wilhelm Fliess, confessing that "I am actually not at all a man of science, not an observer, not an experimenter, not a thinker. I am by temperament nothing but a conquistador—an adventurer . . . with all the curiosity, daring, and tenacity characteristic of a man of this sort" (Freud, 1985, p. 398).

Although Freud at times may have seen himself as a conquistador, he also believed that he was constructing a scientific theory. How well does that theory meet the six criteria for a useful theory that we identified in Chapter 1?

Despite serious difficulties in testing Freud's assumptions, researchers have conducted studies that relate either directly or indirectly to psychoanalytic theory. Thus, we rate Freudian theory about average in its ability to *generate research.*

Second, a useful theory should be *falsifiable.* Because much of the research evidence consistent with Freud's ideas can also be explained by other models, Freudian theory is nearly impossible to falsify. A good example of the difficulty of falsifying psychoanalysis is the story of the woman who dreamed that her mother-in-law was coming for a visit. The content of his dream could not be a wish fulfillment because the woman hated her mother-in-law and would not wish for a visit from her. Freud escaped this conundrum by explaining that the woman had the dream merely to spite Freud and to prove to him that not all dreams are wish fulfillments. This kind of reasoning clearly gives Freudian theory a very low rating on its ability to generate falsifiable hypotheses.

A third criterion of any useful theory is its ability to *organize knowledge* into a meaningful framework. Unfortunately, the framework of Freud's personality theory, with its emphasis on the unconscious, is so loose and flexible that seemingly inconsistent data can coexist within its boundaries. Compared with other theories of personality, psychoanalysis ventures more answers to questions concerning why people behave as they do. But only some of these answers come from scientific investigations—most are simply logical extensions of Freud's basic assumptions. Thus, we rate psychoanalysis as having only moderate ability to organize knowledge.

Fourth, a useful theory should serve as *a guide for the solution of practical problems.* Because Freudian theory is unusually comprehensive, many psychoanalytically trained practitioners rely on it to find solutions to practical day-to-day problems. However, psychoanalysis no longer dominates the field of psychotherapy, and most present-day therapists use other theoretical orientations in their practice. Thus, we give psychoanalysis a low rating as a guide to the practitioner.

The fifth criterion of a useful theory deals with *internal consistency,* including operationally defined terms. Psychoanalysis is an internally consistent theory, if one remembers that Freud wrote over a period of more than 40 years and gradually altered the meaning of some concepts during that time. However, at any single point in time, the theory generally possessed internal consistency, although some specific terms were used with less than scientific rigor.

Does psychoanalysis possess a set of operationally defined terms? Here the theory definitely falls short. Such terms as id, ego, superego, conscious, preconscious, unconscious, oral stage, sadistic-anal stage, phallic stage, Oedipus complex, latent level of dreams, and many others are not operationally defined; that is, they are not spelled out in terms of specific operations or behaviors. Researchers must originate their own particular definition of most psychoanalytic terms.

Sixth, psychoanalysis is not a simple or *parsimonious* theory, but considering its comprehensiveness and the complexity of human personality, it is not needlessly cumbersome.

Concept of Humanity

In Chapter 1, we outlined several dimensions for a concept of humanity. Where does Freud's theory fall on these various dimensions?

The first of these is *determinism versus free choice.* On this dimension Freud's views on the nature of human nature would easily fall toward determinism. Freud believed that most of our behavior is determined by past events rather than molded by present goals. Humans have little control over their present actions because many of their behaviors are rooted in unconscious strivings that lie beyond present awareness. Although people usually believe that they are in control of their own lives, Freud insisted that such beliefs are illusions.

Adult personality is largely determined by childhood experiences—especially the Oedipus complex—that have left their residue in the unconscious mind. Freud (1917/1955a) held that humanity in its history has suffered three great blows to its narcissistic ego. The first was the rediscovery by Copernicus that the earth is not the center of the universe; the second was Darwin's discovery that humans are quite similar to other animals; the third, and most damaging blow of all, was Freud's own discovery that we are not in control of our own actions or, as he stated it, "the ego is not master in its own house" (p. 143).

A second and related issue is *pessimism versus optimism*. According to Freud, we come into the world in a basic state of conflict, with life and death forces operating on us from opposing sides. The innate death wish drives us incessantly toward self-destruction or aggression, while the sexual drive causes us to seek blindly after pleasure. The ego experiences a more or less permanent state of conflict, attempting to balance the contradictory demands of the id and superego while at the same time making concessions to the external world. Underneath a thin veneer of civilization, we are savage beasts with a natural tendency to exploit others for sexual and destructive satisfaction. Antisocial behavior lies just underneath the surface of even the most peaceful person, Freud believed. Worse yet, we are not ordinarily aware of the reasons for our behavior nor are we conscious of the hatred we feel for our friends, family, and lovers. For these reasons, psychoanalytic theory is essentially pessimistic.

A third approach for viewing humanity is the dimension of *causality versus teleology*. Freud believed that present behavior is mostly shaped by past causes rather than by people's goals for the future. People do not move toward a self-determined goal; instead, they are helplessly caught in the struggle between Eros and Thanatos. These two powerful drives force people to compulsively repeat primitive patterns of behavior. As adults, their behavior is one long series of reactions. People constantly attempt to reduce tension; to relieve anxieties; to repress unpleasant experiences; to regress to earlier, more secure stages of development; and to compulsively repeat behaviors that are familiar and safe. Therefore, we rate Freud's theory very high on causality.

On the dimension of *conscious versus unconscious,* psychoanalytic theory obviously leans heavily in the direction of unconscious motivation. Freud believed that everything from slips of the tongue to religious experiences is the result of a deep-rooted desire to satisfy sexual or aggressive drives. These motives make us slaves to our unconscious. Although we are aware of our actions, Freud believed that the motivations underlying those actions are deeply embedded in our unconscious and are frequently quite different from what we believe them to be.

A fifth dimension is *social versus biological influences*. As a physician, Freud's medical training disposed him to see human personality from a biological viewpoint. Yet Freud (1913/1953, 1985) frequently speculated about the consequences of prehistoric social units and about the consequences of an individual's early social experiences. Because Freud believed that many infantile fantasies and anxieties are rooted in biology, we rate him low on social influences.

Sixth is the issue of *uniqueness versus similarities*. On this dimension, psychoanalytic theory takes a middle position. Humanity's evolutionary past gives rise to a great many similarities among people. Nevertheless, individual experiences, especially those of early childhood, shape people in a somewhat unique manner and account for many of the differences among personalities.

Key Terms and Concepts

- Freud identified three *levels of mental life*—unconscious, preconscious, and conscious.
- Early childhood experiences that create high levels of anxiety are repressed into the *unconscious,* where they may influence behavior, emotions, and attitudes for years.
- Events that are not associated with anxiety but are merely forgotten make up the contents of the *preconscious.*
- *Conscious* images are those in awareness at any given time.
- Freud recognized three *provinces of the mind*—id, ego, and superego.
- The *id* is unconscious, chaotic, out of contact with reality, and in service of the *pleasure principle.*
- The *ego* is the executive of personality, in contact with the real world, and in service of the *reality principle.*
- The *superego* serves the *moral* and *idealistic principles* and begins to form after the Oedipus complex is resolved.
- All motivation can be traced to sexual and aggressive drives. Childhood behaviors related to *sex* and *aggression* are often punished, which leads to either *repression* or *anxiety.*
- To protect itself against anxiety, the ego initiates various *defense mechanisms,* the most basic of which is repression.
- Freud outlined three major *stages of development*—*infancy, latency*, and a *genital period*—but he devoted most attention to the infantile stage.
- The infantile stage is divided into three substages—*oral, anal,* and *phallic,* the last of which is accompanied by the Oedipus complex.
- During the simple *Oedipal stage,* a child desires sexual union with one parent while harboring hostility for the other.
- Freud believed that *dreams* and *Freudian slips* are disguised means of expressing unconscious impulses.

CHAPTER 3

Adler: Individual Psychology

Adler

In 1937, a young Abraham Maslow was having dinner in a New York restaurant with a somewhat older colleague. The older man was widely known for his earlier association with Sigmund Freud, and many people, including Maslow, regarded him as a disciple of Freud. When Maslow casually asked the older man about being Freud's follower, the older man became quite angry, and according to Maslow, he nearly shouted that

> this was a lie and a swindle for which he blamed Freud entirely, whom he then called names like swindler, sly, schemer. . . . He said that he had never been a student of Freud or a disciple or a follower. He made it clear from the beginning that he didn't agree with Freud and that he had his own opinions. (Maslow, 1962, p. 125)

Maslow, who had known the older man as an even-tempered, congenial person, was stunned by his outburst.

The older man, of course, was Alfred Adler, who battled throughout his professional life to dispel the notion that he had ever been a follower of Freud. Whenever reporters and other people would inquire about his early relationship with Freud, Adler would produce the old faded postcard with Freud's invitation to Adler to join Freud and three other physicians to meet at Freud's home the following Thursday evening. Freud closed the invitation saying, "With hearty greetings as your colleague" (quoted in Hoffman, 1994, p. 42). This friendly remark gave Adler some tangible evidence that Freud considered him to be his equal.

However, the warm association between Adler and Freud came to a bitter end, with both men hurling caustic remarks toward the other. For example, after World War I, when Freud elevated aggression to a basic human drive, Adler, who had long since abandoned the concept, commented sarcastically: "I enriched psychoanalysis by the aggressive drive. I gladly make them a present of it" (quoted in Bottome, 1939, p. 64).

During the acrimonious breakup between the two men, Freud accused Adler of having paranoid delusions and of using terrorist tactics. He told one of his friends that the revolt by Adler was that of "an abnormal individual driven mad by ambition" (quoted in Gay, 1988, p. 223).

Overview of Individual Psychology

Alfred Adler was neither a terrorist nor a person driven mad by ambition. Indeed, his **individual psychology** presents an optimistic view of people while resting heavily on the notion of *social interest,* that is, a feeling of oneness with all humankind. In addition to Adler's more optimistic look at people, several other differences made the relationship between Freud and Adler quite tenuous.

First, Freud reduced all motivation to sex and aggression, whereas Adler saw people as being motivated mostly by social influences and by their striving for superiority or success; second, Freud assumed that people have little or no choice in shaping their personality, whereas Adler believed that people are largely responsible for who they are; third, Freud's assumption that present behavior is caused by past experiences was directly opposed to Adler's notion that present behavior is shaped by people's view of the future; and fourth, in contrast to Freud, who placed very heavy emphasis on unconscious components of behavior, Adler believed that psychologically healthy people are usually aware of what they are doing and why they are doing it.

As we have seen, Adler was an original member of the small clique of physicians who met in Freud's home on Wednesday evenings to discuss psychological topics. However, when theoretical and personal differences between Adler and Freud emerged, Adler left the Freud circle and established an opposing theory, which became known as individual psychology.

Biography of Alfred Adler

Alfred Adler was born on February 7, 1870, in Rudolfsheim, a village near Vienna. His mother, Pauline, was a hard-working homemaker who kept busy with her seven children. His father, Leopold, was a middle-class Jewish grain merchant from Hungary. As a young boy, Adler was weak and sickly and at age 5, he nearly died of pneumonia. He had gone ice-skating with an older boy who abandoned young Alfred. Cold and shivering, Adler managed to find his way home where he immediately fell asleep on the living room couch. As Adler gradually gained consciousness, he heard a doctor say to his parents, "Give yourself no more trouble. The boy is lost" (Hoffman, 1994, p. 8). This experience, along with the death of a younger brother, motivated Adler to become a physician.

Adler's poor health was in sharp contrast to the health of his older brother Sigmund. Several of Adler's earliest memories were concerned with the unhappy competition between his brother's good health and his own illness. Sigmund Adler, the childhood rival whom Adler attempted to surpass, remained a worthy opponent, and in later years he became very successful in business and even helped Alfred financially. By almost any standard, however, Alfred Adler was much more famous than Sigmund Adler. Like many secondborn children, however, Alfred continued the rivalry with his older brother into middle age. He once told one of his biographers, Phyllis Bottome (1939, p. 18), "My eldest brother is a good industrious fellow—he was always ahead of me . . . and he is *still* ahead of me!"

The lives of Freud and Adler have several interesting parallels. Although both men came from middle- or lower-middle-class Viennese Jewish parents, neither was devoutly religious. However, Freud was much more conscious of his Jewishness than was Adler and often believed himself to be persecuted because of his Jewish background. On the other hand, Adler never claimed to have been mistreated, and in 1904, while still a member of Freud's inner circle, he converted to Protestantism. Despite this conversion, he held no deep religious convictions, and in fact, one of his biographers (Rattner, 1983) regarded him as an agnostic.

Like Freud, Adler had a younger brother who died in infancy. This early experience profoundly affected both men but in vastly different ways. Freud, by his own account, had wished unconsciously for the death of his rival and when the infant Julius did in fact die, Freud was filled with guilt and self-reproach, conditions that continued into his adulthood.

In contrast, Adler would seem to have had a more powerful reason to be traumatized by the death of his younger brother Rudolf. At age 4, Adler awoke one morning to find Rudolf dead in the bed next to his. Rather than being terrified or feeling guilty, Adler saw this experience, along with his own near death from pneumonia, as a challenge to overcome death. Thus, at age 5, he decided that his goal in life would be to conquer death. Because medicine offered some chance to forestall death, Adler decided at that early age to become a physician (Hoffman, 1994).

Although Freud was surrounded by a large family, including seven younger brothers and sisters, two grown half-brothers, and a nephew and niece about his age, he felt more emotionally attached to his parents, especially his mother, than to these other family members. In contrast, Adler was more interested in social relationships, and his siblings and peers played a pivotal role in his childhood development. Personality differences between Freud and Adler continued throughout adulthood, with Freud preferring intense one-to-one relationships and Adler feeling more comfortable in group situations. These personality differences were also reflected in their professional organizations. Freud's Vienna Psychoanalytic Society and International Psychoanalytic Association were highly structured in pyramid fashion, with an inner circle of six of Freud's trusted friends forming a kind of oligarchy at the top. Adler, by comparison, was more democratic, often meeting with colleagues and friends in Vienna coffeehouses where they played a piano and sang songs. Adler's Society for Individual Psychology, in fact, suffered from a loose organization, and Adler had a relaxed attitude toward business details that did not enhance his movement (Ellenberger, 1970).

Adler attended elementary school with neither difficulty nor distinction. However, when he entered the Gymnasium in preparation for medical school, he did so poorly that his father threatened to remove him from school and apprentice him to a shoemaker (Grey, 1998). As a medical student he once again completed work with no special honors, probably because his interest in patient care conflicted with his professors' interest in precise diagnoses (Hoffman, 1994). When he received his medical degree near the end of 1895, he had realized his childhood goal of becoming a physician.

Because his father had been born in Hungary, Adler was a Hungarian citizen and was thus obliged to serve a tour of military duty in the Hungarian army. He fulfilled that obligation immediately after receiving his medical degree and then returned to Vienna for postgraduate study. (Adler became an Austrian citizen in 1911). He began private practice as an eye specialist, but gave up that specialization and turned to psychiatry and general medicine.

Scholars disagree on the first meeting of Adler and Freud (Bottome, 1939; Ellenberger, 1970; Fiebert, 1997; Handlbauer, 1998), but all agree that in the late fall of 1902, Freud invited Adler and three other Viennese physicians to attend a meeting in Freud's home to discuss psychology and neuropathology. This group was known as the Wednesday Psychological Society until 1908, when it became the Vienna Psychoanalytic Society. Although Freud led these discussion groups, Adler never considered Freud to be his mentor and believed somewhat naively that he and others could make contributions to psychoanalysis—contributions that would be acceptable to Freud. Although Adler was one of the original members of Freud's inner circle, the two men never shared a warm personal relationship. Neither man was quick to recognize theoretical differences even after Adler's 1907 publication of *Study of Organ Inferiority and Its Psychical Compensation* (1907/1917), which assumed that physical deficiencies—not sex—formed the foundation for human motivation.

During the next few years, Adler became even more convinced that psychoanalysis should be much broader than Freud's view of infantile sexuality. In 1911, Adler, who was then president of the Vienna Psychoanalytic Society, presented his views before the group, expressing opposition to the strong sexual proclivities of psychoanalysis and insisting that the drive for superiority was a more basic motive than sexuality. Both he and Freud finally recognized that their differences were irreconcilable, and in October of 1911 Adler resigned his presidency and membership in the Psychoanalytic Society. Along with nine other former members of the Freudian circle, he formed the Society for Free Psychoanalytic Study, a name that irritated Freud with its implication that Freudian psychoanalysis was opposed to a free expression of ideas. Adler, however, soon changed the name of his organization to the Society for Individual Psychology—a name that clearly indicated he had abandoned psychoanalysis.

Like Freud, Adler was affected by events surrounding World War I. Both men had financial difficulties, and both reluctantly borrowed money from relatives—Freud from his brother-in-law Edward Bernays and Adler from his brother Sigmund. Each man also made important changes in his theory. Freud elevated aggression to the level of sex after viewing the horrors of war, and Adler suggested that social interest and compassion could be the cornerstones of human motivation. The war years also brought a major disappointment to Adler when his application for an unpaid lecture position at the University of Vienna was turned down. Adler wanted this position to gain another forum for spreading his views, but he also desperately desired to attain the same prestigious position that Freud had held for more than a dozen years. Adler never attained this position, but after the war he was able to advance his theories through lecturing, establishing child guidance clinics, and training teachers.

During the last several years of his life, Adler frequently visited the United States, where he taught individual psychology at Columbia University and the New School for Social Research. By 1932, he was a permanent resident of the United States and held the position of Visiting Professor for Medical Psychology at Long Island College of Medicine, now Downstate Medical School, State University of New York. Unlike Freud, who disliked Americans and their superficial understanding of psychoanalysis, Adler was impressed by Americans and admired their optimism and open-mindedness. His popularity as a speaker in the United States during the mid-1930s had few rivals, and he aimed his last several books toward a receptive American market (Hoffman, 1994).

Adler married a fiercely independent Russian woman, Raissa Epstein, in December of 1897. Raissa was an early feminist and much more political than her husband. In later years, while Adler lived in New York, she remained mostly in Vienna and worked to promote Marxist-Leninist views that were quite different from Adler's notion of individual freedom and responsibility. After several years of requests by her husband to move to New York, Raissa finally came to stay in New York only a few months before Adler's death. Ironically, Raissa, who did not share her husband's love for America, continued to live in New York until her own death, nearly a quarter of a century after Adler had died (Hoffman, 1994).

Raissa and Alfred had four children: Alexandra and Kurt, who became psychiatrists and continued their father's work; Valentine (Vali), who died as a political prisoner of the Soviet Union in about 1942; and Cornelia (Nelly), who aspired to be an actress.

Adler's favorite relaxation was music, but he also maintained an active interest in art and literature. In his work he often borrowed examples from fairy tales, the Bible, Shakespeare, Goethe, and numerous other literary works. He identified himself closely with the common person, and his manner and appearance were consistent with that identification. His patients included a high percentage of people from the lower and middle classes, a rarity among psychiatrists of his time. His personal qualities included an optimistic attitude toward the human condition, an intense competitiveness coupled with friendly congeniality, and a strong belief in the basic gender equality, which combined with a willingness to forcefully advocate women's rights.

From middle childhood until after his 67th birthday, Adler enjoyed robust health. Then, in the early months of 1937, while concerned with the fate of his daughter Vali who had disappeared somewhere in Moscow, Adler felt chest pains while on a speaking tour in the Netherlands. Ignoring the doctor's advice to rest, he continued on to Aberdeen, Scotland, where on May 28, 1937, he died of a heart attack. Freud, who was 14 years older than Adler, had outlived his longtime adversary. On hearing of Adler's death, Freud (as quoted in E. Jones, 1957) sarcastically remarked, "For a Jew boy out of a Viennese suburb a death in Aberdeen is an unheard-of career in itself and a proof of how far he had got on. The world really rewarded him richly for his service in having contradicted psychoanalysis" (p. 208).

Introduction to Adlerian Theory

Although Alfred Adler has had a profound effect on such later theorists as Harry Stack Sullivan, Karen Horney, Julian Rotter, Abraham H. Maslow, Carl Rogers, Albert Ellis, Rollo May, and others (Mosak & Maniacci, 1999), his name is less well known than that of either Freud or Carl Jung. At least three reasons account for this. First, Adler did not establish a tightly run organization to perpetuate his theories. Second, he was not a particularly gifted writer, and most of his books were compiled by a series of editors using Adler's scattered lectures. Third, many of his views were incorporated into the works of such later theorists as Maslow, Rogers, and Ellis and thus are no longer associated with Adler's name.

Although his writings revealed great insight into the depth and complexities of human personality, Adler evolved a basically simple and parsimonious theory. To Adler, people are born with weak, inferior bodies—a condition that leads to *feelings* of inferiority and a consequent dependence on other people. Therefore, a feeling of unity with others (social interest) is inherent in people and the ultimate standard for psychological health. More specifically, the main tenets of Adlerian theory can be stated in outline form. The following is adapted from a list that represents the final statement of individual psychology (Adler, 1964).

1. The one dynamic force behind people's behavior is the *striving for success or superiority.*

2. People's *subjective perceptions* shape their behavior and personality.
3. Personality is *unified and self-consistent.*
4. The value of all human activity must be seen from the viewpoint of *social interest.*
5. The self-consistent personality structure develops into a person's *style of life.*
6. Style of life is molded by people's *creative power.*

Striving for Success or Superiority

The first tenet of Adlerian theory is: *The one dynamic force behind people's behavior is the striving for success or superiority.*

Adler reduced all motivation to a single drive—the striving for success or superiority. Adler's own childhood was marked by physical deficiencies and strong feelings of competitiveness with his older brother. Individual psychology holds that everyone begins life with physical deficiencies that activate feelings of inferiority—feelings that motivate a person to strive for either superiority or success. Psychologically unhealthy individuals strive for personal superiority, whereas psychologically healthy people seek success for all humanity.

Early in his career, Adler believed that *aggression* was the dynamic power behind all motivation, but he soon became dissatisfied with this term. After rejecting aggression as a single motivational force, Adler used the term *masculine protest,* which implied will to power or a domination of others. However, he soon abandoned masculine protest as a universal drive while continuing to give it a limited role in his theory of abnormal development.

Next, Adler called the single dynamic force *striving for superiority.* In his final theory, however, he limited striving for superiority to those people who strive for personal superiority over others and introduced the term *striving for success* to describe actions of people who are motivated by highly developed social interest (Adler, 1956). Regardless of the motivation for striving, each individual is guided by a final goal.

The Final Goal

According to Adler (1956), people strive toward a final goal of either personal superiority or the goal of success for all humankind. In either case, the final goal is fictional and has no objective existence. Nevertheless, the final goal has great significance because it unifies personality and renders all behavior comprehensible.

Each person has the power to create a personalized fictional goal, one constructed out of the raw materials provided by heredity and environment. However, the goal is neither genetically nor environmentally determined. Rather, it is the product of the *creative power,* that is, people's ability to freely shape their behavior and create their own personality. By the time children reach 4 or 5 years of age, their creative power has developed to the point that they can set their final goal. Even infants have an innate drive toward growth, completion, or success. Because infants are small, incomplete, and weak, they feel inferior and powerless. To compensate for this deficiency, they set a fictional goal to be big, complete, and strong. Thus, a person's final goal reduces the pain of inferiority feelings and points that person in the direction of either superiority or success.

If children feel neglected or pampered, their goal remains largely unconscious. Adler (1964) hypothesized that children will compensate for feelings of inferiority in devious ways that have no apparent relationship to their fictional goal. The goal of superiority for a pampered girl, for example, may be to make permanent her parasitic relationship with her mother. As an adult, she may appear dependent and self-deprecating, and such behavior may seem inconsistent with a goal of superiority. However, it is quite consistent with her unconscious and misunderstood goal of being a parasite that she set at age 4 or 5, a time when her mother appeared large and powerful, and attachment to her became a natural means of attaining superiority.

Conversely, if children experience love and security, they set a goal that is largely conscious and clearly understood. Psychologically secure children strive toward superiority defined in terms of success and social interest. Although their goal never becomes completely conscious, these healthy individuals understand and pursue it with a high level of awareness.

In striving for their final goal, people create and pursue many preliminary goals. These subgoals are often conscious, but the connection between them and the final goal usually remains unknown. Furthermore, the relationship among preliminary goals is seldom realized. From the point of view of the final goal, however, they fit together in a self-consistent pattern. Adler (1956) used the analogy of the playwright who builds the characteristics and the subplots of the play according to the final goal of the drama. When the final scene is known, all dialogue and every subplot acquire new meaning. When an individual's final goal is known, all actions make sense and each subgoal takes on new significance.

The Striving Force as Compensation

People strive for superiority or success as a means of compensation for feelings of inferiority or weakness. Adler (1930) believed that all humans are "blessed" at birth with small, weak, and inferior bodies. These physical deficiencies ignite feelings of inferiority only because people, by their nature, possess an innate tendency toward completion or wholeness. People are continually pushed by the need to overcome inferiority feelings and pulled by the desire for completion. The minus and plus situations exist simultaneously and cannot be separated because they are two dimensions of a single force.

The striving force itself is innate, but its nature and direction are due both to feelings of inferiority and to the goal of superiority. Without the innate movement toward perfection, children would never feel inferior; but without feelings of inferiority, they would never set a goal of superiority or success. The goal, then, is set as compensation for the deficit feeling, but the deficit feeling would not exist unless a child first possessed a basic tendency toward completion (Adler, 1956).

Although the striving for success is innate, it must be developed. At birth it exists as potentiality, not actuality; each person must actualize this potential in his or her own manner. At about age 4 or 5, children begin this process by setting a direction to the striving force and by establishing a goal either of personal superiority or of social success. The goal provides guidelines for motivation, shaping psychological development and giving it an aim.

As a creation of the individual, the goal may take any form. It is not necessarily a mirror image of the deficiency, even though it is a compensation for it. For example, a person with a weak body will not necessarily become a robust athlete but instead may become an artist, an actor, or a writer. Success is an individualized concept and all people formulate their own definition of it. Although creative power is swayed by the forces of heredity and environment, it is ultimately responsible for people's personality. Heredity establishes the potentiality, whereas environment contributes to the development of social interest and courage. The forces of nature and nurture can never deprive a person of the power to set a unique goal or to choose a unique style of reaching for the goal (Adler, 1956).

In his final theory, Adler identified two general avenues of striving. The first is the socially nonproductive attempt to gain personal superiority; the second involves social interest and is aimed at success or perfection for everyone.

Striving for Personal Superiority

Some people strive for superiority with little or no concern for others. Their goals are personal ones, and their strivings are motivated largely by exaggerated feelings of personal inferiority, or the presence of an **inferiority complex.** Murderers, thieves, and con artists are obvious examples of people who strive for personal gain. Some people create clever disguises for their personal striving and may consciously or unconsciously hide their self-centeredness behind the cloak of social concern. A college teacher, for example, may appear to have a great interest in his students because he establishes a personal relationship with many of them. By conspicuously displaying much sympathy and concern, he encourages vulnerable students to talk to him about their personal problems. This teacher possesses a private intelligence that allows him to believe that he is the most accessible and dedicated teacher in his college. To a casual observer, he may appear to be motivated by social interest, but his actions are largely self-serving and motivated by overcompensation for his exaggerated feelings of personal superiority.

Striving for Success

In contrast to people who strive for personal gain are those psychologically healthy people who are motivated by social interest and the success of all humankind. These healthy individuals are concerned with goals beyond themselves, are capable of helping others without demanding or expecting a personal payoff, and are able to see others not as opponents but as people with whom they can cooperate for social benefit. Their own success is not gained at the expense of others but is a natural tendency to move toward completion or perfection.

People who strive for success rather than personal superiority maintain a sense of self, of course, but they see daily problems from the view of society's development rather than from a strictly personal vantage point. Their sense of personal worth is tied closely to their contributions to human society. Social progress is more important to them than personal credit (Adler, 1956).

Subjective Perceptions

Adler's second tenet is: *People's subjective perceptions shape their behavior and personality.*

People strive for superiority or success to compensate for feelings of inferiority, but the manner in which they strive is not shaped by reality but by their subjective perceptions of reality, that is, by their **fictions,** or expectations of the future.

Fictionalism

Our most important fiction is the goal of superiority or success, a goal we created early in life and may not clearly understand. This subjective, fictional final goal guides our style of life, gives unity to our personality. Adler's ideas on fictionalism originated with Hans Vaihinger's book *The Philosophy of "As If"* (1911/1925). Vaihinger believed that fictions are ideas that have no real existence, yet they influence people *as if* they really existed. One example of a fiction might be: "Men are superior to women." Although this notion is a fiction, many people, both men and women, act as if it were a reality. A second example might be: "Humans have a free will that enables them to make choices." Again, many people act *as if* they and others have a free will and are thus responsible for their choices. No one can prove that free will exists, yet this fiction guides the lives of most of us. People are motivated not by what is true but by their subjective perceptions of what is true. A third example of a fiction might be a belief in an omnipotent God who rewards good and punishes evil. Such a belief guides the daily lives of millions of people and helps shape many of their actions. Whether true or false, fictions have a powerful influence on people's lives.

Adler's emphasis on fictions is consistent with his strongly held teleological view of motivation. *Teleology* is an explanation of behavior in terms of its final purpose or aim. It is opposed to *causality,* which considers behavior as springing from a specific cause. Teleology is usually concerned with future goals or ends, whereas causality ordinarily deals with past experiences that produce some present effect. Freud's view of motivation was basically causal; he believed that people are driven by past events that activate present behavior. In contrast, Adler adopted a teleological view, one in which people are motivated by present perceptions of the future. As fictions, these perceptions need not be conscious or understood. Nevertheless, they bestow a purpose on all of people's actions and are responsible for a consistent pattern that runs throughout their life.

 Beyond Biography   **Why did Adler really break with Freud? For motivations behind the Adler-Freud breakup, see our website at** *www.mhhe.com/feist7*

Physical Inferiorities

Because people begin life small, weak, and inferior, they develop a fiction or belief system about how to overcome these physical deficiencies and become big, strong, and superior. But even after they attain size, strength, and superiority, they may act *as if* they are still small, weak, and inferior.

Adler (1929/1969) insisted that the whole human race is "blessed" with organ inferiorities. These physical handicaps have little or no importance by themselves but become meaningful when they stimulate subjective feelings of inferiority, which serve as an impetus toward perfection or completion. Some people compensate for these feelings of inferiority by moving toward psychological health and a useful style of life, whereas others overcompensate and are motivated to subdue or retreat from other people.

History provides many examples of people like Demosthenes or Beethoven overcoming a handicap and making significant contributions to society. Adler himself was weak and sickly as a child, and his illness moved him to overcome death by becoming a physician and by competing with his older brother and with Sigmund Freud.

Adler (1929/1969) emphasized that physical deficiencies alone do not *cause* a particular style of life; they simply provide present motivation for reaching future goals. Such motivation, like all aspects of personality, is unified and self-consistent.

Unity and Self-Consistency of Personality

The third tenet of Adlerian theory is: *Personality is unified and self-consistent.*

In choosing the term *individual psychology,* Adler wished to stress his belief that each person is unique and indivisible. Thus, individual psychology insists on the fundamental unity of personality and the notion that inconsistent behavior does not exist. Thoughts, feelings, and actions are all directed toward a single goal and serve a single purpose. When people behave erratically or unpredictably, their behavior forces other people to be on the defensive, to be watchful so as not to be confused by capricious actions. Although behaviors may appear inconsistent, when they are viewed from the perspective of a final goal, they appear as clever but probably unconscious attempts to confuse and subordinate other people. This confusing and seemingly inconsistent behavior gives the erratic person the upper hand in an interpersonal relationship. Although erratic people are often successful in their attempt to gain superiority over others, they usually remain unaware of their underlying motive and may stubbornly reject any suggestion that they desire superiority over other people.

Adler (1956) recognized several ways in which the entire person operates with unity and self-consistency. The first of these he called organ jargon, or organ dialect.

Organ Dialect

According to Adler (1956), the whole person strives in a self-consistent fashion toward a single goal, and all separate actions and functions can be understood only as parts of this goal. The disturbance of one part of the body cannot be viewed in isolation; it affects the entire person. In fact, the deficient organ expresses the direction of the individual's goal, a condition known as **organ dialect.** Through organ dialect, the body's organs "speak a language which is usually more expressive and discloses the individual's opinion more clearly than words are able to do" (Adler, 1956, p. 223).

One example of organ dialect might be a man suffering from rheumatoid arthritis in his hands. His stiff and deformed joints voice his whole style of life. It is as if they cry out, "See my deformity. See my handicap. You can't expect me to do manual work." Without an audible sound, his hands speak of his desire for sympathy from others.

Adler (1956) presented another example of organ dialect—the case of a very obedient boy who wet the bed at night to send a message that he does not wish to obey parental wishes. His behavior is "really a creative expression, for the child is speaking with his bladder instead of his mouth" (p. 223).

Conscious and Unconscious

A second example of a unified personality is the harmony between conscious and unconscious actions. Adler (1956) defined the unconscious as that part of the goal that is neither clearly formulated nor completely understood by the individual. With this definition, Adler avoided a dichotomy between the unconscious and the conscious, which he saw as two cooperating parts of the same unified system. Conscious thoughts are those that are understood and regarded by the individual as helpful in striving for success, whereas unconscious thoughts are those that are not helpful.

> We cannot oppose "consciousness" to "unconsciousness" as if they were antagonistic halves of an individual's existence. The conscious life becomes unconscious as soon as we fail to understand it—and as soon as we understand an unconscious tendency it has already become conscious. (Adler, 1929/1964, p. 163)

Whether people's behaviors lead to a healthy or an unhealthy style of life depends on the degree of social interest that they developed during their childhood years.

Social Interest

The fourth of Adler's tenets is: *The value of all human activity must be seen from the viewpoint of social interest.*

Social interest is Adler's somewhat misleading translation of his original German term, ***Gemeinschaftsgefühl.*** A better translation might be "social feeling" or "community feeling," but *Gemeinschaftsgefühl* actually has a meaning that is not fully expressed by any English word or phrase. Roughly, it means a feeling of oneness with all humanity; it implies membership in the social community of all people. A person with well-developed *Gemeinschaftsgefühl* strives not for personal superiority but for perfection for all people in an ideal community. Social interest can be defined as an attitude of relatedness with humanity in general as well as an empathy for each member of the human community. It manifests itself as cooperation with others for social advancement rather than for personal gain (Adler, 1964).

Social interest is the natural condition of the human species and the adhesive that binds society together (Adler, 1927). The natural inferiority of individuals necessitates their joining together to form a society. Without protection and nourishment from a father or mother, a baby would perish. Without protection from the family or clan, our ancestors would have been destroyed by animals that were stronger,

Both mother and father can contribute powerfully to the developing social interest of their children.

more ferocious, or endowed with keener senses. Social interest, therefore, is a necessity for perpetuating the human species.

Origins of Social Interest

Social interest is rooted as potentiality in everyone, but it must be developed before it can contribute to a useful style of life. It originates from the mother-child relationship during the early months of infancy. Every person who has survived infancy was kept alive by a mothering person who possessed some amount of social interest. Thus, every person has had the seeds of social interest sown during those early months.

Adler believed that marriage and parenthood is a task for two. However, the two parents may influence a child's social interest in somewhat different ways. The mother's job is to develop a bond that encourages the child's mature social interest and fosters a sense of cooperation. Ideally, she should have a genuine and deep-rooted love for her child—a love that is centered on the child's well-being, not on her own needs or wants. This healthy love relationship develops from a true caring for her child, her husband, and other people. If the mother has learned to give and receive love from others, she will have little difficulty broadening her child's social interest. But if she favors the child over the father, her child may become pampered and spoiled. Conversely, if she favors her husband or society, the child will feel neglected and unloved.

The father is a second important person in a child's social environment. He must demonstrate a caring attitude toward his wife as well as to other people. The ideal father cooperates on an equal footing with the child's mother in caring for the child and treating the child as a human being. According to Adler's (1956) standards, a successful father avoids the dual errors of emotional detachment and paternal authoritarianism. These errors may represent two attitudes, but they are often found in the same father. Both prevent the growth and spread of social interest in a child. A father's emotional detachment may influence the child to develop a warped sense of social interest, a feeling of neglect, and possibly a parasitic attachment to the mother. A child who experiences paternal detachment creates a goal of personal superiority rather than one based on social interest. The second error—paternal authoritarianism—may also lead to an unhealthy style of life. A child who sees the father as a tyrant learns to strive for power and personal superiority.

Adler (1956) believed that the effects of the early social environment are extremely important. The relationship a child has with the mother and father is so powerful that it smothers the effects of heredity. Adler believed that after age 5, the effects of heredity become blurred by the powerful influence of the child's social environment. By that time, environmental forces have modified or shaped nearly every aspect of a child's personality.

Importance of Social Interest

Social interest was Adler's yardstick for measuring psychological health and is thus "the sole criterion of human values" (Adler, 1927, p. 167). To Adler, social interest is the only gauge to be used in judging the worth of a person. As the barometer of normality, it is the standard to be used in determining the usefulness of a life. To the degree that people possess social interest, they are psychologically mature. Immature people lack *Gemeinschaftsgefühl,* are self-centered, and strive for personal power and superiority over others. Healthy individuals are genuinely concerned about people and have a goal of success that encompasses the well-being of all people.

Social interest is not synonymous with charity and unselfishness. Acts of philanthropy and kindness may or may not be motivated by *Gemeinschaftsgefühl.* A wealthy woman may regularly give large sums of money to the poor and needy, not because she feels a oneness with them, but, quite to the contrary, because she wishes to maintain a separateness from them. The gift implies, "You are inferior, I am superior, and this charity is proof of my superiority." Adler believed that the worth of all such acts can only be judged against the criterion of social interest.

In summary, people begin life with a basic striving force that is activated by ever-present physical deficiencies. These organic weaknesses lead inevitably to feelings of inferiority. Thus, all people possess feelings of inferiority, and all set a final goal at around age 4 or 5. However, psychologically unhealthy individuals develop exaggerated feelings of inferiority and attempt to compensate by setting a goal of personal superiority. They are motivated by personal gain rather than by social interest, whereas healthy people are motivated by normal feelings of incompleteness and high levels of social interest. They strive toward the goal of success, defined in terms of perfection and completion for everyone. Figure 3.1 illustrates how the innate striving force combines with inevitable physical deficiencies to produce universal feelings of inferiority, which can be either exaggerated or normal. Exaggerated feelings of inferiority lead to a neurotic style of life, whereas normal feelings of incompletion result in a healthy style of life. Whether a person forms a useless style of life or a socially useful one depends on how that person views these inevitable feelings of inferiority.

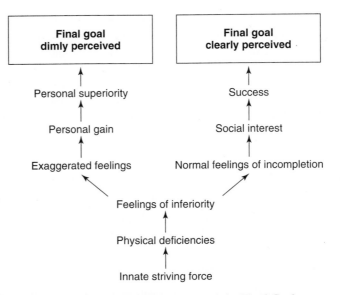

FIGURE 3.1   *Two Basic Methods of Striving toward the Final Goal.*

Style of Life

Adler's fifth tenet is: *The self-consistent personality structure develops into a person's style of life.*

Style of life is the term Adler used to refer to the flavor of a person's life. It includes a person's goal, self-concept, feelings for others, and attitude toward the world. It is the product of the interaction of heredity, environment, and a person's creative power. Adler (1956) used a musical analogy to elucidate style of life. The separate notes of a composition are meaningless without the entire melody, but the melody takes on added significance when we recognize the composer's style or unique manner of expression.

A person's style of life is fairly well established by age 4 or 5. After that time, all our actions revolve around our unified style of life. Although the final goal is singular, style of life need not be narrow or rigid. Psychologically unhealthy individuals often lead rather inflexible lives that are marked by an inability to choose new ways of reacting to their environment. In contrast, psychologically healthy people behave in diverse and flexible ways with styles of life that are complex, enriched, and changing. Healthy people see many ways of striving for success and continually seek to create new options for themselves. Even though their final goal remains constant, the way in which they perceive it continually changes. Thus, they can choose new options at any point in life.

People with a healthy, socially useful style of life express their social interest through *action.* They actively struggle to solve what Adler regarded as the three major problems of life—neighborly love, sexual love, and occupation—and they do so through cooperation, personal courage, and a willingness to make a contribution to the welfare of another. Adler (1956) believed that people with a socially useful style of life represent the highest form of humanity in the evolutionary process and are likely to populate the world of the future.

Creative Power

The final tenet of Adlerian theory is: *Style of life is molded by people's creative power.*

Each person, Adler believed, is empowered with the freedom to create her or his own style of life. Ultimately, all people are responsible for who they are and how they behave. Their **creative power** places them in control of their own lives, is responsible for their final goal, determines their method of striving for that goal, and contributes to the development of social interest. In short, creative power makes each person a free individual. Creative power is a dynamic concept implying *movement,* and this movement is the most salient characteristic of life. All psychic life involves movement toward a goal, movement with a direction (Adler, 1964).

Adler (1956) acknowledged the importance of heredity and environment in forming personality. Except for identical twins, every child is born with a unique genetic makeup and soon comes to have social experiences different from those of any other human. People, however, are much more than a product of heredity and environment. They are creative beings who not only react to their environment but also act on it and cause it to react to them.

Each person uses heredity and environment as the bricks and mortar to build personality, but the architectural design reflects that person's own style. Of primary importance is not what people have been given, but how they put those materials to use. The building materials of personality are secondary. We are our own architect and can build either a useful or a useless style of life. We can choose to construct a gaudy façade or to expose the essence of the structure. We are not compelled to grow in the direction of social interest, inasmuch as we have no inner nature that forces us to be good. Conversely, we have no inherently evil nature from which we must escape. We are who we are because of the use we have made of our bricks and mortar.

Adler (1929/1964) used an interesting analogy, which he called "the law of the low doorway." If you are trying to walk through a doorway four feet high, you have two basic choices. First, you can use your creative power to bend down as you approach the doorway, thereby successfully solving the problem. This is the manner in which the psychologically healthy individual solves most of life's problems. Conversely, if you bump your head and fall back, you must still solve the problem correctly or continue bumping your head. Neurotics often choose to bump their head on the realities of life. When approaching the low doorway, you are neither compelled to stoop nor forced to bump your head. You have a creative power that permits you to follow either course.

Abnormal Development

Adler believed that people are what they make of themselves. The creative power endows humans, within certain limits, with the freedom to be either psychologically healthy or unhealthy and to follow either a useful or useless style of life.

General Description

According to Adler (1956), the one factor underlying all types of maladjustments is *underdeveloped social interest.* Besides lacking social interest, neurotics tend to (1) set their goals too high, (2) live in their own private world, and (3) have a rigid and dogmatic style of life. These three characteristics follow inevitably from a lack of social interest. In short, people become failures in life because they are overconcerned with themselves and care little about others. Maladjusted people set extravagant goals as an overcompensation for exaggerated feelings of inferiority. These lofty goals lead to dogmatic behavior, and the higher the goal, the more rigid the striving. To compensate for deeply rooted feelings of inadequacy and basic insecurity, these individuals narrow their perspective and strive compulsively and rigidly for unrealistic goals.

The exaggerated and unrealistic nature of neurotics' goals sets them apart from the community of other people. They approach the problems of friendship, sex, and occupation from a personal angle that precludes successful solutions. Their view of the world is not in focus with that of other individuals and they possess what Adler (1956) called "private meaning" (p. 156). These people find everyday living to be hard work, requiring great effort. Adler (1929/1964) used an analogy to describe how these people go through life.

> In a certain popular music hall, the "strong" man comes on and lifts an enormous weight with care and intense difficulty. Then, during the hearty applause of the audience, a child comes in and gives away the fraud by carrying the dummy weight off with one hand. There are plenty of neurotics who swindle us with such weights, and who are adepts at appearing overburdened. They could really dance with the load under which they stagger. (p. 91)

External Factors in Maladjustment

Why do some people create maladjustments? Adler (1964) recognized three contributing factors, any one of which is sufficient to contribute to abnormality: (1) exaggerated physical deficiencies, (2) a pampered style of life, and (3) a neglected style of life.

Exaggerated Physical Deficiencies

Exaggerated physical deficiencies, whether congenital or the result of injury or disease, are not sufficient to lead to maladjustment. They must be accompanied by accentuated feelings of inferiority. These subjective feelings may be greatly encouraged by a defective body, but they are the progeny of the creative power.

Each person comes into the world "blessed" with physical deficiencies, and these deficiencies lead to feelings of inferiority. People with exaggerated physical deficiencies sometimes develop exaggerated feelings of inferiority because they overcompensate for their inadequacy. They tend to be overly concerned with themselves and lack consideration for others. They feel as if they are living in enemy country, fear defeat more than they desire success, and are convinced that life's major problems can be solved only in a selfish manner (Adler, 1927).

Pampered Style of Life

A pampered style of life lies at the heart of most neuroses. Pampered people have weak social interest but a strong desire to perpetuate the pampered, parasitic relationship they originally had with one or both of their parents. They expect others to look after them, overprotect them, and satisfy their needs. They are characterized by extreme discouragement, indecisiveness, oversensitivity, impatience, and exaggerated emotion, especially anxiety. They see the world with private vision and believe that they are entitled to be first in everything (Adler, 1927, 1964).

Pampered children have not received too much love; rather, they feel unloved. Their parents have demonstrated a lack of love by doing too much for them and by treating them as if they were incapable of solving their own problems. Because these children *feel* pampered and spoiled, they develop a pampered style of life. Pampered children may also feel neglected. Having been protected by a doting parent, they are fearful when separated from that parent. Whenever they must fend for themselves, they feel left out, mistreated, and neglected. These experiences add to the pampered child's stockpile of inferiority feelings.

Neglected Style of Life

The third external factor contributing to maladjustment is neglect. Children who feel unloved and unwanted are likely to borrow heavily from these feelings in creating a neglected style of life. Neglect is a relative concept. No one feels totally neglected or completely unwanted. The fact that a child survived infancy is proof that someone cared for that child and that the seed of social interest has been planted (Adler, 1927).

Abused and mistreated children develop little social interest and tend to create a neglected style of life. They have little confidence in themselves and tend to overestimate difficulties connected with life's major problems. They are distrustful of other people and are unable to cooperate for the common welfare. They see society as enemy country, feel alienated from all other people, and experience a strong sense of envy toward the success of others. Neglected children have many of the characteristics of pampered ones, but generally they are more suspicious and more likely to be dangerous to others (Adler, 1927).

Safeguarding Tendencies

Adler believed that people create patterns of behavior to protect their exaggerated sense of self-esteem against public disgrace. These protective devices, called **safeguarding tendencies,** enable people to hide their inflated self-image and to maintain their current style of life.

Adler's concept of safeguarding tendencies can be compared to Freud's concept of defense mechanisms. Basic to both is the idea that symptoms are formed as a protection against anxiety. However, there are important differences between the two concepts. Freudian defense mechanisms operate unconsciously to protect the ego against anxiety, whereas Adlerian safeguarding tendencies are largely conscious and shield a person's fragile self-esteem from public disgrace. Also, Freud's defense mechanisms are common to everyone, but Adler (1956) discussed safeguarding tendencies only with reference to the construction of neurotic symptoms. Excuses, aggression, and withdrawal are three common safeguarding tendencies, each designed to protect a person's present style of life and to maintain a fictional, elevated feeling of self-importance (Adler, 1964).

Excuses

The most common of the safeguarding tendencies are **excuses,** which are typically expressed in the "Yes, but" or "If only" format. In the "Yes, but" excuse, people first state what they claim they would like to do—something that sounds good to others—then they follow with an excuse. A woman might say, "Yes, I would like to go to college, *but* my children demand too much of my attention." An executive explains, "Yes, I agree with your proposal, *but* company policy will not allow it."

The "If only" statement is the same excuse phrased in a different way. "*If only* my husband were more supportive, I would have advanced faster in my profession." "*If only* I did not have this physical deficiency, I could compete successfully for a job." These excuses protect a weak—but artificially inflated—sense of self-worth and deceive people into believing that they are more superior than they really are (Adler, 1956).

Aggression

Another common safeguarding tendency is **aggression.** Adler (1956) held that some people use aggression to safeguard their exaggerated superiority complex, that is, to protect their fragile self-esteem. Safeguarding through aggression may take the form of depreciation, accusation, or self-accusation.

Depreciation is the tendency to undervalue other people's achievements and to overvalue one's own. This safeguarding tendency is evident in such aggressive behaviors as criticism and gossip. "The only reason Kenneth got the job I applied for is because he is an African American." "If you look closely, you'll notice that Jill works hardest at avoiding work." The intention behind each act of depreciation is to belittle another so that the person, by comparison, will be placed in a favorable light.

Accusation, the second form of an aggressive safeguarding device, is the tendency to blame others for one's failures and to seek revenge, thereby safeguarding one's own tenuous self-esteem. "I wanted to be an artist, but my parents forced me to go to medical school. Now I have a job that makes me miserable." Adler (1956) believed that there is an element of aggressive accusation in all unhealthy lifestyles. Unhealthy people invariably act to cause the people around them to suffer more than they do.

The third form of neurotic aggression, **self-accusation,** is marked by self-torture and guilt. Some people use self-torture, including masochism, depression, and suicide, as means of hurting people who are close to them. Guilt is often aggressive, self-accusatory behavior. "I feel distressed because I wasn't nicer to my grandmother while she was still living. Now, it's too late."

Self-accusation is the converse of depreciation, although both are aimed toward gaining personal superiority. With depreciation, people who feel inferior devalue others to make themselves look good. With self-accusation, people devalue themselves in order to inflict suffering on others while protecting their own magnified feelings of self-esteem (Adler, 1956).

Withdrawal

Personality development can be halted when people run away from difficulties. Adler referred to this tendency as **withdrawal,** or safeguarding through distance. Some people unconsciously escape life's problems by setting up a distance between themselves and those problems.

Adler (1956) recognized four modes of safeguarding through withdrawal: (1) moving backward, (2) standing still, (3) hesitating, and (3) constructing obstacles.

Moving backward is the tendency to safeguard one's fictional goal of superiority by psychologically reverting to a more secure period of life. Moving backward is similar to Freud's concept of regression in that both involve attempts to return to earlier, more comfortable phases of life. Whereas regression takes place unconsciously and protects people against anxiety-filled experiences, moving backward may sometimes be conscious and is directed at maintaining an inflated goal of superiority. Moving backward is designed to elicit sympathy, the deleterious attitude offered so generously to pampered children.

Psychological distance can also be created by **standing still.** This withdrawal tendency is similar to moving backward but, in general, it is not as severe. People who stand still simply do not move in any direction; thus, they avoid all responsibility by ensuring themselves against any threat of failure. They safeguard their fictional aspirations because they never do anything to prove that they cannot accomplish their goals. A person who never applies to graduate school can never be denied entrance; a child who shies away from other children will not be rejected by them. By doing nothing, people safeguard their self-esteem and protect themselves against failure.

Closely related to standing still is **hesitating.** Some people hesitate or vacillate when faced with difficult problems. Their procrastinations eventually give them the excuse "It's too late now." Adler believed that most compulsive behaviors are attempts to waste time. Compulsive hand washing, retracing one's steps, behaving in an obsessive orderly manner, destroying work already begun, and leaving work unfinished are examples of hesitation. Although hesitating may appear to other people to be self-defeating, it allows neurotic individuals to preserve their inflated sense of self-esteem.

The least severe of the withdrawal safeguarding tendencies is **constructing obstacles.** Some people build a straw house to show that they can knock it down. By overcoming the obstacle, they protect their self-esteem and their prestige. If they fail to hurdle the barrier, they can always resort to an excuse.

In summary, safeguarding tendencies are found in nearly everyone, but when they become overly rigid, they lead to self-defeating behaviors. Overly sensitive people create safeguarding tendencies to buffer their fear of disgrace, to eliminate their exaggerated inferiority feelings, and to attain self-esteem. However, safeguarding tendencies are self-defeating because their built-in goals of self-interest and personal superiority actually block them from securing authentic feelings of self-esteem. Many people fail to realize that their self-esteem would be better safeguarded if they gave up their self-interest and developed a genuine caring for other people. Adler's idea of safeguarding tendencies and Freud's notion of defense mechanisms are compared in Table 3.1.

Masculine Protest

In contrast to Freud, Adler (1930, 1956) believed that the psychic life of women is essentially the same as that of men and that a male-dominated society is not natural but rather an artificial product of historical development. According to Adler, cultural and social practices—not anatomy—influence many men and women to overemphasize the importance of being manly, a condition he called the **masculine protest.**

Origins of the Masculine Protest

In many societies, both men and women place an inferior value on being a woman. Boys are frequently taught early that being masculine means being courageous, strong, and dominant. The epitome of success for boys is to win, to be powerful, to be on top. In contrast, girls often learn to be passive and to accept an inferior position in society.

Some women fight against their feminine roles, developing a masculine orientation and becoming assertive and competitive; others revolt by adopting a passive role, becoming exceedingly helpless and obedient; still others become resigned to the belief that they are inferior human beings, acknowledging men's privileged position by shifting responsibilities to them. Each of these modes of adjustment results from cultural and social influences, not from inherent psychic difference between the two genders.

Adler, Freud, and the Masculine Protest

In the previous chapter we saw that Freud (1924/1961) believed that "anatomy is destiny" (p. 178), and that he regarded women as the "'dark continent' for psychology" (Freud 1926/1959b, p. 212). Moreover, near the end of his life, he was still asking, "What does a woman want?" (E. Jones, 1955, p. 421). According to Adler, these attitudes toward women would be evidence of a person with a strong masculine

---

TABLE 3.1

Comparison of Safeguarding Tendencies with Defense Mechanisms

Adler's Safeguarding Tendencies	Freud's Defense Mechanisms
1. Limited mostly to the construction of a neurotic style of life	1. Found in everyone
2. Protect the person's fragile self-esteem from public disgrace	2. Protect the ego from the pain of anxiety
3. Can be partly conscious	3. Operate only on an unconscious level

4. Common types include:
A. excuses
B. aggression
  (1) depreciation
  (2) accusation
  (3) self-accusation
C. withdrawal
  (1) moving backward
  (2) standing still
  (3) hesitating
  (4) constructing obstacles
	4. Common types include:
	A. repression
	B. reaction formation
	C. displacement
	D. fixation
	E. regression
	F. projection
	G. introjection
	H. sublimation

protest. In contrast to Freud's views on women, Adler assumed that women—because they have the same physiological and psychological needs as men—want more or less the same things that men want.

These opposing views on femininity were magnified in the women Freud and Adler chose to marry. Martha Bernays Freud was a subservient housewife dedicated to her children and husband, but she had no interest in her husband's professional work. In contrast, Raissa Epstein Adler was an intensely independent woman who abhorred the traditional domestic role, preferring a politically active career.

During the early years of their marriage, Raissa and Alfred Adler had somewhat compatible political views, but in time, these views diverged. Alfred became more of a capitalist, advocating personal responsibility, while Raissa became involved in the dangerous Communist politics of her native Russia. Such independence pleased Adler, who was as much a feminist as his strong-willed wife.

Applications of Individual Psychology

We have divided the practical applications of individual psychology into four areas: (1) family constellation, (2) early recollections, (3) dreams, and (4) psychotherapy.

Family Constellation

In therapy, Adler almost always asked patients about their family constellation, that is, their birth order, the gender of their siblings, and the age spread between them. Although people's perception of the situation into which they were born is more important than numerical rank, Adler did form some general hypotheses about birth order.

Firstborn children, according to Adler (1931), are likely to have intensified feelings of power and superiority, high anxiety, and overprotective tendencies. (Recall that Freud was his mother's firstborn child.) Firstborn children occupy a unique position, being an only child for a time and then experiencing a traumatic dethronement when a younger sibling is born. This event dramatically changes the situation and the child's view of the world.

If firstborn children are age 3 or older when a baby brother or sister is born, they incorporate this dethronement into a previously established style of life. If they have already developed a self-centered style of life, they likely will feel hostility and resentment toward the new baby, but if they have formed a cooperating style, they will eventually adopt this same attitude toward the new sibling. If firstborn children are less than 3 years old, their hostility and resentment will be largely unconscious, which makes these attitudes more resistant to change in later life.

According to Adler, secondborn children (such as himself) begin life in a better situation for developing cooperation and social interest. To some extent, the personalities of secondborn children are shaped by their perception of the older child's attitude toward them. If this attitude is one of extreme hostility and vengeance, the second child may become highly competitive or overly discouraged. The typical second child, however, does not develop in either of these two directions. Instead, the secondborn child matures toward moderate competitiveness, having a healthy desire to overtake the older rival. If some success is achieved, the child is likely to develop

Siblings may feel superior or inferior and may adopt different attitudes toward the world depending in part on their order of birth.

a revolutionary attitude and feel that any authority can be challenged. Again, children's interpretations are more important than their chronological position.

Youngest children, Adler believed, are often the most pampered and, consequently, run a high risk of being problem children. They are likely to have strong feelings of inferiority and to lack a sense of independence. Nevertheless, they possess many advantages. They are often highly motivated to exceed older siblings and to become the fastest runner, the best musician, the most skilled athlete, or the most ambitious student.

Only children are in a unique position of competing, not against brothers and sisters, but against father and mother. Living in an adult world, they often develop an exaggerated sense of superiority and an inflated self-concept. Adler (1931) stated that only children may lack well-developed feelings of cooperation and social interest, possess a parasitic attitude, and expect other people to pamper and protect them. Typical positive and negative traits of oldest, second, youngest, and only children are shown in Table 3.2.

Early Recollections

To gain an understanding of patients' personality, Adler would ask them to reveal their **early recollections** (ERs). Although he believed that the recalled memories yield clues for understanding patients' style of life, he did not consider these memories to have a causal effect. Whether the recalled experiences correspond with objective reality or are complete fantasies is of no importance. People reconstruct the

TABLE 3.2

Adler's View of Some Possible Traits by Birth Order

Positive Traits	Negative Traits
Oldest Child	
Nurturing and protective of others	Highly anxious
Good organizer	Exaggerated feelings of power
	Unconscious hostility
	Fights for acceptance
	Must always be "right," whereas others are always "wrong"
	Highly critical of others
	Uncooperative
Second Child	
Highly motivated	Highly competitive
Cooperative	Easily discouraged
Moderately competitive	
Youngest Child	
Realistically ambitious	Pampered style of life
	Dependent on others
	Wants to excel in everything
	Unrealistically ambitious
Only Child	
Socially mature	Exaggerated feelings of superiority
	Low feelings of cooperation
	Inflated sense of self
	Pampered style of life

events to make them consistent with a theme or pattern that runs throughout their lives.

Adler (1929/1969, 1931) insisted that early recollections are always consistent with people's present style of life and that their subjective account of these experiences yields clues to understanding both their final goal and their present style of life. One of Adler's earliest recollections was of the great contrast between his brother Sigmund's good health and his own sickly condition. As an adult, Adler reported that

> One of my earliest recollections is of sitting on a beach . . . bandaged up on account of rickets, with my healthier elder brother sitting opposite me. He could run, jump, and move about quite effortlessly, while for me movement of any sort was a strain. . . . Everyone went to great pains to help me. (Bottome, 1957, p. 30)

If Adler's assumption that early recollections are a valid indicator of a person's style of life, then this memory should yield clues about Adler's adult style of life.

First, it tells us that he must have seen himself as an underdog, competing valiantly against a powerful foe. However, this early recollection also indicates that he believed he had the help of others. Receiving aid from other people would have given Adler the confidence to compete against such a powerful rival. This confidence coupled with a competitive attitude likely carried over to his relationship with Sigmund Freud, making that association tenuous from the beginning.

Adler (1929/1964) presented another example of the relationship between early recollections and style of life. During therapy an outwardly successful man who greatly distrusted women reported the following early memory: "I was going with my mother and little brother to market. Suddenly it began to rain and my mother took me in her arms, and then, remembering that I was the older, she put me down and took up my younger brother" (p. 123). Adler saw that this recollection related directly to the man's current distrust of women. Having initially gained a favorite position with his mother, he eventually lost it to his younger brother. Although others may claim to love him, they will soon withdraw their love. Note that Adler did not believe that the early childhood experiences *caused* the man's current distrust of women, but rather that his current distrustful style of life shapes and colors his early recollections.

Adler believed that highly anxious patients will often project their current style of life onto their memory of childhood experiences by recalling fearful and anxiety-producing events, such as being in a motor vehicle crash, losing parents either temporarily or permanently, or being bullied by other children. In contrast, self-confident people tend to recall memories that include pleasant relations with other people. In either case the early experience does not determine the style of life. Adler believed that the opposite was true; that is, recollections of early experiences are simply shaped by present style of life.

Dreams

Although dreams cannot foretell the future, they can provide clues for solving future problems. Nevertheless, the dreamer frequently does not wish to solve the problem in a productive manner. Adler (1956) reported the dream of a 35-year-old man who was considering marriage. In the dream, the man "crossed the border between Austria and Hungary, and they wanted to imprison me" (p. 361). Adler interpreted this dream to mean that the dreamer wants to come to a standstill because he would be defeated if he went on. In other words, the man wanted to limit his scope of activity and had no deep desire to change his marital status. He did not wish to be "imprisoned" by marriage. Any interpretation of this or any dream must be tentative and open to reinterpretation. Adler (1956) applied the golden rule of individual psychology to dream work, namely, "Everything can be different" (p. 363). If one interpretation doesn't feel right, try another.

Immediately before Adler's first trip to the United States in 1926, he had a vivid and anxious dream that related directly to his desire to spread his individual psychology to a new world and to free himself from the constraints of Freud and Vienna. The night before he was to depart for America, Adler dreamed that he was on board the ship when

> suddenly it capsized and sunk. All of Adler's worldly possessions were on it and were destroyed by the raging waves. Hurled into the ocean, Adler was forced to

swim for his life. Alone he thrashed and struggled through the choppy water. But through the force of will and determination, he finally reached land in safety. (Hoffman, 1994, p. 151)

Adler interpreted this dream to mean that he had to muster the courage to venture into a new world and to break from old worldly possessions.

Although Adler believed that he could easily interpret this dream, he contended that most dreams are self-deceptions and not easily understood by the dreamer. Dreams are disguised to deceive the dreamer, making self-interpretation difficult. The more an individual's goal is inconsistent with reality, the more likely that person's dreams will be used for self-deception. For example, a man may have the goal of reaching the top, being above, or becoming an important military figure. If he also possesses a dependent style of life, his ambitious goal may be expressed in dreams of being lifted onto another person's shoulders or being shot from a cannon. The dream unveils the style of life, but it fools the dreamer by presenting him with an unrealistic, exaggerated sense of power and accomplishment. In contrast, a more courageous and independent person with similar lofty ambitions may dream of unaided flying or reaching a goal without help, much as Adler had done when he dreamed of escaping from a sinking ship.

Psychotherapy

Adlerian theory postulates that psychopathology results from lack of courage, exaggerated feelings of inferiority, and underdeveloped social interest. Thus, the chief purpose of Adlerian psychotherapy is to enhance courage, lessen feelings of inferiority, and encourage social interest. This task, however, is not easy because patients struggle to hold on to their existing, comfortable view of themselves. To overcome this resistance to change, Adler would sometimes ask patients, "What would you do if I cured you immediately?" Such a question usually forced patients to examine their goals and to see that responsibility for their current misery rests with them.

Adler often used the motto "Everybody can accomplish everything." Except for certain limitations set by heredity, he strongly believed this maxim and repeatedly emphasized that what people do with what they have is more important than what they have (Adler, 1925/1968, 1956). Through the use of humor and warmth, Adler tried to increase the patient's courage, self-esteem, and social interest. He believed that a warm, nurturing attitude by the therapist encourages patients to expand their social interest to each of the three problems of life: sexual love, friendship, and occupation.

Adler innovated a unique method of therapy with problem children by treating them in front of an audience of parents, teachers, and health professionals. When children receive therapy in public, they more readily understand that their problems are community problems. Adler (1964) believed that this procedure would enhance children's social interest by allowing them to feel that they belong to a community of concerned adults. Adler was careful not to blame the parents for a child's misbehavior. Instead, he worked to win the parents' confidence and to persuade them to change their attitudes toward the child.

Although Adler was quite active in setting the goal and direction of psychotherapy, he maintained a friendly and permissive attitude toward the patient. He established himself as a congenial coworker, refrained from moralistic preaching, and placed great value on the human relationship. By cooperating with their thera-pists, patients establish contact with another person. The therapeutic relationship awakens their social interest in the same manner that children gain social interest from their parents. Once awakened, the patients' social interest must spread to fam-ily, friends, and people outside the therapeutic relationship (Adler, 1956).

Related Research

Adlerian theory continues to generate a moderate amount of research on such topics as career choice, eating disorders, binge drinking, and other important issues. Each of these topics can provide a potentially rich source for understanding various Adler-ian concepts.

Early Recollections and Career Choice

Do early recollections predict career choice among young students? Adler believed that career choices reflect a person's personality. "If ever I am called on for voca-tional guidance, I always ask the individual what he was interested in during his first years. His memories of this period show conclusively what he has trained himself for most continuously" (Adler, 1958, as quoted in Kasler & Nevo, 2005, p. 221). Re-searchers inspired by Adler therefore predicted that the kind of career one chooses as an adult is often reflected in one's earliest recollections.

In order to test this hypothesis, Jon Kasler and Ofra Nevo (2005) gathered ear-liest memories from 130 participants. These recollections were then coded by two judges on the kind of career the memory reflected. The recollections were classified using Holland's (1973) vocational interest types, namely Realistic, Investigative, Artistic, Social, Enterprising, and Conventional (see Table 3.3 for description of these interest types). For example, an early recollection that reflects a social career interest later in life was: "I went to nursery school for the first time in my life at the age of four or five. I don't remember my feelings that day but I went with my mother and the moment I arrived I met my first friend, a boy by the name of P. I remember a clear picture of P playing on the railings and somehow I joined him. I had fun all day" (Kasler & Nevo, 2005, p. 226). This early recollection centers around social in-teraction and relationships. An example of an early recollection that reflects a real-istic career interest was: "When I was a little boy, I used to like to take things apart, especially electrical appliances. One day I wanted to find out what was inside the tel-evision, so I decided to take a knife and break it open. Because I was so small I didn't have the strength and anyway my father caught me and yelled at me" (Kasler & Nevo, 2005, p. 225).

Career interest of participants was assessed by a self-report measure, the Self-Directed Search (SDS) questionnaire (Holland, 1973). The SDS measures vocational interests, which were independently categorized into the same six Holland types that early recollections were placed into. The researchers therefore had early recollec-tions and adult career interests both classified into the six career types, and they wanted to examine whether early recollections matched career interest.

Kasler and Nevo (2005) found that early recollections in childhood did match career type as an adult, at least for the three career types that were well represented

TABLE 3.3

Qualities of Holland's Six Career Types: Realistic, Investigative, Artistic, Social, Enterprising, and Conventional

Realistic

- Likes to work with animals, tools, or machines; generally avoids social activities like teaching, healing, and informing others;
- Has good skills in working with tools, mechanical or electrical drawings, machines, or plants and animals;
- Values practical things you can see, touch, and use like plants and animals, tools, equipment, or machines; and
- Sees self as practical, mechanical, and realistic.

Investigative

- Likes to study and solve math or science problems; generally avoids leading, selling, or persuading people;
- Is good at understanding and solving science and math problems;
- Values science; and
- Sees self as precise, scientific, and intellectual.

Artistic

- Likes to do creative activities like art, drama, crafts, dance, music, or creative writing; generally avoids highly ordered or repetitive activities;
- Has good artistic abilities—in creative writing, drama, crafts, music, or art;
- Values the creative arts—like drama, music, art, or the works of creative writers; and
- Sees self as expressive, original, and independent.

Social

- Likes to do things to help people—like teaching, nursing, or giving first aid, providing information; generally avoids using machines, tools, or animals to achieve a goal;
- Is good at teaching, counseling, nursing, or giving information;
- Values helping people and solving social problems; and
- Sees self as helpful, friendly, and trustworthy.

Enterprising

- Likes to lead and persuade people, and to sell things and ideas; generally avoids activities that require careful observation and scientific, analytical thinking;
- Is good at leading people and selling things or ideas;
- Values success in politics, leadership, or business; and
- Sees self as energetic, ambitious, and sociable.

Conventional

- Likes to work with numbers, records, or machines in a set, orderly way; generally avoids ambiguous, unstructured activities;
- Is good at working with written records and numbers in a systematic, orderly way;
- Values success in business; and
- Sees self as orderly, and good at following a set plan.

in their sample (Realistic, Artistic, and Social). The general direction of a participant's career path could be identified from themes seen in early recollections. These vignettes are consistent with Alder's view of early recollections and demonstrate how style of life may relate to occupational choice.

Early Childhood and Health-Related Issues

Psychologists have been studying health-related issues for a number of years, but only recently have these topics become of interest to Adlerian psychologists. As it turns out, Adler's theory of inferiority, superiority, and social feeling can be applied to explain health-related behaviors such as eating disorders and binge drinking.

According to Susan Belangee (2006), dieting, overeating, and bulimia can be viewed as common ways of expressing inferiority feelings. Belangee cites a report by Lowes and Tiggeman (2003), who looked at body satisfaction in 135 children 5 to 8 years old and found that 59% of them wanted to be thinner. Other research found that 35% of young dieters progressed to pathological dieting. Adlerian psychologists have recognized this progression and have seen it as a means of compensating for inferiority or a sense of worthlessness. In other words, the eating disorder and its striving toward superiority are an unhealthy means of compensating for inferiority. Moreover, eating disorders suggest that a person's *Gemeinschaftsgefühl,* or social feeling, is out of whack. Rather than being focused on helping others and feeling compassion for others, persons with eating disorders are very much focused on their own lives and difficulties (Belangee, 2007).

Adlerian theory can also shed light on another health-related behavior—binge drinking. Although heavy drinking among college students has a long and destructive history, this pattern of alcohol consumption has increased in recent years with male students being more likely than female students to engage in excessive drinking over a relatively short period of time (Brannon & Feist, 2007). College men and women between the ages of 18 and 30 have the highest risk for heavy drinking. However, drinking rates among these students have not been analyzed according to birth order, gender of siblings, ethnicity, and other Adlerian topics.

Recently, however, Teresa Laird and Andrea Shelton (2006) examined the issue of binge drinking and birth order among men and women attending college. These researchers found significant differences among students with regard to family dynamics, alcohol consumption, and drinking patterns. That is, the youngest children in a family were more likely to binge drink, whereas older children demonstrated more drinking restraint. The authors explained this association using Adlerian theory: Youngest children are more dependent upon others, and when people who are dependent are stressed, they are more likely to cope by heavy drinking.

Early Recollections and Counseling Outcomes

If early recollections are fictional constructions amenable to present shifts in a person's style of life, then early recollections should change as style of life changes. This hypothesis is difficult to test because researchers would need to (1) measure early recollections, (2) assess current style of life, (3) bring about changes in style of life, and (4) reassess early recollections. If changes in early recollections tend to track changes in personality variables, then ERs could be used as criteria for measures of psychotherapy outcomes.

Some evidence exists that early recollections do change through the course of counseling. For example, Gary Savill and Daniel Eckstein (1987) obtained early recollections and mental status of psychiatric patients both before and after counseling and compared them to ERs and mental status of a matched group of control participants. They found significant changes in both mental status and early recollections for the counseling group but not for the controls. Consistent with Adlerian theory, this finding indicates that when counseling is successful, patients change their early recollections.

Similarly, Jane Statton and Bobbie Wilborn (1991) looked at the three earliest recollections of 5- to 12-year-old children after each of 10 weekly counseling sessions and compared them with the early recollections of a control group of children that did not receive counseling. The researchers found that the counseling group showed greater changes in the theme, character, setting, amount of detail, and level of affect of their early memories. In addition, they reported one dramatic example of how early recollections can change as style of life changes. One young child recalled that

> my uncle and dad took me fishing. They were fishing and my uncle got his line hung on a tree stump in the water. He yanked on the pole and the hook came back and hooked me in the head. . . . I waited for them to pull it out of my head. (p. 341)

After counseling, the child recast this passive early recollection in a more active light.

> I went fishing when I was about 5. . . . I caught a fish . . . and my uncle threw his line out and he got it hung on a tree stump and he yanked it back and the hook came back and got me in the head. . . . I pulled it out. (p. 344)

This research is intriguing because it suggests that early recollections may change as a result of psychotherapy or some other life-altering experience. These results tend to support Adler's teleological approach to personality; namely, early childhood experiences are less important than the adult's view of those experiences.

Critique of Adler

Adler's theory, like that of Freud, produced many concepts that do not easily lend themselves to either verification or falsification. For example, although research has consistently shown a relationship between early childhood recollections and a person's present style of life (Clark, 2002), these results do not verify Adler's notion that present style of life shapes one's early recollections. An alternate, causal explanation is also possible; that is, early experiences may cause present style of life. Thus, one of Adler's most important concepts—the assumption that present style of life determines early memories rather than vice versa—is difficult to either verify or falsify.

Another function of a useful theory is to *generate research,* and on this criterion we rate Adler's theory above average. Much of the research suggested by individual psychology has investigated early recollections, social interest, and style of life. Arthur J. Clark (2002), for example, cites evidence showing that early recollections relate to myriad personality factors, including dimensions or personality clinical disorders, vocational choice, explanatory style, and psychotherapy processes and outcomes. In addition, Adler's theory has encouraged researchers to construct several social interest scales, for example, the Social Interest Scale (Crandall, 1975, 1981), the Social Interest Index (Greever, Tseng, & Friedland, 1973), and the Sulliman Scale of Social Interest (Sulliman, 1973). Research activity on these scales and on birth order, early recollections, and style of life gives Adlerian theory a moderate to high rating on its *ability to generate research.*

How well does Adlerian theory *organize knowledge* into a meaningful framework? In general, individual psychology is sufficiently broad to encompass possible explanations for much of what is known about human behavior and development. Even seemingly self-defeating and inconsistent behaviors can be fit into the framework of striving for superiority. Adler's practical view of life's problems allows us to rate his theory high on its ability to make sense out of what we know about human behavior.

We also rate Adlerian theory high on its ability to *guide action.* The theory serves the psychotherapist, the teacher, and the parent with guidelines for the solution to practical problems in a variety of settings. Adlerian practitioners gather information through reports on birth order, dreams, early recollections, childhood difficulties, and physical deficiencies. They then use this information to understand a person's style of life and to apply those specific techniques that will both increase that person's individual responsibility and broaden his or her freedom of choice.

Is individual psychology *internally consistent?* Does it include a set of operationally defined terms? Although Adlerian theory is a model for self-consistency, it suffers from a lack of *precise operational definitions.* Terms such as *goal of superiority* and *creative power* have no scientific definition. Nowhere in Adler's works are they operationally defined, and the potential researcher will look in vain for precise definitions that lend themselves to rigorous study. The term *creative power* is an especially illusory one. Just what is this magical force that takes the raw materials of heredity and environment and molds a unique personality? How does the creative power transform itself into specific actions or operations needed by the scientist to carry out an investigation? Unfortunately, individual psychology is somewhat philosophical—even moralistic—and does not provide answers to these questions.

The concept of creative power is a very appealing one. Probably most people prefer to believe that they are composed of something more than the interactions of heredity and environment. Many people intuitively feel that they have some agent (soul, ego, self, creative power) within them that allows them to make choices and to create their style of life. As inviting as it is, however, the concept of creative power is simply a fiction and cannot be scientifically studied. Due to lack of operational definitions, therefore, we rate individual psychology low on internal consistency.

The final criterion of a useful theory is simplicity, or *parsimony.* On this standard we rate individual psychology about average. Although Adler's awkward and unorganized writings distract from the theory's rating on parsimony, the work of Ansbacher and Ansbacher (Adler, 1956, 1964) has made individual psychology more parsimonious.

Concept of Humanity

Adler believed that people are basically self-determined and that they shape their personalities from the meaning they give to their experiences. The building material of personality is provided by heredity and environment, but the creative power shapes this material and puts it to use. Adler frequently emphasized that the use that people make of their abilities is more important than the quantity of those abilities. Heredity endows people with certain abilities and environment gives them some opportunity to enhance those abilities, but we are ultimately responsible for the use they make of these abilities.

Adler also believed that people's interpretations of experiences are more important than the experiences themselves. Neither the past nor the future determines present behavior. Instead, people are motivated by their present perceptions of the past and their present expectations of the future. These perceptions do not necessarily correspond with reality, and as Adler (1956) stated, "meanings are not determined by situations, but we determine ourselves by the meanings we give to situations" (p. 208).

People are forward moving, motivated by future goals rather than by innate instincts or causal forces. These future goals are often rigid and unrealistic, but people's personal freedom allows them to reshape their goals and thereby change their lives. People create their personalities and are capable of altering them by learning new attitudes. These attitudes encompass an understanding that change can occur, that no other person or circumstance is responsible for what a person is, and that personal goals must be subordinated to social interest.

Although our final goal is relatively fixed during early childhood, we remain free to change our style of life at any time. Because the goal is fictional and unconscious, we can set and pursue temporary goals. These momentary goals are not rigidly circumscribed by the final goal but are created by us merely as partial solutions. Adler (1927) expressed this idea as follows: "We must understand that the reactions of the human soul are not final and absolute: Every response is but a partial response, valid temporarily, but in no way to be considered a final solution of a problem" (p. 24). In other words, even though our final goal is set during childhood, we are capable of change at any point in life. However, Adler maintained that not all our choices are conscious and that style of life is created through both conscious and unconscious choices.

Adler believed that ultimately people are responsible for their own personalities. People's creative power is capable of transforming feelings of inadequacy into either social interest or into the self-centered goal of personal superiority. This capacity means that people remain free to choose between psychological health and neuroticism. Adler regarded self-centeredness as pathological and established social interest as the standard of psychological maturity. Healthy people have a high level of social interest, but throughout their lives, they remain free to accept or reject normality and to become what they will.

On the six dimensions of a concept of humanity listed in Chapter 1, we rate Adler very high on *free choice and optimism;* very low on *causality;* moderate on *unconscious influences;* and high on *social factors* and on the *uniqueness* of individuals. In summary, Adler held that people are self-determining social creatures, forward moving and motivated by present fictions to strive toward perfection for themselves and society.

Key Terms and Concepts

- People begin life with both an innate striving force and physical deficiencies, which combine to produce *feelings of inferiority.*
- These feelings stimulate people to set a *goal* of overcoming their inferiority.
- People who see themselves as having more than their share of physical deficiencies or who experience a pampered or neglected style of life *overcompensate* for these deficiencies and are likely to have exaggerated feelings of inferiority, strive for personal gain, and set unrealistically high goals.
- People with normal feelings of inferiority *compensate* for these feelings by cooperating with others and developing a high level of social interest.
- *Social interest,* or a deep concern for the welfare of other people, is the sole criterion by which human actions should be judged.
- The three major problems of life—*neighborly love, work,* and *sexual love*—can only be solved through social interest.
- All behaviors, even those that appear to be incompatible, are *consistent with a person's final goal.*
- Human behavior is shaped neither by past events nor by objective reality, but rather by people's *subjective perception* of a situation.
- Heredity and environment provide the building material of personality, but people's *creative power* is responsible for their style of life.
- All people, but especially neurotics, make use of various *safeguarding tendencies*—such as excuses, aggression, and withdrawal—as conscious or unconscious attempts to protect inflated feelings of superiority against public disgrace.
- *The masculine protest*—the belief that men are superior to women—is a fiction that lies at the root of many neuroses, both for men and for women.
- Adlerian therapy uses *birth order, early recollections,* and *dreams* to foster courage, self-esteem, and social interest.

CHAPTER 4

Jung: Analytical Psychology

Jung

The middle-aged doctor sat at his desk in deep contemplation and concern. A 6-year relationship with an older friend and mentor had recently ended on bitter terms, and the doctor felt frustrated and uncertain of his future. He no longer had confidence in his manner of treating patients and had begun to simply allow them to talk, not offering any specific advice or treatment.

For some months the doctor had been having bizarre, inexplicable dreams and seeing strange, mysterious visions. None of this seemed to make sense to him. He felt lost and disoriented—unsure whether or not the work he had been trained to do was indeed science.

A moderately gifted artist, he had begun to illustrate his dreams and visions with little or no comprehension of what the finished product might mean. He had also been writing down his fantasies without really trying to understand them.

On this particular day, he began to ponder: "What am I really doing?" He doubted if his work was science but was uncertain about what it was. Suddenly, to his astonishment, he heard a clear, distinct feminine voice from within him say, "It is art." He recognized the voice as that of a gifted female patient who had strong, positive feelings for him. He protested to the voice that his work was not art, but no answer was immediately forthcoming. Then, returning to his writing, he again heard the voice say, "That is art." When he tried to argue with the voice, no answer came. He reasoned that the "woman from within" had no speech center so he suggested that she use his. This she did, and a lengthy conversation followed.

The middle-aged doctor who talked to the "woman from within" was Carl Gustav Jung, and the time was the winter of 1913–1914. Jung had been an early admirer and friend of Sigmund Freud, but when theoretical differences arose, their personal relationship broke up, leaving Jung with bitter feelings and a deep sense of loss.

The above story is but one of many strange and bizarre occurrences experienced by Jung during his midlife "confrontation with the unconscious." An interesting account of his unusual journey into the recesses of his psyche is found in Jung's autobiography *Memories, Dreams, Reflections* (Jung, 1961).

Overview of Analytical Psychology

An early colleague of Freud, Carl Gustav Jung broke from orthodox psychoanalysis to establish a separate theory of personality called **analytical psychology,** which rests on the assumption that occult phenomena can and do influence the lives of everyone. Jung believed that each of us is motivated not only by repressed experiences but also by certain emotionally toned experiences inherited from our ancestors. These inherited images make up what Jung called the *collective unconscious.* The collective unconscious includes those elements that we have never experienced individually but which have come down to us from our ancestors.

Some elements of the collective unconscious become highly developed and are called *archetypes.* The most inclusive archetype is the notion of self-realization, which can be achieved only by attaining a balance between various opposing forces of personality. Thus, Jung's theory is a compendium of opposites. People are both introverted and extraverted; rational and irrational; male and female; conscious and unconscious; and pushed by past events while being pulled by future expectations.

This chapter looks with some detail into the long and colorful life of Carl Jung and uses fragments from his life history to illustrate his concepts and theories. Jung's notion of a collective unconscious makes his theory one of the most intriguing of all conceptions of personality.

Biography of Carl Jung

Carl Gustav Jung was born on July 26, 1875, in Kesswil, a town on Lake Constance in Switzerland. His paternal grandfather, the elder Carl Gustav Jung, was a prominent physician in Basel and one of the best-known men of that city. A local rumor suggested that the elder Carl Jung was the illegitimate son of the great German poet Goethe. Although the elder Jung never acknowledged the rumor, the younger Jung, at least sometimes, believed himself to be the great-grandson of Goethe (Ellenberger, 1970).

Both of Jung's parents were the youngest of 13 children, a situation that may have contributed to some of the difficulties they had in their marriage. Jung's father, Johann Paul Jung, was a minister in the Swiss Reformed Church, and his mother, Emilie Preiswerk Jung, was the daughter of a theologian. In fact, eight of Jung's maternal uncles and two of his paternal uncles were pastors, so both religion and medicine were prevalent in his family. Jung's mother's family had a tradition of spiritualism and mysticism, and his maternal grandfather, Samuel Preiswerk, was a believer in the occult and often talked to the dead. He kept an empty chair for the ghost of his first wife and had regular and intimate conversations with her. Quite understandably, these practices greatly annoyed his second wife.

Jung's parents had three children, a son born before Carl but who lived only 3 days and a daughter 9 years younger than Carl. Thus, Jung's early life was that of an only child.

Jung (1961) described his father as a sentimental idealist with strong doubts about his religious faith. He saw his mother as having two separate dispositions. On one hand, she was realistic, practical, and warmhearted, but on the other, she was unstable, mystical, clairvoyant, archaic, and ruthless. An emotional and sensitive child, Jung identified more with this second side of his mother, which he called her No. 2 or night personality (Alexander, 1990). At age 3 years, Jung was separated from his mother, who had to be hospitalized for several months, and this separation deeply troubled young Carl. For a long time after, he felt distrustful whenever the word "love" was mentioned. Years later he still associated "woman" with unreliability, whereas the word "father" meant reliable—but powerless (Jung, 1961).

Before Jung's fourth birthday, his family moved to a suburb of Basel. It is from this period that his earliest dream stems. This dream, which was to have a profound effect on his later life and on his concept of a collective unconscious, will be described later.

During his school years, Jung gradually became aware of two separate aspects of his self, and he called these his No. 1 and No. 2 personalities. At first he saw both personalities as parts of his own personal world, but during adolescence he became aware of the No. 2 personality as a reflection of something other than himself—an old man long since dead. At that time Jung did not fully comprehend these separate powers, but in later years he recognized that No. 2 personality had been in touch with feelings and intuitions that No. 1 personality did not perceive. In *Memories, Dreams, Reflections,* Jung (1961) wrote of his No. 2 personality:

> I experienced him and his influence in a curiously unreflective manner; when he was present, No. 1 personality paled to the point of nonexistence, and when the ego that became increasingly identical with No. 1 personality dominated the scene, the old man, if remembered at all, seemed a remote and unreal dream. (p. 68)

Between his 16th and 19th years, Jung's No. 1 personality emerged as more dominant and gradually "repressed the world of intuitive premonitions" (Jung, 1961, p. 68). As his conscious, everyday personality prevailed, he could concentrate on school and career. In Jung's own theory of attitudes, his No. 1 personality was extraverted and in tune to the objective world, whereas his No. 2 personality was introverted and directed inward toward his subjective world. Thus, during his early school years, Jung was mostly introverted, but when the time came to prepare for a profession and meet other objective responsibilities, he became more extraverted, an attitude that prevailed until he experienced a midlife crisis and entered a period of extreme introversion.

Jung's first choice of a profession was archeology, but he was also interested in philology, history, philosophy, and the natural sciences. Despite a somewhat aristocratic background, Jung had limited financial resources (Noll, 1994). Forced by lack of money to attend a school near home, he enrolled in Basel University, a school without an archeology teacher. Having to select another field of study, Jung chose natural science because he twice dreamed of making important discoveries in the natural world (Jung, 1961). His choice of a career eventually narrowed to medicine. That choice was narrowed further when he learned that psychiatry deals with subjective phenomena (Singer, 1994).

While Jung was in his first year of medical school, his father died, leaving him in care of his mother and sister. Also while still in medical school, Jung began to attend a series of seances with relatives from the Preiswerk family, including his first cousin Helene Preiswerk, who claimed she could communicate with dead people. Jung attended these seances mostly as a family member, but later, when he wrote his medical dissertation on the occult phenomenon, he reported that these seances had been controlled experiments (McLynn, 1996).

After completing his medical degree from Basel University in 1900, Jung became a psychiatric assistant to Eugene Bleuler at Burghöltzli Mental Hospital in Zürich, possibly the most prestigious psychiatric teaching hospital in the world at that time. During 1902–1903, Jung studied for 6 months in Paris with Pierre Janet, successor to Charcot. When he returned to Switzerland in 1903, he married Emma Rauschenbach, a young sophisticated woman from a wealthy Swiss family. Two years later, while continuing his duties at the hospital, he began teaching at the University of Zürich and seeing patients in his private practice.

Jung had read Freud's *Interpretation of Dreams* (Freud, 1900/1953) soon after it appeared, but he was not much impressed with it (Singer, 1994). When he reread the book a few years later, he had a better understanding of Freud's ideas and was moved to begin interpreting his own dreams. In 1906, Jung and Freud began a steady correspondence (see McGuire & McGlashan, 1994, for the Freud/Jung letters). The following year, Freud invited Carl and Emma Jung to Vienna. Immediately, both Freud and Jung developed a strong mutual respect and affection for one another, talking during their first meeting for 13 straight hours and well into the early morning hours. During this marathon conversation, Martha Freud and Emma Jung busied themselves with polite conversation (Ferris, 1997).

Freud believed that Jung was the ideal person to be his successor. Unlike other men in Freud's circle of friends and followers, Jung was neither Jewish nor Viennese. In addition, Freud had warm personal feelings for Jung and regarded him as a man of great intellect. These qualifications prompted Freud to select Jung as the first president of the International Psychoanalytic Association.

In 1909, G. Stanley Hall, the president of Clark University and one of the first psychologists in the United States, invited Jung and Freud to deliver a series of lectures at Clark University in Worcester, Massachusetts. Together with Sándor Ferenczi, another psychoanalyst, the two men journeyed to America, the first of Jung's nine visits to the United States (Bair, 2003). During their 7-week trip and while they were in daily contact, an underlying tension between Jung and Freud slowly began to simmer. This personal tension was not diminished when the two now-famous psychoanalysts began to interpret each other's dreams, a pastime likely to strain any relationship.

In *Memories, Dreams, Reflections,* Jung (1961) claimed that Freud was unwilling to reveal details of his personal life—details Jung needed in order to interpret one of Freud's dreams. According to Jung's account, when asked for intimate details, Freud protested, "But I cannot risk my authority!" (Jung, 1961, p. 158). At that moment, Jung concluded, Freud indeed had lost his authority. "That sentence burned itself into my memory, and in it the end of our relationship was already foreshadowed" (p. 158).

Jung also asserted that, during the trip to America, Freud was unable to interpret Jung's dreams, especially one that seemed to contain rich material from Jung's collective unconscious. Later, we discuss this dream in more detail, but here we merely present those aspects of the dream that may relate to some of the lifelong problems Jung had with women. In this dream, Jung and his family were living on the second floor of his house when he decided to explore hitherto unknown levels of his house. At the bottom level of his dwelling, he came upon a cave where he found "two human skulls, very old and half disintegrated" (p. 159).

After Jung described the dream, Freud became interested in the two skulls, but not as collective unconscious material. Instead, he insisted that Jung associate the skulls to some wish. Whom did Jung wish dead? Not yet completely trusting his own judgment and knowing what Freud expected, Jung answered, "My wife and my sister-in-law—after all, I had to name someone whose death was worth the wishing!"

"I was newly married at the time and knew perfectly well that there was nothing within myself which pointed to such wishes" (Jung, 1961, pp. 159–160).

Although Jung's interpretation of this dream may be more accurate than Freud's, it is quite possible that Jung did indeed wish for the death of his wife. At that time, Jung was not "newly married" but had been married for nearly 7 years, and for the previous 5 of those years he was deeply involved in an intimate relationship with a former patient named Sabina Spielrein. Frank McLynn (1996) claimed that Jung's "mother complex" caused him to harbor animosity toward his wife, but a more likely explanation is that Jung needed more than one woman to satisfy the two aspects of his personality.

However, the two women who shared Jung's life for nearly 40 years were his wife Emma and another former patient named Antonia (Toni) Wolff (Bair, 2003). Emma Jung seemed to have related better to Jung's No. 1 personality while Toni Wolff was more in touch with his No. 2 personality. The three-way relationship was not always amiable, but Emma Jung realized that Toni Wolff could do more for Carl than she (or anyone else) could, and she remained grateful to Wolff (Dunne, 2000).

Although Jung and Wolff made no attempt to hide their relationship, the name Toni Wolff does not appear in Jung's posthumously published autobiography, *Memories, Dreams, Reflections*. Alan Elms (1994) discovered that Jung had written a whole chapter on Toni Wolff, a chapter that was never published. The absence of Wolff's name in Jung's autobiography is probably due to the lifelong resentments Jung's children had toward her. They remembered when she had carried on openly with their father, and as adults with some veto power over what appeared in their father's autobiography, they were not in a generous mood to perpetuate knowledge of the affair.

In any event, little doubt exists that Jung needed women other than his wife. In a letter to Freud dated January 30, 1910, Jung wrote: "The prerequisite for a good marriage, it seems to me, is the license to be unfaithful" (McGuire, 1974, p. 289).

Almost immediately after Jung and Freud returned from their trip to the United States, personal as well as theoretical differences became more intense as their friendship cooled. In 1913, they terminated their personal correspondence and the following year, Jung resigned the presidency and shortly afterward withdrew his membership in the International Psychoanalytic Association.

Jung's break with Freud may have been related to events not discussed in *Memories, Dreams, Reflections* (Jung, 1961). In 1907, Jung wrote to Freud of his "boundless admiration" for him and confessed that his veneration "has something of the character of a 'religious' crush" and that it had an "undeniable erotic undertone" (McGuire, 1974, p. 95). Jung continued his confession, saying: "This abominable feeling comes from the fact that as a boy I was the victim of a sexual assault by a man I once worshipped" (p. 95). Jung was actually 18 years old at the time of the sexual assault and saw the older man as a fatherly friend in whom he could confide nearly everything. Alan Elms (1994) contended that Jung's erotic feelings toward Freud—coupled with his early experience of the sexual assault by an older man he once worshipped—may have been one of the major reasons why Jung eventually broke from Freud. Elms further suggested that Jung's rejection of Freud's sexual theories may have stemmed from his ambivalent sexual feelings toward Freud.

The years immediately following the break with Freud were filled with loneliness and self-analysis for Jung. From December of 1913 until 1917, he underwent the most profound and dangerous experience of his life—a trip through the underground of his own unconscious psyche. Marvin Goldwert (1992) referred to this time in Jung's life as a period of "creative illness," a term Henri Ellenberger (1970) had used to describe Freud in the years immediately following his father's death. Jung's period of "creative illness" was similar to Freud's self-analysis. Both men began their search for self while in their late 30s or early 40s: Freud, as a reaction to the death of his father; Jung, as a result of his split with his spiritual father, Freud.

Both underwent a period of loneliness and isolation and both were deeply changed by the experience.

Although Jung's journey into the unconscious was dangerous and painful, it was also necessary and fruitful. By using dream interpretation and active imagination to force himself through his underground journey, Jung eventually was able to create his unique theory of personality.

During this period he wrote down his dreams, drew pictures of them, told himself stories, and then followed these stories wherever they moved. Through these procedures he became acquainted with his *personal* unconscious. (See Jung, 1979, and Dunne, 2000, for a collection of many of his paintings during this period.) Prolonging the method and going more deeply, he came upon the contents of the *collective* unconscious—the archetypes. He heard his anima speak to him in a clear feminine voice; he discovered his shadow, the evil side of his personality; he spoke with the wise old man and the great mother archetypes; and finally, near the end of his journey, he achieved a kind of psychological rebirth called *individuation* (Jung, 1961).

Although Jung traveled widely in his study of personality, he remained a citizen of Switzerland, residing in Küsnacht, near Zürich. He and his wife, who was also an analyst, had five children, four girls and a boy. Jung was a Christian, but did not attend church. His hobbies included wood carving, stone cutting, and sailing his boat on Lake Constance. He also maintained an active interest in alchemy, archeology, gnosticism, Eastern philosophies, history, religion, mythology, and ethnology.

In 1944, he became professor of medical psychology at the University of Basel, but poor health forced him to resign his position the following year. After his wife died in 1955, he was mostly alone, the "wise old man of Küsnacht." He died June 6, 1961, in Zürich, a few weeks short of his 86th birthday. At the time of his death, Jung's reputation was worldwide, extending beyond psychology to include philosophy, religion, and popular culture (Brome, 1978).

Levels of the Psyche

Jung, like Freud, based his personality theory on the assumption that the mind, or psyche, has both a conscious and an unconscious level. Unlike Freud, however, Jung strongly asserted that the most important portion of the unconscious springs not from personal experiences of the individual but from the distant past of human existence, a concept Jung called the *collective unconscious.* Of lesser importance to Jungian theory are the *conscious* and the *personal unconscious.*

Conscious

According to Jung, **conscious** images are those that are sensed by the ego, whereas unconscious elements have no relationship with the ego. Jung's notion of the **ego** is more restrictive than Freud's. Jung saw the ego as the center of consciousness, but not the core of personality. Ego is not the whole personality, but must be completed by the more comprehensive *self,* the center of personality that is largely unconscious. In a psychologically healthy person, the ego takes a secondary position to the unconscious self (Jung, 1951/1959a). Thus, consciousness plays a relatively minor role in analytical psychology, and an overemphasis on expanding one's conscious psyche can lead to psychological imbalance. Healthy individuals are in contact with their conscious world, but they also allow themselves to experience their unconscious self and thus to achieve *individuation,* a concept we discuss in the section titled Self-Realization.

Personal Unconscious

The **personal unconscious** embraces all repressed, forgotten, or subliminally perceived experiences of one particular individual. It contains repressed infantile memories and impulses, forgotten events, and experiences originally perceived below the threshold of our consciousness. Our personal unconscious is formed by our individual experiences and is therefore unique to each of us. Some images in the personal unconscious can be recalled easily, some remembered with difficulty, and still others are beyond the reach of consciousness. Jung's concept of the personal unconscious differs little from Freud's view of the unconscious and preconscious combined (Jung, 1931/1960b).

Contents of the personal unconscious are called **complexes.** A complex is an emotionally toned conglomeration of associated ideas. For example, a person's experiences with Mother may become grouped around an emotional core so that the person's mother, or even the word "mother," sparks an emotional response that blocks the smooth flow of thought. Complexes are largely personal, but they may also be partly derived from humanity's collective experience. In our example, the mother complex comes not only from one's personal relationship with mother but also from the entire species' experiences with mother. In addition, the mother complex is partly formed by a person's conscious image of mother. Thus, complexes may be partly conscious and may stem from both the personal and the collective unconscious (Jung, 1928/1960).

Collective Unconscious

In contrast to the personal unconscious, which results from individual experiences, the **collective unconscious** has roots in the ancestral past of the entire species. It represents Jung's most controversial, and perhaps his most distinctive, concept. The physical contents of the collective unconscious are inherited and pass from one generation to the next as psychic potential. Distant ancestors' experiences with universal concepts such as God, mother, water, earth, and so forth have been transmitted through the generations so that people in every clime and time have been influenced by their primitive ancestors' primordial experiences (Jung, 1937/1959). Therefore, the contents of the collective unconscious are more or less the same for people in all cultures (Jung, 1934/1959).

The contents of the collective unconscious do not lie dormant but are active and influence a person's thoughts, emotions, and actions. The collective unconscious is responsible for people's many myths, legends, and religious beliefs. It also produces "big dreams," that is, dreams with meaning beyond the individual dreamer and that are filled with significance for people of every time and place (Jung, 1948/1960b).

The collective unconscious does not refer to inherited ideas but rather to humans' innate tendency to react in a particular way whenever their experiences stimulate a biologically inherited response tendency. For example, a young mother may unexpectedly react with love and tenderness to her newborn infant, even though she previously had negative or neutral feelings toward the fetus. The tendency to respond was part of the woman's innate potential or inherited blueprint, but such innate potential requires an individual experience before it will become activated. Humans, like other animals, come into the world with inherited predispositions to act or react in certain ways if their present experiences touch on these biologically based predispositions. For example, a man who falls in love at first sight may be greatly surprised and perplexed by his own reactions. His beloved may not resemble his conscious ideal of a woman, yet something within him moves him to be attracted to her. Jung would suggest that the man's collective unconscious contained biologically based impressions of woman and that these impressions were activated when the man first saw his beloved.

How many biologically based predispositions do humans have? Jung said that people have as many of these inherited tendencies as they have typical situations in life. Countless repetitions of these typical situations have made them part of the human biological constitution. At first, they are "*forms without content,* representing merely the possibility of a certain type of perception and action" (Jung, 1937/1959, p. 48). With more repetition these forms begin to develop some content and to emerge as relatively autonomous *archetypes.*

Archetypes

Archetypes are ancient or archaic images that derive from the collective unconscious. They are similar to complexes in that they are emotionally toned collections of associated images. But whereas complexes are individualized components of the personal unconscious, archetypes are generalized and derive from the contents of the collective unconscious.

Archetypes should also be distinguished from *instincts.* Jung (1948/1960a) defined an **instinct** as an unconscious physical impulse toward action and saw the archetype as the psychic counterpart to an instinct. In comparing archetypes to instincts, Jung (1975) wrote:

> As animals of the same kind show the same instinctual phenomena all over the world, man also shows the same archetypal forms no matter where he lives. As animals have no need to be taught their instinctive activities, so man also possesses his primordial psychic patterns and repeats them spontaneously, independently of any kind of teaching. Inasmuch as man is conscious and capable of introspection, it is quite possible that he can perceive his instinctual patterns in the form of archetypal representations. (p. 152)

In summary, both archetypes and instincts are unconsciously determined, and both can help shape personality.

Archetypes have a biological basis but originate through the repeated experiences of humans' early ancestors. The potential for countless numbers of archetypes exists within each person, and when a personal experience corresponds to the latent primordial image, the archetype becomes activated.

The archetype itself cannot be directly represented, but when activated, it expresses itself through several modes, primarily dreams, fantasies, and delusions.

During his midlife encounter with his unconscious, Jung had many archetypal dreams and fantasies. He frequently initiated fantasies by imagining that he was descending into a deep cosmic abyss. He could make little sense of his visions and dreams at that time, but later, when he began to understand that dream images and fantasy figures were actually archetypes, these experiences took on a completely new meaning (Jung, 1961).

Dreams are the main source of archetypal material, and certain dreams offer what Jung considered proof for the existence of the archetype. These dreams produce motifs that could not have been known to the dreamer through personal experience. The motifs often coincide with those known to ancient people or to natives of contemporary aboriginal tribes.

Jung believed that hallucinations of psychotic patients also offered evidence for universal archetypes (Bair, 2003). While working as a psychiatric assistant at Burghöltzli, Jung observed a paranoid schizophrenic patient looking through a window at the sun. The patient begged the young psychiatrist to also observe.

> He said I must look at the sun with eyes half shut, and then I could see the sun's phallus. If I moved my head from side to side the sun-phallus would move too, and that was the origin of the wind. (Jung, 1931/1960b, p. 150)

Four years later Jung came across a book by the German philologist Albrecht Dieterich that had been published in 1903, several years after the patient was committed. The book, written in Greek, dealt with a liturgy derived from the so-called Paris magic papyrus, which described an ancient rite of the worshippers of Mithras, the Persian god of light. In this liturgy, the initiate was asked to look at the sun until he could see a tube hanging from it. The tube, swinging toward the east and west, was the origin of the wind. Dieterich's account of the sun-phallus of the Mithraic cult was nearly identical to the hallucination of the mental patient who, almost certainly, had no personal knowledge of the ancient initiation rite. Jung (1931/1960b) offered many similar examples as proof of the existence of archetypes and the collective unconscious.

As noted in Chapter 2, Freud also believed that people collectively inherit predispositions to action. His concept of *phylogenetic endowment,* however, differs somewhat from Jung's formulation. One difference was that Freud looked first to the personal unconscious and resorted to the phylogenetic endowment only when individual explanations failed—as he sometimes did when explaining the Oedipus complex (Freud, 1933/1964). In contrast, Jung placed primary emphasis on the collective unconscious and used personal experiences to round out the total personality.

The major distinction between the two, however, was Jung's differentiation of the collective unconscious into autonomous forces called *archetypes*, each with a life and a personality of its own. Although a great number of archetypes exist as vague images, only a few have evolved to the point where they can be conceptualized. The most notable of these include the persona, shadow, anima, animus, great mother, wise old man, hero, and self.

Persona

The side of personality that people show to the world is designated as the **persona.** The term is well chosen because it refers to the mask worn by actors in the early theater. Jung's concept of the persona may have originated from experiences with his

No. 1 personality, which had to make accommodations to the outside world. Each of us, Jung believed, should project a particular role, one that society dictates to each of us. A physician is expected to adopt a characteristic "bedside manner," a politician must show a face to society that can win the confidence and votes of the people; an actor exhibits the style of life demanded by the public (Jung, 1950/1959).

Although the persona is a necessary side of our personality, we should not confuse our public face with our complete self. If we identify too closely with our persona, we remain unconscious of our individuality and are blocked from attaining *self-realization.* True, we must acknowledge society, but if we over identify with our persona, we lose touch with our inner self and remain dependent on society's expectations of us. To become psychologically healthy, Jung believed, we must strike a balance between the demands of society and what we truly are. To be oblivious of one's persona is to underestimate the importance of society, but to be unaware of one's deep individuality is to become society's puppet (Jung, 1950/1959).

During Jung's near break with reality from 1913 to 1917, he struggled hard to remain in touch with his persona. He knew that he must maintain a normal life, and his work and family provided that contact. He was frequently forced to tell himself, "I have a medical diploma from a Swiss university, I must help my patients, I have a wife and five children, I live at 228 Seestrasse in Küsnacht" (Jung, 1961, p. 189). Such self-talk kept Jung's feet rooted to the ground and reassured him that he really existed.

Shadow

The **shadow,** the archetype of darkness and repression, represents those qualities we do not wish to acknowledge but attempt to hide from ourselves and others. The shadow consists of morally objectionable tendencies as well as a number of constructive and creative qualities that we, nevertheless, are reluctant to face (Jung, 1951/1959a).

Jung contended that, to be whole, we must continually strive to know our shadow and that this quest is our *first test of courage.* It is easier to project the dark side of our personality onto others, to see in them the ugliness and evil that we refuse to see in ourselves. To come to grips with the darkness within ourselves is to achieve the "realization of the shadow." Unfortunately, most of us never realize our shadow but identify only with the bright side of our personality. People who never realize their shadow may, nevertheless, come under its power and lead tragic lives, constantly running into "bad luck" and reaping harvests of defeat and discouragement for themselves (Jung, 1954/1959a).

In *Memories, Dreams, Reflections,* Jung (1961) reported a dream that took place at the time of his break from Freud. In this dream his shadow, a brown-skinned savage, killed the hero, a man named Siegfried, who represented the German people. Jung interpreted the dream to mean that he no longer needed Sig Freud (Siegfried); thus, his shadow performed the constructive task of eradicating his former hero.

Anima

Like Freud, Jung believed that all humans are psychologically bisexual and possess both a masculine and a feminine side. The feminine side of men originates in the collective unconscious as an archetype and remains extremely resistant to consciousness. Few men become well acquainted with their **anima** because this task requires great courage and is even more difficult than becoming acquainted with their shadow. To master the projections of the anima, men must overcome intellectual barriers, delve into the far recesses of their unconscious, and realize the feminine side of their personality.

As we reported in the opening vignette in this chapter, Jung first encountered his own anima during his journey through his unconscious psyche soon after his break with Freud. The process of gaining acquaintance with his anima was Jung's *second test of courage.* Like all men, Jung could recognize his anima only after learning to feel comfortable with his shadow (Jung, 1954/1959a, 1954/1959b).

In *Memories, Dreams, Reflections,* Jung vividly described this experience. Intrigued by this "woman from within," Jung (1961) concluded that

> she must be the "soul," in the primitive sense, and I began to speculate on the reasons why the name "anima" was given to the soul. Why was it thought of as feminine? Later I came to see that this inner feminine figure plays a typical, or archetypal, role in the unconscious of a man, and I called her the "anima." The corresponding figure in the unconscious of woman I called the "animus." (p. 186)

Jung believed that the anima originated from early men's experiences with women—mothers, sisters, and lovers—that combined to form a generalized picture of woman. In time, this global concept became embedded in the collective unconscious of all men as the anima archetype. Since prehistoric days, every man has come into the world with a predetermined concept of woman that shapes and molds all his relationships with individual women. A man is especially inclined to project his anima onto his wife or lover and to see her not as she really is but as his personal and collective unconscious have determined her. This anima can be the source of much misunderstanding in male-female relationships, but it may also be responsible for the alluring mystique woman has in the psyche of men (Hayman, 2001; Hillman, 1985).

A man may dream about a woman with no definite image and no particular identity. The woman represents no one from his personal experience, but enters his dream from the depths of his collective unconscious. The anima need not appear in dreams as a woman, but can be represented by a feeling or mood (Jung, 1945/1953). Thus, the anima influences the feeling side in man and is the explanation for certain irrational moods and feelings. During these moods a man almost never admits that his feminine side is casting her spell; instead, he either ignores the irrationality of the feelings or tries to explain them in a very rational masculine manner. In either event he denies that an autonomous archetype, the anima, is responsible for his mood.

The anima's deceptive qualities were elucidated by Jung (1961) in his description of the "woman from within" who spoke to him during his journey into the unconscious and while he was contemplating whether his work was science.

> What the anima said seemed to me full of a deep cunning. If I had taken these fantasies of the unconscious as art, they would have carried no more conviction than visual perceptions, as if I were watching a movie. I would have felt no moral obligation toward them. The anima might then have easily seduced me into believing that I was a misunderstood artist, and that my so-called artistic nature gave me the right to neglect reality. If I had followed her voice, she would in all probability have said to me one day, "Do you imagine the nonsense you're engaged in is really art? Not a bit." Thus the insinuations of the anima, the mouthpiece of the unconscious, can utterly destroy a man. (p. 187)

Animus

The masculine archetype in women is called the **animus.** Whereas the anima represents irrational moods and feelings, the animus is symbolic of thinking and reasoning. It is capable of influencing the thinking of a woman, yet it does not actually belong to her. It belongs to the collective unconscious and originates from the encounters of prehistoric women with men. In every female-male relationship, the woman runs a risk of projecting her distant ancestors' experiences with fathers, brothers, lovers, and sons onto the unsuspecting man. In addition, of course, her personal experiences with men, buried in her personal unconscious, enter into her relationships with men. Couple these experiences with projections from the man's anima and with images from his personal unconscious, and you have the basic ingredients of any female-male relationship.

Jung believed that the animus is responsible for thinking and opinion in women just as the anima produces feelings and moods in men. The animus is also the explanation for the irrational thinking and illogical opinions often attributed to women. Many opinions held by women are objectively valid, but according to Jung, close analysis reveals that these opinions were not thought out, but existed ready-made. If a woman is dominated by her animus, no logical or emotional appeal can shake her from her prefabricated beliefs (Jung, 1951/1959a). Like the anima, the animus appears in dreams, visions, and fantasies in a personified form.

Great Mother

Two other archetypes, the great mother and the wise old man, are derivatives of the anima and animus. Everyone, man or woman, possesses a **great mother** archetype. This preexisting concept of mother is always associated with both positive and negative feelings. Jung (1954/1959c), for example, spoke of the "loving and terrible mother" (p. 82). The great mother, therefore, represents two opposing forces—fertility and nourishment on the one hand and power and destruction on the other. She is capable of producing and sustaining life (fertility and nourishment), but she may also devour or neglect her offspring (destruction). Recall that Jung saw his own mother as having two personalities—one loving and nurturing; the other uncanny, archaic, and ruthless.

Jung (1954/1959c) believed that our view of a personal loving and terrible mother is largely overrated. "All those influences which the literature describes as being exerted on the children do not come from the mother herself, but rather from the archetype projected upon her, which gives her a mythological background" (p. 83). In other words, the strong fascination that mother has for both men and women, often in the absence of a close personal relationship, was taken by Jung as evidence for the great mother archetype.

The fertility and nourishment dimension of the great mother archetype is symbolized by a tree, garden, plowed field, sea, heaven, home, country, church, and hollow objects such as ovens and cooking utensils. Because the great mother also represents power and destruction, she is sometimes symbolized as a godmother, the Mother of God, Mother Nature, Mother Earth, a stepmother, or a witch. One example of the opposing forces of fertility and destruction is the story of Cinderella, whose fairy godmother is able to create for her a world of horses, carriages, fancy balls, and a charming prince. However, the powerful godmother could also destroy that world at the strike of midnight. Legends, myths, religious beliefs, art, and literary stories are filled with other symbols of the great mother, a person who is both nurturing and destructive.

Fertility and power combine to form the concept of *rebirth,* which may be a separate archetype, but its relation to the great mother is obvious. Rebirth is represented by such processes as reincarnation, baptism, resurrection, and individuation or self-realization. People throughout the world are moved by a desire to be reborn: that is, to reach self-realization, nirvana, heaven, or perfection (Jung, 1952/1956, 1954/1959c).

Wise Old Man

The **wise old man,** archetype of wisdom and meaning, symbolizes humans' preexisting knowledge of the mysteries of life. This archetypal meaning, however, is unconscious and cannot be directly experienced by a single individual. Politicians and others who speak authoritatively—but not authentically—often sound sensible and wise to others who are all too willing to be misled by their own wise old man archetypes. Similarly, the wizard in L. Frank Baum's *Wizard of Oz* was an impressive and captivating speaker whose words, however, rang hollow. A man or woman dominated by the wise old man archetype may gather a large following of disciples by using verbiage that sounds profound but that really makes little sense because the collective unconscious cannot directly impart its wisdom to an individual. Political, religious, and social prophets who appeal to reason as well as emotion (archetypes are always emotionally tinged) are guided by this unconscious archetype. The danger to society comes when people become swayed by the pseudoknowledge of a powerful prophet and mistake nonsense for real wisdom. Recall that Jung saw the preachings of his own father (a pastor) as hollow pontifications, not backed by any strong religious conviction.

The wise old man archetype is personified in dreams as father, grandfather, teacher, philosopher, guru, doctor, or priest. He appears in fairy tales as the king, the sage, or the magician who comes to the aid of the troubled protagonist and, through superior wisdom, he helps the protagonist escape from myriad misadventures. The wise old man is also symbolized by life itself. Literature is replete with stories of young people leaving home, venturing out into the world, experiencing the trials and sorrows of life, and in the end acquiring a measure of wisdom (Jung, 1954/1959a).

Hero

The **hero** archetype is represented in mythology and legends as a powerful person, sometimes part god, who fights against great odds to conquer or vanquish evil in the form of dragons, monsters, serpents, or demons. In the end, however, the hero often is undone by some seemingly insignificant person or event (Jung, 1951/1959b). For example, Achilles, the courageous hero of the Trojan War, was killed by an arrow in his only vulnerable spot—his heel. Similarly, Macbeth was a heroic figure with a single tragic flaw—ambition. This ambition was also the source of his greatness, but it contributed to his fate and his downfall. Heroic deeds can be performed only by someone who is vulnerable, such as Achilles or the comic book character Superman,

The hero archetype has a tragic flaw. With Superman, the fatal weakness was kryptonite.

whose only weakness was the chemical element kryptonite. An immortal person with no weakness cannot be a hero.

The image of the hero touches an archetype within us, as demonstrated by our fascination with the heroes of movies, novels, plays, and television programs. When the hero conquers the villain, he or she frees us from feelings of impotence and misery; at the same time, serving as our model for the ideal personality (Jung, 1934/1954a).

The origin of the hero motif goes back to earliest human history—to the dawn of consciousness. In conquering the villain, the hero is symbolically overcoming the darkness of prehuman unconsciousness. The achievement of consciousness was one of our ancestors' greatest accomplishments, and the image of the archetypal conquering hero represents victory over the forces of darkness (Jung, 1951/1959b).

Self

Jung believed that each person possesses an inherited tendency to move toward growth, perfection, and completion, and he called this innate disposition the **self.** The most comprehensive of all archetypes, the self is the *archetype of archetypes* because it pulls together the other archetypes and unites them in the process of **self-realization.** Like the other archetypes, it possesses conscious and personal unconscious components, but it is mostly formed by collective unconscious images.

As an archetype, the self is symbolized by a person's ideas of perfection, completion, and wholeness, but its ultimate symbol is the **mandala,** which is depicted as a circle within a square, a square within a circle, or any other concentric figure. It represents the strivings of the collective unconscious for unity, balance, and wholeness.

The self includes both personal and collective unconscious images and thus should not be confused with the ego, which represents consciousness only. In Figure 4.1, consciousness (the ego) is represented by the outer circle and is only a small part of total personality; the personal unconscious is depicted by the middle circle; the collective unconscious is represented by the inner circle; and totality of all three circles symbolizes the self. Only four archetypes—persona, shadow, animus, and anima—have been drawn in this mandala, and each has been idealistically depicted as being the same size. For most people the persona is more conscious than the shadow, and the shadow may be more accessible to consciousness than either the anima or the animus. As shown in Figure 4.1, each archetype is partly conscious, partly personal unconscious, and partly collective unconscious.

The balance shown in Figure 4.1 between consciousness and the total self is also somewhat idealistic. Many people have an overabundance of consciousness and thus lack the "soul spark" of personality; that is, they fail to realize the richness and vitality of their personal unconscious and especially of their collective unconscious.

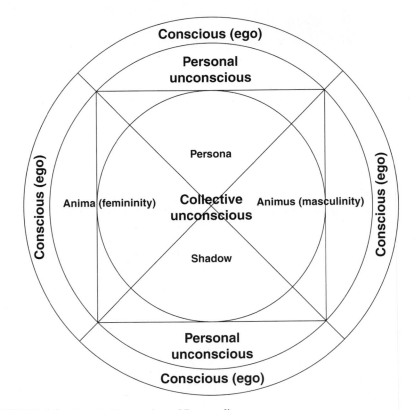

FIGURE 4.1   *Jung's Conception of Personality.*

On the other hand, people who are overpowered by their unconscious are often pathological, with one-sided personalities (Jung, 1951/1959a).

Although the self is almost never perfectly balanced, each person has in the collective unconscious a concept of the perfect, unified self. The mandala represents the perfect self, the archetype of order, unity, and totality. Because self-realization involves completeness and wholeness, it is represented by the same symbol of perfection (the mandala) that sometimes signifies divinity. In the collective unconscious, the self appears as an ideal personality, sometimes taking the form of Jesus Christ, Buddha, Krishna, or other deified figures.

Jung found evidence for the self archetype in the mandala symbols that appear in dreams and fantasies of contemporary people who have never been conscious of their meaning. Historically, people produced countless mandalas without appearing to have understood their full significance. Jung (1951/1959a) believed that psychotic patients experience an increasing number of mandala motifs in their dreams at the exact time that they are undergoing a period of serious psychic disorder and that this experience is further evidence that people strive for order and balance. It is as if the unconscious symbol of order counterbalances the conscious manifestation of disorder.

In summary, the self includes both the conscious and unconscious mind, and it unites the opposing elements of psyche—male and female, good and evil, light and dark forces. These opposing elements are often represented by the yang and yin (see Figure 4.2), whereas the self is usually symbolized by the mandala. This latter motif stands for unity, totality, and order—that is, *self-realization.* Complete self-realization is seldom if ever achieved, but as an ideal it exists within the collective unconscious of everyone. To actualize or fully experience the self, people must overcome their

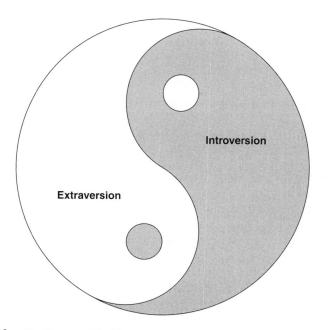

FIGURE 4.2   *The Yang and the Yin.*

fear of the unconscious; prevent their persona from dominating their personality; recognize the dark side of themselves (their shadow); and then muster even greater courage to face their anima or animus.

On one occasion during his midlife crisis, Jung had a vision in which he confronted a bearded old man who was living with a beautiful blind young girl and a large black snake. The old man explained that he was Elijah and that the young girl was Salome, both biblical figures. Elijah had a certain, sharp intelligence, although Jung did not clearly understand him. Salome gave Jung a feeling of distinct suspiciousness, while the serpent showed a remarkable fondness for Jung. At the time he experienced this vision, Jung was unable to comprehend its meaning, but many years later he came to see the three figures as archetypes. Elijah represented the wise old man, seemingly intelligent, but not making a good deal of sense; the blind Salome was an anima figure, beautiful and seductive, but unable to see the meaning of things; and the snake was the counterpart of the hero, showing an affinity for Jung, the hero of the vision. Jung (1961) believed that he had to identify these unconscious images in order to maintain his own identity and not lose himself to the powerful forces of the collective unconscious. He later wrote:

> The essential thing is to differentiate oneself from these unconscious contents by personifying them, and at the same time to bring them into relationship with consciousness. That is the technique for stripping them of their power. It is not too difficult to personify them, as they always possess a certain degree of autonomy, a separate identity of their own. Their autonomy is a most uncomfortable thing to reconcile oneself to, and yet the very fact that the unconscious presents itself in that way gives us the best means of handling it. (p. 187)

Dynamics of Personality

In this section on the dynamics of personality, we look at Jung's ideas on *causality* and *teleology* and on *progression* and *regression.*

Causality and Teleology

Does motivation spring from past causes or from teleological goals? Jung insisted that it comes from both. *Causality* holds that present events have their origin in previous experiences. Freud relied heavily on a causal viewpoint in his explanations of adult behavior in terms of early childhood experiences (see Chapter 2). Jung criticized Freud for being one-sided in his emphasis on causality and insisted that a causal view could not explain all motivation. Conversely, *teleology* holds that present events are motivated by goals and aspirations for the future that direct a person's destiny. Adler held this position, insisting that people are motivated by conscious and unconscious perceptions of fictional final goals (see Chapter 3). Jung was less critical of Adler than of Freud, but he insisted that human behavior is shaped by *both* causal and teleological forces and that causal explanations must be balanced with teleological ones.

Jung's insistence on balance is seen in his conception of dreams. He agreed with Freud that many dreams spring from past events; that is, they are caused by earlier experiences. On the other hand, Jung claimed that some dreams can help a person make decisions about the future, just as dreams of making important discoveries in the natural sciences eventually led to his own career choice.

Progression and Regression

To achieve self-realization, people must adapt not only to their outside environment but to their inner world as well. Adaptation to the outside world involves the forward flow of psychic energy and is called **progression,** whereas adaptation to the inner world relies on a backward flow of psychic energy and is called **regression.** Both progression and regression are essential if people are to achieve individual growth or self-realization.

Progression inclines a person to react consistently to a given set of environmental conditions, whereas regression is a necessary backward step in the successful attainment of a goal. Regression activates the unconscious psyche, an essential aid in the solution of most problems. Alone, neither progression nor regression leads to development. Either can bring about too much one-sidedness and failure in adaptation; but the two, working together, can activate the process of healthy personality development (Jung, 1928/1960).

Regression is exemplified in Jung's midlife crisis, during which time his psychic life was turned inward toward the unconscious and away from any significant outward accomplishments. He spent most of his energy becoming acquainted with his unconscious psyche and did little in the way of writing or lecturing. Regression dominated his life while progression nearly ceased. Subsequently, he emerged from this period with a greater balance of the psyche and once again became interested in the extraverted world. However, his regressive experiences with the introverted world had left him permanently and profoundly changed. Jung (1961) believed that the regressive step is necessary to create a balanced personality and to grow toward self-realization.

Psychological Types

Besides the levels of the psyche and the dynamics of personality, Jung recognized various psychological types that grow out of a union of two basic *attitudes*—introversion and extraversion—and four separate *functions*—thinking, feeling, sensing, and intuiting.

Attitudes

Jung (1921/1971) defined an **attitude** as a predisposition to act or react in a characteristic direction. He insisted that each person has both an *introverted* and an *extraverted* attitude, although one may be conscious while the other is unconscious. Like other opposing forces in analytical psychology, introversion and extraversion serve in a compensatory relationship to one another and can be illustrated by the yang and yin motif (see Figure 4.2).

Introversion

According to Jung, **introversion** is the turning inward of psychic energy with an orientation toward the subjective. Introverts are tuned in to their inner world with all its biases, fantasies, dreams, and individualized perceptions. These people perceive the external world, of course, but they do so selectively and with their own subjective view (Jung, 1921/1971).

The story of Jung's life shows two episodes when introversion was clearly the dominant attitude. The first was during early adolescence when he became cognizant of a No. 2 personality, one beyond awareness to his extraverted personality. The second episode was during his midlife confrontation with his unconscious when he carried on conversations with his anima, experienced bizarre dreams, and induced strange visions that were the "stuff of psychosis" (Jung, 1961, p. 188). During his nearly completely introverted midlife crisis, his fantasies were individualized and subjective. Other people, including even Jung's wife, could not accurately comprehend what he was experiencing. Only Toni Wolff seemed capable of helping him emerge from his confrontation with the unconscious. During that introverted confrontation, Jung suspended or discontinued much of his extraverted or objective attitude. He stopped actively treating his patients, resigned his position as lecturer at the University of Zürich, ceased his theoretical writing, and for 3 years, found himself "utterly incapable of reading a scientific book" (p. 193). He was in the process of discovering the introverted pole of his existence.

Jung's voyage of discovery, however, was not totally introverted. He knew that unless he retained some hold on his extraverted world, he would risk becoming absolutely possessed by his inner world. Afraid that he might become completely psychotic, he forced himself to continue as much of a normal life as possible with his family and his profession. By this technique, Jung eventually emerged from his inner journey and established a balance between introversion and extraversion.

Extraversion

In contrast to introversion, **extraversion** is the attitude distinguished by the turning outward of psychic energy so that a person is oriented toward the objective and away from the subjective. Extraverts are more influenced by their surroundings than by their inner world. They tend to focus on the objective attitude while suppressing the subjective. Like Jung's childhood No. 1 personality, they are pragmatic and well rooted in the realities of everyday life. At the same time, they are overly suspicious of the subjective attitude, whether their own or that of someone else.

In summary, people are neither completely introverted nor completely extraverted. Introverted people are like an unbalanced teeter-totter with a heavy weight on one end and a very light weight on the other (see Figure 4.3 A). Conversely, extraverted people are unbalanced in the other direction, with a heavy extraverted attitude and a very light introverted one (see Figure 4.3 B). However, psychologically healthy people attain a balance of the two attitudes, feeling equally comfortable with their internal and their external worlds (see Figure 4.3 C).

In Chapter 3, we said that Adler developed a theory of personality that was quite opposite to that of Freud. Where did Jung place these two theories on the extraversion/introversion pole? Jung (1921/1971) said that "Freud's view is essentially extraverted, Adler's introverted" (p. 62). Our biographical sketches of Freud and

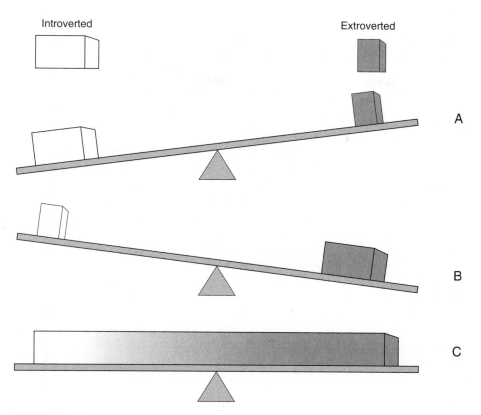

FIGURE 4.3   *The Balance of Introversion and Extraversion.*

Adler reveal that the opposite appears to be true: Freud was personally somewhat introverted, in tune to his dreams and fantasy life, whereas Adler was personally extraverted, feeling most comfortable in group settings, singing songs and playing the piano in the coffeehouses of Vienna. Yet Jung held that Freud's *theory* was extraverted because it reduced experiences to the external world of sex and aggression, Conversely, Jung believed that Adler's *theory* was introverted because it emphasized fictions and subjective perceptions. Jung, of course, saw his own theory as balanced, able to accept both the objective and the subjective.

Functions

Both introversion and extraversion can combine with any one or more of four functions, forming eight possible orientations, or **types.** The four functions—sensing, thinking, feeling, and intuiting—can be briefly defined as follows: Sensing tells people that something exists; thinking enables them to recognize its meaning; feeling tells them its value or worth; and intuition allows them to know about it without knowing how they know.

Thinking

Logical intellectual activity that produces a chain of ideas is called **thinking.** The thinking type can be either extraverted or introverted, depending on a person's basic attitude.

Extraverted thinking people rely heavily on concrete thoughts, but they may also use abstract ideas if these ideas have been transmitted to them from without, for example, from parents or teachers. Mathematicians and engineers make frequent use of extraverted thinking in their work. Accountants, too, are extraverted thinking types because they must be objective and not subjective in their approach to numbers. Not all objective thinking, however, is productive. Without at least some individual interpretation, ideas are merely previously known facts with no originality or creativity (Jung, 1921/1971).

Introverted thinking people react to external stimuli, but their interpretation of an event is colored more by the internal meaning they bring with them than by the objective facts themselves. Inventors and philosophers are often introverted thinking types because they react to the external world in a highly subjective and creative manner, interpreting old data in new ways. When carried to an extreme, introverted thinking results in unproductive mystical thoughts that are so individualized that they are useless to any other person (Jung, 1921/1971).

Feeling

Jung used the term **feeling** to describe the process of evaluating an idea or event. Perhaps a more accurate word would be *valuing,* a term less likely to be confused with either sensing or intuiting. For example, when people say, "This surface feels smooth," they are using their sensing function, and when they say, "I have a feeling that this will be my lucky day," they are intuiting, not feeling.

The feeling function should be distinguished from emotion. Feeling is the evaluation of every conscious activity, even those valued as indifferent. Most of these evaluations have no emotional content, but they are capable of becoming emotions if their intensity increases to the point of stimulating physiological changes within the person. Emotions, however, are not limited to feelings; any of the four functions can lead to emotion when their strength is increased.

Extraverted feeling people use objective data to make evaluations. They are not guided so much by their subjective opinion, but by external values and widely accepted standards of judgment. They are likely to be at ease in social situations, knowing on the spur of the moment what to say and how to say it. They are usually well liked because of their sociability, but in their quest to conform to social standards, they may appear artificial, shallow, and unreliable. Their value judgments will have an easily detectable false ring. Extraverted feeling people often become businesspeople or politicians because these professions demand and reward the making of value judgments based on objective information (Jung, 1921/1971).

Introverted feeling people base their value judgments primarily on subjective perceptions rather than objective facts. Critics of the various art forms make much use of introverted feeling, making value judgments on the basis of subjective individualized data. These people have an individualized conscience, a taciturn demeanor, and an unfathomable psyche. They ignore traditional opinions and beliefs, and their nearly complete indifference to the objective world (including people) often causes persons around them to feel uncomfortable and to cool their attitude toward them (Jung, 1921/1971).

Sensing

The function that receives physical stimuli and transmits them to perceptual consciousness is called **sensation.** Sensing is not identical to the physical stimulus but is simply the individual's perception of sensory impulses. These perceptions are not dependent on logical thinking or feeling but exist as absolute, elementary facts within each person.

Extraverted sensing people perceive external stimuli objectively, in much the same way that these stimuli exist in reality. Their sensations are not greatly influenced by their subjective attitudes. This facility is essential in such occupations as proofreader, house painter, wine taster, or any other job demanding sensory discriminations congruent with those of most people (Jung, 1921/1971).

Introverted sensing people are largely influenced by their subjective sensations of sight, sound, taste, touch, and so forth. They are guided by their interpretation of sense stimuli rather than the stimuli themselves. Portrait artists, especially those whose paintings are extremely personalized, rely on an introverted-sensing attitude. They give a subjective interpretation to objective phenomena yet are able to communicate meaning to others. When the subjective sensing attitude is carried to its extreme, however, it may result in hallucinations or esoteric and incomprehensible speech (Jung, 1921/1971).

Intuiting

Intuition involves perception beyond the workings of consciousness. Like sensing, it is based on the perception of absolute elementary facts, ones that provide the raw material for thinking and feeling. Intuiting differs from sensing in that it is more creative, often adding or subtracting elements from conscious sensation.

Extraverted intuitive people are oriented toward facts in the external world. Rather than fully sensing them, however, they merely perceive them subliminally. Because strong sensory stimuli interfere with intuition, intuitive people suppress many of their sensations and are guided by hunches and guesses contrary to sensory data. An example of an extraverted intuitive type might be inventors who must inhibit distracting sensory data and concentrate on unconscious solutions to objective problems. They may create things that fill a need few other people realized existed.

Introverted intuitive people are guided by unconscious perception of facts that are basically subjective and have little or no resemblance to external reality. Their subjective intuitive perceptions are often remarkably strong and capable of motivating decisions of monumental magnitude. Introverted intuitive people, such as mystics, prophets, surrealistic artists, or religious fanatics, often appear peculiar to people of other types who have little comprehension of their motives. Actually, Jung (1921/1971) believed that introverted intuitive people may not clearly understand their own motivations, yet they are deeply moved by them. (See Table 4.1 for the eight Jungian types with some possible examples of each.)

The four functions usually appear in a hierarchy, with one occupying a *superior* position, another a *secondary position,* and the other two *inferior* positions. Most people cultivate only one function, so they characteristically approach a situation relying on the one dominant or superior function. Some people develop two functions, and a few very mature individuals have cultivated three. A person who has

TABLE 4.1

Examples of the Eight Jungian Types

Functions	Attitudes	
	Introversion	Extraversion
Thinking	Philosophers, theoretical scientists, some inventors	Research scientists, accountants, mathematicians
Feeling	Subjective movie critics, art appraisers	Real estate appraisers, objective movie critics
Sensation	Artists, classical musicians	Wine tasters, proofreaders, popular musicians, house painters
Intuition	Prophets, mystics, religious fanatics	Some inventors, religious reformers

theoretically achieved self-realization or individuation would have all four functions highly developed.

Development of Personality

Jung believed that personality develops through a series of stages that culminate in individuation, or self-realization. In contrast to Freud, he emphasized the second half of life, the period after age 35 or 40, when a person has the opportunity to bring together the various aspects of personality and to attain self-realization. However, the opportunity for degeneration or rigid reactions is also present at that time. The psychological health of middle-aged people is related to their ability in achieving balance between the poles of the various opposing processes. This ability is proportional to the success achieved in journeying through the previous stages of life.

Stages of Development

Jung grouped the stages of life into four general periods—*childhood, youth, middle life,* and *old age.* He compared the trip through life to the journey of the sun through the sky, with the brightness of the sun representing consciousness. The early morning sun is childhood, full of potential, but still lacking in brilliance (consciousness); the morning sun is youth, climbing toward the zenith, but unaware of the impending decline; the early afternoon sun is middle life, brilliant like the late morning sun, but obviously headed for the sunset; the evening sun is old age, its once bright consciousness now markedly dimmed (see Figure 4.4). Jung (1931/1960a) argued that values, ideals, and modes of behavior suitable for the morning of life are inappropriate for the second half, and that people must learn to find new meaning in their declining years of life.

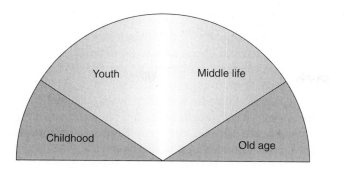

FIGURE 4.4   *Jung Compares the Stages of Life to the Sun's Journey through the Sky, with the Brilliance of the Sun Representing Consciousness.*

Childhood

Jung divided childhood into three substages: (1) the anarchic, (2) the monarchic, and (3) the dualistic. The *anarchic phase* is characterized by chaotic and sporadic consciousness. "Islands of consciousness" may exist, but there is little or no connection among these islands. Experiences of the anarchic phase sometimes enter consciousness as primitive images, incapable of being accurately verbalized.

The *monarchic phase* of childhood is characterized by the development of the ego and by the beginning of logical and verbal thinking. During this time children see themselves objectively and often refer to themselves in the third person. The islands of consciousness become larger, more numerous, and inhabited by a primitive ego. Although the ego is perceived as an object, it is not yet aware of itself as perceiver.

The ego as perceiver arises during the *dualistic phase* of childhood when the ego is divided into the objective and subjective. Children now refer to themselves in the first person and are aware of their existence as separate individuals. During the dualistic period, the islands of consciousness become continuous land, inhabited by an ego-complex that recognizes itself as both object and subject (Jung, 1931/1960a).

Youth

The period from puberty until middle life is called youth. Young people strive to gain psychic and physical independence from their parents, find a mate, raise a family, and make a place in the world. According to Jung (1931/1960a), youth is, or should be, a period of increased activity, maturing sexuality, growing consciousness, and recognition that the problem-free era of childhood is gone forever. The major difficulty facing youth is to overcome the natural tendency (found also in middle and later years) to cling to the narrow consciousness of childhood, thus avoiding problems pertinent to the present time of life. This desire to live in the past is called the *conservative principle.*

A middle-aged or elderly person who attempts to hold on to youthful values faces a crippled second half of life, handicapped in the capacity to achieve self-realization and impaired in the ability to establish new goals and seek new meaning to life (Jung, 1931/1960a).

Middle Life

Jung believed that middle life begins at approximately age 35 or 40, by which time the sun has passed its zenith and begins its downward descent. Although this decline can present middle-aged people with increasing anxieties, middle life is also a period of tremendous potential.

If middle-aged people retain the social and moral values of their early life, they become rigid and fanatical in trying to hold on to their physical attractiveness and agility. Finding their ideals shifting, they may fight desperately to maintain their youthful appearance and lifestyle. Most of us, wrote Jung (1931/1960a), are unprepared to "take the step into the afternoon of life; worse still, we take this step with the false assumption that our truths and ideals will serve us as hitherto. . . . We cannot live in the afternoon of life according to the programme of life's morning; for what was great in the morning will be little at evening, and what in the morning was true will at evening have become a lie" (p. 399).

How can middle life be lived to its fullest? People who have lived youth by neither childish nor middle-aged values are well prepared to advance to middle life and to live fully during that stage. They are capable of giving up the extraverted goals of youth and moving in the introverted direction of expanded consciousness. Their psychological health is not enhanced by success in business, prestige in society, or satisfaction with family life. They must look forward to the future with hope and anticipation, surrender the lifestyle of youth, and discover new meaning in middle life. This step often, but not always, involves a mature religious orientation, especially a belief in some sort of life after death (Jung, 1931/1960a).

Old Age

As the evening of life approaches, people experience a diminution of consciousness just as the light and warmth of the sun diminish at dusk. If people fear life during the early years, then they will almost certainly fear death during the later ones. Fear of death is often taken as normal, but Jung believed that death is the goal of life and that life can be fulfilling only when death is seen in this light. In 1934, during his 60th year, Jung wrote:

> Ordinarily we cling to our past and remain stuck in the illusion of youthfulness. Being old is highly unpopular. Nobody seems to consider that not being able to grow old is just as absurd as not being able to outgrow child's-size shoes. A still infantile man of thirty is surely to be deplored, but a youthful septuagenarian— isn't that delightful? And yet both are perverse, lacking in style, psychological monstrosities. A young man who does not fight and conquer has missed the best part of his youth, and an old man who does not know how to listen to the secrets of the brooks, as they tumble down from the peaks to the valleys, makes no sense; he is a spiritual mummy who is nothing but a rigid relic of the past. (Jung, 1934/1960, p. 407)

Most of Jung's patients were middle aged or older, and many of them suffered from a backward orientation, clinging desperately to goals and lifestyles of the past and going through the motions of life aimlessly. Jung treated these people by helping them establish new goals and find meaning in living by first finding meaning in death. He accomplished this treatment through dream interpretation, because the dreams of elderly people are often filled with symbols of rebirth, such as long journeys or changes in location. Jung used these and other symbols to determine patients' unconscious attitudes toward death and to help them discover a meaningful philosophy of life (Jung, 1934/1960).

Self-Realization

Psychological rebirth, also called *self-realization* or **individuation,** is the process of becoming an individual or whole person (Jung, 1939/1959, 1945/1953). Analytical psychology is essentially a psychology of opposites, and self-realization is the process of integrating the opposite poles into a single homogeneous individual. This process of "coming to selfhood" means that a person has all psychological components functioning in unity, with no psychic process atrophying. People who have gone through this process have achieved realization of the self, minimized their persona, recognized their anima or animus, and acquired a workable balance between introversion and extraversion. In addition, these self-realized individuals have elevated all four of the functions to a superior position, an extremely difficult accomplishment.

Self-realization is extremely rare and is achieved only by people who are able to assimilate their unconscious into their total personality. To come to terms with the unconscious is a difficult process that demands courage to face the evil nature of one's shadow and even greater fortitude to accept one's feminine or masculine side. This process is almost never achieved before middle life and then only by men and women who are able to remove the ego as the dominant concern of personality and replace it with the self. The self-realized person must allow the unconscious self to become the core of personality. To merely expand consciousness is to inflate the ego and to produce a one-sided person who lacks the soul spark of personality. The self-realized person is dominated neither by unconscious processes nor by the conscious ego but achieves a balance between all aspects of personality.

Self-realized people are able to contend with both their external and their internal worlds. Unlike psychologically disturbed individuals, they live in the real world and make necessary concessions to it. However, unlike average people, they are aware of the regressive process that leads to self-discovery. Seeing unconscious images as potential material for new psychic life, self-realized people welcome these images as they appear in dreams and introspective reflections (Jung, 1939/1959; 1945/1953).

Jung's Methods of Investigation

Jung looked beyond psychology in his search for data to build his conception of humanity. He made no apologies for his ventures into the fields of sociology, history, anthropology, biology, physics, philology, religion, mythology, and philosophy. He strongly believed that the study of personality was not the prerogative of any single discipline and that the whole person could be understood only by pursuing knowledge wherever it existed. Like Freud, Jung persistently defended himself as a scientific investigator, eschewing the labels of mystic and philosopher. In a letter to Calvin Hall, dated October 6, 1954, Jung argued: "If you call me an occultist because I am seriously investigating *religious, mythological, folkloristic and philosophical fantasies* in modern individuals and ancient texts, then you are bound to diagnose *Freud as a sexual pervert* since he is doing likewise with sexual fantasies" (Jung, 1975, p. 186). Nevertheless, Jung asserted that the psyche could not be understood by the intellect alone but must be grasped by the total person. Along the same line, he once said, "Not everything I bring forth is written out of my head, but much of it comes from the heart also" (Jung, 1943/1953, p. 116).

Jung gathered data for his theories from extensive reading in many disciplines, but he also gathered data from his use of the word association test, dream analysis, active imagination, and psychotherapy. This information was then combined with readings on medieval *alchemy,* occult phenomena, or any other subject in an effort to confirm the hypotheses of analytical psychology.

Word Association Test

Jung was not the first to use the word association test, but he can be credited with helping develop and refine it. He originally used the technique as early as 1903 when he was a young psychiatric assistant at Burghöltzli, and he lectured on the word association test during his trip with Freud to the United States in 1909. However, he seldom employed it in his later career. In spite of this inattention, the test continues to be closely linked with Jung's name.

His original purpose in using the word association test was to demonstrate the validity of Freud's hypothesis that the unconscious operates as an autonomous process. However, the basic purpose of the test in Jungian psychology today is to uncover feeling-toned complexes. As noted in the section of levels of the psyche, a complex is an individualized, emotionally toned conglomeration of images grouped around a central core. The word association test is based on the principle that complexes create measurable emotional responses.

In administering the test, Jung typically used a list of about 100 stimulus words chosen and arranged to elicit an emotional reaction. He instructed the person to respond to each stimulus word with the first word that came to mind. Jung recorded each verbal response, time taken to make a response, rate of breathing, and galvanic skin response. Usually, he would repeat the experiment to determine test-retest consistency.

Certain types of reactions indicate that the stimulus word has touched a complex. Critical responses include restricted breathing, changes in the electrical conductivity of the skin, delayed reactions, multiple responses, disregard of instructions, inability to pronounce a common word, failure to respond, and inconsistency on test-retest. Other significant responses include blushing, stammering, laughing, coughing, sighing, clearing the throat, crying, excessive body movement, and repetition of the stimulus word. Any one or combination of these responses might indicate that a complex has been reached (Jung, 1935/1968; Jung & Riklin, 1904/1973).

Dream Analysis

Jung agreed with Freud that dreams have meaning and that they should be taken seriously. He also agreed with Freud that dreams spring from the depths of the unconscious and that their latent meaning is expressed in symbolic form. However, he objected to Freud's notion that nearly all dreams are wish fulfillments and that most dream symbols represent sexual urges. Jung (1964) believed that people used symbols to represent a variety of concepts—not merely sexual ones—to try to comprehend the "innumerable things beyond the range of human understanding" (p. 21). Dreams are our unconscious and spontaneous attempt to know the unknowable, to comprehend a reality that can only be expressed symbolically.

The purpose of Jungian dream interpretation is to uncover elements from the personal and collective unconscious and to integrate them into consciousness in order to facilitate the process of self-realization. The Jungian therapist must realize that dreams are often compensatory; that is, feelings and attitudes not expressed during waking life will find an outlet through the dream process. Jung believed that the natural condition of humans is to move toward completion or self-realization. Thus, if a person's conscious life is incomplete in a certain area, then that person's unconscious self will strive to complete that condition through the dream process. For example, if the anima in a man receives no conscious development, she will express herself through dreams filled with self-realization motifs, thus balancing the man's masculine side with his feminine disposition (Jung, 1916/1960).

Jung felt that certain dreams offered proof for the existence of the collective unconscious. These dreams included *big dreams,* which have special meaning for all people; *typical dreams,* which are common to most people; and *earliest dreams remembered.*

In *Memories, Dreams, Reflections,* Jung (1961) wrote about a big dream he had while traveling to the United States with Freud in 1909. In this dream—briefly mentioned in our biographical sketch of Jung—Jung was living in the upper floor of a two-story house. This floor had an inhabited atmosphere, although its furnishings were somewhat old. In the dream, Jung realized that he did not know what the ground floor was like, so he decided to explore it. After descending the stairs, he noticed that all the furnishings were medieval and dated to the 15th or 16th century. While exploring this floor, he discovered a stone stairway that led down into a cellar. "Descending again, I found myself in a beautifully vaulted room which looked exceedingly ancient. . . . As soon as I saw this I knew that the walls dated from Roman times" (Jung, 1961, p. 159). While exploring the floor of this cellar, Jung noticed a ring on one of the stone slabs. When he lifted it, he saw another narrow stairway leading to an ancient cave. There, he saw broken pottery, scattered animal bones, and two very old human skulls. In his own words, he had "discovered the world of the primitive man within myself—a world which can scarcely be reached or illuminated by consciousness" (Jung, 1961, p. 160).

Jung later accepted this dream as evidence for different levels of the psyche. The upper floor had an inhabited atmosphere and represented consciousness, the top layer of the psyche. The ground floor was the first layer of the unconscious—old but not as alien or ancient as the Roman artifacts in the cellar, which symbolized a deeper layer of the personal unconscious. In the cave, Jung discovered two human skulls—the ones for which Freud insisted Jung harbored death wishes. Jung, however, saw these ancient human skulls as representing the depths of his collective unconscious.

Beyond Biography   **Did Jung wish for the death of his wife?
For insight into Jung's relationship with women and to see how one
of his big dreams may have reflected a wish for his wife's death, see
our website at *www.mhhe.com/feist7***

The second kind of collective dreams is the typical dreams, those that are common to most people. These dreams include archetypal figures, such as mother, father, God, devil, or wise old man. They may also touch on archetypal events, such as birth, death, separation from parents, baptism, marriage, flying, or exploring a cave. They may also include archetypal objects, such as sun, water, fish, snakes, or predatory animals.

The third category includes earliest dreams remembered. These dreams can be traced back to about age 3 or 4 and contain mythological and symbolic images and motifs that could not have reasonably been experienced by the individual child. These early childhood dreams often contain archetypal motifs and symbols such as the hero, the wise old man, the tree, the fish, and the mandala. Jung (1948/1960b) wrote of these images and motifs: "Their frequent appearance in individual case material, as well as their universal distribution, prove that the human psyche is unique and subjective or personal only in part, and for the rest is collective and objective" (p. 291).

Jung (1961) presented a vivid illustration in one of his earliest dreams, which took place before his 4th birthday. He dreamed he was in a meadow when suddenly he saw a dark rectangular hole in the ground. Fearfully, he descended a flight of stairs and at the bottom encountered a doorway with a round arch covered by a heavy green curtain. Behind the curtain was a dimly lit room with a red carpet running from the entrance to a low platform. On the platform was a throne and on the throne was an elongated object that appeared to Jung to be a large tree trunk. "It was a huge thing, reaching almost to the ceiling. But it was of a curious composition: It was made of skin and naked flesh, and on top there was something like a rounded head with no face and no hair. On the very top of the head was a single eye, gazing motionlessly upward" (p. 12). Filled with terror, the young boy heard his mother say, "Yes, just look at him. That is the man-eater!" This comment frightened him even more and jolted him awake.

Jung thought often about the dream, but 30 years would pass before the obvious phallus became apparent to him. An additional number of years were required before he could accept the dream as an expression of his collective unconscious rather than the product of a personal memory trace. In his own interpretation of the dream, the rectangular hole represented death; the green curtain symbolized the mystery of Earth with her green vegetation; the red carpet signified blood; and the tree, resting majestically on a throne, was the erect penis, anatomically accurate in every detail. After interpreting the dream, Jung was forced to conclude that no $3\frac{1}{2}$-year-old boy could produce such universally symbolic material solely from his own experiences. A collective unconscious, common to the species, was his explanation (Jung, 1961).

Active Imagination

A technique Jung used during his own self-analysis as well as with many of his patients was **active imagination.** This method requires a person to begin with any impression—a dream image, vision, picture, or fantasy—and to concentrate until the

Carl Jung, the wise old man of Küsnacht.

impression begins to "move." The person must follow these images to wherever they lead and then courageously face these autonomous images and freely communicate with them.

The purpose of active imagination is to reveal archetypal images emerging from the unconscious. It can be a useful technique for people who want to become better acquainted with their collective and personal unconscious and who are willing to overcome the resistance that ordinarily blocks open communication with the unconscious. Jung believed that active imagination has an advantage over dream analysis in that its images are produced during a conscious state of mind, thus making them more clear and reproducible. The feeling tone is also quite specific, and ordinarily a person has little difficulty reproducing the vision or remembering the mood (Jung, 1937/1959).

As a variation to active imagination, Jung sometimes asked patients who were so inclined to draw, paint, or express in some other nonverbal manner the progression of their fantasies. Jung relied on this technique during his own self-analysis, and many of these reproductions, rich in universal symbolism and often exhibiting the mandala, are scattered throughout his books. *Man and His Symbols* (1964), *Word and Image* (1979), *Psychology and Alchemy* (1952/1968), and Claire Dunne's (2000) illustrated biography, *Carl Jung: Wounded Healer of the Soul,* are especially prolific sources for these drawings and photographs.

In 1961, Jung wrote about his experiences with active imagination during his midlife confrontation with the unconscious:

> When I look back upon it all today and consider what happened to me during the period of my work on the fantasies, it seems as though a message had come to me with overwhelming force. There were things in the images which concerned not only myself but many others also. It was then that I ceased to belong to myself alone, ceased to have the right to do so. From then on, my life belonged to the generality. . . . It was then that I dedicated myself to service of the psyche: I loved it and hated it, but it was my greatest wealth. My delivering myself over to it, as it were, was the only way by which I could endure my existence and live it as fully as possible. (p. 192)

Psychotherapy

Jung (1931/1954b) identified four basic approaches to therapy, representing four developmental stages in the history of psychotherapy. The first is confession of a pathogenic secret. This is the cathartic method practiced by Josef Breuer and his patient Anna O. For patients who merely have a need to share their secrets, catharsis is effective. The second stage involves interpretation, explanation, and elucidation. This approach, used by Freud, gives the patients insight into the causes of their neuroses, but may still leave them incapable of solving social problems. The third stage, therefore, is the approach adopted by Adler and includes the education of patients as social beings. Unfortunately, says Jung, this approach often leaves patients merely socially well adjusted.

To go beyond these three approaches, Jung suggested a fourth stage, **transformation.** By transformation, he meant that the therapist must first be transformed into a healthy human being, preferably by undergoing psychotherapy. Only after transformation and an established philosophy of life is the therapist able to help patients move toward individuation, wholeness, or self-realization. This fourth stage is especially employed with patients who are in the second half of life and who are concerned with realization of the inner self, with moral and religious problems, and with finding a unifying philosophy of life (Jung, 1931/1954b).

Jung was quite eclectic in his theory and practice of psychotherapy. His treatment varied according to the age, stage of development, and particular problem of the patient. About two thirds of Jung's patients were in the second half of life, and a great many of them suffered from a loss of meaning, general aimlessness, and a fear of death. Jung attempted to help these patients find their own philosophical orientation.

The ultimate purpose of Jungian therapy is to help neurotic patients become healthy and to encourage healthy people to work independently toward self-realization. Jung sought to achieve this purpose by using such techniques as dream analysis and active imagination to help patients discover personal and collective unconscious material and to balance these unconscious images with their conscious attitude (Jung, 1931/1954a).

Although Jung encouraged patients to be independent, he admitted the importance of *transference,* particularly during the first three stages of therapy. He regarded both positive and negative transference as a natural concomitant to patients' revelation of highly personal information. He thought it quite all right that a number of male patients referred to him as "Mother Jung" and quite understandable that others saw him as God or savior. Jung also recognized the process of **countertransference,** a term used to describe a therapist's feelings toward the patient. Like transference, countertransference can be either a help or a hindrance to treatment, depending on whether it leads to a better relationship between doctor and patient, something that Jung felt was indispensable to successful psychotherapy.

Because Jungian psychotherapy has many minor goals and a variety of techniques, no universal description of a person who has successfully completed analytical treatment is possible. For the mature person, the goal may be to find meaning in life and strive toward achieving balance and wholeness. The self-realized person is able to assimilate much of the unconscious self into consciousness but, at the same time, remains fully aware of the potential dangers hidden in the far recess of the unconscious psyche. Jung once warned against digging too deeply in land not properly surveyed, comparing this practice to a person digging for an artesian well and running the risk of activating a volcano.

Related Research

Jung's approach to personality was very influential in the early development of personality psychology. In recent times, however, its influence has waned, even though there are still a few institutions around the world dedicated to analytical psychology. Today, most research related to Jung focuses on his descriptions of personality types. The Myers-Briggs Type Indicator (MBTI; Myers, 1962) is the most frequently used measure of Jung's personality types and is often used by school counselors to direct students toward rewarding avenues of study. For example, research has found that people high on the intuition and feeling dimensions are likely to find teaching rewarding (Willing, Guest, & Morford, 2001). More recently, researchers have extended work on the usefulness of Jungian personality types by exploring the role of types in how people manage their personal finances and the kinds of careers they pursue.

Personality Type and Investing Money

Research on personality is not only conducted by personality psychologists. Because personality is the study of the uniqueness of each person, it is relevant to any person and any place. For example, although research on psychology and finance do not typically cross paths, personality can be a common factor in both areas because unique aspects of individuals are important in both areas. Recently, business finance researchers were interested in studying how personality affected the way people invest their money (Filbeck, Hatfield, & Horvath, 2005). Specifically, Filbeck and colleagues (2005) wanted to better understand the level of risk individuals are willing to tolerate when it comes to investing money. Investments are often quite volatile. It is true that you can make a lot of money playing the stock market, but you can also lose everything. Some people have natural tolerance for wide fluctuations in their investments, whereas others do not. What kinds of people are willing to take such risks?

Filbeck and colleagues (2005) used the MBTI to determine which of Jung's personality types were more likely to tolerate risk when investing money. The MBTI is a self-report measure with items that assess each of the eight Jungian personality types outlined in Table 4.1. To measure risk tolerance when investing money, the researchers used a questionnaire on which people were presented with several different hypothetical situations of either increasing or decreasing their wealth. Based on responses to these hypothetical situations, the researchers were able to determine at which point (i.e., what percentage gain/loss) people felt their investments were too volatile and risky. The researchers recruited a sample of students and adults to complete the MBTI and risk tolerance questionnaire and then tested their hypothesis that some personality types would tolerate more risk than others.

Their findings revealed that the MBTI is a good predictor of who is willing to tolerate risk and who is not. Specifically, the researchers found that those who are of the thinking type have a high tolerance for risk, whereas those of the feeling type have a relatively low tolerance for the same level of risk. Surprisingly, the extraversion-introversion dimension was not a good predictor of risk tolerance, so it is difficult to predict what specific type of thinkers and feelers (e.g., extraverted or introverted) are most tolerant or intolerant of risk. Still, the findings are informative and in line with Jungian types. For example, the thinking personality type (provided one is not of the extremely extraverted or extremely introverted type) is one who places importance on logical intellectual activity. Logically speaking, stock markets go up and down, and therefore it is wise to tolerate risk even when investments are down because they will likely go back up (eventually) as the economy strengthens. The feeling personality type describes the way people evaluate information, and this evaluation is not necessarily circumscribed by the rules of logic and reason. Therefore, the feeling type is more likely to base their risk tolerance on their own personal evaluation of the situation, which may or may not be in line with the logical trends of the stock market. Though not all of the Jungian personality types were related to risk tolerance in this study, the researchers concluded that personality of investors is an important factor for financial advisors to consider when creating an investment portfolio that best meets the needs and personal values of the investor.

Personality Type and Interest in and Attrition From Engineering

Attrition from engineering seems to be a particularly acute problem given that nearly 50% of the students who start the major do not graduate in it. The two most common explanations are poor performance in "weeding out" courses and poor self-perceived fit with the typical engineer. A study in the *Journal of Psychological Type* examined whether personality type and fit predicted interest in and attrition from engineering in a sample of engineering majors at Georgia Tech (Thomas, Benne, Marr, Thomas, & Hume, 2000). The researchers looked at 195 students (72% male) enrolled in a known "weeding out" engineering class (electricity and magnetism), where 30% of the students traditionally received grades below a C. The students completed the Myers-Briggs Type Indicator (MBTI) in a laboratory session. Thomas and colleagues predicted MBTI scores would be related to scores on the final exam, grade for the course, and withdrawing from the course.

As might be expected, results showed that as a group, the sample was over-represented by the Thinking (75%), Introversion (57%), and Judging (56%) types and was almost evenly split on Intuitive-Sensing (51% Sensing). More importantly, students who withdrew from the course had high scores on the Extraversion and Feeling scales, with 96% of the dropouts scoring high on at least one of those scales. Interestingly, personality type was not related to course grades. In addition, Thomas et al. found that students who were most likely to drop out were exactly the opposite types of those who were least likely to enter engineering to begin with. This result supports the congruency or fit theory of persons and organizations, which states that those who do best in certain professions are those whose personality type matches closest with those already in the profession (Schneider, 1987).

Critique of Jung

Carl Jung's writings continue to fascinate students of humanity. Despite its subjective and philosophical quality, Jungian psychology has attracted a wide audience of both professional and lay people. His study of religion and mythology may resonate with some readers but repel others. Jung, however, regarded himself as a scientist and insisted that his scientific study of religion, mythology, folklore, and philosophical fantasies did not make him a mystic any more than Freud's study of sex made Freud a sexual pervert (Jung, 1975).

Nevertheless, analytical psychology, like any theory, must be evaluated against the six criteria of a useful theory established in Chapter 1. First, a useful theory must generate *testable hypotheses* and *descriptive research,* and second, it must have the capacity for either verification or *falsification.* Unfortunately, Jung's theory, like Freud's, is nearly impossible to either verify or falsify. The collective unconscious, the core of Jung's theory, remains a difficult concept to test empirically.

Much of the evidence for the concepts of archetype and the collective unconscious has come from Jung's own inner experiences, which he admittedly found difficult to communicate to others, so that acceptance of these concepts rests more on faith than on empirical evidence. Jung (1961) claimed that "archetypal statements are based upon instinctive preconditions and have nothing to do with reason; they are neither rationally grounded nor can they be banished by rational argument" (p. 353). Such a statement may be acceptable to the artist or the theologian, but it is not likely to win adherents among scientific researchers faced with the problems of designing studies and formulating hypotheses.

On the other hand, that part of Jung's theory concerned with classification and typology, that is, the functions and attitudes, can be studied and tested and have *generated a moderate amount of research.* Because the Myers-Briggs Type Indicator has yielded a great number of investigations, we give Jung's theory a moderate rating on its ability to generate research.

Third, a useful theory should *organize observations* into a meaningful framework. Analytical psychology is unique because it adds a new dimension to personality theory, namely, the collective unconscious. Those aspects of human personality dealing with the occult, the mysterious, and the parapsychological are not touched on by most other personality theories. Even though the collective unconscious is not the only possible explanation for these phenomena, and other concepts could be postulated to account for them, Jung is the only modern personality theorist to make a serious attempt to include such a broad scope of human activity within a single theoretical framework. For these reasons, we have given Jung's theory a moderate rating on its ability to organize knowledge.

A fourth criterion of a useful theory is its *practicality*. Does the theory aid therapists, teachers, parents, or others in solving everyday problems? The theory of psychological types or attitudes and the MBTI are used by many clinicians, but the usefulness of most analytical psychology is limited to those therapists who subscribe to basic Jungian tenets. The concept of a collective unconscious does not easily lend itself to empirical research, but it may have some usefulness in helping people understand cultural myths and adjust to life's traumas. Overall, however, we can give Jung's theory only a low rating in practicality.

Is Jung's theory of personality *internally consistent?* Does it possess a set of operationally defined terms? The first question receives a qualified affirmative answer; the second, a definite negative one. Jung generally used the same terms consistently, but he often employed several terms to describe the same concept. The words *regression* and *introverted* are so closely related that they can be said to describe the same process. This is also true of *progression* and *extraverted,* and the list could be expanded to include several other terms such as *individuation* and *self-realization,* which also are not clearly differentiated. Jung's language is often arcane, and many of his terms are not adequately defined. As for operational definitions, Jung, like other early personality theorists, did not define terms operationally. Therefore, we rate his theory as low on internal consistency.

The final criterion of a useful theory is *parsimony.* Jung's psychology is not simple, but neither is human personality. However, because it is more cumbersome than necessary, we can give it only a low rating on parsimony. Jung's proclivity for searching for data from a variety of disciplines and his willingness to explore his own unconscious, even beneath the personal level, contribute to the great complexities and the broad scope of his theory. The law of parsimony states, "When two theories are equally useful, the simpler one is preferred." In fact, of course, no two are ever equal, but Jung's theory, while adding a dimension to human personality not greatly dealt with by others, is probably more complex than necessary.

👥 Concept of Humanity

Jung saw humans as complex beings with many opposing poles. His view of humanity was neither *pessimistic* nor *optimistic,* neither *deterministic* nor *purposive.* To him, people are motivated partly by *conscious* thoughts, partly by images from their personal *unconscious,* and partly by latent memory traces inherited from their ancestral past. Their motivation comes from both *causal* and *teleological* factors.

The complex makeup of humans invalidates any simple or one-sided description. According to Jung, each person is a composition of opposing forces. No one is completely introverted or totally extraverted; all male or all female; solely a thinking, feeling, sensing, or intuitive person; and no one proceeds invariably in the direction of either progression or regression.

The persona is but a fraction of an individual. What one wishes to show others is usually only the socially acceptable side of personality. Every person has a dark side, a shadow, and most try to conceal it from both society and themselves. In addition, each man possesses an anima and every woman an animus.

The various complexes and archetypes cast their spell over people and are responsible for many of their words and actions and most of their dreams and fantasies. Although people are not masters in their own houses, neither are they completely dominated by forces beyond their control. People have some limited capacity to determine their lives. Through strong will and with great courage, they can explore the hidden recesses of their psyche. They can recognize their shadow as their own, become partially conscious of their feminine or masculine side, and cultivate more than a single function. This process, which Jung called individuation or self-realization, is not easy and demands more fortitude than most people can muster. Ordinarily, a person who has achieved self-realization has reached middle life and has lived successfully through the stages of childhood and youth. During middle age, they must be willing to set aside the goals and behaviors of youth and adopt a new style appropriate to their stage of psychic development.

Even after people have achieved individuation, made an acquaintance with their inner world, and brought the various opposing forces into balance, they remain under the influence of an impersonal collective unconscious that controls many of their prejudices, interests, fears, dreams, and creative activities.

On the dimension of *biological versus social* aspects of personality, Jung's theory leans strongly in the direction of biology. The collective unconscious, which is responsible for so many actions, is part of our biological inheritance. Except for the therapeutic potential of the doctor-patient relationship, Jung had little to say about differential effects of specific social practices. In fact, in his studies of various cultures, he found the differences to be superficial, the similarities profound. Thus, analytical psychology can also be rated high on *similarities* among people and low on *individual differences*.

Key Terms and Concepts

- The *personal unconscious* is formed by the repressed experiences of one particular individual and is the reservoir of the complexes.
- Humans inherit a *collective unconscious* that helps shape many of their attitudes, behaviors, and dreams.
- *Archetypes* are contents of the collective unconscious. Typical archetypes include persona, shadow, anima, animus, great mother, wise old man, hero, and self.
- The *persona* represents the side of personality that people show to the rest of the world. Psychologically healthy people recognize their persona but do not mistake it for the whole of personality.

- The *anima* is the feminine side of men and is responsible for many of their irrational moods and feelings.
- The *animus,* the masculine side of women, is responsible for irrational thinking and illogical opinions in women.
- The *great mother* is the archetype of fertility and destruction.
- The *wise old man* archetype is the intelligent but deceptive voice of accumulated experience.
- The *hero* is the unconscious image of a person who conquers an evil foe but who also has a tragic flaw.
- The *self* is the archetype of completeness, wholeness, and perfection.
- The two attitudes of *introversion* and *extraversion* can combine with any one or more of the four functions—*thinking, feeling, sensation,* and *intuition*—to produce eight basic types.
- A healthy *middle life* and *old age* depend on proper solutions to the problems of *childhood* and *youth.*
- Jungian therapists use *dream analysis* and *active imagination* to discover the contents of patients' collective unconscious.

CHAPTER 5

Klein: Object Relations Theory

Klein

Melanie Klein, the woman who developed a theory that emphasized the nurturing and loving relationship between parent and child, had neither a nurturant nor a loving relationship to her own daughter Melitta. The rift between mother and daughter began early. Melitta was the oldest of three children born to parents who did not particularly like one another. When Melitta was 15, her parents separated, and Melitta blamed her mother for this separation and for the divorce that followed. As Melitta matured, her relationship with her mother became more acrimonious.

After Melitta received a medical degree, underwent a personal analysis, and presented scholarly papers to the British Psycho-Analytical Society, she was officially a member of that society, professionally equal to her mother.

Her analyst, Edward Glover, was a bitter rival of Melanie Klein. Glover, who encouraged Melitta's independence, was at least indirectly responsible for Melitta's virulent attacks on her mother. The animosity between mother and daughter became even more intense when Melitta married Walter Schmideberg, another analyst who strongly opposed Klein and who openly supported Anna Freud, Klein's most bitter rival.

Despite being a full member of the British Psycho-Analytical Society, Melitta Schmideberg felt that her mother saw her as an appendage, not a colleague. In a strongly worded letter to her mother in the summer of 1934, Melitta wrote:

> I hope you will . . . also allow me to give you some advice. . . . I am very different from you. I already told you years ago that nothing causes a worse reaction in me than trying to force feelings into me—it is the surest way to kill all feelings. . . . I am now grown up and must be independent. I have my own life, my husband. (quoted in Grosskurth, 1986, p. 199.)

Melitta went on to say that she would no longer relate to her mother in the neurotic manner of her younger years. She now had a shared profession with her mother and insisted that she be treated as an equal.

The story of Melanie Klein and her daughter takes on a new perspective in light of the emphasis that object relations theory places on the importance of the mother-child relationship.

Overview of Object Relations Theory

The **object relations theory** of Melanie Klein was built on careful observations of young children. In contrast to Freud, who emphasized the first 4 to 6 years of life, Klein stressed the importance of the first 4 to 6 *months* after birth. She insisted that the infant's drives (hunger, sex, and so forth) are directed to an object—a breast, a penis, a vagina, and so on. According to Klein, the child's relation to the breast is fundamental and serves as a prototype for later relations to whole objects, such as mother and father. The very early tendency of infants to relate to partial objects gives their experiences an unrealistic or fantasy-like quality that affects all later interpersonal relations. Thus, Klein's ideas tend to shift the focus of psychoanalytic theory from organically based stages of development to the role of early fantasy in the formation of interpersonal relationships.

In addition to Klein, other theorists have speculated on the importance of a child's early experiences with the mother. Margaret Mahler believed that children's sense of identity rests on a three-step relationship with their mother. First, infants have basic needs cared for by their mother; next, they develop a safe symbiotic relationship with an all-powerful mother; and finally, they emerge from their mother's protective circle and establish their separate individuality. Heinz Kohut theorized that children develop a sense of self during early infancy when parents and others treat them as if they had an individualized sense of identity. John Bowlby investigated infants' attachment to their mother as well as the negative consequences of being separated from their mother. Mary Ainsworth and her colleagues developed a technique for measuring the type of attachment style an infant develops toward its caregiver.

Biography of Melanie Klein

Melanie Reizes Klein was born March 30, 1882, in Vienna, Austria. The youngest of four children born to Dr. Moriz Reizes and his second wife, Libussa Deutsch Reizes, Klein believed that her birth was unplanned—a belief that led to feelings of being rejected by her parents. She felt especially distant to her father, who favored his oldest daughter, Emilie (Sayers, 1991). By the time Melanie was born, her father had long since rebelled against his early Orthodox Jewish training and had ceased to practice any religion. As a consequence, Klein grew up in a family that was neither proreligious nor antireligious.

During her childhood Klein observed both parents working at jobs they did not enjoy. Her father was a physician who struggled to make a living in medicine and eventually was relegated to working as a dental assistant. Her mother ran a shop selling plants and reptiles, a difficult, humiliating, and fearful job for someone who abhorred snakes (H. Segal, 1979). Despite her father's meager income as a doctor, Klein aspired to become a physician.

Klein's early relationships were either unhealthy or ended in tragedy. She felt neglected by her elderly father, whom she saw as cold and distant, and although she loved and idolized her mother, she felt suffocated by her. Klein had a special fondness for her older sister Sidonie, who was 4 years older and who taught Melanie arithmetic and reading. Unfortunately, when Melanie was 4 years old, Sidonie died. In later years, Klein confessed that she never got over grieving for Sidonie (H. Segal, 1992). After her sister's death, Klein became deeply attached to her only brother, Emmanuel, who was nearly 5 years older and who became her close confidant. She idolized her brother, and this infatuation may have contributed to her later difficulties in relating to men. Like Sidonie earlier, Emmanuel tutored Melanie, and his excellent instructions helped her pass the entrance examinations of a reputable preparatory school (Petot, 1990).

When Klein was 18, her father died, but a greater tragedy occurred 2 years later when her beloved brother, Emmanuel, died. Emmanuel's death left Klein devastated. While still in mourning over her brother's death, she married Arthur Klein, an engineer who had been Emmanuel's close friend. Melanie believed that her marriage at age 21 prevented her from becoming a physician, and for the rest of her life, she regretted that she had not reached that goal (Grosskurth, 1986).

Unfortunately, Klein did not have a happy marriage; she dreaded sex and abhorred pregnancy (Grosskurth, 1986). Nevertheless, her marriage to Arthur produced three children: Melitta, born in 1904; Hans, born in 1907; and Erich, born in 1914. In 1909, the Kleins moved to Budapest, where Arthur had been transferred. There, Klein met Sandor Ferenczi, a member of Freud's inner circle and the person who introduced her into the world of psychoanalysis. When her mother died in 1914, Klein became depressed and entered analysis with Ferenczi, an experience that served as a turning point in her life. That same year she read Freud's *On Dreams* (1901/1953) "and realized immediately that was what I was aiming at, at least during those years when I was so very keen to find out what would satisfy me intellectually and emotionally" (quoted in Grosskurth, 1986, p. 69). At about the same time that she discovered Freud, her youngest child, Erich, was born. Klein was deeply taken by psychoanalysis and trained her son according to Freudian principles. As part of this training, she began to psychoanalyze Erich from the time he was very young. In addition, she also attempted to analyze Melitta and Hans, both of whom eventually went to other analysts. Melitta, who became a psychoanalyst, was analyzed by Karen Horney (see Chapter 6) as well as by others (Grosskurth, 1986). An interesting parallel between Horney and Klein is that Klein later analyzed Horney's two youngest daughters when they were 12 and 9 years old. (Horney's oldest daughter was 14 and refused to be analyzed.) Unlike Melitta's voluntary analysis by Horney, the two Horney children were compelled to attend analytic sessions, not for treatment of any neurotic disorder but as a preventive measure (Quinn, 1987).

Klein separated from her husband in 1919 but did not obtain a divorce for several years. After the separation, she established a psychoanalytic practice in Berlin and made her first contributions to the psychoanalytic literature with a paper dealing with her analysis of Erich, who was not identified as her son until long after Klein's death (Grosskurth, 1998). Not completely satisfied with her own analysis by Ferenczi, she ended the relationship and began an analysis with Karl Abraham, another member of Freud's inner circle. After only 14 months, however, Klein experienced another tragedy when Abraham died. At this point of her life, Klein decided to begin a self-analysis, one that continued for the remainder of her life. Before 1919, psychoanalysts, including Freud, based their theories of child development on their therapeutic work with *adults*. Freud's only case study of a child was Little Hans, a boy whom he saw as a patient only once. Melanie Klein changed that situation by psychoanalyzing children directly. Her work with very young children, including her own, convinced her that children internalize both positive and negative feelings toward their mother and that they develop a superego much earlier than Freud had believed. Her slight divergence from standard psychoanalytic theory brought much criticism from her colleagues in Berlin, causing her to feel increasingly uncomfortable in that city. Then, in 1926, Ernest Jones invited her to London to analyze his children and to deliver a series of lectures on child analysis. These lectures later resulted in her first book, *The Psycho-Analysis of Children* (Klein, 1932). In 1927, she took up permanent residency in England, remaining there until her death on September 22, 1960. On the day of her memorial service, her daughter Melitta delivered a final posthumous insult by giving a professional lecture wearing flamboyant red boots, which scandalized many in her audience (Grosskurth, 1986).

Klein's years in London were marked by division and controversy. Although she continued to regard herself as a Freudian, neither Freud nor his daughter Anna accepted her emphasis on the importance of very early childhood or her analytic technique with children. Her differences with Anna Freud began while the Freuds were still living in Vienna, but they climaxed after Anna moved with her father and mother to London in 1938. Before the arrival of Anna Freud, the English school of psychoanalysis was steadily becoming the "Kleinian School," and Klein's battles were limited mostly to those with her daughter, Melitta, and these battles were both fierce and personal.

In 1934, Klein's older son, Hans, was killed in a fall. Melitta, who had recently moved to London with her psychoanalyst husband, Walter Schmideberg, maintained that her brother had committed suicide, and she blamed her mother for his death. During that same year, Melitta began an analysis with Edward Glover, one of Klein's rivals in the British Society. Klein and her daughter then became even more personally estranged and professionally antagonistic, and Melitta maintained her animosity even after her mother's death.

Although Melitta Schmideberg was not a supporter of Anna Freud, her persistent antagonism toward Klein increased the difficulties of Klein's struggle with Anna Freud, who never recognized the possibility of analyzing young children (King & Steiner, 1991; Mitchell & Black, 1995). The friction between Klein and Anna Freud never abated, with each side claiming to be more "Freudian" than the other (Hughes, 1989). Finally, in 1946 the British Society accepted three training procedures—the traditional one of Melanie Klein, the one advocated by Anna Freud, and a Middle Group that accepted neither training school but was more eclectic in its approach. By such a division, the British Society remained intact, albeit with an uneasy alliance.

Introduction to Object Relations Theory

Object relations theory is an offspring of Freud's instinct theory, but it differs from its ancestor in at least three general ways. First, object relations theory places less emphasis on biologically based drives and more importance on consistent patterns of interpersonal relationships. Second, as opposed to Freud's rather paternalistic theory that emphasizes the power and control of the father, object relations theory tends to be more maternal, stressing the intimacy and nurturing of the mother. Third, object relations theorists generally see human contact and relatedness—not sexual pleasure—as the prime motive of human behavior.

More specifically, however, the concept of object relations has many meanings, just as there are many object relations theorists. This chapter concentrates primarily on Melanie Klein's work, but it also briefly discusses the theories of Margaret S. Mahler, Heinz Kohut, John Bowlby, and Mary Ainsworth. In general, Mahler's work was concerned with the infant's struggle to gain autonomy and a sense of self; Kohut's, with the formation of the self; Bowlby's, with the stages of separation anxiety; and Ainsworth's, with styles of attachment.

If Klein is the mother of object relations theory, then Freud himself is the father. Recall from Chapter 2 that Freud (1915/1957a) believed instincts or drives have an *impetus,* a *source,* an *aim,* and an *object,* with the latter two having the greater psychological significance. Although different drives may seem to have separate aims, their underlying aim is always the same—to reduce tension: that is, to achieve pleasure. In Freudian terms, the **object** of the drive is any person, part of a person, or thing through which the aim is satisfied. Klein and other object relations theorists begin with this basic assumption of Freud and then speculate on how the infant's real or fantasized early relations with the mother or the breast become a model for all later interpersonal relationships. Adult relationships, therefore, are not always what they seem. An important portion of any relationship is the internal psychic representations of early significant objects, such as the mother's breast or the father's penis, that have been *introjected,* or taken into the infant's psychic structure, and then *projected* onto one's partner. These internal pictures are not accurate representations of the other person but are remnants of each person's earlier experiences.

Although Klein continued to regard herself as a Freudian, she extended psychoanalytic theory beyond the boundaries set by Freud. For his part, Freud chose mostly to ignore Klein. When pressed for an opinion on her work, Freud had little to say. For example, in 1925 when Ernest Jones wrote to him praising Klein's "valuable work" with childhood analysis and play therapy, Freud simply replied that "Melanie Klein's work has aroused considerable doubt and controversy here in Vienna" (Steiner, 1985, p. 30).

Psychic Life of the Infant

Whereas Freud emphasized the first few years of life, Klein stressed the importance of the first 4 or 6 *months.* To her, infants do not begin life with a blank slate but with an inherited predisposition to reduce the anxiety they experience as a result of the conflict produced by the forces of the life instinct and the power of the death instinct. The infant's innate readiness to act or react presupposes the existence of *phylogenetic endowment,* a concept that Freud also accepted.

Phantasies

One of Klein's basic assumptions is that the infant, even at birth, possesses an active phantasy life. These phantasies are psychic representations of unconscious id instincts; they should not be confused with the conscious fantasies of older children and adults. In fact, Klein intentionally spelled phantasy this way to make it distinguishable. When Klein (1932) wrote of the dynamic phantasy life of infants, she did not suggest that neonates could put thoughts into words. She simply meant that they possess unconscious images of "good" and "bad." For example, a full stomach is good; an empty one is bad. Thus, Klein would say that infants who fall asleep while sucking on their fingers are phantasizing about having their mother's good breast inside themselves. Similarly, hungry infants who cry and kick their legs are phantasizing that they are kicking or destroying the bad breast. This idea of a good breast and a bad breast is comparable to Sullivan's notion of a good mother and a bad mother (see Chapter 8 for Sullivan's theory).

As the infant matures, unconscious phantasies connected with the breast continue to exert an impact on psychic life, but newer ones emerge as well. These later unconscious phantasies are shaped by both reality and by inherited predispositions. One of these phantasies involves the Oedipus complex, or the child's wish to destroy one parent and sexually possess the other. (Klein's notion of the Oedipus complex is discussed more fully in the section titled Internalizations.) Because these phantasies are unconscious, they can be contradictory. For example, a little boy can phantasize both beating his mother and having babies with her. Such phantasies spring partly from the boy's experiences with his mother and partly from universal predispositions to destroy the bad breast and to incorporate the good one.

Objects

Klein agreed with Freud that humans have innate drives or instincts, including a *death instinct.* Drives, of course, must have some object. Thus, the hunger drive has the good breast as its object, the sex drive has a sexual organ as its object, and so on. Klein (1948) believed that from early infancy children relate to these external objects, both in fantasy and in reality. The earliest object relations are with the mother's breast, but "very soon interest develops in the face and in the hands which attend to his needs and gratify them" (Klein, 1991, p 757). In their active fantasy, infants *introject,* or take into their psychic structure, these external objects, including their father's penis, their mother's hands and face, and other body parts. Introjected objects are more than internal thoughts about external objects; they are fantasies of internalizing the object in concrete and physical terms. For example, children who have introjected their mother believe that she is constantly inside their own body. Klein's notion of internal objects suggests that these objects have a power of their own, comparable to Freud's concept of a superego, which assumes that the father's or mother's conscience is carried within the child.

Positions

Klein (1946) saw human infants as constantly engaging in a basic conflict between the life instinct and the death instinct, that is, between good and bad, love and hate, creativity and destruction. As the ego moves toward integration and away from disintegration, infants naturally prefer gratifying sensations over frustrating ones.

In their attempt to deal with this dichotomy of good and bad feelings, infants organize their experiences into **positions,** or ways of dealing with both internal and external objects. Klein chose the term "position" rather than "stage of development" to indicate that positions alternate back and forth; they are not periods of time or phases of development through which a person passes. Although she used psychiatric or pathological labels, Klein intended these positions to represent *normal* social growth and development. The two basic positions are the *paranoid-schizoid position* and the *depressive position.*

Paranoid-Schizoid Position

During the earliest months of life, an infant comes into contact with both the good breast and the bad breast. These alternating experiences of gratification and frustration threaten the very existence of the infant's vulnerable ego. The infant desires to control the breast by devouring and harboring it. At the same time, the infant's innate destructive urges create fantasies of damaging the breast by biting, tearing, or annihilating it. In order to tolerate both these feelings toward the same object at the same time, the ego splits itself, retaining parts of its life and death instincts while deflecting parts of both instincts onto the breast. Now, rather than fearing its own death instinct, the infant fears the *persecutory breast.* But the infant also has a relationship with the *ideal breast,* which provides love, comfort, and gratification. The infant desires to keep the ideal breast inside itself as a protection against annihilation by persecutors. To control the good breast and to fight off its persecutors, the infant adopts what Klein (1946) called the **paranoid-schizoid position,** a way of organizing experiences that includes both paranoid feelings of being persecuted and a splitting of internal and external objects into the good and the bad.

According to Klein, infants develop the paranoid-schizoid position during the first 3 or 4 months of life, during which time the ego's perception of the external world is subjective and fantastic rather than objective and real. Thus, the persecutory feelings are considered to be paranoid; that is, they are not based on any real or immediate danger from the outside world. The child must keep the good breast and bad breast separate, because to confuse them would be to risk annihilating the good breast and losing it as a safe harbor. In the young child's schizoid world, rage and destructive feelings are directed toward the bad breast, while feelings of love and comfort are associated with the good breast.

Infants, of course, do not use language to identify the good and bad breast. Rather, they have a biological predisposition to attach a positive value to nourishment and the life instinct and to assign a negative value to hunger and the death instinct. This preverbal splitting of the world into good and bad serves as a prototype for the subsequent development of ambivalent feelings toward a single person. For example, Klein (1946) compared the infantile paranoid-schizoid position to transference feelings that therapy patients often develop toward their therapist.

> Under pressure of ambivalence, conflict and guilt, the patient often splits the figure of the analyst, then the analyst may at certain moments be loved, at other moments hated. Or the analyst may be split in such a way that he remains the good (or bad) figure while someone else becomes the opposite figure. (p. 19)

Ambivalent feelings, of course, are not limited to therapy situations. Most people have both positive and negative feelings toward their loved ones. Conscious ambivalence, however, does not capture the essence of the paranoid-schizoid position. When adults adopt the paranoid-schizoid position, they do so in a primitive, unconscious fashion. As Ogden (1990) pointed out, they may experience themselves as a passive object rather than an active subject. They are likely to say "He's dangerous" instead of saying "I am aware that he is dangerous to me." Other people may project their unconscious paranoid feelings onto others as a means of avoiding their own destruction by the malevolent breast. Still others may project their unconscious positive feelings onto another person and see that person as being perfect while viewing themselves as empty or worthless.

Depressive Position

Beginning at about the 5th or 6th month, an infant begins to view external objects as whole and to see that good and bad can exist in the same person. At that time, the infant develops a more realistic picture of the mother and recognizes that she is an independent person who can be both good and bad. Also, the ego is beginning to mature to the point at which it can tolerate some of its own destructive feelings rather than projecting them outward. However, the infant also realizes that the mother might go away and be lost forever. Fearing the possible loss of the mother, the infant desires to protect her and keep her from the dangers of its own destructive forces, those cannibalistic impulses that had previously been projected onto her. But the infant's ego is mature enough to realize that it lacks the capacity to protect the mother, and thus the infant experiences guilt for its previous destructive urges toward the mother. The feelings of anxiety over losing a loved object coupled with a sense of guilt for wanting to destroy that object constitute what Klein called the **depressive position.**

Children in the depressive position recognize that the loved object and the hated object are now one and the same. They reproach themselves for their previous destructive urges toward their mother and desire to make *reparation* for these attacks. Because children see their mother as whole and also as being endangered, they are able to feel *empathy* for her, a quality that will be beneficial in their future interpersonal relations.

The depressive position is resolved when children fantasize that they have made reparation for their previous transgressions and when they recognize that their mother will not go away permanently but will return after each departure. When the depressive position is resolved, children close the split between the good and the bad mother. They are able not only to experience love *from* their mother, but also to display their own love *for* her. However, an incomplete resolution of the depressive position can result in lack of trust, morbid mourning at the loss of a loved one, and a variety of other psychic disorders.

Psychic Defense Mechanisms

Klein (1955) suggested that, from very early infancy, children adopt several psychic defense mechanisms to protect their ego against the anxiety aroused by their own destructive fantasies. These intense destructive feelings originate with oral-sadistic anxieties concerning the breast—the dreaded, destructive breast on the one hand and the satisfying, helpful breast on the other. To control these anxieties, infants use several psychic defense mechanisms, such as *introjection, projection, splitting,* and *projective identification.*

Introjection

By **introjection,** Klein simply meant that infants fantasize taking into their body those perceptions and experiences that they have had with the external object, originally the mother's breast. Introjection begins with an infant's first feeding, when there is an attempt to incorporate the mother's breast into the infant's body. Ordinarily, the infant tries to introject good objects, to take them inside itself as a protection against anxiety. However, sometimes the infant introjects bad objects, such as the bad breast or the bad penis, in order to gain control over them. When dangerous objects are introjected, they become internal persecutors, capable of terrifying the infant and leaving frightening residues that may be expressed in dreams or in an interest in fairy tales such as "The Big Bad Wolf" or "Snow White and the Seven Dwarfs."

Introjected objects are not accurate representations of the real objects but are colored by children's fantasies. For example, infants will fantasize that their mother is constantly present; that is, they feel that their mother is always inside their body. The real mother, of course, is not perpetually present, but infants nevertheless devour her in fantasy so that she becomes a constant internal object.

Projection

Just as infants use introjection to take in both good and bad objects, they use *projection* to get rid of them. Projection is the fantasy that one's own feelings and impulses actually reside in another person and not within one's body. By projecting unmanageable destructive impulses onto external objects, infants alleviate the unbearable anxiety of being destroyed by dangerous internal forces (Klein, 1935).

Children project both bad and good images onto external objects, especially their parents. For example, a young boy who desires to castrate his father may instead project these castration fantasies onto his father, thus turning his castration wishes around and blaming his father for wanting to castrate him. Similarly, a young girl might fantasize devouring her mother but projects that fantasy onto her mother, who she fears will retaliate by persecuting her.

People can also project good impulses. For example, infants who feel good about their mother's nurturing breast will attribute their own feelings of goodness onto the breast and imagine that the breast is good. Adults sometimes project their own feelings of love onto another person and become convinced that the other person loves them. Projection thus allows people to believe that their own subjective opinions are true.

Splitting

Infants can only manage the good and bad aspects of themselves and of external objects by **splitting** them, that is, by keeping apart incompatible impulses. In order to separate bad and good objects, the ego must itself be split. Thus, infants develop a picture of both the "good me" and the "bad me" that enables them to deal with both pleasurable and destructive impulses toward external objects.

Splitting can have either a positive or a negative effect on the child. If it is not extreme and rigid, it can be a positive and useful mechanism not only for infants but also for adults. It enables people to see both positive and negative aspects of themselves, to evaluate their behavior as good or bad, and to differentiate between likable and unlikable acquaintances. On the other hand, excessive and inflexible splitting can lead to pathological repression. For instance, if children's egos are too rigid to be split into good me and bad me, then they cannot introject bad experiences into the good ego. When children cannot accept their own bad behavior, they must then deal with destructive and terrifying impulses in the only way they can—by repressing them.

Projective Identification

A fourth means of reducing anxiety is **projective identification,** a psychic defense mechanism in which infants split off unacceptable parts of themselves, project them into another object, and finally introject them back into themselves in a changed or distorted form. By taking the object back into themselves, infants feel that they have become like that object; that is, they identify with that object. For example, infants typically split off parts of their destructive impulse and project them into the bad, frustrating breast. Next, they identify with the breast by introjecting it, a process that permits them to gain control over the dreaded and wonderful breast.

Projective identification exerts a powerful influence on adult interpersonal relations. Unlike simple projection, which can exist wholly in phantasy, projective identification exists only in the world of real interpersonal relationships. For example, a husband with strong but unwanted tendencies to dominate others will project those feelings into his wife, whom he then sees as domineering. The man subtly tries to get his wife to *become* domineering. He behaves with excessive submissiveness in an attempt to force his wife to display the very tendencies that he has deposited in her.

Internalizations

When object relations theorists speak of **internalizations,** they mean that the person takes in (introjects) aspects of the external world and then organizes those introjections into a psychologically meaningful framework. In Kleinian theory, three important internalizations are the ego, the superego, and the Oedipus complex.

Ego

Klein (1930, 1946) believed that the ego, or one's sense of self, reaches maturity at a much earlier stage than Freud had assumed. Although Freud hypothesized that the ego exists at birth, he did not attribute complex psychic functions to it until about the 3rd or 4th year. To Freud, the young child is dominated by the id. Klein, however, largely ignored the id and based her theory on the ego's early ability to sense both destructive and loving forces and to manage them through splitting, projection, and introjection.

Klein (1959) believed that although the ego is mostly unorganized at birth, it nevertheless is strong enough to feel anxiety, to use defense mechanisms, and to form early object relations in both phantasy and reality. The ego begins to evolve with the infant's first experience with feeding, when the good breast fills the infant not only with milk but with love and security. But the infant also experiences the bad breast—the one that is not present or does not give milk, love, or security. The infant introjects both the good breast and the bad breast, and these images provide a focal point for further expansion of the ego. All experiences, even those not connected with feeding, are evaluated by the ego in terms of how they relate to the good breast and the bad breast. For example, when the ego experiences the good breast, it expects similar good experiences with other objects, such as its own fingers, a pacifier, or the father. Thus, the infant's first object relation (the breast) becomes the prototype not only for the ego's future development but for the individual's later interpersonal relations.

However, before a unified ego can emerge, it must first become split. Klein assumed that infants innately strive for integration, but at the same time, they are forced to deal with the opposing forces of life and death, as reflected in their experience with the good breast and the bad breast. To avoid disintegration, the newly emerging ego must split itself into the good me and the bad me. The good me exists when infants are being enriched with milk and love; the bad me is experienced when they do not receive milk and love. This dual image of self allows them to manage the good and bad aspects of external objects. As infants mature, their perceptions become more realistic, they no longer see the world in terms of partial objects, and their egos become more integrated.

Superego

Klein's picture of the superego differs from Freud's in at least three important respects. First, it emerges much earlier in life; second, it is *not* an outgrowth of the Oedipus complex; and third, it is much more harsh and cruel. Klein (1933) arrived at these differences through her analysis of young children, an experience Freud did not have.

> There could be no doubt that a super-ego had been in full operation for some time in my small patients of between two-and-three-quarters and four years of age, whereas according to the accepted [Freudian] view the super-ego would not begin to be activated until the Oedipus complex had died down—i.e. until about the fifth year of life. Furthermore, my data showed that this early super-ego was immeasurably harsher and more cruel than that of the older child or adult, and that it literally crushed down the feeble ego of the small child. (p. 267)

Recall that Freud conceptualized the superego as consisting of two subsystems: an ego-ideal that produces inferiority feelings and a conscience that results in guilt feelings. Klein would concur that the more mature superego produces feelings of inferiority and guilt, but her analysis of young children led her to believe that the *early superego* produces not guilt but *terror.*

To Klein, young children fear being devoured, cut up, and torn into pieces—fears that are greatly out of proportion to any realistic dangers. Why are the children's superegos so drastically removed from any actual threats by their parents? Klein (1933) suggested that the answer resides with the infant's own destructive instinct, which is experienced as anxiety. To manage this anxiety, the child's ego mobilizes libido (life instinct) against the death instinct. However, the life and death instincts cannot be completely separated, so the ego is forced to defend itself against its own actions. This early ego defense lays the foundation for the development of the superego, whose extreme violence is a reaction to the ego's aggressive self-defense against its own destructive tendencies. Klein believed that this harsh, cruel superego is responsible for many antisocial and criminal tendencies in adults.

Klein would describe a 5-year-old child's superego in much the same way Freud did. By the 5th or 6th year, the superego arouses little anxiety but a great measure of guilt. It has lost most of its severity while gradually being transformed into a realistic conscience. However, Klein rejected Freud's notion that the superego is a consequence of the Oedipus complex. Instead, she insisted that it grows along with the Oedipus complex and finally emerges as realistic guilt after the Oedipus complex is resolved.

Oedipus Complex

Although Klein believed that her view of the Oedipus complex was merely an extension and not a refutation of Freud's ideas, her conception departed from the Freudian one in several ways. First, Klein (1946, 1948, 1952) held that the Oedipus complex begins at a much earlier age than Freud had suggested. Freud believed that the Oedipus complex took place during the phallic stage, when children are about 4 or 5 years old and after they have experienced an oral and anal stage. In contrast, Klein held that the Oedipus complex begins during the earliest months of life, overlaps with the oral and anal stages, and reaches its climax during the **genital stage** at around age 3 or 4. (Klein preferred the term "genital" stage rather than "phallic," because the latter suggests a masculine psychology.) Second, Klein believed that a significant part of the Oedipus complex is children's fear of retaliation from their parent for their fantasy of emptying the parent's body. Third, she stressed the importance of children retaining positive feelings toward *both* parents during the Oedipal years. Fourth, she hypothesized that during its early stages, the Oedipus complex serves the same need for both genders, that is, to establish a positive attitude with the good or gratifying object (breast or penis) and to avoid the bad or terrifying object (breast or penis). In this position, children of either gender can direct their love either alternately or simultaneously toward each parent. Thus, children are capable of both homosexual and heterosexual relations with both parents. Like Freud, Klein assumed that girls and boys eventually come to experience the Oedipus complex differently.

Female Oedipal Development

At the beginning of the female Oedipal development—during the first months of life—a little girl sees her mother's breast as both "good and bad. Then around 6 months of age, she begins to view the breast as more positive than negative. Later, she sees her whole mother as full of good things, and this attitude leads her to imagine how babies are made. She fantasizes that her father's penis feeds her mother with riches, including babies. Because the little girl sees the father's penis as the giver of children, she develops a positive relationship to it and fantasizes that her father will fill her body with babies. If the female Oedipal stage proceeds smoothly, the little girl adopts a "feminine" position and has a positive relationship with both parents.

However, under less ideal circumstances, the little girl will see her mother as a rival and will fantasize robbing her mother of her father's penis and stealing her mother's babies. The little girl's wish to rob her mother produces a paranoid fear that her mother will retaliate against her by injuring her or taking away her babies. The little girl's principal anxiety comes from a fear that the inside of her body has been injured by her mother, an anxiety that can be alleviated only when she later gives birth to a healthy baby. According to Klein (1945), penis envy stems from the little girl's wish to internalize her father's penis and to receive a baby from him. This fantasy precedes any desire for an external penis. Contrary to Freud's view, Klein could find no evidence that the little girl blames her mother for bringing her into the world without a penis. Instead, Klein contended that the girl retains a strong attachment to her mother throughout the Oedipal period.

Male Oedipal Development

Like the young girl, the little boy sees his mother's breast as both good and bad (Klein, 1945). Then, during the early months of Oedipal development, a boy shifts some of his oral desires from his mother's breast to his father's penis. At this time the little boy is in his *feminine position;* that is, he adopts a passive homosexual attitude toward his father. Next, he moves to a heterosexual relationship with his mother, but because of his previous homosexual feeling for his father, he has no fear that his father will castrate him. Klein believed that this passive homosexual position is a prerequisite for the boy's development of a healthy heterosexual relationship with his mother. More simply, the boy must have a good feeling about his father's penis before he can value his own.

As the boy matures, however, he develops oral-sadistic impulses toward his father and wants to bite off his penis and to murder him. These feelings arouse castration anxiety and the fear that his father will retaliate against him by biting off his penis. This fear convinces the little boy that sexual intercourse with his mother would be extremely dangerous to him.

The boy's Oedipus complex is resolved only partially by his castration anxiety. A more important factor is his ability to establish positive relationships with both parents at the same time. At that point, the boy sees his parents as whole objects, a condition that enables him to work through his depressive position.

For both girls and boys, a healthy resolution of the Oedipus complex depends on their ability to allow their mother and father to come together and to have sexual intercourse with each other. No remnant of rivalry remains. Children's positive feelings toward both parents later serve to enhance their adult sexual relations.

In summary, Klein believed that people are born with two strong drives—the life instinct and the death instinct. Infants develop a passionate caring for the good breast and an intense hatred for the bad breast, leaving a person to struggle a lifetime to reconcile these unconscious psychic images of good and bad, pleasure and pain. The most crucial stage of life is the first few months, a time when relationships with mother and other significant objects form a model for later interpersonal relations. A person's adult ability to love or to hate originates with these early object relations.

Later Views on Object Relations

Since Melanie Klein's bold and insightful descriptions, a number of other theorists have expanded and modified object relations theory. Among the more prominent of these later theorists are Margaret Mahler, Heinz Kohut, John Bowlby, and Mary Ainsworth.

Margaret Mahler's View

Margaret Schoenberger Mahler (1897–1985) was born in Sopron, Hungary, and received a medical degree from the University of Vienna in 1923. In 1938, she moved to New York, where she was a consultant to the Children's Service of the New York State Psychiatric Institute. She later established her own observational studies at the Masters Children's Center in New York. From 1955 to 1974, she was clinical professor of psychiatry at Albert Einstein College of Medicine.

Mahler was primarily concerned with the psychological birth of the individual that takes place during the first 3 years of life, a time when a child gradually surrenders security for autonomy. Originally, Mahler's ideas came from her observation of the behaviors of disturbed children interacting with their mothers. Later, she

observed normal babies as they bonded with
their mothers during the first 36 months of life
(Mahler, 1952).

To Mahler, an individual's psychological
birth begins during the first weeks of postnatal
life and continues for the next 3 years or so. By
psychological birth, Mahler meant that the child
becomes an *individual* separate from his or her
primary caregiver, an accomplishment that leads
ultimately to a *sense of identity.*

To achieve psychological birth and individuation, a child proceeds through a series of
three major developmental stages and four substages (Mahler, 1967, 1972; Mahler, Pine, &
Bergman, 1975). The first major developmental
stage is **normal autism,** which spans the period
from birth until about age 3 or 4 weeks. To describe the normal autism stage, Mahler (1967)

Margaret Mahler

borrowed Freud's (1911/1958) analogy that compared psychological birth with an
unhatched bird egg. The bird is able to satisfy its nutritional needs autistically (without regard to external reality) because its food supply is enclosed in its shell. Similarly, a newborn infant satisfies various needs within the all-powerful protective orbit
of a mother's care. Neonates have a sense of omnipotence, because, like unhatched
birds, their needs are cared for automatically and without their having to expend any
effort. Unlike Klein, who conceptualized a newborn infant as being terrified, Mahler
pointed to the relatively long periods of sleep and general lack of tension in a
neonate. She believed that this stage is a period of absolute primary narcissism in
which an infant is unaware of any other person. Thus, she referred to normal autism
as an "objectless" stage, a time when an infant naturally searches for the mother's
breast. She disagreed with Klein's notion that infants incorporate the good breast and
other objects into their ego.

As infants gradually realize that they cannot satisfy their own needs, they
begin to recognize their primary caregiver and to seek a symbiotic relationship with
her, a condition that leads to **normal symbiosis,** the second developmental stage in
Mahler's theory. Normal symbiosis begins around the 4th or 5th week of age but
reaches its zenith during the 4th or 5th month. During this time, "the infant behaves
and functions as though he and his mother were an omnipotent system—a dual unity
within one common boundary" (Mahler, 1967, p. 741). In the analogy of the bird
egg, the shell is now beginning to crack, but a psychological membrane in the form
of a symbiotic relationship still protects the newborn. Mahler recognized that this relationship is not a true symbiosis because, although the infant's life is dependent on
the mother, the mother does not absolutely need the infant. The symbiosis is characterized by a mutual cuing of infant and mother. The infant sends cues to the mother
of hunger, pain, pleasure, and so forth, and the mother responds with her own cues,
such as feeding, holding, or smiling. By this age the infant can recognize the
mother's face and can perceive her pleasure or distress. However, object relations
have not yet begun—mother and others are still "preobjects." Older children and

even adults sometimes regress to this stage, seeking the strength and safety of their mother's care.

The third major developmental stage, **separation-individuation,** spans the period from about the 4th or 5th month of age until about the 30th to 36th month. During this time, children become psychologically separated from their mothers, achieve a sense of individuation, and begin to develop feelings of personal identity. Because children no longer experience a dual unity with their mother, they must surrender their delusion of omnipotence and face their vulnerability to external threats. Thus, young children in the separation-individuation stage experience the external world as being more dangerous than it was during the first two stages.

Mahler divided the separation-individuation stage into four overlapping substages. The first is *differentiation,* which lasts from about the 5th month until the 7th to 10th month of age and is marked by a bodily breaking away from the mother-infant symbiotic orbit. For this reason, the differentiation substage is analogous to the hatching of an egg. At this age, Mahler observed, infants smile in response to their own mother, indicating a bond with a specific other person. Psychologically healthy infants who expand their world beyond the mother will be curious about strangers and will inspect them; unhealthy infants will fear strangers and recoil from them.

As infants physically begin to move away from their mothers by crawling and walking, they enter the *practicing* substage of separation-individuation, a period from about the 7th to 10th month of age to about the 15th or 16th month. During this subphase, children easily distinguish their body from their mother's, establish a specific bond with their mother, and begin to develop an autonomous ego. Yet, during the early stages of this period, they do not like to lose sight of their mother; they follow her with their eyes and show distress when she is away. Later, they begin to walk and to take in the outside world, which they experience as fascinating and exciting.

From about 16 to 25 months of age, children experience a *rapprochement* with their mother; that is, they desire to bring their mother and themselves back together, both physically and psychologically. Mahler noticed that children of this age want to share with their mother every new acquisition of skill and every new experience. Now that they can walk with ease, children are more physically separate from the mother, but paradoxically, they are more likely to show separation anxiety during the rapprochement stage than during the previous period. Their increased cognitive skills make them more aware of their separateness, causing them to try various ploys to regain the dual unity they once had with their mother. Because these attempts are never completely successful, children of this age often fight dramatically with their mother, a condition called the *rapprochement crisis.*

The final subphase of the separation-individuation process is *libidinal object constancy,* which approximates the 3rd year of life. During this time, children must develop a constant inner representation of their mother so that they can tolerate being physically separate from her. If this libidinal object constancy is not developed, children will continue to depend on their mother's physical presence for their own security. Besides gaining some degree of object constancy, children must consolidate their individuality; that is, they must learn to function without their mother and to develop other object relationships (Mahler et al., 1975).

The strength of Mahler's theory is its elegant description of psychological birth based on empirical observations that she and her colleagues made on child-mother interactions. Although many of her tenets rely on inferences gleaned from reactions of preverbal infants, her ideas can easily be extended to adults. Any errors made during the first 3 years—the time of psychological birth—may result in later regressions to a stage when a person had not yet achieved separation from the mother and thus a sense of personal identity.

Heinz Kohut's View

Heinz Kohut (1913–1981) was born in Vienna to educated and talented Jewish parents (Strozier, 2001). On the eve of World War II, he emigrated to England and, a year later, he moved to the United States, where he spent most of his professional life. He was a professional lecturer in the Department of Psychiatry at the University of Chicago, a member of the faculty at the Chicago Institute for Psychoanalysis, and visiting professor of psychoanalysis at the University of Cincinnati. A neurologist and a psychoanalyst, Kohut upset many psychoanalysts in 1971 with his publication of *The Analysis of the Self,* which replaced the ego with the concept of self. In addition to this book, aspects of his self psychology are found in *The Restoration of the Self* (1977) and *The Kohut Seminars* (1987), edited by Miriam Elson and published after Kohut's death.

More than the other object relations theorists, Kohut emphasized the process by which the *self* evolves from a vague and undifferentiated image to a clear and precise sense of individual identity. As did other object relations theorists, he focused on the early mother-child relationship as the key to understanding later development. Kohut believed that human relatedness, not innate instinctual drives, are at the core of human personality.

According to Kohut, infants require adult caregivers not only to gratify physical needs but also to satisfy basic psychological needs. In caring for both physical and psychological needs, adults, or **selfobjects,** treat infants as if they had a sense of self. For example, parents will act with warmth, coldness, or indifference depending in part on their infant's behavior. Through the process of empathic interaction, the infant takes in the selfobject's responses as pride, guilt, shame, or envy—all attitudes that eventually form the building blocks of the self. Kohut (1977) defined the self as "the center of the individual's psychological universe" (p. 311). The self gives unity and consistency to one's experiences, remains relatively stable over time, and is "the center of initiative and a recipient of impressions" (p. 99). The self is also the child's focus of interpersonal relations, shaping how he or she will relate to parents and other selfobjects.

Kohut (1971, 1977) believed that infants are naturally narcissistic. They are self-centered, looking out exclusively for their own welfare and wishing to be admired for who they are and what they do. The early self becomes crystallized

Heinz Kohut

around two basic *narcissistic needs:* (1) the need to exhibit the grandiose self and (2) the need to acquire an idealized image of one or both parents. The *grandiose-exhibitionistic self* is established when the infant relates to a "mirroring" selfobject who reflects approval of its behavior. The infant thus forms a rudimentary self-image from messages such as "If others see me as perfect, then I am perfect." The *idealized parent image* is opposed to the grandiose self because it implies that someone else is perfect. Nevertheless, it too satisfies a narcissistic need because the infant adopts the attitude "You are perfect, but I am part of you."

Both narcissistic self-images are necessary for healthy personality development. Both, however, must change as the child grows older. If they remain unaltered, they result in a pathologically narcissistic adult personality. Grandiosity must change into a realistic view of self, and the idealized parent image must grow into a realistic picture of the parents. The two self-images should not entirely disappear; the healthy adult continues to have positive attitudes toward self and continues to see good qualities in parents or parent substitutes. However, a narcissistic adult does not transcend these infantile needs and continues to be self-centered and to see the rest of the world as an admiring audience. Freud believed that such a narcissistic person was a poor candidate for psychoanalysis, but Kohut held that psychotherapy could be effective with these patients.

John Bowlby's Attachment Theory

John Bowlby (1907–1990) was born in London, where his father was a well-known surgeon. From an early age, Bowlby was interested in natural science, medicine, and psychology—subjects he studied at Cambridge University. After receiving a medical degree, he started his practice in psychiatry and psychoanalysis in 1933. At about the same time, he began training in child psychiatry under Melanie Klein. During World War II, Bowlby served as an army psychiatrist, and in 1946 he was appointed direc-

tor of the Department for Children and Parents of the Tavistock Clinic. During the late 1950s, Bowlby spent some time at Stanford's Center for the Advanced Study in the Behavioral Sciences but returned to London, where he remained until his death in 1990 (van Dijken, 1998).

In the 1950s, Bowlby became dissatisfied with the object relations perspective, primarily for its inadequate theory of motivation and its lack of empiricism. With his knowledge of **ethology** and evolutionary theory (especially Konrad Lorenz's idea of early bonding to a mother-figure), he realized that object relations theory could be integrated with an evolutionary perspective. By forming such an integration he felt he could correct the empirical shortcomings of the theory and extend it in a new direction. Bowlby's *attachment theory* also departed from psychoanalytic thinking by taking childhood as

John Bowlby

its starting point and then extrapolating forward to adulthood (Bowlby, 1969/1982, 1988). Bowlby firmly believed that the attachments formed during childhood have an important impact on adulthood. Because childhood attachments are crucial to later development, Bowlby argued that investigators should study childhood directly and not rely on distorted retrospective accounts from adults.

The origins of attachment theory came from Bowlby's observations that both human and primate infants go through a clear sequence of reactions when separated from their primary caregivers. Bowlby observed three stages of this **separation anxiety.** When their caregiver is first out of sight, infants will cry, resist soothing by other people, and search for their caregiver. This stage is the *protest* stage. As separation continues, infants become quiet, sad, passive, listless, and apathetic. This second stage is called *despair.* The last stage—the only one unique to humans—is *detachment.* During this stage, infants become emotionally detached from other people, including their caregiver. If their caregiver (mother) returns, infants will disregard and avoid her. Children who become detached are no longer upset when their mother leaves them. As they become older, they play and interact with others with little emotion but appear to be sociable. However, their interpersonal relations are superficial and lack warmth.

From such observations, Bowlby developed his attachment theory, which he published in a trilogy titled *Attachment and Loss* (1969/1982, 1973, 1980). Bowlby's theory rests on two fundamental assumptions: First, a responsive and accessible caregiver (usually the mother) must create a secure base for the child. The infant needs to know that the caregiver is accessible and dependable. If this dependability is present, the child is better able to develop confidence and security in exploring the world. This bonding relationship serves the critical function of attaching the caregiver to the infant, thereby making survival of the infant, and ultimately the species, more likely.

A second assumption of attachment theory is that a bonding relationship (or lack thereof) becomes internalized and serves as a mental working model on which future friendships and love relationships are built. The first bonding attachment is therefore the most critical of all relationships. However, for bonding to take place, an infant must be more than a mere passive receptor to the caregiver's behavior, even if that behavior radiates accessibility and dependability. Attachment style is a *relationship* between two people and not a trait given to the infant by the caregiver. It is a two-way street—the infant and the caregiver must be responsive to each other and each must influence the other's behavior.

Mary Ainsworth and the *Strange Situation*

Mary Dinsmore Salter Ainsworth (1919–1999) was born in Glendale, Ohio, the daughter of the president of an aluminum goods business. She received her BA, MA, and PhD, all from the University of Toronto, where she also served as instructor and lecturer. During her long career, she taught and conducted research at several universities and institutes in Canada, the United States, the United Kingdom, and Uganda.

Influenced by Bowlby's theory, Ainsworth and her associates (Ainsworth, Blehar, Waters, & Wall, 1978) developed a technique for measuring the type of

Mary Ainsworth

attachment style that exists between caregiver and infant, known as the *Strange Situation.* This procedure consists of a 20-minute laboratory session in which a mother and infant are initially alone in a playroom. Then a stranger comes into the room, and after a few minutes the stranger begins a brief interaction with the infant. The mother then goes away for two separate 2-minute periods. During the first period, the infant is left alone with the stranger; during the second period, the infant is left completely alone. The critical behavior is how the infant reacts when the mother returns; this behavior is the basis of the attachment style rating. Ainsworth and her associates found three attachment style ratings: secure, anxious-resistant, and avoidant.

In a *secure attachment,* when their mother returns, infants are happy and enthusiastic and initiate contact; for example, they will go over to their mother and want to be held. All securely attached infants are confident in the accessibility and responsiveness of their caregiver, and this security and dependability provides the foundation for play and exploration.

In an *anxious-resistant attachment* style, infants are ambivalent. When their mother leaves the room, they become unusually upset, and when their mother returns they seek contact with her but reject attempts at being soothed. With the anxious-resistant attachment style, infants give very conflicted messages. On the one hand, they seek contact with their mother, while on the other hand, they squirm to be put down and may throw away toys that their mother has offered them.

The third attachment style is *anxious-avoidant.* With this style, infants stay calm when their mother leaves; they accept the stranger, and when their mother returns, they ignore and avoid her. In both kinds of insecure attachment (anxious-resistant and anxious-avoidant), infants lack the ability to engage in effective play and exploration.

Psychotherapy

Klein, Mahler, Kohut, and Bowlby were all psychoanalysts trained in orthodox Freudian practices. However, each modified psychoanalytic treatment to fit her or his own theoretical orientation. Because these theorists varied among themselves on therapeutic procedures, we will limit our discussion of therapy to the approach used by Melanie Klein.

Klein's pioneering use of psychoanalysis with children was not well accepted by other analysts during the 1920s and 1930s. Anna Freud was especially resistive to the notion of childhood psychoanalysis, contending that young children who were still attached to their parents could not develop a transference to the therapist because they have no unconscious fantasies or images. Therefore, she claimed, young children could not profit from psychoanalytic therapy. In contrast, Klein believed that both disturbed and healthy children should be psychoanalyzed; disturbed children would receive the benefit of therapeutic treatment, whereas healthy children would profit from a prophylactic analysis. Consistent with this belief, she insisted that her own children be analyzed. She also insisted that negative transference was an essential step toward successful treatment, a view not shared by Anna Freud and many other psychoanalysts.

To foster negative transference and aggressive fantasies, Klein provided each child with a variety of small toys, pencil and paper, paint, crayons, and so forth. She substituted *play therapy* for Freudian dream analysis and free association, believing that young children express their conscious and unconscious wishes through play therapy. In addition to expressing negative transference feelings as means of play, Klein's young patients often attacked her verbally, which gave her an opportunity to interpret the unconscious motives behind these attacks (Klein, 1943).

The aim of Kleinian therapy is to reduce depressive anxieties and persecutory fears and to mitigate the harshness of internalized objects. To accomplish this aim, Klein encouraged her patients to reexperience early emotions and fantasies but this time with the therapist pointing out the differences between reality and fantasy, between conscious and unconscious. She also allowed patients to express both positive and negative transference, a situation that is essential for patients' understanding of how unconscious fantasies connect with present everyday situations. Once this connection is made, patients feel less persecuted by internalized objects, experience reduced depressive anxiety, and are able to project previously frightening internal objects onto the outer world.

Related Research

Both object relations theory and attachment continue to spark some empirical research. For example, object relations has been used to explain the formation of eating disorders. This research rests on the assumption that having an unresponsive or inconsistent caregiver leads to children's inability to reduce anxiety and frustration. As applied to eating disorders, when these individuals feel anxious, they look for comfort in external sources; and food is a primary means of soothing and regulating their anxiety. Prior research has supported these assumptions, primarily in women. For instance, Smolak and Levine (1993) found that bulimia was associated with overseparation (detachment) from parents, whereas anorexia was associated with high levels of guilt and conflict over separation from parents.

Object Relations and Eating Disorders

More recently, this line of theory and research has been applied to both men and women. Steven Huprich and colleagues (Huprich, Stepp, Graham, & Johnson, 2004), for instance, examined the connection between disturbed object relations and eating disorders in a nearly equal number of female and male college students. Because eating disorders are much more common in women than in men (Brannon & Feist,

2007), the investigation by Huprich and colleagues was an important addition to the research on eating disorders of both men and women. The researchers administered three measures of object relations and three measures of eating disorders to the participants to see whether the association between object relations and eating problems could be found in men as well as women.

The experimenters used three measures of object relations: (1) interpersonal dependency; (2) separation-individuation; and (3) a general measure of object relations, which assessed alienation, insecure attachment, egocentricity, and social incompetence. The three measures of eating disorder assessed (1) anorexic tendencies, (2) bulimic tendencies, and (3) a person's sense of control and self-efficacy over compulsive eating. Results showed gender differences on one object relations measure (the Interpersonal Dependency Scale). With regard to measures of eating disorder, men scored lower than women on all three measures of disordered eating. In other words, men have less trouble with binge and compulsive eating than women and are less interpersonally dependent than women. Nevertheless, some overlap existed between college males and females, which suggests that gender differences, though usually significant, do not neatly divide men from women on such measures as interpersonal dependency and its relationship to eating disorders. For example, Huprich and colleagues found that both men and women who were insecurely attached and self-focused (egocentric) had greater difficulty in controlling their compulsive eating than those who were more securely attached and less self-focused. In other words, when insecurely attached people of either gender are threatened, "they turn to an external object (food) as a means by which to comfort themselves" (Huprich et al., 2004, p. 808).

Attachment Theory and Adult Relationships

Attachment theory as originally conceptualized by John Bowlby emphasized the relationship between parent and child. Since the 1980s, however, researchers have begun to systematically examine attachment relationships in adults, especially in romantic relationships.

A classic study of adult attachment was conducted by Cindy Hazan and Phil Shaver (1987), who predicted that different types of early attachment styles would distinguish the kind, duration, and stability of adult love relationships. More specifically, these investigators expected that people who had secure early attachments with their caregivers would experience more trust, closeness, and positive emotions in their adult love relationships than would people in either of the two insecure groups. Likewise, they predicted that avoidant adults would fear closeness and lack trust, whereas anxious-ambivalent adults would be preoccupied with and obsessed by their relationships.

Using college students and other adults, Hazan and Shaver found support for each of these predictions. Securely attached adults did experience more trust and closeness in their love relationships than did avoidant or anxious-ambivalent adults. Moreover, the researchers found that securely attached adults were more likely than insecure adults to believe that romantic love can be long lasting. In addition, securely attached adults were less cynical about love in general, had longer lasting relationships, and were less likely to divorce than either avoidant or anxious-ambivalent adults.

Other researchers have continued to extend the research on attachment and adult romantic relationships. Steven Rholes and colleagues, for example, tested the idea that attachment style is related to the type of information people seek or avoid regarding their relationship and romantic partner (Rholes, Simpson, Tran, Martin, & Friedman, 2007). The researchers predicted that avoidant individuals would not seek out additional information about their partner's intimate feelings and dreams, whereas anxious individuals would express a strong desire to gain more information about their romantic partner. Avoidant individuals typically strive to maintain emotional independence and therefore do not want any information that could increase closeness. Closeness subverts their goal of independence. Conversely, anxious individuals tend to be chronically worried about the state of their relationship and want to strengthen emotional bonds by seeking out as much information about their partner's most intimate feelings as possible.

To test their predictions, Rholes and colleagues recruited couples who had been dating for a while and had them come in to a psychology lab to complete measures of attachment and information seeking. Attachment style was measured using a standard questionnaire containing self-report items about how anxious or avoidant the person feels within their romantic relationship. Information seeking was measured using a clever (and bogus) computerized task whereby each participant independently completed several items about their relationship including each partner's intimate feelings and goals for the future. Participants were told that the computer would then generate a profile of their relationship that both dating partners could view at the end of the study. The researchers then were able to measure how much of the information provided by the relationship profile each partner read about the other. In accord with their predictions, and attachment theory more generally, the avoidant individuals showed less interest in reading information about their partner contained in the relationship profile, whereas anxious individuals sought more information about their partner's intimacy-related issues and goals for the future.

Attachment style is not only related to parents and romantic partners. Recent research has explored the role of attachment style in the relationships between leaders and their followers (military officers and their soldiers, for example; Davidovitz, Mikulincer, Shaver, Izsak, & Popper, 2007; Popper & Mayseless, 2003). The theory is that attachment style is relevant in leader-follower relationships because leaders or authority figures can occupy the role of caregiver and be a source of security in a manner similar to the support offered by parents and romantic partners. Researchers predicted that leaders with a secure attachment style (neither anxious nor avoidant) are more effective than insecurely attached (anxious or avoidant) leaders.

To explore the role of attachment in leadership, Rivka Davidovitz and colleagues (2007) studied a group of military officers and the soldiers in their charge. Officers completed the same measure of attachment used in the previously discussed study on attachment and information seeking (Rholes et al., 2007), but rather than reporting on their attachment within a romantic relationship they reported on their close relationships more generally. Soldiers then completed measures of the effectiveness of their officer's leadership, cohesiveness of their military unit, and measures of psychological well-being.

The results provided further support of the generality and importance of attachment style in multiple types of relationships. The units of officers who had an avoidant attachment style were less cohesive and the soldiers expressed lower psychological well-being compared to members of other units. Most likely, these effects of leaders' avoidant attachment style are due to the avoidant officers' desire to avoid information about the social and emotional well-being of their unit. Anxiously attached officers led units that were rated low on instrumental functioning (degree to which soldiers take their work seriously). Yet, those same units were rated high on socioemotional functioning (degree to which soldiers feel free to express their thoughts and feelings). This last finding regarding socioemotional functioning was surprising to the researchers but makes sense when considering the findings of Rholes and colleagues discussed above (Rholes et al., 2007): The anxiously attached officers were likely more interested in seeking out information about how their soldiers were feeling and how they were getting along with others.

Attachment is a construct in personality psychology that continues to generate a substantial amount of research. While the work on attachment theory began as a way to understand differences in parent-child relationships, recent research has shown that those same dynamics (secure, avoidant, and anxious attachment styles) are important to understanding a wide range of adult relationships—from romantic partners to military leaders and soldiers.

Critique of Object Relations Theory

Currently, object relations theory continues to be more popular in the United Kingdom than it is in the United States. The "British School," which included not only Melanie Klein but also W. R. D. Fairbairn and D. W. Winnicott, has exerted a strong influence on psychoanalysts and psychiatrists in the United Kingdom. In the United States, however, the influence of object relations theorists, while growing, has been less direct.

How does object relations theory rate in generating research? In 1986, Morris Bell and colleagues published the Bell Object Relations Inventory (BORI), a self-report questionnaire that identifies four main aspects of object relations: Alienation, Attachment, Egocentricity, and Social Incompetence. To date, only a few studies have used the BORI to empirically investigate object relations. However, attachment theory is currently generating much research. Thus, we rate object relations theory low on its ability to generate research, but we judge attachment theory moderate to high on this criterion for a useful theory.

Because object relations theory grew out of orthodox psychoanalytic theory, it suffers from some of the same *falsifications* that confront Freud's theory. Most of its tenets are based on what is happening inside the infant's psyche, and thus these assumptions cannot be falsified. The theory does not lend itself to falsifications because it generates very few testable hypotheses. Attachment theory, on the other hand, rates somewhat higher on falsification.

Perhaps the most useful feature of object relations theory is its *ability to organize* information about the behavior of infants. More than most other personality theorists, object relations theorists have speculated on how humans gradually come to acquire a sense of identity. Klein, and especially Mahler, Bowlby, and Ainsworth, built their theories on careful observations of the mother-child relationship. They watched the interactions between infant and mother and drew inferences based on what they saw. However, beyond the early childhood years, object relations theory lacks usefulness as an organizer of knowledge.

As a *guide to the practitioner,* the theory fares somewhat better than it does in organizing data or suggesting testable hypotheses. Parents of young infants can learn of the importance of a warm, accepting, and nurturing caregiver. Psychotherapists may find object relations theory useful not only in understanding the early development of their clients but also in understanding and working with the transference relationship that clients form with the therapist, whom they view as a substitute parent.

On the criterion of consistency, each of the theories discussed in this chapter has a high level of *internal consistency,* but the different theorists disagree among themselves on a number of points. Even though they all place primary importance on human relationships, the differences among them far exceed the similarities.

In addition, we rate object relations theory low on the criterion of *parsimony.* Klein, especially, used needlessly complex phrases and concepts to express her theory.

Concept of Humanity

Object relations theorists generally see human personality as a product of the early mother-child relationship. The interaction between mother and infant lays the foundation for future personality development because that early interpersonal experience serves as a prototype for subsequent interpersonal relations. Klein saw the human psyche as "unstable, fluid, constantly fending off psychotic anxieties" (Mitchell & Black, 1995, p. 87). Moreover, "each of us struggles with the deep terrors of annihilation . . . and utter abandonment" (p. 88).

Because they emphasize the mother-child relationship and view these experiences as crucial to later development, object relations theorists rate high on *determinism* and low on free choice.

For the same reason, these theorists can be either *pessimistic* or *optimistic,* depending on the quality of the early mother-infant relationship. If that relationship is healthy, then a child will grow into a psychologically healthy adult; if it is not, the child will acquire a pathological, self-absorbed personality.

On the dimension of *causality versus teleology,* object relations theory tends to be more causal. Early experiences are the primary shapers of personality. Expectations of the future play a very minor role in object relations theory.

We rate object relations theory high on *unconscious determinants of behavior* because most of the theorists trace the prime determinants of behavior to very early infancy, a time before verbal language. Thus, people acquire many personal traits and attitudes on a preverbal level and remain unaware of the complete nature of these traits and attitudes. In addition, Klein's acceptance of an innately acquired phylogenetic endowment places her theory even further in the direction of unconscious determinants.

The emphasis that Klein placed on the death instinct and phylogenetic endowment would seem to suggest that she saw biology as more important than environment in shaping personality. However, Klein shifted the emphasis from Freud's biologically based infantile stages to an interpersonal one. Because the intimacy and nurturing that infants receive from their mother are environmental experiences, Klein and other object relations theorists lean more toward *social determinants* of personality.

On the dimension of *uniqueness versus similarities,* object relations theorists tend more toward similarities. As clinicians dealing mostly with disturbed patients, Klein, Mahler, Kohut, and Bowlby limited their discussions to the distinction between healthy personalities and pathological ones and were little concerned with differences among psychologically healthy personalities.

Key Terms and Concepts

- Object relations theories assume that the *mother-child relationship* during the first 4 or 5 months is the most critical time for personality development.
- Klein believed that an important part of any relationship is the *internal psychic representations* of early significant objects, such as the mother's breast or the father's penis.
- Infants *introject* these psychic representations into their own psychic structure and then *project* them onto an external object, that is, another person. These internal pictures are not accurate representations of the other person but are remnants of earlier interpersonal experiences.
- The *ego,* which exists at birth, can sense both destructive and loving forces, that is, both a nurturing and a frustrating breast.
- To deal with the nurturing breast and the frustrating breast, infants *split* these objects into good and bad while also splitting their own ego, giving them a *dual image* of self.
- Klein believed that the *superego* comes into existence much earlier than Freud had speculated and that it grows along with the Oedipal process rather than being a product of it.
- During the early female Oedipus complex, the little girl adopts a *feminine position* toward both parents. She has a positive feeling both for her mother's breasts and for her father's penis, which she believes will feed her with babies.
- Sometimes the little girl develops hostility toward her mother, who she fears will retaliate against her and rob her of her babies.
- With most girls, however, the female Oedipus complex is resolved without any antagonism or jealousy toward their mother.

- The little boy also adopts a feminine position during the early Oedipal years. At that time, he has no fear of being castrated as punishment for his sexual feelings for his mother.
- Later, the boy projects his destructive drive onto his father, who he fears will bite or castrate him.
- The male Oedipus complex is resolved when the boy establishes good relations with both parents and feels comfortable about his parents having sexual intercourse with one another.

CHAPTER 6

Horney: Psychoanalytic Social Theory

Horney

Please Mark These "True" or "False" as They Apply to You.

1. T F It's very important to me to please other people.
2. T F When I feel distressed, I seek out an emotionally strong person to tell my troubles to.
3. T F I prefer routine more than change.
4. T F I enjoy being in a powerful leadership position.
5. T F I believe in and follow the advice: "Do unto others before they can do unto me."
6. T F I enjoy being the life of the party.
7. T F It's very important to me to be recognized for my accomplishments.
8. T F I enjoy seeing the achievements of my friends.
9. T F I usually end relationships when they begin to get too close.
10. T F It's very difficult for me to overlook my own mistakes and personal flaws.

These questions represent 10 important needs proposed by Karen Horney. We discuss these items in the section on neurotic needs. Please know that marking an item in the direction of neurotic needs does not indicate that you are emotionally unstable or driven by neurotic needs.

Overview of Psychoanalytic Social Theory

The **psychoanalytic social theory** of Karen Horney (pronounced Horn-eye) was built on the assumption that social and cultural conditions, especially childhood experiences, are largely responsible for shaping personality. People who do not have their needs for love and affection satisfied during childhood develop *basic hostility* toward their parents and, as a consequence, suffer from *basic anxiety*. Horney theorized that people combat basic anxiety by adopting one of three fundamental styles of relating to others: (1) moving toward people, (2) moving against people, or (3) moving away from people. Normal individuals may use any of these modes of relating to other people, but neurotics are compelled to rigidly rely on only one. Their compulsive behavior generates a basic *intrapsychic conflict* that may take the form of either an idealized self-image or self-hatred. The idealized self-image is expressed as (1) neurotic search for glory, (2) neurotic claims, or (3) neurotic pride. Self-hatred is expressed as either self-contempt or alienation from self.

Although Horney's writings are concerned mostly with the neurotic personality, many of her ideas can also be applied to normal individuals. This chapter looks at Horney's basic theory of neurosis, compares her ideas to those of Freud, examines her views on feminine psychology, and briefly discusses her ideas on psychotherapy.

As with other personality theorists, Horney's views on personality are a reflection of her life experiences. Bernard Paris (1994) wrote that "Horney's insights were derived from her efforts to relieve her own pain, as well as that of her patients. If her suffering had been less intense, her insights would have been less profound" (p. xxv). We look now at the life of this often-troubled woman.

Biography of Karen Horney

The biography of Karen Horney has several parallels with the life of Melanie Klein (see Chapter 5). Each was born during the 1880s, the youngest child of a 50-year-old father and his second wife. Each had older siblings who were favored by the parents, and each felt unwanted and unloved. Also, each had wanted to become a physician, but only Horney fulfilled that ambition. Finally, both Horney and Klein engaged in an extended self-analysis—Horney's, beginning with her diaries from age 13 to 26, continuing with her analysis by Karl Abraham, and culminating with her book *Self-Analysis* (Quinn, 1987).

Karen Danielsen Horney was born in Eilbek, a small town near Hamburg, Germany, on September 15, 1885. She was the only daughter of Berndt (Wackels) Danielsen, a sea captain, and Clothilda van Ronzelen Danielsen, a woman nearly 18 years younger than her husband. The only other child of this marriage was a son, about 4 years older than Karen. However, the old sea captain had been married earlier and had four other children, most of whom were adults by the time Horney was born. The Danielsen family was an unhappy one, in part because Karen's older half-siblings turned their father against his second wife. Karen felt great hostility toward her stern, devoutly religious father and regarded him as a religious hypocrite. However, she idolized her mother, who both supported and protected her against the stern old sea captain. Nevertheless, Karen was not a happy child. She resented the favored treatment given to her older brother, and in addition, she worried about the bitterness and discord between her parents.

When she was 13, Horney decided to become a physician, but at that time no university in Germany admitted women. By the time she was 16, this situation had changed. So Horney—over the objections of her father, who wanted her to stay home and take care of the household—entered the gymnasium, a school that would lead to a university and then to medical school. On her own for the first time, Karen was to remain independent for the rest of her life. According to Paris (1994), however, Horney's independence was mostly superficial. On a deeper level, she retained a compulsive need to merge with a great man. This morbid dependency, which typically included idealization and fear of inciting angry rejection, haunted Horney during her relationships with a series of men.

In 1906, she entered the University of Freiburg, becoming one of the first women in Germany to study medicine. There she met Oskar Horney, a political science student. Their relationship began as a friendship, but it eventually became a romantic one. After their marriage in 1909, the couple settled in Berlin, where Oskar, now with a PhD, worked for a coal company and Karen, not yet with an MD, specialized in psychiatry.

By this time, Freudian psychoanalysis was becoming well established, and Karen Horney became familiar with Freud's writings. Early in 1910, she began an analysis with Karl Abraham, one of Freud's close associates and a man who later analyzed Melanie Klein. After Horney's analysis was terminated, she attended Abraham's evening seminars, where she became acquainted with other psychoanalysts. By 1917, she had written her first paper on psychoanalysis, "The Technique of Psychoanalytic Therapy" (Horney, 1917/1968), which reflected the orthodox Freudian view and gave little indication of Horney's subsequent independent thinking.

The early years of her marriage were filled with many notable personal experiences for Horney. Her father and mother, who were now separated, died within less than a year of each other; she gave birth to three daughters in 5 years; she received her MD degree in 1915 after 5 years of psychoanalysis; and, in her quest for the right man, she had several love affairs (Paris, 1994; Quinn, 1987).

After World War I, the Horneys lived a prosperous, suburban lifestyle with several servants and a chauffeur. Oskar did well financially while Karen enjoyed a thriving psychiatric practice. This idyllic scene, however, soon ended. The inflation and economic disorder of 1923 cost Oskar his job, and the family was forced to move back to an apartment in Berlin. In 1926, Karen and Oskar separated but did not officially divorce until 1938 (Paris, 1994).

The early years following her separation from Oskar were the most productive of Horney's life. In addition to seeing patients and caring for her three daughters, she became more involved with writing, teaching, traveling, and lecturing. Her papers now showed important differences with Freudian theory. She believed that culture, not anatomy, was responsible for psychic differences between men and women. When Freud reacted negatively to Horney's position, she became even more outspoken in her opposition.

In 1932, Horney left Germany for a position as associate director of the newly established Chicago Psychoanalytic Institute. Several factors contributed to her decision to immigrate—the anti-Jewish political climate in Germany (although Horney was not Jewish), increasing opposition to her unorthodox views, and an opportunity to extend her influence beyond Berlin. During the 2 years she spent in Chicago, she met Margaret Mead, John Dollard, and many of the same scholars who had influenced Harry Stack Sullivan (see Chapter 8). In addition, she renewed acquaintances with Erich Fromm and his wife, Frieda Fromm-Reichmann, whom she had known in Berlin. During the next 10 years, Horney and Fromm were close friends, greatly influencing one another and eventually becoming lovers (Hornstein, 2000).

After 2 years in Chicago, Horney moved to New York, where she taught at the New School for Social Research. While in New York, she became a member of the Zodiac group that included Fromm, Fromm-Reichmann, Sullivan, and others. Although Horney was a member of the New York Psychoanalytic Institute, she seldom agreed with the established members. Moreover, her book *New Ways in Psychoanalysis* (1939) made her the leader of an opposition group. In this book, Horney called for abandoning the instinct theory and placing more emphasis on ego and social influences. In 1941, she resigned from the institute over issues of dogma and orthodoxy and helped form a rival organization—the Association for the Advancement of Psychoanalysis (AAP). This new group, however, also quickly suffered from internal strife. In 1943, Fromm (whose intimate relationship with Horney had recently ended) and several others resigned from the AAP, leaving that organization without its strongest members. Despite this rift, the association continued, but under a new name—the Karen Horney Psychoanalytic Institute. In 1952, Horney established the Karen Horney Clinic.

In 1950, Horney published her most important work, *Neurosis and Human Growth*. This book sets forth theories that were no longer merely a reaction to Freud but rather were an expression of her own creative and independent thinking. After a short illness, Horney died of cancer on December 4, 1952. She was 65 years old.

Introduction to Psychoanalytic Social Theory

The early writings of Karen Horney, like those of Adler, Jung, and Klein, have a distinctive Freudian flavor. Like Adler and Jung, she eventually became disenchanted with orthodox psychoanalysis and constructed a revisionist theory that reflected her own personal experiences—clinical and otherwise.

Although Horney wrote nearly exclusively about neuroses and neurotic personalities, her works suggest much that is appropriate to normal, healthy development. Culture, especially early childhood experiences, plays a leading role in shaping human personality, either neurotic or healthy. Horney, then, agreed with Freud that early childhood traumas are important, but she differed from him in her insistence that social rather than biological forces are paramount in personality development.

Horney and Freud Compared

Horney criticized Freud's theories on several accounts. First, she cautioned that strict adherence to orthodox psychoanalysis would lead to stagnation in both theoretical thought and therapeutic practice (Horney, 1937). Second, Horney (1937, 1939) objected to Freud's ideas on feminine psychology, a subject we return to later. Third, she stressed the view that psychoanalysis should move beyond instinct theory and emphasize the importance of cultural influences in shaping personality. "Man is ruled not by the pleasure principle alone but by two guiding principles: safety and satisfaction" (Horney, 1939, p. 73). Similarly, she claimed that neuroses are not the result of instincts but rather of the person's "attempt to find paths through a wilderness full of unknown dangers" (p. 10). This wilderness is created by society and not by instincts or anatomy.

Despite becoming increasingly critical of Freud, Horney continued to recognize his perceptive insights. Her main quarrel with Freud was not so much the accuracy of his observations but the validity of his interpretations. In general terms, she held that Freud's explanations result in a pessimistic concept of humanity based on innate instincts and the stagnation of personality. In contrast, her view of humanity is an optimistic one and is centered on cultural forces that are amenable to change (Horney, 1950).

The Impact of Culture

Although Horney did not overlook the importance of genetic factors, she repeatedly emphasized cultural influences as the primary bases for both neurotic and normal personality development. Modern culture, she contended, is based on *competition* among individuals. "Everyone is a real or potential competitor of everyone else" (Horney, 1937, p. 284). Competitiveness and the *basic hostility* it spawns result in feelings of *isolation*. These feelings of being alone in a potentially hostile world lead to intensified *needs for affection,* which, in turn, cause people to overvalue love. As a result, many people see love and affection as the solution for all their problems. Genuine love, of course, can be a healthy, growth-producing experience; but the desperate need for love (such as that shown by Horney herself) provides a fertile ground for the development of neuroses. Rather than benefiting from the need for love, neurotics strive in pathological ways to find it. Their self-defeating attempts result in low self-esteem, increased hostility, basic anxiety, more competitiveness, and a continuous excessive need for love and affection.

According to Horney, Western society contributes to this vicious circle in several respects. First, people of this society are imbued with the cultural teachings of kinship and humility. These teachings, however, run contrary to another prevailing attitude, namely, aggressiveness and the drive to win or be superior. Second, society's demands for success and achievement are nearly endless, so that even when people achieve their material ambitions, additional goals are continually being placed before them. Third, Western society tells people that they are free, that they can accomplish anything through hard work and perseverance. In reality, however, the freedom of most people is greatly restricted by genetics, social position, and the competitiveness of others.

These contradictions—all stemming from cultural influences rather than biological ones—provide intrapsychic conflicts that threaten the psychological health of normal people and provide nearly insurmountable obstacles for neurotics.

The Importance of Childhood Experiences

Horney believed that neurotic conflict can stem from almost any developmental stage, but childhood is the age from which the vast majority of problems arise. A variety of traumatic events, such as sexual abuse, beatings, open rejection, or pervasive neglect, may leave their impressions on a child's future development; but Horney (1937) insisted that these debilitating experiences can almost invariably be traced to lack of genuine warmth and affection. Horney's own lack of love from her father and her close relationship with her mother must have had a powerful effect on her personal development as well as on her theoretical ideas.

Horney (1939) hypothesized that a difficult childhood is primarily responsible for neurotic needs. These needs become powerful because they are the child's only means of gaining feelings of safety. Nevertheless, no single early experience is responsible for later personality. Horney cautioned that "the sum total of childhood experiences brings about a certain character structure, or rather, starts its development" (p. 152). In other words, the totality of early relationships molds personality development. "Later attitudes to others, then, are not repetitions of infantile ones but emanate from the character structure, the basis of which is laid in childhood" (p. 87).

Although later experiences can have an important effect, especially in normal individuals, childhood experiences are primarily responsible for personality development. People who rigidly repeat patterns of behavior do so because they interpret new experiences in a manner consistent with those established patterns.

Basic Hostility and Basic Anxiety

Horney (1950) believed that each person begins life with the potential for healthy development, but like other living organisms, people need favorable conditions for growth. These conditions must include a warm and loving environment yet one that is not overly permissive. Children need to experience both genuine love and healthy discipline. Such conditions provide them with feelings of *safety* and *satisfaction* and permit them to grow in accordance with their real self.

Unfortunately, a multitude of adverse influences may interfere with these favorable conditions. Primary among these is the parents' inability or unwillingness to love their child. Because of their own neurotic needs, parents often dominate, neglect, overprotect, reject, or overindulge. If parents do not satisfy the child's needs for safety and satisfaction, the child develops feelings of **basic hostility** toward the parents. However, children seldom overtly express this hostility as rage; instead, they repress their hostility toward their parents and have no awareness of it. Repressed hostility then leads to profound feelings of insecurity and a vague sense of apprehension. This condition is called **basic anxiety,** which Horney (1950) defined as "a feeling of being isolated and helpless in a world conceived as potentially hostile" (p. 18). Earlier, she gave a more graphic description, calling basic anxiety "a feeling of being small, insignificant, helpless, deserted, endangered, in a world that is out to abuse, cheat, attack, humiliate, betray, envy" (Horney, 1937, p. 92).

Horney (1937, p. 75) believed that basic hostility and basic anxiety are "inextricably interwoven." Hostile impulses are the principal source of basic anxiety, but basic anxiety can also contribute to feelings of hostility. As an example of how basic hostility can lead to anxiety, Horney (1937) wrote about a young man with repressed hostility who went on a hiking trip in the mountains with a young woman with whom he was deeply in love. His repressed hostility, however, also led him to become jealous of the woman. While walking on a dangerous mountain pass, the young man suddenly suffered a severe "anxiety attack" in the form of rapid heart rate and heavy breathing. The anxiety resulted from a seemingly inappropriate but conscious impulse to push the young woman over the edge of the mountain pass.

In this case, basic hostility led to severe anxiety, but anxiety and fear can also lead to strong feelings of hostility. Children who feel threatened by their parents develop a reactive hostility in defense of that threat. This reactive hostility, in turn, may create additional anxiety, thus completing the interactive circle between hostility and anxiety. Horney (1937) contended that "it does not matter whether anxiety or hostility has been the primary factor" (p. 74). The important point is that their reciprocal influence may intensify a neurosis without a person's experiencing any additional outside conflict.

Basic anxiety itself is not a neurosis, but "it is the nutritive soil out of which a definite neurosis may develop at any time" (Horney, 1937, p. 89). Basic anxiety is constant and unrelenting, needing no particular stimulus such as taking a test in school or giving a speech. It permeates all relationships with others and leads to unhealthy ways of trying to cope with people.

Although she later amended her list of defenses against basic anxiety, Horney (1937) originally identified four general ways that people protect themselves against this feeling of being alone in a potentially hostile world. The first is *affection,* a strategy that does not always lead to authentic love. In their search for affection, some people may try to purchase love with self-effacing compliance, material goods, or sexual favors.

The second protective device is *submissiveness.* Neurotics may submit themselves either to people or to institutions such as an organization or a religion. Neurotics who submit to another person often do so in order to gain affection.

Neurotics may also try to protect themselves by striving for power, prestige, or possession. *Power* is a defense against the real or imagined hostility of others and takes the form of a tendency to dominate others; *prestige* is a protection against humiliation and is expressed as a tendency to humiliate others; *possession* acts as a buffer against destitution and poverty and manifests itself as a tendency to deprive others.

The fourth protective mechanism is *withdrawal.* Neurotics frequently protect themselves against basic anxiety either by developing an independence from others or by becoming emotionally detached from them. By psychologically withdrawing, neurotics feel that they cannot be hurt by other people.

These protective devices did not necessarily indicate a neurosis, and Horney believed that all people use them to some extent. They become unhealthy when people feel compelled to rely on them and are thus unable to employ a variety of interpersonal strategies. Compulsion, then, is the salient characteristic of all neurotic drives.

Compulsive Drives

Neurotic individuals have the same problems that affect normal people, except neurotics experience them to a greater degree. Everyone uses the various protective devices to guard against the rejection, hostility, and competitiveness of others. But whereas normal individuals are able to use a variety of defensive maneuvers in a somewhat useful way, neurotics compulsively repeat the same strategy in an essentially unproductive manner.

Horney (1942) insisted that neurotics do not enjoy misery and suffering. They cannot change their behavior by free will but must continually and compulsively protect themselves against basic anxiety. This defensive strategy traps them in a vicious circle in which their compulsive needs to reduce basic anxiety lead to behaviors that perpetuate low self-esteem, generalized hostility, inappropriate striving for power, inflated feelings of superiority, and persistent apprehension, all of which result in more basic anxiety.

Neurotic Needs

At the beginning of this chapter, we asked you to select either "True" or "False" for each of 10 items that might suggest a neurotic need. For each item except number 8, a "True" response parallels one of Horney's neurotic needs. For number 8, a "False" answer is consistent with the neurotic need for self-centeredness. Remember that endorsing most or even all of these statements in the "neurotic" direction is no indication of emotional instability, but these items may give you a better understanding of what Horney meant by neurotic needs.

Horney tentatively identified 10 categories of **neurotic needs** that characterize neurotics in their attempts to combat basic anxiety. These needs were more specific than the four protective devices discussed earlier, but they describe the same basic defensive strategies. The 10 categories of neurotic needs overlapped one another, and a single person might employ more than one. Each of the following neurotic needs relates in some way or another to other people.

1. *The neurotic need for affection and approval.* In their quest for affection and approval, neurotics attempt indiscriminately to please others. They try to live up to the expectations of others, tend to dread self-assertion, and are quite uncomfortable with the hostility of others as well as the hostile feelings within themselves.

2. *The neurotic need for a powerful partner.* Lacking self-confidence, neurotics try to attach themselves to a powerful partner. This need includes an overvaluation of love and a dread of being alone or deserted. Horney's own life story reveals a strong need to relate to a great man, and she had a series of such relationships during her adult life.

3. *The neurotic need to restrict one's life within narrow borders.* Neurotics frequently strive to remain inconspicuous, to take second place, and to be content with very little. They downgrade their own abilities and dread making demands on others.

4. *The neurotic need for power.* Power and affection are perhaps the two greatest neurotic needs. The need for power is usually combined with the needs for prestige and possession and manifests itself as the need to control others and to avoid feelings of weakness or stupidity.

5. *The neurotic need to exploit others.* Neurotics frequently evaluate others on the basis of how they can be used or exploited, but at the same time, they fear being exploited by others.

6. *The neurotic need for social recognition or prestige.* Some people combat basic anxiety by trying to be first, to be important, or to attract attention to themselves.

7. *The neurotic need for personal admiration.* Neurotics have a need to be admired for what they are rather than for what they possess. Their inflated self-esteem must be continually fed by the admiration and approval of others.

8. *The neurotic need for ambition and personal achievement.* Neurotics often have a strong drive to be the best—the best salesperson, the best bowler, the best lover. They must defeat other people in order to confirm their superiority.

9. *The neurotic need for self-sufficiency and independence.* Many neurotics have a strong need to move away from people, thereby proving that they can get along without others. The playboy who cannot be tied down by any woman exemplifies this neurotic need.

10. *The neurotic need for perfection and unassailability.* By striving relentlessly for perfection, neurotics receive "proof" of their self-esteem and personal superiority. They dread making mistakes and having personal flaws, and they desperately attempt to hide their weaknesses from others.

Neurotic Trends

As her theory evolved, Horney began to see that the list of 10 neurotic needs could be grouped into three general categories, each relating to a person's basic attitude toward self and others. In 1945, she identified the three basic attitudes, or **neurotic trends,** as (1) *moving toward people,* (2) *moving against people,* and (3) *moving away from people.*

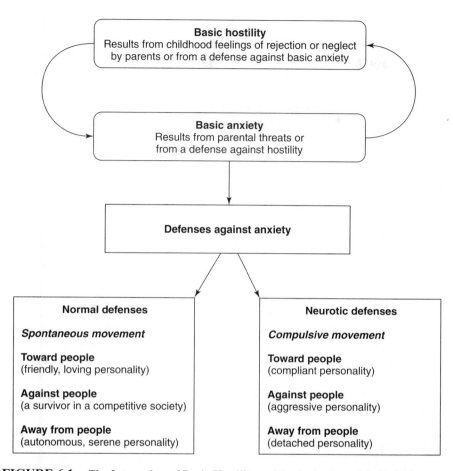

FIGURE 6.1   *The Interaction of Basic Hostility and Basic Anxiety with the Defenses against Anxiety.*

Although these neurotic trends constitute Horney's theory of neurosis, they also apply to normal individuals. There are, of course, important differences between normal and neurotic attitudes. Whereas normal people are mostly or completely conscious of their strategies toward other people, neurotics are unaware of their basic attitude; although normals are free to choose their actions, neurotics are forced to act; whereas normals experience mild conflict, neurotics experience severe and insoluble conflict; and whereas normals can choose from a variety of strategies, neurotics are limited to a single trend. Figure 6.1 shows Horney's conception of the mutual influence of basic hostility and basic anxiety as well as both normal and neurotic defenses against anxiety.

People can use each of the neurotic trends to solve basic conflict, but unfortunately, these solutions are essentially nonproductive or neurotic. Horney (1950) used the term **basic conflict** because very young children are driven in all three directions—toward, against, and away from people.

In healthy children, these three drives are not necessarily incompatible. But the feelings of isolation and helplessness that Horney described as *basic anxiety* drive some children to act compulsively, thereby limiting their repertoire to a single neurotic trend. Experiencing basically contradictory attitudes toward others, these children attempt to solve this basic conflict by making one of the three neurotic trends consistently dominant. Some children move *toward* people by behaving in a *compliant* manner as a protection against feelings of *helplessness;* other children move *against* people with acts of *aggression* in order to circumvent the *hostility* of others; and still other children move *away from* people by adopting a *detached* manner, thus alleviating feelings of *isolation* (Horney, 1945).

Moving Toward People

Horney's concept of **moving toward people** does *not* mean moving toward them in the spirit of genuine love. Rather, it refers to a neurotic need to protect oneself against feelings of helplessness.

In their attempts to protect themselves against feelings of *helplessness,* compliant people employ either or both of the first two neurotic needs; that is, they desperately strive for affection and approval of others, or they seek a powerful partner who will take responsibility for their lives. Horney (1937) referred to these needs as "morbid dependency," a concept that anticipated the term "codependency."

The neurotic trend of moving toward people involves a complex of strategies. It is "a whole way of thinking, feeling, acting—a whole way of life" (Horney, 1945, p. 55). Horney also called it a philosophy of life. Neurotics who adopt this philosophy are likely to see themselves as loving, generous, unselfish, humble, and sensitive to other people's feelings. They are willing to subordinate themselves to others, to see others as more intelligent or attractive, and to rate themselves according to what others think of them.

Moving Against People

Just as compliant people assume that everyone is nice, aggressive people take for granted that everyone is *hostile.* As a result, they adopt the strategy of **moving against people.** Neurotically aggressive people are just as compulsive as compliant people are, and their behavior is just as much prompted by basic anxiety. Rather than moving toward people in a posture of submissiveness and dependence, these people move against others by appearing tough or ruthless. They are motivated by a strong need to exploit others and to use them for their own benefit. They seldom admit their mistakes and are compulsively driven to appear perfect, powerful, and superior.

Five of the 10 neurotic needs are incorporated in the neurotic trend of moving against people. They include the need to be powerful, to exploit others, to receive recognition and prestige, to be admired, and to achieve. Aggressive people play to win rather than for the enjoyment of the contest. They may appear to be hard working and resourceful on the job, but they take little pleasure in the work itself. Their basic motivation is for power, prestige, and personal ambition.

In the United States, the striving for these goals is usually viewed with admiration. Compulsively aggressive people, in fact, frequently come out on top in many endeavors valued by American society. They may acquire desirable sex partners, high-paying jobs, and the personal admiration of many people. Horney (1945) said that it is not to the credit of American society that such characteristics are rewarded while love, affection, and the capacity for true friendship—the very qualities that aggressive people lack—are valued less highly.

Moving toward others and moving against others are, in many ways, polar opposites. The compliant person is compelled to receive affection from everyone, whereas the aggressive person sees everyone as a potential enemy. For both types, however, "the center of gravity lies outside the person" (Horney, 1945, p. 65). Both need other people. Compliant people need others to satisfy their feelings of helplessness; aggressive people use others as a protection against real or imagined hostility. With the third neurotic trend, in contrast, other people are of lesser importance.

Moving Away From People

In order to solve the basic conflict of *isolation,* some people behave in a detached manner and adopt a neurotic trend of **moving away from people.** This strategy is an expression of needs for privacy, independence, and self-sufficiency. Again, each of these needs can lead to positive behaviors, with some people satisfying these needs in a healthy fashion. However, these needs become neurotic when people try to satisfy them by compulsively putting emotional distance between themselves and other people.

Many neurotics find associating with others an intolerable strain. As a consequence, they are compulsively driven to move away from people, to attain autonomy and separateness. They frequently build a world of their own and refuse to allow anyone to get close to them. They value freedom and self-sufficiency and often appear to be aloof and unapproachable. If married, they maintain their detachment even from their spouse. They shun social commitments, but their greatest fear is to need other people.

All neurotics possess a need to feel superior, but detached persons have an intensified need to be strong and powerful. Their basic feelings of isolation can be

Moving away from people is a neurotic trend that many people use in an attempt to solve the basic conflict of isolation.

TABLE 6.1

Summary of Horney's Neurotic Trends

	Neurotic Trends		
	Toward People The Compliant Personality	**Against People** The Aggressive Personality	**Away from People** The Detached Personality
Basic conflict or source of neurotic trend	Feelings of helplessness	Protection against hostility of others	Feelings of isolation
Neurotic needs	1. Affection and approval 2. Powerful partner 3. Narrow limits to life	4. Power 5. Exploitation 6. Recognition and unassailability 7. Personal admiration 8. Personal achievement	9. Self-sufficiency and independence 10. Perfection and prestige
Normal analog	Friendly, loving	Ability to survive in a competitive society	Autonomous and serene

tolerated only by the self-deceptive belief that they are perfect and therefore beyond criticism. They dread competition, fearing a blow to their illusory feelings of superiority. Instead, they prefer that their hidden greatness be recognized without any effort on their part (Horney, 1945).

In summary, each of the three neurotic trends has an analogous set of characteristics that describe normal individuals. In addition, each of 10 neurotic needs can be easily placed within the three neurotic trends. Table 6.1 summarizes the three *neurotic trends,* the *basic conflicts* that give rise to them, the *outstanding characteristics* of each, the 10 *neurotic needs* that compose them, and the three *analogous* traits that characterize normal people.

Intrapsychic Conflicts

The neurotic trends flow from basic anxiety, which in turn, stems from a child's relationships with other people. To this point, our emphasis has been on culture and interpersonal conflict. However, Horney did not neglect the impact of intrapsychic factors in the development of personality. As her theory evolved, she began to place greater emphasis on the inner conflicts that both normal and neurotic individuals experience. Intrapsychic processes originate from interpersonal experiences; but as they become part of a person's belief system, they develop a life of their own—an existence separate from the interpersonal conflicts that gave them life.

This section looks at two important intrapsychic conflicts: *the idealized self-image* and *self-hatred.* Briefly, the **idealized self-image** is an attempt to solve conflicts by painting a godlike picture of oneself. **Self-hatred** is an interrelated yet equally irrational and powerful tendency to despise one's real self. As people build an idealized image of their self, their real self lags farther and farther behind. This gap creates a growing alienation between the real self and the idealized self and leads neurotics to hate and despise their actual self because it falls so short in matching the glorified self-image (Horney, 1950).

The Idealized Self-Image

Horney believed that human beings, if given an environment of discipline and warmth, will develop feelings of security and self-confidence and a tendency to move toward *self-realization.* Unfortunately, early negative influences often impede people's natural tendency toward self-realization, a situation that leaves them with feelings of isolation and inferiority. Added to this failure is a growing sense of alienation from themselves.

Feeling alienated from themselves, people need desperately to acquire a stable *sense of identity.* This dilemma can be solved only by creating an idealized self-image, an extravagantly positive view of themselves that exists only in their personal belief system. These people endow themselves with infinite powers and unlimited capabilities; they see themselves as "a hero, a genius, a supreme lover, a saint, a god" (Horney, 1950, p. 22). The idealized self-image is not a global construction. Neurotics glorify and worship themselves in different ways. Compliant people see themselves as good and saintly; aggressive people build an idealized image of themselves as strong, heroic, and omnipotent; and detached neurotics paint their self-portraits as wise, self-sufficient, and independent.

As the idealized self-image becomes solidified, neurotics begin to believe in the reality of that image. They lose touch with their real self and use the idealized self as the standard for self-evaluation. Rather than growing toward self-realization, they move toward actualizing their idealized self.

Horney (1950) recognized three aspects of the idealized image: (1) the neurotic search for glory, (2) neurotic claims, and (3) neurotic pride.

The Neurotic Search for Glory

As neurotics come to believe in the reality of their idealized self, they begin to incorporate it into all aspects of their lives—their goals, their self-concept, and their relations with others. Horney (1950) referred to this comprehensive drive toward actualizing the ideal self as the **neurotic search for glory.**

In addition to *self-idealization,* the neurotic search for glory includes three other elements: the need for perfection, neurotic ambition, and the drive toward a vindictive triumph.

The *need for perfection* refers to the drive to mold the whole personality into the idealized self. Neurotics are not content to merely make a few alterations; nothing short of complete perfection is acceptable. They try to achieve perfection by erecting a complex set of "shoulds" and "should nots." Horney (1950) referred to this drive as the **tyranny of the should.** Striving toward an imaginary picture of perfection, neurotics unconsciously tell themselves: "Forget about the disgraceful creature you actually *are;* this is how you *should be*" (p. 64).

A second key element in the neurotic search for glory is *neurotic ambition,* that is, the compulsive drive toward superiority. Although neurotics have an exaggerated need to excel in everything, they ordinarily channel their energies into those activities that are most likely to bring success. This drive, therefore, may take several different forms during a person's lifetime (Horney, 1950). For example, while still in school, a girl may direct her neurotic ambition toward being the best student in school. Later, she may be driven to excel in business or to raise the very best show dogs. Neurotic ambition may also take a less materialistic form, such as being the most saintly or most charitable person in the community.

The third aspect of the neurotic search for glory is the *drive toward a vindictive triumph,* the most destructive element of all. The need for a vindictive triumph may be disguised as a drive for achievement or success, but "its chief aim is to put others to shame or defeat them through one's very success; or to attain the power . . . to inflict suffering on them—mostly of a humiliating kind" (Horney, 1950, p. 27). Interestingly, in Horney's personal relationship with men, she seemed to take pleasure in causing them to feel ashamed and humiliated (Hornstein, 2000).

The drive for a vindictive triumph grows out of the childhood desire to take revenge for real or imagined humiliations. No matter how successful neurotics are in vindictively triumphing over others, they never lose their drive for a vindictive triumph—instead, they increase it with each victory. Every success raises their fear of defeat and increases their feelings of grandeur, thus solidifying their need for further vindictive triumphs.

Neurotic Claims

A second aspect of the idealized image is **neurotic claims.** In their search for glory, neurotics build a fantasy world—a world that is out of sync with the real world. Believing that something is wrong with the outside world, they proclaim that they are special and therefore entitled to be treated in accordance with their idealized view of themselves. Because these demands are very much in accord with their idealized self-image, they fail to see that their claims of special privilege are unreasonable.

Neurotic claims grow out of normal needs and wishes, but they are quite different. When normal wishes are not fulfilled, people become understandably frustrated; but when neurotic claims are not met, neurotics become indignant, bewildered, and unable to comprehend why others have not granted their claims. The difference between normal desires and neurotic claims is illustrated by a situation in which many people are waiting in line for tickets for a popular movie. Most people near the end of the line might wish to be up front, and some of them may even try some ploy to get a better position. Nevertheless, these people know that they don't really deserve to cut ahead of others. Neurotic people, on the other hand, truly

Self-hatred is sometimes expressed through abuse of alcohol.

believe that they are entitled to be near the front of the line, and they feel no guilt or remorse in moving ahead of others.

Neurotic Pride

The third aspect of an idealized image is **neurotic pride,** a false pride based not on a realistic view of the true self but on a spurious image of the idealized self. Neurotic pride is qualitatively different from healthy pride or realistic self-esteem. Genuine self-esteem is based on realistic attributes and accomplishments and is generally expressed with quiet dignity. Neurotic pride, on the other hand, is based on an idealized image of self and is usually loudly proclaimed in order to protect and support a glorified view of one's self (Horney, 1950).

Neurotics imagine themselves to be glorious, wonderful, and perfect, so when others fail to treat them with special consideration, their neurotic pride is hurt. To prevent the hurt, they avoid people who refuse to yield to their neurotic claims, and instead, they try to become associated with socially prominent and prestigious institutions and acquisitions.

Self-Hatred

People with a neurotic search for glory can never be happy with themselves because when they realize that their real self does not match the insatiable demands of their idealized self, they will begin to hate and despise themselves:

> The glorified self becomes not only a *phantom* to be pursued; it also becomes a measuring rod with which to measure his actual being. And this actual being is such an embarrassing sight when viewed from the perspective of a godlike perfection that he cannot but despise it. (Horney, 1950, p. 110)

Horney (1950) recognized six major ways in which people express self-hatred. First, self-hatred may result in *relentless demands on the self,* which are exemplified by the tyranny of the should. For example, some people make demands on themselves that don't stop even when they achieve a measure of success. These people continue to push themselves toward perfection because they believe they should be perfect.

The second mode of expressing self-hatred is *merciless self-accusation.* Neurotics constantly berate themselves. "If people only knew me, they would realize that I'm pretending to be knowledgeable, competent, and sincere. I'm really a fraud, but no one knows it but me." Self-accusation may take a variety of forms—from obviously grandiose expressions, such as taking responsibility for natural disasters, to scrupulously questioning the virtue of their own motivations.

Third, self-hatred may take the form of *self-contempt,* which might be expressed as belittling, disparaging, doubting, discrediting, and ridiculing oneself. Self-contempt prevents people from striving for improvement or achievement. A young man may say to himself, "You conceited idiot! What makes you think you can get a date with the best-looking woman in town?" A woman may attribute her successful career to "luck." Although these people may be aware of their behavior, they have no perception of the self-hatred that motivates it.

A fourth expression of self-hatred is *self-frustration.* Horney (1950) distinguished between healthy self-discipline and neurotic self-frustration. The former involves postponing or forgoing pleasurable activities in order to achieve reasonable goals. Self-frustration stems from self-hatred and is designed to actualize an inflated self-image. Neurotics are frequently shackled by taboos against enjoyment. "I don't deserve a new car." "I must not wear nice clothes because many people around the world are in rags." "I must not strive for a better job because I'm not good enough for it."

Fifth, self-hatred may be manifested as *self-torment,* or self-torture. Although self-torment can exist in each of the other forms of self-hatred, it becomes a separate category when people's main intention is to inflict harm or suffering on themselves. Some people attain masochistic satisfaction by anguishing over a decision, exaggerating the pain of a headache, cutting themselves with a knife, starting a fight that they are sure to lose, or inviting physical abuse.

The sixth and final form of self-hatred is *self-destructive actions and impulses,* which may be either physical or psychological, conscious or unconscious, acute or chronic, carried out in action or enacted only in the imagination. Overeating, abusing alcohol and other drugs, working too hard, driving recklessly, and suicide are common expressions of physical self-destruction. Neurotics may also attack themselves psychologically, for example, quitting a job just when it begins to be fulfilling, breaking off a healthy relationship in favor of a neurotic one, or engaging in promiscuous sexual activities.

Horney (1950) summarized the neurotic search for glory and its attendant self-hatred with these descriptive words:

> Surveying self-hate and its ravaging force, we cannot help but see in it a great tragedy, perhaps the greatest tragedy of the human mind. Man in reaching out for the Infinite and Absolute also starts destroying himself. When he makes a pact with the devil, who promises him glory, he has to go to hell—to the hell within himself. (p. 154)

Feminine Psychology

As a woman trained in the promasculine psychology of Freud, Horney gradually realized that the traditional psychoanalytic view of women was skewed. She then set forth her own theory, one that rejected several of Freud's basic ideas.

For Horney, psychic differences between men and women are not the result of anatomy but rather of cultural and social expectations. Men who subdue and rule women and women who degrade or envy men do so because of the neurotic competitiveness that is rampant in many societies. Horney (1937) insisted that basic anxiety is at the core of men's need to subjugate women and women's wish to humiliate men.

Although Horney (1939) recognized the existence of the *Oedipus complex,* she insisted that it was due to certain environmental conditions and not to biology. If it were the result of anatomy, as Freud contended, then it would be universal (as Freud indeed believed). However, Horney (1967) saw no evidence for a universal Oedipus complex. Instead, she held that it is found only in some people and is an expression of the neurotic need for love. The neurotic need for affection and the neurotic need for aggression usually begin in childhood and are two of the three basic neurotic trends. A child may passionately cling to one parent and express jealousy toward the other, but these behaviors are means of alleviating basic anxiety and not manifestations of an anatomically based Oedipus complex. Even when there is a sexual aspect to these behaviors, the child's main goal is security, not sexual intercourse.

Horney (1939) found the concept of *penis envy* even less tenable. She contended that here is no more anatomical reason why girls should be envious of the penis than boys should desire a breast or a womb. In fact, boys sometimes do express a desire to have a baby, but this desire is not the result of a universal male "womb envy."

Horney agreed with Adler that many women possess a *masculine protest;* that is, they have a pathological belief that men are superior to women. This perception easily leads to the neurotic desire to be a man. The desire, however, is not an expression of penis envy but rather "a wish for all those qualities or privileges which in our culture are regarded as masculine" (Horney, 1939, p. 108). (This view is nearly identical to that expressed by Erikson and discussed in Chapter 9).

In 1994, Bernard J. Paris published a talk that Horney had delivered in 1935 to a professional and business women's club in which she summarized her ideas on feminine psychology. By that time Horney was less interested in differences between men and women than in a general psychology of both genders. Because culture and society are responsible for psychological differences between women and men, Horney felt that "it was not so important to try to find the answer to the question about differences as to understand and analyze the real significance of this keen interest in feminine 'nature'" (Horney, 1994, p. 233). Horney concluded her speech by saying that

> once and for all we should stop bothering about what is feminine and what is not. Such concerns only undermine our energies. Standards of masculinity and femininity are artificial standards. All that we definitely know at present about sex differences is that we do not know what they are. Scientific differences between the two sexes certainly exist, but we shall never be able to discover what they are until we have first developed our potentialities as human beings. Paradoxical as it

may sound, we shall find out about these differences only if we forget about them. (p. 238)

Psychotherapy

Horney believed that neuroses grow out of basic conflict that usually begins in childhood. As people attempt to solve this conflict, they are likely to adopt one of the three neurotic trends: namely, moving toward, against, or away from others. Each of these tactics can produce temporary relief, but eventually they drive the person farther away from actualizing the real self and deeper into a neurotic spiral (Horney, 1950).

The general goal of Horneyian therapy is to help patients gradually grow in the direction of self-realization. More specifically, the aim is to have patients give up their idealized self-image, relinquish their neurotic search for glory, and change self-hatred to an acceptance of the real self. Unfortunately, patients are usually convinced that their neurotic solutions are correct, so they are reluctant to surrender their neurotic trends. Even though patients have a strong investment in maintaining the status quo, they do not wish to remain ill. They find little pleasure in their sufferings and would like to be free of them. Unfortunately, they tend to resist change and cling to those behaviors that perpetuate their illness. The three neurotic trends can be cast in favorable terms such as "love," "mastery," or "freedom." Because patients usually see their behaviors in these positive terms, their actions appear to them to be healthy, right, and desirable (Horney, 1942, 1950).

The therapist's task is to convince patients that their present solutions are perpetuating rather than alleviating the core neurosis, a task that takes much time and hard work. Patients may look for quick cures or solutions, but only the long, laborious process of self-understanding can effect positive change. Self-understanding must go beyond information; it must be accompanied by an emotional experience. Patients must understand their pride system, their idealized image, their neurotic search for glory, their self-hatred, their shoulds, their alienation from self, and their conflicts. Moreover, they must see how all these factors are interrelated and operate to preserve their basic neurosis.

Although a therapist can help encourage patients toward self-understanding, ultimately successful therapy is built on self-analysis (Horney, 1942, 1950). Patients must understand the difference between their idealized self-image and their real self. Fortunately, people possess an inherent curative force that allows them to move inevitably in the direction of self-realization once self-understanding and self-analysis are achieved.

As to techniques, Horneyian therapists use many of the same ones employed by Freudian therapists, especially dream interpretation and free association. Horney saw dreams as attempts to solve conflicts, but the solutions can be either neurotic or healthy. When therapists provide a correct interpretation, patients are helped toward a better understanding of their real self. "From dreams . . . the patient can catch a glimpse, even in the initial phase of analysis, of a world operating within him which is peculiarly his own and which is more true of his feelings than the world of his illusions" (Horney, 1950, p. 349).

With the second major technique, free association, patients are asked to say everything that comes to mind regardless of how trivial or embarrassing it may seem (Horney, 1987). They are also encouraged to express whatever feelings may arise from the associations. As with dream interpretation, free association eventually reveals patients' idealized self-image and persistent but unsuccessful attempts at accomplishing it.

When therapy is successful, patients gradually develop confidence in their ability to assume responsibility for their psychological development. They move toward self-realization and all those processes that accompany it; they have a deeper and clearer understanding of their feelings, beliefs, and wishes; they relate to others with genuine feelings instead of using people to solve basic conflicts; at work, they take a greater interest in the job itself rather than seeing it as a means to perpetuate a neurotic search for glory.

Related Research

Horney's psychoanalytic social theory has not directly inspired a great deal of research in modern personality psychology. Her musings on neurotic trends however are quite relevant to much of the research being conducted today on neuroticism.

The Neurotic Compulsion to Avoid the Negative

Most research on neuroticism highlights its negative side. High levels of neuroticism are associated with experiencing more negative emotion and being more likely to develop generalized anxiety disorder (Borkovec & Sharpless, 2004). Neuroticism is also associated with setting avoidance goals, in which a person avoids negative outcomes, rather than setting approach goals in which a person approaches positive outcomes (Elliot & Thrash, 2002). In Horney's (1942) view, neurotics are compulsively protecting themselves against basic anxiety and this defensive strategy traps them in a negative cycle. Setting goals that are framed as approaching positive outcomes is generally considered to be a healthier way of life than being preoccupied with avoiding negative outcomes, but neurotics are generally unable to break free from their avoidance mindset (Elliot & Thrash, 2002). These findings would not be too surprising to Horney as they fit quite well into her model of neurotic trends. Whether it's the constant battle with basic anxiety or just being stuck in a frame of mind focused on avoiding negative outcomes, neurotic defenses are not the path to a strong sense of positive well-being.

Can Neuroticism Ever Be a Good Thing?

Horney's theory, as well as most of the work in personality psychology, paints neuroticism rather negatively. Based on the research reviewed in the previous section on neuroticism and avoidance goals and the associated negative outcomes, the negative bias toward neuroticism is understandable. Some recent research has begun investigating conditions under which neuroticism might not be all negative and, ironically, may actually have some benefits.

Michael Robinson and colleagues (Robinson, Ode, Wilkowski, & Amodio, 2007) asked the question "How could one be a successful neurotic?" For sure it's tough to be a successful neurotic. People high in neuroticism are constantly drawn toward avoidance goals and dealing with basic anxiety by using all the detrimental neurotic defenses described by Horney. But there may be some cases where neuroticism is good, specifically in detecting threats. Neurotics are predisposed to avoid threats (and any negative outcome). Therefore, Robinson and colleagues designed a study to investigate the relationship between neuroticism, recognition of threats, and mood. They predicted that for those high in neuroticism, the ability to accurately recognize threats in the environment would be related to decreased negative mood. In other words, the neurotic sensitivity to threat would serve a purpose in that such people could recognize problems, and presumably avoid them, and that successful avoidance would make them feel better.

To test this hypothesis, Robinson and colleagues (2007) had 181 students come into the lab and complete a self-report measure of neuroticism and then engage in a computer task that measured their ability to accurately detect threats and assessed what they did upon making an error in detecting a threat. If a person makes an error, the adaptive thing to do would be to slow down and assess the situation more carefully. But not everyone does this, and the computer task used by Robinson and colleagues measured whether people exhibited the appropriate response to making an error. The computer task consisted of a word appearing on a computer screen and then the participant, as quickly as possible, had to determine whether or not the word represented a threat. For example, the word "stench" does not represent a threat, but the word "knife" does. The computer kept track of how long participants took at deciding whether or not the word was a threat and whether or not the participant correctly identified the threat. Additionally, when the participant made an error, the computer also kept track of how long a participant took to determine whether or not the next word to appear on the screen represented a threat. Once the researchers had each participant's neuroticism score and a good measure of how they detected threats and reacted to errors, participants were asked to keep track of their mood over the next 7 days.

Interestingly, Robinson and colleagues found that there actually is a way to be a "successful neurotic." Specifically, they discovered that for those who are predisposed toward being neurotic, the ability to react adaptively to errors (i.e., to slow down and think carefully) while assessing threat was related to experiencing less negative mood in daily life (Robinson et al., 2007).

Generally speaking, it may not be a positive thing to be neurotic and constantly obsessed with avoiding negative outcomes, but there is only so much about our personality that is in our control. Neurotic people cannot simply wake up one day and stop being neurotic. Neurotic trends and related defenses outlined by Horney are stable and durable aspects of individuals' personalities that are not likely to change suddenly. Therefore, it is important to realize that, though much research shows the dark side of neuroticism, it is not all bad news. Many neurotic people are quite skilled at avoiding negative outcomes, and the avoidance of these outcomes does indeed make them feel better on a daily basis.

Critique of Horney

Horney's social psychoanalytic theory provides interesting perspectives on the nature of humanity, but it suffers from lack of current research that might support her suppositions. The strength of Horney's theory is her lucid portrayal of the neurotic personality. No other personality theorist has written so well (or so much) about neuroses. Her comprehensive descriptions of neurotic personalities provide an excellent framework for understanding unhealthy people. However, her nearly exclusive concern with neurotics is a serious limitation to her theory. Her references to the normal or healthy personality are general and not well explicated. She believed that people by their very nature will strive toward self-realization, but she suggested no clear picture of what self-realization would be.

Horney's theory falls short on its power both to *generate research* and to submit to the criterion of *falsifiability*. Speculations from the theory do not easily yield testable hypotheses and therefore lack both verifiability and falsifiability. Horney's theory was based largely on clinical experiences that put her in contact mostly with neurotic individuals. To her credit, she was reluctant to make specific assumptions about psychologically healthy individuals. Because her theory deals mostly with neurotics, it is rated high on its ability to *organize knowledge* of neurotics but very low on its capacity to explain what is known about people in general.

As a *guide to action,* Horney's theory fares somewhat better. Teachers, therapists, and especially parents can use her assumptions concerning the development of neurotic trends to provide a warm, safe, and accepting environment for their students, patients, or children. Beyond these provisions, however, the theory is not specific enough to give the practitioner a clear and detailed course of action. On this criterion, the theory receives a low rating.

Is Horney's theory *internally consistent,* with clearly defined terms used uniformly? In Horney's book *Neurosis and Human Growth* (1950), her concepts and formulations are precise, consistent, and unambiguous. However, when all her works are examined, a different picture emerges. Through the years, she used terms such as "neurotic needs" and "neurotic trends" sometimes separately and sometimes interchangeably. Also, the terms "basic anxiety" and "basic conflict" were not always clearly differentiated. These inconsistencies render her entire work somewhat inconsistent, but again, her final theory (1950) is a model of lucidity and consistency.

Another criterion of a useful theory is *parsimony,* and Horney's final theory, as expressed in the last chapter of *Neurosis and Human Growth* (Horney, 1950, Chap. 15), would receive a high mark on this standard. This chapter, which provides a useful and concise introduction to Horney's theory of neurotic development, is relatively simple, straightforward, and clearly written.

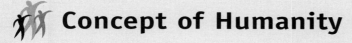 # Concept of Humanity

Horney's concept of humanity was based almost entirely on her clinical experiences with neurotic patients; therefore, her view of human personality is strongly colored by her concept of neurosis. According to Horney, the prime difference between a healthy person and a neurotic individual is the degree of compulsivity with which each moves toward, against, or away from people.

The compulsive nature of neurotic trends suggests that Horney's concept of humanity is deterministic. However, a healthy person would have a large element of free choice. Even a neurotic individual, through psychotherapy and hard work, can wrest some control over those intrapsychic conflicts. For this reason, Horney's psychoanalytic social theory is rated slightly higher on *free choice* than on determinism.

On the same basis, Horney's theory is somewhat more *optimistic* than pessimistic. Horney believed that people possess inherent curative powers that lead them toward self-realization. If basic anxiety (the feeling of being alone and helpless in a potentially hostile world) can be avoided, people will feel safe and secure in their interpersonal relations and consequently will develop healthy personalities.

> My own belief is that man has the capacity as well as the desire to develop his potentialities and become a decent human being, and that these deteriorate if his relationship to others and hence to himself is, and continues to be, disturbed. I believe that man can change and go on changing as long as he lives. (Horney, 1945, p. 19)

On the dimension of *causality versus teleology,* Horney adopted a middle position. She stated that the natural goal for people is self-realization, but she also believed that childhood experiences can block that movement. "The past in some way or other is always contained in the present" (Horney, 1939, p. 153). Included in people's past experiences, however, is the formation of a philosophy of life and a set of values that give both their present and their future some direction

Although Horney adopted a middle stance regarding *conscious versus unconscious motivation,* she believed that most people have only limited awareness of their motives. Neurotics, especially, have little understanding of themselves and do not see that their behaviors guarantee the continuation of their neuroses. They mislabel their personal characteristics, couching them in socially acceptable terms, while remaining largely unaware of their basic conflict, their self-hate, their neurotic pride and neurotic claims, and their need for a vindictive triumph.

Horney's concept of personality strongly emphasized *social influences* more than biological ones. Psychological differences between men and women, for example, are due more to cultural and societal expectations than to anatomy. To Horney, the Oedipus complex and penis envy are not inevitable consequences of biology but rather are shaped by social forces. Horney did not neglect biological factors completely, but her main emphasis was on social influences.

Because Horney's theory looks almost exclusively at neuroses, it tends to highlight *similarities among people* more than uniqueness. Not all neurotics are alike, of course, and Horney described three basic types—the helpless, the hostile, and the detached. However, she placed little emphasis on individual differences within each of these categories.

Key Terms and Concepts

- Horney insisted that *social and cultural influences* were more important than biological ones.
- Children who lack warmth and affection fail to meet their *needs for safety and satisfaction.*

- These feelings of isolation and helplessness trigger *basic anxiety,* or feelings of isolation and helplessness in a potentially hostile world.
- The inability of people to use different tactics in their relationships with others generates *basic conflict:* that is, the incompatible tendency to move toward, against, and away from people.
- Horney called the tendencies to move toward, against, or away from people the three *neurotic trends.*
- Healthy people solve their basic conflict by using all three neurotic trends, whereas neurotics compulsively adopt only one of these trends.
- The three neurotic trends (moving toward, against, or away from people) are a combination of 10 neurotic trends that Horney had earlier identified.
- Both healthy and neurotic people experience *intrapsychic conflicts* that have become part of their belief system. The two major intrapsychic conflicts are the idealized self-image and self-hatred.
- The *idealized self-image* results in neurotics' attempts to build a godlike picture of themselves.
- *Self-hatred* is the tendency for neurotics to hate and despise their real self.
- Any psychological *differences between men and women* are due to cultural and social expectations and not to biology.
- The goal of Horneyian *psychotherapy* is to bring about growth toward actualization of the real self.

CHAPTER 7

Fromm: Humanistic Psychoanalysis

Fromm

Why war? Why can't nations get along? Why can't people from different countries relate to one another, if not in a respectful manner at least in an acceptable one? How can people avoid the violence that leads to and perpetuates slaughter on the battlefield?

As the young boy pondered these questions, a war raged throughout his homeland. This war that he saw firsthand was World War I, the Great War, the War to End All Wars. He saw that the people of his country—Germany—hated people of the opposing countries—mostly France and England, and he was sure that the people of France and England hated the people of Germany. The war made no sense. Why would normally friendly and rational people revert to such senseless killing?

These questions weren't the first to have bothered the young boy. He was also at a loss in trying to understand the suicide of a beautiful young artist who killed herself immediately after the death of her father—an event that left the 12-year-old boy confused and perplexed. The young woman—a friend of the boy's family—was both beautiful and talented, whereas her father was old and unattractive. Yet she left a suicide note stating that she wished to be buried with her father. The young boy could make no sense of either her wish or her actions. The beautiful artist seemed to have had much to live for, but she chose death rather than a life without her father. How could the young woman make such a decision?

A third experience that helped shape the young man's early life was his training by Talmudic teachers. He was especially moved by the compassionate and redemptive tone of the Old Testament prophets Isaiah, Hosea, and Amos. Although he later abandoned organized religion, these early experiences with the Talmudic scholars, combined with his distaste for war and his puzzlement over the suicide of the young artist, contributed substantially to the humanistic views of Erich Fromm.

Overview of Humanistic Psychoanalysis

Erich Fromm's basic thesis is that modern-day people have been torn away from their prehistoric union with nature and also with one another, yet they have the power of reasoning, foresight, and imagination. This combination of lack of animal instincts and presence of rational thought makes humans the freaks of the universe. Self-awareness contributes to feelings of loneliness, isolation, and homelessness. To escape from these feelings, people strive to become reunited with nature and with their fellow human beings.

Trained in Freudian psychoanalysis and influenced by Karl Marx, Karen Horney, and other socially oriented theorists, Fromm developed a theory of personality that emphasizes the influence of sociobiological factors, history, economics, and class structure. His **humanistic psychoanalysis** assumes that humanity's separation from the natural world has produced feelings of loneliness and isolation, a condition called *basic anxiety.*

Fromm was more than a personality theorist. He was a social critic, psychotherapist, philosopher, biblical scholar, cultural anthropologist, and psychobiographer. His humanistic psychoanalysis looks at people from a historical and cultural perspective rather than a strictly psychological one. It is less concerned with the individual and more concerned with those characteristics common to a culture.

Fromm takes an evolutionary view of humanity. When humans emerged as a separate species in animal evolution, they lost most of their animal instincts but gained "an increase in brain development that permitted self-awareness, imagination, planning, and doubt" (Fromm, 1992, p. 5). This combination of weak instincts and a highly developed brain makes humans distinct from all other animals.

A more recent event in human history has been the rise of capitalism, which on one hand has contributed to the growth of leisure time and personal freedom, but on the other hand, it has resulted in feelings of anxiety, isolation, and powerlessness. The cost of freedom, Fromm maintained, has exceeded its benefits. The isolation wrought by capitalism has been unbearable, leaving people with two alternatives: (1) to escape from freedom into interpersonal dependencies, or (2) to move to self-realization through productive love and work.

Biography of Erich Fromm

Like the views of all personality theorists, Erich Fromm's view of human nature was shaped by childhood experiences. For Fromm, a Jewish family life, the suicide of a young woman, and the extreme nationalism of the German people contributed to his conception of humanity.

Fromm was born on March 23, 1900, in Frankfurt, Germany, the only child of middle-class Orthodox Jewish parents. His father, Naphtali Fromm, was the son of a rabbi and the grandson of two rabbis. His mother, Rosa Krause Fromm, was the niece of Ludwig Krause, a well-known Talmudic scholar. As a boy, Erich studied the Old Testament with several prominent scholars, men who were regarded as "humanists of extraordinary tolerance" (Landis & Tauber, 1971, p. xi). Fromm's humanistic psychology can be traced to the reading of these prophets, "with their vision of universal peace and harmony, and their teachings that there are ethical aspects to history—that nations can do right and wrong, and that history has its moral laws" (p. x).

Fromm's early childhood was less than ideal. He recalled that he had "very neurotic parents" and that he was "probably a rather unbearably neurotic child" (Evans, 1966, p. 56). He saw his father as being moody and his mother as prone to depression. Moreover, he grew up in two very distinct worlds, one the traditional Orthodox Jewish world, the other the modern capitalist world. This split existence created tensions that were nearly unendurable, but it generated in Fromm a lifelong tendency to see events from more than one perspective (Fromm, 1986; Hausdorff, 1972).

The chapter opening vignette chronicled the shocking and puzzling suicide of an attractive artistic young woman who killed herself so she could be buried with her father, who had just died. How was it possible that this young woman could prefer death to being "alive to the pleasures of life and painting"? (Fromm, 1962, p. 4). This question haunted Fromm for the next 10 years and eventually led to an interest in Sigmund Freud and psychoanalysis. As Fromm read Freud, he began to learn about the Oedipus complex and to understand how such an event might be possible. Later, Fromm would interpret the young woman's irrational dependence on her father as a nonproductive symbiotic relationship, but in those early years he was content with the Freudian explanation.

Fromm was 14 when World War I began, too young to fight but not too young to be impressed by the irrationality of the German nationalism that he had observed firsthand. He was sure that the British and French were equally irrational, and once again he was struck by a troubling question: How could normally rational and peaceful people become so driven by national ideologies, so intent on killing, so ready to die? "When the war ended in 1918, I was a deeply troubled young man who was obsessed by the question of how war was possible, by the wish to understand the irrationality of human mass behavior, by a passionate desire for peace and international understanding" (Fromm, 1962, p. 9).

During adolescence, Fromm was deeply moved by the writings of Freud and Karl Marx, but he was also stimulated by differences between the two. As he studied more, he began to question the validity of both systems. "My main interest was clearly mapped out. I wanted to understand the laws that govern the life of the individual man, and the laws of society" (Fromm, 1962, p. 9).

After the war, Fromm became a socialist, although at that time, he refused to join the Socialist Party. Instead, he concentrated on his studies in psychology, philosophy, and sociology at the University of Heidelberg, where he received his PhD in sociology at either age 22 or 25. [Fromm was such a private person that his biographers do not agree on many facts of his life (Hornstein, 2000).]

Still not confident that his training could answer such troubling questions as the suicide of the young woman or the insanity of war, Fromm turned to psychoanalysis, believing that it promised answers to questions of human motivation not offered in other fields. From 1925 until 1930 he studied psychoanalysis, first in Munich, then in Frankfurt, and finally at the Berlin Psychoanalytic Institute, where he was analyzed by Hanns Sachs, a student of Freud. Although Fromm never met Freud, most of his teachers during those years were strict adherents of Freudian theory (Knapp, 1989).

In 1926, the same year that he repudiated Orthodox Judaism, Fromm married Frieda Reichmann, his analyst, who was more than 10 years his senior. Reichmann would later obtain an international reputation for her work with schizophrenic patients. G. P. Knapp (1989) claimed that Reichmann was clearly a mother figure to Fromm and that she even resembled his mother. Gail Hornstein (2000) added that Fromm seemed to have gone directly from being his mother's darling to relationships with a number of older women who doted on him. In any event, the marriage of Fromm and Fromm-Reichmann was not a happy one. They separated in 1930 but were not divorced until much later, after both had emigrated to the United States.

In 1930, Fromm and several others founded the South German Institute for Psychoanalysis in Frankfurt, but with the Nazi threat becoming more intense, he soon moved to Switzerland where he joined the newly founded International Institute of Social Research in Geneva. In 1933, he accepted an invitation to deliver a series of lectures at the Chicago Psychoanalytic Institute. The following year he emigrated to the United States and opened a private practice in New York City.

In both Chicago and New York, Fromm renewed his acquaintance with Karen Horney, whom he had known casually at the Berlin Psychoanalytic Institute. Horney, who was 15 years older than Fromm, eventually became a strong mother figure and mentor to him (Knapp, 1989). Fromm joined Horney's newly formed Association for the Advancement of Psychoanalysis (AAP) in 1941. Although he and Horney had been lovers, by 1943 dissension within the association had made them rivals. When students requested that Fromm, who did not hold an MD degree, teach a clinical course, the organization split over his qualifications. With Horney siding against him, Fromm, along with Harry Stack Sullivan, Clara Thompson, and several other members, quit the association and immediately made plans to begin an alternative organization (Quinn, 1987). In 1946, this group established the William Alanson White Institute of Psychiatry, Psychoanalysis, and Psychology, with Fromm chairing both the faculty and the training committee.

In 1944, Fromm married Henny Gurland, a woman two years younger than Fromm and whose interest in religion and mystical thought furthered Fromm's own inclinations toward Zen Buddhism. In 1951, the couple moved to Mexico for a more favorable climate for Gurland, who suffered from rheumatoid arthritis. Fromm joined the faculty at the National Autonomous University in Mexico City, where he established a psychoanalytic department at the medical school. After his wife died in 1952, he continued to live in Mexico and commuted between his home in Cuernavaca and the United States, where he held various academic positions, including professor of psychology at Michigan State University from 1957 to 1961 and adjunct professor at New York University from 1962 to 1970. While in Mexico, he met Annis Freeman, whom he married in 1953. In 1968, Fromm suffered a serious heart attack and was forced to slow down his busy schedule. In 1974 and still ill, he and his wife moved to Muralto, Switzerland, where he died March 18, 1980, a few days short of his 80th birthday.

What kind of person was Erich Fromm? Apparently, different people saw him in quite different ways. Hornstein (2000) listed a number of opposing traits that have been used to describe his personality. According to this account, Fromm was authoritarian, gentle, pretentious, arrogant, pious, autocratic, shy, sincere, phony, and brilliant.

Fromm began his professional career as a psychotherapist using orthodox psychoanalytic technique, but after 10 years he became "bored" with the Freudian approach and developed his own more active and confrontational methods (Fromm, 1986, 1992; Sobel, 1980). Over the years, his cultural, social, economic, and psychological ideas have attained a wide audience. Among his best-known books are *Escape from Freedom* (1941), *Man for Himself* (1947), *Psychoanalysis and Religion* (1950), *The Sane Society* (1955), *The Art of Loving* (1956), *Marx's Concept of Man* (1961), *The Heart of Man* (1964), *The Anatomy of Human Destructiveness* (1973), *To Have or Be* (1976), and *For the Love of Life* (1986).

Fromm's theory of personality borrows from myriad sources and is, perhaps, the most broadly based theory in this book. Landis and Tauber (1971) listed five important influences on Fromm's thinking: (1) the teachings of the humanistic rabbis; (2) the revolutionary spirit of Karl Marx; (3) the equally revolutionary ideas of Sigmund Freud; (4) the rationality of Zen Buddhism as espoused by D. T. Suzuki; and (5) the writings of Johann Jakob Bachofen (1815–1887) on matriarchal societies.

Fromm's Basic Assumptions

Fromm's most basic assumption is that individual personality can be understood only in the light of human history. "The discussion of the human situation must precede that of personality, [and] psychology must be based on an anthropologic-philosophical concept of human existence" (Fromm, 1947, p. 45).

Fromm (1947) believed that humans, unlike other animals, have been "torn away" from their prehistoric union with nature. They have no powerful instincts to adapt to a changing world; instead, they have acquired the facility to reason—a condition Fromm called the **human dilemma.** People experience this basic dilemma because they have become separate from nature and yet have the capacity to be aware of themselves as isolated beings. The human ability to reason, therefore, is both a blessing and a curse. On one hand, it permits people to survive, but on the other, it forces them to attempt to solve basic insoluble dichotomies. Fromm referred to these as "existential dichotomies" because they are rooted in people's very existence. Humans cannot do away with these existential dichotomies; they can only react to these dichotomies relative to their culture and their individual personalities.

The first and most fundamental dichotomy is that between life and death. Self-awareness and reason tell us that we will die, but we try to negate this dichotomy by postulating life after death, an attempt that does not alter the fact that our lives end with death.

A second existential dichotomy is that humans are capable of conceptualizing the goal of complete self-realization, but we also are aware that life is too short to reach that goal. "Only if the life span of the individual were identical with that of mankind could he participate in the human development which occurs in the historical process" (Fromm, 1947, p. 42). Some people try to solve this dichotomy by assuming that their own historical period is the crowning achievement of humanity, while others postulate a continuation of development after death.

The third existential dichotomy is that people are ultimately alone, yet we cannot tolerate isolation. They are aware of themselves as separate individuals, and at the same time, they believe that their happiness depends on uniting with their fellow human beings. Although people cannot completely solve the problem of aloneness versus union, they must make an attempt or run the risk of insanity.

Human Needs

As animals, humans are motivated by such physiological needs as hunger, sex, and safety; but they can never resolve their human dilemma by satisfying these animal needs. Only the distinctive *human needs* can move people toward a reunion with the natural world. These **existential needs** have emerged during the evolution of human culture, growing out of their attempts to find an answer to their existence and to avoid becoming insane. Indeed, Fromm (1955) contended that one important difference between mentally healthy individuals and neurotic or insane ones is that healthy people find answers to their existence—answers that more completely correspond to their total human needs. In other words, healthy individuals are better able to find ways of reuniting to the world by productively solving the human needs of *relatedness, transcendence, rootedness, a sense of identity,* and *a frame of orientation.*

Relatedness

The first human, or existential, need is **relatedness,** the drive for union with another person or other persons. Fromm postulated three basic ways in which a person may relate to the world: (1) submission, (2) power, and (3) love. A person can submit to another, to a group, or to an institution in order to become one with the world. "In this way he transcends the separateness of his individual existence by becoming part of somebody or something bigger than himself and experiences his identity in connection with the power to which he has submitted" (Fromm, 1981, p. 2).

Whereas submissive people search for a relationship with domineering people, power seekers welcome submissive partners. When a submissive person and a domineering person find each other, they frequently establish a *symbiotic relationship,* one that is satisfying to both partners. Although such symbiosis may be gratifying, it blocks growth toward integrity and psychological health. The two partners "live on each other and from each other, satisfying their craving for closeness, yet suffering from the lack of inner strength and self-reliance which would require freedom and independence" (Fromm, 1981, p. 2).

People in symbiotic relationships are drawn to one another not by love but by a desperate need for relatedness, a need that can never be completely satisfied by such a partnership. Underlying the union are unconscious feelings of hostility. People in symbiotic relationships blame their partners for not being able to completely satisfy their needs. They find themselves seeking additional submission or power, and as a result, they become more and more dependent on their partners and less and less of an individual.

Fromm believed that **love** is the only route by which a person can become united with the world and, at the same time, achieve individuality and integrity. He defined love as a "union with somebody, or something outside oneself *under the condition of retaining the separateness and integrity of one's own self*" (Fromm, 1981, p. 3). Love involves sharing and communion with another, yet it allows a person the

Relatedness can take the form of submission, power, or love.

freedom to be unique and separate. It enables a person to satisfy the need for relatedness without surrendering integrity and independence. In love, two people become one yet remain two.

In *The Art of Loving,* Fromm (1956) identified care, responsibility, respect, and knowledge as four basic elements common to all forms of genuine love. Someone who loves another person must *care* for that person and be willing to take care of him or her. Love also means *responsibility,* that is, a willingness and ability to respond. A person who loves others responds to their physical and psychological needs, respects them for who they are, and avoids the temptation of trying to change them. But people can respect others only if they have *knowledge* of them. To know others means to see them from their own point of view. Thus, care, responsibility, respect, and knowledge are all entwined in a love relationship.

Transcendence

Like other animals, humans are thrown into the world without their consent or will and then removed from it—again without their consent or will. But unlike other animals, human beings are driven by the need for **transcendence,** defined as the urge to rise above a passive and accidental existence and into "the realm of purposefulness and freedom" (Fromm, 1981, p. 4). Just as relatedness can be pursued through either productive or nonproductive methods, transcendence can be sought through either positive or negative approaches. People can transcend their passive nature by either creating life or by destroying it. Although other animals can create life through reproduction, only humans are aware of themselves as creators. Also, humans can be creative in other ways. They can create art, religions, ideas, laws, material production, and love.

To create means to be active and to care about that which we create. But we can also transcend life by destroying it and thus rising above our slain victims. In *The Anatomy of Human Destructiveness,* Fromm (1973) argued that humans are the only species to use **malignant aggression:** that is, to kill for reasons other than survival. Although malignant aggression is a dominant and powerful passion in some individuals and cultures, it is not common to all humans. It apparently was unknown to many prehistoric societies as well as some contemporary "primitive" societies.

Rootedness

A third existential need is for **rootedness,** or the need to establish roots or to feel at home again in the world. When humans evolved as a separate species, they lost their home in the natural world. At the same time, their capacity for thought enabled them to realize that they were without a home, without roots. The consequent feelings of isolation and helplessness became unbearable.

Rootedness, too, can be sought in either productive or nonproductive strategies. With the productive strategy, people are weaned from the orbit of their mother and become fully born; that is, they actively and creatively relate to the world and become whole or integrated. This new tie to the natural world confers security and reestablishes a sense of belongingness and rootedness. However, people may also seek rootedness through the nonproductive strategy of **fixation**—a tenacious reluctance to move beyond the protective security provided by one's mother. People who strive for rootedness through fixation are "afraid to take the next step of birth, to be weaned from the mother's breast. [They] . . . have a deep craving to be mothered, nursed, protected by a motherly figure; they are the externally dependent ones, who are frightened and insecure when motherly protection is withdrawn" (Fromm, 1955, p. 40).

Rootedness can also be seen phylogenetically in the evolution of the human species. Fromm agreed with Freud that incestuous desires are universal, but he disagreed with Freud's belief that they are essentially sexual. According to Fromm (1955, pp. 40–41), incestuous feelings are based in "the deep-seated craving to remain in, or to return to, the all-enveloping womb, or to the all-nourishing breasts." Fromm was influenced by Johann Jakob Bachofen's (1861/1967) ideas on early matriarchal societies. Unlike Freud, who believed that early societies were patriarchal, Bachofen held that the mother was the central figure in these ancient social groups. It was she who provided roots for her children and motivated them either to develop their individuality and reason or to become fixated and incapable of psychological growth.

Fromm's (1997) strong preference for Bachofen's mother-centered theory of the Oedipal situation over Freud's father-centered conception is consistent with his preference for older women. Fromm's first wife, Frieda Fromm-Reichmann, was more than 10 years older than Fromm, and his long-time lover, Karen Horney, was 15 years his senior. Fromm's conception of the Oedipus complex as a desire to return to the mother's womb or breast or to a person with a mothering function should be viewed in light of his attraction to older women.

Sense of Identity

The fourth human need is for a **sense of identity,** or the capacity to be aware of ourselves as a separate entity. Because we have been torn away from nature, we need to form a concept of our self, to be able to say, "I am I," or "I am the subject of my actions." Fromm (1981) believed that primitive people identified more closely with their clan and did not see themselves as individuals existing apart from their group. Even during medieval times, people were identified largely by their social role in the feudal hierarchy. In agreement with Marx, Fromm believed that the rise of capitalism has given people more economic and political freedom. However, this freedom has given only a minority of people a true sense of "I." The identity of most people still resides in their attachment to others or to institutions such as nation, religion, occupation, or social group.

> Instead of the pre-individualistic clan identity, a new herd identity develops in which the sense of identity rests on the sense of an unquestionable belonging to the crowd. That this uniformity and conformity are often not recognized as such, and are covered by the illusion of individuality, does not alter the facts. (p. 9)

Without a sense of identity, people could not retain their sanity, and this threat provides a powerful motivation to do almost anything to acquire a sense of identity. Neurotics try to attach themselves to powerful people or to social or political institutions. Healthy people, however, have less need to conform to the herd, less need to give up their sense of self. They do not have to surrender their freedom and individuality in order to fit into society because they possess an authentic sense of identity.

Frame of Orientation

A final human need is for a **frame of orientation.** Being split off from nature, humans need a road map, a frame of orientation, to make their way through the world. Without such a map, humans would be "confused and unable to act purposefully and consistently" (Fromm, 1973, p. 230). A frame of orientation enables people to organize the various stimuli that impinge on them. People who possess a solid frame of orientation can make sense of these events and phenomena, but those who lack a reliable frame of orientation will, nevertheless, strive to put these events into some sort of framework in order to make sense of them. For example, an American with a shaky frame of orientation and a poor understanding of history may attempt to understand the events of September 11, 2001, by blaming them on "evil" or "bad" people.

Every person has a philosophy, a consistent way of looking at things. Many people take for granted this philosophy or frame of reference so that anything at odds with their view is judged as "crazy" or "unreasonable." Anything consistent with it is seen simply as "common sense." People will do nearly anything to acquire and retain a frame of orientation, even to the extreme of following irrational or bizarre philosophies such as those espoused by fanatical political and religious leaders.

A road map without a *goal* or destination is worthless. Humans have the mental capacity to imagine many alternative paths to follow. To keep from going insane, however, they need a final goal or "object of devotion" (Fromm, 1976, p. 137). According to Fromm, this goal or object of devotion focuses people's energies in a single direction, enables us to transcend our isolated existence, and confers meaning to their lives.

Summary of Human Needs

In addition to physiological or animal needs, people are motivated by five distinctively human needs—relatedness, transcendence, rootedness, a sense of identity, and a frame of orientation. These needs have evolved from human existence as a separate species and are aimed at moving people toward a reunion with the natural world. Fromm believed that lack of satisfaction of any of these needs is unbearable and results in insanity. Thus, people are strongly driven to fulfill them in some way or another, either positively or negatively.

Table 7.1 shows that relatedness can be satisfied through submission, domination, or love, but only love produces authentic fulfillment; transcendence can be satisfied by either destructiveness or creativeness, but only the latter permits joy; rootedness can be satisfied either by fixation to the mother or by moving forward into full birth and wholeness; the sense of identity can be based on adjustment to the group, or it can be satisfied through creative movement toward individuality; and a frame of orientation may be either irrational or rational, but only a rational philosophy can serve as a basis for the growth of total personality (Fromm, 1981).

TABLE 7.1

Summary of Fromm's Human Needs

	Negative Components	Positive Components
Relatedness	Submission or domination	Love
Transcendence	Destructiveness	Creativeness
Rootedness	Fixation	Wholeness
Sense of identity	Adjustment to a group	Individuality
Frame of orientation	Irrational goals	Rational goals

The Burden of Freedom

The central thesis of Fromm's writings is that humans have been torn from nature, yet they remain part of the natural world, subject to the same physical limitations as other animals. As the only animal possessing self-awareness, imagination, and reason, humans are "the freak[s] of the universe" (Fromm, 1955, p. 23). Reason is both a curse and a blessing. It is responsible for feelings of isolation and loneliness, but it is also the process that enables humans to become reunited with the world.

Historically, as people gained more and more economic and political freedom, they came to feel increasingly more isolated. For example, during the Middle Ages people had relatively little personal freedom. They were anchored to prescribed roles in society, roles that provided security, dependability, and certainty. Then, as they acquired more *freedom to* move both socially and geographically, they found that they were *free from* the security of a fixed position in the world. They were no longer tied to one geographic region, one social order, or one occupation. They became separated from their roots and isolated from one another.

A parallel experience exists on a personal level. As children become more independent of their mothers, they gain more *freedom to* express their individuality, to move around unsupervised, to choose their friends, clothes, and so on. At the same time, they experience the burden of freedom; that is, they are *free from* the security of being one with the mother. On both a social and an individual level, this burden of freedom results in **basic anxiety,** the feeling of being alone in the world.

Mechanisms of Escape

Because basic anxiety produces a frightening sense of isolation and aloneness, people attempt to flee from freedom through a variety of escape mechanisms. In *Escape from Freedom,* Fromm (1941) identified three primary mechanisms of escape—authoritarianism, destructiveness, and conformity. Unlike Horney's *neurotic* trends (see Chapter 6), Fromm's mechanisms of escape are the driving forces in normal people, both individually and collectively.

Authoritarianism

Fromm (1941) defined **authoritarianism** as the "tendency to give up the independence of one's own individual self and to fuse one's self with somebody or something outside oneself, in order to acquire the strength which the individual is lacking"

The negative qualities of receptive people include passivity, submissiveness, and lack of self-confidence. Their positive traits are loyalty, acceptance, and trust.

Exploitative

Like receptive people, **exploitative characters** believe that the source of all good is outside themselves. Unlike receptive people, however, they aggressively take what they desire rather than passively receive it. In their social relationships, they are likely to use cunning or force to take someone else's spouse, ideas, or property. An exploitative man may "fall in love" with a married woman, not so much because he is truly fond of her, but because he wishes to exploit her husband. In the realm of ideas, exploitative people prefer to steal or plagiarize rather than create. Unlike receptive characters, they are willing to express an opinion, but it is usually an opinion that has been pilfered.

On the negative side, exploitative characters are egocentric, conceited, arrogant, and seducing. On the positive side, they are impulsive, proud, charming, and self-confident.

Hoarding

Rather than valuing things outside themselves, **hoarding characters** seek to save that which they have already obtained. They hold everything inside and do not let go of anything. They keep money, feelings, and thoughts to themselves. In a love relationship, they try to possess the loved one and to preserve the relationship rather than allowing it to change and grow. They tend to live in the past and are repelled by anything new. They are similar to Freud's anal characters in that they are excessively orderly, stubborn, and miserly. Fromm (1964), however, believed that hoarding characters' anal traits are not the result of sexual drives but rather are part of their general interest in all that is not alive, including the feces.

Negative traits of the hoarding personality include rigidity, sterility, obstinacy, compulsivity, and lack of creativity; positive characteristics are orderliness, cleanliness, and punctuality.

Marketing

The **marketing character** is an outgrowth of modern commerce in which trade is no longer personal but carried out by large, faceless corporations. Consistent with the demands of modern commerce, marketing characters see themselves as commodities, with their personal value dependent on their exchange value, that is, their ability to sell themselves.

Marketing, or exchanging, personalities must see themselves as being in constant demand; they must make others believe that they are skillful and salable. Their personal security rests on shaky ground because they must adjust their personality to that which is currently in fashion. They play many roles and are guided by the motto "'I am as you desire me'" (Fromm, 1947, p. 73).

Marketing people are without a past or a future and have no permanent principles or values. They have fewer positive traits than the other orientations because they are basically empty vessels waiting to be filled with whatever characteristic is most marketable.

Negative traits of marketing characters are aimless, opportunistic, inconsistent, and wasteful. Some of their positive qualities include changeability, open-mindedness, adaptability, and generosity.

The Productive Orientation

The single productive orientation has three dimensions—working, loving, and reasoning. Because productive people work toward positive freedom and a continuing realization of their potential, they are the most healthy of all character types. Only through productive activity can people solve the basic human dilemma: that is, to unite with the world and with others while retaining uniqueness and individuality. This solution can be accomplished only through productive work, love, and thought.

Healthy people value *work* not as an end in itself, but as a means of creative self-expression. They do not work to exploit others, to market themselves, to withdraw from others, or to accumulate needless material possessions. They are neither lazy nor compulsively active, but use work as a means of producing life's necessities.

Productive *love* is characterized by the four qualities of love discussed earlier—care, responsibility, respect, and knowledge. In addition to these four characteristics, healthy people possess **biophilia:** that is, a passionate love of life and all that is alive. Biophilic people desire to further all life—the life of people, animals, plants, ideas, and cultures. They are concerned with the growth and development of themselves as well as others. Biophilic individuals want to influence people through love, reason, and example—not by force.

Fromm believed that love of others and self-love are inseparable but that self-love must come first. All people have the capacity for productive love, but most do not achieve it because they cannot first love themselves.

Productive *thinking,* which cannot be separated from productive work and love, is motivated by a concerned interest in another person or object. Healthy people see others as they are and not as they would wish them to be. Similarly, they know themselves for who they are and have no need for self-delusion.

Fromm (1947) believed that healthy people rely on some combination of all five character orientations. Their survival as healthy individuals depends on their ability to *receive* things from other people, to *take* things when appropriate, to *preserve* things, to *exchange* things, and to *work, love,* and *think* productively.

Personality Disorders

If healthy people are able to work, love, and think productively, then unhealthy personalities are marked by problems in these three areas, especially failure to love productively. Fromm (1981) held that psychologically disturbed people are incapable of love and have failed to establish union with others. He discussed three severe personality disorders—*necrophilia, malignant narcissism,* and *incestuous symbiosis.*

Necrophilia

The term "necrophilia" means love of death and usually refers to a sexual perversion in which a person desires sexual contact with a corpse. However, Fromm (1964, 1973) used **necrophilia** in a more generalized sense to denote any attraction to death. Necrophilia is an alternative character orientation to *biophilia*. People naturally love life, but when social conditions stunt biophilia, they may adopt a necrophilic orientation.

Necrophilic personalities hate humanity; they are racists, warmongers, and bullies; they love bloodshed, destruction, terror, and torture; and they delight in destroying life. They are strong advocates of law and order; love to talk about sickness, death, and burials; and they are fascinated by dirt, decay, corpses, and feces. They prefer night to day and love to operate in darkness and shadow.

Necrophilous people do not simply *behave* in a destructive manner; rather, their destructive behavior is a reflection of their basic *character.* All people behave aggressively and destructively at times, but the entire lifestyle of the necrophilous person revolves around death, destruction, disease, and decay.

Malignant Narcissism

Just as all people display some necrophilic behavior, so too do all have some narcissistic tendencies. Healthy people manifest a benign form of **narcissism,** that is, an interest in their own body. However, in its malignant form, narcissism impedes the perception of reality so that everything belonging to a narcissistic person is highly valued and everything belonging to another is devalued.

Narcissistic individuals are preoccupied with themselves, but this concern is not limited to admiring themselves in a mirror. Preoccupation with one's body often leads to **hypochondriasis,** or an obsessive attention to one's health. Fromm (1964) also discussed **moral hypochondriasis,** or a preoccupation with *guilt* about previous transgressions. People who are fixated on themselves are likely to internalize experiences and to dwell on both physical health and moral virtues.

Narcissistic people possess what Horney (see Chapter 6) called "neurotic claims." They achieve security by holding on to the distorted belief that their extraordinary personal qualities give them superiority over everyone else. Because what they *have*—looks, physique, wealth—is so wonderful, they believe that they need not *do* anything to prove their value. Their sense of worth depends on their narcissistic self-image and not on their achievements. When their efforts are criticized by others, they react with anger and rage, frequently striking out against their critics, trying to destroy them. If the criticism is overwhelming, they may be unable to destroy it, and so they turn their rage inward. The result is *depression,* a feeling of worthlessness. Although depression, intense guilt, and hypochondriasis may appear to be anything but self-glorification, Fromm believed that each of these could be symptomatic of deep underlying narcissism.

Incestuous Symbiosis

A third pathological orientation is **incestuous symbiosis,** or an extreme dependence on the mother or mother surrogate. Incestuous symbiosis is an exaggerated form of the more common and more benign *mother fixation.* Men with a mother fixation need a woman to care for them, dote on them, and admire them; they feel somewhat anxious and depressed when their needs are not fulfilled. This condition is relatively normal and does not greatly interfere with their daily life.

With incestuous symbiosis, however, people are inseparable from the *host* person; their personalities are blended with the other person and their individual identities are lost. Incestuous symbiosis originates in infancy as a natural attachment to the mothering one. The attachment is more crucial and fundamental than any sexual interest that may develop during the Oedipal period. Fromm agreed more with Harry Stack Sullivan (see Chapter 8) than with Freud in suggesting that attachment to the mother rests on the need for security and not for sex. "Sexual strivings are not the cause of the fixation to mother, but the *result*" (Fromm, 1964, p. 99).

People living in incestuous symbiotic relationships feel extremely anxious and frightened if that relationship is threatened. They believe that they cannot live without their mother substitute. (The host need not be another human—it can be a family, a business, a church, or a nation.) The incestuous orientation distorts reasoning powers, destroys the capacity for authentic love, and prevents people from achieving independence and integrity.

Some pathologic individuals possess all three personality disorders; that is, they are attracted to death (necrophilia), take pleasure in destroying those whom they regard as inferiors (malignant narcissism), and possess a neurotic symbiotic relationship with their mother or mother substitute (incestuous symbiosis). Such people formed what Fromm called the *syndrome of decay*. He contrasted these pathological people with those who are marked by the *syndrome of growth*, which is made up of the opposite qualities: namely, biophilia, love, and positive freedom. As shown in Figure 7.1, both the syndrome of decay and the syndrome of growth are extreme forms of development; most people have average psychological health.

Psychotherapy

Fromm was trained as an orthodox Freudian analyst but became bored with standard analytic techniques. "With time I came to see that my boredom stemmed from the fact that I was not in touch with the life of my patients" (Fromm, 1986, p. 106). He then evolved his own system of therapy, which he called *humanistic psychoanalysis*. Compared with Freud, Fromm was much more concerned with the interpersonal aspects of a therapeutic encounter. He believed that the aim of therapy is for patients to come to know themselves. Without knowledge of ourselves, we cannot know any other person or thing.

Fromm believed that patients come to therapy seeking satisfaction of their basic human needs—relatedness, transcendence, rootedness, a sense of identity, and a frame of orientation. Therefore, therapy should be built on a personal relationship between therapist and patient. Because accurate communication is essential to therapeutic growth, the therapist must relate "as one human being to another with utter concentration and utter sincerity" (Fromm, 1963, p. 184). In this spirit of relatedness, the patient will once again feel at one with another person. Although *transference* and even *countertransference* may exist within this relationship, the important point is that two real human beings are involved with one another.

As part of his attempt to achieve shared communication, Fromm asked patients to reveal their dreams. He believed that dreams, as well as fairy tales and myths, are expressed in symbolic language—the only universal language humans have developed (Fromm, 1951). Because dreams have meaning beyond the individual dreamer, Fromm would ask for the patient's associations to the dream material. Not all dream symbols, however, are universal; some are accidental and depend on the dreamer's

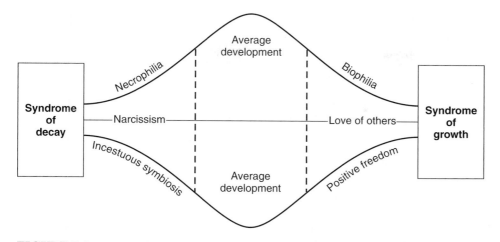

FIGURE 7.1 *Three pathological orientations—necrophilia, narcissism, and incestuous symbiosis—converge to form the syndrome of decay, whereas three healthy orientations—biophilia, love of others, and positive freedom—converge in the syndrome of growth. Most people have average development and are motivated by neither the syndrome of decay nor the syndrome of growth.*

mood before going to sleep; others are regional or national and depend on climate, geography, and dialect. Many symbols have several meanings because of the variety of experiences that are connected with them. For example, fire may symbolize warmth and home to some people but death and destruction to others. Similarly, the sun may represent a threat to desert people, but growth and life to people in cold climates.

Fromm (1963) believed that therapists should not try to be too scientific in understanding a patient. Only with the attitude of relatedness can another person be truly understood. The therapist should not view the patient as an illness or a thing but as a person with the same human needs that all people possess.

Fromm's Methods of Investigation

Fromm gathered data on human personality from many sources, including psychotherapy, cultural anthropology, and psychohistory. In this section, we look briefly at his anthropological study of life in a Mexican village and his psychobiographical analysis of Adolf Hitler.

Social Character in a Mexican Village

Beginning in the late 1950s and extending into the mid-1960s, Fromm and a group of psychologists, psychoanalysts, anthropologists, physicians, and statisticians studied social character in Chiconcuac, a Mexican village about 50 miles south of Mexico City. The team interviewed every adult and half the children in this isolated farming village of 162 households and about 800 inhabitants. The people of the village were mostly farmers, earning a living from small plots of fertile land. As Fromm and Michael Maccoby (1970) described them:

> They are selfish, suspicious of each others' motives, pessimistic about the future, and fatalistic. Many appear submissive and self-deprecatory, although they have the potential for rebelliousness and revolution. They feel inferior to city people, more stupid, and less cultured. There is an overwhelming feeling of powerlessness to influence either nature or the industrial machine that bears down on them. (p. 37)

Could one expect to find Fromm's character orientations in such a society? After living among the villagers and gaining their acceptance, the research team employed an assortment of techniques designed to answer this and other questions. Included among the research tools were extensive interviews, dream reports, detailed questionnaires, and two projective techniques—the Rorschach inkblot test and the Thematic Apperception Test.

Fromm believed that the *marketing character* was a product of modern commerce and that it is most likely to exist in societies where trade is no longer personal and where people regard themselves as commodities. Not surprisingly, the research team found that the marketing orientation did not exist among these peasant villagers.

However, the researchers did find evidence for several other character types, the most common of which was the *nonproductive-receptive* type. People of this orientation tended to look up to others and devoted much energy in trying to please those whom they regarded as superiors. On paydays, working men who belonged to this type would accept their pay in servile fashion, as if somehow they had not earned it.

The second most frequently found personality type was the *productive-hoarding* character. People of this type were hardworking, productive, and independent. They usually farmed their own plot of land and relied on saving part of each crop for seed and for food in the event of a future crop failure. Hoarding, rather than consuming, was essential to their lives.

The *nonproductive-exploitative* personality was identified as a third character orientation. Men of this type were most likely to get into knife or pistol fights, whereas the women tended to be malicious gossipmongers (Fromm & Maccoby, 1970). Only about 10% of the population was predominantly exploitative, a surprisingly small percentage considering the extreme poverty of the village.

An even smaller number of inhabitants were described as *productive-exploitative*—no more than 15 individuals in the whole village. Among them were the richest and most powerful men in the village—men who had accumulated capital by taking advantage of new agricultural technology as well as a recent increase in tourism. They had also taken advantage of the nonproductive-receptive villagers by keeping them economically dependent.

In general, Fromm and Maccoby (1970) reported a remarkable similarity between character orientations in this Mexican village and the theoretical orientations Fromm had suggested some years earlier. This anthropological study, of course, cannot be considered a confirmation of Fromm's theory. As one of the study's principal investigators, Fromm may simply have found what he had expected to find.

A Psychohistorical Study of Hitler

Following Freud (see Chapter 2), Fromm examined historical documents in order to sketch a psychological portrait of a prominent person, a technique called *psychohistory* or *psychobiography*. The subject of Fromm's most complete psychobiographical study was Freud (Fromm, 1959), but Fromm (1941, 1973, 1986) also wrote at length on the life of Adolf Hitler.

Fromm regarded Hitler as the world's most conspicuous example of a person with the *syndrome of decay,* possessing a combination of necrophilia, malignant narcissism, and incestuous symbiosis. Hitler displayed all three pathological disorders. He was attracted to death and destruction; narrowly focused on self-interests; and driven by an incestuous devotion to the Germanic "race," being fanatically dedicated to preventing its blood from being polluted by Jews and other "non-Aryans."

Unlike some psychoanalysts who look only to early childhood for clues to adult personality, Fromm believed that each stage of development is important and that nothing in Hitler's early life bent him inevitably toward the syndrome of decay.

As a child, Hitler was somewhat spoiled by his mother, but her indulgence did not cause his later pathology. It did, however, foster narcissistic feelings of self-importance. "Hitler's mother never became to him a person to whom he was lovingly or tenderly attached. She was a symbol of the protecting and admiring goddesses, but also of the goddess of death and chaos" (Fromm, 1973, p. 378).

Hitler was an above-average student in elementary school, but a failure in high school. During adolescence, he experienced some conflict with his father, who wanted him to be more responsible and to take a reliable civil service job. Hitler, on the other hand, somewhat unrealistically desired to be an artist. Also during this time, he began increasingly to lose himself in fantasy. His narcissism ignited a burning passion for greatness as an artist or architect, but reality brought him failure after

Adolf Hitler personified for Fromm the syndrome of decay.

failure in this area. "Each failure caused a graver wound to his narcissism and a deeper humiliation than the previous one" (Fromm, 1973, p. 395). As his failures grew in number, he became more involved in his fantasy world, more resentful of others, more motivated for revenge, and more necrophilic.

Hitler's terrible realization of his failure as an artist was blunted by the outbreak of World War I. His fierce ambition could now be channeled into being a great war hero fighting for his homeland. Although he was no great hero, he was a responsible, disciplined, and dutiful soldier. After the war, however, he experienced more failure. Not only had his beloved nation lost, but revolutionaries within Germany had "attacked everything that was sacred to Hitler's reactionary nationalism, and they won. . . . The victory of the revolutionaries gave Hitler's destructiveness its final and ineradicable form" (Fromm, 1973, p. 394).

Necrophilia does not simply refer to behavior; it pervades a person's entire character. And so it was with Hitler. After he came to power, he demanded that his enemies not merely surrender, but that they be annihilated as well. His necrophilia was expressed in his mania for destroying buildings and cities, his orders to kill "defective" people, his boredom, and his slaughter of millions of Jews.

Another trait Hitler manifested was *malignant narcissism.* He was interested only in himself, his plans, and his ideology. His conviction that he could build a "Thousand-Year Reich" shows an inflated sense of self-importance. He had no interest in anyone unless that person was of service to him. His relations to women lacked love and tenderness; he seemed to have used them solely for perverted personal pleasure, especially for voyeuristic satisfaction.

According to Fromm's analysis, Hitler also possessed an *incestuous symbiosis,* manifested by his passionate devotion not to his real mother but to the Germanic "race." Consistent with this trait, he also was sadomasochistic, withdrawn, and lacking in feelings of genuine love or compassion. All these characteristics, Fromm contended, did not make Hitler psychotic. They did, however, make him a sick and dangerous man.

Insisting that people not see Hitler as inhuman, Fromm (1973) concluded his psychohistory with these words: "Any analysis that would distort Hitler's picture by depriving him of his humanity would only intensify the tendency to be blind to the potential Hitlers unless they wear horns" (p. 433).

Related Research

Although Erich Fromm's writings are stimulating and insightful, his ideas have produced very little empirical research in the field of personality psychology. One reason for this may be due to the broad approach Fromm takes. In many ways his ideas are more sociological than psychological in that his theory deals with alienation from culture and nature in general, two topics that are more typically covered in a sociology class than a psychology class. This does not mean, however, that such broad topics are not important to personality psychology. Quite the contrary, because though broad and sociological, estrangement from one's culture is a topic that can be studied at the individual level in psychological studies and can have implications for well-being.

Estrangement From Culture and Well-Being

Recall that the central theme to Erich Fromm's theory of personality involves estrangement and alienation: Humans have become removed from the natural environment they were designed to inhabit and distanced from one another. Furthermore, according to Fromm, the material wealth created by capitalism has created so much freedom that quite frankly we do not know what to do with ourselves. Anxiety and isolation, ironically, result from too much freedom. Mark Bernard and colleagues (2006) sought to test these central components of Fromm's theory through the use of self-report measures in a sample of undergraduate students in Great Britain. Specifically, the researchers wanted to test whether or not discrepancies between a person's own beliefs and the way the person perceived the beliefs of his or her society led to feelings of estrangement.

Seventy-two participants completed a questionnaire consisting of several values that had been identified by previous research as being present in many different cultures (such as the importance of freedom, wealth, spirituality, etc.). First, participants rated each value for how much it was a guiding principle in their lives, and then they rated the same values on how much each was a guiding principle for their society. Administering the questionnaire in this manner allowed the researchers to compute the extent to which each participant held values that were different from their society in general. Second, estrangement was assessed by having participants complete a questionnaire with items that asked them how much they felt different from their society and the extent to which they felt they were not "normal" in their culture.

The findings of the study were as predicted. The more a person reported that his or her values were discrepant from society in general, the more likely he or she was to have a strong feeling of estrangement (Bernard, Gebauer, & Maio, 2006). This is not surprising. Basically, if your values are different from those of your society or culture, you feel as though you are different and not normal. This is also precisely what Fromm's theory predicts. The more distant people feel from those around them in their community, the more people are likely to feel isolated.

To further test Fromm's ideas, Bernard and colleagues (2006) next examined whether having a feeling of estrangement from one's culture was related to increased feelings of anxiety and depression. The same participants who completed the self-report measures of values discrepancies and estrangement also completed a measure of anxiety and depression. Just as the researchers predicted, and as Fromm's theory contends, the more estranged from society people felt in general, the more anxious and depressed they were. Although estrangement from society in general was detrimental to well-being, there was a specific type of estrangement that was bad for people. Those who felt a sense of estrangement from their friends reported increased feelings of anxiety and depression. This finding suggests that feeling estranged from society in general may make people more susceptible to feelings of depression, but these feelings can be lessened if a person can find a group of people who share their beliefs, even if those are not the beliefs of the society in general. It is particularly harmful, however, if people feel estranged not only from society in general, but also from those closest to them.

Taken together, these findings clearly support the ideas of Erich Fromm. The modern society in which we live provides us with innumerable conveniences and benefits. But those conveniences do come at a cost. Personal freedom and a sense of individuality are important, but when those forces lead people to be estranged from their community, it can be harmful to their well-being.

The Burden of Freedom and Political Persuasions

One area of research where Fromm's ideas also continue to be influential is in the development of political beliefs (de Zavala & Van Bergh, 2007; Jost, Glaser, Kruglanski, & Sulloway, 2003; Oesterreich, 2005). Fromm's mechanisms of escape as a response to the burden of freedom are implicated in political beliefs, particularly in authoritarianism and conformity. Authoritarianism, for example, involves acquiring strength by uniting with a person or a belief system that is more powerful than the individual seeking strength (Fromm, 1941). Being devoutly loyal to one political party is a way to unite with a system more powerful than the individual. Similarly, conformity involves giving up one's individuality and becoming whatever other people desire one to be. Conformity often involves giving up independent thought by going along with the beliefs and stance of one particular political party.

For personality psychologists, one interesting aspect of political beliefs is to examine how people develop the political persuasions they do and whether personality can predict which type of political party any given individual will be drawn to. Fromm (1941) articulated how people might be drawn to strongly endorse one political party over another, but his theory does not clearly articulate which party an individual will be drawn to. In the United States, there are two big political parties: the Republicans (conservative) and the Democrats (liberal). Yet, what kind of person is more likely to become a Republican or a Democrat?

Jack and Jeanne Block (2006) conducted a longitudinal study in which they assessed the personality of a group of preschoolers. Almost 20 years later, they followed up with these participants (many of whom were now in or had recently graduated from college) and asked about their political beliefs. When the participants were in preschool, they were evaluated on a variety of personality dimensions by their preschool teachers who had been trained in personality assessment.

Twenty years after preschool, the researchers asked these now young adults to complete some self-report questionnaires assessing political beliefs. Children who were described by their teachers 20 years previously as being easily offended, indecisive, fearful, and rigid were more likely to be politically conservative in their twenties. Children who had been described as being self-reliant, energetic, somewhat dominating, and relatively undercontrolled in preschool grew up to be more liberal. This research shows not only how people grow up to deal with their "burden of freedom" differently, to use Fromm's words, but it also shows the remarkably powerful predictive ability of personality, even when personality is measured at a very young age.

Critique of Fromm

Erich Fromm was perhaps the most brilliant essayist of all personality theorists. He wrote beautiful essays on international politics (Fromm, 1961); on the relevance of biblical prophets for people today (Fromm, 1986); on the psychological problems of the aging (Fromm, 1981); on Marx, Hitler, Freud, and Christ; and on myriad other topics. Regardless of the topic, at the core of all Fromm's writings can be found an unfolding of the essence of human nature.

Like other psychodynamic theorists, Fromm tended to take a global approach to theory construction, erecting a grand, highly abstract model that was more philosophical than scientific. His insights into human nature strike a responsive chord, as evidenced by the popularity of his books. Unfortunately, his essays and arguments are not as popularly known today as they were 50 years ago. Paul Roazen (1996) stated that, during the mid-1950s, a person could not be considered educated without having read Fromm's eloquently written *Escape from Freedom.* Today, however, Fromm's books are seldom required reading on college campuses.

Eloquence, of course, does not equal science. From a scientific perspective, we must ask how Fromm's ideas rate on the six criteria of a useful theory. First, Fromm's imprecise and vague terms have rendered his ideas nearly sterile as a *generator of empirical research.* Indeed, our search of the last 45 years of psychology literature yielded fewer than a dozen empirical studies that directly tested Fromm's theoretical assumptions. This paucity of scientific investigations places him among the least empirically validated of all the theorists covered in this book.

Second, Fromm's theory is too philosophical to be either *falsifiable* or verifiable. Nearly any empirical findings generated by Fromm's theory (if they existed) could be explained by alternative theories.

Third, the breadth of Fromm's theory enables it to *organize and explain* much of what is known about human personality. Fromm's social, political, and historical perspective provides both breadth and depth for understanding the human condition; but his theory's lack of precision makes prediction difficult and falsification impossible.

Fourth, as a *guide to action,* the chief value of Fromm's writings is to stimulate readers to think productively. Unfortunately, however, neither the researcher nor the therapist receives much practical information from Fromm's essays.

Fifth, Fromm's views are *internally consistent* in the sense that a single theme runs throughout his writings. However, the theory lacks a structured taxonomy, a set of operationally defined terms, and a clear limitation of scope. Therefore, it rates low on internal consistency.

Finally, because Fromm was reluctant to abandon earlier concepts or to relate them precisely to his later ideas, his theory lacks simplicity and unity. For these reasons, we rate Fromm's theory low on the criterion of *parsimony.*

Concept of Humanity

More than any other personality theorist, Erich Fromm emphasized the differences between humans and the other animals. The essential nature of humans rests on their unique experience of *"being in nature* and subject to all its laws, and simultaneously *transcending nature"* (Fromm, 1992, p. 24). He believed that only humans are aware of themselves and their existence.

More specifically, Fromm's view of humanity is summed up in his definition of the species: *"The human species can be defined as the primate who emerged at that point of evolution where instinctive determinism had reached a minimum and the development of the brain a maximum"* (Fromm, 1976, p. 137). Human beings, then, are the freaks of nature, the only species ever to have evolved this combination of minimal instinctive powers and maximal brain development. "Lacking the capacity to act by the command of instincts while possessing the capacity for self-awareness, reason, and imagination . . . the human species needed a frame of orientation and an object of devotion in order to survive" (p. 137).

Human survival, however, has been paid for by the price of basic anxiety, loneliness, and powerlessness. In every age and culture, people have been faced with the same fundamental problem: how to escape from feelings of isolation and find unity with nature and with other people.

In general, Fromm was both *pessimistic* and *optimistic.* On one hand, he believed that most people do not accomplish a reunion with nature or other people and that few people achieve positive freedom. He also had a rather negative attitude toward modern capitalism, which he insisted was responsible for most people's feeling isolated and alone while clinging desperately to the illusion of independence and freedom. On the other hand, Fromm was hopeful enough to believe that some people will achieve reunion and will therefore realize their human potential. He also believed that humans can achieve a sense of identity, positive freedom, and growing individuality within the confines of a capitalistic society. In *Man for Himself* (1947), he wrote: "I have become increasingly impressed by . . . the strength of the strivings for happiness and health, which are part of the natural equipment of [people]" (p. x).

On the dimension of *free choice versus determinism,* Fromm took a middle position, insisting that this issue cannot be applied to the entire species. Instead, he believed that individuals have degrees of inclinations toward freely chosen action, even though they are seldom aware of all the possible alternatives. Nevertheless, their ability to reason enables people to take an active part in their own fate.

On the dimension of *causality versus teleology,* Fromm tended to slightly favor teleology. He believed that people constantly strive for a frame of orientation, a road map, by which to plan their lives into the future.

Fromm took a middle stance regarding *conscious versus unconscious motivation,* placing slightly more emphasis on conscious motivation and contending that one of the uniquely human traits is *self-awareness.* Humans are the only animal that can reason, visualize the future, and consciously strive toward self-erected goals. Fromm insisted, however, that self-awareness is a mixed blessing and that many people repress their basic character to avoid mounting anxiety.

On the issue of *social influences* versus *biological ones,* Fromm placed somewhat more importance on the impact of history, culture, and society than on biology. Although he insisted that human personalities are historically and culturally determined, he did not overlook biological factors, defining humans as the freaks of the universe.

Finally, whereas Fromm placed moderate emphasis on *similarities among people,* he also allowed room for some individuality. He believed that although history and culture impinge heavily on personality, people can retain some degree of uniqueness. Humans are one species sharing many of the same human needs, but interpersonal experiences throughout people's lives give them some measure of uniqueness.

Key Terms and Concepts

- People have been torn away from their prehistoric union with nature and also with one another, yet they have the power of reasoning, foresight, and imagination.
- *Self-awareness* contributes to feelings of loneliness, isolation, and homelessness.
- To escape these feelings, people strive to become united with others and with nature.
- Only the uniquely *human needs* of relatedness, transcendence, rootedness, sense of identity, and a frame of orientation can move people toward a reunion with the natural world.
- A sense of *relatedness* drives people to unite with another person through submission, power, or love.
- *Transcendence* is the need for people to rise above their passive existence and create or destroy life.
- *Rootedness* is the need for a consistent structure in people's lives.
- A *sense of identity* gives a person a feeling of "I" or "me."
- A *frame of orientation* is a consistent way of looking at the world.
- *Basic anxiety* is a sense of being alone in the world.
- To relieve basic anxiety, people use various *mechanisms of escape,* especially authoritarianism, destructiveness, and conformity.
- Psychologically healthy people acquire the *syndrome of growth,* which includes (1) *positive freedom,* or the spontaneous activity of a whole, integrated personality; (2) *biophilia,* or a passionate love of life; and (3) *love* for fellow humans.
- Other people, however, live nonproductively and acquire things through passively *receiving* things, *exploiting* others, *hoarding* things, and *marketing* or exchanging things, including themselves.
- Some extremely sick people are motivated by the *syndrome of decay,* which includes (1) *necrophilia,* or the love of death; (2) *malignant narcissism,* or infatuation with self; and (3) *incestuous symbiosis,* or the tendency to remain bound to a mothering person or her equivalents.
- The goal of Fromm's *psychotherapy* is to establish a union with patients so that they can become reunited with the world.

CHAPTER 8

Sullivan:
Interpersonal Theory

Sullivan

The young boy had no friends his age but did have several imaginary playmates. At school, his Irish brogue and quick mind made him unpopular among schoolmates. Then, at age $8^{1}/_{2}$, the boy experienced an intimate relationship with a 13-year-old boy that transformed his life. The two boys remained unpopular with other children, but they developed close bonds with each other. Most scholars (Alexander, 1990, 1995; Chapman, 1976; Havens, 1987) believe that the relationship between these boys—Harry Stack Sullivan and Clarence Bellinger—was at least in some ways homosexual, but others (Perry, 1982) believed that the two boys were never sexually intimate.

Why is it important to know about Sullivan's sexual orientation? This knowledge is important for at least two reasons. First, a personality theorist's early life history, including gender, birth order, religious beliefs, ethnic background, schooling, as well as sexual orientation, all relate to that person's adult beliefs, conception of humanity, and the type of personality theory that that person will develop.

Second, in Sullivan's case, his sexual orientation may have prevented him from gaining the acceptance and recognition he might have had if others had not suspected that he was homosexual. A. H. Chapman (1976) has argued that Sullivan's influence is pervasive yet unrecognized largely because many psychologists and psychiatrists of his day had difficulty accepting the theoretical concepts and therapeutic practices of someone they suspected of being homosexual. Chapman contended that Sullivan's contemporaries might have easily accepted a homosexual artist, musician, or writer, but, when it came to a psychiatrist, they were still guided by the concept "Physician heal thyself." This phrase was so ingrained in American society during Sullivan's time that mental health workers found it very difficult to "admit their indebtedness to a psychiatrist whose homosexuality was commonly known" (Chapman, 1976, p. 12). Thus, Sullivan, who otherwise might have achieved greater fame, was shackled by sexual prejudices that kept him from being regarded as American's foremost psychiatrist of the first half of the 20th century.

Overview of Interpersonal Theory

Harry Stack Sullivan, the first American to construct a comprehensive personality theory, believed that people develop their personality within a social context. Without other people, Sullivan contended, humans would have no personality. "A personality can never be isolated from the complex of interpersonal relations in which the person lives and has his being" (Sullivan, 1953a, p. 10). Sullivan insisted that knowledge of human personality can be gained only through the scientific study of interpersonal relations. His **interpersonal theory** emphasizes the importance of various developmental stages—infancy, childhood, the juvenile era, preadolescence, early adolescence, late adolescence, and adulthood. Healthy human development rests on a person's ability to establish intimacy with another person, but unfortunately, anxiety can interfere with satisfying interpersonal relations at any age. Perhaps the most crucial stage of development is preadolescence—a period when children first possess the capacity for intimacy but have not yet reached an age at which their intimate relationships are complicated by lustful interests. Sullivan believed that people achieve healthy development when they are able to experience both intimacy and lust toward the same other person.

Ironically, Sullivan's own relationships with other people were seldom satisfying. As a child, he was lonely and physically isolated; as an adolescent, he suffered at least one schizophrenic episode; and as an adult, he experienced only superficial and ambivalent interpersonal relationships. Despite, or perhaps because of, these interpersonal difficulties, Sullivan contributed much to an understanding of human personality. In Leston Havens's (1987) language, "He made his contributions walking on one leg . . . he never gained the spontaneity, receptiveness, and capacity for intimacy his own interpersonal school worked to achieve for others" (p. 184).

Biography of Harry Stack Sullivan

Harry Stack Sullivan was born in the small farming town of Norwich, New York, on February 21, 1892, the sole surviving child of poor Irish Catholic parents. His mother, Ella Stack Sullivan, was 32 when she married Timothy Sullivan and 39 when Harry was born. She had given birth to two other sons, neither of whom lived past the first year. As a consequence, she pampered and protected her only child, whose survival she knew was her last chance for motherhood. Harry's father, Timothy Sullivan, was a shy, withdrawn, and taciturn man who never developed a close relationship with his son until after his wife had died and Sullivan had become a prominent physician. Timothy Sullivan had been a farm laborer and a factory worker who moved to his wife's family farm outside the village of Smyrna, some 10 miles from Norwich, before Harry's third birthday. At about this same time, Ella Stack Sullivan was mysteriously absent from the home, and Sullivan was cared for by his maternal grandmother, whose Gaelic accent was not easily understood by the young boy. After more than a year's separation, Harry's mother—who likely had been in a mental hospital—returned home. In effect, Sullivan then had two women to mother him. Even after his grandmother died, he continued to have two mothers because a maiden aunt then came to share in the child-rearing duties.

Although both parents were of poor Irish Catholic descent, his mother regarded the Stack family as socially superior to the Sullivans. Sullivan accepted the social supremacy of the Stacks over the Sullivans until he was a prominent psychiatrist developing an interpersonal theory that emphasized similarities among people rather than differences. He then realized the folly of his mother's claims.

As a preschool child, Sullivan had neither friends nor acquaintances of his age. After beginning school he still felt like an outsider, being an Irish Catholic boy in a Protestant community. His Irish accent and quick mind made him unpopular with his classmates throughout his years of schooling in Smyrna.

When Sullivan was $8^{1}/_{2}$ years old, he formed a close friendship with a 13-year-old boy from a neighboring farm. This chum was Clarence Bellinger, who lived a mile beyond Harry in another school district, but who was now beginning high school in Smyrna. Although the two boys were not peers chronologically, they had much in common socially and intellectually. Both were retarded socially but advanced intellectually; both later became psychiatrists and neither ever married. The relationship between Harry and Clarence had a transforming effect on Sullivan's life. It awakened in him the power of intimacy, that is, the ability to love another who was more or less like himself. In Sullivan's mature theory of personality, he placed heavy emphasis on the therapeutic, almost magical power of an intimate relationship during the preadolescent years. This belief, along with many other Sullivanian hypotheses, seems to have grown out of his own childhood experiences.

Sullivan was interested in books and science, not in farming. Although he was an only child growing up on a farm that required much hard work, Harry was able to escape many of the chores by absentmindedly "forgetting" to do them. This ruse was successful because his indulgent mother completed them for him and allowed Sullivan to receive credit.

A bright student, Sullivan graduated from high school as valedictorian at age 16. He then entered Cornell University intending to become a physicist, although he also had an interest in psychiatry. His academic performance at Cornell was a disaster, however, and he was suspended after 1 year. The suspension may not have been solely for academic deficiencies. He got into trouble with the law at Cornell, possibly for mail fraud. He was probably a dupe of older, more mature students who used him to pick up some chemicals illegally ordered through the mail. In any event, for the next 2 years Sullivan mysteriously disappeared from the scene. Perry (1982) reported he may have suffered a schizophrenic breakdown at this time and was confined to a mental hospital. Alexander (1990), however, surmised that Sullivan spent this time under the guidance of an older male model who helped him overcome his sexual panic and who intensified his interest in psychiatry. Whatever the answer to Sullivan's mysterious disappearance from 1909 to 1911, his experiences seemed to have matured him academically and possibly sexually.

In 1911, with only one very unsuccessful year of undergraduate work, Sullivan enrolled in the Chicago College of Medicine and Surgery, where his grades, though only mediocre, were a great improvement over those he earned at Cornell. He finished his medical studies in 1915 but did not receive his degree until 1917. Sullivan claimed that the delay was because he had not yet paid his tuition in full, but Perry (1982) found evidence that he had not completed all his academic requirements by 1915 and needed, among other requirements, an internship. How was Sullivan able to obtain a medical degree if he lacked all the requirements? None of Sullivan's biographers has a satisfactory answer to this question. Alexander (1990) hypothesized that Sullivan, who had accumulated nearly a year of medically related employment, used his considerable persuasive abilities to convince authorities at Chicago College of Medicine and Surgery to accept that experience in lieu of an internship. Any other deficiency may have been waived if Sullivan agreed to enlist in the military. (The United States had recently entered World War I and was in need of medical officers.)

After the war Sullivan continued to serve as a military officer, first for the Federal Board for Vocational Education and then for the Public Health Service. However, this period in his life was still confusing and unstable, and he showed little promise of the brilliant career that lay just ahead (Perry, 1982).

In 1921, with no formal training in psychiatry, he went to St. Elizabeth Hospital in Washington, DC, where he became closely acquainted with William Alanson White, one of America's best-known neuropsychiatrists. At St. Elizabeth, Sullivan had his first opportunity to work with large numbers of schizophrenic patients. While in Washington, he began an association with the Medical School of the University of Maryland and with the Sheppard and Enoch Pratt Hospital in Towson, Maryland. During this Baltimore period of his life, he conducted intensive studies of schizophrenia, which led to his first hunches about the importance of interpersonal relationships. In trying to make sense out of the speech of schizophrenic patients, Sullivan concluded that their illness was a means of coping with the anxiety generated from social and interpersonal environments. His experiences as a practicing clinician gradually transformed themselves into the beginnings of an interpersonal theory of psychiatry.

Sullivan spent much of his time and energy at Sheppard selecting and training hospital attendants. Although he did little therapy himself, he developed a system in which nonprofessional but sympathetic male attendants treated schizophrenic patients with human respect and care. This innovative program gained him a reputation as a clinical wizard. However, he became disenchanted with the political climate at Sheppard when he was passed over for a position as head of the new reception center that he had advocated. In March of 1930, he resigned from Sheppard.

Later that year, he moved to New York City and opened a private practice, hoping to enlarge his understanding of interpersonal relations by investigating nonschizophrenic disorders, especially those of an obsessive nature (Perry, 1982). Times were hard, however, and his expected wealthy clientele did not come in the numbers he needed to maintain his expenses.

On a more positive note, his residence in New York brought him into contact with several psychiatrists and social scientists with a European background. Among these were Karen Horney, Erich Fromm, and Frieda Fromm-Reichmann who, along with Sullivan, Clara Thompson, and others, formed the Zodiac group, an informal organization that met regularly over drinks to discuss old and new ideas in psychiatry and the related social sciences. Sullivan, who had met Thompson earlier, persuaded her to travel to Europe to take a training analysis under Sandor Ferenczi, a disciple of Freud. Sullivan learned from all members of the Zodiac group, and through Thompson, and Ferenczi, his therapeutic technique was indirectly influenced by Freud. Sullivan also credited two other outstanding practitioners, Adolf Meyer and William Alanson White, as having had an impact on his practice of therapy. Despite some Freudian influence on his therapeutic technique, Sullivan's theory of interpersonal psychiatry is neither psychoanalytic nor neo-Freudian.

During his residence in New York, Sullivan also came under the influence of several noted social scientists from the University of Chicago, which was the center of American sociological study during the 1920s and 1930s. Included among them were social psychologist George Herbert Mead, sociologists Robert Ezra Park and W. I. Thomas, anthropologist Edward Sapir, and political scientist Harold Lasswell. Sullivan, Sapir, and Lasswell were primarily responsible for establishing the William Alanson White Psychiatric Foundation in Washington, DC, for the purpose of joining psychiatry to the other social sciences. Sullivan served as the first president of the foundation and also as editor of the foundation's journal, *Psychiatry*. Under Sullivan's guidance, the foundation began a training institution known as the Washington School of Psychiatry. Because of these activities, Sullivan gave up his New York practice, which was not very lucrative anyway, and moved back to Washington, DC, where he remained closely associated with the school and the journal.

In January 1949, Sullivan attended a meeting of the World Federation for Mental Health in Amsterdam. While on his way home, January 14, 1949, he died of a cerebral hemorrhage in a Paris hotel room, a few weeks short of his 57th birthday. Not uncharacteristically, he was alone at the time.

On the personal side, Sullivan was not comfortable with his sexuality and had ambivalent feelings toward marriage (Perry, 1982). As an adult, he brought into his home a 15-year-old boy who was probably a former patient (Alexander, 1990). This young man—James Inscoe—remained with Sullivan for 22 years, looking after his financial affairs, typing manuscripts, and generally running the household. Although Sullivan never officially adopted Jimmie, he regarded him as a son and even had his legal name changed to James I. Sullivan.

 Beyond Biography   **Was Sullivan a homosexual? For information on Sullivan's sexual orientation, see our website at** *www.mhhe.com/feist7*

Sullivan also had ambivalent attitudes toward his religion. Born to Catholic parents who attended church only irregularly, he abandoned Catholicism early on. In later life, his friends and acquaintances regarded him as nonreligious or even anti-Catholic, but to their surprise, Sullivan had written into his will a request to receive a Catholic burial. Incidentally, this request was granted despite the fact that Sullivan's body had been cremated in Paris. His ashes were returned to the United States, where they were placed inside a coffin and received a full Catholic burial, complete with a requiem mass.

Sullivan's chief contribution to personality theory is his conception of developmental stages. Before turning to Sullivan's ideas on the stages of development, we will explain some of his unique terminology.

Tensions

Like Freud and Jung, Sullivan (1953b) saw personality as an energy system. Energy can exist either as *tension* (potentiality for action) or as actions themselves (*energy transformations*). **Energy transformations** transform tensions into either covert or overt behaviors and are aimed at satisfying needs and reducing anxiety. **Tension** is a potentiality for action that may or may not be experienced in awareness. Thus, not all tensions are consciously felt. Many tensions, such as anxiety, premonitions, drowsiness, hunger, and sexual excitement, are felt but not always on a conscious level. In fact, probably all felt tensions are at least partial distortions of reality. Sullivan recognized two types of tensions: *needs* and *anxiety*. Needs usually result in productive actions, whereas anxiety leads to nonproductive or disintegrative behaviors.

Needs

Needs are tensions brought on by biological imbalance between a person and the physiochemical environment, both inside and outside the organism. Needs are episodic—once they are satisfied, they temporarily lose their power, but after a time, they are likely to recur. Although needs originally have a biological component, many of them stem from the interpersonal situation. The most basic *interpersonal need* is **tenderness.** An infant develops a need to receive tenderness from its primary caretaker (called by Sullivan "the mothering one"). Unlike some needs, tenderness requires actions from at least two people. For example, an infant's need *to receive* tenderness may be expressed as a cry, smile, or coo, whereas the mother's need *to give* tenderness may be transformed into touching, fondling, or holding. In this example, the need for tenderness is satisfied through the use of the infant's *mouth* and the mother's *hands*.

Tenderness is a *general need* because it is concerned with the overall well-being of a person. General needs, which also include oxygen, food, and water, are opposed to *zonal needs*, which arise from a particular area of the body. Several areas of the body are instrumental in satisfying both general and zonal needs. For example, the mouth satisfies general needs by taking in food and oxygen, but it also satisfies the zonal need for oral activity. Also, the hands may be used to help satisfy the general need of tenderness, but they can likewise be used to satisfy the zonal need for manual activity. Similarly, other body zones, such as the anus and the genitals, can be used to satisfy both kinds of needs.

Very early in life, the various zones of the body begin to play a significant and lasting role in interpersonal relations. While satisfying general needs for food, water, and so forth, an infant expends more energy than necessary, and the excess energy is transformed into consistent characteristic modes of behavior, which Sullivan called *dynamisms*.

Anxiety

A second type of tension, **anxiety,** differs from tensions of needs in that it is disjunctive, is more diffuse and vague, and calls forth no consistent actions for its relief. If infants lack food (a need), their course of action is clear; but if they are anxious, they can do little to escape from that anxiety.

How does anxiety originate? Sullivan (1953b) postulated that it is transferred from the parent to the infant through the process of **empathy.** Anxiety in the mothering one inevitably induces anxiety in the infant. Because all mothers have some amount of anxiety while caring for their babies, all infants will become anxious to some degree.

Just as the infant does not have the capacity to reduce anxiety, the parent has no effective means of dealing with the baby's anxiety. Any signs of anxiety or insecurity by the infant are likely to lead to attempts by the parent to satisfy the infant's *needs*. For example, a mother may feed her anxious, crying baby because she mistakes anxiety for hunger. If the baby hesitates in accepting the milk, the mother may become more anxious herself, which generates additional anxiety within the infant. Finally, the baby's anxiety reaches a level at which it interferes with sucking and swallowing. Anxiety, then, operates in opposition to tensions of needs and prevents them from being satisfied.

Anxiety has a deleterious effect on adults too. It is the *chief disruptive force blocking the development of healthy interpersonal relations.* Sullivan (1953b) likened severe anxiety to a blow on the head. It makes people incapable of learning, impairs memory, narrows perception, and may result in complete amnesia. It is unique among the tensions in that it maintains the status quo even to people's overall detriment. Whereas other tensions result in actions directed specifically toward their relief, anxiety produces behaviors that (1) prevent people from learning from their mistakes, (2) keep people pursuing a childish wish for security, and (3) generally ensure that people will not learn from their experiences.

Sullivan insisted that anxiety and loneliness are unique among all experiences in that they are totally unwanted and undesirable. Because anxiety is painful, people have a natural tendency to avoid it, inherently preferring the state of **euphoria,** or complete lack of tension. Sullivan (1954) summarized this concept by stating simply that "*the presence of anxiety is much worse than its absence*" (p. 100).

Sullivan distinguished anxiety from fear in several important ways. First, anxiety usually stems from complex interpersonal situations and is only vaguely represented in awareness; fear is more clearly discerned and its origins more easily pinpointed. Second, anxiety has no positive value. Only when transformed into another tension (anger or fear, for example) can it lead to profitable actions. Third, anxiety blocks the satisfaction of needs, whereas fear sometimes helps people satisfy certain needs. This opposition to the satisfaction of needs is expressed in words that can be considered Sullivan's definition of anxiety: "Anxiety is a tension in opposition to the tensions of needs and to action appropriate to their relief" (Sullivan, 1953b, p. 44).

Energy Transformations

Tensions that are transformed into actions, either overt or covert, are called energy transformations. This somewhat awkward term simply refers to our behaviors that are aimed at satisfying needs and reducing anxiety—the two great tensions. Not all energy transformations are obvious, overt actions; many take the form of emotions, thoughts, or covert behaviors that can be hidden from other people.

Dynamisms

Energy transformations become organized as typical behavior patterns that characterize a person throughout a lifetime. Sullivan (1953b) called these behavior patterns **dynamisms,** a term that means about the same as traits or habit patterns. Dynamisms are of two major classes: first, those related to specific zones of the body, including the mouth, anus, and genitals; and second, those related to tensions. This second class is composed of three categories—the disjunctive, the isolating, and the conjunctive. Disjunctive dynamisms include those destructive patterns of behavior that are related to the concept of *malevolence;* isolating dynamisms include those behavior patterns (such as *lust*) that are unrelated to interpersonal relations; and conjunctive dynamisms include beneficial behavior patterns, such as *intimacy* and the *self-system.*

Malevolence

Malevolence is the disjunctive dynamism of evil and hatred, characterized by the feeling of living among one's enemies (Sullivan, 1953b). It originates around age 2 or 3 years when children's actions that earlier had brought about maternal tenderness are rebuffed, ignored, or met with anxiety and pain. When parents attempt to control their children's behavior by physical pain or reproving remarks, some children will learn to withhold any expression of the need for tenderness and to protect themselves by adopting the malevolent attitude. Parents and peers then find it more and more difficult to react with tenderness, which in turn solidifies the child's negative attitude toward the world. Malevolent actions often take the form of timidity,

Significant intimate relationships prior to puberty are usually boy-boy or girl-girl friendships, according to Sullivan.

mischievousness, cruelty, or other kinds of asocial or antisocial behavior. Sullivan expressed the malevolent attitude with this colorful statement: "Once upon a time everything was lovely, but that was before I had to deal with people" (p. 216).

Intimacy

Intimacy grows out of the earlier need for tenderness but is more specific and involves a close interpersonal relationship between two people who are more or less of equal status. Intimacy must not be confused with sexual interest. In fact, it develops prior to puberty, ideally during preadolescence when it usually exists between two children, each of whom sees the other as a person of equal value. Because intimacy is a dynamism that requires an equal partnership, it does not usually exist in parent-child relationships unless both are adults and see one another as equals.

Intimacy is an integrating dynamism that tends to draw out loving reactions from the other person, thereby decreasing anxiety and loneliness, two extremely painful experiences. Because intimacy helps us avoid anxiety and loneliness, it is a rewarding experience that most healthy people desire (Sullivan, 1953b).

Lust

On the other hand, **lust** is an isolating tendency, requiring no other person for its satisfaction. It manifests itself as autoerotic behavior even when another person is the object of one's lust. Lust is an especially powerful dynamism during adolescence, at which time it often leads to a reduction of self-esteem. Attempts at lustful activity are often rebuffed by others, which increases anxiety and decreases feelings of self-worth. In addition, lust often hinders an intimate relationship, especially during early adolescence when it is easily confused with sexual attraction.

Self-System

The most complex and inclusive of all the dynamisms is the **self-system,** a consistent pattern of behaviors that maintains people's interpersonal security by protecting them from anxiety. Like intimacy, the self-system is a conjunctive dynamism that arises out of the interpersonal situation. However, it develops earlier than intimacy, at about age 12 to 18 months. As children develop intelligence and foresight, they become able to learn which behaviors are related to an increase or decrease in anxiety. This ability to detect slight increases or decreases in anxiety provides the self-system with a built-in warning device.

The warning, however, is a mixed blessing. On one hand, it serves as a signal, alerting people to increasing anxiety and giving them an opportunity to protect themselves. On the other, this desire for protection against anxiety makes the self-system resistant to change and prevents people from profiting from anxiety-filled experiences. Because the primary task of the self-system is to protect people against anxiety, it is "the principal stumbling block to favorable changes in personality" (Sullivan, 1953b, p. 169). Sullivan (1964), however, believed that personality is not static and is especially open to change at the beginning of the various stages of development.

As the self-system develops, people begin to form a consistent image of themselves. Thereafter, any interpersonal experiences that they perceive as contrary to their self-regard threatens their *security.* As a consequence, people attempt to defend themselves against interpersonal tensions by means of **security operations,** the purpose of which is to reduce feelings of insecurity or anxiety that result from endangered self-esteem. People tend to deny or distort interpersonal experiences that conflict with their self-regard. For example, when people who think highly of themselves are called incompetent, they may choose to believe that the name-caller is stupid or, perhaps, merely joking. Sullivan (1953b) called security operations "a powerful brake on personal and human progress" (p. 374).

Two important security operations are *dissociation* and *selective inattention.* **Dissociation** includes those impulses, desires, and needs that a person refuses to allow into awareness. Some infantile experiences become dissociated when a baby's behavior is neither rewarded nor punished, so those experiences simply do not become part of the self-system. Adult experiences that are too foreign to one's standards of conduct can also become dissociated. These experiences do not cease to exist but continue to influence personality on an unconscious level. Dissociated images manifest themselves in dreams, daydreams, and other unintentional activities outside of awareness and are directed toward maintaining interpersonal security (Sullivan, 1953b).

The control of focal awareness, called **selective inattention,** is a refusal to see those things that we do not wish to see. It differs from dissociation in both degree and origin. Selectively inattended experiences are more accessible to awareness and more limited in scope. They originate after we establish a self-system and are triggered by our attempts to block out experiences that are not consistent with our existing self-system. For example, people who regard themselves as scrupulously law-abiding drivers may "forget" about the many occasions when they exceeded the speed limit or the times when they failed to stop completely at a stop sign. Like dissociated experiences, selectively inattended perceptions remain active even though they are not fully conscious. They are crucial in determining which elements of an experience will be attended and which will be ignored or denied (Sullivan, 1953b).

Personifications

Beginning in infancy and continuing throughout the various developmental stages, people acquire certain images of themselves and others. These images, called **personifications,** may be relatively accurate, or because they are colored by people's needs and anxieties, they may be grossly distorted. Sullivan (1953b) described three basic personifications that develop during infancy—the bad-mother, the good-mother, and the me. In addition, some children acquire an eidetic personification (imaginary playmate) during childhood.

Bad-Mother, Good-Mother

Sullivan's notion of the bad-mother and good-mother is similar to Klein's concept of the bad breast and good breast. The *bad-mother personification,* in fact, grows out of the infant's experiences with the bad-nipple: that is, the nipple that does not satisfy hunger needs. Whether the nipple belongs to the mother or to a bottle held by the mother, the father, a nurse, or anyone else is not important. The bad-mother personification is almost completely undifferentiated, inasmuch as it includes everyone involved in the nursing situation. It is not an accurate image of the "real" mother but merely the infant's vague representation of not being properly fed.

After the bad-mother personification is formed, an infant will acquire a *good-mother personification* based on the tender and cooperative behaviors of the mothering one. These two personifications, one based on the infant's perception of an anxious, malevolent mother and the other based on a calm, tender mother, combine to form a complex personification composed of contrasting qualities projected onto the same person. Until the infant develops language, however, these two opposing images of mother can easily coexist (Sullivan, 1953b).

Me Personifications

During midinfancy a child acquires three me personifications (bad-me, good-me, and not-me) that form the building blocks of the self personification. Each is related to the evolving conception of me or my body. The *bad-me personification* is fashioned from experiences of punishment and disapproval that infants receive from their mothering one. The resulting anxiety is strong enough to teach infants that they are bad, but it is not so severe as to cause the experience to be dissociated or selectively inattended. Like all personifications, the bad-me is shaped out of the interpersonal situation; that is, infants can learn that they are bad only from someone else, ordinarily the bad-mother.

The *good-me personification* results from infants' experiences with reward and approval. Infants feel good about themselves when they perceive their mother's expressions of tenderness. Such experiences diminish anxiety and foster the good-me personification. Sudden severe anxiety, however, may cause an infant to form the *not-me personification* and to either dissociate or selectively inattend experiences related to that anxiety. An infant denies these experiences to the me image so that they become part of the not-me personification. These shadowy not-me personifications are also encountered by adults and are expressed in dreams, schizophrenic episodes, and other dissociated reactions. Sullivan believed that these nightmarish experiences are always preceded by a warning. When adults are struck by sudden severe anxiety, they are overcome by *uncanny emotion.* Although this experience incapacitates people in their interpersonal relationships, it serves as a valuable signal for approaching schizophrenic reactions. Uncanny emotion may be experienced in dreams or may take the form of awe, horror, loathing, or a "chilly crawling" sensation (Sullivan, 1953b).

Eidetic Personifications

Not all interpersonal relations are with real people; some are **eidetic personifications:** that is, unrealistic traits or imaginary friends that many children invent in order to protect their self-esteem. Sullivan (1964) believed that these *imaginary friends* may be as significant to a child's development as real playmates.

Eidetic personifications, however, are not limited to children; most adults see fictitious traits in other people. Eidetic personifications can create conflict in interpersonal relations when people project onto others imaginary traits that are remnants from previous relationships. They also hinder communication and prevent people from functioning on the same level of cognition.

Levels of Cognition

Sullivan divided cognition into three levels or modes of experience: *prototaxic, parataxic,* and *syntaxic.* Levels of cognition refer to ways of perceiving, imagining, and conceiving. Experiences on the prototaxic level are impossible to communicate; parataxic experiences are personal, prelogical, and communicated only in distorted form; and syntaxic cognition is meaningful interpersonal communication.

Prototaxic Level

The earliest and most primitive experiences of an infant take place on a **prototaxic** level. Because these experiences cannot be communicated to others, they are difficult to describe or define. One way to understand the term is to imagine the earliest subjective experiences of a newborn baby. These experiences must, in some way, relate to different zones of the body. A neonate feels hunger and pain, and these prototaxic experiences result in observable action, for example, sucking or crying. The infant does not know the reason for the actions and sees no relationship between these actions and being fed. As undifferentiated experiences, prototaxic events are beyond conscious recall.

In adults, prototaxic experiences take the form of momentary sensations, images, feelings, moods, and impressions. These primitive images of dream and waking life are dimly perceived or completely unconscious. Although people are incapable of communicating these images to others, they can sometimes tell another person that they have just had a strange sensation, one that they cannot put into words.

Parataxic Level

Parataxic experiences are prelogical and usually result when a person assumes a cause-and-effect relationship between two events that occur coincidentally. Parataxic cognitions are more clearly differentiated than prototaxic experiences, but their meaning remains private. Therefore, they can be communicated to others only in a distorted fashion.

An example of parataxic thinking takes place when a child is conditioned to say "please" in order to receive candy. If "candy and "please" occur together a number of times, the child may eventually reach the illogical conclusion that her supplications caused the candy's appearance. This conclusion is a **parataxic distortion,** or an illogical belief that a cause-and-effect relationship exists between two events in close temporal proximity. However, uttering the word "please" does not, by itself, cause the candy to appear. A dispensing person must be present who hears the word and is able and willing to honor the request. When no such person is present, a child may ask God or imaginary people to grant favors. A good bit of adult behavior comes from similar parataxic thinking.

Syntaxic Level

Experiences that are consensually validated and that can be symbolically communicated take place on a **syntaxic** level. Consensually validated experiences are those on whose meaning two or more persons agree. Words, for example, are consensually validated because different people more or less agree on their meaning. The most common symbols used by one person to communicate with another are those of language, including words and gestures.

Sullivan hypothesized that the first instance of syntaxic cognition appears whenever a sound or gesture begins to have the same meaning for parents as it does for a child. The syntaxic level of cognition becomes more prevalent as the child begins to develop formal language, but it never completely supplants prototaxic and parataxic cognition. Adult experience takes place on all three levels.

In summary, Sullivan identified two kinds of experience—*tensions* and *energy transformations.* Tensions, or potentiality for action, include *needs* and *anxiety.* Whereas needs are helpful or conjunctive when satisfied, anxiety is always disjunctive, interfering with the satisfaction of needs and disrupting interpersonal relations. Energy transformations literally involve the transformation of potential energy into actual energy (behavior) for the purpose of satisfying needs or reducing anxiety. Some of these behaviors form consistent patterns of behavior called *dynamisms.* Sullivan also recognized three levels of cognition—*prototaxic, parataxic,* and *syntaxic.* Table 8.1 summarizes Sullivan's concept of personality.

TABLE 8.1

Summary of Sullivan's Theory of Personality

   I.   *Tensions* (potential for action)
   - A. *Needs* (conjunctive; they help integrate personality)
       1. General needs (facilitate the overall well-being of a person)
          - a. Interpersonal (tenderness, intimacy, and love)
          - b. Physiological (food, oxygen, water, and so forth)
       2. Zonal needs (may also satisfy general needs)
          - a. Oral
          - b. Genital
          - c. Manual
   - B. *Anxiety* (disjunctive; it interferes with the satisfaction of needs)

   II. *Energy Transformations* (overt or covert actions designed to satisfy needs or to reduce anxiety. Some energy transformations become relatively consistent patterns of behavior called dynamisms)

   III. *Dynamisms* **(traits or behavioral patterns)**
   - A. *Malevolence* (a feeling of living in enemy country)
   - B. *Intimacy* (an integrating experience marked by a close personal relationship with another person who is more or less of equal status)
   - C. *Lust* (an isolating dynamism characterized by an impersonal sexual interest in another person)

   IV. **Levels of Cognitions** (ways of perceiving, imagining, and conceiving)
   - A. *Prototaxic* (undifferentiated experiences that are completely personal)
   - B. *Parataxic* (prelogical experiences that are communicated to others only in a distorted fashion)
   - C. *Syntaxic* (consensually validated experiences that can be accurately communicated to others)

Stages of Development

Sullivan (1953b) postulated seven epochs or stages of development, each crucial to the formation of human personality. The thread of interpersonal relations runs throughout the stages; other people are indispensable to a person's development from infancy to mature adulthood.

Personality change can take place at any time, but it is most likely to occur during the transition from one stage to the next. In fact, these threshold periods are more crucial than the stages themselves. Experiences previously dissociated or selectively inattended may enter into the self-system during one of the transitional periods. Sullivan hypothesized that, "as one passes over one of these more-or-less determinable thresholds of a developmental era, everything that has gone before becomes reasonably open to influence" (p. 227). His seven stages are infancy, childhood, the juvenile era, preadolescence, early adolescence, late adolescence, and adulthood.

Infancy

Infancy begins at birth and continues until a child develops articulate or syntaxic speech, usually at about age 18 to 24 months. Sullivan believed that an infant becomes human through tenderness received from the mothering one. The satisfaction of nearly every human need demands the cooperation of another person. Infants cannot survive without a mothering one to provide food, shelter, moderate temperature, physical contact, and the cleansing of waste materials.

The emphatic linkage between mother and infant leads inexorably to the development of anxiety for the baby. Being human, the mother enters the relationship with some degree of previously learned anxiety. Her anxiety may spring from any one of a variety of experiences, but the infant's first anxiety is always associated with the nursing situation and the oral zone. Unlike that of the mother, the infant's repertoire of behaviors is not adequate to handle anxiety. So, whenever infants feel anxious (a condition originally transmitted to it by the mother), they try whatever means available to reduce anxiety. These attempts typically include rejecting the nipple, but this neither reduces anxiety nor satisfies the need for food. An infant's rejection of the nipple, of course, is not responsible for the mother's original anxiety but now adds to it. Eventually the infant discriminates between the good-nipple and the bad-nipple: the former being associated with relative euphoria in the feeding process; the latter, with enduring anxiety (Sullivan, 1953b).

An infant expresses both anxiety and hunger through crying. The mothering one may mistake anxiety for hunger and force the nipple onto an anxious (but not hungry) infant. The opposite situation may also take place when a mother, for whatever reason, fails to satisfy the baby's needs. The baby then will experience rage, which increases the mother's anxiety and interferes with her ability to cooperate with her baby. With mounting tension, the infant loses the capacity to receive satisfaction, but the need for food, of course, continues to increase. Finally, as tension approaches terror, the infant experiences difficulty with breathing. The baby may even stop breathing and turn a bluish color, but the built-in protections of **apathy** and **somnolent detachment** keep the infant from death. Apathy and somnolent detachment allow the infant to fall asleep despite the hunger (Sullivan, 1953b).

During the feeding process, the infant not only receives food but also satisfies some *tenderness* needs. The tenderness received by the infant at this time demands the cooperation of the mothering one and introduces the infant to the various strategies required by the interpersonal situation. The mother-infant relationship, however, is like a two-sided coin. The infant develops a dual personification of mother, seeing her as both good and bad; the mother is good when she satisfies the baby's needs and bad when she stimulates anxiety.

Around midinfancy, infants begin to learn how to communicate through language. In the beginning, their language is not consensually validated but takes place on an individualized or parataxic level. This period of infancy is characterized by **autistic language,** that is, private language that makes little or no sense to other people. Early communication takes place in the form of facial expressions and the sounding of various phonemes. Both are learned through imitation, and eventually gestures and speech sounds have the same meaning for the infant as they do for other people. This communication marks the beginning of syntaxic language and the end of infancy.

Childhood

The era of childhood begins with the advent of syntaxic language and continues until the appearance of the need for playmates of an equal status. The age of childhood varies from culture to culture and from individual to individual, but in Western society it covers the period from about age 18 to 24 months until about age 5 or 6 years.

During this stage, the mother remains the most significant other person, but her role is different from what it was in infancy. The dual personifications of mother are now fused into one, and the child's perception of the mother is more congruent with the "real" mother. Nevertheless, the good-mother and bad-mother personifications are usually retained on a parataxic level. In addition to combining the mother personifications, the child differentiates the various persons who previously formed the concept of the mothering one, separating mother and father and seeing each as having a distinct role.

At about the same time, children are fusing the me-personifications into a single self-dynamism. Once they establish syntaxic language, they can no longer consciously deal with the bad-me and good-me at the same time; now they label behaviors as good or bad in imitation of their parents. However, these labels differ from the old personifications of infancy because they are symbolized on a syntaxic level and originate from children's behavior rather than from decreases or increases in their anxiety. Also, good and bad now imply social or moral value and no longer refer to the absence or presence of that painful tension called anxiety.

During childhood, emotions become reciprocal; a child is able to give tenderness as well as receive it. The relationship between mother and child becomes more personal and less one-sided. Rather than seeing the mother as good or bad based on how she satisfied hunger needs, the child evaluates the mother syntaxically according to whether she shows reciprocal tender feelings, develops a relationship based on the mutual satisfaction of needs, or exhibits a rejecting attitude.

Besides their parents, preschool-aged children often have one other significant relationship—an *imaginary playmate*. This eidetic friend enables children to have a safe, secure relationship that produces little anxiety. Parents sometimes observe their preschool-aged children talking to an imaginary friend, calling the friend by name, and possibly even insisting that an extra place be set at the table or space be made available in the car or the bed for this playmate. Also, many adults can recall their own childhood experiences with imaginary playmates. Sullivan insisted that having an imaginary playmate is not a sign of instability or pathology but a positive event that helps children become ready for intimacy with real friends during the preadolescence stage. These playmates offer children an opportunity to interact with another "person" who is safe and who will not increase their level of anxiety. This comfortable, nonthreatening relationship with an imaginary playmate permits children to be more independent of parents and to make friends in later years.

Sullivan (1953b) referred to childhood as a period of rapid acculturation. Besides acquiring language, children learn cultural patterns of cleanliness, toilet training, eating habits, and sex-role expectancies. They also learn two other important processes: *dramatizations* and *preoccupations*. Dramatizations are attempts to act like or sound like significant authority figures, especially mother and father. Preoccupations are strategies for avoiding anxiety and fear-provoking situations by remaining occupied with an activity that has earlier proved useful or rewarding.

The malevolent attitude reaches a peak during the preschool years, giving some children an intense feeling of living in a hostile or enemy country. At the same time, children learn that society has placed certain restraints on their freedom. From these restrictions and from experiences with approval and disapprobation, children evolve their self-dynamism, which helps them handle anxiety and stabilize their personality. In fact, the self-system introduces so much stability that it makes future changes exceedingly difficult.

Juvenile Era

The juvenile era begins with the appearance of the need for peers or playmates of equal status and ends when one finds a single chum to satisfy the need for intimacy. In the United States, the juvenile stage is roughly parallel to the first 3 years of school, beginning around age 5 or 6 and ending at about age $8^{1}/_{2}$. (It is interesting that Sullivan was so specific with the age at which this period ends and the preadolescent stage begins. Remember that Sullivan was $8^{1}/_{2}$ when he began an intimate relationship with a 13-year-old boy from a nearby farm.)

During the juvenile stage, Sullivan believed, a child should learn to compete, compromise, and cooperate. The degree of *competition* found among children of this

During the juvenile stage, children need to learn competition, cooperation, and compromise.

age varies with the culture, but Sullivan believed that people in the United States have generally overemphasized competition. Many children believe that they must be competitive to be successful. *Compromise,* too, can be overdone. A 7-year-old child who learns to continually give in to others is handicapped in the socialization process, and this yielding trait may continue to characterize the person in later life. *Cooperation* includes all those processes necessary to get along with others. The juvenile-age child must learn to cooperate with others in the real world of interpersonal relationships. Cooperation is a critical step in becoming socialized and is the most important task confronting children during this stage of development.

During the juvenile era, children associate with other children who are of equal standing. One-to-one relationships are rare, but if they exist, they are more likely to be based on convenience than on genuine intimacy. Boys and girls play with one another with little regard for the gender of the other person. Although permanent dyadic (two-person) relationships are still in the future, children of this age are beginning to make discriminations among themselves and to distinguish among adults. They see one teacher as kinder than another, one parent as more indulgent. The real world is coming more into focus, allowing them to operate increasingly on the syntaxic level.

By the end of the juvenile stage, a child should have developed an orientation toward living that makes it easier to consistently handle anxiety, satisfy zonal and tenderness needs, and set goals based on memory and foresight. This *orientation toward living* readies a person for the deeper interpersonal relationships to follow (Sullivan, 1953b).

Preadolescence

Preadolescence, which begins at age $8\frac{1}{2}$ and ends with adolescence, is a time for intimacy with one particular person, usually a person of the same gender. All preceding stages have been egocentric, with friendships being formed on the basis of self-interest. A preadolescent, for the first time, takes a genuine interest in the other person. Sullivan (1953a) called this process of becoming a social being the "quiet miracle of preadolescence" (p. 41), a likely reference to the personality transformation he experienced during his own preadolescence.

The outstanding characteristic of preadolescence is the genesis of the capacity to love. Previously, all interpersonal relationships were based on personal need satisfaction, but during preadolescence, intimacy and love become the essence of friendships. Intimacy involves a relationship in which the two partners consensually validate one another's personal worth. Love exists "when the satisfaction or the security of another person becomes as significant to one as is one's own satisfaction or security" (Sullivan, 1953a, pp. 42–43).

A preadolescent's intimate relationship ordinarily involves another person of the same gender and of approximately the same age or social status. Infatuations with teachers or movie stars are not intimate relationships because they are not consensually validated. The significant relationships of this age are typically boy-boy or girl-girl chumships. To be liked by one's peers is more important to the preadolescent than to be liked by teachers or parents. Chums are able to freely express opinions and emotions to one another without fear of humiliation or embarrassment. This free exchange of personal thoughts and feelings initiates the preadolescent into the world of intimacy. Each chum becomes more fully human, acquires an expanded personality, and develops a wider interest in the humanity of all people.

Sullivan believed that preadolescence is the most untroubled and carefree time of life. Parents are still significant, even though they have been reappraised in a more realistic light. Preadolescents can experience unselfish love that has not yet been complicated by lust. The cooperation they acquired during the juvenile era evolves into collaboration or the capacity to work with another, not for self-prestige, but for the well-being of that other.

Experiences during preadolescence are critical for the future development of personality. If children do not learn intimacy at this time, they are likely to be seriously stunted in later personality growth. However, earlier negative influences can be extenuated by the positive effects of an intimate relationship. Even the malevolent attitude can be reversed, and many other juvenile problems, such as loneliness and self-centeredness, are diminished by the achievement of intimacy. In other words, mistakes made during earlier stages of development can be overcome during preadolescence, but mistakes made during preadolescence are difficult to surmount during later stages. The relatively brief and uncomplicated period of preadolescence is shattered by the onset of puberty.

Early Adolescence

Early adolescence begins with puberty and ends with the need for sexual love with one person. It is marked by the eruption of genital interest and the advent of lustful relationships. In the United States, early adolescence is generally parallel with the middle-school years. As with most other stages, however, Sullivan placed no great emphasis on chronological age.

The need for intimacy achieved during the preceding stage continues during early adolescence, but is now accompanied by a parallel but separate need—lust. In addition, security, or the need to be free from anxiety, remains active during early adolescence. Thus, intimacy, lust, and security often collide with one another, bringing stress and conflict to the young adolescent in at least three ways. First, lust interferes with security operations because genital activity in American culture is frequently ingrained with anxiety, guilt, and embarrassment. Second, intimacy also can threaten security, as when young adolescents seek intimate friendships with other-gender adolescents. These attempts are fraught with self-doubt, uncertainty, and ridicule from others, which may lead to loss of self-esteem and an increase in anxiety. Third, intimacy and lust are frequently in conflict during early adolescence. Although intimate friendships with peers of equal status are still important, powerful genital tensions seek outlet without regard for the intimacy need. Therefore, young adolescents may retain their intimate friendships from preadolescence while feeling lust for people they neither like nor even know.

Because the lust dynamism is biological, it bursts forth at puberty regardless of the individual's interpersonal readiness for it. A boy with no previous experience with intimacy may see girls as sex objects, while having no real interest in them. An early adolescent girl may sexually tease boys but lack the ability to relate to them on an intimate level.

The early adolescent's search for intimacy can increase anxiety and threaten security.

Sullivan (1953b) believed that early adolescence is a turning point in personality development. The person either emerges from this stage in command of the intimacy and lust dynamisms or faces serious interpersonal difficulties during future stages. Although sexual adjustment is important to personality development, Sullivan felt that the real issue lies in getting along with other people.

Late Adolescence

Late adolescence begins when young people are able to feel both lust and intimacy toward the same person, and it ends in adulthood when they establish a lasting love relationship. Late adolescence embraces that period of self-discovery when adolescents are determining their preferences in genital behavior, usually during secondary school years, or about ages 15 to 17 or 18.

The outstanding feature of late adolescence is the fusion of intimacy and lust. The troubled attempts at self-exploration of early adolescence evolve into a stable pattern of sexual activity in which the loved one is also the object of lustful interest. People of the other gender are no longer desired solely as sex objects but as people who are capable of being loved nonselfishly. Unlike the previous stage that was ushered in by biological changes, late adolescence is completely determined by interpersonal relations.

Successful late adolescence includes a growing syntaxic mode. At college or in the workplace, late adolescents begin exchanging ideas with others and having their opinions and beliefs either validated or repudiated. They learn from others how to live in the adult world, but a successful journey through the earlier stages facilitates this adjustment. If previous developmental epochs were unsuccessful, young

During late adolescence, young people feel both lust and intimacy toward one other person.

people come to late adolescence with no intimate interpersonal relations, inconsistent patterns of sexual activity, and a great need to maintain security operations. They rely heavily on the parataxic mode to avoid anxiety and strive to preserve self-esteem through selective inattention, dissociation, and neurotic symptoms. They face serious problems in bridging the gulf between society's expectations and their own inability to form intimate relations with persons of the other gender. Believing that love is a universal condition of young people, they are often pressured into "falling in love." However, only the mature person has the capacity to love; others merely go through the motions of being "in love" in order to maintain security (Sullivan, 1953b).

Adulthood

The successful completion of late adolescence culminates in adulthood, a period when people can establish a love relationship with at least one significant other person. Writing of this love relationship, Sullivan (1953b) stated that "this really highly developed intimacy with another is not the principal business of life, but is, perhaps, the principal source of satisfaction in life" (p. 34).

Sullivan had little to say about this final stage because he believed that mature adulthood was beyond the scope of interpersonal psychiatry; people who have achieved the capacity to love are not in need of psychiatric counsel. His sketch of the mature person, therefore, was not founded on clinical experience but was an extrapolation from the preceding stages.

Mature adults are perceptive of other people's anxiety, needs, and security. They operate predominantly on the syntaxic level, and find life interesting and exciting (Sullivan, 1953b).

Table 8.2 summarizes the first six Sullivanian stages of development and shows the importance of interpersonal relationships at each stage.

TABLE 8.2

Summary of Sullivan's Stages of Development

Stage	Age	Significant Others	Interpersonal Process	Important Learnings
Infancy	0 to 2	Mothering one	Tenderness	Good mother/bad mother; good me/bad me
Childhood	2 to 6	Parents	Protect security through imaginary playmates	Syntaxic language
Juvenile era	6 to 8½	Playmates of equal status	Orientation toward living in the world of peers	Competition, compromise, cooperation
Preadolescence	8½ to 13	Single chum	Intimacy	Affection and respect from peers
Early adolescence	13 to 15	Several chums	Intimacy and lust toward different persons	Balance of lust, intimacy and security operations
Late adolescence	15 —	Lover	Fusion of intimacy and lust	Discovery of self and the world outside of self

Psychological Disorders

Sullivan believed that all psychological disorders have an interpersonal origin and can be understood only with reference to the patient's social environment. He also held that the deficiencies found in psychiatric patients are found in every person, but to a lesser degree. There is nothing unique about psychological difficulties; they are derived from the same kind of interpersonal troubles faced by all people. Sullivan (1953a) insisted that "everyone is much more simply human than unique, and that no matter what ails the patient, he is *mostly* a person like the psychiatrist" (p. 96).

Most of Sullivan's early therapeutic work was with schizophrenic patients, and many of his subsequent lectures and writings dealt with schizophrenia. Sullivan (1962) distinguished two broad classes of schizophrenia. The first included all those symptoms that originate from organic causes and are therefore beyond the study of interpersonal psychiatry. The second class included all schizophrenic disorders grounded in situational factors. These disorders were the only ones of concern to Sullivan because they are the only ones amenable to change through interpersonal psychiatry.

Dissociated reactions, which often precede schizophrenia, are characterized by loneliness, low self-esteem, the uncanny emotion, unsatisfactory relations with others, and ever-increasing anxiety (Sullivan, 1953b). People with a dissociated personality, in common with all people, attempt to minimize anxiety by building an elaborate self-system that blocks out those experiences that threaten their security. Whereas normal individuals feel relatively secure in their interpersonal relations and do not need to constantly rely on dissociation as a means of protecting self-esteem, mentally disordered individuals dissociate many of their experiences from their self-system. If this strategy becomes persistent, these people will begin to increasingly operate in their own private worlds, with increasing parataxic distortions and decreasing consensually validated experiences (Sullivan, 1956).

Psychotherapy

Because he believed that psychic disorders grow out of interpersonal difficulties, Sullivan based his therapeutic procedures on an effort to improve a patient's relationship with others. To facilitate this process, the therapist serves as a *participant observer,* becoming part of an interpersonal, face-to-face relationship with the patient and providing the patient an opportunity to establish syntaxic communication with another human being.

While at St. Elizabeth Hospital, Sullivan devised a then radical means of treating seriously disturbed patients. His supervisors agreed to grant him a ward for his own patients and to allow him to select and train paraprofessional workers who could treat the patients as fellow human beings. At that time, most schizophrenic and other psychotic patients were warehoused and regarded as subhuman. But Sullivan's experiment worked. A high rate of his patients got better. Erich Fromm (1994) regarded Sullivan's near miraculous results as evidence that a psychosis is not merely a physical disorder and that the personal relationship of one human being to another is the essence of psychological growth.

In general terms, Sullivanian therapy is aimed at uncovering patients' difficulties in relating to others. To accomplish this goal, the therapist helps patients to give up some security in dealing with other people and to realize that they can achieve mental health only through consensually validated personal relations. The therapeutic ingredient in this process is the face-to-face relationship between therapist and patients, which permits patients to reduce anxiety and to communicate with others on the syntaxic level.

Although they are participants in the interview, Sullivanian therapists avoid getting personally involved. They do not place themselves on the same level with the patient; on the contrary, they try to convince the patient of their expert abilities. In other words, friendship is not a condition of psychotherapy—therapists must be trained as experts in the difficult business of making discerning observations of the patient's interpersonal relations (Sullivan, 1954).

Sullivan was primarily concerned with understanding patients and helping them improve foresight, discover difficulties in interpersonal relations, and restore their ability to participate in consensually validated experiences. To accomplish these goals, he concentrated his efforts on answering three continuing questions: Precisely what is the patient saying to me? How can I best put into words what I wish to say to the patient? What is the general pattern of communication between us?

Related Research

Sullivan's interpersonal theory of personality rests on the assumption that unhealthy personality development results from interpersonal conflicts and difficulties. Beginning around the age of 6, and especially by the age of 9, children's relationships with peers their own age become increasingly important for personality development. Sullivan particularly emphasized the importance of same-sex friends and used the term "chums" to describe this specific category of peers. In this section we review some recent research on the dynamics of same-sex friendships in childhood and how they can be simultaneously helpful and harmful for healthy development depending on certain factors.

The Pros and Cons of "Chums" for Girls and Boys

Harry Stack Sullivan, like countless other psychologists, considered friends during childhood and adolescence to be crucial to developing into a healthy adult. Friends are a source of social support, and it is comforting to lean on them when times are tough or when you're having a bad day. Friends may be particularly important during childhood because children do not have the same advanced coping mechanisms that adults have and sometimes struggle to deal with issues like being rejected by a peer. In situations like these it is important to have a friend, or a "chum" to use Sullivan's language, to talk to. But recently, psychologists have begun investigating the potentially harmful aspects of social support in childhood. It may seem counterintuitive to suggest that having friends can be a bad thing, but sometimes the dynamics of a particular friendship can actually be damaging.

Rumination is one such dynamic that can have a negative impact on children's well-being. Ruminating is the act of dwelling on a negative event or negative aspects of an otherwise neutral or even positive event and is generally considered to be harmful as it is associated with an increase in depression. When rumination occurs in the context of a friendship, it is called co-rumination, which is defined as excessively discussing personal problems within a relationship (Rose, Carlson, & Waller, 2007). While generally speaking, Sullivan had it right when he emphasized the importance of childhood friendships in his interpersonal theory of personality, one of the most important attributes of science is to question previously held assumptions.

And this is exactly what Amanda Rose and her colleagues have begun doing in their research on how, in some cases, friendships can be damaging. Specifically, Rose and colleagues are interested in the negative impact of co-rumination in childhood friendships (Rose, 2002; Rose et al., 2007).

To investigate the existence of co-rumination in childhood relationships and the impact of co-rumination on children's well-being, Amanda Rose and colleagues conducted a longitudinal study of children in elementary and middle school. The researchers went into local schools and recruited almost 1,000 children in third, fifth, seventh, and ninth grades to participate in the study. Toward the beginning of the school year, all participants completed self-report measures of depression and anxiety and also rated their friendships on overall quality and co-rumination. The items for co-rumination within friendships consisted of statements like "When we talk about a problem that one of us has, we usually talk about that problem every day even if nothing new has happened" and "When we talk about a problem that one of us has, we try to figure out everything about the problem, even if there are parts that we may never understand" (Rose et al., 2007, p. 1022). As these sample items demonstrate, co-rumination is not a constructive process by which a child works through a problem with a friend. Rather, co-rumination involves dwelling on the negative even when there is no solution to be found and no good that can come of it.

The researchers returned to the schools toward the end of the school year and once again had participants complete measures of depression, anxiety, and friendship quality. Nearly all of the children reported that their closest friends were same-sex (or "chums" as Sullivan would call them), so the researchers focused on these friendships. Overall, co-rumination in same-sex friendships was related to increased feelings of depression and anxiety but was also related to greater friendship quality (Rose et al., 2007). In other words, although co-rumination did increase negative feelings, it was not all negative because it was also a sign of a good friendship. This makes sense because constantly dwelling on negative events will understandably lead one to feel more depressed, but disclosing your feelings to friends can make you feel closer to that person and generally improve the relationship.

The researchers were also interested in whether co-rumination functions differently in boys and girls. Are girls more likely to engage in co-rumination than boys? Is co-rumination better for girls than boys or vice versa? Before her study on co-rumination, Rose and a colleague conducted a review of research on the friendships of boys and girls (Rose & Rudolph, 2006). What they found was that boys and girls engage in very different activities within their friendships on a daily basis. For example, girls spend more time talking, and particularly engaging in self-disclosure, whereas boys are more likely to engage in rough-and-tumble play together. Girls also report placing a greater importance on their friendships than do boys. These findings indicate that there are different dynamics within same-sex friendships for girls and boys.

Returning to the longitudinal study of children and their same-sex friends, Rose and colleagues looked for sex differences in the effects of co-rumination on depression, anxiety, and overall friendship quality. What they found was quite interesting because co-rumination was particularly bad for girls but not so bad for boys. For girls, the overall effects previously described held up: Co-rumination was associated with increased depression and anxiety but also with better friendships. For boys, however, co-rumination was associated with better friendships but was not related to increased depression or anxiety. These findings make clear that there are very different dynamics functioning in the same-sex friendships of boys and girls and that the implications can be profound.

Many times when a parent, therapist, or school counselor evaluates whether or not a child is at risk for depression or other psychological issues, they check to make sure the child has a supportive friend group or "chums." Amanda Rose's research shows that for boys, having a supportive friend may well be sufficient to ward off depression and anxiety. For girls, however, the research paints a different picture: If girls are engaging in co-rumination with their friends, then no matter how supportive those friends are and no matter how good the friendship is, girls are at increased risk for developing depression.

Imaginary Friends

More than any other personality theorist, Sullivan recognized the importance of having an imaginary friend, especially during the childhood stage. He believed that these friendships can facilitate independence from parents and help children build real relationships. In support of Sullivan's notion, research has found that children do tend to view imaginary friends as a source of nurturance (Gleason, 2002; Gleason & Hohmann, 2006). Moreover, evidence supports Sullivan's theory that children who develop imaginary friends—in contrast to those who do not—are more creative, imaginary, intelligent, friendly, and sociable (Fern, 1991; Gleason, 2002). Of course it's hard to get by on imaginary friends alone, but there is some evidence that suggests imaginary friends are just as important as real friends, at least in the eyes of children (Gleason & Hohmann, 2006).

To explore how children view imaginary friends in relation to their real friends, Tracy Gleason and Lisa Hohmann (2006) conducted a study of preschool-age children. The researchers had 84 children enrolled in preschool complete an activity in which they listed who their friends were at preschool, described their imaginary friend if they had one, and rated each friend (including the imaginary ones) on several dimensions. Specifically, the children rated how much they liked playing with each friend, whether they told secrets to one another, how much they liked each friend in general, and how good each friend made them feel about their own abilities. Of course, because the participants in this study were young children, they could not respond to a standard self-report measure. Instead, the questions were read aloud to each child, and the questions were carefully worded to use language that preschoolers could easily understand. Additionally, because children can get confused easily, their responses had to be corroborated by their parents and preschool teachers.

What Gleason and Hohmann (2006) found was generally supportive of Sullivan's notion that imaginary friends are important and help to model how real friendships should work. Twenty-six percent of the preschoolers sampled reported having an imaginary friend and that their imaginary friend was a source of real support and one of their highest rated sources of enjoyment (Gleason & Hohmann, 2006). The researchers were also able to compare children's ratings of imaginary friends with those of their real friends and found that imaginary friends very closely modeled the enjoyment derived from reciprocal friendships but not that derived from friendships that were essentially one-way. That is, relationships with imaginary friends were enjoyable at about the same level as those friendships in which both children described each other as friends (a reciprocal friendship), but not in which one child says the other is a friend but the other one does not reciprocate (one-way friendships).

In summary, research tends to support Sullivan's assumptions that having an imaginary playmate is a normal, healthy experience It is neither a sign of pathology nor a result of feelings of loneliness and alienation from other children. Indeed, imaginary friends not only may serve as a source of enjoyment but also may have the more important purpose of modeling for children what a truly good, mutually enjoyable friendship should be so that they can avoid bad relationships as they grow and mature into healthy adults.

Critique of Sullivan

Although Sullivan's theory of personality is quite comprehensive, it is not as popular among academic psychologists as the theories of Freud, Adler, Jung, or Erik Erikson (see Chapter 9). However, the ultimate value of any theory does not rest on its popularity but on the six criteria enumerated in Chapter 1.

The first criterion of a useful theory is its ability to *generate research.* Currently, few researchers are actively investigating hypotheses specifically drawn from Sullivan's theory. One possible explanation for this deficiency is Sullivan's lack of popularity among researchers most apt to conduct research—the academicians. This lack of popularity might be accounted for by Sullivan's close association with psychiatry, his isolation from any university setting, and the relative lack of organization in his writings and speeches.

Second, a useful theory must be *falsifiable;* that is, it must be specific enough to suggest research that may either support or fail to support its major assumptions. On this criterion, Sullivan's theory, like those of Freud, Jung, and Fromm, must receive a very low mark. Sullivan's notion of the importance of interpersonal relations for psychological health has received a moderate amount of indirect support. However, alternative explanations are possible for most of these findings.

Third, how well does Sullivanian theory provide an organization for all that is known about human personality? Despite its many elaborate postulates, the theory can receive only a moderate rating on its ability to *organize knowledge.* Moreover, the theory's extreme emphasis on interpersonal relations subtracts from its ability to organize knowledge, because much of what is presently known about human behavior has a biological basis and does not easily fit into a theory restricted to interpersonal relations.

The relative lack of testing of Sullivan's theory diminishes its usefulness as a *practical guide* for parents, teachers, psychotherapists, and others concerned with the care of children and adolescents. However, if one accepts the theory without supporting evidence, then many practical problems can be managed by resorting to Sullivanian theory. As a guide to action, then, the theory receives a fair to moderate rating.

Is the theory *internally consistent?* Sullivan's ideas suffer from his inability to write well, but the theory itself is logically conceptualized and holds together as a unified entity. Although Sullivan used some unusual terms, he did so in a consistent fashion throughout his writings and speeches. Overall, his theory is consistent, but it lacks the organization he might have achieved if he had committed more of his ideas to the printed page.

Finally, is the theory *parsimonious,* or simple? Here Sullivan must receive a low rating. His penchant for creating his own terms and the awkwardness of his writing add needless bulk to a theory that, if streamlined, would be far more useful.

Concept of Humanity

Sullivan's basic conception of humanity is summed up in his *one-genus hypothesis,* which states that *"everyone is much more simply human than otherwise"* (1953b, p. 32). This hypothesis was his way of saying that similarities among people are much more important than differences. People are more like people than anything else.

> In other words, the differences between any two instances of human personality— from the lowest-grade imbecile to the highest-grade genius—are much less striking than the difference between the least-gifted human being and a member of the nearest other biological genus. (p. 33)

Sullivan's ability to successfully treat schizophrenic patients undoubtedly was greatly enhanced by his deeply held belief that they shared a common humanity with the therapist. Having experienced at least one schizophrenic episode himself, Sullivan was able to form an empathic bond with these patients through his role as a participant observer.

The one influence separating humans from all other creatures is interpersonal relations. People are born biological organisms—animals with no human qualities except the potential for participation in interpersonal relations. Soon after birth, they begin to realize their potential when interpersonal experiences transform them into human beings. Sullivan believed that the mind contains nothing except what was put there through interpersonal experiences. People are not motivated by instincts but by those environmental influences that come through interpersonal relationships.

Children begin life with a somewhat one-sided relationship with a mothering one who both cares for their needs and increases their anxiety. Later, they become able to reciprocate feelings for the mothering one, and this relationship between child and parent serves as a foundation on which subsequent interpersonal relations are built. At about the time children enter the first grade at school, they are exposed to competition, cooperation, and compromise with other children. If they handle these tasks successfully, they obtain the tools necessary for intimacy and love that come later. Through their intimate and love relationships, they become healthy personalities. However, an absence of healthy interpersonal relationships leads to stunted psychological growth.

Personal individuality is an illusion; people exist only in relation to other people and have as many personalities as they have interpersonal relations. Thus, the concepts of *uniqueness* and *individuality* are of little concern to Sullivan's interpersonal theory.

Anxiety and interpersonal relations are tied together in a cyclic manner, which makes significant personality changes difficult. Anxiety interferes with interpersonal relations, and unsatisfactory interpersonal relations lead to the use of rigid behaviors that may temporarily buffer anxiety. But because these inflexible behaviors do not solve the basic problem, they eventually lead to higher levels of anxiety, which lead to further deterioration in interpersonal relations. The increasing anxiety must then be held in check by an ever-rigid self-system. For this reason, we rate Sullivan's theory as *neither optimistic nor pessimistic* concerning the potential for growth and change. Interpersonal relations can transform a person into either a healthy personality or one marked by anxiety and a rigid self-structure.

Because Sullivan believed that personality is built solely on interpersonal relations, we rate his theory *very high on social influence.* Interpersonal relations are responsible for both positive and negative characteristics in people. Infants who have their needs satisfied by the mothering one will not be greatly disturbed by their mother's anxiety, will receive genuine feelings of tenderness, can avoid being a malevolent personality, and have the ability to develop tender feelings toward others. However, unsatisfactory interpersonal relations may trigger malevolence and leave some children with the feeling that people cannot be trusted and that they are essentially alone among their enemies.

Key Terms and Concepts

- People develop their personality through *interpersonal relationships.*
- Experience takes place on three levels—*prototaxic* (primitive, presymbolic), *parataxic* (not accurately communicated to others), and *syntaxic* (accurate communication).
- Two aspects of experience are *tensions* (potential for action) and *energy transformations* (actions or behaviors).
- Tensions are of two kinds—needs and anxiety.
- *Needs* are conjunctive in that they facilitate interpersonal development.
- *Anxiety* is disjunctive in that it interferes with the satisfaction of needs and is the primary obstacle to establishing healthy interpersonal relationships.
- Energy transformations become organized into consistent traits or behavior patterns called *dynamisms.*
- Typical dynamisms include *malevolence* (a feeling of living in enemy country), *intimacy* (a close interpersonal relationship with a peer of equal status, and *lust* (impersonal sexual desires).
- Sullivan's chief contribution to personality was his concept of various *developmental stages.*
- The first developmental stage is *infancy* (from birth to the development of syntaxic language), a time when an infant's primary interpersonal relationship is with the mothering one.
- During *childhood* (from syntaxic language to the need for playmates of equal status), the mother continues as the most important interpersonal relationship, although children of this age often have an imaginary playmate.
- The third stage is the *juvenile era* (from the need for playmates of equal status to the development of intimacy), a time when children should learn

competition, compromise, and cooperation—skills that will enable them to move successfully through later stages of development.

- The most crucial stage of development is *preadolescence* (from intimacy with a best friend to the beginning of puberty). Mistakes made during this phase are difficult to overcome later.
- During *early adolescence* young people are motivated by both intimacy (usually for someone of the same gender) and lust (ordinarily for a person of the opposite gender).
- People reach *late adolescence* when they are able to direct their intimacy and lust toward one other person.
- The successful completion of late adolescence culminates in *adulthood,* a stage marked by a stable love relationship.
- With Sullivan's *psychotherapy,* the therapist serves as a participant observer and attempts to improve patients' interpersonal relations.

Erikson: Post-Freudian Theory

Erikson

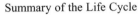

As a child, Erik Salomonsen had many questions but few answers about his biological father. He knew who his mother was—a beautiful Jewish Dane whose family tried hard to appear Danish rather than Jewish. But who was his father?

Born into a single-parent family, the young boy held three separate beliefs regarding his origins. At first, he believed that his mother's husband, a physician named Theodor Homburger, was his biological father. However, as Erik matured, he began to realize that this was incorrect because his blond hair and blue eyes did not match the dark features of either parent. He pressed his mother for an explanation, but she lied to him and said that a man named Valdemar Salomonsen—her first husband—was his biological father and that he abandoned her after she became pregnant with Erik. However, Erik didn't quite believe this second story either because he learned that Salomonsen had left his mother 4 years before Erik was born. Finally, Erik chose to believe that he was the outcome of a sexual liaison between his mother and an artistically gifted aristocratic Dane. For nearly the remainder of his life, Erik believed this third story. Nevertheless, he continued to search for his own identity while seeking the name of his biological father.

During his school days, Erik's Scandinavian features contributed to his identity confusion. When he attended temple, his blue eyes and blond hair made him appear to be an outsider. At public school, his Aryan classmates referred to him as a Jew, so Erik felt out of place in both arenas. Throughout his life, he had difficulty accepting himself as either a Jew or a Gentile.

When his mother died, Erik, then 58 years old, feared he would never know the identity of his biological father. But he persevered in his search. Finally, more than 30 years later and as his mind and body began to deteriorate, Erik lost interest in learning his father's name. However, he continued to show some identity confusion. For example, he spoke mostly in German—the language of his youth—and rarely spoke in English, his primary language for more than 60 years. In addition, he retained a long-held affinity for Denmark and the Danish people and took perverted pride in displaying the flag of Denmark, a country in which he never lived.

Overview of Post-Freudian Theory

The person we introduced in the opening vignette, of course, was Erik Erikson, the person who coined the term *identity crisis*. Erikson had no college degree of any kind, but this lack of formal training did not prevent him from gaining world fame in an impressive variety of fields including psychoanalysis, anthropology, psychohistory, and education.

Unlike earlier psychodynamic theorists who severed nearly all ties to Freudian psychoanalysis, Erikson intended his theory of personality to extend rather than repudiate Freud's assumptions and to offer a new "way of looking at things" (Erikson, 1963, p. 403). His **post-Freudian theory** extended Freud's infantile developmental stages into adolescence, adulthood, and old age. Erikson suggested that at each stage a specific *psychosocial struggle* contributes to the formation of personality. From adolescence on, that struggle takes the form of an **identity crisis**—a turning point in one's life that may either strengthen or weaken personality.

Erikson regarded his post-Freudian theory as an extension of psychoanalysis, something Freud might have done in time. Although he used Freudian theory as the foundation for his *life-cycle* approach to personality, Erikson differed from Freud in several respects. In addition to elaborating on psychosexual stages beyond childhood, Erikson placed more emphasis on both *social* and *historical* influences.

Erikson's post-Freudian theory, like those of other personality theorists, is a reflection of his background, a background that included art, extensive travels, experiences with a variety of cultures, and a lifelong search for his own identity, which we mentioned briefly in our opening story.

Biography of Erik Erikson

Who was Erik Erikson? Was he a Dane, a German, or an American? Jew or Gentile? Artist or psychoanalyst? Erikson himself had difficulty answering these questions, and he spent nearly a lifetime trying to determine who he was.

Born June 15, 1902, in southern Germany, Erikson was brought up by his mother and stepfather, but he remained uncertain of the true identity of his biological father. To discover his niche in life, Erikson ventured away from home during late adolescence, adopting the life of a wandering artist and poet. After nearly 7 years of drifting and searching, he returned home confused, exhausted, depressed, and unable to sketch or paint. At this time, a fortuitous event changed his life: He received a letter from his friend Peter Blos inviting him to teach children in a new school in Vienna. One of the founders of the school was Anna Freud, who became not only Erikson's employer, but his psychoanalyst as well.

While undergoing analytic treatment, he stressed to Anna Freud that his most difficult problem was searching for the identity of his biological father. However, Ms. Freud was less than empathic and told Erikson that he should stop fantasizing about his absent father. Although Erikson usually obeyed his psychoanalyst, he could not take Freud's advice to stop trying to learn his father's name.

While in Vienna, Erikson met and, with Anna Freud's permission, married Joan Serson, a Canadian-born dancer, artist, and teacher who had also undergone psychoanalysis. With her psychoanalytic background and her facility with the English language, she became a valuable editor and occasional coauthor of Erikson's books.

The Eriksons had four children: sons Kai, Jon, and Neil, and daughter Sue. Kai and Sue pursued important professional careers, but Jon, who shared his father's experience as a wandering artist, worked as a laborer and never felt emotionally close to his parents.

Erikson's search for identity took him through some difficult experiences during his adult developmental stage (Friedman, 1999). According to Erikson, this stage requires a person to take care of children, products, and ideas that he or she has generated. On this issue, Erikson was deficient in meeting his own standards. He failed to take good care of his son Neil, who was born with Down syndrome. At the hospital while Joan was still under sedation, Erik agreed to place Neil in an institution. Then he went home and told his three older children that their brother had died at birth. He lied to them much as his mother had lied to him about the identity of his biological father. Later, he told his oldest son, Kai, the truth, but he continued to deceive the two younger children, Jon and Sue. Although his mother's lie had distressed him greatly, he failed to understand that his lie about Neil might later distress his other children. In deceiving his children the way he did, Erikson violated two of his own principles: "Don't lie to people you should care for," and "Don't pit one family member against another." To compound the situation, when Neil died at about age 20, the Eriksons, who were in Europe at the time, called Sue and Jon and instructed them to handle all the funeral arrangements for a brother they had never met and who they only recently knew existed (Friedman, 1999).

Erikson also sought his identity through the myriad changes of jobs and places of residence. Lacking any academic credentials, he had no specific professional identity and was variously known as an artist, a psychologist, a psychoanalyst, a clinician, a professor, a cultural anthropologist, an existentialist, a psychobiographer, and a public intellectual.

In 1933, with fascism on the rise in Europe, Erikson and his family left Vienna for Denmark, hoping to gain Danish citizenship. When Danish officials refused his request, he left Copenhagen and immigrated to the United States.

In America, he changed his name from Homburger to Erikson. This change was a crucial turning point in his life because it represented a retreat from his earlier Jewish identification. Originally, Erikson resented any implication that he was abandoning his Jewish identity by changing his name. He countered these charges by pointing out that he used his full name—Erik Homburger Erikson—in his books and essays. However, as time passed, he dropped his middle name and replaced it with the initial H. Thus, this person who at the end of life was known as Erik H. Erikson had previously been called Erik Salomonsen, Erik Homburger, and Erik Homburger Erikson.

In America, Erikson continued his pattern of moving from place to place. He first settled in the Boston area where he set up a modified psychoanalytic practice. With neither medical credentials nor any kind of college degree, he accepted research positions at Massachusetts General Hospital, Harvard Medical School, and the Harvard Psychological Clinic.

Wanting to write but needing more time than his busy schedule in Boston and Cambridge allowed, Erikson took a position at Yale in 1936, but after $2^{1}/_{2}$ years, he moved to the University of California at Berkeley, but not before living among and studying people of the Sioux nation on the Pine Ridge reservation in South Dakota. He later lived with people of the Yurok nation in northern California, and these experiences in cultural anthropology added to the richness and completeness of his concept of humanity.

During his California period, Erikson gradually evolved a theory of personality, separate from but not incompatible with Freud's. In 1950, Erikson published *Childhood and Society,* a book that at first glance appears to be a hodgepodge of unrelated chapters. Erikson himself originally had some difficulty finding a common theme underlying such topics as childhood in two Native American tribes, the growth of the ego, the eight stages of human development, and Hitler's childhood. Eventually, however, he recognized that the influence of psychological, cultural, and historical factors on *identity* was the underlying element that held the various chapters together. *Childhood and Society,* which became a classic and gave Erikson an international reputation as an imaginative thinker, remains the finest introduction to his post-Freudian personality theory.

In 1949, the University of California officials demanded that faculty members sign an oath pledging loyalty to the United States. Such a demand was not uncommon during those days when Senator Joseph McCarthy convinced many Americans that Communists and Communist sympathizers were poised to overthrow the U.S. government. Erikson was not a Communist, but as a matter of principle he refused to sign the oath. Although the Committee on Privilege and Tenure recommended that he retain his position, Erikson left California and returned to Massachusetts, where he worked as a therapist at Austen Riggs, a treatment center for psychoanalytic training and research located in Stockbridge. In 1960, he returned to Harvard and, for the next 10 years, held the position of professor of human development. After retirement, Erikson continued an active career—writing, lecturing, and seeing a few patients. During the early years of his retirement, he lived in Marin County, California; Cambridge, Massachusetts; and Cape Cod. Through all these changes, Erikson continued to seek his father's name. He died May 12, 1994, at the age of 91.

Who was Erik Erikson? Although he himself may not have been able to answer this question, other people can learn about the person known as Erik Erikson through his brilliantly constructed books, lectures, and essays.

Erikson's best-known works include *Childhood and Society* (1950, 1963, 1985); *Young Man Luther* (1958); *Identity: Youth and Crisis* (1968); *Gandhi's Truth* (1969), a book that won both the Pulitzer Prize and the National Book Award; *Dimensions of a New Identity* (1974); *Life History and the Historical Moment* (1975); *Identity and the Life Cycle* (1980); and *The Life Cycle Completed* (1982). Stephen Schlein compiled many of his papers in *A Way of Looking at Things* (Erikson, 1987).

The Ego in Post-Freudian Theory

In Chapter 2, we pointed out that Freud used the analogy of a rider on horseback to describe the relationship between the ego and the id. The rider (ego) is ultimately at the mercy of the stronger horse (id). The ego has no strength of its own but must borrow its energy from the id. Moreover, the ego is constantly attempting to balance blind demands of the superego against the relentless forces of the id and the realistic opportunities of the external world. Freud believed that, for psychologically healthy people, the ego is sufficiently developed to rein in the id, even though its control is still tenuous and id impulses might erupt and overwhelm the ego at any time.

In contrast, Erikson held that our ego is a positive force that creates a self-identity, a sense of "I." As the center of our personality, our ego helps us adapt to the various conflicts and crises of life and keeps us from losing our individuality to the leveling forces of society. During childhood, the ego is weak, pliable, and fragile; but by adolescence it should begin to take form and gain strength. Throughout our life, it unifies personality and guards against indivisibility. Erikson saw the ego as a partially unconscious organizing agency that synthesizes our present experiences with past self-identities and also with anticipated images of self. He defined the ego as a person's ability to unify experiences and actions in an adaptive manner (Erikson, 1963).

Erikson (1968) identified three interrelated aspects of ego: the body ego, the ego ideal, and ego identity. The *body ego* refers to experiences with our body; a way of seeing our physical self as different for other people. We may be satisfied or dissatisfied with the way our body looks and functions, but we recognize that it is the only body we will ever have. The *ego ideal* represents the image we have of ourselves in comparison with an established ideal; it is responsible for our being satisfied or dissatisfied not only with our physical self but with our entire personal identity. *Ego identity* is the image we have of ourselves in the variety of social roles we play. Although adolescence is ordinarily the time when these three components are changing most rapidly, alterations in body ego, ego ideal, and ego identity can and do take place at any stage of life.

Society's Influence

Although inborn capacities are important in personality development, the ego emerges from and is largely shaped by society. Erikson's emphasis on social and historical factors was in contrast with Freud's mostly biological viewpoint. To Erikson, the ego exists as potential at birth, but it must emerge from within a cultural environment. Different societies, with their variations in child-rearing practices, tend to shape personalities that fit the needs and values of their culture. For example, Erikson (1963) found that prolonged and permissive nursing of infants of the Sioux nation (sometimes for as long as 4 or 5 years) resulted in what Freud would call "oral" personalities: that is, people who gain great pleasure through functions of the mouth. The Sioux place great value on generosity, and Erikson believed that the reassurance resulting from unlimited breast-feeding lays the foundation for the virtue of generosity. However, Sioux parents quickly suppress biting, a practice that may contribute to the child's fortitude and ferocity. On the other hand, people of the Yurok nation set strict regulations concerning elimination of urine and feces, practices that tend to develop "anality," or compulsive neatness, stubbornness, and miserliness. In European American societies, orality and anality are often considered undesirable traits or neurotic symptoms. Erikson (1963), however, argued that orality among the Sioux hunters and anality among the Yurok fishermen are adaptive characteristics that help both the individual and the culture. The fact that European American culture views orality and anality as deviant traits merely displays its own ethnocentric view of other societies. Erikson (1968, 1974) argued that historically all tribes or nations, including the United States, have developed what he called a **pseudospecies:** that is, an illusion perpetrated and perpetuated by a particular society that it is somehow chosen to be *the* human species. In past centuries, this belief has aided the survival of the tribe, but with modern means of world annihilation, such a prejudiced perception (as demonstrated by Nazi Germany) threatens the survival of every nation.

One of Erikson's principal contributions to personality theory was his extension of the Freudian early stages of development to include school age, youth, adulthood, and old age. Before looking more closely at Erikson's theory of ego development, we discuss his view of how personality develops from one stage to the next.

Epigenetic Principle

Erikson believed that the ego develops throughout the various stages of life according to an **epigenetic principle,** a term borrowed from embryology. Epigenetic development implies a step-by-step growth of fetal organs. The embryo does not begin as a completely formed little person, waiting to merely expand its structure and

Children crawl before they walk, walk before they run, and run before they jump.

form. Rather, it develops, or should develop, according to a predetermined rate and in a fixed sequence. If the eyes, liver, or other organs do not develop during that critical period for their development, then they will never attain proper maturity.

In similar fashion, the ego follows the path of epigenetic development, with each stage developing at its proper time. One stage emerges from and is built upon a previous stage, but it does not replace that earlier stage. This epigenetic development is analogous to the physical development of children, who crawl before they walk, walk before they run, and run before they jump. When children are still crawling, they are developing the potential to walk, run, and jump; and after they are mature enough to jump, they still retain their ability to run, walk, and crawl. Erikson (1968) described the epigenetic principle by saying that "anything that grows has a ground plan, and that out of this ground plan the parts arise, each part having its time of special ascendancy, until all parts have arisen to form a functioning whole" (p. 92). More succinctly, "Epigenesis means that one characteristic develops on top of another in space and time" (Evans, 1967, pp. 21–22).

The epigenetic principle is illustrated in Figure 9.1, which depicts the first three Eriksonian stages. The sequence of stages (1, 2, 3) and the development of their component parts (A, B, C) are shown in the heavily lined boxes along the diagonal. Figure 9.1 shows that each part exists before its critical time (at least as biological potential), emerges at its proper time, and finally, continues to develop during subsequent stages. For example, component part B of Stage 2 (early childhood) exists during Stage 1 (infancy) as shown in Box 1_B. Part B reaches its full ascendance during Stage 2 (Box 2_B), but continues into Stage 3 (Box 3_B). Similarly, all components

Parts

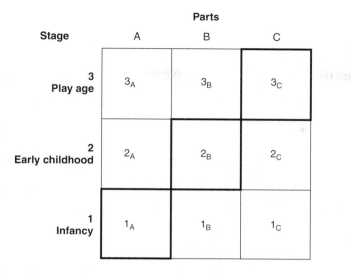

FIGURE 9.1   *Three Eriksonian Stages, Depicting the Epigenetic Principle.*

Reprinted from *The Life Cycle Completed: A Review* by Erik H. Erikson, by permission of W. W. Norton & Company, Inc. Copyright © 1982 by Rikan Enterprises, Ltd.

of Stage 3 exist during Stages 1 and 2, reach full development during Stage 3, and continue throughout all later stages (Erikson, 1982).

Stages of Psychosocial Development

Comprehension of Erikson's eight stages of psychosocial development requires an understanding of several basic points. First, growth takes place according to the *epigenetic principle*. That is, one component part arises out of another and has its own time of ascendancy, but it does not entirely replace earlier components.

Second, in every stage of life there is an *interaction of opposites*—that is, a conflict between a **syntonic** (harmonious) element and a **dystonic** (disruptive) element. For example, during infancy *basic trust* (a syntonic tendency) is opposed to *basic mistrust* (a dystonic tendency). Both trust and mistrust, however, are necessary for proper adaptation. An infant who learns only to trust becomes gullible and is ill prepared for the realities encountered in later development, whereas an infant who learns only to mistrust becomes overly suspicious and cynical. Similarly, during each of the other seven stages, people must have both harmonious (syntonic) and disruptive (dystonic) experiences.

Third, at each stage, the conflict between the dystonic and syntonic elements produces an ego quality or ego strength, which Erikson referred to as a **basic strength.** For instance, from the antithesis between trust and mistrust emerges hope, an ego quality that allows an infant to move into the next stage. Likewise, each of the other stages is marked by a basic ego strength that emerges from the clash between the harmonious and the disruptive elements of that stage.

Fourth, too little basic strength at any one stage results in a **core pathology** for that stage. For example, a child who does not acquire sufficient hope during infancy will develop the antithesis or opposite of hope, namely, *withdrawal.* Again, each stage has a potential core pathology.

Fifth, although Erikson referred to his eight stages as *psychosocial stages,* he never lost sight of the biological aspect of human development.

Sixth, events in earlier stages do not cause later personality development. Ego identity is shaped by a *multiplicity of conflicts and events*—past, present, and anticipated.

Seventh, during each stage, but especially from adolescence forward, personality development is characterized by an *identity crisis,* which Erikson (1968) called "a turning point, a crucial period of increased vulnerability and heightened potential" (p. 96). Thus, during each crisis, a person is especially susceptible to major modifications in identity, either positive or negative. Contrary to popular usage, an identity crisis is not a catastrophic event but rather an opportunity for either adaptive or maladaptive adjustment.

Erikson's eight stages of psychosocial development are shown in Figure 9.2. The boldfaced capitalized words are the ego qualities or basic strengths that emerge from the conflicts or psychosocial crises that typify each period. The "vs." separating syntonic and dystonic elements signifies not only an antithetical relationship but also a complementary one. Only the boxes along the diagonal are filled in; that is, Figure 9.2 highlights only the basic strengths and psychosocial crises that are most characteristic of each stage of development. However, the epigenetic principle suggests that all the other boxes would be filled (as in Figure 9.1), though with other items less characteristic of their stage of psychosocial development. Each item in the ensemble is vital to personality development, and each is related to all the others.

Infancy

The first psychosocial stage is **infancy,** a period encompassing approximately the first year of life and paralleling Freud's oral phase of development. However, Erikson's model adopts a broader focus than Freud's oral stage, which was concerned almost exclusively with the mouth. To Erikson (1963, 1989), infancy is a time of *incorporation,* with infants "taking in" not only through their mouth but through their various sense organs as well. Through their eyes, for example, infants take in visual stimuli. As they take in food and sensory information, infants learn to either trust or mistrust the outside world, a situation that gives them realistic hope. Infancy, then, is marked by the *oral-sensory* psychosexual mode, the psychosocial crisis of *basic trust versus basic mistrust,* and the basic strength of *hope.*

Oral-Sensory Mode

Erikson's expanded view of infancy is expressed in the term **oral-sensory,** a phrase that includes infants' principal *psychosexual* mode of adapting. The oral-sensory stage is characterized by two modes of incorporation—receiving and accepting what is given. Infants can receive even in the absence of other people; that is, they can take in air through the lungs and can receive sensory data without having to manipulate others. The second mode of incorporation, however, implies a social context. Infants not only must *get,* but they also must get someone else to *give.* This early training in interpersonal relations helps them learn to eventually become givers. In getting other

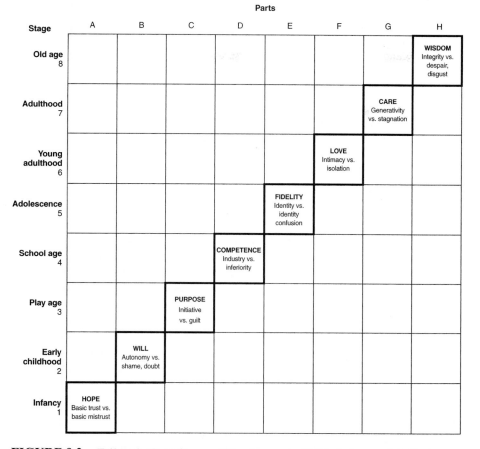

Parts

Stage	A	B	C	D	E	F	G	H
Old age 8								**WISDOM** Integrity vs. despair, disgust
Adulthood 7							**CARE** Generativity vs. stagnation	
Young adulthood 6						**LOVE** Intimacy vs. isolation		
Adolescence 5					**FIDELITY** Identity vs. identity confusion			
School age 4				**COMPETENCE** Industry vs. inferiority				
Play age 3			**PURPOSE** Initiative vs. guilt					
Early childhood 2		**WILL** Autonomy vs. shame, doubt						
Infancy 1	**HOPE** Basic trust vs. basic mistrust							

FIGURE 9.2   *Erikson's Eight Stages of Development with Their Appropriate Basic Strengths and Psychosocial Crises.*

Reprinted from *The Life Cycle Completed: A Review* by Erik H. Erikson, by permission of W. W. Norton & Company, Inc. Copyright © 1982 by Rikan Enterprises, Ltd.

people to give, they learn to trust or mistrust other people, thus setting up the basic *psychosocial crisis* of infancy, namely, basic trust versus basic mistrust.

Basic Trust Versus Basic Mistrust

Infants' most significant interpersonal relations are with their primary caregiver, ordinarily their mother. If they realize that their mother will provide food regularly, then they begin to learn *basic trust;* if they consistently hear the pleasant, rhythmic voice of their mother, then they develop more basic trust; if they can rely on an exciting visual environment, then they solidify basic trust even more. In other words, if their pattern of accepting things corresponds with culture's way of giving things, then infants learn basic trust. In contrast, they learn *basic mistrust* if they find no correspondence between their oral-sensory needs and their environment.

Basic trust is ordinarily syntonic, and basic mistrust, dystonic. Nevertheless, infants must develop both attitudes. Too much trust makes them gullible and vulnerable to the vagaries of the world, whereas too little trust leads to frustration, anger, hostility, cynicism, or depression.

Both trust and mistrust are inevitable experiences of infants. All babies who have survived have been fed and otherwise cared for and therefore have some reason to trust. In addition, all have been frustrated by pain, hunger, or discomfort, and thus have a reason to mistrust. Erikson believed that some ratio of trust and mistrust is critical to people's ability to adapt. He told Richard Evans (1967) that "when we enter a situation, we must be able to differentiate how much we can trust and how much we must mistrust, and I use mistrust in the sense of a readiness for danger and an anticipation of discomfort" (p. 15).

The inevitable clash between basic trust and basic mistrust results in people's first psychosocial crisis. If people successfully solve this crisis, they acquire their first basic strength—*hope.*

Hope: The Basic Strength of Infancy

Hope emerges from the conflict between basic trust and basic mistrust. Without the antithetical relationship between trust and mistrust, people cannot develop hope. Infants must experience hunger, pain, and discomfort as well as the alleviation of these unpleasant conditions. By having both painful and pleasurable experiences, infants learn to expect that future distresses will meet with satisfactory outcomes.

If infants do not develop sufficient hope during infancy, they will demonstrate the antithesis or the opposite of hope—*withdrawal,* the *core pathology* of infancy. With little to hope for, they will retreat from the outside world and begin the journey toward serious psychological disturbance.

Early Childhood

The second psychosocial stage is **early childhood,** a period paralleling Freud's anal stage and encompassing approximately the 2nd and 3rd years of life. Again, some differences exist between the views of Freud and Erikson. In Chapter 2, we explained that Freud regarded the anus as the primary erogenous zone during this period and that during the early sadistic-anal phase, children receive pleasure in destroying or losing objects, while later they take satisfaction in defecating.

Once again, Erikson took a broader view. To him, young children receive pleasure not only from mastering the sphincter muscle but also from mastering other body functions such as urinating, walking, throwing, holding, and so on. In addition, children develop a sense of control over their interpersonal environment, as well as a measure of self-control. However, early childhood is also a time of experiencing doubt and shame as children learn that many of their attempts at autonomy are unsuccessful.

Anal-Urethral-Muscular Mode

During the 2nd year of life, children's primary psychosexual adjustment is the **anal-urethral-muscular** mode. At this time, children learn to control their body, especially in relation to cleanliness and mobility. Early childhood is more than a time of toilet training; it is also a time of learning to walk, run, hug parents, and hold on to toys and other objects. With each of these activities, young children are likely to display some stubborn tendencies. They may retain their feces or eliminate them at will, snuggle up to their mother or suddenly push her away, delight in hoarding objects or ruthlessly discard them.

Early childhood is a time of contradiction, a time of stubborn rebellion and meek compliance, a time of *impulsive* self-expression and *compulsive* deviance, a time of loving cooperation and hateful resistance. This obstinate insistence on conflicting impulses triggers the major psychosocial crisis of childhood—autonomy versus shame and doubt (Erikson, 1968).

Autonomy Versus Shame and Doubt

If early childhood is a time for self-expression and *autonomy,* then it is also a time for *shame and doubt.* As children stubbornly express their anal-urethral-muscular mode, they are likely to find a culture that attempts to inhibit some of their self-expression. Parents may shame their children for soiling their pants or for making a mess with their food. They may also instill doubt by questioning their children's ability to meet their standards. The conflict between autonomy and shame and doubt becomes the major psychosocial crisis of early childhood.

Ideally, children should develop a proper ratio between autonomy and shame and doubt, and the ratio should be in favor of autonomy, the syntonic quality of early childhood. Children who develop too little autonomy will have difficulties in subsequent stages, lacking the basic strengths of later stages.

According to Erikson's epigenetic diagrams (see Figures 9.1 and 9.2), autonomy grows out of basic trust; and if basic trust has been established in infancy, then children learn to have faith in themselves, and their world remains intact while they experience a mild psychosocial crisis. Conversely, if children do not develop basic trust during infancy, then their attempts to gain control of their anal, urethral, and muscular organs during early childhood will be met with a strong sense of shame and doubt, setting up a serious psychosocial crisis. *Shame* is a feeling of self-consciousness, of being looked at and exposed. *Doubt,* on the other hand, is the feeling of not being certain, the feeling that something remains hidden and cannot be seen. Both shame and doubt are dystonic qualities, and both grow out of the basic mistrust that was established in infancy.

Will: The Basic Strength of Early Childhood

The basic strength of *will* or willfulness evolves from the resolution of the crisis of autonomy versus shame and doubt. This step is the beginning of free will and willpower—but only a beginning. Mature willpower and a significant measure of free will are reserved for later stages of development, but they originate in the rudimentary will that emerges during early childhood. Anyone who has spent much time around 2-year-olds knows how willful they can be. Toilet training often epitomizes the conflict of wills between adult and child, but willful expression is not limited to this area. The basic conflict during early childhood is between the child's striving for autonomy and the parent's attempts to control the child through the use of shame and doubt.

Children develop will only when their environment allows them some self-expression in their control of sphincters and other muscles. When their experiences result in too much shame and doubt, children do not adequately develop this second important basic strength. Inadequate will is expressed as *compulsion,* the core pathology of early childhood. Too little will and too much compulsivity carry forward into the play age as lack of purpose and into the school age as lack of confidence.

Play Age

Erikson's third stage of development is the **play age,** a period covering the same time as Freud's phallic phase—roughly ages 3 to 5 years. Again, differences emerge between the views of Freud and Erikson. Whereas Freud placed the Oedipus complex at the core of the phallic stage, Erikson believed that the Oedipus complex is but one of several important developments during the play age. Erikson (1968) contended that, in addition to identifying with their parents, preschool-age children are developing locomotion, language skills, curiosity, imagination, and the ability to set goals.

Genital-Locomotor Mode

The primary psychosexual mode during the play age is **genital-locomotor.** Erikson (1982) saw the Oedipal situation as a prototype "of the lifelong power of human playfulness" (p. 77). In other words, the Oedipus complex is a drama played out in the child's imagination and includes the budding understanding of such basic concepts as reproduction, growth, future, and death. The Oedipus and castration complexes, therefore, are not always to be taken literally. A child may play at being a mother, a father, a wife, or a husband; but such play is an expression not only of the genital mode but also of the child's rapidly developing locomotor abilities. A little girl may envy boys, not because boys possess a penis, but rather because society grants more prerogatives to children with a penis. A little boy may have anxiety about losing something, but this anxiety refers not only to the penis but also to other body parts. The Oedipus complex, then, is both more than and less than what Freud believed, and infantile sexuality is "a mere promise of things to come" (Erikson, 1963, p. 86). Unless sexual interest is provoked by cultural sex play or by adult sexual abuse, the Oedipus complex produces no harmful effects on later personality development.

The interest that play-age children have in genital activity is accompanied by their increasing facility at locomotion. They can now move with ease, running, jumping, and climbing with no conscious effort; and their play shows both initiative and imagination. Their rudimentary will, developed during the preceding stage, is now evolving into activity with a *purpose.* Children's cognitive abilities enable them to manufacture elaborate fantasies that include Oedipal fantasies but also include imagining what it is like to be grown up, to be omnipotent, or to be a ferocious animal. These fantasies, however, also produce guilt and thus contribute to the psychosocial crisis of the play age, namely, initiative versus guilt.

Initiative Versus Guilt

As children begin to move around more easily and vigorously and as their genital interest awakens, they adopt an intrusive head-on mode of approaching the world. Although they begin to adopt *initiative* in their selection and pursuit of goals, many goals, such as marrying their mother or father or leaving home, must be either repressed or delayed. The consequence of these taboo and inhibited goals is *guilt*. The conflict between initiative and guilt becomes the dominant psychosocial crisis of the play age.

Again, the ratio between these two should favor the syntonic quality—initiative. Unbridled initiative, however, may lead to chaos and a lack of moral principles. On the other hand, if guilt is the dominant element, children may become compulsively moralistic or overly inhibited. *Inhibition,* which is the antipathy of purpose, constitutes the core pathology of the play age.

Purpose: The Basic Strength of the Play Age

The conflict of initiative versus guilt produces the basic strength of *purpose*. Children now play with a purpose, competing at games in order to win or to be on top. Their genital interests have a direction, with mother or father being the object of their sexual desires. They set goals and pursue them with purpose. Play age is also the stage in which children are developing a conscience and beginning to attach labels such as right and wrong to their behavior. This youthful conscience becomes the "cornerstone of morality" (Erikson, 1968, p. 119).

School Age

Erikson's concept of **school age** covers development from about age 6 to approximately age 12 or 13 and matches the latency years of Freud's theory. At this age, the social world of children is expanding beyond family to include peers, teachers, and other adult models. For school-age children, their wish to know becomes strong and is tied to their basic striving for competence. In normal development, children strive industriously to read and write, to hunt and fish, or to learn the skills required by their culture. School age does not necessarily mean formalized schools. In contemporary literate cultures, schools and professional teachers play a major part in children's education, whereas in preliterate societies, adults use less formalized but equally effective methods to instruct children in the ways of society.

Latency

Erikson agreed with Freud that school age is a period of psychosexual **latency.** Sexual latency is important because it allows children to divert their energies to learning the technology of their culture and the strategies of their social interactions. As children work and play to acquire these essentials, they begin to form a picture of themselves as competent or incompetent. These self images are the origin of *ego identity*—that feeling of "I" or "me-ness" that evolves more fully during adolescence.

Industry Versus Inferiority

Although school age is a period of little *sexual* development, it is a time of tremendous *social* growth. The psychosocial crisis of this stage is industry versus inferiority. *Industry,* a syntonic quality, means industriousness, a willingness to remain busy with something and to finish a job. School-age children learn to work and play at activities directed toward acquiring job skills and toward learning the rules of cooperation.

As children learn to do things well, they develop a sense of industry, but if their work is insufficient to accomplish their goals, they acquire a sense of *inferiority*—the dystonic quality of the school age. Earlier inadequacies can also contribute to children's feelings of inferiority. For example, if children acquire too much guilt and too little purpose during the play age, they will likely feel inferior and incompetent during the school age. However, failure is not inevitable. Erikson was optimistic in suggesting that people can successfully handle the crisis of any given stage even though they were not completely successful in previous stages.

The ratio between industry and inferiority should, of course, favor industry; but inferiority, like the other dystonic qualities, should not be avoided. As Alfred Adler (Chapter 3) pointed out, inferiority can serve as an impetus to do one's best. Conversely, an oversupply of inferiority can block productive activity and stunt one's feelings of competence.

Competence: The Basic Strength of the School Age

From the conflict of industry versus inferiority, school-age children develop the basic strength of c*ompetence:* that is, the confidence to use one's physical and cognitive abilities to solve the problems that accompany school age. Competence lays the foundation for "co-operative participation in productive adult life" (Erikson, 1968, p. 126).

If the struggle between industry and inferiority favors either inferiority or an overabundance of industry, children are likely to give up and regress to an earlier stage of development. They may become preoccupied with infantile genital and Oedipal fantasies and spend most of their time in nonproductive play. This regression is called *inertia,* the antithesis of competence and the core pathology of the school age.

Adolescence

Adolescence, the period from puberty to young adulthood, is one of the most crucial developmental stages because, by the end of this period, a person must gain a firm sense of *ego identity.* Although ego identity neither begins nor ends during adolescence, the crisis between *identity* and *identity confusion* reaches its ascendance during this stage. From this crisis of identity versus identity confusion emerges *fidelity,* the basic strength of adolescence.

Erikson (1982) saw adolescence as a period of *social* latency, just as he saw school age as a time of *sexual* latency. Although adolescents are developing sexually and cognitively, in most Western societies they are allowed to postpone lasting commitment to an occupation, a sex partner, or an adaptive philosophy of life. They are permitted to experiment in a variety of ways and to try out new roles and beliefs while seeking to establish a sense of ego identity. Adolescence, then, is an adaptive phase of personality development, a period of trial and error.

Puberty

Puberty, defined as genital maturation, plays a relatively minor role in Erikson's concept of adolescence. For most young people, genital maturation presents no major sexual crisis. Nevertheless, puberty is important psychologically because it triggers expectations of adult roles yet ahead—roles that are essentially social and can be filled only through a struggle to attain ego identity.

Identity Versus Identity Confusion

The search for ego *identity* reaches a climax during adolescence as young people strive to find out who they are and who they are not. With the advent of puberty, adolescents look for new roles to help them discover their sexual, ideological, and occupational identities. In this search, young people draw from a variety of earlier self-images that have been accepted or rejected. Thus, the seeds of identity begin to sprout during infancy and continue to grow through childhood, the play age, and the school age. Then during adolescence, identity strengthens into a crisis as young people learn to cope with the psychosocial conflict of identity versus identity confusion.

A crisis should not suggest a threat or catastrophe but rather "a turning point, a crucial period of increased vulnerability and heightened potential" (Erikson, 1968, p. 96). An identity crisis may last for many years and can result in either greater or lesser ego strength.

According to Erikson (1982), identity emerges from two sources: (1) adolescents' affirmation or repudiation of childhood identifications, and (2) their historical and social contexts, which encourage conformity to certain standards. Young people frequently reject the standards of their elders, preferring instead the values of a peer

The late adolescent's search for identity includes a discovery of sexual identity.

group or gang. In any event, the society in which they live plays a substantial role in shaping their identity.

Identity is defined both positively and negatively, as adolescents are deciding what they want to become and what they believe while also discovering what they *do not* wish to be and what they *do not* believe. Often they must either repudiate the values of parents or reject those of the peer group, a dilemma that may intensify their *identity confusion.*

Identity confusion is a syndrome of problems that includes a divided self-image, an inability to establish intimacy, a sense of time urgency, a lack of concentration on required tasks, and a rejection of family or community standards. As with the other dystonic tendencies, some amount of identity confusion is both normal and necessary. Young people must experience some doubt and confusion about who they are before they can evolve a stable identity. They may leave home (as Erikson did) to wander alone in search of self; experiment with drugs and sex; identify with a street gang; join a religious order; or rail against the existing society, with no alternative answers. Or they may simply and quietly consider where they fit into the world and what values they hold dear.

Once again, Erikson's theory is consistent with his own life. At age 18 and feeling alienated from the standards of his bourgeois family, Erikson set about searching for a different style of life. Gifted at sketching and with more identity confusion than identity, he spent the next 7 years wandering through southern Europe in search of an identity as an artist. Erikson (1975) referred to this stage of his life as a time of discontent, rebellion, and identity confusion.

Although identity confusion is a necessary part of our search for identity, too much confusion can lead to pathological adjustment in the form of regression to earlier stages of development. We may postpone the responsibilities of adulthood and drift aimlessly from one job to another, from one sex partner to another, or from one ideology to another. Conversely, if we develop the proper ratio of identity to identity confusion, we will have (1) faith in some sort of ideological principle, (2) the ability to freely decide how we should behave, (3) trust in our peers and adults who give us advice regarding goals and aspirations, and (4) confidence in our choice of an eventual occupation.

Fidelity: The Basic Strength of Adolescence

The basic strength emerging from adolescent identity crises is *fidelity,* or faith in one's ideology. After establishing their internal standards of conduct, adolescents are no longer in need of parental guidance but have confidence in their own religious, political, and social ideologies.

The trust learned in infancy is basic for fidelity in adolescence. Young people must learn to trust others before they can have faith in their own view of the future. They must have developed hope during infancy, and they must follow hope with the other basic strengths—will, purpose, and competence. Each is a prerequisite for fidelity, just as fidelity is essential for acquiring subsequent ego strengths.

The pathological counterpart of fidelity is **role repudiation,** the core pathology of adolescence that blocks one's ability to synthesize various self-images and values into a workable identity. Role repudiation can take the form of either diffidence or defiance (Erikson, 1982). *Diffidence* is an extreme lack of self-trust or self-confidence and is expressed as shyness or hesitancy to express oneself. In contrast, defiance is the act of rebelling against authority. Defiant adolescents stubbornly hold to socially unacceptable beliefs and practices simply because these beliefs and practices are unacceptable. Some amount of role repudiation, Erikson believed, is necessary, not only because it allows adolescents to evolve their personal identity, but also because it injects some new ideas and new vitality into the social structure.

Young Adulthood

After achieving a sense of identity during adolescence, people must acquire the ability to fuse that identity with the identity of another person while maintaining their sense of individuality. **Young adulthood**—a time from about age 19 to 30—is circumscribed not so much by time as by the acquisition of *intimacy* at the beginning of the stage and the development of *generativity* at the end. For some people, this stage is a relatively short time, lasting perhaps only a few years. For others, young adulthood may continue for several decades. Young adults should develop mature *genitality,* experience the conflict between *intimacy* and *isolation,* and acquire the basic strength of *love.*

Genitality

Much of the sexual activity during adolescence is an expression of one's search for identity and is basically self-serving. True **genitality** can develop only during young adulthood when it is distinguished by mutual trust and a stable sharing of sexual satisfactions with a loved person. It is the chief psychosexual accomplishment of young adulthood and exists only in an intimate relationship (Erikson, 1963).

Intimacy Versus Isolation

Young adulthood is marked by the psychosocial crisis of intimacy versus isolation. **Intimacy** is the ability to fuse one's identity with that of another person without fear of losing it. Because intimacy can be achieved only after people have formed a stable ego, the infatuations often found in young adolescents are not true intimacy. People who are unsure of their identity may either shy away from psychosocial intimacy or desperately seek intimacy through meaningless sexual encounters.

In contrast, mature intimacy means an ability and willingness to share a mutual trust. It involves sacrifice, compromise, and commitment within a relationship of two equals. It should be a requirement for marriage, but many marriages lack intimacy because some young people marry as part of their search for the identity that they failed to establish during adolescence.

The psychosocial counterpart to intimacy is **isolation,** defined as "the incapacity to take chances with one's identity by sharing true intimacy" (Erikson, 1968, p. 137). Some people become financially or socially successful, yet retain a sense of isolation because they are unable to accept the adult responsibilities of productive work, procreation, and mature love.

Again, some degree of isolation is essential before one can acquire mature love. Too much togetherness can diminish a person's sense of ego identity, which leads that person to a psychosocial regression and an inability to face the next developmental stage. The greater danger, of course, is too much isolation, too little intimacy, and a deficiency in the basic strength of love.

Love: The Basic Strength of Young Adulthood

Love, the basic strength of young adulthood, emerges from the crisis of intimacy versus isolation. Erikson (1968, 1982) defined love as mature devotion that overcomes basic differences between men and women. Although love includes intimacy, it also contains some degree of isolation, because each partner is permitted to retain a separate identity. Mature love means commitment, sexual passion, cooperation, competition, and friendship. It is the basic strength of young adulthood, enabling a person to cope productively with the final two stages of development.

The antipathy of love is **exclusivity,** the core pathology of young adulthood. Some exclusivity, however, is necessary for intimacy; that is, a person must be able to exclude certain people, activities, and ideas in order to develop a strong sense of identity. Exclusivity becomes pathological when it blocks one's ability to cooperate, compete, or compromise—all prerequisite ingredients for intimacy and love.

Adulthood

The seventh stage of development is **adulthood,** that time when people begin to take their place in society and assume responsibility for whatever society produces. For most people, this is the longest stage of development, spanning the years from about age 31 to 60. Adulthood is characterized by the psychosexual mode of *procreativity,* the psychosocial crisis of *generativity versus stagnation,* and the basic strength of *care.*

Procreativity

Erikson's psychosexual theory assumes an instinctual drive to perpetuate the species. This drive is the counterpart of an adult animal's instinct toward procreation and is an extension of the genitality that marks young adulthood (Erikson, 1982). However, **procreativity** refers to more than genital contact with an intimate partner. It includes assuming responsibility for the care of offspring that result from that sexual contact. Ideally, procreation should follow from the mature intimacy and love established during the preceding stage. Obviously, people are physically capable of producing offspring before they are psychologically ready to care for the welfare of these children.

Mature adulthood demands more than procreating offspring; it includes caring for one's children as well as other people's children. In addition, it encompasses working productively to transmit culture from one generation to the next.

Generativity Versus Stagnation

The syntonic quality of adulthood is *generativity,* defined as "the generation of new beings as well as new products and new ideas" (Erikson, 1982, p. 67). Generativity, which is concerned with establishing and guiding the next generation, includes the procreation of children, the production of work, and the creation of new things and ideas that contribute to the building of a better world.

People have a need not only to learn but also to instruct. This need extends beyond one's own children to an altruistic concern for other young people. Generativity grows out of earlier syntonic qualities such as intimacy and identity. As noted earlier, intimacy calls for the ability to fuse one's ego to that of another person without fear of losing it. This unity of ego identities leads to a gradual expansion of interests. During adulthood, one-to-one intimacy is no longer enough. Other people, especially children, become part of one's concern. Instructing others in the ways of culture is a practice found in all societies. For the mature adult, this motivation is not merely an obligation or a selfish need but an evolutionary drive to make a contribution to succeeding generations and to ensure the continuity of human society as well.

The antithesis of generativity is *self-absorption and stagnation.* The generational cycle of productivity and creativity is crippled when people become too absorbed in themselves, too self-indulgent. Such an attitude fosters a pervading sense of stagnation. Some elements of stagnation and self-absorption, however, are necessary. Creative people must, at times, remain in a dormant stage and be absorbed with themselves in order to eventually generate new growth. The interaction of generativity and stagnation produces care, the basic strength of adulthood.

Care: The Basic Strength of Adulthood

Erikson (1982) defined **care** as "a widening commitment to *take care of* the persons, the products, and the ideas one has learned to *care for*" (p. 67). As the basic strength of adulthood, care arises from each earlier basic ego strength. One must have hope, will, purpose, competence, fidelity, and love in order to take care of that which one cares for. Care is not a duty or obligation but a natural desire emerging from the conflict between generativity and stagnation or self-absorption.

The antipathy of care is *rejectivity,* the core pathology of adulthood. Rejectivity is the unwillingness to take care of certain persons or groups (Erikson, 1982). Rejectivity is manifested as self-centeredness, provincialism, or *pseudospeciation:* that is, the belief that other groups of people are inferior to one's own. It is responsible for much of human hatred, destruction, atrocities, and wars. As Erikson said, rejectivity "has far-reaching implications for the survival of the species as well as for every individual's psychosocial development" (p. 70).

Old Age

The eighth and final stage of development is **old age.** Erikson was in his early 40s when he first conceptualized this stage and arbitrarily defined it as the period from about age 60 to the end of life. Old age need not mean that people are no longer generative. Procreation, in the narrow sense of producing children, may be absent, yet old people can remain productive and creative in other ways. They can be caring grandparents to their own grandchildren as well as to other younger members of society. Old age can be a time of joy, playfulness, and wonder; but it is also a time of senility, depression, and despair. The psychosexual mode of old age is *generalized sensuality;* the psychosocial crisis is *integrity versus despair,* and the basic strength is *wisdom.*

Erikson's stages of development extend into old age.

Generalized Sensuality

The final psychosexual stage is *generalized sensuality*. Erikson had little to say about this mode of psychosexual life, but one may infer that it means to take pleasure in a variety of different physical sensations—sights, sounds, tastes, odors, embraces, and perhaps genital stimulation. Generalized sensuality may also include a greater appreciation for the traditional lifestyle of the opposite sex. Men become more nurturant and more acceptant of the pleasures of nonsexual relationships, including those with their grandchildren and great-grandchildren. Women become more interested and involved in politics, finance, and world affairs (Erikson, Erikson, & Kivnick, 1986). A generalized sensual attitude, however, is dependent on one's ability to hold things together, that is, to maintain integrity in the face of despair.

Integrity Versus Despair

A person's final identity crisis is *integrity versus despair.* At the end of life, the dystonic quality of despair may prevail, but for people with a strong ego identity who have learned intimacy and who have taken care of both people and things, the syntonic quality of integrity will predominate. Integrity means a feeling of wholeness and coherence, an ability to hold together one's sense of "I-ness" despite diminishing physical and intellectual powers.

   Beyond Biography   **Who was Erik Erikson? For information on Erikson's lifelong search for his own identity, please go to our website at *www.mhhe.com/feist7***

Ego integrity is sometimes difficult to maintain when people see that they are losing familiar aspects of their existence: for example, spouse, friends, physical health, body strength, mental alertness, independence, and social usefulness. Under such pressure, people often feel a pervading sense of despair, which they may express as disgust, depression, contempt for others, or any other attitude that reveals a nonacceptance of the finite boundaries of life.

Despair literally means to be without hope. A reexamination of Figure 9.2 reveals that despair, the last dystonic quality of the life cycle, is in the opposite corner from hope, a person's first basic strength. From infancy to old age, hope can exist. Once hope is lost, despair follows and life ceases to have meaning.

Wisdom: The Basic Strength of Old Age

Some amount of despair is natural and necessary for psychological maturity. The inevitable struggle between integrity and despair produces *wisdom,* the basic strength of old age. Erikson (1982) defined wisdom as "informed and detached concern with life itself in the face of death itself" (p. 61). People with detached concern do not lack concern; rather, they exhibit an active but dispassionate interest. With mature wisdom, they maintain their integrity in spite of declining physical and mental abilities. Wisdom draws from and contributes to the traditional knowledge passed from generation to generation. In old age, people are concerned with ultimate issues, including nonexistence (Erikson, Erikson, & Kivnick, 1986).

The antithesis of wisdom and the core pathology of old age is *disdain,* which Erikson (1982, p. 61) defined as "a reaction to feeling (and seeing others) in an increasing state of being finished, confused, helpless." Disdain is a continuation of rejectivity, the core pathology of adulthood.

As Erikson himself aged, he became less optimistic about old age, and he and his wife began to describe a ninth stage—a period of very old age when physical and mental infirmities rob people of their generative abilities and reduce them to waiting for death. Joan, especially, was interested in this ninth stage as she watched her husband's health rapidly deteriorate during the last few years of his life. Unfortunately, Joan herself died before she could complete this ninth stage.

Summary of the Life Cycle

Erikson's cycle of life is summarized in Table 9.1. Each of the eight stages is characterized by a psychosexual mode as well as a psychosocial crisis. The psychosocial crisis is stimulated by a conflict between the predominating syntonic element and its antithetical dystonic element. From this conflict emerges a basic strength, or ego quality. Each basic strength has an underlying antipathy that becomes the core pathology of that stage. Humans have an ever-increasing radius of significant relations, beginning with the maternal person in infancy and ending with an identification with all humanity during old age.

Personality always develops during a particular historical period and within a given society. Nevertheless, Erikson believed that the eight developmental stages transcend chronology and geography and are appropriate to nearly all cultures, past and present.

Erikson's Methods of Investigation

Erikson insisted that personality is a product of history, culture, and biology; and his diverse methods of investigation reflect this belief. He employed anthropological, historical, sociological, and clinical methods to learn about children, adolescents, mature adults, and elderly people. He studied middle-class Americans, European children, people of the Sioux and Yurok nations of North America, and even sailors

TABLE 9.1

Summary of Erikson's Eight Stages of the Life Cycle

Stage	Psychosexual Mode	Psychosocial Crisis	Basic Strength	Core Pathology	Significant Relations
8 Old age	Generalization of sensual modes	Integrity vs. despair	Wisdom	Disdain	All humanity
7 Adulthood	Procreativity	Generativity vs. stagnation	Care	Rejectivity	Divided labor and shared household
6 Young adulthood	Genitality	Intimacy vs. isolation	Love	Exclusivity	Sexual partners, friends
5 Adolescence	Puberty	Identity vs. identity confusion	Fidelity	Role repudiation	Peer groups
4 School age	Latency	Industry vs. inferiority	Competence	Inertia	Neighborhood, school
3 Play age	Infantile genital-locomotor	Initiative vs. guilt	Purpose	Inhibition	Family
2 Early childhood	Anal-urethral-muscular	Autonomy vs. shame, doubt	Will	Compulsion	Parents
1 Infancy	Oral-respiratory: sensory-kinesthetic	Basic trust vs. basic mistrust	Hope	Withdrawal	The mothering one

on a submarine. He wrote biographical portraits of Adolf Hitler, Maxim Gorky, Martin Luther, and Mohandas K. Gandhi, among others. In this section, we present two approaches Erikson used to explain and describe human personality—anthropological studies and psychohistory.

Anthropological Studies

In 1937, Erikson made a field trip to the Pine Ridge Indian Reservation in South Dakota to investigate the causes of apathy among Sioux children. Erikson (1963) reported on early Sioux training in terms of his newly evolving theories of psychosexual and psychosocial development. He found that apathy was an expression of an extreme dependency the Sioux had developed as a result of their reliance on various federal government programs. At one time, they had been courageous buffalo hunters, but by 1937, the Sioux had lost their group identity as hunters and were trying halfheartedly to scrape out a living as farmers. Child-rearing practices, which in the past had trained young boys to be hunters and young girls to be helpers and mothers of future hunters, were no longer appropriate for an agrarian society. As a consequence, the Sioux children of 1937 had great difficulty achieving a sense of ego identity, especially after they reached adolescence.

Two years later, Erikson made a similar field trip to northern California to study people of the Yurok nation, who lived mostly on salmon fishing. Although the Sioux and Yurok had vastly divergent cultures, each tribe had a tradition of training its youth in the virtues of its society. Yurok people were trained to catch fish, and therefore they possessed no strong national feeling and had little taste for war. Obtaining and retaining provisions and possessions were highly valued among people of the Yurok nation. Erikson (1963) was able to show that early childhood training was consistent with this strong cultural value and that history and society helped shape personality.

Psychohistory

The discipline called **psychohistory** is a controversial field that combines psychoanalytic concepts with historical methods. Freud (1910/1957) originated psychohistory with an investigation of Leonardo da Vinci and later collaborated with American ambassador William Bullitt to write a book-length psychological study of American president Woodrow Wilson (Freud & Bullitt, 1967). Although Erikson (1975) deplored this latter work, he took up the methods of psychohistory and refined them, especially in his study of Martin Luther (Erikson, 1958, 1975) and Mahatma Gandhi (Erikson, 1969, 1975). Both Luther and Gandhi had an important impact on history because each was an exceptional person with the right personal conflict living during a historical period that needed to resolve collectively what could not be resolved individually (E. Hall, 1983).

Erikson (1974) defined psychohistory as "the study of individual and collective life with the combined methods of psychoanalysis and history" (p. 13). He used psychohistory to demonstrate his fundamental beliefs that each person is a product of his or her historical time and that those historical times are influenced by exceptional leaders experiencing a personal identity conflict.

As an author of psychohistory, Erikson believed that he should be emotionally involved in his subject. For example, he developed a strong emotional attachment to Gandhi, which he attributed to his own lifelong search for the father he had never seen (Erikson, 1975). In *Gandhi's Truth,* Erikson (1969) revealed strong positive feelings for Gandhi as he attempted to answer the question of how healthy individuals such as Gandhi work through conflict and crisis when other people are debilitated by lesser strife. In searching for an answer, Erikson examined Gandhi's entire life cycle but concentrated on one particular crisis, which climaxed when a middle-aged Gandhi first used self-imposed fasting as a political weapon.

As a child, Gandhi was close to his mother but experienced conflict with his father. Rather than viewing this situation as an Oedipal conflict, Erikson saw it as Gandhi's opportunity to work out conflict with authority figures—an opportunity Gandhi was to have many times during his life.

Gandhi was born October 2, 1869, in Porbandar, India. As a young man, he studied law in London and was inconspicuous in manner and appearance. Then, dressed like a proper British subject, he returned to India to practice law. After 2 years of unsuccessful practice, he went to South Africa, which, like India, was a

According to Erikson, Mahatma Gandhi developed basic strengths from his several identity crises.

British colony. He intended to remain for a year, but his first serious identity crisis kept him there for more than 20 years.

A week after a judge excluded him from a courtroom, Gandhi was thrown off a train when he refused to give up his seat to a "white" man. These two experiences with racial prejudice changed Gandhi's life. By the time he resolved this identity crisis, his appearance had changed dramatically. No longer attired in silk hat and black coat, he dressed in the cotton loincloth and shawl that were to become familiar to millions of people throughout the world. During those years in South Africa, he evolved the technique of passive resistance known as *Satyagraha* and used it to solve his conflicts with authorities. *Satyagraha* is a Sanskirt term meaning a tenacious, stubborn method of gathering the truth.

After returning to India, Gandhi experienced another identity crisis when, in 1918, at age 49, he became the central figure in a workers' strike against the mill owners at Ahmedabad. Erikson referred to the events surrounding the strike as "The Event" and devoted the core of *Gandhi's Truth* to this crisis. Although this strike was only a minor event in the history of India and received only scant attention in Gandhi's autobiography, Erikson (1969) saw it as having a great impact on Gandhi's identity as a practitioner of militant nonviolence.

The mill workers had pledged to strike if their demands for a 35% pay increase were not met. But the owners, who had agreed among themselves to offer no more than a 20% increase, locked out the workers and tried to break their solidarity by offering the 20% increase to those who would come back to work. Gandhi, the workers' spokesperson, agonized over this impasse. Then, somewhat impetuously, he pledged to eat no more food until the workers' demands were met. This, the first of his 17 "fasts to the death," was not undertaken as a threat to the mill owners but to demonstrate to the workers that a pledge must be kept. In fact, Gandhi feared that the mill owners might surrender out of sympathy for him rather than from recognition of the workers' desperate plight. Indeed, on the third day, the workers and owners reached a compromise that allowed both to save face—the workers would work one day for a 35% increase, one day for a 20% increase, and then for whatever amount an arbitrator decided. The next day Gandhi ended his hunger strike, but his passive resistance had helped shape his identity and had given him a new tool for peaceful political and social change.

Unlike neurotic individuals whose identity crises result in core pathologies, Gandhi had developed strength from this and other crises. Erikson (1969) described the difference between conflicts in great people, such as Gandhi, and psychologically disturbed people: "This, then, is the difference between a case history and a life-history: patients, great or small, are increasingly debilitated by their inner conflicts, but in historical actuality inner conflict only adds an indispensable momentum to all superhuman effort" (p. 363).

Related Research

One of Erikson's major contributions was to extend personality development into adulthood. By expanding Freud's notion of development all the way into old age, Erikson challenged the idea that psychological development stops with childhood. Erikson's most influential legacy has been his theory of development and, in particular, the stages from adolescence into old age. He was one of the first theorists to emphasize the critical period of adolescence and the conflicts revolving around one's search for an identity. Adolescents and young adults often ask: Who am I? Where am I going? And what do I want to do with the rest of my life? How they answer these questions plays an important role in what kinds of relationships they develop, who they marry, and what career paths they follow.

In contrast to most other psychodynamic theorists, Erikson stimulated quite a bit of empirical research, much of it on adolescence, young adulthood, and adulthood. Here we discuss recent research on development in middle adulthood, specifically the stage of generativity.

Generativity and Parenting

Erikson (1982) defined generativity as "the generation of new beings as well as products and new ideas" (p. 67). Generativity is typically expressed not only in bringing up children and fostering growth in young people but also in teaching, mentoring, creating, and storytelling activities that bring new knowledge into existence and pass on old knowledge to the next generation. Dan McAdams and his colleagues (McAdams, 1999; McAdams & de St. Aubin, 1992; Bauer & McAdams, 2004b) have been major figures in research on generativity and have developed the Loyola Generativity Scale (LGS) to measure it. The LGS includes items such as "I have important skills that I try to teach others" and "I do not volunteer to work for a charity." The scale measures several aspects of generativity, including concern for the next generation; creating and maintaining objects and things; and person narration: that is, the subjective story or theme that an adult creates about providing for the next generation.

Using the LGS scale, researchers have investigated the impact of parental generativity on the development of children. Theoretically, parents who have a high sense of generativity should put a great deal of effort and care into raising children and therefore produce offspring who are well-adjusted and happy. Bill Peterson tested this idea in a study of college students and their parents (Peterson, 2006). Peterson predicted that the children of generative parents would not only be happier but also possess a high level of future time perspective, which is a technical way to say the children of generative parents will look toward the future more and do so with an optimistic view of things to come. To test these predictions, parents completed the LGS and students completed a measure of well-being that included items about general happiness, sense of freedom, and confidence in one's self. Students also completed a measure of future time perspective whereby they rated how much they typically think about the next day, next month, the next year, and 10 years from now.

The results were supportive of the general notion that having a sense of generativity is important to effective parenting. The children of highly generative parents had more confidence in themselves, had a stronger sense of freedom, and were just generally happier with life. Additionally, the children of highly generative parents had a stronger future time orientation meaning they spent time thinking about their future and, based on the overall well-being measure, felt pretty good about it. When these findings are considered within Erikson's framework, they make perfect sense. The opposite of generativity is self-absorption and stagnation. If parents are overly self-absorbed and self-indulgent, then they are spending less time being concerned about the well-being of their children. Conversely, if parents are highly generative, then they are concerned about the development of their children and will do everything within their power to provide a stimulating and supportive environment in which children will thrive.

Generativity Versus Stagnation

Like all stages, adulthood consists of two interacting conflicts, generativity and stagnation. Erikson generally considered stagnation and generativity to be opposite ends of the same continuum. In other words, a person who is high on generativity tends to be low on stagnation and vice versa. But recently, researchers have begun to question how opposing these two aspects of adult development really are and have explored stagnation and generativity as somewhat independent constructs (Van Hiel, Mervielde, & De Fruyt, 2006). One reason for this switch from Erikson's model is that it might be possible for people to be both generative and stagnant. Such a situation could happen if a person really wants to be generative and understands the importance of being generative but, for whatever reason, cannot overcome his or her own self-involvement. He or she may realize that generativity is the next stage in development but just cannot get there.

One way to determine the independence of these two constructs is to measure both separately and then measure several outcomes. If they are opposite levels of the same continuum, then when generativity positively predicts an outcome such as mental health, stagnation should negatively predict mental health. But if they do not always match, then the two constructs might be separate concepts. Because stagnation had never been measured separate from generativity before, the researchers had to create a measure from scratch. Based on the description of stagnation provided by other scholars (e.g., Bradley & Marcia, 1998), Van Hiel and colleagues (2006) created a self-report measure consisting of items such as "I often keep a distance between myself and my children" and "It is hard to say what my goals are." To measure generativity, the researchers used the LGS previously described and used in most research on generativity. To see how these two constructs match up to important outcomes, the researchers selected a broad measure of mental health that included the assessment of symptoms related to various personality disorders such as the inability to regulate emotions and intimacy issues.

The results of this study supported the new proposition that stagnation and generativity should be considered independently. For example, stagnation and generativity did not predict mental health outcomes in the same way. Those who were high on stagnation tended to be less able to regulate their emotions; yet, at the same time, generativity was not related to emotion regulation. If only generativity had been measured (and not stagnation separately), then these researchers would not have uncovered the important finding that stagnation is related to problems in emotional regulation. The researchers also found that there are individuals who are high on both generativity and stagnation and that such a personality profile is not healthy in terms of mental and emotional well-being. Compared to people who are high on generativity but low on stagnation, people who are high on both dimensions are less able to regulate their emotions and experience more intimacy difficulties. Both of these qualities are considered to be components of a maladaptive personality.

Conceptually, this research does not differ a great deal from Erikson's model (stagnation and generativity are still included). It does show, however, that for the practical purposes of research and in order to understand personality in adulthood more fully, stagnation and generativity can and sometimes do operate separately and independently in adult development.

Critique of Erikson

Erikson built his theory largely on ethical principles and not necessarily on scientific data. He came to psychology from art and acknowledged that he saw the world more through the eyes of an artist than through those of a scientist. He once wrote that he had nothing to offer except "a way of looking at things" (Erikson, 1963, p. 403). His books are admittedly subjective and personal, which undoubtedly adds to their appeal. Nevertheless, Erikson's theory must be judged by the standards of science, not ethics or art.

The first criterion of a useful theory is its ability to *generate research,* and by this standard, we rate Erikson's theory somewhat higher than average. For example, the topic of ego identity alone has generated several hundred studies, and other aspects of Erikson's developmental stages, such as intimacy versus isolation (Gold & Rogers, 1995) and generativity (Arnett, 2000; Pratt, Norris, Arnold, & Filyer, 1999), as well as the entire life cycle (Whitbourne, Zuschlag, Elliot, & Waterman, 1992), have stimulated active empirical investigations.

Despite this active research, we rate Erikson's theory only average on the criterion of *falsifiability.* Many findings from this body of research can be explained by theories other than Erikson's developmental stages theory.

In its ability to *organize knowledge,* Erikson's theory is limited mostly to developmental stages. It does not adequately address such issues as personal traits or motivation, a limitation that subtracts from the theory's ability to shed meaning on much of what is currently known about human personality. The eight stages of development remain an eloquent statement of what the life cycle should be, and research findings in these areas usually can be fit into an Eriksonian framework. However, the theory lacks sufficient scope to be rated high on this criterion.

As a *guide to action,* Erikson's theory provides many general guidelines, but offers little specific advice. Compared to other theories discussed in this book, it ranks near the top in suggesting approaches to dealing with middle-aged and older adults. Erikson's views on aging have been helpful to people in the field of gerontology, and his ideas on ego identity are nearly always cited in adolescent psychology textbooks. In addition, his concepts of intimacy versus isolation and generativity versus stagnation have much to offer to marriage counselors and others concerned with intimate relationships among young adults.

We rate Erikson's theory high on *internal consistency,* mostly because the terms used to label the different psychosocial crises, basic strengths, and core pathologies are very carefully chosen. English was not Erikson's first language, and his extensive use of a dictionary while writing increased the precision of his terminology. Yet concepts like hope, will, purpose, love, care, and so on are not operationally defined. They have little scientific usefulness, although they rank high in both literary and emotional value. On the other hand, Erikson's epigenetic principle and the eloquence of his description of the eight stages of development mark his theory with conspicuous internal consistency.

On the criterion of simplicity, or *parsimony,* we give the theory a moderate rating. The precision of its terms is a strength, but the descriptions of psychosexual stages and psychosocial crises, especially in the later stages, are not always clearly differentiated. In addition, Erikson used different terms and even different concepts to fill out the 64 boxes that are mostly vacant in Figure 9.2. Such inconsistency subtracts from the theory's simplicity.

🏃 Concept of Humanity

In contrast to Freud, who believed that anatomy was destiny, Erikson suggested that other factors might be responsible for differences between women and men. Citing some of his own research, Erikson (1977) suggested that, although girls and boys have different methods of play, these differences are at least partly a result of different socialization practices. Does this conclusion mean that Erikson agreed with Freud that anatomy is destiny? Erikson's answer was yes, anatomy is destiny, but he quickly qualified that dictum to read: "Anatomy, history, and personality are our combined destiny" (Erikson, 1968, p. 285). In other words, anatomy alone does not determine destiny, but it combines with past events, including social and various personality dimensions such as temperament and intelligence, to determine who a person will become.

How does Erikson's theory conceptualize humanity in terms of the six dimensions we introduced in Chapter 1? First, is the life cycle determined by *external forces* or do people have some *choice* in molding their personalities and shaping their lives? Erikson was not as deterministic as Freud, but neither did he believe strongly in free choice. His position was somewhere in the middle. Although personality is molded in part by culture and history, people retain some limited control over their destiny. People can search for their own identities and are not completely constrained by culture and history. Individuals, in fact, can change history and alter their environment. The two subjects of Erikson's most extensive psychohistories, Martin Luther and Mahatma Gandhi, each had a profound effect on world history and on his own immediate surroundings. Similarly, each of us has the power to determine his or her own life cycles, even though our global impact may be on a lesser scale.

On the dimension of *pessimism versus optimism*, Erikson tended to be somewhat optimistic. Even though core pathologies may predominate early stages of development, humans are not inevitably doomed to continue a pathological existence in later stages. Although weaknesses in early life make it more difficult to acquire basic strengths later on, people remain capable of changing at any stage of life. Each psychosocial conflict consists of a syntonic and a dystonic quality. Each crisis can be resolved in favor of the syntonic, or harmonious element, regardless of past resolutions.

Erikson did not specifically address the issue of *causality versus teleology,* but his view of humanity suggests that people are influenced more by biological and social forces than by their view of the future. People are a product of a particular historical moment and a specific social setting. Although we can set goals and actively strive to achieve these goals, we cannot completely escape the powerful causal forces of anatomy, history, and culture. For this reason, we rate Erikson high on causality.

On the fourth dimension, *conscious versus unconscious determinants,* Erikson's position is mixed. Prior to adolescence, personality is largely shaped by unconscious motivation. Psychosexual and psychosocial conflicts during the first four developmental stages occur before children have firmly established their identity. We seldom are clearly aware of these crises and the ways in which they mold our personalities. From adolescence forward, however, people ordinarily are aware of their actions and most of the reasons underlying those actions.

Erikson's theory, of course, is more *social* than biological, although it does not overlook anatomy and other physiological factors in personality development. Each psychosexual mode has a clear biological component. However, as people advance through the eight stages, social influences become increasingly more powerful. Also, the radius of social relations expands from the single maternal person to a global identification with all humanity.

The sixth dimension for a concept of humanity is *uniqueness versus similarities.* Erikson tended to place more emphasis on individual differences than on universal characteristics. Although people in different cultures advance through the eight developmental stages in the same order, myriad differences are found in the pace of that journey. Each person resolves psychosocial crises in a unique manner, and each uses the basic strengths in a way that is peculiarly theirs.

Key Terms and Concepts

- Erikson's stages of development rest on an *epigenetic principle,* meaning that each component proceeds in a step-by-step fashion with later growth building on earlier development.
- During every stage, people experience an interaction of opposing *syntonic* and *dystonic* attitudes, which leads to a conflict, or *psychosocial crisis.*
- Resolution of this crisis produces a *basic strength* and enables a person to move to the next stage.
- Biological components lay a ground plan for each individual, but a multiplicity of historical and cultural events also shapes *ego identity.*
- Each basic strength has an underlying antipathy that becomes the *core pathology* of that stage.
- The first stage of development is *infancy,* characterized by the *oral-sensory mode,* the psychosocial crisis of basic *trust versus mistrust,* the basic strength of *hope,* and the core pathology of *withdrawal.*
- During *early childhood,* children experience the *anal, urethral, and muscular* psychosexual mode; the psychosocial conflict of *autonomy versus shame and doubt;* the basic strength of *will;* and the core pathology of *compulsion.*
- During the *play age,* children experience *genital-locomotor* psychosexual development and undergo a psychosocial crisis of *initiative versus guilt,* with either the basic strength of *purpose* or the core pathology of *inhibition.*
- *School-age* children are in a period of *sexual latency* but face the psychosocial crisis of *industry versus inferiority,* which produces either the basic strength of *competence* or the core pathology of *inertia.*
- *Adolescence,* or puberty, is a crucial stage because a person's sense of *identity* should emerge from this period. However, *identity confusion* may dominate the psychosocial crisis, thereby postponing identity. *Fidelity* is the basic strength of adolescence; *role repudiation* is its core pathology.
- *Young adulthood,* the time from about age 18 to 30, is characterized by the psychosexual mode of *genitality,* the psychosocial crisis of *intimacy versus isolation,* the basic strength of *love,* and the core pathology of *exclusivity.*
- *Adulthood* is a time when people experience the psychosexual mode of *procreativity,* the psychosocial crisis of *generativity versus stagnation,* the basic strength of *care,* and the core pathology of *rejectivity.*
- *Old age* is marked by the psychosexual mode of *generalized sensuality,* the crisis of *integrity versus despair,* and the basic strength of wisdom or the core pathology of *disdain.*
- Erikson used *psychohistory* (a combination of psychoanalysis and history) to study the identity crises of Martin Luther, Mahatma Gandhi, and others.

PART THREE

Humanistic/ Existential Theories

Maslow: Holistic-Dynamic Theory

Maslow

College professors and students have long recognized that some intellectually "average" students are able to make good grades, whereas some intellectually superior students make only average grades, and some bright students actually flunk out of school. What factors account for this situation? Motivation is one likely suspect. Personal health, death in the immediate family, and too many jobs are other possibilities.

Some years ago, a brilliant young college student was struggling through his third school. Although he performed reasonably well in courses that aroused his interest, his work was so poor in other classes that he was placed on academic probation. Later, this young man took an IQ test on which he scored 195, a score so high that it can be achieved by only about one person in several million. Therefore, lack of intellectual ability was not the reason for this young man's lackluster college performance.

Like some other young men, this student was deeply in love, a condition that made it difficult to concentrate on school work. Being hopelessly shy, the young man could not muster the courage to approach his beloved in any romantic fashion. Interestingly, the young woman who was the object of his affections was also his first cousin. This situation allowed him to visit his cousin on the pretext of calling on his aunt. He loved his cousin in a distant, bashful sort of way, having never touched her nor expressed his feelings. Then, suddenly a fortuitous event changed his life. While visiting his aunt, his cousin's older sister shoved the young man toward his cousin, virtually ordering him to kiss her. He did, and to his surprise his cousin did not fight back. She kissed him, and from that time on his life became meaningful.

The bashful young man in this story was Abraham Maslow, and his cousin was Bertha Goodman. After the fortuitous first kiss, Abe and Bertha were quickly married, and this marriage changed him from a mediocre college student to a brilliant scholar who eventually shaped the course of humanistic psychology in the United States. This story should not be seen as a recommendation for marrying one's first cousin, but it does illustrate how brilliant people sometimes need only a small shove to reach their potential.

Overview of Holistic-Dynamic Theory

The personality theory of Abraham Maslow has variously been called humanistic theory, transpersonal theory, the third force in psychology, the fourth force in personality, needs theory, and self-actualization theory. However, Maslow (1970) referred to it as a **holistic-dynamic theory** because it assumes that the whole person is constantly being motivated by one need or another and that people have the potential to grow toward psychological health, that is, *self-actualization.* To attain self-actualization, people must satisfy lower level needs such as hunger, safety, love, and esteem. Only after they are relatively satisfied in each of these needs can they reach self-actualization.

The theories of Maslow, Gordon Allport, Carl Rogers, Rollo May, and others are sometimes thought of as the **third force** in psychology. (The first force was psychoanalysis and its modifications; the second was behaviorism and its various forms). Like these other theorists, Maslow accepted some of the tenets of psychoanalysis and behaviorism. As a graduate student, he had studied Freud's

Interpretation of Dreams (Freud, 1900/1953) and became keenly interested in psychoanalysis. In addition, his graduate-level research with primates was greatly influenced by the work of John B. Watson (Watson, 1925). In his mature theory, however, Maslow criticized both psychoanalysis and behaviorism for their limited views of humanity and their inadequate understanding of the psychologically healthy person. Maslow believed that humans have a higher nature than either psychoanalysis or behaviorism would suggest; and he spent the latter years of his life trying to discover the nature of psychologically healthy individuals.

Biography of Abraham H. Maslow

Abraham Harold (Abe) Maslow had, perhaps, the most lonely and miserable childhood of any person discussed in this book. Born in Manhattan, New York, on April 1, 1908, Maslow spent his unhappy childhood in Brooklyn. Maslow was the oldest of seven children born to Samuel Maslow and Rose Schilosky Maslow. As a child, Maslow's life was filled with intense feelings of shyness, inferiority, and depression.

Maslow was not especially close to either parent, but he tolerated his often-absent father, a Russian-Jewish immigrant who made a living preparing barrels. Toward his mother, however, Maslow felt hatred and deep-seated animosity, not only during his childhood, but until the day she died just a couple of years before Maslow's own death. Despite several years of psychoanalysis, he never overcame the intense hatred of his mother and refused to attend her funeral, despite pleas from his siblings who did not share his hateful feelings for their mother. A year before his own death, Maslow (1969) entered this reflection in his diary:

> What I had reacted against and totally hated and rejected was not only her
> physical appearance, but also her values and world view, her stinginess, her total
> selfishness, her lack of love for anyone else in the world, even her own husband
> and children . . . her assumption that anyone was wrong who disagreed with her,
> her lack of concern for her grandchildren, her lack of friends, her sloppiness and
> dirtiness, her lack of family feeling for her own parents and siblings. . . . I've
> always wondered where my Utopianism, ethical stress, humanism, stress on
> kindness, love, friendship, and all the rest came from. I knew certainly of the
> direct consequences of having no mother-love. But the whole thrust of my life-
> philosophy and all my research and theorizing also has its roots in a hatred for
> and revulsion against everything she stood for. (p. 958)

Edward Hoffman (1988) reported a story that vividly describes Rose Maslow's cruelty. One day young Maslow found two abandoned kittens in the neighborhood. Moved with pity, he brought the kittens home, put them in the basement, and fed them milk from a dish. When his mother saw the kittens, she became furious and, as the young boy watched, she smashed the kittens' heads against the basement walls until they were dead.

Maslow's mother was also a very religious woman who often threatened young Maslow with punishment from God. As a young boy, Maslow decided to test his mother's threats by intentionally misbehaving. When no divine retribution befell him, he reasoned that his mother's warnings were not scientifically sound. From such experiences, Maslow learned to hate and mistrust religion and to become a committed atheist.

Despite his atheistic views, he felt the sting of anti-Semitism not only in childhood but also during his adult years. Possibly as a defense against the anti-Semitic attitudes of his classmates, he turned to books and scholarly pursuits. He loved to read, but to reach the safety of the public library, he had to avoid the anti-Semitic gangs that roamed his Brooklyn neighborhood and that needed no excuse to terrorize young Maslow and other Jewish boys.

Being intellectually gifted, Abe found some solace during his years at Boys High School in Brooklyn, where his grades were only slightly better than average. At the same time, he developed a close friendship with his cousin Will Maslow, an outgoing, socially active person. Through this relationship, Abe himself developed some social skills and was involved in several school activities (Hoffman, 1988).

After Maslow graduated from Boys High School, his cousin Will encouraged him to apply to Cornell University, but lacking self-confidence, Maslow selected the less prestigious City College of New York. At about this time, his parents divorced and he and his father became less emotionally distant. Maslow's father had wanted his oldest son to be a lawyer, and while attending City College, Maslow enrolled in law school. However, he walked out of law classes one night, leaving his books behind. Significantly, he felt that law dealt too much with evil people and was not sufficiently concerned with the good. His father, although initially disappointed, eventually accepted Maslow's decision to quit law school (M. H. Hall, 1968).

As a student at City College, Maslow did well in philosophy and other courses that sparked his interest. However, in courses he did not like, he performed so poorly that he was placed on academic probation. After three semesters, he transferred to Cornell University in upstate New York partly to be closer to his cousin Will, who attended that school, but also to distance himself from his first cousin Bertha Goodman, with whom he was falling in love (Hoffman, 1988). At Cornell, too, Maslow's scholastic work was only mediocre. His introductory psychology professor was Edward B. Titchener, a renowned pioneer in psychology who taught all his classes in full academic robes. Maslow was not impressed. He regarded Titchener's approach to psychology as cold, "bloodless," and having nothing to do with people.

After one semester at Cornell, Maslow returned to the City College of New York, now to be nearer to Bertha. After the fortuitious event described in the opening vignette, Abe and Bertha were soon married but not before overcoming his parents' resistance. Maslow's parents objected to the marriage partly because he was only 20 and she 19. However, their strongest fear was that a marriage between first cousins might result in hereditary defects in any possible offspring. This fear was ironic in light of the fact that Maslow's parents themselves were first cousins and had six healthy children. (One daughter died during infancy but not because of any genetic defect.)

One semester before his marriage, Maslow had enrolled at the University of Wisconsin, from which he received a BA degree in philosophy. In addition, he was quite interested in John B. Watson's behaviorism, and this interest prompted him to take enough psychology courses to meet prerequisites for a PhD in psychology. As a graduate student, he worked closely with Harry Harlow, who was just beginning his research with monkeys. Maslow's dissertation research on dominance and sexual behavior of monkeys suggested that social dominance was a more powerful motive than sex, at least among primates (Blum, 2002).

In 1934, Maslow received his doctorate, but he could not find an academic position, partly because of the Great Depression and partly because of an anti-Semitic prejudice still strong on many American campuses in those years. Consequently, he continued to teach at Wisconsin for a short time and even enrolled in medical school there. However, he was repulsed by the cold and dispassionate attitude of surgeons who could cut off diseased body parts with no discernible emotion. To Maslow, medical school—like law school—reflected an unemotional and negative view of people, and he was both disturbed and bored by his experiences in medical school. Whenever Maslow became bored with something, he usually quit it, and medical school was no exception (Hoffman, 1988).

The following year he returned to New York to become E. L. Thorndike's research assistant at Teachers College, Columbia University. Maslow, a mediocre student during his days at City College and Cornell, scored 195 on Thorndike's intelligence test, prompting Thorndike to give his assistant free rein to do as he wished. Maslow's fertile mind thrived in this situation; but after a year and a half of doing research on human dominance and sexuality, he left Columbia to join the faculty of Brooklyn College, a newly established school whose students were mostly bright, young adolescents from working-class homes, much like Maslow himself 10 years earlier (Hoffman, 1988).

Living in New York during the 1930s and 1940s afforded Maslow an opportunity to come into contact with many of the European psychologists who had escaped Nazi rule. In fact, Maslow surmised that, of all the people who had ever lived, he had the best teachers (Goble, 1970). Among others, he met and learned from Erich Fromm, Karen Horney, Max Wertheimer, and Kurt Goldstein. He was influenced by each of these people, most of whom conducted lectures at the New School for Social Research. Maslow also became associated with Alfred Adler, who was living in New York at that time. Adler held seminars in his home on Friday nights, and Maslow was a frequent visitor to these sessions, as was Julian Rotter (see Chapter 17).

Another of Maslow's mentors was Ruth Benedict, an anthropologist at Columbia University. In 1938, Benedict encouraged Maslow to conduct anthropological studies among the Northern Blackfoot Indians of Alberta, Canada. His work among these Native Americans taught him that differences among cultures were superficial and that the Northern Blackfoot were first people and only second were they Blackfoot Indians. This insight helped Maslow in later years to see that his famous hierarchy of needs applied equally to everyone.

During the mid-1940s, Maslow's health began to deteriorate. In 1946, at age 38, he suffered a strange illness that left him weak, faint, and exhausted. The next year he took a medical leave and, with Bertha and their two daughters, moved to Pleasanton, California, where, in name only, he was plant manager of a branch of the Maslow Cooperage Corporation. His light work schedule enabled him to read biographies and histories in a search for information on self-actualizing people. After a year, his health had improved and he went back to teaching at Brooklyn College.

In 1951, Maslow took a position as chairman of the psychology department at the recently established Brandeis University in Waltham, Massachusetts. During his Brandeis years, he began writing extensively in his journals, jotting down at irregular intervals his thoughts, opinions, feelings, social activities, important conversations, and concerns for his health (Maslow, 1979).

Despite achieving fame during the 1960s, Maslow became increasingly disenchanted with his life at Brandeis. Some students rebelled against his teaching methods, demanding more experiential involvement and less of an intellectual and scientific approach.

In addition to work-related problems, Maslow suffered a severe but nonfatal heart attack in December of 1967. He then learned that his strange malady more than 20 years earlier had been an undiagnosed heart attack. Now in poor health and disappointed with the academic atmosphere at Brandeis, Maslow accepted an offer to join the Saga Administrative Corporation in Menlo Park, California. He had no particular job there and was free to think and write as he wished. He enjoyed that freedom, but on June 8, 1970, he suddenly collapsed and died of a massive heart attack. He was 62.

Maslow received many honors during his lifetime, including his election to the presidency of the American Psychological Association for the year 1967–1968. At the time of his death, he was well known, not only within the profession of psychology, but among educated people generally, particularly in business management, marketing, theology, counseling, education, nursing, and other health-related fields.

Maslow's personal life was filled with pain, both physical and psychological. As an adolescent, he was terribly shy, unhappy, isolated, and self-rejecting. In later years, he was often in poor physical health, suffering from a series of ailments, including chronic heart problems. His journals (Maslow, 1979) are sprinkled with references to poor health. In his last journal entry (May 7, 1970), a month before his death, he complained about people expecting him to be a courageous leader and spokesperson. He wrote: "I am not temperamentally 'courageous.' My courage is really an *overcoming* of all sorts of inhibitions, politeness, gentleness, timidities—and it always cost me a lot in fatigue, tension, apprehension, bad sleep" (p. 1307).

Maslow's View of Motivation

Maslow's theory of personality rests on several basic assumptions regarding motivation. First, Maslow (1970) adopted a *holistic approach to motivation:* That is, the whole person, not any single part or function, is motivated.

Second, *motivation is usually complex,* meaning that a person's behavior may spring from several separate motives. For example, the desire for sexual union may be motivated not only by a genital need but also by needs for dominance, companionship, love, and self-esteem. Moreover, the motivation for a behavior may be unconscious or unknown to the person. For example, the motivation for a college student to make a high grade may mask the need for dominance or power. Maslow's acceptance of the importance of unconscious motivation represents one important way in which he differed from Gordon Allport (Chapter 13). Whereas Allport might say that a person plays golf just for the fun of it, Maslow would look beneath the surface for underlying and often complex reasons for playing golf.

A third assumption is that *people are continually motivated by one need or another.* When one need is satisfied, it ordinarily loses its motivational power and is then replaced by another need. For example, as long as people's hunger needs are frustrated, they will strive for food; but when they do have enough to eat, they move on to other needs such as safety, friendship, and self-worth.

Another assumption is that *all people everywhere are motivated by the same basic needs.* The *manner* in which people in different cultures obtain food, build shelters, express friendship, and so forth may vary widely, but the fundamental needs for food, safety, and friendship are common to the entire species.

A final assumption concerning motivation is that *needs can be arranged on a hierarchy* (Maslow, 1943, 1970).

Hierarchy of Needs

Maslow's **hierarchy of needs** concept assumes that lower level needs must be satisfied or at least relatively satisfied before higher level needs become motivators. The five needs composing this hierarchy are **conative needs,** meaning that they have a striving or motivational character. These needs, which Maslow often referred to as *basic needs,* can be arranged on a hierarchy or staircase, with each ascending step representing a higher need but one less basic to survival (see Figure 10.1). Lower level needs have *prepotency* over higher level needs; that is, they must be satisfied or mostly satisfied before higher level needs become activated. For example, anyone motivated by esteem or self-actualization must have previously satisfied needs for food and safety. Hunger and safety, therefore, have prepotency over both esteem and self-actualization.

Maslow (1970) listed the following needs in order of their prepotency: physiological, safety, love and belongingness, esteem, and self-actualization.

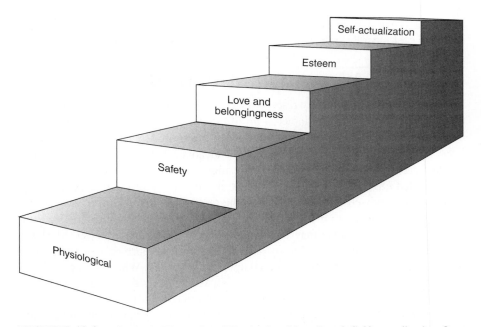

FIGURE 10.1   *Maslow's Hierarchy of Needs. One Must Reach Self-actualization One Step at a Time.*

Physiological Needs

The most basic needs of any person are **physiological needs,** including food, water, oxygen, maintenance of body temperature, and so on. Physiological needs are the most prepotent of all. Perpetually hungry people are motivated to eat—not to make friends or gain self-esteem. They do not see beyond food, and as long as this need remains unsatisfied, their primary motivation is to obtain something to eat.

In affluent societies, most people satisfy their hunger needs as a matter of course. They usually have enough to eat, so when they say they are hungry, they are really speaking of appetites, not hunger. A truly hungry person will not be overly particular about taste, smell, temperature, or texture of the food.

Maslow (1970) said: "It is quite true that man lives by bread alone—when there is no bread" (p. 38). When people do not have their physiological needs satisfied, they live primarily for those needs and strive constantly to satisfy them. Starving people become preoccupied with food and are willing to do nearly anything to obtain it (Keys, Brozek, Henschel, Mickelsen, & Taylor, 1950).

Physiological needs differ from other needs in at least two important respects. First, they are the only needs that can be completely satisfied or even overly satisfied. People can get enough to eat so that food completely loses its motivational power. For someone who has just finished a large meal, the thought of more food can even have a nauseating effect. A second characteristic peculiar to physiological needs is their recurring nature. After people have eaten, they will eventually become hungry again; they constantly need to replenish their food and water supply; and one breath of air must be followed by another. Other level needs, however, do not constantly recur. For example, people who have at least partially satisfied their love and esteem needs will remain confident that they can continue to satisfy their love and esteem needs.

Safety Needs

When people have partially satisfied their physiological needs, they become motivated by **safety needs,** including physical security, stability, dependency, protection, and freedom from threatening forces such as war, terrorism, illness, fear, anxiety, danger, chaos, and natural disasters. The needs for law, order, and structure are also safety needs (Maslow, 1970).

Safety needs differ from physiological needs in that they cannot be overly satiated; people can never be completely protected from meteorites, fires, floods, or the dangerous acts of others.

In societies not at war, most healthy adults satisfy their safety needs most of the time, thus making these needs relatively unimportant. Children, however, are more often motivated by safety needs because they live with such threats as darkness, animals, strangers, and punishments from parents. Also, some adults also feel relatively unsafe because they retain irrational fears from childhood that cause them to act as if they were afraid of parental punishment. They spend far more energy than do healthy people trying to satisfy safety needs, and when they are not successful in their attempts, they suffer from what Maslow (1970) called **basic anxiety.**

Love and Belongingness Needs

After people partially satisfy their physiological and safety needs, they become motivated by **love and belongingness needs,** such as the desire for friendship; the wish for a mate and children; the need to belong to a family, a club, a neighborhood, or a

In addition to physiological and safety needs, children have love and belongingness needs.

nation. Love and belongingness also include some aspects of sex and human contact as well as the need to both give and receive love (Maslow, 1970).

People who have had their love and belongingness needs adequately satisfied from early years do not panic when denied love. These people have confidence that they are accepted by those who are important to them, so when other people reject them, they do not feel devastated.

A second group of people consists of those who have never experienced love and belongingness, and, therefore, they are incapable of giving love. They have seldom or never been hugged, or cuddled nor experienced any form of verbal love. Maslow believed that these people will eventually learn to devalue love and to take its absence for granted.

A third category includes those people who have received love and belongingness only in small doses. Because they receive only a taste of love and belongingness, they will be strongly motivated to seek it. In other words, people who have received only a little amount of love have stronger needs for affection and acceptance than do people who have received either a healthy amount of love or no love at all (Maslow, 1970).

Children need love in order to grow psychologically, and their attempts to satisfy this need are usually straightforward and direct. Adults, too, need love, but their attempts to attain it are sometimes cleverly disguised. These adults often engage in self-defeating behaviors, such as pretending to be aloof from other people or adopting a cynical, cold, and calloused manner in their interpersonal relationships. They may give the appearance of self-sufficiency and independence, but in reality they have a strong need to be accepted and loved by other people. Other adults whose love needs remain largely unsatisfied adopt more obvious ways of trying to satisfy them, but they undermine their own success by striving too hard. Their constant supplications for acceptance and affection leave others suspicious, unfriendly, and impenetrable.

Esteem Needs

To the extent that people satisfy their love and belongingness needs, they are free to pursue **esteem needs,** which include self-respect, confidence, competence, and the knowledge that others hold them in high esteem. Maslow (1970) identified two levels of esteem needs—reputation and self-esteem. Reputation is the perception of the prestige, recognition, or fame a person has achieved in the eyes of others, whereas self-esteem is a person's own feelings of worth and confidence. Self-esteem is based on more than reputation or prestige; it reflects a "desire for strength, for achievement, for adequacy, for mastery and competence, for confidence in the face of the world, and for independence and freedom" (p. 45). In other words, self-esteem is based on real competence and not merely on others' opinions. Once people meet their esteem needs, they stand on the threshold of self-actualization, the highest need recognized by Maslow.

Self-Actualization Needs

When lower level needs are satisfied, people proceed more or less automatically to the next level. However, once esteem needs are met, they do not always move to the level of self-actualization. Originally, Maslow (1950) assumed that self-actualization needs become potent whenever esteem needs have been met. However, during the 1960s, he realized that many of the young students at Brandeis and other campuses around the country had all their lower needs gratified, including reputation and self-esteem, and yet they did not become self-actualizing (Frick, 1982; Hoffman, 1988; Maslow, 1971). Why some people step over the threshold from esteem to self-actualization and others do not is a matter of whether or not they embrace the B-values (B-values will be discussed in the section titled Self-Actualization). People who highly respect such values as truth, beauty, justice, and the other B-values become self-actualizing after their esteem needs are met, whereas people who do not embrace these values are frustrated in their self-actualization needs even though they have satisfied each of their other basic needs.

Although not necessarily artistic, self-actualizers are creative in their own ways.

Self-actualization needs include self-fulfillment, the realization of all one's potential, and a desire to become creative in the full sense of the word (Maslow, 1970). People who have reached the level of self-actualization become fully human, satisfying needs that others merely glimpse or never view at all. They are natural in the same sense that animals and infants are natural; that is, they express their basic human needs and do not allow them to be suppressed by culture.

Self-actualizing people maintain their feelings of self-esteem even when scorned, rejected, and dismissed by other people. In other words, self-actualizers are not dependent on the satisfaction of either love or esteem needs; they become independent from the lower level needs that gave them birth. (We present a more complete sketch of self-actualizing people in the section titled Self-Actualization.)

In addition to these five conative needs, Maslow identified three other categories of needs—*aesthetic, cognitive,* and *neurotic.* The satisfaction of aesthetic and cognitive needs is consistent with psychological health, whereas the deprivation of these two needs results in pathology. Neurotic needs, however, lead to pathology whether or not they are satisfied.

Aesthetic Needs

Unlike conative needs, **aesthetic needs** are not universal, but at least some people in every culture seem to be motivated by the need for beauty and aesthetically pleasing experiences (Maslow, 1967). From the days of the cave dwellers down to the present time, some people have produced art for art's sake.

People with strong aesthetic needs desire beautiful and orderly surroundings, and when these needs are not met, they become sick in the same way that they become sick when their conative needs are frustrated. People prefer beauty to ugliness, and they may even become physically and spiritually ill when forced to live in squalid, disorderly environments (Maslow, 1970).

Cognitive Needs

Most people have a desire to know, to solve mysteries, to understand, and to be curious. Maslow (1970) called these desires **cognitive needs.** When cognitive needs are blocked, all needs on Maslow's hierarchy are threatened; that is, knowledge is necessary to satisfy each of the five conative needs. People can gratify their physiological needs by knowing how to secure food, safety needs by knowing how to build a shelter, love needs by knowing how to relate to people, esteem needs by knowing how to acquire some level of self-confidence, and self-actualization by fully using their cognitive potential.

Maslow (1968b, 1970) believed that healthy people desire to know more, to theorize, to test hypotheses, to uncover mysteries, or to find out how something works just for the satisfaction of knowing. However, people who have not satisfied their cognitive needs, who have been consistently lied to, have had their curiosity stifled, or have been denied information, become pathological, a pathology that takes the form of skepticism, disillusionment, and cynicism.

Neurotic Needs

The satisfaction of conative, aesthetic, and cognitive needs is basic to one's physical and psychological health, and their frustration leads to some level of illness. However, **neurotic needs** lead only to stagnation and pathology (Maslow, 1970).

By definition, neurotic needs are nonproductive. They perpetuate an unhealthy style of life and have no value in the striving for self-actualization. Neurotic needs are usually reactive; that is, they serve as compensation for unsatisfied basic needs. For example, a person who does not satisfy safety needs may develop a strong desire to hoard money or property. The hoarding drive is a neurotic need that leads to pathology whether or not it is satisfied. Similarly, a neurotic person may be able to establish a close relationship with another person, but that relationship may be a neurotic, symbiotic one that leads to a pathological relationship rather than genuine love. Maslow (1970) presented yet another example of a neurotic need. A person strongly motivated by power can acquire nearly unlimited power, but that does not make the person less neurotic or less demanding of additional power. "It makes little difference for ultimate health whether a neurotic need be gratified or frustrated" (Maslow, 1970, p. 274).

General Discussion of Needs

Maslow (1970) estimated that the hypothetical average person has his or her needs satisfied to approximately these levels: physiological, 85%; safety, 70%; love and belongingness, 50%; esteem, 40%; and self-actualization, 10%. The more a lower level need is satisfied, the greater the emergence of the next level need. For example, if love needs are only 10% satisfied, then esteem needs may not be active at all. But if love needs are 25% satisfied, then esteem may emerge 5% as a need. If love is 75% satisfied, then esteem may emerge 50%, and so on. Needs, therefore, emerge gradually, and a person may be simultaneously motivated by needs from two or more levels. For example, a self-actualizing person may be the honorary guest at a dinner given by close friends in a peaceful restaurant. The act of eating gratifies a physiological need; but at the same time, the guest of honor may be satisfying safety, love, esteem, and self-actualization needs.

Reversed Order of Needs

Even though needs are generally satisfied in the hierarchical order shown in Figure 10.1, occasionally they are reversed. For some people, the drive for creativity (a self-actualization need) may take precedence over safety and physiological needs. An enthusiastic artist may risk safety and health to complete an important work. For years, the late sculptor Korczak Ziolkowski endangered his health and abandoned companionship to work on carving a mountain in the Black Hills into a monument to Chief Crazy Horse.

Reversals, however, are usually more apparent than real, and some seemingly obvious deviations in the order of needs are not variations at all. If we understood the *unconscious motivation* underlying the behavior, we would recognize that the needs are not reversed.

Unmotivated Behavior

Maslow believed that even though all behaviors have a cause, some behaviors are not motivated. In other words, not all determinants are motives. Some behavior is not caused by needs but by other factors such as conditioned reflexes, maturation, or drugs. Motivation is limited to the striving for the satisfaction of some need. Much of what Maslow (1970) called "expressive behavior" is unmotivated.

Expressive and Coping Behavior

Maslow (1970) distinguished between expressive behavior (which is often unmotivated) and coping behavior (which is always motivated and aimed at satisfying a need).

Expressive behavior is often an end in itself and serves no other purpose than to be. It is frequently unconscious and usually takes place naturally and with little effort. It has no goals or aim but is merely the person's mode of expression. Expressive behavior includes such actions as slouching, looking stupid, being relaxed, showing anger, and expressing joy. Expressive behavior can continue even in the absence of reinforcement or reward. For example, a frown, a blush, or a twinkle of the eye is not ordinarily specifically reinforced.

Expressive behaviors also include one's gait, gestures, voice, and smile (even when alone). A person, for example, may express a methodical, compulsive personality simply because she is what she is and not because of any need to do so. Other examples of expression include art, play, enjoyment, appreciation, wonder, awe, and excitement. Expressive behavior is usually unlearned, spontaneous, and determined by forces within the person rather than by the environment.

On the other hand, *coping behavior* is ordinarily conscious, effortful, learned, and determined by the external environment. It involves the individual's attempts to cope with the environment; to secure food and shelter; to make friends; and to receive acceptance, appreciation, and prestige from others. Coping behavior serves some aim or goal (although not always conscious or known to the person), and it is always motivated by some deficit need (Maslow, 1970).

Deprivation of Needs

Lack of satisfaction of any of the basic needs leads to some kind of pathology. Deprivation of physiological needs results in malnutrition, fatigue, loss of energy, obsession with sex, and so on. Threats to one's safety lead to fear, insecurity, and dread. When love needs go unfulfilled, a person becomes defensive, overly aggressive, or socially timid. Lack of esteem results in the illnesses of self-doubt, self-depreciation, and lack of confidence. Deprivation of self-actualization needs also leads to pathology, or more accurately, **metapathology.** Maslow (1967) defined metapathology as the absence of values, the lack of fulfillment, and the loss of meaning in life.

Instinctoid Nature of Needs

Maslow (1970) hypothesizes that some human needs are innately determined even though they can be modified by learning. He called these needs **instinctoid needs.** Sex, for example, is a basic physiological need, but the manner in which it is expressed depends on learning. For most people, then, sex is an instinctoid need.

One criterion for separating instinctoid needs from noninstinctoid needs is the level of pathology upon frustration. The thwarting of instinctoid needs produces pathology, whereas the frustration of noninstinctoid needs does not. For example, when people are denied sufficient love, they become sick and are blocked from achieving psychological health. Likewise, when people are frustrated in satisfying their physiological, safety, esteem, and self-actualization needs, they become sick. Therefore, these needs are instinctoid. On the other hand, the need to comb one's hair or to speak one's native tongue is learned, and the frustration of these needs does not ordinarily produce illness. If one would become psychologically ill as the result of not being able to comb one's hair or to speak one's native language, then the frustrated need is actually a basic instinctoid need, perhaps love and belongingness or possibly esteem.

A second criterion for distinguishing between instinctoid and noninstinctoid needs is that instinctoid needs are persistent and their satisfaction leads to psychological health. Noninstinctoid needs, in contrast, are usually temporary and their satisfaction is not a prerequisite for health.

A third distinction is that instinctoid needs are species-specific. Therefore, animal instincts cannot be used as a model for studying human motivation. Only humans can be motivated by esteem and self-actualization.

Fourth, though difficult to change, instinctoid needs can be molded, inhibited, or altered by environmental influences. Because many instinctoid needs (e.g., love) are weaker than cultural forces (e.g., aggression in the form of crime or war), Maslow (1970) insisted that society should "protect the weak, subtle, and tender instinctoid needs if they are not to be overwhelmed by the tougher more powerful culture" (p. 82). Stated another way, even though instinctoid needs are basic and unlearned, they can be changed and even destroyed by the more powerful forces of civilization. Hence, a healthy society should seek ways in which its members can receive satisfaction not only for physiological and safety needs but for love, esteem, and self-actualization needs as well.

Comparison of Higher and Lower Needs

Important similarities and differences exist between higher level needs (love, esteem, and self-actualization) and lower level needs (physiological and safety). Higher needs are similar to lower ones in that they are instinctoid. Maslow (1970) insisted that love, esteem, and self-actualization are just as biological as thirst, sex, and hunger.

Differences between higher needs and lower ones are those of degree and not of kind. First, higher level needs are later on the phylogenetic or evolutionary scale. For instance, only humans (a relatively recent species) have the need for self-actualization. Also, higher needs appear later during the course of individual development; lower level needs must be cared for in infants and children before higher level needs become operative.

Second, higher level needs produce more happiness and more peak experiences, although satisfaction of lower level needs may produce a degree of pleasure. Hedonistic pleasure, however, is usually temporary and not comparable to the quality of happiness produced by the satisfaction of higher needs. Also, the satisfaction of higher level needs is more subjectively desirable to those people who have experienced both higher and lower level needs. In other words, a person who has reached the level of self-actualization would have no motivation to return to a lower stage of development (Maslow, 1970).

Self-Actualization

Maslow's ideas on self-actualization began soon after he received his PhD, when he became puzzled about why two of his teachers in New York City—anthropologist Ruth Benedict and psychologist Max Wertheimer—were so different from average people. To Maslow, these two people represented the highest level of human development, and he called this level "self-actualization."

Maslow's Quest for the Self-Actualizing Person

What traits made Wertheimer and Benedict so special? To answer this question, Maslow began to take notes on these two people; and he hoped to find others whom he could call a "Good Human Being." However, he had trouble finding them. The young students in his classes were willing volunteers, but none of them seemed to match Wertheimer and Benedict as Good Human Beings, causing Maslow to wonder if 20-year-old college students could be Good Human Beings (Hoffman, 1988).

Maslow found a number of older people who seemed to have some of the characteristics for which he was searching, but when he interviewed these people to learn what made them special, he was almost always disappointed. Typically, he found them to be "well-adjusted . . . but they have no flame, spark, excitement, good dedication, feeling of responsibility" (Lowry, 1973, p. 87). Maslow was forced to conclude that emotional security and good adjustment were not dependable predictors of a Good Human Being.

Maslow faced additional handicaps in his quest for whom he now called the "self-actualizing person." First, he was trying to find a personality syndrome that had never been clearly identified. Second, many of the people he believed to be self-actualizing refused to participate in his search. They weren't much interested in what Professor Maslow was trying to do. Maslow (1968a) later commented that not one single person he identified as definitely self-actualizing would agree to be tested. They seemed to value their privacy too much to share themselves with the world.

Rather than being discouraged by his inability to find self-actualizing people, Maslow decided to take a different approach—he began reading biographies of famous people to see if he could find self-actualizing people among the saints, sages, national heroes, and artists. While learning about the lives of Thomas Jefferson, Abraham Lincoln (in his later years), Albert Einstein, William James, Albert Schweitzer, Benedict de Spinoza, Jane Addams, and other great people, Maslow suddenly had an "Aha" experience. Rather than asking "What makes Max Wertheimer and Ruth Benedict self-actualizing?" he turned the question around and asked, "Why are we not all self-actualizing?" This new slant on the problem gradually changed Maslow's conception of humanity and expanded his list of self-actualizing people.

Once he had learned to ask the right questions, Maslow continued his quest for the self-actualizing person. To facilitate his search, he identified a syndrome for psychological health. After selecting a sample of potentially healthy individuals, he carefully studied those people to build a personality syndrome. Next, he refined his original definition and then reselected potential self-actualizers, retaining some, eliminating others, and adding new ones. Then he repeated the entire procedure with the second group, making some changes in the definition and the criteria of self-actualization. Maslow (1970) continued this cyclical process to a third or fourth selection group or until he was satisfied that he had refined a vague, unscientific concept into a precise and scientific definition of the self-actualizing person.

Criteria for Self-Actualization

What criteria did these and other self-actualizing people possess? First, *they were free from psychopathology.* They were neither neurotic nor psychotic nor did they have a tendency toward psychological disturbances. This point is an important negative criterion because some neurotic and psychotic individuals have some things in common with self-actualizing people: namely, such characteristics as a heightened sense of reality, mystical experiences, creativity, and detachment from other people. Maslow eliminated from the list of possible self-actualizing people anyone who showed clear signs of psychopathology—excepting some psychosomatic illnesses.

Second, these *self-actualizing people had progressed through the hierarchy of needs* and therefore lived above the subsistence level of existence and had no ever-present threat to their safety. Also, they experienced love and had a well-rooted sense of self-worth. Because they had their lower level needs satisfied, self-actualizing people were better able to tolerate the frustration of these needs, even in the face of criticism and scorn. They are capable of loving a wide variety of people but have no obligation to love everyone.

Maslow's third criterion for self-actualization was the *embracing of the B-values.* His self-actualizing people felt comfortable with and even demanded truth, beauty, justice, simplicity, humor, and each of the other B-values that we discuss later.

The final criterion for reaching self-actualization was "full use and exploitation of talents, capacities, potentialities, etc." (Maslow, 1970, p. 150). In other words, his self-actualizing individuals *fulfilled their needs to grow, to develop, and to increasingly become what they were capable of becoming.*

Values of Self-Actualizers

Maslow (1971) held that self-actualizing people are motivated by the "eternal verities," what he called **B-values.** These "Being" values are indicators of psychological health and are opposed to deficiency needs, which motivate non-self-actualizers. B-values are not needs in the same sense that food, shelter, or companionship are. Maslow termed B-values "metaneeds" to indicate that they are the ultimate level of needs. He distinguished between ordinary need motivation and the motives of self-actualizing people, which he called **metamotivation.**

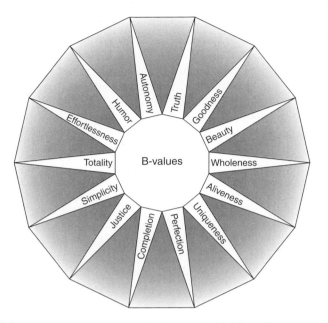

FIGURE 10.2   *Maslow's B-values: A Single Jewel with Many Facets.*

Metamotivation is characterized by expressive rather than coping behavior and is associated with the B-values. It differentiates self-actualizing people from those who are not. In other words, metamotivation was Maslow's tentative answer to the problem of why some people have their lower needs satisfied, are capable of giving and receiving love, possess a great amount of confidence and self-esteem, and yet fail to pass over the threshold to self-actualization. The lives of these people are meaningless and lacking in B-values. Only people who live among the B-values are self-actualizing, and they alone are capable of metamotivation.

Maslow (1964, 1970) identified 14 B-values, but the exact number is not important because ultimately all become one, or at least all are highly correlated. The values of self-actualizing people include *truth, goodness, beauty, wholeness* or the *transcendence of dichotomies, aliveness* or *spontaneity, uniqueness, perfection, completion, justice and order, simplicity, richness* or *totality, effortlessness, playfulness* or *humor,* and *self-sufficiency* or *autonomy* (see Figure 10.2).

These values distinguish self-actualizing people from those whose psychological growth is stunted after they reach esteem needs. Maslow (1970) hypothesized that when people's metaneeds are not met, they experience illness, an existential illness. All people have a holistic tendency to move toward completeness or totality; and when this movement is thwarted, they suffer feelings of inadequacy, disintegration, and unfulfillment. Absence of the B-values leads to pathology just as surely as lack of food results in malnutrition. When denied the truth, people suffer from paranoia; when they live in ugly surroundings, they become physically ill; without justice and order, they experience fear and anxiety; without playfulness and humor, they become stale, rigid, and somber. Deprivation of any of the B-values results in *metapathology,* or the lack of a meaningful philosophy of life.

Characteristics of Self-Actualizing People

Maslow believed that all humans have the potential for self-actualization. Then why are we not all self-actualizing? To be self-actualizing, Maslow believed, people must be regularly satisfied in their other needs and must also embrace the B-values. Using these two criteria, he guessed that the psychologically healthiest 1% of the adult population of the United States would be self-actualizing.

 Beyond Biography   What prompted Maslow to look for self-actualizing people? For information on Maslow's quest for the self-actualizing person, see our website at *www.mhhe.com/feist7*

Maslow (1970) listed 15 tentative qualities that characterize self-actualizing people to at least some degree.

More Efficient Perception of Reality

Self-actualizing people can more easily detect phoniness in others. They can discriminate between the genuine and the fake not only in people but also in literature, art, and music. They are not fooled by facades and can see both positive and negative underlying traits in others that are not readily apparent to most people. They perceive ultimate values more clearly than other people do and are less prejudiced and less likely to see the world as they wish it to be.

Also, self-actualizing people are less afraid and more comfortable with the unknown. They not only have a greater tolerance of ambiguity, but they actively seek it and feel comfortable with problems and puzzles that have no definite right or wrong solution. They welcome doubt, uncertainty, indefiniteness, and uncharted paths, a quality that makes self-actualizing people particularly well suited to be philosophers, explorers, or scientists.

Acceptance of Self, Others, and Nature

Self-actualizing people can accept themselves the way they are. They lack defensiveness, phoniness, and self-defeating guilt; have good hearty animal appetites for food, sleep, and sex; are not overly critical of their own shortcomings; and are not burdened by undue anxiety or shame. In similar fashion, they accept others and have no compulsive need to instruct, inform, or convert. They can tolerate weaknesses in others and are not threatened by others' strengths. They accept nature, including human nature, as it is and do not expect perfection either in themselves or in others. They realize that people suffer, grow old, and die.

Spontaneity, Simplicity, and Naturalness

Self-actualizing people are spontaneous, simple, and natural. They are unconventional but not compulsively so; they are highly ethical but may appear unethical or nonconforming. They usually behave conventionally, either because the issue is not of great importance or out of deference to others. But when the situation warrants it, they can be unconventional and uncompromising even at the price of ostracism and censure. The similarity between self-actualizing people and children and animals is in their spontaneous and natural behavior. They ordinarily live simple lives in the sense that they have no need to erect a complex veneer designed to deceive the world. They are unpretentious and not afraid or ashamed to express joy, awe, elation, sorrow, anger, or other deeply felt emotions.

Problem-Centering

A fourth characteristic of self-actualizing people is their interest in problems outside themselves. Non-self-actualizing people are self-centered and tend to see all the world's problems in relation to themselves, whereas self-actualizing people are task-oriented and concerned with problems outside themselves. This interest allows self-actualizers to develop a mission in life, a purpose for living that spreads beyond self-aggrandizement. Their occupation is not merely a means to earning a living but a vocation, a calling, an end in itself.

Self-actualizing people extend their frame of reference far beyond self. They are concerned with eternal problems and adopt a solid philosophical and ethical basis for handling these problems. They are unconcerned with the trivial and the petty. Their realistic perception enables them to clearly distinguish between the important and the unimportant issues in life.

The Need for Privacy

Self-actualizing people have a quality of detachment that allows them to be alone without being lonely. They feel relaxed and comfortable when they are either with people or alone. Because they have already satisfied their love and belongingness needs, they have no desperate need to be surrounded by other people. They can find enjoyment in solitude and privacy.

Self-actualizing people may be seen as aloof or uninterested, but in fact, their disinterest is limited to minor matters. They have a global concern for the welfare of others without becoming entangled in minute and insignificant problems. Because they spend little energy attempting to impress others or trying to gain love and acceptance, they have more ability to make responsible choices. They are self-movers, resisting society's attempts to make them adhere to convention.

Autonomy

Self-actualizing people are autonomous and depend on themselves for growth even though at some time in their past they had to have received love and security from others. No one is born autonomous, and therefore no one is completely independent of people. Autonomy can be achieved only through satisfactory relations with others.

However, the confidence that one is loved and accepted without conditions or qualifications can be a powerful force in contributing to feelings of self-worth. Once that confidence is attained, a person no longer depends on others for self-esteem. Self-actualizing people have that confidence and therefore a large measure of autonomy that allows them to be unperturbed by criticism as well as unmoved by flattery. This independence also gives them an inner peace and serenity not enjoyed by those who live for the approval of others.

Continued Freshness of Appreciation

Maslow (1970) wrote that "self-actualizing people have the wonderful capacity to appreciate again and again, freshly and naively, the basic goods of life, with awe, pleasure, wonder, and even ecstasy" (p. 163). They are keenly aware of their good physical health, friends and loved ones, economic security, and political freedom. Unlike other people who take their blessings for granted, self-actualizing individuals see with a fresh vision such everyday phenomena as flowers, food, and friends. They have an appreciation of their possessions and do not waste time complaining about a boring, uninteresting existence. In short, they "retain their constant sense of good fortune and gratitude for it" (Maslow, 1970, p. 164).

The Peak Experience

As Maslow's study of self-actualizers continued, he made the unexpected discovery that many of his people had had experiences that were mystical in nature and that somehow gave them a feeling of transcendence. Originally, he thought that these so-called **peak experiences** were far more common among self-actualizers than among non-self-actualizers. Later, however, Maslow (1971) stated that "most people, or almost all people, have peak experiences, or ecstasies" (p. 175).

Not all peak experiences are of equal intensity; some are only mildly sensed, others moderately felt, and some are quite intensely experienced. In their mild form, these peak experiences probably occur in everyone, although they are seldom noticed. For example, long-distance runners often report a sort of transcendence, a loss of self, or a feeling of being separated from their body. Sometimes, during periods of intense pleasure or satisfaction, people will experience mystical or peak experiences. Viewing a sunset or some other grandeur of nature may precipitate a peak experience, but these experiences cannot be brought on by an act of the will; often they occur at unexpected, quite ordinary moments.

What is it like to have a peak experience? Maslow (1964) described several guidelines that may help answer this question. First, peak experiences are quite natural and are part of human makeup. Second, people having a peak experience see the whole universe as unified or all in one piece, and they see clearly their place in that universe. Also, during this mystical time, peakers feel both more humble and more powerful at the same time. They feel passive, receptive, more desirous of listening, and more capable of hearing. Simultaneously, they feel more responsible for their activities and perceptions, more active, and more self-determined. Peakers experience a loss of fear, anxiety, and conflict and become more loving, accepting, and spontaneous. Although peakers often report such emotions as awe, wonder, rapture, ecstasy, reverence, humility, and surrender, they are not likely to want to get something practical from the experience. They often experience a disorientation in time and space, a loss of self-consciousness, an unselfish attitude, and an ability to transcend everyday polarities.

The peak experience is unmotivated, nonstriving, and nonwishing, and during such an experience, a person experiences no needs, wants, or deficiencies. In addition, Maslow (1964) says, "The peak experience is seen only as beautiful, good, desirable, worthwhile, etc., and is never experienced as evil or undesirable" (p. 63). Maslow also believed that the peak experience often has a lasting effect on a person's life.

Gemeinschaftsgefühl

Self-actualizing people possess *Gemeinschaftsgefühl,* Adler's term for social interest, community feeling, or a sense of oneness with all humanity. Maslow found that his self-actualizers had a kind of caring attitude toward other people. Although they often feel like aliens in a foreign land, self-actualizers nevertheless identify with all other people and have a genuine interest in helping others—strangers as well as friends.

Self-actualizers may become angry, impatient, or disgusted with others; but they retain a feeling of affection for human beings in general. More specifically, Maslow (1970) stated that self-actualizing people are "often saddened, exasperated, and even enraged by the shortcomings of the average person" (p. 166), but nevertheless, they continue to feel a basic kinship with that person.

Profound Interpersonal Relations

Related to *Gemeinschaftsgefühl* is a special quality of interpersonal relations that involves deep and profound feelings for individuals. Self-actualizers have a nurturant feeling toward people in general, but their close friendships are limited to only a few. They have no frantic need to be friends with everyone, but the few important interpersonal relationships they do have are quite deep and intense. They tend to choose healthy people as friends and avoid intimate interpersonal relationships with dependent or infantile people, although their social interest allows them to have a special feeling of empathy for these less healthy persons.

Self-actualizers are often misunderstood and sometimes despised by others. On the other hand, many are greatly loved and attract a large group of admirers and even worshipers, especially if they have made a notable contribution to their business or professional field. Those healthy people studied by Maslow felt uneasy and embarrassed by this veneration, preferring instead relationships that were mutual rather than one-sided.

The Democratic Character Structure

Maslow found that all his self-actualizers possessed democratic values. They could be friendly and considerate with other people regardless of class, color, age, or gender, and in fact, they seemed to be quite unaware of superficial differences among people.

Beyond this democratic attitude, self-actualizers have a desire and an ability to learn from anyone. In a learning situation, they recognize how little they know in relation to what they could know. They realize that less healthy individuals have much to offer them, and they are respectful and even humble before these people. However, they do not passively accept evil behavior in others; rather, they fight against evil people and evil behavior.

Discrimination Between Means and Ends

Self-actualizing people have a clear sense of right and wrong conduct and have little conflict about basic values. They set their sights on ends rather than means and have an unusual ability to distinguish between the two. What other people consider to be a means (e.g., eating or exercising), self-actualizing people often see as an end in itself. They enjoy doing something for its own sake and not just because it is a means to some other end. Maslow (1970) described his self-actualizing people by saying that "they can often enjoy for its own sake the getting to some place as well as the arriving. It is occasionally possible for them to make out of the most trivial and routine activity an intrinsically enjoyable game" (p. 169).

Philosophical Sense of Humor

Another distinguishing characteristic of self-actualizing people is their philosophical, nonhostile sense of humor. Most of what passes for humor or comedy is basically hostile, sexual, or scatological. The laugh is usually at someone else's expense. Healthy people see little humor in put-down jokes. They may poke fun at themselves, but not masochistically so. They make fewer tries at humor than others, but their attempts serve a purpose beyond making people laugh. They amuse, inform, point out ambiguities, provoke a smile rather than a guffaw.

The humor of a self-actualizing person is intrinsic to the situation rather than contrived; it is spontaneous rather than planned. Because it is situation-dependent, it usually cannot be repeated. For those who look for examples of a philosophical sense of humor, disappointment is inevitable. A retelling of the incident almost invariably loses its original quality of amusement. One must "be there" to appreciate it.

Creativeness

All self-actualizing people studied by Maslow were creative in some sense of the word. In fact, Maslow suggested that creativity and self-actualization may be one and the same. Not all self-actualizers are talented or creative in the arts, but all are creative in their own way. They have a keen perception of truth, beauty, and reality— ingredients that form the foundation of true creativity.

Self-actualizing people need not be poets or artists to be creative. In speaking of his mother-in-law (who was also his aunt), Maslow (1968a) vividly pointed out that creativity can come from almost anywhere. He said that whereas his self-actualizing mother-in-law had no special talents as a writer or artist, she was truly creative in preparing homemade soup. Maslow remarked that first-rate soup was more creative than second-rate poetry!

Resistance to Enculturation

A final characteristic identified by Maslow was resistance to enculturation. Self-actualizing people have a sense of detachment from their surroundings and are able to transcend a particular culture. They are neither antisocial nor consciously nonconforming. Rather, they are autonomous, following their own standards of conduct and not blindly obeying the rules of others.

Self-actualizing people do not waste energy fighting against insignificant customs and regulations of society. Such folkways as dress, hair style, and traffic laws are relatively arbitrary, and self-actualizing people do not make a conspicuous show of defying these conventions. Because they accept conventional style and dress, they are not too different in appearance from anyone else. However, on important matters, they can become strongly aroused to seek social change and to resist society's attempts to enculturate them. Self-actualizing people do not merely have different social mores, but, Maslow (1970) hypothesized, they are "less enculturated, less flattened out, less molded" (p. 174).

For this reason, these healthy people are more individualized and less homogenized than others. They are not all alike. In fact, the term "self-actualization" means to become everything that one can become, to actualize or fulfill all of one's potentials. When people can accomplish this goal, they become more unique, more heterogeneous, and less shaped by a given culture (Maslow, 1970).

Love, Sex, and Self-Actualization

Before people can become self-actualizing, they must satisfy their love and belongingness needs. It follows then that self-actualizing people are capable of both giving and receiving love and are no longer motivated by the kind of deficiency love (**D-love**) common to other people. Self-actualizing people are capable of **B-love,** that is, love for the essence or "Being" of the other. B-love is mutually felt and shared and not motivated by a deficiency or incompleteness within the lover. In fact, it is unmotivated, expressive behavior. Self-actualizing people do not love because they expect something in return. They simply love and are loved. Their love is never harmful. It is the kind of love that allows lovers to be relaxed, open, and nonsecretive (Maslow, 1970).

Because self-actualizers are capable of a deeper level of love, Maslow (1970) believed that sex between two B-lovers often becomes a kind of mystical experience. Although they are lusty people, fully enjoying sex, food, and other sensuous pleasures, self-actualizers are not dominated by sex. They can more easily tolerate the absence of sex (as well as other basic needs), because they have no deficiency need for it. Sexual activity between B-lovers is not always a heightened emotional experience; sometimes it is taken quite lightly in the spirit of playfulness and humor. But this approach is to be expected, because playfulness and humor are B-values, and like the other B-values, they are an important part of a self-actualizer's life.

Philosophy of Science

Maslow's philosophy of science and his research methods are integral to an understanding of how he arrived at his concept of self-actualization. Maslow (1966) believed that value-free science does not lead to the proper study of human personality. Maslow argued for a different philosophy of science, a humanistic, holistic approach that is not value free and that has scientists who *care* about the people and topics they investigate. For example, Maslow was motivated to search for self-actualizing people because he idolized and greatly admired Max Wertheimer and Ruth Benedict, his two original models for self-actualization. But he also expressed affection and admiration for Abraham Lincoln, Eleanor Roosevelt, and other self-actualizing people (Maslow, 1968a).

Maslow agreed with Allport (see Chapter 13) that psychological science should place more emphasis on the study of the individual and less on the study of large groups. Subjective reports should be favored over rigidly objective ones, and people should be allowed to tell about themselves in a holistic fashion instead of the more orthodox approach that studies people in bits and pieces. Traditional psychology has dealt with sensations, intelligence, attitudes, stimuli, reflexes, test scores, and hypothetical constructs from an external point of view. It has not been much concerned with the whole person as seen from that person's subjective view.

When Maslow attended medical school, he was shocked by the impersonal attitude of surgeons who nonchalantly tossed recently removed body parts onto a table. His observation of such a cold and calloused procedure led Maslow to originate the concept of **desacralization:** that is, the type of science that lacks emotion, joy, wonder, awe, and rapture (Hoffman, 1988). Maslow believed that orthodox science has no ritual or ceremony; and he called for scientists to put values, creativity, emotion, and ritual back into their work. Scientists must be willing to **resacralize** science or to instill it with human values, emotion, and ritual. Astronomers must not only study the stars; they must be awestruck by them. Psychologists must not only study human personality; they must do so with enjoyment, excitement, wonder, and affection.

Maslow (1966) argued for a **Taoistic attitude** for psychology, one that would be noninterfering, passive, and receptive. This new psychology would abolish prediction and control as the major goals of science and replace them with sheer fascination and the desire to release people from controls so that they can grow and become less predictable. The proper response to mystery, Maslow said, is not analysis but awe.

Maslow insisted that psychologists must themselves be healthy people, able to tolerate ambiguity and uncertainty. They must be intuitive, nonrational, insightful, and courageous enough to ask the right questions. They must also be willing to flounder, to be imprecise, to question their own procedures, and to take on the important problems of psychology. Maslow (1966) contended that there is no need to do well that which is not worth doing. Rather, it is better to do poorly that which is important.

In his study of self-actualizing people and peak experiences, Maslow employed research methods consistent with his philosophy of science. He began intuitively, often "skating on thin ice," then attempted to verify his hunches using idiographic and subjective methods. He often left to others the technical work of gathering evidence. His personal preference was to "scout out ahead," leaving one area when he grew tired of it and going on to explore new ones (M. H. Hall, 1968).

Measuring Self-Actualization

Everett L. Shostrom (1974) developed the **Personal Orientation Inventory** (POI) in an attempt to measure the values and behaviors of self-actualizing people. This inventory consists of 150 forced-choice items, such as (a) "I can feel comfortable with less than a perfect performance" versus (b) "I feel uncomfortable with anything less than a perfect performance"; (a) "Two people will get along best if each concentrates on pleasing the other" versus (b) "Two people can get along best if each person feels free to express himself"; and (a) "My moral values are dictated by society" versus (b) "My moral values are self-determined" (Shostrom, 1963). Respondents are asked to choose either statement (a) or statement (b), but they may leave the answer blank if neither statement applies to them or if they do not know anything about the statement.

The POI has 2 major scales and 10 subscales. The first major scale—the Time Competence/Time Incompetence scale—measures the degree to which people are present oriented. The second major scale—the Support scale—is "designed to measure whether an individual's mode of reaction is characteristically 'self' oriented or 'other' oriented" (Shostrom, 1974, p. 4). The 10 subscales assess levels of (1) self-actualization values, (2) flexibility in applying values, (3) sensitivity to one's own needs and feelings, (4) spontaneity in expressing feelings behaviorally, (5) self-regard, (6) self-acceptance, (7) positive view of humanity, (8) ability to see opposites of life as meaningfully related, (9) acceptance of aggression, and (10) capacity for intimate contact. High scores on the 2 major scales and the 10 subscales indicate some level of self-actualization; low scores do not necessarily suggest pathology but give clues concerning a person's self-actualizing values and behaviors.

The POI seems to be quite resistant to faking—unless one is familiar with Maslow's description of a self-actualizing person. In the POI manual, Shostrom (1974) cited several studies in which the examinees were asked to "fake good" or "make a favorable impression" in filling out the inventory. When participants followed these instructions, they generally scored lower (in the direction away from self-actualization) than they did when responding honestly to the statements.

This finding, indeed, is an interesting one. Why should people lower their scores when trying to look good? The answer lies in Maslow's concept of self-actualization. Statements that might be true for self-actualizers are not necessarily socially desirable and do not always conform to cultural standards. For example, items such as "I can overcome any obstacles as long as I believe in myself" or "My basic responsibility is to be aware of others' needs" may seem like desirable goals to someone trying to simulate self-actualization, but a self-actualizing person probably would not endorse either of these items. On the other hand, a truly self-actualizing person may choose such items as "I do not always need to live by the rules and standards of society" or "I do not feel obligated when a stranger does me a favor" (Shostrom, 1974, p. 22). Because one of the characteristics of self-actualizing people is resistance to enculturation, it should not be surprising that attempts to make a good impression will usually result in failure.

Interestingly, Maslow himself seemed to have answered the questions honestly when he filled out the inventory. Despite the fact that he helped in the construction of the POI, Maslow's own scores were only in the direction of self-actualization and not nearly as high as the scores of people who were definitely self-actualizing (Shostrom, 1974).

Even though the POI has demonstrated reasonable reliability and validity, some researchers (Weiss, 1991; Whitson & Olczak, 1991) have criticized the inventory for failing to distinguish between known self-actualizers and non-self-actualizers. Furthermore, the POI has two practical problems; first, it is long, taking most participants 30 to 45 minutes to complete; and second, the two-item forced-choice format can engender hostility in the participants, who feel frustrated by the limitations of a forced-choice option. To overcome these two practical limitations, Alvin Jones and Rick Crandall (1986) created the Short Index of Self-Actualization, which borrows 15 items from the POI that are most strongly correlated with the total self-actualization score. Items on the Short Index are on a 6-point Likert scale (from *strongly disagree* to *strongly agree*). Research (Compton, Smith, Cornish, & Qualls, 1996; Rowan, Compton, & Rust, 1995; Runco, Ebersole, & Mraz, 1991) on the Short Index of the POI has indicated that it is a useful scale for assessing self-actualization.

A third measure of self-actualization is the Brief Index of Self-Actualization, developed by John Sumerlin and Charles Bundrick (1996, 1998). The original Brief Index (Sumerlin & Bundrick, 1996) comprised 40 items placed on a 6-point Likert scale and thus yields scores from 40 to 240. Factor analysis yielded four factors of self-actualization, but because some items were placed in more than one factor, the authors (Sumerlin & Bundrick, 1998) revised the Brief Index of Self-Actualization by eliminating eight items so that no single item was found on more than one factor. This inventory yields four factors: (I) Core Self-Actualization, or the full use of one's potentials; (II) Autonomy; (III) Openness to Experience; and (IV) Comfort with Solitude. Typical items include "I enjoy my achievements" (Core Self-Actualization), "I fear that I will not live up to my potential" (a reversed scored item measuring Autonomy), "I am sensitive to the needs of others" (Openness to Experience), and "I enjoy my solitude" (Comfort with Solitude). The reliability, validity, and usefulness of the Brief Index have not yet been fully determined.

The Jonah Complex

According to Maslow (1970), everyone is born with a will toward health, a tendency to grow toward self-actualization, but few people reach it. What prevents people from achieving this high level of health? Growth toward normal, healthy personality can be blocked at each of the steps in the hierarchy of needs. If people cannot provide for food and shelter, they remain at the level of physiological and safety needs. Others remain blocked at the level of love and belongingness needs, striving to give and receive love and to develop feelings of belongingness. Still others satisfy their love needs and gain self-esteem, but do not advance to the level of self-actualization because they fail to embrace the B-values (Maslow, 1970).

Another obstacle that often blocks people's growth toward self-actualization is the **Jonah complex,** or the fear of being one's best (Maslow, 1979). The Jonah complex is characterized by attempts to run away from one's destiny just as the biblical Jonah tried to escape from his fate. The Jonah complex, which is found in nearly everyone, represents a fear of success, a fear of being one's best, and a feeling of awesomeness in the presence of beauty and perfection. Maslow's own life story demonstrated his Jonah complex. Despite an IQ of 195, he was only an average student, and, as a world-famous psychologist, he frequently experienced panic when called on to deliver a talk.

Why do people run away from greatness and self-fulfillment? Maslow (1971, 1996) offered the following rationale. First, the human body is simply not strong enough to endure the ecstasy of fulfillment for any length of time, just as peak experiences and sexual orgasms would be overly taxing if they lasted too long. Therefore, the intense emotion that accompanies perfection and fulfillment carries with it a shattering sensation such as "This is too much" or "I can't stand it anymore."

Maslow (1971) listed a second explanation for why people evade greatness. Most people, he reasoned, have private ambition to be great, to write a great novel, to be a movie star, to become a world-famous scientist, and so on. However, when they compare themselves with those who have accomplished greatness, they are appalled by their own arrogance: "Who am I to think I could do as well as this great person?" As a defense against this grandiosity or "sinful pride," they lower their aspirations, feel stupid and humble, and adopt the self-defeating approach of running away from the realization of their full potentials.

Although the Jonah complex stands out most sharply in neurotic people, nearly everyone has some timidity toward seeking perfection and greatness. People allow false humility to stifle creativity, and thus they prevent themselves from becoming self-actualizing.

Psychotherapy

To Maslow (1970), the aim of therapy would be for clients to embrace the Being-values, that is, to value truth, justice, goodness, simplicity, and so forth. To accomplish this aim, clients must be free from their dependency on others so that their natural impulse toward growth and self-actualization could become active. Psychotherapy cannot be value free but must take into consideration the fact that everyone has an inherent tendency to move toward a better, more enriching condition, namely self-actualization.

The goals of psychology follow from the client's position on the hierarchy of needs. Because physiological and safety needs are prepotent, people operating on these levels will not ordinarily be motivated to seek psychotherapy. Instead, they will strive to obtain nourishment and protection.

Most people who seek therapy have these two lower level needs relatively well satisfied but have some difficulty achieving love and belongingness needs. Therefore, psychotherapy is largely an interpersonal process. Through a warm, loving, interpersonal relationship with the therapist, the client gains satisfaction of love and belongingness needs and thereby acquires feelings of confidence and self-worth. A healthy interpersonal relationship between client and therapist is therefore the best psychological medicine. This accepting relationship gives clients a feeling of being worthy of love and facilitates their ability to establish other healthy relationships outside of therapy. This view of psychotherapy is nearly identical to that of Carl Rogers, as we discuss in Chapter 11.

Related Research

As you just read, one of the most notable aspects of Maslow's theory of personality is the concept of a hierarchy of needs. Some needs such as physiological and safety needs are lower order needs, whereas needs like esteem and self-actualization are higher order. Generally speaking, according to Maslow's theory the lower order needs must be met early in life, whereas the higher order needs such as self-actualization tend to be fulfilled later in life.

Recently, researchers have tested this aspect of Maslow's theory by measuring need fulfillment in a sample of 1,749 people of all age groups (Reiss &

Havercamp, 2006). In this study, participants completed a questionnaire that asked about their fulfillment of needs. These needs were divided into two types of motivation: lower motivation (e.g., eating and physical exercise) and higher motivation (e.g., honor, family, and idealism). The results supported Maslow's theory. The researchers found that the lower motives were stronger in younger people, whereas the higher motives were stronger in older people. Recall that in order to focus on fulfilling the highest order needs such as esteem and self-actualization, people must first have fulfilled the lower order needs. Therefore, as Maslow theorized and as Reiss and Havercamp (2006) found, if people can secure the most basic needs early in life, they have more time and energy to focus on achieving the highest reaches of human existence later in life.

Positive Psychology

Positive psychology is a relatively new field of psychology that combines an emphasis on hope, optimism, and well-being with scientific research and assessment. Many of the questions examined by positive psychologists stem directly from humanistic theorists such as Abraham Maslow and Carl Rogers (see Chapter 11). Like Maslow and Rogers, positive psychologists are critical of traditional psychology, which has resulted in a model of the human being as lacking the positive features that make life worth living. Hope, wisdom, creativity, future mindedness, courage, spirituality, responsibility, and positive experiences are ignored (Seligman & Csikszentmihalyi, 2000).

One area of positive psychology where Maslow's ideas have been particularly influential is in the role of positive experiences in people's lives. Maslow referred to extremely positive experiences that involve a sense of awe, wonder, and reverence as peak experiences. While such experiences are more common among self-actualizers, they can be experienced to various degrees by other people as well. Recently, researchers have investigated the potential benefits that come from reexperiencing, through writing or thinking, such positive experiences. In one such study, participants were instructed to write about a positive experience or experiences for 20 minutes each day for 3 consecutive days (Burton & King, 2004). Instructions given to participants before starting were derived directly from Maslow's writings on peak experiences, and they asked participants to write about their "happiest moments, ecstatic moments, moments of rapture, perhaps from being in love, from listening to music or suddenly 'being hit' by a book or painting or from some great creative moment" (p. 155). Experiencing such positive awe-inspiring events will undoubtedly enhance positive emotion, and, as this study tested, perhaps simply recalling such events from the past by writing about them can also enhance positive emotion. The experience of positive emotion is generally a good thing and has been associated with enhanced coping resources, better health, creativity, and prosocial behaviors (Lyubomirsky, King, & Diener, 2005). Therefore, Burton and King predicted that writing about these peak or intensely positive experiences would be associated with better physical health in the months following the writing exercise. Indeed, Burton and King (2004) found that those who wrote about positive experiences, compared to those in a control condition who wrote about nonemotional topics such as a description of their bedroom, visited the doctor fewer times for illness during the 3 months after writing.

Other researchers have followed up on the health effects of writing about extremely positive experiences. Sonja Lyubomirsky and colleagues investigated whether or not just thinking about past positive experiences would have benefits comparable to or even greater than the benefits derived from writing about such experiences (Lyubomirsky, Sousa, & Dickerhoof, 2006). Although they did not find physical health benefits for thinking about positive experiences, they did find that those who were instructed to simply think about these experiences for 15 minutes a day for 3 consecutive days reported greater well-being 1 month later than those who wrote about such experiences for the same time period. These results suggest that you do not need to overanalyze or pick apart positive experiences to derive benefits. Rather, casually recalling the experience in your head and remembering how good the positive experience made you feel is enough to experience greater well-being.

These studies demonstrate the importance of reflecting and reliving the most positive or "peak" experiences in our lives. Recall from earlier in the chapter that Abraham Maslow predicted that peak experiences often have a lasting impact on people's lives. The recent research in the area of positive psychology reviewed in this section certainly supports this aspect of Maslow's theory.

Personality Development, Growth, and Goals

Implicit in Maslow's concept of self-actualization is the assumption that people acquire greater levels of psychological health as they become older. Children and young adults struggling to acquire an education, a job, and a mate are not likely to have achieved the criteria for reaching self-actualization. Does empirical research support this assumption?

Jack Bauer and Dan McAdams (2004a) assumed the existence of two kinds of approaches to growth and development—extrinsic and intrinsic. Extrinsic development is primarily cognitive and revolves around one's ability to think complexly about one's life goals, whereas intrinsic development is primarily emotional and revolves around one's ability to feel better about one's life. More specifically, extrinsic growth focuses on fame, money, physical appearance, status, and power. By contrast, intrinsic goals focus on satisfaction, happiness, personal growth, and healthy interpersonal relationships. Cognitive-extrinsic growth and emotional-intrinsic growth seem to be unrelated to one another; that is, one can be cognitively complex about one's life and not be happy or satisfied.

In their research on growth goals, Bauer and McAdams predicted a positive relationship between age and personality development and psychological well-being. But they predicted the relationship between personality development and well-being would change depending on whether one was striving toward intrinsic or extrinsic goals. In other words, only people with intrinsic growth goals would see how getting older results in greater ego and personality development and well-being. Similarly, for those with extrinsic growth goals, getting older would not lead to greater personality development and psychological health.

Participants in Bauer and McAdams's study included both college students and volunteers from the community. The former had a mean age of about 20 years, whereas the latter had a mean age of about 52 years, and both groups were about

70% female. Life goals were coded from responses to a task that asked participants to write a paragraph each about their two most important life goals. The goals themselves were not coded but, rather, the reasons for the goals. Specifically, goals were coded on whether they were intrinsic, extrinsic, or exploratory. Intrinsic goals were those that included making a contribution to society, enhancing interpersonal relationships, improving feelings of happiness, and fostering advancement toward personal growth. Extrinsic goals included wanting to gain money, status, approval, or some other nonintrinsic goals. Exploratory goals included those designed to understand and to seek conceptual challenges.

As predicted, intrinsic and exploratory goals were positively correlated with maturity and personality development. People who are driven by happiness and need for conceptual understanding tend to be higher in ego-development and well-being. But there were also more specific associations: People high in exploratory growth goals were especially high in ego-development, and those high in intrinsic growth goals were especially high in well-being.

With regard to age and personality growth, results generally showed that older people were indeed higher in ego-development and well-being than younger people, and that this relationship was strongest for those with intrinsic growth goals. In other words, older adults had higher life satisfaction than younger adults. This was in part explained by older adults' being more likely to have intrinsic goals and concerns.

Bauer and McAdams (2004a) concluded that growth goals, particularly when studied in narrative form, open a window for researchers and therapists to understand whether people's intentions are likely to lead in personally desirable directions—namely, toward a more complex understanding of their lives and toward a heightened sense of well-being. This conclusion is consistent with Maslow's (1968b) argument that people generally take either a safety or a growth orientation in their everyday lives and that a growth orientation more readily facilitates psychological health and well-being.

Critique of Maslow

Maslow's search for the self-actualizing person did not end with his empirical studies. In his later years, he would frequently speculate about self-actualization with little evidence to support his suppositions. Although this practice opens the door for criticizing Maslow, he was unconcerned about desacralized, or orthodox, science.

Nevertheless, we use the same criteria to evaluate holistic-dynamic personality theory as we do with the other theories. First, how does Maslow's theory rate on its ability to *generate research?* On this criterion, we rate Maslow's theory a little above average. Self-actualization remains a popular topic with researchers, and the tests of self-actualization have facilitated efforts to investigate this illusive concept. However, Maslow's notions about metamotivation, the hierarchy of needs, the Jonah complex, and instinctoid needs have received less research interest.

On the criterion of falsifiability, we must rate Maslow's theory low. Researchers remained handicapped in their ability to falsify or confirm Maslow's means of identifying self-actualizing people. Maslow said that his self-actualizing people refused to take any tests that might assess self-actualization. If this is true, then the various inventories that purport to measure self-actualization may be incapable of identifying the truly self-actualizing person. However, if researchers wish to follow Maslow's lead and use personal interviews, they will have few guidelines to direct them. Because Maslow failed to provide an operational definition of self-actualization and a full description of his sampling procedures, researchers cannot be certain that they are replicating Maslow's original study or that they are identifying the same syndrome of self-actualization. Maslow left future researchers with few clear guidelines to follow when attempting to replicate his studies on self-actualization. Lacking operational definitions of most of Maslow's concepts, researchers are able to neither verify nor falsify much of his basic theory.

Nevertheless, Maslow's hierarchy of needs framework gives his theory excellent flexibility to *organize what is known about human behavior.* Maslow's theory is also quite consistent with common sense. For example, common sense suggests that a person must have enough to eat before being motivated by other matters. Starving people care little about political philosophy. Their primary motivation is to obtain food, not to sympathize with one political philosophy or another. Similarly, people living under threat to their physical well-being will be motivated mostly to secure safety, and people who have physiological and safety needs relatively satisfied will strive to be accepted and to establish a love relationship.

Does Maslow's theory serve as *a guide to the practitioner?* On this criterion, we rate the theory as highly useful. For example, psychotherapists who have clients with threatened safety needs must provide a safe and secure environment for those clients. Once clients have satisfied their safety needs, the therapist can work to provide them with feelings of love and belongingness. Likewise, personnel managers in business and industry can use Maslow's theory to motivate workers. The theory suggests that increases in pay cannot satisfy any needs beyond the physiological and safety levels. Because physiological and safety needs are already largely gratified for the average worker in the United States, wage increases per se will not permanently increase worker morale and productivity. Pay raises can satisfy higher level needs only when workers see them as recognition for a job well done. Maslow's theory suggests that business executives should allow workers more responsibility and freedom, tap into their ingenuity and creativity in solving problems, and encourage them to use their intelligence and imagination on the job.

Is the theory *internally consistent?* Unfortunately, Maslow's arcane and often unclear language makes important parts of his theory ambiguous and inconsistent. Apart from the problem of idiosyncratic language, however, Maslow's theory ranks high on the criterion of internal consistency. The hierarchy of needs concept follows a logical progression, and Maslow hypothesized that the order of needs is the same for everyone, although he does not overlook the possibility of certain reversals. Aside from some deficiencies in his scientific methods, Maslow's theory has a consistency and precision that give it popular appeal.

Is Maslow's theory *parsimonious,* or does it contain superfluous fabricated concepts and models? At first glance, the theory seems quite simplistic. A hierarchy of needs model with only five steps gives the theory a deceptive appearance of simplicity. A full understanding of Maslow's total theory, however, suggests a far more complex model. Overall, the theory is moderately parsimonious.

✯ Concept of Humanity

Maslow believed that all of us can be self-actualizing; our human nature carries with it a tremendous potential for being a Good Human Being. If we have not yet reached this high level of functioning, it is because we are in some manner crippled or pathological. We fail to satisfy our self-actualization needs when our lower level needs become blocked: that is, when we cannot satisfy our needs for food, safety, love and belongingness, and esteem. This insight led Maslow to postulate a hierarchy of basic needs that must be regularly satisfied before we become fully human.

Maslow concluded that true human nature is seen only in self-actualized people, and that "there seems no *intrinsic* reason why everyone should not be this way. Apparently, every baby has possibilities for self-actualization, but most get it knocked out of them" (Lowry, 1973, p. 91). In other words, self-actualizing people are not ordinary people with something added, but rather as ordinary people with nothing taken away. That is, if food, safety, love, and esteem are not taken away from people, then those people will move naturally toward self-actualization.

Maslow was generally *optimistic* and hopeful about humans, but he recognized that people are capable of great evil and destruction. Evil, however, stems from the frustration or thwarting of basic needs, not from the essential nature of people. When basic needs are not met, people may steal, cheat, lie, or kill.

Maslow believed that society, as well as individuals, can be improved, but growth for both is slow and painful. Nevertheless, these small forward steps seem to be part of humanity's evolutionary history. Unfortunately, most people "are doomed to wish for what they do not have" (Maslow, 1970, p. 70). In other words, although all people have the potential for self-actualization, most will live out their lives struggling for food, safety, or love. Most societies, Maslow believed, emphasize these lower level needs and base their educational and political systems on an invalid concept of humanity.

Truth, love, beauty, and the like are instinctoid and are just as basic to human nature as are hunger, sex, and aggression. All people have the potential to strive toward self-actualization, just as they have the motivation to seek food and protection. Because Maslow held that basic needs are structured the same for all people and that people satisfy these needs at their own rate, his holistic-dynamic theory of personality places moderate emphasis on both *uniqueness* and *similarities*.

From both a historical and an individual point of view, humans are an evolutionary animal, in the process of becoming more and more fully human. That is, as evolution progresses, humans gradually become more motivated by metamotivations and by the B-values. High level needs exist, at least as potentiality, in everyone. Because people aim toward self-actualization, Maslow's view can be considered *teleological and purposive*.

Maslow's view of humanity is difficult to classify on such dimensions as determinism versus free choice, conscious versus unconscious, or biological versus social determinants of personality. In general, the behavior of people motivated by physiological and safety needs is *determined by outside forces*, whereas the behavior of self-actualizing people is at least partially shaped by *free choice*.

On the dimension of *consciousness versus unconsciousness*, Maslow held that self-actualizing people are ordinarily more aware than others of what they are doing and why. However, motivation is so complex that people may be driven by several needs at the same time, and even healthy people are not always fully aware of all the reasons underlying their behavior.

As for *biological versus social influences*, Maslow would have insisted that this dichotomy is a false one. Individuals are shaped by both biology *and* society, and the two cannot be separated. Inadequate genetic endowment does not condemn a person to an unfulfilled life, just as a poor social environment does not preclude growth. When people achieve self-actualization, they experience a wonderful synergy among the biological, social, and spiritual aspects of their lives. Self-actualizers receive more physical enjoyment from the sensuous pleasures; they experience deeper and richer interpersonal relationships; and they receive pleasure from spiritual qualities such as beauty, truth, goodness, justice, and perfection.

Key Terms and Concepts

- Maslow assumed that *motivation* affects the whole person; it is complete, often unconscious, continual, and applicable to all people.
- People are motivated by four dimensions of needs: *conative* (willful striving), *aesthetic* (the need for order and beauty), *cognitive* (the need for curiosity and knowledge), and *neurotic* (an unproductive pattern of relating to other people).
- The conative needs can be arranged on a *hierarchy*, meaning that one need must be relatively satisfied before the next need can become active.
- The five conative needs are *physiological, safety, love and belongingness, esteem,* and *self-actualization.*
- Occasionally, needs on the hierarchy can be *reversed*, and they are frequently *unconscious*.
- *Coping behavior* is motivated and is directed toward the satisfaction of basic needs.
- *Expressive behavior* has a cause but is not motivated; it is simply one's way of expressing oneself.
- Conative needs, including self-actualization, are *instinctoid;* that is, their deprivation leads to pathology.
- The frustration of self-actualization needs results in *metapathology* and a rejection of the B-values.
- Acceptance of the *B-values* (truth, beauty, humor, etc.) is the criterion that separates self-actualizing people from those who are merely healthy but mired at the level of esteem.
- The *characteristics of self-actualizers* include (1) a more efficient perception of reality; (2) acceptance of self, others, and nature;

(3) spontaneity, simplicity, and naturalness; (4) a problem-centered approach to life; (5) the need for privacy; (6) autonomy; (7) freshness of appreciation; (8) peak experiences; (9) social interest; (10) profound interpersonal relations; (11) a democratic attitude; (12) the ability to discriminate means from ends; (13) a philosophical sense of humor; (14) creativeness; and (15) resistance to enculturation.

- In his philosophy of science, Maslow argued for a *Taoistic attitude,* one that is noninterfering, passive, receptive, and subjective.
- The *Personal Orientation Inventory* (POI) is a standardized test designed to measure self-actualizing values and behavior.
- The *Jonah complex* is the fear of being or doing one's best.
- *Psychotherapy* should be directed at the need level currently being thwarted, in most cases love and belongingness needs.

CHAPTER 11

Rogers: Person-Centered Theory

Rogers

He shared his elementary school days in Oak Park, Illinois, with Ernest Hemingway and the children of Frank Lloyd Wright, but he had no aspirations for either literature or for architecture. Instead, he wanted to be a farmer, a scientific farmer who cared about plants and animals and how they grew and developed.

Although he was from a large family, he was quite shy and lacking in social skills. A sensitive boy, he was easily hurt by the teasing he received from classmates and siblings.

At the beginning of his high school years, his parents—hoping for a more wholesome and religious atmosphere—moved their family to a farm about 45 miles west of Chicago. The move met his parents' purpose. In this isolated atmosphere, the family developed close ties with one another but not with young people from other families. Reading the Bible, working hard, and taking care of farm animals and plants occupied much of his time. Although he believed that his parents cared very much for their children, he also believed that they were quite controlling in their child-rearing practices. As a result, the children grew up in a home that included almost no social life and an abundance of hard work. Dancing, playing cards, drinking carbonated beverages, and attending the theater were all forbidden.

In this environment, the young man developed a scientific attitude toward farming, taking detailed notes on his observations. These notes taught him about the "necessary and sufficient" conditions for the optimal growth of plants and animals. Throughout his high school years and into his college days, he retained a passionate interest in scientific agriculture. However, he never did become a farmer. After two years of college, he changed his life goal from agriculture to the ministry and later to psychology.

But devotion to the scientific method was to remain with Carl Rogers for a lifetime, and his research on the "necessary and sufficient" conditions for human psychological growth was at least partially responsible for his winning the first Distinguished Scientific Contribution Award granted by the American Psychological Association.

Overview of Client-Centered Theory

Although he is best known as the founder of **client-centered therapy,** Carl Rogers developed a humanistic theory of personality that grew out of his experiences as a practicing psychotherapist. Unlike Freud, who was primarily a theorist and secondarily a therapist, Rogers was a consummate therapist but only a reluctant theorist (Rogers, 1959). He was more concerned with helping people than with discovering why they behaved as they did. He was more likely to ask "How can I help this person grow and develop?" than to ponder the question "What caused this person to develop in this manner?"

Like many personality theorists, Rogers built his theory on the scaffold provided by experiences as a therapist. Unlike most of these other theorists, however, he continually called for empirical research to support both his personality theory and his therapeutic approach. Perhaps more than any other therapist-theorist, Rogers (1986) advocated a balance between tender-minded and hardheaded studies that would expand knowledge of how humans feel and think.

Even though he formulated a rigorous, internally consistent theory of personality, Rogers did not feel comfortable with the notion of theory. His personal preference was to be a helper of people and not a constructor of theories. To him, theories seemed to make things too cold and external, and he worried that his theory might imply a measure of finality.

During the 1950s, at a midpoint in his career, Rogers was invited to write what was then called the "client-centered" theory of personality, and his original statement is found in Volume 3 of Sigmund Koch's *Psychology: A Study of a Science* (see Rogers, 1959). Even at that time, Rogers realized that 10 or 20 years hence, his theories would be different; but unfortunately, throughout the intervening years, he never systematically reformulated his theory of personality. Although many of his subsequent experiences altered some of those earlier ideas, his final theory of personality rests on that original foundation spelled out in the Koch series.

Biography of Carl Rogers

Carl Ransom Rogers was born on January 8, 1902, in Oak Park, Illinois, the fourth of six children born to Walter and Julia Cushing Rogers. Carl was closer to his mother than to his father who, during the early years, was often away from home working as a civil engineer. Walter and Julia Rogers were both devoutly religious, and Carl became interested in the Bible, reading from it and other books even as a preschool child. From his parents, he also learned the value of hard work—a value that, unlike religion, stayed with him throughout his life.

Rogers had intended to become a farmer, and after he graduated from high school, he entered the University of Wisconsin as an agriculture major. However, he soon became less interested in farming and more devoted to religion. By his third year at Wisconsin, Rogers was deeply involved with religious activities on campus and spent 6 months traveling to China to attend a student religious conference. This trip made a lasting impression on Rogers. The interaction with other young religious leaders changed him into a more liberal thinker and moved him toward independence from the religious views of his parents. These experiences with his fellow leaders also gave him more self-confidence in social relationships. Unfortunately, he returned from the journey with an ulcer.

Although his illness prevented him from immediately going back to the university, it did not keep him from working: He spent a year recuperating by laboring on the farm and at a local lumberyard before eventually returning to Wisconsin. There, he joined a fraternity, displayed more self-confidence, and in general, was a changed student from his pre-China days.

In 1924, Rogers entered the Union Theological Seminary in New York with the intention of becoming a minister. While at the seminary, he enrolled in several psychology and education courses at neighboring Columbia University. He was influenced by the progressive education movement of John Dewey, which was then strong at Teachers College, Columbia. Gradually, Rogers became disenchanted with the doctrinaire attitude of religious work. Even though Union Theological Seminary was quite liberal, Rogers decided that he did not wish to express a fixed set of beliefs but desired more freedom to explore new ideas. Finally, in the fall of 1926, he left the seminary to attend Teachers College on a full-time basis with a major in clinical and educational psychology. From that point on, he never returned to formal religion. His life would now take a new direction—toward psychology and education.

In 1927, Rogers served as a fellow at the new Institute for Child Guidance in New York City and continued to work there while completing his doctoral degree. At the institute, he gained an elementary knowledge of Freudian psychoanalysis, but he was not much influenced by it, even though he tried it out in his practice. He also attended a lecture by Alfred Adler, who shocked Rogers and the other staff members with his contention that an elaborate case history was unnecessary for psychotherapy.

Rogers received a PhD from Columbia in 1931 after having already moved to New York to work with the Rochester Society for the Prevention of Cruelty to Children. During the early phase of his professional career, Rogers was strongly influenced by the ideas of Otto Rank, who had been one of Freud's closest associates before his dismissal from Freud's inner circle. In 1936, Rogers invited Rank to Rochester for a 3-day seminar to present his new post-Freudian practice of psychotherapy. Rank's lectures provided Rogers with the notion that therapy is an emotional growth-producing relationship, nurtured by the therapist's empathic listening and unconditional acceptance of the client.

Rogers spent 12 years at Rochester, working at a job that might easily have isolated him from a successful academic career. He had harbored a desire to teach in a university after a rewarding teaching experience during the summer of 1935 at Teachers College and after having taught courses in sociology at the University of Rochester. During this period, he wrote his first book, *The Clinical Treatment of the Problem Child* (1939), the publication of which led to a teaching offer from Ohio State University. Despite his fondness for teaching, he might have turned down the offer if his wife had not urged him to accept and if Ohio State had not agreed to start him at the top, with the academic rank of full professor. In 1940, at the age of 38, Rogers moved to Columbus to begin a new career.

Pressed by his graduate students at Ohio State, Rogers gradually conceptualized his own ideas on psychotherapy, not intending them to be unique and certainly not controversial. These ideas were put forth in *Counseling and Psychotherapy,* published in 1942. In this book, which was a reaction to the older approaches to therapy, Rogers minimized the causes of disturbances and the identification and labeling of disorders. Instead, he emphasized the importance of growth within the patient (called by Rogers the "client").

In 1944, as part of the war effort, Rogers moved back to New York as director of counseling services for the United Services Organization. After 1 year, he took a position at the University of Chicago, where he established a counseling center and was allowed more freedom to do research on the process and outcome of psychotherapy. The years 1945 to 1957 at Chicago were the most productive and creative of his career. His therapy evolved from one that emphasized methodology, or what in the early 1940s was called the "nondirective" technique, to one in which the sole emphasis was on the client-therapist relationship. Always the scientist, Rogers, along with his students and colleagues, produced groundbreaking research on the process and effectiveness of psychotherapy.

Wanting to expand his research and his ideas to psychiatry, Rogers accepted a position at the University of Wisconsin in 1957. However, he was frustrated with his stay at Wisconsin because he was unable to unite the professions of psychiatry and psychology and because he felt that some members of his own research staff had engaged in dishonest and unethical behavior (Milton, 2002).

Disappointed with his job at Wisconsin, Rogers moved to California where he joined the Western Behavioral Sciences Institute (WBSI) and became increasingly interested in encounter groups.

Rogers resigned from WBSI when he felt it was becoming less democratic and, along with about 75 others from the institute, formed the Center for Studies of the Person. He continued to work with encounter groups but extended his person-centered methods to education (including the training of physicians) and to international politics. During the last years of his life, he led workshops in such countries as Hungary, Brazil, South Africa, and the former Soviet Union (Gendlin, 1988). He died February 4, 1987, following surgery for a broken hip.

The personal life of Carl Rogers was marked by change and openness to experience. As an adolescent, he was extremely shy, had no close friends, and was "socially incompetent in any but superficial contacts" (Rogers, 1973, p. 4). He did, however, have an active fantasy life, which he later believed would have been diagnosed as "schizoid" (Rogers, 1980, p. 30). His shyness and social ineptitude greatly restricted his experiences with women. When he originally entered the University of Wisconsin, he had only enough courage to ask out a young lady whom he had known in elementary school in Oak Park—Helen Elliott. Helen and Carl were married in 1924 and had two children—David and Natalie. Despite his early problems with interpersonal relationships, Rogers grew to become a leading proponent of the notion that the interpersonal relationship between two individuals is a powerful ingredient that cultivates psychological growth within both persons. However, the transition was not easy. He abandoned the formalized religion of his parents, gradually shaping a humanistic/existential philosophy that he hoped would bridge the gap between Eastern and Western thought.

Rogers received many honors during his long professional life. He was the first president of the American Association for Applied Psychology and helped bring that organization and the American Psychological Association (APA) back together. He served as president of APA for the year 1946–1947 and served as first president of the American Academy of Psychotherapists. In 1956, he was cowinner of the first Distinguished Scientific Contribution Award presented by APA. This award was especially satisfying to Rogers because it highlighted his skill as a researcher, a skill he learned well as a farm boy in Illinois (O'Hara, 1995).

Rogers originally saw little need for a theory of personality. But under pressure from others and also to satisfy an inner need to be able to explain the phenomena he was observing, he evolved his own theory, which was first tentatively expressed in his APA presidential address (Rogers, 1947). His theory was more fully espoused in *Client-Centered Therapy* (1951) and was expressed in even greater detail in the Koch series (Rogers, 1959). However, Rogers always insisted that the theory should remain tentative, and it is with this thought that one should approach a discussion of Rogerian personality theory.

Person-Centered Theory

Although Rogers's concept of humanity remained basically unchanged from the early 1940s until his death in 1987, his therapy and theory underwent several changes in name. During the early years, his approach was known as "nondirective," an unfortunate term that remained associated with his name for far too long. Later, his approach was variously termed "client-centered," "person-centered," "student-centered," "group-centered," and "person to person." We use the label *client-centered* in reference to Rogers's therapy and the more inclusive term **person-centered** to refer to Rogerian personality *theory*.

In Chapter 1, we said that clearly formulated theories often are stated in an *if-then* framework. Of all the theories in this book, Rogers's person-centered theory comes closest to meeting this standard. An example of an if-then construction is: *If* certain conditions exist, *then* a process will occur; *if* this process occurs, *then* certain outcomes can be expected. A more specific example is found in therapy: *If* the therapist is congruent and communicates unconditional positive regard and accurate empathy to the client, *then* therapeutic change will occur; *if* therapeutic change occurs, *then* the client will experience more self-acceptance, greater trust of self, and so on. (We discuss congruence, unconditional positive regard, and empathy more fully in the section titled Psychotherapy.)

Basic Assumptions

What are the basic assumptions of person-centered theory? Rogers postulated two broad assumptions—the formative tendency and the actualizing tendency.

Formative Tendency

Rogers (1978, 1980) believed that there is a tendency for all matter, both organic and inorganic, to evolve from simpler to more complex forms. For the entire universe, a creative process, rather than a disintegrative one, is in operation. Rogers called this process the **formative tendency** and pointed to many examples from nature. For instance, complex galaxies of stars form from a less well-organized mass; crystals such as snowflakes emerge from formless vapor; complex organisms develop from single cells; and human consciousness evolves from a primitive unconsciousness to a highly organized awareness.

Actualizing Tendency

An interrelated and more pertinent assumption is the **actualizing tendency,** or the tendency within all humans (and other animals and plants) to move toward completion or fulfillment of potentials (Rogers, 1959, 1980). This tendency is the only motive people possess. The need to satisfy one's hunger drive, to express deep emotions when they are felt, and to accept one's self are all examples of the single motive of actualization. Because each person operates as one complete organism, actualization involves the whole person—physiological and intellectual, rational and emotional, conscious and unconscious.

Tendencies to maintain and to enhance the organism are subsumed within the actualizing tendency. The need for **maintenance** is similar to the lower steps on Maslow's hierarchy of needs (see Chapter 10). It includes such basic needs as food, air, and safety; but it also includes the tendency to resist change and to seek the status quo. The conservative nature of maintenance needs is expressed in people's desire to protect their current, comfortable self-concept. People fight against new ideas; they distort experiences that do not quite fit; they find change painful and growth frightening.

Even though people have a strong desire to maintain the status quo, they are willing to learn and to change. This need to become more, to develop, and to achieve growth is called **enhancement.** The need for enhancing the self is seen in people's willingness to learn things that are not immediately rewarding. Other than enhancement, what motivates a child to walk? Crawling can satisfy the need for mobility, whereas walking is associated with falling and with pain. Rogers's position is that people are willing to face threat and pain because of a biologically based tendency for the organism to fulfill its basic nature.

Enhancement needs are expressed in a variety of forms, including curiosity, playfulness, self-exploration, friendship, and confidence that one can achieve psychological growth. People have within themselves the creative power to solve problems, to alter their self-concepts, and to become increasingly self-directed. Individuals perceive their experiences as reality, and they know their reality better than anyone else. They do not need to be directed, controlled, exhorted, or manipulated in order to spur them toward actualization.

The actualization tendency is not limited to humans. Other animals and even plants have an inherent tendency to grow toward reaching their genetic potential—provided certain conditions are present. For example, in order for a bell pepper plant to reach its full productive potential, it must have water, sunlight, and a nutrient soil. Similarly, a human's actualization tendency is realized only under certain *conditions.* Specifically, people must be involved in a relationship with a partner who is *congruent,* or *authentic,* and who demonstrates *empathy* and *unconditional positive regard.* Rogers (1961) emphasized that having a partner who possesses these three qualities does not *cause* people to move toward constructive personal change. It does, however, permit them to actualize their innate tendency toward self-fulfillment.

Rogers contended that whenever congruence, unconditional positive regard, and empathy are present in a relationship, psychological growth will invariably occur. For this reason, he regarded these three conditions as both *necessary* and *sufficient* conditions for becoming a fully functioning or self-actualizing person. Although people share the actualizing tendency with plants and other animals, only humans have a concept of self and thus a potential for *self-actualization.*

The Self and Self-Actualization

According to Rogers (1959), infants begin to develop a vague concept of self when a portion of their experience becomes personalized and differentiated in *awareness* as "I" or "me" experiences. Infants gradually become aware of their own identity as they learn what tastes good and what tastes bad, what feels pleasant and what does not. They then begin to evaluate experiences as positive or negative, using as a criterion the actualizing tendency. Because nourishment is a requirement for actualization, infants value food and devalue hunger. They also value sleep, fresh air, physical contact, and health because each of these is needed for actualization.

Once infants establish a rudimentary self structure, their tendency to actualize the self begins to evolve. **Self-actualization** is a subset of the actualization tendency and is therefore not synonymous with it. The *actualization tendency* refers to organismic experiences of the individual; that is, it refers to the whole person—conscious and unconscious, physiological and cognitive. On the other hand, *self-actualization* is the tendency to actualize the self as *perceived in awareness*. When the organism and the perceived self are in harmony, the two actualization tendencies are nearly identical; but when people's organismic experiences are not in harmony with their view of self, a discrepancy exists between the actualization tendency and the self-actualization tendency. For example, if a man's organismic experience is one of anger toward his wife, and if anger toward spouse is contrary to his perception of self, then his actualization tendency and his self-actualization are incongruent and he will experience conflict and inner tension. Rogers (1959) postulated two self subsystems, the *self-concept* and the *ideal self.*

The Self-Concept

The **self-concept** includes all those aspects of one's being and one's experiences that are perceived in awareness (though not always accurately) by the individual. The self-concept is not identical with the **organismic self.** Portions of the organismic self may be beyond a person's awareness or simply not owned by that person. For example, the stomach is part of the organismic self, but unless it malfunctions and causes concern, it is not likely to be part of one's self-concept. Similarly, people can disown

Incongruence between the ideal self and the perceived self can result in conflict and unhappiness.

certain aspects of their selves, such as experiences of dishonesty, when such experiences are not consistent with their self-concept.

Thus, once people form their self-concept, they find change and significant learnings quite difficult. Experiences that are inconsistent with their self-concept usually are either denied or accepted only in distorted forms.

An established self-concept does not make change impossible, merely difficult. Change most readily occurs in an atmosphere of acceptance by others, which allows a person to reduce anxiety and threat and to take ownership of previously rejected experiences.

The Ideal Self

The second subsystem of the self is the **ideal self,** defined as one's view of self as one wishes to be. The ideal self contains all those attributes, usually positive, that people aspire to possess. A wide gap between the ideal self and the self-concept indicates **incongruence** and an unhealthy personality. Psychologically healthy individuals perceive little discrepancy between their self-concept and what they ideally would like to be.

Awareness

Without awareness the self-concept and the ideal self would not exist. Rogers (1959) defined *awareness* as "the symbolic representation (not necessarily in verbal symbols) of some portion of our experience" (p. 198). He used the term synonymously with both consciousness and symbolization.

Levels of Awareness

Rogers (1959) recognized three levels of awareness. First, some events are experienced below the threshold of awareness and are either *ignored* or *denied.* An ignored experience can be illustrated by a woman walking down a busy street, an activity that presents many potential stimuli, particularly of sight and sound. Because she cannot attend to all of them, many remain *ignored.* An example of *denied* experience might be a mother who never wanted children, but out of guilt she becomes overly solicitous to them. Her anger and resentment toward her children may be hidden to her for years, never reaching consciousness but yet remaining a part of her experience and coloring her conscious behavior toward them.

Second, Rogers (1959) hypothesized that some experiences are *accurately symbolized* and freely admitted to the self-structure. Such experiences are both nonthreatening and consistent with the existing self-concept. For example, if a pianist who has full confidence in his piano-playing ability is told by a friend that his playing is excellent, he may hear these words, accurately symbolize them, and freely admit them to his self-concept.

A third level of awareness involves experiences that are perceived in a *distorted* form. When our experience is not consistent with our view of self, we reshape or distort the experience so that it can be assimilated into our existing self-concept. If the gifted pianist were to be told by a distrusted competitor that his playing was excellent, he might react very differently than he did when he heard the same words from a trusted friend. He may hear the remarks but distort their meaning because he feels threatened. "Why is this person trying to flatter me? This doesn't make sense." His experiences are inaccurately symbolized in awareness and therefore can be distorted so that they conform to an existing self-concept that, in part, says, "I am a person who does not trust my piano-playing competitors, especially those who are trying to trick me."

Denial of Positive Experiences

Our example of the gifted pianist illustrates that it is not only the negative or derogatory experiences that are distorted or denied to awareness; many people have difficulty accepting genuine compliments and positive feedback, even when deserved. A student who feels inadequate but yet makes a superior grade might say to herself, "I know this grade should be evidence of my scholastic ability, but somehow I just don't feel that way. This class was the easiest one on campus. The other students just didn't try. My teacher did not know what she was doing." Compliments, even those genuinely dispensed, seldom have a positive influence on the self-concept of the recipient. They may be distorted because the person distrusts the giver, or they may be denied because the recipient does not feel deserving of them; in all cases, a compliment from another also implies the right of that person to criticize or condemn, and thus the compliment carries an implied threat (Rogers, 1961).

Becoming a Person

Rogers (1959) discussed the processes necessary to becoming a person. First, an individual must make *contact*—positive or negative—with another person. This contact is the minimum experience necessary for becoming a person. In order to survive, an infant must experience some contact from a parent or other caregiver.

As children (or adults) become aware that another person has some measure of regard for them, they begin to value positive regard and devalue negative regard. That is, the person develops a need to be loved, liked, or accepted by another person, a need that Rogers (1959) referred to as **positive regard.** If we perceive that others, especially significant others, care for, prize, or value us, then our need to receive positive regard is at least partially satisfied.

Positive regard is a prerequisite for **positive self-regard,** defined as the experience of prizing or valuing one's self. Rogers (1959) believed that receiving positive regard from others is necessary for positive self-regard, but once positive self-regard is established, it becomes independent of the continual need to be loved. This conception is quite similar to Maslow's (see Chapter 10) notion that we must satisfy our love and belongingness needs before self-esteem needs can become active, but once we begin to feel confident and worthy, we no longer require a replenishing supply of love and approval from others.

The source of positive self-regard, then, lies in the positive regard we receive from others, but once established, it is autonomous and self-perpetuating. As Rogers (1959) stated it, the person then "becomes in a sense his [or her] own significant social other" (p. 224).

Barriers to Psychological Health

Not everyone becomes a psychologically healthy person. Rather, most people experience conditions of worth, incongruence, defensiveness, and disorganization.

Conditions of Worth

Instead of receiving unconditional positive regard, most people receive **conditions of worth;** that is, they perceive that their parents, peers, or partners love and accept them only if they meet those people's expectations and approval. "A condition of worth arises when the positive regard of a significant other is conditional, when the individual feels that in some respects he [or she] is prized and in others not" (Rogers, 1959, p. 209).

Conditions of worth become the criterion by which we accept or reject our experiences. We gradually assimilate into our self-structure the attitudes we perceive others expressing toward us, and in time we begin to evaluate experiences on this basis. If we see that others accept us regardless of our actions, then we come to believe that we are prized unconditionally. But if we perceive that some of our behaviors are approved and some disapproved, then we see that our worth is conditional. Eventually, we may come to believe those appraisals of others that are consistent with our negative view of self, ignore our own sensory and visceral perceptions, and gradually become estranged from our real or organismic self.

From early childhood forward, most of us learn to disregard our own organismic valuations and to look beyond ourselves for direction and guidance. To the degree that we introject the values of others, that is, accept conditions of worth, we tend to be incongruent or out of balance. Other people's values can be assimilated only in distorted fashion or at the risk of creating disequilibrium and conflict within the self.

Our perceptions of other people's view of us are called **external evaluations.** These evaluations, whether positive or negative, do not foster psychological health but, rather, prevent us from being completely open to our own experiences. For example, we may reject pleasurable experiences because we believe that other people do not approve of them. When our own experiences are distrusted, we distort our awareness of them, thus solidifying the discrepancy between our organismic evaluation and the values we have introjected from others. As a result, we experience incongruence (Rogers, 1959).

Incongruence

We have seen that the organism and the self are two separate entities that may or may not be congruent with one another. Also recall that actualization refers to the organism's tendency to move toward fulfillment, whereas self-actualization is the desire of the perceived self to reach fulfillment. These two tendencies are sometimes at variance with one another.

Psychological disequilibrium begins when we fail to recognize our organismic experiences as self-experiences: that is, when we do not accurately symbolize organismic experiences into awareness because they appear to be inconsistent with our emerging self-concept. This *incongruence* between our self-concept and our organismic experience is the source of psychological disorders. Conditions of worth that we received during early childhood lead to a somewhat false self-concept, one based on distortions and denials. The self-concept that emerges includes vague perceptions that are not in harmony with our organismic experiences, and this incongruence between self and experience leads to discrepant and seemingly inconsistent behaviors. Sometimes we behave in ways that maintain or enhance our actualizing tendency, and at other times, we may behave in a manner designed to maintain or enhance a self-concept founded on other people's expectations and evaluations of us.

Vulnerability   The greater the incongruence between our perceived self (self-concept) and our organismic experience, the more vulnerable we are. Rogers (1959) believed that people are **vulnerable** when they are unaware of the discrepancy between their organismic self and their significant experience. Lacking awareness of their incongruence, vulnerable people often behave in ways that are incomprehensible not only to others but also to themselves.

Anxiety and Threat   Whereas vulnerability exists when we have no awareness of the incongruence within our self, anxiety and threat are experienced as we gain awareness of such an incongruence. When we become dimly aware that the discrepancy between our organismic experience and our self-concept may become conscious, we feel anxious. Rogers (1959) defined **anxiety** as "a state of uneasiness or tension whose cause is unknown" (p. 204). As we become more aware of the incongruence between our organismic experience and our perception of self, our anxiety begins to evolve into threat: that is, an awareness that our self is no longer whole or congruent. Anxiety and **threat** can represent steps toward psychological health because they signal to us that our organismic experience is inconsistent with our self-concept. Nevertheless, they are not pleasant or comfortable feelings.

Defensiveness

In order to prevent this inconsistency between our organismic experience and our perceived self, we react in a defensive manner. **Defensiveness** is the protection of the self-concept against anxiety and threat by the denial or distortion of experiences inconsistent with it (Rogers, 1959). Because the self-concept consists of many self-descriptive statements, it is a many-faceted phenomenon. When one of our experiences is inconsistent with one part of our self-concept, we will behave in a defensive manner in order to protect the current structure of our self-concept.

The two chief defenses are *distortion* and *denial*. With **distortion,** we misinterpret an experience in order to fit it into some aspect of our self-concept. We perceive the experience in awareness, but we fail to understand its true meaning. With **denial,** we refuse to perceive an experience in awareness, or at least we keep some aspect of it from reaching symbolization. Denial is not as common as distortion because most experiences can be twisted or reshaped to fit the current self-concept. According to Rogers (1959), both distortion and denial serve the same purpose—they keep our perception of our organismic experiences consistent with our self-concept—which allows us to ignore or block out experiences that otherwise would cause unpleasant anxiety or threat.

Disorganization

Most people engage in defensive behavior, but sometimes defenses fail and behavior becomes disorganized or psychotic. But why would defenses fail to function?

To answer this question, we must trace the course of disorganized behavior, which has the same origins as normal defensive behavior, namely a discrepancy between people's organismic experience and their view of self. Denial and distortion are adequate to keep normal people from recognizing this discrepancy, but when the incongruence between people's perceived self and their organismic experience is either too obvious or occurs too suddenly to be denied or distorted, their behavior becomes disorganized. Disorganization can occur suddenly, or it can take place gradually over a long period of time. Ironically, people are particularly vulnerable to disorganization during therapy, especially if a therapist accurately interprets their actions and also insists that they face the experience prematurely (Rogers, 1959).

In a state of disorganization, people sometimes behave consistently with their organismic experience and sometimes in accordance with their shattered self-concept. An example of the first case is a previously prudish and proper woman who suddenly begins to use language explicitly sexual and scatological. The second case can be illustrated by a man who, because his self-concept is no longer a gestalt or unified whole, begins to behave in a confused, inconsistent, and totally unpredictable manner. In both cases, behavior is still consistent with the self-concept, but the self-concept has been broken and thus the behavior appears bizarre and confusing.

Although Rogers was even more tentative than usual when he first put forth his views of disorganized behavior in 1959, he made no important revisions in this portion of his theory. He never wavered in his disdain for using diagnostic labels to describe people. Traditional classifications such as those found in the *Diagnostic and Statistical Manual of Mental Disorders, Fourth Edition* (DSM-IV) (American Psychiatric Association, 1994) have never been part of the vocabulary of person-centered theory. In fact, Rogers always remained uncomfortable with the terms "neurotic" and "psychotic," preferring instead to speak of "defensive" and "disorganized" behaviors, terms that more accurately convey the idea that psychological maladjustment is on a continuum from the slightest discrepancy between self and experience to the most incongruent.

Behavior can become disorganized or even psychotic when one's defenses fail to operate properly.

Psychotherapy

Client-centered therapy is deceptively simple in statement but decidedly difficult in practice. Briefly, the client-centered approach holds that in order for vulnerable or anxious people to grow psychologically, they must come into contact with a therapist who is congruent and whom they perceive as providing an atmosphere of unconditional acceptance and accurate empathy. But therein lies the difficulty. The qualities of congruence, unconditional positive regard, and empathic understanding are not easy for a counselor to attain.

Like person-centered theory, the client-centered counseling approach can be stated in an if-then fashion. If the *conditions* of therapist congruence, unconditional positive regard, and empathic listening are present in a client-counselor relationship, then the *process* of therapy will transpire. If the process of therapy takes place, then certain *outcomes* can be predicted. Rogerian therapy, therefore, can be viewed in terms of conditions, process, and outcomes.

Conditions

Rogers (1959) postulated that in order for therapeutic growth to take place, the following conditions are necessary and sufficient. First, an anxious or vulnerable client must come into contact with a congruent therapist who also possesses *empathy* and unconditional positive regard for that client. Next, the client must perceive these characteristics in the therapist. Finally, the contact between client and therapist must be of some duration.

The significance of the Rogerian hypothesis is revolutionary. With nearly any psychotherapy, the first and third conditions are present; that is, the client, or patient, is motivated by some sort of tension to seek help, and the relationship between the client and the therapist will last for some period of time. Client-centered therapy is unique in its insistence that the conditions of *counselor congruence, unconditional positive regard,* and *empathic listening* are both necessary and sufficient (Rogers, 1957).

Even though all three conditions are necessary for psychological growth, Rogers (1980) believed that congruence is more basic than either unconditional positive regard or empathic listening. Congruence is a general quality possessed by the therapist, whereas the other two conditions are specific feelings or attitudes that the therapist has for an individual client.

Counselor Congruence

The first necessary and sufficient condition for therapeutic change is a congruent therapist. **Congruence** exists when a person's organismic experiences are matched by an awareness of them and by an ability and willingness to openly express these feelings (Rogers, 1980). To be congruent means to be real or genuine, to be whole or integrated, to be what one truly is. Rogers (1995) spoke about congruence in these words:

> In my relationships with persons I have found that it does not help, in the long run, to act as though I were something that I am not. . . . It does not help to act

calm and pleasant when actually I am angry and critical. It does not help to act as though I were permissive when I am really feeling that I would like to set limits. . . . It does not help to act as though I were acceptant of another person when underneath that exterior I feel rejection. (p. 9)

A congruent counselor, then, is not simply a kind and friendly person but rather a complete human being with feelings of joy, anger, frustration, confusion, and so on. When these feelings are experienced, they are neither denied nor distorted but flow easily into awareness and are freely expressed. A congruent therapist, therefore, is not passive, not aloof, and definitely *not* "nondirective."

Congruent therapists are not static. Like most other people, they are constantly exposed to new organismic experiences, but unlike most people, they accept these experiences into awareness, which contributes to their psychological growth. They wear no mask, do not attempt to fake a pleasant facade, and avoid any pretense of friendliness and affection when these emotions are not truly felt. Also, they do not fake anger, toughness, or ignorance, nor do they cover up feelings of joy, elation, or happiness. In addition, they are able to match feelings with awareness and both with honest expression.

Because congruence involves (1) feelings, (2) awareness, and (3) expression, incongruence can arise from either of the two points dividing these three experiences. First, there can be a breakdown between feelings and awareness. A person may be feeling angry, and the anger may be obvious to others; but the angry person is unaware of the feeling. "I'm not angry. How dare you say I'm angry!" The second source of incongruence is a discrepancy between awareness of an experience and the ability or willingness to express it to another. "I know I'm feeling bored by what is being said, but I don't dare verbalize my disinterest because my client will think that I am not a good therapist." Rogers (1961) stated that therapists will be more effective if they communicate genuine feelings, even when those feelings are negative or threatening. To do otherwise would be dishonest, and clients

Effective client-centered therapy requires a congruent counselor who feels empathy and unconditional positive regard for the client.

will detect—though not necessarily consciously—any significant indicators of incongruence.

Although congruence is a necessary ingredient in successful therapy, Rogers (1980) did not believe that it is necessary for a therapist to be congruent in all relationships outside the therapeutic process. One can be less than perfect and yet become an effective psychotherapist. Also, a therapist need not be absolutely congruent in order to facilitate some growth within a client. As with unconditional positive regard and empathic listening, different degrees of congruence exist. The more the client perceives each of these qualities as characterizing the therapist, the more successful will be the therapeutic process.

Unconditional Positive Regard

Positive regard is the need to be liked, prized, or accepted by another person. When this need exists without any conditions or qualifications, **unconditional positive regard** occurs (Rogers, 1980). Therapists have unconditional positive regard when they are "experiencing a warm, positive and accepting attitude toward what is the client" (Rogers, 1961, p. 62). The attitude is without possessiveness, without evaluations, and without reservations.

A therapist with unconditional positive regard toward a client will show a nonpossessive warmth and acceptance, not an effusive, effervescent persona. To have nonpossessive warmth means to care about another without smothering or owning that person. It includes the attitude "Because I care about you, I can permit you to be autonomous and independent of my evaluations and restrictions. You are a separate person with your own feelings and opinions regarding what is right or wrong. The fact that I care for you does not mean that I must guide you in making choices, but that I can allow you to be yourself and to decide what is best for you." This kind of permissive attitude earned for Rogers the undeserved reputation of being passive or nondirective in therapy, but a client-centered therapist must be actively involved in a relationship with the client.

Unconditional positive regard means that therapists accept and prize their clients without any restrictions or reservations and without regard to the clients' behavior. Although therapists may value some client behaviors more than others, their positive regard remains constant and unwavering. Unconditional positive regard also means that therapists do not evaluate clients, nor do they accept one action and reject another. External evaluation, whether positive or negative, leads to clients' defensiveness and prevents psychological growth.

Although unconditional positive regard is a somewhat awkward term, all three words are important. "Regard" means that there is a close relationship and that the therapist sees the client as an important person; "positive" indicates that the direction of the relationship is toward warm and caring feelings; and "unconditional" suggests that the positive regard is no longer dependent on specific client behaviors and does not have to be continually earned.

Empathic Listening

The third necessary and sufficient condition of psychological growth is **empathic listening.** Empathy exists when therapists accurately sense the feelings of their clients and are able to communicate these perceptions so that clients know that another person has entered their world of feelings without prejudice, projection, or evaluation. To Rogers (1980), empathy "means temporarily living in the other's life, moving about in it delicately without making judgments" (p. 142). Empathy does not involve interpreting clients' meanings or uncovering their unconscious feelings, procedures that would entail an external frame of reference and a threat to clients. In contrast, empathy suggests that a therapist sees things from the client's point of view and that the client feels safe and unthreatened.

Client-centered therapists do not take empathy for granted; they check the accuracy of their sensings by trying them out on the client. "You seem to be telling me that you feel a great deal of resentment toward your father." Valid empathic understanding is often followed by an exclamation from the client along these lines: "Yes, that's it exactly! I really do feel resentful."

Empathic listening is a powerful tool, which along with genuineness and caring, facilitates personal growth within the client. What precisely is the role of empathy in psychological change? How does an empathic therapist help a client move toward wholeness and psychological health? Rogers's (1980) own words provide the best answer to these questions.

> When persons are perceptively understood, they find themselves coming in closer touch with a wider range of their experiencing. This gives them an expanded referent to which they can turn for guidance in understanding themselves and directing their behavior. If the empathy has been accurate and deep, they may also be able to unblock a flow of experiencing and permit it to run its uninhibited course. (p. 156)

Empathy is effective because it enables clients to listen to themselves and, in effect, become their own therapists.

Empathy should not be confused with sympathy. The latter term suggests a feeling *for* a client, whereas empathy connotes a feeling *with* a client. Sympathy is never therapeutic, because it stems from external evaluation and usually leads to clients' feeling sorry for themselves. Self-pity is a deleterious attitude that threatens a positive self-concept and creates disequilibrium within the self-structure. Also, empathy does not mean that a therapist has the same feelings as the client. A therapist does not feel anger, frustration, confusion, resentment, or sexual attraction at the same time a client experiences them. Rather, a therapist is experiencing the depth of the client's feeling while permitting the client to be a separate person. A therapist has an emotional as well as a cognitive reaction to a client's feelings, but *the feelings belong to the client,* not the therapist. A therapist does not take ownership of a client's experiences but is able to convey to the client an understanding of what it means to be the client at that particular moment (Rogers, 1961).

Process

If the conditions of therapist congruence, unconditional positive regard, and empathy are present, then the process of therapeutic change will be set in motion. Although each person seeking psychotherapy is unique, Rogers (1959) believed that a certain lawfulness characterizes the process of therapy.

Stages of Therapeutic Change

The process of constructive personality change can be placed on a continuum from most defensive to most integrated. Rogers (1961) arbitrarily divided this continuum into seven stages.

Stage 1 is characterized by an unwillingness to communicate anything about oneself. People at this stage ordinarily do not seek help, but if for some reason they come to therapy, they are extremely rigid and resistant to change. They do not recognize any problems and refuse to own any personal feelings or emotions.

In *Stage 2,* clients become slightly less rigid. They discuss external events and other people, but they still disown or fail to recognize their own feelings. However, they may talk about personal feelings as if such feelings were objective phenomena.

As clients enter into *Stage 3,* they more freely talk about self, although still as an object. "I'm doing the best I can at work, but my boss still doesn't like me." Clients talk about feelings and emotions in the past or future tense and avoid present feelings. They refuse to accept their emotions, keep personal feelings at a distance from the here-and-now situation, only vaguely perceive that they can make personal choices, and deny individual responsibility for most of their decisions.

Clients in *Stage 4* begin to talk of deep feelings but not ones presently felt. "I was really burned up when my teacher accused me of cheating." When clients do express present feelings, they are usually surprised by this expression. They deny or distort experiences, although they may have some dim recognition that they are capable of feeling emotions in the present. They begin to question some values that have been introjected from others, and they start to see the incongruence between their perceived self and their organismic experience. They accept more freedom and responsibility than they did in Stage 3 and begin to tentatively allow themselves to become involved in a relationship with the therapist.

By the time clients reach *Stage 5,* they have begun to undergo significant change and growth. They can express feelings in the present, although they have not yet accurately symbolized those feelings. They are beginning to rely on an internal locus of evaluation for their feelings and to make fresh and new discoveries about themselves. They also experience a greater differentiation of feelings and develop more appreciation for nuances among them. In addition, they begin to make their own decisions and to accept responsibility for their choices.

People at *Stage 6* experience dramatic growth and an irreversible movement toward becoming fully functioning or self-actualizing. They freely allow into awareness those experiences that they had previously denied or distorted. They become more congruent and are able to match their present experiences with awareness and with open expression. They no longer evaluate their own behavior from an external viewpoint but rely on their organismic self as the criterion for evaluating experiences. They begin to develop unconditional self-regard, which means that they have a feeling of genuine caring and affection for the person they are becoming.

An interesting concomitant to this stage is a physiological loosening. These people experience their whole organismic self, as their muscles relax, tears flow, circulation improves, and physical symptoms disappear.

Persons of tomorrow are confident in
themselves and comfortable with change.

In many ways, Stage 6 signals an end to therapy. Indeed, if therapy were to be terminated at this point, clients would still progress to the next level.

Stage 7 can occur outside the therapeutic encounter, because growth at Stage 6 seems to be irreversible. Clients who reach Stage 7 become fully functioning "persons of tomorrow" (a concept more fully explained in the section titled The Person of Tomorrow). They are able to generalize their in-therapy experiences to their world beyond therapy. They possess the confidence to be themselves at all times, to own and to feel deeply the totality of their experiences, and to live those experiences in the present. Their organismic self, now unified with the self-concept, becomes the locus for evaluating their experiences. People at Stage 7 receive pleasure in knowing that these evaluations are fluid and that change and growth will continue. In addition, they become congruent, possess *unconditional positive self-regard,* and are able to be loving and empathic toward others.

Theoretical Explanation for Therapeutic Change

What theoretical formulation can explain the dynamics of therapeutic change? Rogers's (1980) explanation follows this line of reasoning. When persons come to experience themselves as prized and unconditionally accepted, they realize, perhaps for the first time, that they are lovable. The example of the therapist enables them to prize and accept themselves, to have unconditional positive self-regard. As clients perceive that they are emphatically understood, they are freed to listen to themselves more accurately, to have empathy for their own feelings. As a consequence, when these persons come to prize themselves and to accurately understand themselves, their perceived self becomes more congruent with their organismic experiences. They now possess the same three therapeutic characteristics as any effective helper, and in effect, they become their own therapist.

Outcomes

If the process of therapeutic change is set in motion, then certain observable outcomes can be expected. The most basic outcome of successful client-centered therapy is a congruent client who is less defensive and more open to experience. Each of the remaining outcomes is a logical extension of this basic one.

As a result of being more congruent and less defensive, clients have a clearer picture of themselves and a more realistic view of the world. They are better able to assimilate experiences into the self on the symbolic level; they are more effective in solving problems; and they have a higher level of positive self-regard.

Being realistic, they have a more accurate view of their potentials, which permits them to narrow the gap between self-ideal and real self. Typically, this gap is narrowed because both the ideal self and the true self show some movement. Because clients are more realistic, they lower their expectations of what they should be or would like to be; and because they have an increase in positive self-regard, they raise their view of what they really are.

Because their ideal self and their real self are more congruent, clients experience less physiological and psychological tension, are less vulnerable to threat, and have less anxiety. They are less likely to look to others for direction and less likely to use others' opinions and values as the criteria for evaluating their own experiences. Instead, they become more self-directed and more likely to perceive that the locus of evaluation resides within themselves. They no longer feel compelled to please other people and to meet external expectations. They feel sufficiently safe to

---

TABLE 11.1

Rogers's Theory of Therapeutic Change

If the following conditions exist:	*Then* therapeutic change occurs and the client will
1. A vulnerable or anxious client	1. **become more congruent;**
2. contacts a counselor who possesses	2. **be less defensive;**
3. **congruence in the relationship,**	3. **become more open to experiences;**
4. **unconditional positive regard for the client,** and	4. have a more realistic view of the world;
5. **empathic understanding for the client's internal frame of reference,** and	5. develop positive self-regard;
6. the client perceives Conditions 3, 4, and 5—the three necessary and sufficient conditions for therapeutic growth;	6. narrow the gap between ideal self and real self;
	7. be less vulnerable to threat;
	8. become less anxious;
	9. take ownership of experiences;
	10. become more accepting of others;
	11. become more congruent in relationships with others.

Note: Boldfaced phrases represent the key therapeutic conditions and the most basic outcomes.

take ownership of an increasing number of their experiences and comfortable enough with themselves to lessen their need for denial and distortion.

Their relationships with others are also changed. They become more accepting of others, make fewer demands, and simply allow others to be themselves. Because they have less need to distort reality, they have less desire to force others to meet their expectations. They are also perceived by others as being more mature, more likable, and more socialized. Their genuineness, positive self-regard, and empathic understanding are extended beyond therapy, and they become better able to participate in other growth-facilitating relationships (Rogers, 1959, 1961). Table 11.1 illustrates Rogers's theory of therapy.

The Person of Tomorrow

The interest shown by Rogers in the psychologically healthy individual is rivaled only by that of Maslow (see Chapter 10). Whereas Maslow was primarily a researcher, Rogers was first of all a psychotherapist whose concern with psychologically healthy people grew out of his general theory of therapy. In 1951, Rogers first briefly put forward his "characteristics of the altered personality"; then he enlarged on the concept of the **fully functioning person** in an unpublished paper (Rogers, 1953). In 1959, his theory of the healthy personality was expounded in the Koch series, and he returned to this topic frequently during the early 1960s (Rogers, 1961, 1962, 1963). Somewhat later, he described both the world of tomorrow and the **person of tomorrow** (Rogers, 1980).

If the three necessary and sufficient therapeutic conditions of congruence, unconditional positive regard, and empathy are optimal, then what kind of person would emerge? Rogers (1961, 1962, 1980) listed several possible characteristics.

First, psychologically healthy people would be *more adaptable*. Thus, from an evolutionary viewpoint, they would be more likely to survive—hence the title "persons of tomorrow." They would not merely adjust to a static environment but would realize that conformity and adjustment to a fixed condition have little long-term survival value.

Second, persons of tomorrow would be *open to their experiences,* accurately symbolizing them in awareness rather than denying or distorting them. This simple statement is pregnant with meaning. For people who are open to experience, all stimuli, whether stemming from within the organism or from the external environment, are freely received by the self. Persons of tomorrow would listen to themselves and hear their joy, anger, discouragement, fear, and tenderness.

A related characteristic of persons of tomorrow would be a *trust in their organismic selves.* These fully functioning people would not depend on others for guidance because they would realize that their own experiences are the best criteria for making choices; they would do what feels right for them because they would trust their own inner feelings more than the pontifications of parents or the rigid rules of society. However, they would also perceive clearly the rights and feelings of other people, which they would take into consideration when making decisions.

A third characteristic of persons of tomorrow would be a tendency to *live fully in the moment.* Because these people would be open to their experiences, they would experience a constant state of fluidity and change. What they experience in each moment would be new and unique, something never before experienced by their evolving self. They would see each experience with a new freshness and appreciate it fully in the present moment. Rogers (1961) referred to this tendency to live in the moment as **existential living.** Persons of tomorrow would have no need to deceive themselves and no reason to impress others. They would be young in mind and spirit, with no preconceptions about how the world should be. They would discover what an experience means to them by living that experience without the prejudice of prior expectations.

Fourth, persons of tomorrow would remain confident of their own ability to experience *harmonious relations with others.* They would feel no need to be liked or loved by everyone, because they would know that they are unconditionally prized and accepted by someone. They would seek intimacy with another person who is probably equally healthy, and such a relationship itself would contribute to the continual growth of each partner. Persons of tomorrow would be authentic in their relations with others. They would be what they appear to be, without deceit or fraud, without defenses and facades, without hypocrisy and sham. They would care about others, but in a nonjudgmental manner. They would seek meaning beyond themselves and would yearn for the spiritual life and inner peace.

Fifth, persons of tomorrow would be *more integrated,* more whole, with no artificial boundary between conscious processes and unconscious ones. Because they would be able to accurately symbolize all their experiences in awareness, they would see clearly the difference between what is and what should be; because they would use their organismic feelings as criteria for evaluating their experiences, they would bridge the gap between their real self and their ideal self; because they would have no need to defend their self-importance, they would present no facades to other people; and because they would have confidence in who they are, they could openly express whatever feelings they are experiencing.

Sixth, persons of tomorrow would have a *basic trust of human nature.* They would not harm others merely for personal gain; they would care about others and be ready to help when needed; they would experience anger but could be trusted not to strike out unreasonably against others; they would feel aggression but would channel it in appropriate directions.

Finally, because persons of tomorrow are open to all their experiences, they would enjoy a *greater richness in life* than do other people. They would neither distort internal stimuli nor buffer their emotions. Consequently, they would feel more deeply than others. They would live in the present and thus participate more richly in the ongoing moment.

Philosophy of Science

Rogers was first a scientist; second, a therapist; and third, a personality theorist. Because his scientific attitude permeates both his therapy and his theory of personality, we look briefly at his philosophy of science.

According to Rogers (1968), science begins and ends with the subjective experience, although everything in between must be objective and empirical. Scientists must have many of the characteristics of the person of tomorrow; that is, they must be inclined to look within, to be in tune with internal feelings and values, to be intuitive and creative, to be open to experiences, to welcome change, to have a fresh outlook, and to possess a solid trust in themselves.

Rogers (1968) believed that scientists should be completely involved in the phenomena being studied. For example, people who conduct research on psychotherapy must first have had long careers as therapists. Scientists must care about and care for newly born ideas and nurture them lovingly through their fragile infancy.

Science begins when an intuitive scientist starts to perceive patterns among phenomena. At first, these dimly seen relationships may be too vague to be communicated to others, but they are nourished by a caring scientist until eventually they can be formulated into testable hypotheses. These hypotheses, then, are the consequence of an open-minded scientist and not the result of preexisting stereotypical thought.

At this point, methodology enters the picture. Although the creativity of a scientist may yield innovative methods of research, these procedures themselves must be rigorously controlled, empirical, and objective. Precise methods prevent the scientist from self-deception and from intentionally or unintentionally manipulating the observations. But this precision should not be confused with science. It is only the *method* of science that is precise and objective.

The scientist then communicates findings from that method to others, but the communication itself is subjective. The people receiving the communication bring their own degrees of open-mindedness or defensiveness into this process. They have varying levels of readiness to receive the findings, depending on the prevailing climate of scientific thought and the personal subjective experiences of each individual.

The Chicago Studies

Consistent with his philosophy of science, Rogers did not permit methodology to dictate the nature of his research. In his investigations of the outcomes of client-centered psychotherapy, first at the Counseling Center of the University of Chicago (Rogers & Dymond, 1954) and then with schizophrenic patients at the University of Wisconsin (Rogers, Gendlin, Kiesler, & Truax, 1967), he and his colleagues allowed the problem to take precedence over methodology and measurement. They did not formulate hypotheses simply because the tools for testing them were readily available. Instead, they began by sensing vague impressions from clinical experience and gradually forming these into testable hypotheses. It was only then that Rogers and his colleagues dealt with the task of finding or inventing instruments by which these hypotheses could be tested.

The purpose of the Chicago Studies was to investigate both the process and the outcomes of client-centered therapy. The therapists were of a "journeyman" level. They included Rogers and other faculty members, but graduate students also served as therapists. Though they ranged widely in experience and ability, all were basically client centered in approach (Rogers, 1961; Rogers & Dymond, 1954).

Hypotheses

Research at the University of Chicago Counseling Center was built around the basic client-centered hypothesis, which states that all persons have within themselves the capacity, either active or latent, for self-understanding as well as the capacity and tendency to move in the direction of self-actualization and maturity. This tendency will become realized provided the therapist creates the proper psychological atmosphere. More specifically, Rogers (1954) hypothesized that during therapy, clients would assimilate into their self-concepts those feelings and experiences previously denied to awareness. He also predicted that during and after therapy the discrepancy between real self and ideal self would diminish and that the observed behavior of clients would become more socialized, more self-accepting, and more accepting of others. These hypotheses, in turn, became the foundation for several more specific hypotheses, which were operationally stated and then tested.

Method

Because the hypotheses of the study dictated that subtle subjective personality changes be measured in an objective fashion, the selection of measuring instruments was a difficult one. To assess change from an external viewpoint, the researchers used the Thematic Apperception Test (TAT), the Self-Other Attitude Scale (S-O Scale), and the Willoughby Emotional Maturity Scale (E-M Scale). The TAT, a projective personality test developed by Henry Murray (1938), was used to test hypotheses that called for a standard clinical diagnosis; the S-O Scale, an instrument compiled at the Counseling Center from several earlier sources, measures antidemocratic trends and ethnocentrism; the E-M Scale was used to compare descriptions of clients' behavior and emotional maturity as seen by two close friends and by the clients themselves.

To measure change from the client's point of view, the researchers relied on the **Q sort** technique developed by William Stephenson of the University of Chicago (Stephenson, 1953). The Q sort technique begins with a universe of 100 self-referent statements printed on 3-by-5 cards, which participants are requested to sort into nine piles from "most like me" to "least like me." Researchers asked the participants to sort the cards into piles of 1, 4, 11, 21, 26, 21, 11, 4, and 1. The resulting distribution approximates a normal curve and allows for statistical analysis. At various points throughout the study, participants were requested to sort the cards to describe their self, their ideal self, and the ordinary person.

Participants for the study were 18 men and 11 women who had sought therapy at the Counseling Center. More than half were university students and the others were from the surrounding community. These clients—called the experimental or *therapy group*—received at least six therapeutic interviews, and each session was electronically recorded and transcribed, a procedure Rogers had pioneered as early as 1938.

The researchers used two different methods of control. First, they asked half the people in the therapy group to wait 60 days before they would receive therapy. These participants, known as the own-control or *wait group,* were required to wait before receiving therapy in order to determine if motivation to change rather than the

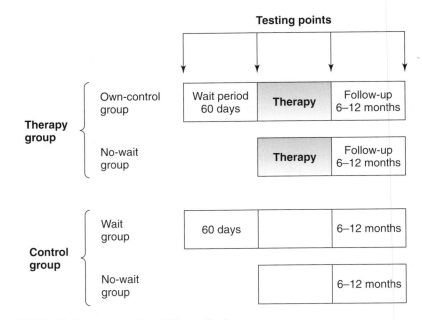

FIGURE 11.1 *Design of the Chicago Study.*

From C. R. Rogers and R. F. Dymond, *Psychotherapy and Personality Change,* 1954. Copyright © 1954 The University of Chicago Press, Chicago, IL. Reprinted by permission.

therapy itself might cause people to get better. The other half of the therapy group, called the *no-wait group,* received therapy immediately.

The second control consisted of a separate group of "normals," who had volunteered to serve as participants in a "research on personality" study. This comparison group allowed researchers to determine the effects of such variables as passage of time, knowledge that one is part of an experiment (the **placebo effect**), and the impact of repeated testing. The participants in this *control group* were divided into a *wait group* and a *no-wait group,* which corresponded to the wait and no-wait therapy groups. Researchers tested both the therapy wait group and the control wait group four times: at the beginning of the 60-day wait period, prior to therapy, immediately after therapy, and after a 6- to 12-month follow-up period. They administered the no-wait groups the same tests on the same occasions, except, of course, prior to the wait period. The overall design of the study is shown in Figure 11.1.

Findings

The researchers found that the therapy group showed less discrepancy between self and ideal self after therapy than before, and they retained almost all those gains throughout the follow-up period. As expected, the "normal" controls had a higher level of congruence than the therapy group at the beginning of the study, but in contrast to the therapy group, they showed almost no change in congruence between self and self-ideal from the initial testing until the final follow-up.

In addition, the therapy group changed their self-concept more than they changed their perception of the ordinary person. This finding suggests that, although clients showed little change in their notion of what the average person was like, they manifested marked change in their perceptions of self. In other words, intellectual insight does not result in psychological growth (Rudikoff, 1954).

Does therapy bring about noticeable changes in clients' behavior as perceived by close friends? Participants in both the therapy and the control groups were asked to supply the experimenters with names of two intimate friends who would be in a position to judge overt behavioral changes.

In general, the friends reported no significant behavioral changes in the clients from the pretherapy period to posttherapy. However, this global rating of no change was due to a counterbalancing effect. Clients judged by their therapists as being most improved received higher posttherapy maturity scores from their friends, whereas those rated as least improved received lower scores from their friends. Interestingly, before therapy, clients typically rated themselves less mature than their friends rated them, but as therapy progressed, they began to rate themselves higher and, therefore, more in agreement with their friends' ratings. Participants in the control group showed no changes throughout the study in emotional maturity as judged by friends (Rogers & Dymond, 1954).

Summary of Results

The Chicago Studies demonstrated that people receiving client-centered therapy generally showed some growth or improvement. However, improvement fell short of the optimum. The therapy group began treatment as less healthy than the control group, showed growth during therapy, and retained most of that improvement throughout the follow-up period. However, they never attained the level of psychological health demonstrated by "normal" people in the control group.

Looking at these outcomes another way, the typical person receiving client-centered therapy probably never approaches Stage 7 hypothesized by Rogers and discussed earlier. A more realistic expectation might be for clients to advance to Stage 3 or 4. Client-centered therapy is effective, but it does not result in the fully functioning person.

Related Research

Compared to Maslow's theory, Rogers's ideas on the power of unconditional positive regard generated quite a bit of empirical research. Indeed, Rogers's own research on the three necessary and sufficient conditions for psychological growth were precursors to positive psychology and have been further supported by modern research (Cramer, 1994, 2002, 2003a). Moreover, Rogers's notion of incongruence between real and ideal self and motivation to pursue goals have sparked continued interest from researchers.

Self-Discrepancy Theory

Rogers also proposed that the cornerstone of mental health was the congruency between how we really view ourselves and how we ideally would like to be. If these two self-evaluations are congruent, then one is relatively adjusted and healthy. If not, then one experiences various forms of mental discomfort, such as anxiety, depression, and low self-esteem.

In the 1980s, E. Tory Higgins developed a version of Rogers's theory that continues to be influential in personality and social psychological research. Higgins's version of the theory is called self-discrepancy theory and argues not only for the real self–ideal self discrepancy but also for real self–ought self discrepancy (Higgins, 1987). One difference between Rogers and Higgins is the more specific nature of Higgins's theory. By proposing at least two distinct forms of discrepancy, he predicted distinct negative outcomes from each. For instance, real-ideal discrepancy should lead to dejection-related emotions (e.g., depression, sadness, disappointment), whereas real-ought discrepancy should lead to agitation-related emotions (e.g., anxiety, fear, threat). Although more specific, Higgins's theory nonetheless has essentially the same form and assumptions of Rogers's theory: Individuals with high levels of self-discrepancy are most likely to experience high levels of negative affect in their lives, such as anxiety and depression.

Higgins's theory has garnered much empirical attention since the mid-1980s. Some of the recent research has sought to clarify the conditions under which self-discrepancies predict emotional experience (Phillips & Silvia, 2005). For example, Ann Phillips and Paul Silvia predicted that the negative emotion experienced from either real-ideal or real-ought discrepancies would be most extreme when people are more self-focused or self-aware. Being in a state of self-focus not only makes one more aware of his or her self-relevant traits, but also makes a person more likely to detect discrepancies and therefore be more interested in being congruent.

To test their prediction, Phillips and Silvia brought participants into a lab and induced self-awareness in half of the participants by having them complete questionnaires about self-discrepancies and mood in front of a mirror. The other half of the sample completed the same questionnaires but while sitting at a normal desk without a mirror present. For obvious reasons, if you are answering questions about yourself while looking at yourself in a mirror, you are more likely to be self-aware. As predicted, the phenomenon of experiencing negative emotion as a result of self-discrepancies occurred only among those participants who were highly self-aware (i.e., those who completed the questionnaires in front of the mirror).

In other research involving Higgins's self-discrepancy theory, researchers have applied the theory to health-related variables such as alcohol consumption (Wolfe & Maisto, 2000), eating disorders (Veale, Kinderman, Riley, & Lambrou, 2003), and mental health in general (Liao & Fan, 2003). For instance, Wendy Wolfe and Stephen Maisto (2000) tested the prediction that higher real-ideal self-discrepancy would be related to greater alcohol consumption in a sample of university students. Wolfe and Maisto reasoned that people who have large real-ideal self-discrepancies look to relieve their negative affective states (anxiety, depression) by turning to alcohol. As was the case in the research by Phillips and Silvia on self-awareness and self-discrepancy, the researchers also reasoned that this effect should be even stronger on those dimensions of self-concept that are particularly important and salient to the individual. In other words, they believed both the magnitude of the discrepancy and the salience of the discrepancy (i.e., self-awareness) should be related to alcohol consumption.

To test their prediction, Wolfe and Maisto studied university students who were moderate drinkers. In an experimental design, they assigned half the students to a high salience condition and the other half to a low salience condition. The first session consisted of participants completing pre-screening and real-ideal self-discrepancy measures. For the latter, participants rated 35 personality dimensions twice: first, as they really are and second, as they ideally would like to be. The researchers also evaluated how important each dimension was. The second session primarily consisted of a mood assessment, the salience manipulation, and alcohol consumption. Baseline mood was first assessed by a short questionnaire. Participants in the high salience condition were instructed to think of and list possible reasons for the discrepancies between real and ideal self from the first session. By focusing attention on their discrepancy, just like the participants in the Phillips and Silvia study completing their questionnaires in front of a mirror, this procedure was expected to increase negative self-evaluations and negative mood. Participants in the low salience condition simply completed a filler task during this time by crossing out letters in a document. Mood was again assessed to examine whether those in the high salience condition experience greater negative mood. Finally, alcohol consumption was assessed by having each participant take part in a "taste testing" session. They were given three different carafes of wine and three different carafes of seltzer. Next, they were instructed to rate each drink on its palatability on seven adjective pairs (e.g., weak-strong). They were given 30 minutes and informed they could drink as much or as little of each in order to make the evaluations.

After controlling for a gender effect (men drank more than women), results showed no overall effect of real-ideal self-discrepancy on wine consumption. There was, however, a positive relationship between discrepancy and amount of wine consumed for the low salience (filler task) group—only the greater the discrepancy, the more wine consumed. For the high salience group, surprisingly, the researchers found a small negative relationship—the greater the discrepancy, the less wine consumed. This last finding was unexpected, and Wolfe and Maisto suggested that it may be due to the salience manipulation not performing as predicted. Most importantly, based on evaluation of mood ratings, high salience participants actually showed a decrease in negative mood (anxiety), not an increase as expected. Clearly the salience manipulation used here was not as powerful as the self-awareness manipulation (completing questionnaires in front of mirror) used by Phillips and Silvia but, in one sense, the theory was supported: Decreasing negative mood should and did lead to less alcohol consumption. The researchers simply did not expect the salience manipulation to decrease negative mood. In general, these results supported Rogers's notion that people whose ideal self is at variance with their real self may turn to alcohol or other unhealthy behaviors as a means of coping with this discrepancy.

Motivation and Pursuing One's Goals

One area of research where Rogers's ideas continue to be influential is goal pursuit. Setting and pursuing goals is a way for people to organize their lives in a way that leads to desirable outcomes and adds meaning to daily activities. Setting goals is easy, but setting the right goals can be more difficult than it seems. According to Rogers, a source of psychological distress is incongruence, or when one's ideal self does not sufficiently overlap with his or her self-concept and this incongruence can be represented in the goals the person chooses to pursue. For example, a person may pursue the goal to do well in biology but does not even like biology or may not even need it for her or his goal of being an architect. Perhaps this person's parents are biologists and it was always expected he or she would do the same even though the person feels that architecture is more exciting and fulfilling. In this example, biology is a part of the person's self-concept, but architecture is a part of his or her ideal self. The incongruence between the two can be a source of distress. Fortunately, Rogers (1951) expanded on these ideas to propose that we all have an **organismic valuing process (OVP)**—that is, a natural instinct directing us toward the most fulfilling pursuits. In the above example, the OVP would be represented as a visceral or unexplainable gut feeling that architecture, not biology, is the right path.

Ken Sheldon and colleagues (2003) have explored the existence of an OVP in college students by designing studies that ask students to rate the importance of several goals repeatedly over the course of multiple weeks. Any time people rate the same thing (for example, goals) over time, there is bound to be fluctuation in their ratings. Sheldon and colleagues, however, predicted that the fluctuation in the importance of several goals would have a distinct pattern. If people truly possess an OVP as Rogers theorized, then over time they will rate goals that are inherently more fulfilling as more desirable than goals that lead only to materialistic gains. To test their prediction, Sheldon and colleagues had undergraduate students rate multiple pre-selected goals (some of which were inherently more fulfilling than others). Six weeks later, participants rated the same goals again, and then one final time 6 weeks after that. What the researchers found was that, in line with the prediction that people possess an OVP, the participants tended to rate the more fulfilling goals with increasing importance over time and the materialistic goals with decreasing importance.

Although the study discussed above on the role of the OVP in goal pursuit is a direct test of Rogers's ideas, there is other modern personality research inspired by the potential for incongruence that uses a different terminology. For example, personality researchers talk about goals being either intrinsically or extrinsically motivated. Intrinsic goals are goals a person finds satisfying and fulfilling; these goals are part of the ideal self, and people will be directed toward them by their OVP. The pursuit of intrinsic goals does not need to be encouraged by rewards such as money, grades, or treats. Simply pursuing the goal is a rewarding experience in its own right. Extrinsic goals, conversely, are goals that are not experienced as inherently rewarding; these goals can be represented in one's self-concept but are not necessarily part of the ideal self. Extrinsic goals are typically motivated by factors such as money and prestige. A simple test to see if one of your goals is intrinsic or extrinsic is to ask yourself if you would pursue the goal even if you never received any material compensation for it. If the answer is yes, then the goal is intrinsic, but if the answer is no, then the goal is likely to be extrinsically motivated.

Intrinsically motivated activities generally make people happier and more fulfilled. Intrinsic motivation and fulfillment are connected because intrinsically motivated activities represent the ideal self. Recent research has explored the extent to which having more self-realizing experiences in which people are allowed to express who they really are (similar to Rogers's ideal self) is related to experiencing more intrinsic motivation (Schwartz & Waterman, 2006). Schwartz and Waterman designed a longitudinal study in which at Time 1 participants listed several activities that were important to them. Then, at subsequent time points scattered over the course of a semester, the researchers checked in with participants to evaluate to what extent engagement in the activities participants listed at Time 1 led to greater feelings of self-realization (i.e., opportunities to develop one's best potentials) and to what extent the activities fostered intrinsic motivation. The results of this longitudinal study indicated that, just as Carl Rogers would have predicted, the more the activities people engage in reflect self-realization, the more likely those activities are to be interesting, self-expressive, and lead to an experience of "flow." Flow is the experience of being fully immersed and engaged in an experience to the point of losing track of time and one's sense of self (Csikszentmihalyi, 1990).

Carl Rogers clearly had keen insight into the human condition, and his ideas continue to be supported by the most modern research. If you engage in experiences that are part of your ideal self, you will be led to pursuits that are more engaging, enriching, interesting, and rewarding (Schwartz & Waterman, 2006). But what if you don't know what specific pursuits you will find the most rewarding? Fortunately, as Rogers predicted and as Sheldon and colleagues (2003) found in their study of college students, people have a built-in system (the OVP) that will direct them toward fulfilling pursuits. All you have to do is listen to your gut.

Critique of Rogers

How well does Rogerian theory satisfy the six criteria of a useful theory? First, does it *generate research* and suggest testable hypotheses? Although Rogerian theory has produced much research in the realm of psychotherapy and classroom learning (see Rogers, 1983), it has been only moderately productive outside these two areas and thus receives only an average rating on its ability to spark research activity within the general field of personality.

Second, we rate Rogerian theory high on *falsification.* Rogers was one of only a few theorists who spelled out his theory in an if-then framework, and such a paradigm lends itself to either confirmation or disconfirmation. His precise language facilitated research at the University of Chicago and later at the University of Wisconsin that exposed his theory of therapy to falsification. Unfortunately, since Rogers's death, many humanistically oriented followers have failed to put his more general theory to test.

Third, does person-centered theory *organize knowledge* into a meaningful framework? Although much of the research generated by the theory has been limited to interpersonal relations, Rogerian theory nevertheless can be extended to a relatively wide range of human personality. Rogers's interests went beyond the consulting room and included group dynamics, classroom learning, social problems, and international relations. Therefore, we rate person-centered theory high on its ability to explain what is currently known about human behavior.

Fourth, how well does person-centered theory serve as a *guide for the solution of practical problems?* For the psychotherapist, the answer is unequivocal. To bring about personality change, the therapist must possess congruence and be able to demonstrate empathic understanding and unconditional positive regard for the client. Rogers suggested that these three conditions are both necessary and sufficient to affect growth in any interpersonal relationship, including those outside of therapy.

Fifth, is person-centered theory *internally consistency,* with a set of operational definitions. We rate person-centered theory very high for its consistency and its carefully worked-out operational definitions. Future theory builders can learn a valuable lesson from Rogers's pioneering work in constructing a theory of personality.

Finally, is Rogerian theory *parsimonious* and free from cumbersome concepts and difficult language? The theory itself is unusually clear and economical, but some of the language is awkward and vague. Concepts such as "organismic experiencing," "becoming," "positive self-regard," "need for self-regard," "unconditional self-regard," and "fully functioning" are too broad and imprecise to have clear scientific meaning. This criticism is a small one, however, in comparison with the overall tightness and parsimony of person-centered theory.

Concept of Humanity

Rogers's concept of humanity was clearly stated in his famous debates with B. F. Skinner during the mid-1950s and early 1960s. Perhaps the most famous debates in the history of American psychology, these discussions consisted of three face-to-face confrontations between Rogers and Skinner regarding the issue of freedom and control (Rogers & Skinner, 1956). Skinner (see Chapter 15) argued that people are always controlled, whether they realize it or not. Because we are controlled mostly by haphazard contingencies that have no grand design or plan, we often have the illusion that we are free (Skinner, 1971).

Rogers, however, contended that people have some degree of *free choice* and some capacity to be self-directed. Admitting that some portion of human behavior is controlled, predictable, and lawful, Rogers argued that the important values and choices are within the scope of personal control.

Throughout his long career, Rogers remained cognizant of the human capacity for great evil, yet his concept of humanity is realistically *optimistic.* He believed that people are essentially forward moving and that, under proper conditions, they will grow toward self-actualization. People are basically trustworthy, socialized, and constructive. They ordinarily know what is best for themselves and will strive for completion provided they are prized and understood by another healthy individual. However, Rogers (1959) was also aware that people can be quite brutal, nasty, and neurotic:

> I do not have a Pollyanna view of human nature. I am quite aware that out of defensiveness and inner fear individuals can and do behave in ways which are horribly destructive, immature, regressive, anti-social, hurtful. Yet, one of the most refreshing and invigorating parts of my experience is to work with such individuals and to discover the strongly positive directional tendencies which exist in them, as in all of us, at the deepest levels. (p. 21)

This tendency toward growth and self-actualization has a biological basis. Just as plants and animals have an innate tendency toward growth and fulfillment, so too do human beings. All organisms actualize themselves, but only humans can become self-actualizing. Humans are different from plants and animals primarily because they have self-awareness. To the extent that we have awareness, we are able to make free choices and to play an active role in forming our personalities.

Rogers's theory is also high on *teleology,* maintaining that people strive with purpose toward goals that they freely set for themselves. Again, under proper therapeutic conditions, people consciously desire to become more fully functioning, more open to their experiences, and more accepting of self and others.

Rogers placed more emphasis on individual differences and *uniqueness* than on similarities. If plants have individual potential for growth, people have even greater uniqueness and individuality. Within a nurturant environment, people can grow in their own fashion toward the process of being more fully functioning.

Although Rogers did not deny the importance of unconscious processes, his primary emphasis was on the ability of people to *consciously* choose their own course of action. Fully functioning people are ordinarily aware of what they are doing and have some understanding of their reasons for doing it.

On the dimension of *biological versus social influences,* Rogers favored the latter. Psychological growth is not automatic. In order to move toward actualization, one must experience empathic understanding and unconditional positive regard from another person who is genuine or congruent. Rogers firmly held that, although much of our behavior is determined by heredity and environment, we have within us the capacity to choose and to become self-directed. Under nurturant conditions, this choice "always seems to be in the direction of greater socialization, improved relationships with others" (Rogers, 1982, p. 8).

Rogers (1982) did not claim that, if left alone, people would be righteous, virtuous, or honorable. However, in an atmosphere without threat, people are free to become what they potentially can be. No evaluation in terms of morality applies to the nature of humanity. People simply have the potential for growth, the need for growth, and the desire for growth. By nature, they will strive for completion even under unfavorable conditions, but under poor conditions they do not realize their full potential for psychological health. However, under the most nurturant and favorable conditions, people will become more self-aware, trustworthy, congruent, and self-directed, qualities that will move them toward becoming persons of tomorrow.

Key Terms and Concepts

- The *formative tendency* states that all matter, both organic and inorganic, tends to evolve from simple to more complex forms.
- Humans and other animals possess an *actualization tendency:* that is, the predisposition to move toward completion or fulfillment.
- *Self-actualization* develops after people evolve a self-system and refers to the tendency to move toward becoming a fully functional person.

- An individual becomes a person by making *contact* with a caregiver whose *positive regard* for that individual fosters *positive self-regard.*
- *Barriers to psychological growth* exist when a person experiences conditions of worth, incongruence, defensiveness, and disorganization.
- *Conditions of worth* and *external evaluation* lead to *vulnerability, anxiety,* and *threat* and prevent people from experiencing unconditional positive regard.
- *Incongruence* develops when the organismic self and the perceived self do not match.
- When the organismic self and perceived self are incongruent, people will become *defensive* and use *distortion* and *denial* as attempts to reduce incongruence.
- People become *disorganized* whenever distortion and denial are insufficient to block out incongruence.
- Vulnerable people are unaware of their incongruence and are likely to become *anxious, threatened,* and defensive.
- When vulnerable people come in contact with a therapist who is *congruent* and who has *unconditional positive regard* and *empathy,* the process of personality change begins.
- This *process* of therapeutic personality change ranges from extreme defensiveness, or an unwillingness to talk about self, to a final stage in which clients become their own therapists and are able to continue psychological growth outside the therapeutic setting.
- The basic *outcomes* of client-centered counseling are congruent clients who are open to experiences and who have no need to be defensive.
- Theoretically, successful clients will become *persons of tomorrow,* or *fully functioning persons.*

CHAPTER 12

May: Existential Psychology

May

Twice married, twice divorced, Philip was struggling through yet another difficult relationship—this time with Nicole, a writer in her mid-40s. Philip could offer Nicole both love and financial security, but their relationship did not seem to be working.

Six months after Philip met Nicole, the two spent an idyllic summer together at his retreat. Nicole's two small sons were with their father and Philip's three children were by then young adults who could care for themselves. At the beginning of the summer, Nicole talked about the possibility of marriage, but Philip replied that he was against it, citing his two previous unsuccessful marriages as his reason. Aside from this brief disagreement, the time they spent together that summer was completely pleasurable. Their intellectual discussions were gratifying to Philip and their lovemaking was the most satisfying he had ever experienced, often bordering on ecstasy.

At the end of this romantic summer, Nicole returned home alone to put her children in school. The day after she arrived home, Philip telephoned her, but somehow her voice seemed strange. The next morning he called again and got the feeling that someone else was with Nicole. That afternoon he called several more times but kept getting a busy signal. When he finally got through, he asked her if someone had been with her that morning. Without hesitation, Nicole reported that Craig, an old friend from her college days, was staying with her and that she had fallen in love with him. Moreover, she planned to marry Craig at the end of the month and move to another part of the country.

Philip was devastated. He felt betrayed and abandoned. He lost weight, resumed smoking, and suffered from insomnia. When he saw Nicole again, he expressed his anger at her "crazy" plan. This outburst of rage was rare for Philip. He seldom showed anger, perhaps for fear of losing the one he loved. To complicate matters, Nicole said she still loved Philip, and she continued to see him whenever Craig was not available. Eventually, Nicole lost her infatuation with Craig and told Philip that, as he well knew, she could never leave him. This comment confused Philip because he knew no such thing.

Overview of Existential Psychology

We return to Philip's story at several points in this chapter. But first, we present a brief overview of existential psychology.

Shortly after World War II, a new psychology—existential psychology—began to spread from Europe to the United States. Existential psychology is rooted in the philosophy of Søren Kierkegaard, Friedrich Nietzsche, Martin Heidegger, Jean-Paul Sartre, and other European philosophers. The first existential psychologists and psychiatrists were also Europeans, and these included Ludwig Binswanger, Medard Boss, Victor Frankl, and others.

For nearly 50 years, the foremost spokesperson for existential psychology in the United States was Rollo May. During his years as a psychotherapist, May evolved a new way of looking at human beings. His approach was not based on any controlled scientific research but rather on clinical experience. He saw people as living in the world of present experiences and ultimately being responsible for who they become. May's penetrating insights and profound analyses of the human condition made him a popular writer among laypeople as well as professional psychologists.

Many people, May believed, lack the courage to face their destiny, and in the process of fleeing from it, they give up much of their freedom. Having negated their freedom, they likewise run away from their responsibility. Not being willing to make choices, they lose sight of who they are and develop a sense of insignificance and alienation. In contrast, healthy people challenge their destiny, cherish their freedom, and live authentically with other people and with themselves. They recognize the inevitability of death and have the courage to live life in the present.

Biography of Rollo May

Rollo Reese May was born April 21, 1909, in Ada, Ohio, the first son of the six children born to Earl Tittle May and Matie Boughton May. Neither parent was very well educated, and May's early intellectual climate was virtually nonexistent. In fact, when his older sister had a psychotic breakdown some years later, May's father attributed it to too much education (Bilmes, 1978)!

At an early age, May moved with his family to Marine City, Michigan, where he spent most of his childhood. As a young boy, May was not particularly close to either of his parents, who frequently argued with each other and eventually separated. May's father, a secretary for the Young Men's Christian Association, moved frequently during May's youth. May's mother often left the children to care for themselves and, according to May's description, was a "bitch-kitty on wheels" (Rabinowitz, Good, & Cozad, 1989, p. 437). May attributed his own two failed marriages to his mother's unpredictable behavior and to his older sister's psychotic episode.

During his childhood, May found solitude and relief from family strife by playing on the shores of the St. Clair River. The river became his friend, a serene place to swim during the summer and to ice skate during the winter. He claimed to have learned more from the river than from the school he attended in Marine City (Rabinowitz et al., 1989). As a youth, he acquired an interest in art and literature, interests that never left him. He first attended college at Michigan State University, where he majored in English. However, he was asked to leave school soon after he became editor of a radical student magazine. May then transferred to Oberlin College in Ohio, from which he received a bachelor's degree in 1930.

For the next 3 years, May followed a course very similar to the one traveled by Erik Erikson some 10 years earlier (see Chapter 9). He roamed throughout eastern and southern Europe as an artist, painting pictures and studying native art (Harris, 1969). Actually, the nominal purpose for May's trip was to tutor English at Anatolia College in Saloniki, Greece. This job provided him time to work as an itinerant artist in Turkey, Poland, Austria, and other countries. However, by his second year, May was beginning to become lonely. As a consequence, he poured himself into his work as a teacher, but the harder he worked, the less effective he became.

> Finally in the spring of that second year I had what is called, euphemistically, a nervous breakdown. Which meant simply that the rules, principles, values, by which I used to work and live simply did not suffice anymore. I got so completely fatigued that I had to go to bed for two weeks to get enough energy to continue my teaching. I had learned enough psychology at college to know that these

> symptoms meant that something was wrong with my whole way of life. I had to
> find some new goals and purposes for my living and to relinquish my moralistic,
> somewhat rigid way of existence. (May, 1985, p. 8)

From that point on, May began to listen to his inner voice, the one that spoke to him of beauty. "It seems it had taken a collapse of my whole former way of life for this voice to make itself heard" (p. 13).

A second experience in Europe also left a lasting impression on him, namely, his attendance at Alfred Adler's 1932 summer seminars at a resort in the mountains above Vienna. May greatly admired Adler and learned much about human behavior and about himself during that time (Rabinowitz et al., 1989).

After May returned to the United States in 1933, he enrolled at Union Theological Seminary in New York, the same seminary Carl Rogers had attended 10 years earlier. Unlike Rogers, however, May did not enter the seminary to become a minister but rather to ask the ultimate questions concerning the nature of human beings (Harris, 1969). While at the Union Theological Seminary, he met the renowned existential theologian and philosopher Paul Tillich, then a recent refugee from Germany and a faculty member at the seminary. May learned much of his philosophy from Tillich, and the two men remained friends for more than 30 years.

Although May had not gone to the seminary to be a preacher, he was ordained as a Congregational minister in 1938 after receiving a Master of Divinity degree. He then served as a pastor for 2 years, but finding parish work meaningless, he quit to pursue his interest in psychology. He studied psychoanalysis at the William Alanson White Institute of Psychiatry, Psychoanalysis, and Psychology while working as a counselor to male students at City College of New York. At about this time, he met Harry Stack Sullivan (see Chapter 8), president and cofounder of the William Alanson White Institute. May was impressed with Sullivan's notion that the therapist is a participant observer and that therapy is a human adventure capable of enhancing the life of both patient and therapist. He also met and was influenced by Erich Fromm (see Chapter 7), who at that time was a faculty member at the William Alanson White Institute.

In 1946, May opened his own private practice and, 2 years later, joined the faculty of the William Alanson White Institute. In 1949, at the relatively advanced age of 40, he earned a PhD in clinical psychology from Columbia University. He continued to serve as assistant professor of psychiatry at the William Alanson White Institute until 1974.

Prior to receiving his doctorate, May underwent the most profound experience of his life. While still in his early thirties, he contracted tuberculosis and spent 3 years at the Saranac Sanitarium in upstate New York. At that time, no medication for tuberculosis was available, and for a year and a half, May did not know whether he would live or die. He felt helpless and had little to do except wait for the monthly X-ray that would tell whether the cavity in his lung was getting larger or smaller (May, 1972).

At that point, he began to develop some insight into the nature of his illness. He realized that the disease was taking advantage of his helpless and passive attitude. He saw that the patients around him who accepted their illness were the very ones who tended to die, whereas those who fought against their condition tended to survive. "Not until I developed some 'fight,' some sense of personal responsibility for the fact that it was I who had the tuberculosis, an assertion of my own will to live, did I make lasting progress" (May, 1972, p. 14).

As May learned to listen to his body, he discovered that healing is an active, not a passive, process. The person who is sick, be it physiologically or psychologically, must be an active participant in the therapeutic process. May realized this truth for himself as he recovered from tuberculosis, but it was only later that he was able to see that his psychotherapy patients also had to fight against their disturbance in order to get better (May, 1972).

During his illness and recovery, May was writing a book on anxiety. To better understand the subject, he read both Freud and Søren Kierkegaard, the great Danish existential philosopher and theologian. He admired Freud, but he was more deeply moved by Kierkegaard's view of anxiety as a struggle against *nonbeing,* that is, loss of consciousness (May, 1969a).

After May recovered from his illness, he wrote his dissertation on the subject of anxiety and the next year published it under the title *The Meaning of Anxiety* (May, 1950). Three years later, he wrote *Man's Search for Himself* (May, 1953), the book that gained him some recognition not only in professional circles but among other educated people as well. In 1958, he collaborated with Ernest Angel and Henri Ellenberger to publish *Existence: A New Dimension in Psychiatry and Psychology.* This book introduced American psychotherapists to the concepts of existential therapy and continued the popularity of the existential movement. May's best-known work, *Love and Will* (1969b), became a national best-seller and won the 1970 Ralph Waldo Emerson Award for humane scholarship. In 1971, May won the American Psychological Association's Distinguished Contribution to the Science and Profession of Clinical Psychology Award. In 1972, the New York Society of Clinical Psychologists presented him with the Dr. Martin Luther King, Jr. Award for his book *Power and Innocence* (1972), and in 1987, May received the American Psychological Foundation Gold Medal Award for Lifetime Contributions to Professional Psychology.

During his career, May was a visiting professor at both Harvard and Princeton and lectured at such institutions as Yale, Dartmouth, Columbia, Vassar, Oberlin, and the New School for Social Research. In addition, he was an adjunct professor at New York University, chairman for the Council for the Association of Existential Psychology and Psychiatry, president of the New York Psychological Association, and a member of the Board of Trustees of the American Foundation for Mental Health.

In 1969, May and his first wife, Florence DeFrees, were divorced after 30 years of marriage. He later married Ingrid Kepler Scholl, but that marriage too ended in divorce. On October 22, 1994, after 2 years of declining health, May died in Tiburon, California, where he had made his home since 1975. He was survived by his third wife, Georgia Lee Miller Johnson (a Jungian analyst whom he married in 1988); son, Robert; and twin daughters, Allegra and Carolyn.

Through his books, articles, and lectures, May was the best-known American representative of the existential movement. Nevertheless, he spoke out against the tendency of some existentialists to slip into an antiscientific or even anti-intellectual posture (May, 1962). He was critical of any attempt to dilute existential psychology into a painless method of reaching self-fulfillment. People can aspire to psychological health only through coming to grips with the unconscious core of their existence.

Although he was philosophically aligned with Carl Rogers (see Chapter 11), May took issue with what he saw as Rogers's naive view that evil is a cultural phenomenon. May (1982) regarded human beings as both good and evil and capable of creating cultures that are both good and evil.

Background of Existentialism

Modern existential psychology has roots in the writings of Søren Kierkegaard (1813–1855), Danish philosopher and theologian. Kierkegaard was concerned with the increasing trend in postindustrial societies toward the dehumanization of people. He opposed any attempt to see people merely as objects, but at the same time, he opposed the view that subjective perceptions are one's only reality. Instead, Kierkegaard was concerned with *both* the experiencing person and the person's experience. He wished to understand people as they exist in the world as thinking, active, and willing beings. As May (1967) put it, "Kierkegaard sought to overcome the dichotomy of reason and emotion by turning [people's] attentions to the reality of the immediate experience which underlies both subjectivity and objectivity" (p. 67).

Kierkegaard, like later existentialists, emphasized a balance between *freedom* and *responsibility*. People acquire freedom of action through expanding their self-awareness and then by assuming responsibility for their actions. The acquisition of freedom and responsibility, however, is achieved only at the expense of anxiety. As people realize that, ultimately, they are in charge of their own destiny, they experience the burden of freedom and the pain of responsibility.

Kierkegaard's views had little effect on philosophical thought during his comparatively short lifetime (he died at age 42); but the work of two German philosophers, Friedrich Nietzsche (1844–1900) and Martin Heidegger (1899–1976), helped popularize existential philosophy during the 20th century. Heidegger exerted considerable influence on two Swiss psychiatrists, Ludwig Binswanger and Medard Boss. Binswanger and Boss, along with Karl Jaspers, Victor Frankl, and others, adapted the philosophy of existentialism to the practice of psychotherapy.

Existentialism also permeated 20th-century literature through the work of the French writer Jean-Paul Sartre and the French-Algerian novelist Albert Camus; religion through the writings of Martin Buber, Paul Tillich, and others; and the world of art through the work of Cezanne, Matisse, and Picasso, whose paintings break through the boundaries of realism and demonstrate a freedom of being rather than the freedom of doing (May, 1981).

After World War II, European existentialism in its various forms spread to the United States and became even more diversified as it was taken up by an assorted collection of writers, artists, dissidents, college professors and students, playwrights, clergy, and others.

What Is Existentialism?

Although philosophers and psychologists interpret existentialism in a variety of ways, some common elements are found among most existential thinkers. First, *existence* takes precedence over *essence*. Existence means to emerge or to become; essence implies a static immutable substance. Existence suggests process; essence refers to a product. Existence is associated with growth and change; essence signifies stagnation and finality. Western civilization, and particularly Western science, has traditionally valued essence over existence. It has sought to understand the essential composition of things, including humans. By contrast, existentialists affirm that people's essence is their power to continually redefine themselves through the choices they make.

Second, existentialism opposes the split between subject and object. According to Kierkegaard, people are more than mere cogs in the machinery of an industrialized society, but they are also more than subjective thinking beings living passively through armchair speculation. Instead, people are both subjective and objective and must search for truth by living active and authentic lives.

Third, people search for some meaning to their lives. They ask (though not always consciously) the important questions concerning their being: Who am I? Is life worth living? Does it have a meaning? How can I realize my humanity?

Fourth, existentialists hold that ultimately each of us is responsible for who we are and what we become. We cannot blame parents, teachers, employers, God, or circumstances. As Sartre (1957) said, "Man is nothing else but what he makes of himself. Such is the first principle of existentialism" (p. 15). Although we may associate with others in productive and healthy relationships, in the end, we are each alone. We can choose to become what we can be or we can choose to avoid commitment and choice, but ultimately, it is our choice.

Fifth, existentialists are basically antitheoretical. To them, theories further dehumanize people and render them as objects. As we mentioned in Chapter 1, theories are constructed in part to explain phenomena. Existentialists are generally opposed to this approach. Authentic experience takes precedence over artificial explanations. When experiences are molded into some preexisting theoretical model, they lose their authenticity and become divorced from the individual who experienced them.

Basic Concepts

Before proceeding to Rollo May's view of humanity, we pause to look at two basic concepts of existentialism, namely, being-in-the-world and nonbeing.

Being-in-the-World

Existentialists adopt a phenomenological approach to understanding humanity. To them, we exist in a world that can be best understood from our own perspective. When scientists study people from an external frame of reference, they violate both the subjects and their existential world. The basic unity of person and environment is expressed in the German word **Dasein,** meaning to exist there. Hence, *Dasein* literally means to exist in the world and is generally written as **being-in-the-world.** The hyphens in this term imply a oneness of subject and object, of person and world.

Many people suffer from anxiety and despair brought on by their alienation from themselves or from their world. They either have no clear image of themselves or they feel isolated from a world that seems distant and foreign. They have no sense of *Dasein,* no unity of self and world. As people strive to gain power over nature, they lose touch with their relationship to the natural world. As they come to rely on the products of the industrial revolution, they become more alienated from the stars, the soil, and the sea. Alienation from the world includes being out of touch with one's own body as well. Recall that Rollo May began his recovery from tuberculosis only after realizing that it was he who had the illness.

This feeling of isolation and alienation of self from the world is suffered not only by pathologically disturbed individuals but also by most individuals in modern societies. Alienation is the illness of our time, and it manifests itself in three areas: (1) separation from nature, (2) lack of meaningful interpersonal relations, and (3) alienation from one's authentic self. Thus, people experience three simultaneous modes in their being-in-the-world: *Umwelt,* or the environment around us; *Mitwelt,* or our relations with other people; and *Eigenwelt,* or our relationship with our self.

Umwelt is the world of objects and things and would exist even if people had no awareness. It is the world of nature and natural law and includes biological drives, such as hunger and sleep, and such natural phenomena as birth and death. We cannot escape *Umwelt;* we must learn to live in the world around us and to adjust to changes within this world. Freud's theory, with its emphasis on biology and instincts, deals mostly with *Umwelt.*

But we do not live only in *Umwelt.* We also live in the world with people, that is, *Mitwelt.* We must relate to people as people, not as things. If we treat people as objects, then we are living solely in *Umwelt.* The difference between *Umwelt* and *Mitwelt* can be seen by contrasting sex with love. If a person uses another as an instrument for sexual gratification, then that person is living in *Umwelt,* at least in his or her relationship to that other person. However, love demands that one make a commitment to the other person. Love means respect for the other person's being-in-the-world, an unconditional acceptance of that person. Not every *Mitwelt* relationship, however, necessitates love. The essential criterion is that the *Dasein* of the other person is respected. The theories of Sullivan and Rogers, with their emphasis on interpersonal relations, deal mostly with *Mitwelt.*

Eigenwelt refers to one's relationship with oneself. It is a world not usually explored by personality theorists. To live in *Eigenwelt* means to be aware of oneself as a human being and to grasp who we are as we relate to the world of things and to the world of people. What does this sunset mean to *me?* How is this other person a part of my life? What characteristics of *mine* allow me to love this person? How do *I* perceive this experience?

Healthy people live in *Umwelt, Mitwelt,* and *Eigenwelt* simultaneously (see Figure 12.1). They adapt to the natural world, relate to others as humans, and have a keen awareness of what all these experiences mean to them (May, 1958a).

Nonbeing

Being-in-the-world necessitates an awareness of self as a living, emerging being. This awareness, in turn, leads to the dread of not being: that is, **nonbeing** or **nothingness.** May (1958a) wrote that

> to grasp what it means to exist, one needs to grasp the fact that he might not exist, that he treads at every moment on the sharp edge of possible annihilation and can never escape the fact that death will arrive at some unknown moment in the future. (pp. 47–48)

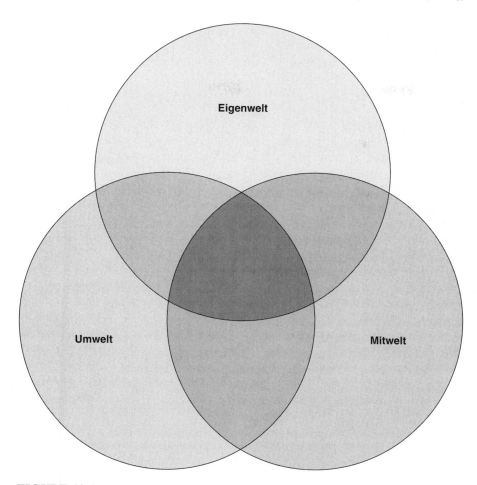

FIGURE 12.1   *Healthy People Live Simultaneously in* **Umwelt, Mitwelt,** *and* **Eigenwelt.**

Death is not the only avenue of nonbeing, but it is the most obvious one. Life becomes more vital, more meaningful when we confront the possibility of our death. Nearly 40 years before his own death, May (1958a) spoke of death as "the one fact of my life which is not relative but absolute, and my awareness of this gives my existence and what I do each hour an absolute quality" (p. 49).

When we do not courageously confront our nonbeing by contemplating death, we nevertheless will experience nonbeing in other forms, including addiction to alcohol or other drugs, promiscuous sexual activity, and other compulsive behaviors. Our nonbeing can also be expressed as blind conformity to society's expectations or as generalized hostility that pervades our relations to others.

The fear of death or nonbeing often provokes us to live defensively and to receive less from life than if we would confront the issue of our nonexistence. As May (1991) said, "we are afraid of nonbeing and so we shrivel up our being" (p. 202). We flee from making active choices; that is, we make choices without considering who we are and what we want. We may try to avoid the dread of nonbeing by dimming

The dread of nonbeing can take the form of isolation and alienation.

our self-awareness and denying our individuality, but such choices leave us with feelings of despair and emptiness. Thus, we escape the dread of nonbeing at the expense of a constricted existence. A healthier alternative is to face the inevitability of death and to realize that nonbeing is an inseparable part of being.

The Case of Philip

Existential psychology is concerned with the individual's struggle to work through life's experiences and to grow toward becoming more fully human. May (1981) described this struggle in a report on one of his patients—Philip, the architect we met in the chapter opening. Here, we continue with Philip's story; and later we use his experiences to illustrate May's concepts of anxiety, intentionality, destiny, psychopathology, and psychotherapy.

When Nicole told Philip that, as he well knew, she could never leave him, Philip was surprised and confused because he knew no such thing. About a year later, Philip learned that Nicole had had another affair; but before he could confront her and break off their relationship, he had to leave for a 5-day business trip. By the time he returned, Philip was able to reason that perhaps he could accept Nicole's right to sleep with other men. Also, Nicole convinced him that the other man didn't mean anything to her and that she loved only Philip.

A little later, Nicole had a third affair, one that she made sure Philip would discover. Once again, Philip was filled with anger and jealousy. But once again, Nicole reassured him that the man meant nothing to her.

On one level, Philip wished to accept Nicole's behavior, but on another, he felt betrayed by her affairs. Yet, he did not seem to be able to leave her and to search for another woman to love. He was paralyzed—unable to change his relationship with Nicole but also unable to break it off. At this point in Philip's life, he sought therapy from Rollo May.

Anxiety

Philip was suffering from neurotic anxiety. Like others who experience neurotic anxiety, he behaved in a nonproductive, self-defeating manner. Although he was deeply hurt by Nicole's unpredictable and "crazy" behavior, he became paralyzed with inaction and could not break off their relationship. Nicole's actions seemed to engender in Philip a sense of duty toward her. Because she obviously needed him, he felt obligated to take care of her.

Before May published *The Meaning of Anxiety* in 1950, most theories of anxiety held that high levels of anxiety were indicative of neuroses or other forms of psychopathology. Just prior to publishing this book, May had experienced a great deal of anxiety while recovering from tuberculosis. He and his first wife and their young son were basically penniless, and he was unsure of his own recovery. In *The Meaning of Anxiety,* May claimed that much of human behavior is motivated by an underlying sense of dread and anxiety. The failure to confront death serves as a temporary escape from the anxiety or dread of nonbeing. But the escape cannot be permanent. Death is the one absolute of life that sooner or later everyone must face.

People experience **anxiety** when they become aware that their existence or some value identified with it might be destroyed. May (1958a) defined anxiety as "the subjective state of the individual's becoming aware that his [or her] existence can be destroyed, that he can become 'nothing'" (p. 50). At another time, May (1967) called anxiety a threat to some important value. Anxiety, then, can spring either from an awareness of one's nonbeing or from a threat to some value essential to one's existence. It exists when one confronts the issue of fulfilling one's potentialities. This confrontation can lead to stagnation and decay, but it can also result in growth and change.

The acquisition of freedom inevitably leads to anxiety. Freedom cannot exist without anxiety, nor can anxiety exist without freedom. May (1981, p. 185) quoted Kierkegaard as saying that "anxiety is the dizziness of freedom." Anxiety, like dizziness, can be either pleasurable or painful, constructive or destructive. It can give people energy and zest, but it can also paralyze and panic them. Moreover, anxiety can be either normal or neurotic.

Normal Anxiety

No one can escape the effects of anxiety. To grow and to change one's values means to experience constructive or normal anxiety. May (1967) defined **normal anxiety** as that "which is proportionate to the threat, does not involve repression, and can be confronted constructively on the conscious level" (p. 80).

As people grow from infancy to old age, their values change, and with each step, they experience normal anxiety. "All growth consists of the anxiety-creating surrender of past values" (May, 1967, p. 80). Normal anxiety is also experienced during those creative moments when an artist, a scientist, or a philosopher suddenly achieves an insight that leads to a recognition that one's life, and perhaps the lives of countless others, will be permanently changed. For example, scientists who witnessed the first atomic bomb tests in Alamogordo, New Mexico, experienced normal anxiety with the realization that, from that moment forward, everything had changed (May, 1981).

Neurotic Anxiety

Normal anxiety, the type experienced during periods of growth or of threat to one's values, is experienced by everyone. It can be constructive provided it remains proportionate to the threat. But anxiety can become neurotic or sick. May (1967) defined **neurotic anxiety** as "a reaction which is disproportionate to the threat, involves repression and other forms of intrapsychic conflict, and is managed by various kinds of blocking-off of activity and awareness" (p. 80).

Whereas normal anxiety is felt whenever values are threatened, neurotic anxiety is experienced whenever values become transformed into dogma. To be absolutely right in one's beliefs provides temporary security, but it is security "bought at the price of surrendering [one's] opportunity for fresh learning and new growth" (May, 1967, p. 80).

Philip's neurotic anxiety was evident in his attachment to unpredictable and "crazy" women, an attachment that began in early childhood. During the first 2 years of his life, his world was inhabited primarily by just two other people—his mother and a sister two years older than Philip. His mother was a borderline schizophrenic whose behavior toward Philip alternated between tenderness and cruelty. His sister was definitely schizophrenic and later spent some time in a mental hospital. So Philip learned early that he had to attach himself to women but also that he had to rescue them as well. "Life, then, for Philip would understandably not be free, but rather would require that he be continuously on guard or on duty" (May, 1981, p. 30).

Philip's neurotic anxiety blocked any new and successful ways of behaving toward Nicole. His approach seemed to be a recapitulation of childhood behaviors toward his mother and sister.

Guilt

Anxiety arises when people are faced with the problem of fulfilling their potentialities. **Guilt** arises when people deny their potentialities, fail to accurately perceive the needs of fellow humans, or remain oblivious to their dependence on the natural world (May, 1958a). Just as May used the term "anxiety" to refer to large issues dealing with one's being-in-the-world, so too did he employ the concept of guilt. In this sense, both anxiety and guilt are *ontological;* that is, they refer to the nature of being and not to feelings arising from specific situations or transgressions.

In all, May (1958a) recognized three forms of ontological guilt, each corresponding to one of the three modes of being-in-the-world, that is, *Umwelt, Mitwelt,* and *Eigenwelt.* To understand the form of guilt that corresponds to *Umwelt,* recall that ontological guilt need not stem from one's own actions or failures to act; it can arise from a lack of awareness of one's being-in-the-world. As civilization advances technologically, people become more and more removed from nature, that is, from *Umwelt.* This alienation leads to a form of ontological guilt that is especially prevalent in "advanced" societies where people live in heated or cooled dwellings, use motorized means of transportation, and consume food gathered and prepared by others. People's undiscerning reliance on others for these and other needs contributes to one's first form of ontological guilt. Because this type of guilt is a result of our separation from nature, May (1958a) also referred to it as *separation guilt,* a concept similar to Fromm's notion of the human dilemma (see Chapter 7).

The second form of guilt stems from our inability to perceive accurately the world of others (*Mitwelt*). We can see other people only through our own eyes and can never perfectly judge the needs of these other people. Thus, we do violence to their true identity. Because we cannot unerringly anticipate the needs of others, we feel inadequate in our relations with them. This then leads to a pervasive condition of guilt, which is experienced by all of us to some extent. May (1958a) wrote that "this is not a question of moral failure . . . it is an inescapable result of the fact that each of us is a separate individuality and has no choice but to look at the world through [our] own eyes" (p. 54).

The third form of ontological guilt is associated with our denial of our own potentialities or with our failure to fulfill them. In other words, this guilt is grounded in our relationship with self (*Eigenwelt*). Again, this form of guilt is universal, because none of us can completely fulfill all our potentials. This third type of guilt is reminiscent of Maslow's concept of the *Jonah complex,* or the fear of being or doing one's best (see Chapter 10).

Like anxiety, ontological guilt can have either a positive or a negative effect on personality. We can use this guilt to develop a healthy sense of humility, to improve our relations with others, and to creatively use our potentialities. However, when we refuse to accept ontological guilt, it becomes neurotic or morbid. Neurotic guilt, like neurotic anxiety, leads to nonproductive or neurotic symptoms such as sexual impotence, depression, cruelty to others, or inability to make a choice.

Intentionality

The ability to make a choice implies some underlying structure upon which that choice is made. The structure that gives meaning to experience and allows people to make decisions about the future is called **intentionality** (May, 1969b). Without intentionality, people could neither choose nor act on their choice. Action implies intentionality, just as intentionality implies action; the two are inseparable.

May used the term "intentionality" to bridge the gap between subject and object. Intentionality is "the structure of meaning which makes it possible for us, subjects that we are, to see and understand the outside world, objective that it is. In intentionality, the dichotomy between subject and object is partially overcome" (May, 1969b, p. 225).

To illustrate how intentionality partially bridges the gap between subject and object, May (1969b) used a simple example of a man (the subject) seated at his desk observing a piece of paper (the object). The man can write on the paper, fold it into a paper airplane for his grandson, or sketch a picture on it. In all three instances, the subject (man) and object (paper) are identical, but the man's actions depend on his intentions and on the meaning he gives to his experience. That meaning is a function of both himself (subject) and his environment (object).

Intentionality is sometimes unconscious. For example, when Philip felt a duty to take care of Nicole despite her unpredictable and "crazy" behavior, he did not see that his actions were in some way connected to his early experiences with his unpredictable mother and his "crazy" sister. He was trapped in his unconscious belief that unpredictable and "crazy" women must be cared for, and this intentionality made it impossible for him to discover new ways of relating to Nicole.

Care, Love, and Will

Philip had a history of taking care of others, especially women. He had given Nicole a "job" with his company that permitted her to work at home and earn enough money to live on. In addition, after she ended her affair with Craig and gave up her "crazy" plan to move across the country, Philip gave her several thousand dollars. He previously had felt a duty to take care of his two wives and, before that, his mother and sister.

In spite of Philip's pattern of taking care of women, he never really learned to care *for* them. To care for someone means to recognize that person as a fellow human being, to identify with that person's pain or joy, guilt or pity. Care is an active process, the opposite of apathy. "Care is a state in which something does *matter*" (May, 1969b, p. 289).

Care is not the same as love, but it is the source of love. To love means to care, to recognize the essential humanity of the other person, to have an active regard for that person's development. May (1953) defined **love** as a "delight in the presence of the other person and an affirming of [that person's] value and development as much as one's own" (p. 206). Without care there can be no love—only empty sentimentality or transient sexual arousal. Care is also the source of will.

May (1969b) called **will** "the capacity to organize one's self so that movement in a certain direction or toward a certain goal may take place" (p. 218). He distinguished between will and wish, saying that

> "will" requires self-consciousness; "wish" does not. "Will" implies some possibility of either/or choice; "wish" does not. "Wish" gives the warmth, the content, the imagination, the child's play, the freshness, and the richness to "will." "Will" gives the self-direction, the maturity to "wish." "Will" protects "wish," permits it to continue without running risks which are too great. (p. 218)

Union of Love and Will

Modern society, May (1969b) claimed, is suffering from an unhealthy division of love and will. Love has become associated with sensual love or sex, whereas will has come to mean a dogged determination or will power. Neither concept captures the true meaning of these two terms. When love is seen as sex, it becomes temporary and lacking in commitment; there is no will, but only wish. When will is seen as will power, it becomes self-serving and lacking in passion; there is no care, but only manipulation.

There are biological reasons why love and will are separated. When children first come into the world, they are at one with the universe (*Umwelt*), their mother (*Mitwelt*), and themselves (*Eigenwelt*). "Our needs are met without self-conscious effort on our part, as, biologically, in the early condition of nursing at the mother's breast. This is the first freedom, the first 'yes'" (May, 1969b, p. 284).

Later, as will begins to develop, it manifests itself as opposition, the first "no." The blissful existence of early infancy is now opposed by the emerging willfulness of late infancy. The "no" should not be seen as a statement against the parents but rather as a positive assertion of self. Unfortunately, parents often interpret the "no" negatively and therefore stifle the child's self-assertion. As a result, children learn to disassociate will from the blissful love they had previously enjoyed.

Our task, said May (1969b, 1990b), is to unite love and will. This task is not easy, but it is possible. Neither blissful love nor self-serving will have a role in the uniting of love and will. For the mature person, both love and will mean a reaching out toward another person. Both involve care, both necessitate choice, both imply action, and both require responsibility.

Forms of Love

May (1969b) identified four kinds of love in Western tradition—sex, eros, philia, and agape.

Sex

Sex is a biological function that can be satisfied through sexual intercourse or some other release of sexual tension. Although it has become cheapened in modern Western societies, "it still remains the power of procreation, the drive which perpetuates the race, the source at once of the human being's most intense pleasure and his [or her] most pervasive anxiety" (May, 1969b, p. 38).

May believed that in ancient times sex was taken for granted, just as eating and sleeping were taken for granted. In modern times, sex has become a problem. First, during the Victorian period, Western societies generally denied sexual feelings, and sex was not a topic of conversation in polite company. Then, during the 1920s, people reacted against this sexual suppression; and sex suddenly came into the open, and much of Western society was preoccupied with it. May (1969b) pointed out that society went from a period when having sex was fraught with guilt and anxiety to a time when not having it brought about guilt and anxiety.

Eros

In the United States, sex is frequently confused with eros. Sex is a physiological need that seeks gratification through the release of tension. **Eros** is a psychological desire that seeks procreation or creation through an enduring union with a loved one. Eros is making love; sex is manipulating organs. Eros is the wish to establish a lasting union; sex is the desire to experience pleasure. Eros "takes wings from human imagination and is forever transcending all techniques, giving the laugh to all the 'how to' books by gaily swinging into orbit above our mechanical rules" (May, 1969b, p. 74).

Eros is built on care and tenderness. It longs to establish an enduring union with the other person, such that both partners experience delight and passion and both are broadened and deepened by the experience. Because the human species could not survive without desire for a lasting union, eros can be regarded as the salvation of sex.

Philia

Eros, the salvation of sex, is built on the foundation of **philia,** that is, an intimate nonsexual friendship between two people. Philia cannot be rushed; it takes time to grow, to develop, to sink its roots. Examples of philia would be the slowly evolving love between siblings or between lifelong friends. "Philia does not require that we do anything for the beloved except accept him, be with him, and enjoy him. It is friendship in the simplest, most direct terms" (May, 1969a, p. 31).

In Chapter 8, we mentioned that Harry Stack Sullivan placed great importance on preadolescence, that developmental epoch characterized by the need for a chum, someone who is more or less like oneself. According to Sullivan, chumship or philia is a necessary requisite for healthy erotic relationships during early and late adolescence. May, who was influenced by Sullivan at the William Alanson White Institute, agreed that philia makes eros possible. The gradual, relaxed development of true friendship is a prerequisite for the enduring union of two people.

Agape

Just as eros depends on philia, so philia needs agape. May (1969b) defined **agape** as "esteem for the other, the concern for the other's welfare beyond any gain that one can get out of it; disinterested love, typically, the love of God for man" (p. 319).

Agape is altruistic love. It is a kind of spiritual love that carries with it the risk of playing God. It does not depend on any behaviors or characteristics of the other person. In this sense, it is undeserved and unconditional.

Agape is altruistic love that requires nothing in return.

In summary, healthy adult relationships blend all four forms of love. They are based on sexual satisfaction, a desire for an enduring union, genuine friendship, and an unselfish concern for the welfare of the other person. Such authentic love, unfortunately, is quite difficult. It requires self-affirmation and the assertion of oneself. "At the same time it requires tenderness, affirmation of the other, relaxing of competition as much as possible, self-abnegation at times in the interests of the loved one, and the age-old virtues of mercy and forgiveness" (May, 1981, p. 147).

Freedom and Destiny

A blend of the four forms of love requires both self-assertion and an affirmation of the other person. It also requires an assertion of one's *freedom* and a confrontation with one's *destiny*. Healthy individuals are able both to assume their freedom and to face their destiny.

Freedom Defined

In an early definition, May (1967) said that "freedom is the individual's capacity to *know that he is the determined one*" (p. 175). The word "determined" in this definition is synonymous with what May (1981) would later call *destiny*. Freedom, then, comes from an understanding of our destiny: an understanding that death is a possibility at any moment, that we are male or female, that we have inherent weaknesses, that early childhood experiences dispose us toward certain patterns of behavior.

Freedom is the possibility of changing, although we may not know what those changes might be. Freedom "entails being able *to harbor different possibilities in one's mind even though it is not clear at the moment which way one must act*" (May, 1981, pp. 10–11). This condition often leads to increases in anxiety, but it is normal anxiety, the kind that healthy people welcome and are able to manage.

Forms of Freedom

May (1981) recognized two forms of freedom—freedom of doing and freedom of being. The first he called *existential freedom;* the latter, *essential freedom.*

Existential Freedom

Existential freedom should not be identified with existential philosophy. It is the freedom of action—the freedom of doing. Most middle-class adult Americans enjoy large measures of existential freedom. They are free to travel across state lines, to choose their associates, to vote for their representatives in government, and so on. On a more trivial scale, they are free to push their shopping carts through a supermarket and select from among thousands of items. Existential freedom, then, is the freedom to act on the choices that one makes.

Essential Freedom

Freedom to act, to move around does not ensure **essential freedom:** that is, freedom of being. In fact, existential freedom often makes essential freedom more difficult. For example, prisoners and inmates in concentration camps often speak enthusiastically of their "inner freedom," despite experiencing very limited existential freedom. Thus, physical confinement or the denial of liberty seems to allow people to face their destiny and to gain their freedom of being. In 1981, May (1981, p. 60) asked: "Do we get to essential freedom only when our everyday existence is interrupted?" May's own answer was "no." One need not be imprisoned to attain essential freedom, that is, freedom of being. Destiny itself is our prison—our concentration camp that allows us to be less concerned with freedom of doing and more concerned with essential freedom.

> Does not the engaging of our destiny—which is the design of our life—hedge us about with the confinement, the sobriety, indeed, often the cruelty, which forces us to look beyond the limits of day-to-day action? Is not the inescapable fact of death . . . the concentration camp of us all? Is not the fact that life is a joy and a bondage at the same time enough to drive us to consider the deeper aspect of being? (May, 1981, p. 61)

What Is Destiny?

May (1981) defined destiny as *"the design of the universe speaking through the design of each one of us"* (p. 90). Our ultimate destiny is death, but on a lesser scale our destiny includes other biological properties such as intelligence, gender, size and strength, and genetic predisposition toward certain illnesses. In addition, psychological and cultural factors contribute to our destiny.

Destiny does not mean preordained or foredoomed. It is our destination, our terminus, our goal. Within the boundaries of our destiny, we have the power to choose, and this power allows us to confront and challenge our destiny. It does not, however, permit any change we wish. We cannot be successful at any job, conquer any illness, enjoy a fulfilling relationship with any person. We cannot erase our destiny, "but we can choose how we shall respond, how we shall live out our talents which confront us" (May, 1981, p. 89).

May suggested that freedom and destiny, like love-hate or life-death, are not antithetical but rather a normal paradox of life. "The paradox is that freedom owes its vitality to destiny, and destiny owes its significance to freedom" (May, 1981, p. 17). Freedom and destiny are thus inexorably intertwined; one cannot exist without the other. Freedom without destiny is unruly license. Ironically, license leads

Destiny is our "concentration camp" that paradoxically defines our essential freedom.

to anarchy and the ultimate destruction of freedom. Without destiny, then, we have no freedom, but without freedom our destiny is meaningless.

Freedom and destiny give birth to each other. As we challenge our destiny, we gain freedom, and as we achieve freedom, we push at the boundaries of destiny.

Philip's Destiny

When Philip, the architect immobilized by his relationship with Nicole, first sought Rollo May as his therapist, he was paralyzed with inaction because he had refused to accept his destiny. He saw no connection between his adult pattern of relating to women and his childhood strategy of getting along in an unpredictable and "crazy" world. His destiny, however, was not fixed by those early experiences. Philip, like other people, had the freedom to change his destiny, but first he had to recognize his biological, social, and psychological limitations; and then he had to possess the courage to make choices within those limitations.

Philip lacked both the understanding and the courage to confront his destiny. Up to the point of seeking therapy, he had tried to compensate for his destiny, to consciously deny it. "He had been searching for someone who would make up for his having been born into an unwelcoming world consisting of a disturbed mother and a schizophrenic sister, a destiny that he did not in the slightest choose" (May, 1981, p. 88). Philip's denial of his destiny left him resentful and confused. His inability or unwillingness to face his destiny robbed him of personal freedom and kept him tied to his mother.

Philip treated his wives and Nicole in the same way that earlier had proven successful with his mother and sister. He could not dare express his anger to women, but instead, he adopted a charming though somewhat possessive and protective attitude toward them. May (1981) insisted that "the freedom of each of us is in proportion to the degree with which we confront and live in relation to our destiny" (p. 89). After several weeks of psychotherapy, Philip was able to stop blaming his mother for not doing what he thought she should have done. When he began to see the positive things she *did* for him, he began to change his attitude toward her. The objective facts of his childhood had not changed, but his subjective perceptions had. As Philip came to terms with his destiny, he began to be able to express his anger, to feel less trapped in his relationship with Nicole, and to become more aware of his possibilities. In other words, he gained his freedom of being.

The Power of Myth

For many years, May was concerned with the powerful effects of **myths** on individuals and cultures—a concern that culminated in his book *The Cry for Myth* (1991). May contended that the people of Western civilization have an urgent need for myths. Lacking myths to believe in, they have turned to religious cults, drug addiction, and popular culture in a vain effort to find meaning in their lives. Myths are not falsehoods; rather, they are conscious and unconscious belief systems that provide explanations for personal and social problems. May (1991) compared myths to the support beams in a house—not visible from the outside, but they hold the house together and make it habitable.

The Oedipus myth holds meaning for people even today because it deals with existential crises common to everyone.

From earliest times and in diverse civilizations, people have found meaning in their lives by the myths they share with others in their culture. Myths are the stories that unify a society; "they are essential to the process of keeping our souls alive and bringing us new meaning in a difficult and often meaningless world" (May, 1991, p. 20).

May believed that people communicate with one another on two levels. The first is rationalistic language, and on this level, truth takes precedence over the people who are communicating. The second is through myths, and on this level, the total human experience is more important than the empirical accuracy of the communication. People use myths and symbols to transcend the immediate concrete situation, to expand self-awareness, and to search for identity.

May (1990a, 1991) believed that the Oedipus story is a powerful myth in our culture because it contains elements of existential crises common to everyone. These crises include (1) birth, (2) separation or exile from parents and home, (3) sexual union with one parent and hostility toward the other, (4) the assertion of independence and the search for identity, and (5) death. The Oedipus myth has meaning for people because it deals with each of these five crises. Like Oedipus, people are removed from their mother and father and are driven by the need for self-knowledge. People's struggle for self-identity, however, is not easy, and it may even result in tragedy, as it did for Oedipus when he insisted on knowing the truth about his origins. After being told that he had killed his father and married his mother, Oedipus put out his eyes, depriving himself of the ability to see, that is, to be aware, to be conscious.

But the Oedipus narration does not end with denial of consciousness. At this point in Sophocles' trilogy, Oedipus once again is exiled, an experience May saw as symbolic of people's own isolation and ostracism. As an old man, Oedipus is seen contemplating his tragic suffering and accepting responsibility for killing his father and marrying his mother. His meditations during old age bring him peace and understanding and the ability to accept death with grace. The central themes of Oedipus's life—birth, exile and separation, identity, incest and patricide, repression of guilt, and finally, conscious meditation and death—touch everyone and make this myth a potentially powerful healing force in people's lives.

May's concept of myths is comparable to Carl Jung's idea of a collective unconscious in that myths are archetypal patterns in the human experience; they are avenues to universal images that lie beyond individual experience (see Chapter 4). And like archetypes, myths can contribute to psychological growth if people will embrace them and allow them to open up a new reality. Tragically, many people deny their universal myths and thus risk alienation, apathy, and emptiness—the principal ingredients of psychopathology.

Psychopathology

According to May, apathy and emptiness—not anxiety and guilt—are the malaise of modern times. When people deny their destiny or abandon their myths, they lose their purpose for being; they become directionless. Without some goal or destination, people become sick and engage in a variety of self-defeating and self-destructive behaviors.

Many people in modern Western societies feel alienated from the world (*Umwelt*), from others (*Mitwelt*), and especially from themselves (*Eigenwelt*). They feel helpless to prevent natural disasters, to reverse industrialization, or to make contact with another human being. They feel insignificant in a world that increasingly dehumanizes the individual. This sense of insignificance leads to *apathy* and to a state of diminished consciousness (May, 1967).

May saw psychopathology as lack of communication—the inability to know others and to share oneself with them. Psychologically disturbed individuals deny their destiny and thus lose their freedom. They erect a variety of neurotic symptoms, not to regain their freedom, but to renounce it. Symptoms narrow the person's phenomenological world to the size that makes coping easier. The compulsive person adopts a rigid routine, thereby making new choices unnecessary.

Symptoms may be temporary, as when stress produces a headache, or they may be relatively permanent, as when early childhood experiences produce apathy and emptiness. Philip's psychopathology was tied to his early environment with a disturbed mother and a schizophrenic sister. These experiences did not *cause* his pathology in the sense that they alone produced it. However, they did set up Philip to learn to adjust to his world by suppressing his anger, by developing a sense of apathy, and by trying to be a "good little boy." Neurotic symptoms, therefore, do not represent a failure of adjustment, but rather a proper and necessary adjustment by which one's *Dasein* can be preserved. Philip's behavior toward his two wives and Nicole represents a denial of his freedom and a self-defeating attempt to escape from his destiny.

Psychotherapy

Unlike Freud, Adler, Rogers, and other clinically oriented personality theorists, May did not establish a school of psychotherapy with avid followers and identifiable techniques. Nevertheless, he wrote extensively on the subject, rejecting the idea that psychotherapy should reduce anxiety and ease feelings of guilt. Instead, he suggested that psychotherapy should make people more human: that is, help them expand their consciousness so that they will be in a better position to make choices (M. H. Hall, 1967). These choices, then, lead to the simultaneous growth of freedom and responsibility.

May believed that the purpose of psychotherapy is to set people free. He argued that therapists who concentrate on a patient's symptoms are missing the more important picture. Neurotic symptoms are simply ways of running away from freedom and an indication that patients' inner possibilities are not being used. When patients become more free, more human, their neurotic symptoms usually disappear, their neurotic anxiety gives way to normal anxiety, and their neurotic guilt is replaced by normal guilt. But these gains are secondary and not the central purpose of therapy. May insisted that psychotherapy must be concerned with helping people experience their existence, and that relieving symptoms is merely a by-product of that experience.

How does a therapist help patients become free, responsible human beings? May did not offer many specific directions for therapists to follow. Existential therapists have no special set of techniques or methods that can be applied to all patients. Instead, they have only themselves, their own humanity to offer. They must establish a one-to-one relationship (*Mitwelt*) that enables patients to become more aware of themselves and to live more fully in their own world (*Eigenwelt*). This approach may mean challenging patients to confront their destiny, to experience despair, anxiety, and guilt. But it also means establishing an I-thou encounter in which both therapist and patient are viewed as subjects rather than objects. In an I-thou relationship, the therapist has empathy for the patient's experience and is open to the patient's subjective world.

May (1991) also described therapy as partly religion, partly science, and partly friendship. The friendship, however, is not an ordinary social relationship; rather, it calls for the therapist to be confronting and to challenge the patient. May believed that the relationship itself is therapeutic, and its transforming effects are independent of anything therapists might say or any theoretical orientation they might have.

> *Our task is to be guide, friend, and interpreter to persons on their journeys through their private hells and purgatories.* Specifically our task is to help patients get to the point where they can decide whether they wish to remain victims . . . or whether they choose to leave this victim-state and venture through purgatory with the hope of achieving some sense of paradise. Our patients often, toward the end, are understandably frightened by the possibility of freely deciding for themselves whether to take their chances by completing the quest they have bravely begun. (May, 1991, p. 165)

Philosophically, May held many of the same beliefs as Carl Rogers (see Chapter 11). Basic to both approaches is the notion of therapy as a human encounter: that is, an I-thou relationship with the potential to facilitate growth within both the therapist and the patient. In practice, however, May was much more likely to ask questions, to delve into a patient's early childhood, and to suggest possible meanings of current behavior.

For example, he explained to Philip that his relationship with Nicole was an attempt to hold on to his mother. Rogers would have rejected such a technique because it emanated from an external (i.e., the therapist's) frame of reference. May, however, believed that these kinds of interpretations can be an effective means of confronting patients with information that they have been hiding from themselves.

Another technique May used with Philip was the suggestion that he hold a fantasy conversation with his dead mother. In this conversation, Philip spoke for both himself and his mother. When talking for his mother, he was able for the first time to empathize with her, to see Philip from his mother's point of view. Speaking for his mother, he said that she was very proud of him and that he had always been her favorite child. Then talking for himself, he told his mother that he appreciated her courage and recalled an incident when her courage saved his eyesight. When Philip finished the fantasy conversation, he said, "'I never in a thousand years would have imagined *that* would come out'" (May, 1981, p. 39).

May also asked Philip to bring a photo of himself when he was a little boy. Philip then had a fantasy conversation with "Little Philip." As the conversation ensued, "Little Philip" explained that he had triumphed over the problem that had most troubled grown Philip, namely, the fear of abandonment. "Little Philip" became Philip's friendly companion and helped him overcome his loneliness and allay his jealousy of Nicole.

At the end of therapy, Philip did not become a new person, but he did become more conscious of a part of himself that had been there all the time. An awareness of new possibilities allowed him to move in the direction of personal freedom. For Philip, the end of therapy was the beginning of "the uniting of himself with that early self that he had had to lock up in a dungeon in order to survive when life was not happy but threatening" (May, 1981, p. 41).

Related Research

Rollo May's existential theory has been moderately influential as a method of psychotherapy, but it has sparked almost no direct empirical research. This state of affairs is no doubt related to the critical stance that May adopted toward objective and quantitative measurement. Any theory that emphasizes the connection between subject and object and the uniqueness of each individual will not be conducive to large sample research with experimental or questionnaire design. In fact, May argued that modern science is too rationalistic, too objective, and that a new science is needed in order to grasp the total, living person.

One existential topic to receive some empirical attention has been existential anxiety. May (1967) defined anxiety as "the apprehension cued off by a threat to some value which the individual holds essential to his [or her] existence as a self" (p. 72). When events threaten our physical or psychological existence, we experience existential anxiety, and strongest among the threats to our existence is death. Indeed, May and Yalom (1989) argued that "a major developmental task is to deal with the terror of obliteration" (p. 367). In a sense, life is the process of coping with and confronting death.

An existential approach to the study of terror and death has carried over into "terror management," a modern experimental offshoot of existential psychology. A conceptual bridge between existential psychology and terror management theory was provided by the American psychiatrist Ernest Becker, who was inspired by Kierkegaard and Otto Rank. A basic argument of these existentialists (as well as writers such as Camus and Sartre) is that humans are first and foremost motivated by fear of death. Moreover, many of these thinkers see human creativity, culture, and meaning as unconscious defenses against mortality. The work of Becker, in particular, has been a major source of inspiration for terror management theorists.

Mortality Salience and Denial of Our Animal Nature

Terror management theory has taken this basic assumption and tested it by conducting some of the more clever and well-designed experimental studies in recent social and personality psychology.

Although humans are part of the animal kingdom and hence mortal, they are unique in understanding of the world and unique in realizing their own uniqueness. Humans have long believed that they are more than just bodies—they have a soul, a spirit, a mind.

Over the centuries, humans have learned to disavow their corporeal selves. For example, bodily functions continue to be among the most taboo and heavily sanctioned of social norms. To be "cultured" is to be in complete control of the biological nature of being human. According to terror management theorists, the crux of the denial of our bodily and animalistic nature stems from the existential fear of death and decay of our bodies. As Sheldon Solomon and colleagues put it, "humans could not function with equanimity if they believed they were not inherently more significant than apes, lizards, and lima beans" (Solomon, Greenberg, & Pyszczynski, 1991, p. 91).

Jamie Goldenberg and colleagues conducted a study to investigate the extent to which mortality salience would lead to greater denial of our animal nature. More specifically, they reasoned: "Cultures promote norms to help distinguish themselves from animals, because this distinction provides the very important psychological function of providing protection against deeply rooted concerns about mortality" (Goldenberg, Pyszczynski, Greenberg, Solomon, Kluck, & Cornwell, 2001, p. 427). Culture, from this perspective, is the mechanism through which awareness of death is regulated. More specifically, cultural worldviews (religion, politics, and social norms) and self-esteem function to defend against thoughts of death so that when death becomes salient through disasters, death of a loved one, or images of death, people respond by clinging more closely to cultural worldviews and bolstering their self-esteem. They do this, for instance, by becoming more patriotic, clinging more firmly to one's in-group, or by wanting to punish more harshly those who violate cultural norms and laws. In addition, in the emotion of disgust, we see most clearly the cultural defenses against our animal nature. Anything that reminds us of our animal nature, and ultimately of death, is responded to with a strong sense of disgust.

Goldenberg and colleagues (2001) were interested in the opposite effect: Does increasing death awareness increase the disgust reaction? In addition, they wondered whether the effect would increase after a delay or distraction because the thoughts of death would be less conscious. To test the prediction that death awareness would increase feelings of disgust and that the effect would increase as it became less conscious, they manipulated death salience in university students (60% female). The outcome variable for the study was how much disgust participants expressed on a questionnaire. The independent variables were whether one's own mortality was made salient or not and whether there was a delay in the disgust measure or not. Disgust was measured by the Disgust Sensitivity scale, without its "death" subscale (Haidt, McCauley, & Rozin, 1994). Responses were made on a 9-point Likert scale, and example items included statements such as "You see maggots on a piece of meat in an outside garbage pail"; "If I see someone vomit, it makes me sick to my stomach"; and "It would bother me." Thoughts of death were made salient by asking participants to write down the feelings that thoughts of their own death aroused in them. They were also asked to write down what they think will happen to them when they physically die. The neutral (nonsalient) condition simply had participants write down what they would feel watching TV. Delay was manipulated by including a word game that took 5 minutes to complete for half of the participants. In the delay condition, participants wrote down thoughts (about death or TV), completed the word game, and then completed the disgust measure. In the immediate condition, the word game preceded the writing about death task.

Results of the manipulation supported the hypothesis. Disgust reactions were greatest after death had been made salient and even more so when there had been a delay between mortality salience and disgust evaluations. Participants in the neutral (TV) and delay condition showed the same level of disgust as the participants in the death salience and immediate condition. Goldenberg and colleagues interpreted these results as support for the basic terror management assumption that people distance themselves from animals because animals remind them of their own physical bodies and death.

Cathy Cox and colleagues have recently extended the findings of Goldenberg and colleagues by investigating a very specific type of disgust reaction related to our animal nature: breast-feeding (Cox, Goldenberg, Arndt, & Pyszczynski, 2007). Cox and colleagues used methods very similar to the previously discussed work on mortality and disgust, where for some participants their own mortality was made salient and for others it was not. However, instead of having the control condition write about what they feel when they watch TV, Cox and colleagues had the control participants write about the anxiety associated with public speaking. This methodological change was included in an effort to control for general, non-death-related anxiety (for many people the idea of public speaking is very anxiety provoking though it is presumably a very different sort of anxiety than that provoked by the idea of death).

What the researchers found supported the conclusions of an increasing number of studies in this area that when their own mortality is made more salient, people tend to be increasingly disgusted by creaturely behaviors such as breast-feeding (Cox, Goldenberg, Arndt, & Pyszczynski, 2007; Cox, Goldenberg, Pyszczynski, & Weise, 2007). The research based on terror management theory and disgust sensitivity has developed into an impressive body of work that points to the general conclusion that human disgust, particularly disgust related to human features that remind us of our animal nature (such as breast-feeding), serves the function of defending against the existential threat posed by our inevitable death.

Fitness as a Defense Against Mortality Awareness

If thoughts of death are so anxiety provoking and defended against, as most every study on terror management has demonstrated, one might think it obvious that if reminded of their mortality, people would then be motivated to do things that decrease the likelihood of dying, such as perform healthy behaviors like exercising.

As implied in the previous section, terror management theory actively argues for two distinct categories of defense against death, namely conscious and unconscious. The conscious defenses are also referred to as proximal defenses and take the form of "not me, not now" and are seen in active suppression of thoughts of death as well as distancing and denying one's vulnerability. When one's death is unconsciously activated, then distal defenses become activated. These involve identifying with and defending cultural beliefs and ideologies and boosting one's self-esteem.

With the distinction between proximal and distal defenses as a guide, Jamie Arndt, Jeff Schimel, and Jamie Goldenberg (2003) reasoned that intention to exercise should be an ideal avenue to study the different effects of both kinds of defense. The intention to exercise is obviously a proximal defense in that people are motivated by the desire to be healthy and avoid disease. It is also a distal defense in that it bolsters self-esteem and body image. In support of this reasoning, health and appearance are often the first and second reasons given in surveys on why people decide to exercise. The study by Arndt and colleagues examined the prediction that mortality salience should therefore increase both reasons for wanting to exercise, namely increasing fitness and looking better (self-esteem). More specifically, Study 1 examined the proximal defense theory (no delay) of exercise, and Study 2 examined a combination of proximal and distal (delay) defenses. Both studies also recruited participants for whom exercise was important to their self-esteem and participants for whom it was not important.

Study 1 was a 2 × 2 design, with two levels of mortality salience (mortality versus dental pain) and two levels of fitness self-esteem. Participants were university students (64% female) who were told they were participating in a study on the relationship between personality and fitness. They were given a packet of questionnaires to complete, which included a similar mortality salience manipulation as those previously described (e.g., Cox, Goldenberg, Arndt, & Pyszczynski, 2007; Goldenberg et al., 2001). But this time the control condition wrote about the pain associated with a minor dental procedure. Dental pain was selected as a control in order to account for the general negativity associated with physical pain. After the mortality salience manipulation, all participants then read a brief article on how exercise promotes longevity and then completed two questions about their intention to exercise. The first was how much they will exercise relative to their own norm over the next month, and the second was how long (30 to 160 minutes) their next exercise will be. Responses to these two questions were standardized and added to create an overall measure of intention to exercise.

Results showed that mortality salience did immediately increase intention to exercise relative to the painful dental procedure condition. Fitness self-esteem also was not related to intention to exercise. The 2 × 2 interaction between mortality salience and fitness self-esteem, contrary to prediction, was also not significant. The authors suggested that the two nonsignificant findings may be the result of everyone getting the information on the health benefits of exercise and thereby making the intention to exercise the socially desirable response. By delaying the fitness intention measure after mortality salience, the fitness as a source of self-esteem should affect the intention to exercise. Study 2 was conducted to test this idea and had the same design as Study 1 (two levels of mortality salience and two levels of fitness self-esteem). But it also had an additional factor of immediacy: Participants assessed their fitness intentions either immediately after the mortality salience manipulation or after a brief delay. Therefore, the second study was a replication and extension of the first and resulted in a 2 × 2 × 2 design.

Participants again were university students (50% female). The main difference in procedures and measures from Study 1 was the inclusion of a filler reading task (five mundane pages from a work by Camus that had no reference to death or other existential issues) for the delay group. In other words, after the mortality salience or dental procedure manipulation, participants either read the Camus passage (delay group) or immediately answered the more elaborate fitness intention questionnaire, consisting of nine rather than two questions. After a factor analysis revealed two of the nine fitness intention questions did not cohere with the others, a final seven-item scale was constructed by standardizing and summing responses to the seven questions. Another difference between the two studies was that no participants were primed by reading about how exercise increases longevity.

Results of the first study were replicated: In the immediate group only, mortality salience led to greater desire for exercise compared to the painful dental procedure. In the second study, however, there was an overall main effect for fitness self-esteem, with participants for whom fitness is important to their overall self-esteem intending to do more exercise following mortality salience than those for whom it was not so important. In addition, again there was a main effect for mortality salience: Regardless of immediacy condition, participants who were made aware of their mortality intended to do more exercise than those who were made to think about undergoing a painful dental procedure. Immediacy also had an overall main effect, with participants who delayed answering questions about their fitness intentions claiming they would exercise more than those who immediately responded. Finally, an interaction was found such that fitness intentions increased after mortality salience only for those participants for whom fitness was an important source of their self-esteem.

Overall, the results of these two studies confirm the importance of distinguishing between proximal (conscious) and distal (unconscious) defenses against death. They also confirm the idea that people may well be motivated to undertake behaviors that fight against death and disease (namely, exercise) when their own mortality is made salient, especially if exercise is a relevant and important source of their self-esteem.

In summary, terror management seems to bolster the fundamental principle of existential psychology that both conscious and unconscious anxiety provoked by thoughts of death is a powerful force behind much of human behavior.

Critique of May

Existentialism in general and May's psychology in particular have been criticized as being anti-intellectual and antitheoretical. May acknowledged the claim that his views did not conform to the traditional concept of theory, but he staunchly defended his psychology against the charge of being anti-intellectual or antiscientific. He pointed to the sterility of conventional scientific methods and their inability to unlock the ontological character of willing, caring, and acting human beings.

May held that a new scientific psychology must recognize such human characteristics as uniqueness, personal freedom, destiny, phenomenological experiences, and especially our capacity to relate to ourselves as both object and subject. A new science of humans must also include ethics. "The actions of living, self-aware human beings are never automatic, but involve some weighing of consequences, some potentiality for good or ill" (May, 1967, p. 199).

Until this new science acquires greater maturity, we must evaluate May's views by the same criteria used for each of the other personality theorists. First, have May's ideas *generated scientific research*? May did not formulate his views in a theoretical structure, and a paucity of hypotheses is suggested by his writings. Some research, such as Jeff Greenberg and associates' investigations on terror management, relates generally to existential psychology, but these studies do not specifically flow from May's theory. On this first criterion of a useful theory, therefore, May's existential psychology receives a very low score.

Second, can May's ideas be verified or *falsified*? Again, existential psychology in general and May's theory in particular must be rated very low on this criterion. The theory is too amorphous to suggest specific hypotheses that could either confirm or disconfirm its major concepts.

Third, does May's philosophically oriented psychology help *organize what is currently known about human nature?* On this criterion, May would receive an average rating. Compared with most theorists discussed in this book, May has more closely followed Gordon Allport's dictum, "Do not forget what you have decided to neglect" (Allport, 1968, p. 23). May did not forget that he excluded discourses on developmental stages, basic motivational forces, and other factors that tend to segment the human experience. May's philosophical writings have reached deep into the far recesses of the human experience and have explored aspects of humanity not examined by other personality theorists. His popularity has been due in part to his ability to touch individual readers, to connect with their humanity. Although his ideas may affect people in ways that other theorists do not, his use of certain concepts was at times inconsistent and confusing. Moreover, he decided to neglect several important topics in human personality: for example, development, cognition, learning, and motivation.

As a *practical guide to action,* May's theory is quite weak. Although he possessed a keen understanding of human personality, May gathered his views more from philosophical than from scientific sources. In fact, he had no objection to being called a philosopher and frequently referred to himself as a philosopher-therapist.

On the criterion of *internal consistency,* May's existential psychology again falls short. He offered a variety of definitions for such concepts as anxiety, guilt, intentionality, will, and destiny. Unfortunately, he never presented operational definitions of these terms. This imprecise terminology has contributed to the lack of research on May's ideas.

The final criterion of a useful theory is *parsimony,* and on this standard, May's psychology receives a moderate rating. His writings at times were cumbersome and awkward, but to his credit, he dealt with complex issues and did not attempt to oversimplify human personality.

✺ Concept of Humanity

Like Erik Erikson (see Chapter 9), May offered a new way of looking at things. His view of humanity is both broader and deeper than the views of most other personality theorists. He saw people as complex beings, capable of both tremendous good and immense evil.

According to May, people have become estranged from the natural world, from other people, and most of all, from themselves. As people become more alienated from other people and from themselves, they surrender portions of their consciousness. They become less aware of themselves as a subject, that is, the person who is aware of the experiencing self. As the subjective self becomes obscured, people lose some of their capacity to make choices. This progression, however, is not inevitable. May believed that people, within the confines of their destiny, have the ability to make free choices. Each choice pushes back the boundaries of determinism and permits new choices. People generally have much more potential for freedom than they realize. However, free choice does not come without anxiety. Choice demands the courage to confront one's destiny, to look within and to recognize the evil as well as the good.

Choice also implies action. Without action, choice is merely a wish, an idle desire. With action comes responsibility. Freedom and responsibility are always commensurable. A person cannot have more freedom than responsibility, nor can one be shackled with more responsibility than freedom. Healthy individuals welcome both freedom and responsibility, but they realize that choice is often painful, anxiety-provoking, and difficult.

May believed that many people have surrendered some of their ability to choose, but that capitulation itself, he insisted, is a choice. Ultimately, each of us is responsible for the choices we make, and those choices define each of us as a unique human being. May, therefore, must be rated high on the dimension of *free choice*.

Is May's theory *optimistic* or *pessimistic*? Although he sometimes painted a rather gloomy picture of humanity, May was not pessimistic. He saw the present age as merely a plateau in humanity's quest for new symbols and new myths that will engender the species with renewed spirit.

Although May recognized the potential impact of childhood experiences on adult personality, he clearly favored *teleology* over causality. Each of us has a particular goal or destiny that we must discover and challenge or else risk alienation and neurosis.

May assumed a moderate stance on the issue of *conscious* versus *unconscious* forces in personality development. By their nature, people have enormous capacity for self-awareness, but often that capacity remains fallow. People sometimes lack the courage to face their destiny or to recognize the evil that exists within their culture as well as within themselves. Consciousness and choices are interrelated. As people make more free choices, they gain more insight into who they are; that is, they develop a greater sense of being. This sharpened sense of being, in turn, facilitates the ability to make further choices. An awareness of self and a capacity for free choice are hallmarks of psychological health.

May also took an intermediate position on *social* versus *biological* influences. Society contributes to personality principally through interpersonal relationships. Our relations with other people can have either a freeing or an enslaving effect. Sick relationships, such as those Philip experienced with his mother and sister, can stifle personal growth and leave us with an inability to participate in a healthy encounter with another person. Without the capacity to relate to people as people, life becomes meaningless and we develop a sense of alienation not only from others but from ourselves as well. Biology also contributes to personality. Biological factors such as gender, physical size, predisposition to illnesses, and ultimately death itself, shape a person's destiny. Everyone must live within the confines of destiny, but those confines can be expanded.

On the dimension of *uniqueness* versus *similarities,* May's view of humanity definitely leans toward uniqueness. Each of us is responsible for shaping our own personality within the limits imposed by destiny. No two of us make the same sequence of choices, and no two develop identical ways of looking at things. May's emphasis on phenomenology implies individual perceptions and therefore unique personalities.

Key Terms and Concepts

- A basic tenet of existentialism is that *existence precedes essence,* meaning that what people do is more important than what they are.
- A second assumption is that *people are both subjective and objective:* that is, they are thinking as well as acting beings.
- *People are motivated to search for answers* to important questions regarding the meaning of life.
- People have an equal degree of both *freedom and responsibility.*
- The unity of people and their phenomenological world is expressed by the term *Dasein,* or *being-in-the-world.*
- Three modes of being-in-the-world are *Umwelt,* one's relationship with the world of things; *Mitwelt,* one's relationship with the world of people; and *Eigenwelt,* one's relationship with oneself.
- *Nonbeing,* or *nothingness,* is an awareness of the possibility of one's not being, through death or loss of awareness.
- People experience *anxiety* when they are aware of the possibility of their nonbeing as well as when they are aware that they are free to choose.
- *Normal anxiety* is experienced by everyone and is proportionate to the threat.
- *Neurotic anxiety* is disproportionate to the threat, involves repression, and is handled in a self-defeating manner.
- People experience *guilt* as a result of their (1) separation from the natural world, (2) inability to judge the needs of others, and (3) denial of their own potentials.

- *Intentionality* is the underlying structure that gives meaning to experience and allows people to make decisions about the future.
- *Love* means taking delight in the presence of the other person and affirming that person's value as much as one's own.
- *Sex,* a basic form of love, is a biological function that seeks satisfaction through the release of sexual tension.
- *Eros,* a higher form of love, seeks an enduring union with a loved one.
- *Philia* is the form of love that seeks a nonsexual friendship with another person.
- *Agape,* the highest form of love, is altruistic and seeks nothing from the other person.
- *Freedom* is gained through confrontation with one's destiny and through an understanding that death or nonbeing is a possibility at any moment.
- *Existential freedom* is freedom of action, freedom to move about, to pursue tangible goals.
- *Essential freedom* is freedom of being, freedom to think, to plan, to hope.
- *Cultural myths* are belief systems, both conscious and unconscious, that provide explanations for personal and social problems.

PART FOUR

Dispositional Theories

Allport: Psychology of the Individual

Allport

In the fall of 1920, a 22-year-old American philosophy and economics student was visiting with an older brother in Vienna. During his visit, the young man penned a note to Sigmund Freud requesting an appointment. Freud, then the world's most famous psychiatrist, agreed to see the young man and suggested a specific time for a meeting.

The young American arrived at No. 19 Berggasse in plenty of time for his appointment with Dr. Freud. At the designated time, Freud opened the door to his consulting room and quietly ushered the young man inside. The American visitor suddenly realized that he had nothing to say. Searching his mind for some incident that might interest Freud, he remembered seeing a small boy on the tram car that day while traveling to Freud's home. The little boy, about 4 years old, displayed an obvious dirt phobia, constantly complaining to his well-starched mother about the filthy conditions on the car. Freud listened silently to the story and then—with a typical Freudian technique—asked his young visitor if he was in reality talking about himself. Feeling guilty, the young man managed to change the subject and to escape without too much further embarrassment.

The American visitor to Freud's consulting room was Gordon Allport, and this encounter was the spark that ignited his interest in personality theory. Back in the United States, Allport began to wonder if there might be room for a third approach to personality, one that borrowed from traditional psychoanalysis and animal-driven learning theories, but also one that adopted a more humanistic stance. Allport quickly completed work for a PhD in psychology and embarked on a long and distinguished career as a staunch advocate for the study of the individual.

Overview of Allport's Psychology of the Individual

More than any other personality theorist, Gordon Allport emphasized the *uniqueness of the individual.* He believed that attempts to describe people in terms of general traits rob them of their unique individuality. For this reason, Allport objected to trait and factor theories that tend to reduce individual behaviors to common traits. He insisted, for example, that one person's stubbornness is different from any other person's stubbornness and the manner in which one person's stubbornness interacts with his or her extraversion and creativity is duplicated by no other individual.

Consistent with Allport's emphasis on each person's uniqueness was his willingness to study in depth a single individual. He called the study of the individual **morphogenic science** and contrasted it with the **nomothetic** methods used by most other psychologists. Morphogenic methods are those that gather data on a *single individual,* whereas nomothetic methods gather data on groups of people. Allport also advocated an **eclectic** approach to theory building. He accepted some of the contributions of Freud, Maslow, Rogers, Eysenck, Skinner, and others; but he believed that no one of these theorists is able to adequately explain the total growing and unique personality. To Allport, a broad, comprehensive theory is preferable to a narrow, specific theory even if it does not generate as many testable hypotheses.

Allport argued against particularism, or theories that emphasize a single aspect of personality. In an important warning to other theorists, he cautioned them not to "forget what you have decided to neglect" (Allport, 1968, p. 23).

In other words, no theory is completely comprehensive, and psychologists should always realize that much of human nature is not included in any single theory. To Allport, a broad, comprehensive theory is preferable to a narrow, specific theory even if it does not generate as many testable hypotheses.

Biography of Gordon Allport

Gordon Willard Allport was born on November 11, 1897, in Montezuma, Indiana, the fourth and youngest son of John E. Allport and Nellie Wise Allport. Allport's father had engaged in a number of business ventures before becoming a physician at about the time of Gordon's birth. Lacking adequate office and clinical facilities, Dr. Allport turned the household into a miniature hospital. Both patients and nurses were found in the home, and a clean, sterile atmosphere prevailed.

Cleanliness of action was extended to cleanliness of thought. In his autobiography, Allport (1967) wrote that his early life "was marked by plain Protestant piety" (p. 4). Floyd Allport, his older brother by 7 years, who also became a famous psychologist, described their mother as a very pious woman who placed heavy emphasis on religion (F. Allport, 1974). As a former schoolteacher, she taught young Gordon the virtues of clean language and proper conduct as well as the importance of searching for ultimate religious answers.

By the time Gordon was 6 years old, the family had moved three times—finally settling in Cleveland, Ohio. Young Allport developed an early interest in philosophical and religious questions and had more facility for words than for games. He described himself as a social "isolate" who fashioned his own circle of activities. Although he graduated second in his high school class of 100, he did not consider himself an inspired scholar (Allport, 1967).

In the fall of 1915, Allport entered Harvard, following in the footsteps of his brother Floyd, who had graduated 2 years earlier and who at that time was a graduate assistant in psychology. In his autobiography, Gordon Allport (1967) wrote: "Almost overnight my world was remade. My basic moral values, to be sure, had been fashioned at home. What was new was the horizon of intellect and culture I was now invited to explore" (p. 5). His enrollment at Harvard also marked the beginning of a 50-year association with that university, which was only twice briefly interrupted. When he received his bachelor's degree in 1919 with a major in philosophy and economics, he was still uncertain about a future career. He had taken undergraduate courses in psychology and social ethics, and both disciplines had made a lasting impression on him. When he received an opportunity to teach in Turkey, he saw it as a chance to find out whether he would enjoy teaching. He spent the academic year 1919–1920 in Europe teaching English and sociology at Robert College in Istanbul.

While in Turkey, Allport was offered a fellowship for graduate study at Harvard. He also received an invitation from his brother Fayette to stay with him in Vienna, where Fayette was working for the U.S. trade commission. In Vienna, Allport had the meeting with Sigmund Freud that we briefly described in the introduction to this chapter. This meeting with Freud greatly influenced Allport's later ideas on personality. With a certain audacity, the 22-year-old Allport wrote to Freud announcing that he was in Vienna and offered the father of psychoanalysis an opportunity to meet with him. The encounter proved to be a fortuitous life-altering event for Allport. Not knowing what to talk about, the young visitor told Freud about seeing a small boy on the tram car earlier that day. The young child complained to his mother about the filthy conditions of the car and announced that he did not want to sit near passengers whom he deemed to be dirty. Allport claimed that he chose this particular incident to get Freud's reaction to a dirt phobia in a child so young, but he was quite flabbergasted when Freud "fixed his kindly therapeutic eyes upon me and said, 'And was that little boy *you?*'" (Allport, 1967, p. 8). Allport said he felt guilty and quickly changed the topic.

Allport told this story many times, seldom changing any words, and never revealing the rest of his lone encounter with Freud. However, Alan Elms has uncovered Allport's written description of what happened next. After realizing that Freud was expecting a professional consultation, Allport then talked about his dislike of cooked raisins:

> I told him I thought it due to the fact that at the age of three, a nurse had told me they were "bugs." Freud asked, "When you recalled this episode, did your dislike vanish?" I said, "No." He replied, "Then you are not at the bottom of it." (Elms, 1994, p. 77)

When Allport returned to the United States, he immediately enrolled in the PhD program at Harvard. After finishing his degree, he spent the following 2 years in Europe studying under the great German psychologists Max Wertheimer, Wolfgang Kohler, William Stern, Heinz Werner, and others in Berlin and Hamburg.

In 1924, he returned again to Harvard to teach, among other classes, a new course in the psychology of personality. In his autobiography, Allport (1967) suggested that this course was the first personality course offered in an American college. The course combined social ethics and the pursuit of goodness and morality with the scientific discipline of psychology. It also reflected Allport's strong personal dispositions of cleanliness and morality.

Two years after beginning his teaching career at Harvard, Allport took a position at Dartmouth College. Four years later, he returned to Harvard and remained there for the rest of his professional career.

In 1925, Allport married Ada Lufkin Gould, whom he had met when both were graduate students. Ada Allport, who received a master's degree in clinical psychology from Harvard, had the clinical training that her husband lacked. She was a valuable contributor to some of Gordon's work, especially his two extensive case studies—the case of Jenny Gove Masterson (discussed in the section titled The Study of the Individual) and the case of Marion Taylor, which was never published (Barenbaum, 1997).

The Allports had one child, Robert, who became a pediatrician and thus sandwiched Allport between two generations of physicians, a fact that seemed to have pleased him in no small measure (Allport, 1967). Allport's awards and honors were many. In 1939, he was elected president of the American Psychological Association (APA). In 1963, he received the Gold Medal Award of the APA; in 1964, he was awarded the Distinguished Scientific Contribution Award of the APA; and in 1966, he was honored as the first Richard Clarke Cabot Professor of Social Ethics at Harvard. On October 9, 1967, Allport, a heavy smoker, died of lung cancer.

Allport's Approach to Personality Theory

Answers to three interrelated questions reveal Allport's approach to personality theory: (1) What is personality? (2) What is the role of *conscious motivation* in personality theory? (3) What are the characteristics of the psychologically healthy person?

What Is Personality?

Few psychologists have been as painstaking and exhaustive as Allport in defining terms. His pursuit of a definition of personality is classic. He traced the etymology of the word *persona* back to early Greek roots, including the Old Latin and Etruscan meanings. As we saw in Chapter 1, the word "personality" probably comes from *persona,* which refers to the theatrical mask used in ancient Greek drama by Roman actors during the first and second centuries B.C.E. After tracing the history of the term, Allport spelled out 49 definitions of personality as used in theology, philosophy, law, sociology, and psychology. He then offered a 50th definition, which in 1937 was *"the dynamic organization within the individual of those psychophysical systems that determine his unique adjustments to his environment"* (Allport, 1937, p. 48). In 1961, he had changed the last phrase to read *"that determine his characteristic behavior and thought"* (Allport, 1961, p. 28). The change was significant and reflected Allport's penchant for accuracy. By 1961, he realized that the phrase "adjustments to his environment" could imply that people merely adapt to their environment. In his later definition, Allport conveyed the idea that behavior is *expressive* as well as adaptive. People not only adjust to their environment, but also reflect on it and interact with it in such a way as to cause their environment to adjust to them.

Allport chose each phrase of his definition carefully so that each word conveys precisely what he wanted to say. The term *dynamic organization* implies an integration or interrelatedness of the various aspects of personality. Personality is organized and patterned. However, the organization is always subject to change: hence, the qualifier "dynamic." Personality is not a static organization; it is constantly growing or changing. The term *psychophysical* emphasizes the importance of both the psychological and the physical aspects of personality.

Another word in the definition that implies action is *determine,* which suggests that "personality is something and does something" (Allport, 1961, p. 29). In other words, personality is not merely the mask we wear, nor is it simply behavior. It refers to the individual behind the facade, the person behind the action.

By *characteristic,* Allport wished to imply "individual" or "unique." The word "character" originally meant a marking or engraving, terms that give flavor to what Allport meant by "characteristic." All persons stamp their unique mark or engraving on their personality, and their characteristic behavior and thought set them apart from all other people. Characteristics are marked with a unique engraving, a stamp or marking, that no one else can duplicate. The words *behavior* and *thought* simply refer to anything the person does. They are omnibus terms meant to include internal behaviors (thoughts) as well as external behaviors such as words and actions.

Allport's comprehensive definition of personality suggests that human beings are both product and process; people have some organized structure while, at the same time, they possess the capability of change. Pattern coexists with growth, order with diversification.

In summary, personality is both physical and psychological; it includes both overt behaviors and covert thoughts; it not only *is* something, but it *does* something. Personality is both substance and change, both product and process, both structure and growth.

What Is the Role of Conscious Motivation?

More than any other personality theorist, Allport emphasized the importance of conscious motivation. Healthy adults are generally aware of what they are doing and their reasons for doing it. His emphasis on conscious motivation goes back to his meeting in Vienna with Freud and his emotional reaction to Freud's question: "And was that little boy *you*?" Freud's response carried the implication that his 22-year-old visitor was unconsciously talking about his own fetish for cleanliness in revealing the story of the clean little boy on the tram car. Allport (1967) insisted that his motivation was quite conscious—he simply wanted to know Freud's ideas about dirt phobia in a child so young.

Whereas Freud would assume an underlying unconscious meaning to the story of the little boy on the tram, Allport was inclined to accept self-reports at face value. "This experience taught me that depth psychology, for all its merits, may plunge too deep, and that psychologists would do well to give full recognition to manifest motives before probing the unconscious" (Allport, 1967, p. 8).

However, Allport (1961) did not ignore the existence or even the importance of unconscious processes. He recognized the fact that some motivation is driven by hidden impulses and sublimated drives. He believed, for example, that most compulsive behaviors are automatic repetitions, usually self-defeating, and motivated by unconscious tendencies. They often originate in childhood and retain a childish flavor into adult years.

What Are the Characteristics of a Healthy Person?

Long before Abraham Maslow (see Chapter 10) made the concept of self-actualization popular, Gordon Allport (1937) hypothesized in depth about the attributes of the mature personality. Allport's interest in the psychologically healthy person goes back to 1922, the year he finished his PhD. Not having any particular skills in mathematics, biology, medicine, or laboratory manipulations, Allport (1967) was forced to "find [his] own way in the humanistic pastures of psychology" (p. 8). Such pastures led to a study of the psychologically mature personality.

A few general assumptions are required to understand Allport's conception of the mature personality. First, psychologically mature people are characterized by **proactive** behavior; that is, they not only react to external stimuli, but they are capable of consciously acting on their environment in new and innovative ways and causing their environment to react to them. Proactive behavior is not merely directed at reducing tensions but also at establishing new ones.

In addition, mature personalities are more likely than disturbed ones to be motivated by conscious processes, which allow them to be more flexible and autonomous than unhealthy people, who remain dominated by unconscious motives that spring from childhood experiences.

Healthy people ordinarily have experienced a relatively trauma-free childhood, even though their later years may be tempered by conflict and suffering. Psychologically healthy individuals are not without the foibles and idiosyncrasies that make them unique. Also, age is not a requisite for maturity, although healthy persons seem to become more mature as they get older.

What, then, are the more specific requirements for psychological health? Allport (1961) identified six criteria for the mature personality.

The first is an *extension of the sense of self.* Mature people continually seek to identify with and participate in events outside themselves. They are not self-centered but are able to become involved in problems and activities that are not centered on themselves. They develop an unselfish interest in work, play, and recreation. Social interest (*Gemeinschaftsgefühl*), family, and spiritual life are important to them. Eventually, these outside activities become part of one's being. Allport (1961) summed up this first criterion by saying: "Everyone has self-love, but only self-extension is the earmark of maturity" (p. 285).

Second, mature personalities are characterized by a *"warm relating of self to others"* (Allport, 1961, p. 285). They have the capacity to love others in an intimate and compassionate manner. Warm relating, of course, is dependent on people's ability to extend their sense of self. Only by looking beyond themselves can mature people love others nonpossessively and unselfishly. Psychologically healthy individuals treat other people with respect, and they realize that the needs, desires, and hopes of others are not completely foreign to their own. In addition, they have a healthy sexual attitude and do not exploit others for personal gratification.

A third criterion is *emotional security* or *self-acceptance.* Mature individuals accept themselves for what they are, and they possess what Allport (1961) called emotional poise. These psychologically healthy people are not overly upset when things do not go as planned or when they are simply "having a bad day." They do not dwell on minor irritations, and they recognize that frustrations and inconveniences are a part of living.

Fourth, psychologically healthy people also possess a *realistic perception* of their environment. They do not live in a fantasy world or bend reality to fit their own wishes. They are problem oriented rather than self-centered, and they are in touch with the world as most others see it.

A fifth criterion is *insight and humor.* Mature people know themselves and, therefore, have no need to attribute their own mistakes and weaknesses to others. They also have a nonhostile sense of humor, which gives them the capacity to laugh at themselves rather than relying on sexual or aggressive themes to elicit laughter from others. Allport (1961) believed that insight and humor are closely related and may be aspects of the same thing, namely self-objectification. Healthy individuals see themselves objectively. They are able to perceive the incongruities and absurdities in life and have no need to pretend or to put on airs.

The final criterion of maturity is a *unifying philosophy of life.* Healthy people have a clear view of the purpose of life. Without this view, their insight would be empty and barren, and their humor would be trivial and cynical. The unifying philosophy of life may or may not be religious, but Allport (1954, 1963), on a personal level, seemed to have felt that a mature religious orientation is a crucial ingredient in the lives of most mature individuals. Although many churchgoing people have an immature religious philosophy and narrow racial and ethnic prejudices, deeply religious people are relatively free of these prejudices. The person with a mature religious attitude and a unifying philosophy of life has a well-developed conscience and, quite likely, a strong desire to serve others.

Structure of Personality

The structure of personality refers to its basic units or building blocks. To Freud, the basic units were instincts; to Eysenck, they were mathematically determined factors. To Allport, the most important structures are those that permit the description of the person in terms of individual characteristics, and he called these individual characteristics *personal dispositions.*

Personal Dispositions

Throughout most of his career, Allport was careful to distinguish between *common traits* and individual traits. **Common traits** are general characteristics held in common by many people. They can be inferred from factor analytic studies such as those conducted by Eysenck and the authors of the Five-Factor Theory (see Chapter 14), or they can be revealed by various personality inventories. Common traits provide the means by which people within a given culture can be compared to one another.

Whereas common traits are important for studies that make comparisons among people, **personal dispositions** are of even greater importance because they permit researchers to study a single individual. Allport (1961) defined a personal disposition as "a generalized neuropsychic structure (peculiar to the individual), with the capacity to render many stimuli functionally equivalent, and to initiate and guide consistent (equivalent) forms of adaptive and stylistic behavior" (p. 373). The most important distinction between a personal disposition and a common trait is indicated by the parenthetical phrase "peculiar to the individual." Personal dispositions are individual; common traits are shared by several people.

To identify personal dispositions, Allport and Henry Odbert (1936) counted nearly 18,000 (17,953, to be exact) personally descriptive words in the 1925 edition of *Webster's New International Dictionary,* about a fourth of which described personality characteristics. Some of these terms, usually referred to as *traits,* describe relatively stable characteristics such as "sociable" or "introverted"; others, usually referred to as *states,* describe temporary characteristics such as "happy" or "angry"; others described evaluative characteristics such as "unpleasant" or "wonderful"; and still others referred to physical characteristics such as "tall" or "obese."

How many personal dispositions does one individual have? This question cannot be answered without reference to the degree of dominance that each personal disposition has in the individual's life. If we count those personal dispositions that are central to a person, then each person probably has 10 or fewer. However, if all tendencies are included, then each person may have hundreds of personal dispositions.

Levels of Personal Dispositions

Allport placed personal dispositions on a continuum from those that are most central to those that are of only peripheral importance to a person.

Cardinal Dispositions Some people possess an eminent characteristic or ruling passion so outstanding that it dominates their lives. Allport (1961) called these personal dispositions **cardinal dispositions.** They are so obvious that they cannot be hidden; nearly every action in a person's life revolves around this one cardinal disposition. Most people do not have a cardinal disposition, but those few people who do are often known by that single characteristic.

Allport identified several historical people and fictional characters who possessed a disposition so outstanding that they have given our language a new word. Some examples of these cardinal dispositions include quixotic, chauvinistic, narcissistic, sadistic, a Don Juan, and so forth. Because personal dispositions are individual and are not shared with any other person, only Don Quixote was truly quixotic; only Narcissus was completely narcissistic; only the Marquis de Sade possessed the cardinal disposition of sadism. When these names are used to describe characteristics in others, they become common traits.

Central Dispositions Few people have cardinal dispositions, but everyone has several **central dispositions,** which include the 5 to 10 most outstanding characteristics around which a person's life focuses. Allport (1961) described central dispositions as those that would be listed in an accurate letter of recommendation written by someone who knew the person quite well. In the section titled The Study of the Individual, we will look at a series of letters written to Gordon and Ada Allport by a woman they called Jenny. The contents of these letters constitute a rich source of information about the writer. We will also see that three separate analyses of these letters revealed that Jenny could be described by about eight central dispositions: that is, characteristics sufficiently strong to be detected by each of these three separate procedures. Similarly, most people, Allport believed, have 5 to 10 central dispositions that their friends and close acquaintances would agree are descriptive of that person.

Secondary Dispositions Less conspicuous but far greater in number than central dispositions are the **secondary dispositions.** Everyone has many secondary dispositions that are not central to the personality yet occur with some regularity and are responsible for much of one's specific behaviors.

The three levels of personal dispositions are, of course, arbitrary points on a continuous scale from most appropriate to least appropriate. Cardinal dispositions, which are exceedingly prominent in a person, shade into central dispositions, which are less dominating but nevertheless mark the person as unique. Central dispositions, which guide much of a person's adaptive and stylistic behavior, blend into secondary dispositions, which are less descriptive of that individual. We cannot say, however, that one person's secondary dispositions are less intense than another person's central dispositions. Interperson comparisons are inappropriate to personal dispositions, and any attempt to make such comparison transforms the personal dispositions into common traits (Allport, 1961).

Motivational and Stylistic Dispositions

All personal dispositions are dynamic in the sense that they have motivational power. Nevertheless, some are much more strongly felt than others, and Allport called these intensely experienced dispositions *motivational dispositions.* These strongly felt dispositions receive their motivation from basic needs and drives. Allport (1961) referred to personal dispositions that are less intensely experienced as *stylistic dispositions,* even though these dispositions possess some motivational power. Stylistic dispositions *guide* action, whereas motivational dispositions *initiate* action. An example of a stylistic disposition might be neat and impeccable personal appearance. People are motivated to dress because of a basic need to stay warm, but the *manner* in which they attire themselves is determined by their stylistic personal dispositions. Motivational dispositions are somewhat similar to Maslow's concept of coping behavior, whereas stylistic dispositions are similar to Maslow's idea of expressive behavior (see Chapter 10).

Unlike Maslow, who drew a clear line between coping and expressive behaviors, Allport saw no distinct division between motivational and stylistic personal dispositions. Although some dispositions are clearly stylistic, others are obviously based on a strongly felt need and are thus motivational. Politeness, for example, is a stylistic disposition, whereas eating is more motivational. How people eat (their style) depends at least partially on how hungry they are, but it also depends on the strength of their stylistic dispositions. A usually polite but hungry person may forego manners while eating alone, but if the politeness disposition is strong enough and if others are present, then the famished person may eat with etiquette and courtesy despite being famished.

Proprium

Whether motivational or stylistic, some personal dispositions are close to the core of personality, whereas others are more on the periphery. Those that are at the center of personality are experienced by the person as being an important part of self. They are characteristics that an individual refers to in such terms as "That is me" or "This is mine." All characteristics that are "peculiarly mine" belong to the *proprium* (Allport, 1955).

Allport used the term **proprium** to refer to those behaviors and characteristics that people regard as warm, central, and important in their lives. The proprium is not the whole personality, because many characteristics and behaviors of a person are not warm and central; rather, they exist on the periphery of personality. These nonpropriate behaviors include (1) basic drives and needs that are ordinarily met and satisfied without much difficulty; (2) tribal customs such as wearing clothes, saying "hello" to people, and driving on the right side of the road; and (3) habitual behaviors, such as smoking or brushing one's teeth, that are performed automatically and that are not crucial to the person's sense of self.

As the warm center of personality, the proprium includes those aspects of life that a person regards as important to a sense of self-identity and self-enhancement (Allport, 1955). The proprium includes a person's values as well as that part of the conscience that is personal and consistent with one's adult beliefs. A generalized conscience—one shared by most people within a given culture—may be only peripheral to a person's sense of personhood and thus outside that person's proprium.

Motivation

Most people, Allport believed, are motivated by present drives rather than by past events and are aware of what they are doing and have some understanding of why they are doing it. He also contended that theories of motivation must consider the differences between peripheral motives and **propriate strivings.** Peripheral motives are those that *reduce a need,* whereas propriate strivings seek to *maintain tension and disequilibrium.* Adult behavior is both reactive and proactive, and an adequate theory of motivation must be able to explain both.

A Theory of Motivation

Allport believed that a useful theory of personality rests on the assumption that people not only react to their environment but also shape their environment and cause it to react to them. Personality is a growing system, allowing new elements to constantly enter into and change the person.

Many older theories of personality, Allport (1960) believed, did not allow for possibilities of growth. Psychoanalysis and the various learning theories are basically homeostatic, or **reactive,** theories because they see people as being motivated primarily by needs to reduce tension and to return to a state of equilibrium.

An adequate theory of personality, Allport contended, must allow for *proactive behavior.* It must view people as consciously acting on their environment in a manner that permits growth toward psychological health. A comprehensive theory must not only include an explanation of reactive theories, but must also include those proactive theories that stress change and growth. In other words, Allport argued for a psychology that, on one hand, studies behavioral patterns and general laws (the subject matter of traditional psychology) and, on the other, growth and individuality.

Sometimes people are motivated to seek tension, not merely reduce it.

Allport claimed that theories of unchanging motives are incomplete because they are limited to an explanation of reactive behavior. The mature person, however, is not motivated merely to seek pleasure and reduce pain but to acquire new systems of motivation that are functionally independent from their original motives.

Functional Autonomy

The concept of **functional autonomy** represents Allport's most distinctive and, at the same time, most controversial postulate. It is Allport's (1961) explanation for the myriad human motives that seemingly are not accounted for by hedonistic or drive-reduction principles. Functional autonomy represents a theory of changing rather than unchanging motives and is the capstone of Allport's ideas on motivation.

In general, the concept of functional autonomy holds that some, but not all, human motives are functionally independent from the original motive responsible for the behavior. If a motive is functionally autonomous, it is the explanation for behavior, and one need not look beyond it for hidden or primary causes. In other words, if hoarding money is a functionally autonomous motive, then the miser's behavior is *not* traceable to childhood experiences with toilet training or with rewards and punishments. Rather, the miser simply *likes* money, and this is the only explanation necessary. This notion that much human behavior is based on present interests and on conscious preferences is in harmony with the commonsense belief of many people who hold that they do things simply because they like to do them.

Functional autonomy is a reaction to what Allport called theories of unchanging motives, namely, Freud's pleasure principle and the drive-reduction hypothesis of stimulus-response psychology. Allport held that both theories are concerned with *historical facts* rather than *functional facts.* He believed that adult motives are built primarily on conscious, self-sustaining, contemporary systems. Functional autonomy represents his attempt to explain these conscious, self-sustaining contemporary motivations.

Admitting that some motivations are unconscious and others are the result of drive reduction, Allport contended that, because some behavior is functionally autonomous, theories of unchanging motives are inadequate. He listed four requirements of an adequate theory of motivation. Functional autonomy, of course, meets each criterion.

1. An adequate theory of motivation *"will acknowledge the contemporaneity of motives."* In other words, "Whatever moves us must move now" (Allport, 1961, p. 220). The past per se is unimportant. The history of an individual is significant only when it has a present effect on motivation.
2. *"It will be a pluralistic theory—allowing for motives of many types"* (Allport, 1961, p. 221). On this point, Allport was critical of Freud and his two-instinct theory, Adler and the single striving for success, and all theories that emphasize self-actualization as the ultimate motive. Allport was emphatically opposed to reducing all human motivation to one master drive. He contended that adults' motives are basically different from those of children and that the motivations of neurotic individuals are not the same as those of normal people. In addition, some motivations are conscious, others unconscious; some are transient, others recurring; some are peripheral,

others propriate; and some are tension reducing, others tension maintaining. Motives that appear to be different really are different, not only in form but also in substance.

3.   *"It will ascribe dynamic force to cognitive processes—e.g., to planning and intention"* (Allport, 1961, p. 222). Allport argued that most people are busy living their lives into the future, but that many psychological theories are "busy tracing these lives backward into the past. And while it seems to each of us that we are spontaneously *active,* many psychologists are telling us that we are only *reactive*" (p. 206). Although intention is involved in all motivation, this third requirement refers more generally to long-range intention. A young woman declines an offer to see a movie because she *prefers* to study anatomy. This preference is consistent with her *purpose* of making good grades at college and relates to her *plans* of being admitted to medical school, which is necessary in order for her to fulfill her *intention* of being a doctor. The lives of healthy adults are future oriented, involving preferences, purposes, plans, and intentions. These processes, of course, are not always completely rational, as when people allow their anger to dominate their plans and intentions.

4.   An adequate theory of motivation is one that *"will allow for the concrete uniqueness of motives"* (Allport, 1961, p. 225). A concrete unique motive is different from an abstract generalized one, the latter being based on a preexistent theory rather than the actual motivation of a real person. An example of a concrete unique motive is Derrick, who is interested in improving his bowling game. His motive is concrete, and his manner of seeking improvement is unique to him. Some theories of motivation may ascribe Derrick's behavior to an aggressive need, others to an inhibited sexual drive, and still others to a secondary drive learned on the basis of a primary drive. Allport would simply say that Derrick wants to improve his bowling game because he wants to improve his bowling game. This is Derrick's unique, concrete, and functionally autonomous motive.

In summary, a functionally autonomous motive is contemporary and self-sustaining; it grows out of an earlier motive but is functionally independent of it. Allport (1961) defined functional autonomy as *"any acquired system of motivation in which the tensions involved are not of the same kind as the antecedent tensions from which the acquired system developed"* (p. 229). In other words, what begins as one motive may grow into a new one that is historically continuous with the original but functionally autonomous from it. For example, a person may originally plant a garden to satisfy a hunger drive but eventually become interested in gardening for its own sake.

Perseverative Functional Autonomy

The more elementary of the two levels of functional autonomy is **perseverative functional autonomy.** Allport borrowed this term from the word "perseveration," which is the tendency of an impression to leave an influence on subsequent experience. Perseverative functional autonomy is found in animals as well as humans and is based on simple neurological principles. An example of perseverative functional autonomy is a rat that has learned to run a maze in order to be fed but then continues to run the maze even after it has become satiated. Why does it continue to run? Allport would say that the rat runs the maze just for the fun of it.

Allport (1961) listed other examples of perseverative functional autonomy that involve human rather than animal motivation. The first is an addiction to alcohol, tobacco, or other drugs when there is no physiological hunger for them. Alcoholics continue to drink although their current motivation is functionally independent from their original motive.

Another example concerns uncompleted tasks. A problem once started but then interrupted will perseverate, creating a new tension to finish the task. This new tension is different from the initial motivation. For example, a college student is offered 10 cents for every piece of a 500-piece jigsaw puzzle she successfully puts together. Assume that she does not have a preexisting interest in solving jigsaw puzzles and that her original motivation was solely for the money. Also assume that her monetary reward is limited to $45, so that after she has completed 450 pieces, she will have maximized her pay. Will this student finish the remaining 50 pieces in the absence of monetary reward? If she does, then a new tension has been created, and her motive to complete the task is functionally autonomous from the original motive of getting paid.

Propriate Functional Autonomy

The master system of motivation that confers unity on personality is **propriate functional autonomy,** which refers to those self-sustaining motives that are related to the proprium. Jigsaw puzzles and alcohol are seldom regarded as "peculiarly mine." They are not part of the proprium but exist only on the periphery of personality. On

A person might begin running to lose weight but continue because running is enjoyable. The motive for continuing to run is then functionally autonomous from the motive for beginning to run.

the other hand, occupations, hobbies, and interests are closer to the core of personality, and many of our motivations concerning them become functionally autonomous. For example, a woman may originally take a job because she needs money. At first, the work is uninteresting, perhaps even distasteful. As the years pass, however, she develops a consuming passion for the job itself, spending some vacation time at work and, perhaps, even developing a hobby that is closely related to her occupation.

Criterion for Functional Autonomy

In general, *a present motive is functionally autonomous to the extent that it seeks new goals,* meaning that the behavior will continue even as the motivation for it changes. For example, a child first learning to walk is motivated by some maturational drive, but later he may walk to increase mobility or to build self-confidence. Similarly, a scientist initially dedicated to finding answers to difficult problems may eventually gain more satisfaction from the search than from the solution. At that point, her motivation becomes functionally independent from her original motive of finding answers. She may then look for another area of inquiry even though the new field is somewhat different from the previous one. New problems may lead her to seek new goals and to set higher levels of aspiration.

Processes That Are Not Functionally Autonomous

Functional autonomy is not an explanation for all human motivation. Allport (1961) listed eight processes that are not functionally autonomous: (1) biological drives, such as eating, breathing, and sleeping; (2) motives directly linked to the reduction of basic drives; (3) reflex actions such as an eye blink; (4) constitutional equipment, namely physique, intelligence, and temperament; (5) habits in the process of being formed; (6) patterns of behavior that require primary reinforcement; (7) sublimations that can be tied to childhood sexual desires; and (8) some neurotic or pathological symptoms.

The eighth process (neurotic or pathological symptoms) may or may not involve functionally autonomous motives. For an example of a compulsive symptom that was not functionally autonomous, Allport (1961) offered the case of a 12-year-girl who had a disturbing habit of smacking her lips several times a minute. This habit had begun about 8 years earlier when the girl's mother told her that when she inhaled it was good air and when she exhaled it was bad air. Because the girl believed that she had made the air bad by bringing it out, she decided to kiss it to make it well. As her habit continued, she repressed the reason for her compulsion and continued "kissing" the bad air, a behavior that took the form of smacking her lips. This behavior was not functionally autonomous, but the result of a compulsive need to keep good air from becoming bad air.

Allport suggested a criterion for differentiating between a functionally autonomous compulsion and one that is not. For example, compulsions that can be eliminated through therapy or behavior modification are not functionally autonomous, whereas those that are extremely resistant to therapy are self-sustaining and thus functionally autonomous. When therapy allowed the 12-year-old girl to discover the reason for her habit, she was able to stop smacking her lips. On the other hand, some pathological symptoms serve a contemporary lifestyle and are functionally autonomous from earlier experiences that instigated the pathology. For example, a second-born child's attempts to overtake his older brother may change into a compulsive lifestyle, one marked by unconscious strivings to overtake or defeat all rivals. Because such a deep-seated neurosis is probably not amenable to therapy, it meets Allport's criterion for being functionally autonomous.

The Study of the Individual

Because psychology has historically dealt with general laws and characteristics that people have in common, Allport repeatedly advocated the development and use of research methods that study the individual. To balance the predominant normative or group approach, he suggested that psychologists employ methods that study the motivational and stylistic behaviors of one person.

Morphogenic Science

Early in his writings, Allport distinguished between two scientific approaches: the *nomothetic,* which seeks general laws, and the **idiographic,** which refers to that which is peculiar to the single case. Because the term "idiographic" was so often misused, misunderstood, and misspelled (being confused with "ideographic," or the representation of ideas by graphic symbols), Allport (1968) abandoned the term in his later writings and spoke of *morphogenic procedures.* Both "idiographic" and "morphogenic" pertain to the individual, but "idiographic" does not suggest structure or pattern. In contrast, "morphogenic" refers to patterned properties of the whole organism and allows for intraperson comparisons. The pattern or structure of one's personal dispositions is important. For example, Tyrone may be intelligent, introverted, and strongly motivated by achievement needs, but the unique manner in which his intelligence is related to his introversion and each of his achievement needs forms a structured pattern. These individual patterns are the subject matter of morphogenic science.

What are the methods of morphogenic psychology? Allport (1962) listed many: some, completely morphogenic; some, partly so. Examples of wholly morphogenic, first-person methods are verbatim recordings, interviews, dreams, confessions; diaries, letters; some questionnaires, expressive documents, projective documents, literary works, art forms, automatic writings, doodles, handshakes, voice patterns, body gestures, handwriting, gait, and autobiographies.

When Allport met Hans Eysenck, the famous British factor analyst and believer in nomothetic science (see Chapter 14), he told Eysenck that one day he (Eysenck) would write his autobiography. Eventually, Eysenck (1997b) did indeed publish an autobiography in which he admitted that Allport was right and that morphogenic methods such as one's description of one's own life and work can have validity.

Semimorphogenic approaches include self-rating scales, such as the adjective checklist; standardized tests in which people are compared to themselves rather than a norm group; the Allport-Vernon-Lindzey *Study of Values* (1960); and the Q sort technique of Stephenson (1953), which we discussed in Chapter 11.

Consistent with common sense, but contrary to many psychologists, Allport was willing to accept at face value the self-disclosure statements of most participants in a study. A psychologist who wishes to learn the personal dynamics of people needs simply to ask them what they think of themselves. Answers to direct questions should be accepted as valid unless the person is a young child, psychotic, or extremely defensive. Allport (1962) said that "too often we fail to consult the richest of all sources of data, namely, the subject's own self-knowledge" (p. 413).

The Diaries of Marion Taylor

During the late 1930s, Allport and his wife, Ada, became acquainted with an extremely rich source of personal data about a woman whom they called Marion Taylor. The core of this data was nearly a lifetime of diaries, but personal information on Marion Taylor also included descriptions of her by her mother, her younger sister, her favorite teacher, two of her friends, and a neighbor as well as notes in a baby book, school records, scores on several psychological tests, autobiographical material, and two personal meetings with Ada Allport.

Nicole Barenbaum (1997) has put together a brief account of Marion Taylor's life. Taylor was born in 1902 in Illinois, moved to California with her parents and younger sister in 1908, and began writing to her diary in 1911. Soon after her 13th birthday, her diary entries became more personal, including fantasies and secret feelings. She eventually graduated from college, earned a master's degree, and became a psychology and biology teacher. She married at age 31 but had no children.

Although a wealth of personal documents on Marion Taylor became available to Ada and Gordon Allport, the Allports chose not to publish an account of her story. Barenbaum (1997) offered some possible reasons for this, but due to major gaps in the correspondence between Marion Taylor and Ada Allport, it is now impossible to know for certain why the Allports did not publish this case history. Their work with Marion Taylor probably helped them organize and publish a second case—the story of Jenny Gove Masterson, another pseudonym.

Letters From Jenny

Allport's morphogenic approach to the study of lives is best illustrated in his famous *Letters from Jenny*. These letters reveal the story of an older woman and her intense love/hate feelings toward her son, Ross. Between March 1926 (when she was 58) and October 1937 (when she died), Jenny wrote a series of 301 letters to Ross's former college roommate, Glenn, and his wife, Isabel, who almost certainly were Gordon and Ada Allport (Winter, 1993). Allport originally published parts of these letters anonymously (Anonymous, 1946) and then later published them in more detail under his own name (Allport, 1965).

Born in Ireland of Protestant parents in 1868, Jenny was the oldest in a family of seven children that included five sisters and a brother. When she was 5 years old, the family moved to Canada; and when she was 18, her father died and Jenny was forced to quit school and go to work to help support her family. After 9 years, her brothers and sisters became self-supporting; and Jenny, who had always been considered rebellious, scandalized her family by marrying a divorced man, a decision that further alienated her from her conservatively religious family.

After only 2 years of marriage, Jenny's husband died. A month or so later, her son, Ross, was born. This was 1897, the same year Gordon Allport, Ross's future college roommate, was born. The next 17 years were somewhat contented ones for Jenny. Her world revolved around her son, and she worked hard to ensure that he had everything he wanted. She told Ross that, aside from art, the world was a miserable place and that it was her duty to sacrifice for him because she was responsible for his existence.

When Ross moved away to attend college, Jenny continued to scrimp in order to pay all his bills. As Ross began to be interested in women, the idyllic mother-son relationship came to an end. The two quarreled often and bitterly over his female friends. Jenny referred to each of them as prostitutes or whores, including the woman Ross married. With that marriage, Jenny and Ross became temporarily estranged.

At about that same time, Jenny began an 11$\frac{1}{2}$-year correspondence with Glenn and Isabel (Gordon and Ada) in which she revealed much about both her life and her personality. The early letters showed that she was deeply concerned with money, death, and Ross. She felt that Ross was ungrateful and that he had abandoned her for another woman, and a prostitute at that! She continued her bitterness toward him until he and his wife were divorced. She then moved into the apartment next to Ross's and for a short time Jenny was happy. But soon Ross was seeing other women, and Jenny inevitably found something wrong with each. Her letters were filled again with animosity for Ross, a suspicious and cynical attitude toward others, and a morbid yet dramatic approach to life.

Three years into the correspondence, Ross suddenly died. After his death, Jenny's letters expressed a somewhat more favorable attitude toward her son. Now she did not have to share him with anyone. Now he was safe—no more prostitutes.

For the next 8 years, Jenny continued writing to Glenn and Isabel, and they usually answered her. However, they served mostly as neutral listeners and not as advisors or confidantes. Jenny continued to be overly concerned with death and money. She increasingly blamed others for her misery and intensified her suspicions and hostility toward her caregivers. After Jenny died, Isabel (Ada) commented that, in the end, Jenny was "the same only more so" (Allport, 1965, p. 156).

These letters represent an unusually rich source of morphogenic material. For years, they were subjected to close analysis and study by Allport and his students, who sought to build the structure of a single personality by identifying personal dispositions that were central to that person. Allport and his students used three techniques to look at Jenny's personality. First, Alfred Baldwin (1942) developed a technique called *personal structure analysis* to analyze approximately one third of the letters. To analyze Jenny's personal structure, Baldwin used two strictly morphogenic procedures, frequency and contiguity, for gathering evidence. The first simply involves a notation of the frequency with which an item appears in the case material. For example, how often did Jenny mention Ross, or money, or herself? Contiguity refers to the proximity of two items in the letters. How often did the category "Ross—unfavorable" occur in close correspondence with "herself—self-sacrificing"? Freud and other psychoanalysts intuitively used this technique of contiguity to discover an association between two items in a patient's unconscious mind. Baldwin, however, refined it by determining statistically those correspondences that occur more frequently than could be expected by chance alone.

Using the personal structure analysis, Baldwin identified three clusters of categories in Jenny's letters. The first related to *Ross, women, the past, and herself—self-sacrificing.* The second dealt with Jenny's *search for a job,* and the third cluster revolved around her attitude toward *money and death.* The three clusters are independent of each other even though a single topic, such as money, may appear in all three clusters.

Second, Jeffrey Paige (1966) used a factor analysis to extract primary personal dispositions revealed by Jenny's letters. In all, Paige identified eight factors: aggression, possessiveness, affiliation, autonomy, familial acceptance, sexuality, sentience, and martyrdom. Paige's study is interesting because he identified eight factors, a number that corresponds very well with the number of central dispositions—5 to 10—that Allport had earlier hypothesized would be found in most people.

The third method of studying Jenny's letters was a commonsense technique used by Allport (1965). His results are quite similar to those of Baldwin and Paige. Allport asked 36 judges to list what they thought were Jenny's essential

TABLE 13.1

Jenny's Central Dispositions Revealed by Clinical and Factor Analytic Techniques

Clinical Technique (Allport)	Factor Analytic Technique (Paige)
Quarrelsome-suspicious	Aggression
Aggressive	
Self-centered (possessive)	Possessiveness
	Need for affiliation
Sentimental	Need for family acceptance
Independent-autonomous	Need for autonomy
Aesthetic-artistic	Sentience
Self-centered (self-pitying)	Martyrdom
(No parallel)	Sexuality
Cynical-morbid	(No parallel)
Dramatic-intense	("Overstate"; that is, the tendency to be dramatic and to overstate her concerns)

characteristics. They recorded 198 descriptive adjectives, many of which were synonymous and overlapping. Allport then grouped the terms into eight clusters: (1) quarrelsome-suspicious, (2) self-centered (possessive), (3) independent-autonomous, (4) dramatic-intense, (5) aesthetic-artistic, (6) aggressive, (7) cynical-morbid, and (8) sentimental.

Comparing this commonsense, clinical approach with Paige's factorial study, Allport (1966) presented some interesting parallels (see Table 13.1). Through Jenny's letters, then, we find that she possessed about eight central traits that characterized the last 12 years of her life—if not her entire life. She was aggressive, suspicious, possessive, aesthetic, sentimental, morbid, dramatic, and self-centered. These central dispositions were sufficiently powerful that she was described in similar terms both by Isabel (Ada Allport), who knew her well, and by independent researchers, who studied her letters (Allport, 1965).

The close agreement between Allport's commonsense clinical approach and Paige's factor analytic method does not prove the validity of either. It does, however, indicate the feasibility of morphogenic studies. Psychologists can analyze one person and identify central dispositions with consistency even when they use different procedures.

Related Research

More than any other personality theorist, Gordon Allport maintained a lifelong active interest in the scientific study of religion and published six lectures on the subject under the title The Individual and His Religion (Allport, 1950). On a personal level, Allport was a devout Episcopalian; and for nearly 30 years, he offered a series of meditations in Appleton Chapel, Harvard University (Allport, 1978).

Intrinsic Versus Extrinsic Religious Orientation

Allport believed that a deep religious commitment was a mark of a mature individual, but he also believed that not all churchgoers have a mature religious orientation. Some, in fact, are highly prejudiced. Allport (1966) offered a possible explanation for this frequently reported observation. He suggested that church and prejudice offer the same safety, security, and status, at least for some people. These people can feel both comfortable and self-righteous with their prejudicial attitudes and their church attendance.

To understand the relationship between church attendance and prejudice, Allport and J. Michael Ross (1967) developed the Religious Orientation Scale (ROS), which is applicable only for churchgoers. The ROS consists of 20 items—11 Extrinsic and 9 Intrinsic. Examples of Extrinsic items are "The primary purpose of prayer is to gain relief and protection"; "What religion offers me most is comfort when sorrow and misfortune strike"; and "One reason for my being a church member is that such membership helps to establish a person in the community." Examples of Intrinsic items include "My religious beliefs are what really lie behind my whole approach to life" and "I try hard to carry my religion over into all my other dealings in life" (p. 436). Allport and Ross assumed that people with an extrinsic orientation have a utilitarian view of religion; that is, they see it as a means to an end. Theirs is a self-serving religion of comfort and social convention. Their beliefs are lightly held and easily reshaped when convenient. In contrast, a second group of people have an intrinsic orientation. These people live their religion and find their master motive in their religious faith. Rather than using religion for some end, they bring other needs into harmony with their religious values. They have an internalized creed and follow it fully.

Previous research has found that, generally speaking, being religious is good for your health. Attending church regularly tends to be associated with feeling better and living longer (Powell, Shahabi, & Thoresen, 2003). But why this is the case is not entirely understood. People who attend church may just tend to take better care of themselves than those who do not. Or maybe there is something unique about religion that encourages better health. One aspect of religion that may affect the connection between religion and health is Allport's concept of religious orientation. Recently, researchers have begun investigating the health implications of having an intrinsic versus extrinsic religious orientation. As we discussed in Chapter 11, intrinsically motivated activities are usually better than those activities that are extrinsically motivated. Therefore, researchers have predicted that those who have internalized their religious values (intrinsic orientation) will be better off than those who use their religion to meet some end (extrinsic orientation).

Kevin Masters and his colleagues (2005) conducted a study looking at religious orientation and cardiovascular health. Blood pressure rises and falls depending on a variety of factors including stressors in the environment, but sometimes people experience chronically high blood pressure. When blood pressure is chronically high, it places increased stress on the heart and is a major health concern for many people, particularly older people, because it makes individuals more susceptible to a variety of heart conditions including heart attacks. To examine the relationship between religious orientation and high blood pressure, Masters and his colleagues (2005) had 75 people between 60 and 80 years old come in to the lab and complete the ROS and some tasks while the researchers carefully monitored their blood pressure.

The tasks were designed to be moderately stressful and likely to raise blood pressure in people who are particularly prone to experiencing high blood pressure. Specifically, the tasks involved completing some math problems and a hypothetical encounter with an insurance company who is refusing to cover a potentially life-saving medical procedure. The researchers found that, as predicted, those who held an intrinsic religious orientation did not experience the same increased blood pressure that those who held an extrinsic orientation did. This research demonstrated that an intrinsic religious orientation serves as a buffer against stressors likely to be experienced in everyday life. Those who have an intrinsic religious orientation likely encounter the same stressors as everybody else, but their bodies react differently and in a healthier manner. There is something about having a deep, intrinsic religious faith that helps people deal with everyday stressors in a way that is not detrimental to physical health.

Researchers have also investigated the relationship between Allport's religious orientation and depression. Generally speaking, being involved in church is related to better overall well-being. This could be for a variety of reasons, one of which may be that being actively involved in any organization integrates individuals into a network of people who can provide social support during times of distress. When experiencing times of distress it is always helpful to have people you can turn to, and members of one's church can be one such group. But being involved in church for the wrong reasons may affect the potential benefits that could otherwise be derived from such a network of people. Timothy Smith and his colleagues (2003) reviewed all the research on the topic of religion and depression in an attempt to conclusively determine whether religion could serve as a buffer against depression. What they found was interesting and generally supported Allport's view that there is a good way and a bad way to be religious. In a review of over 20 studies, intrinsic religious orientation was negatively related to depression but extrinsic religious orientation was positively related (Smith, McCullough, & Poll, 2003). What that means is the more intrinsically oriented toward religion a person is, the less likely he or she will experience depressive symptoms. But the more extrinsically oriented a person is, the more likely he or she will be depressed.

Religion can be good for one's health, but in order to derive health benefits from religion, it is important that people are being religious for the right reasons. It is not enough to just go to church, temple, or synagogue once a week. A person must be attending such services because he or she truly believes in the message of his or her chosen religion and has internalized it as a way of living a good life. It is also important to note that while Allport did consider religious commitment to be a mark of a healthy, mature person, he considered religion to be helpful because it provides a unifying philosophy of life. But religion is not the only means by which one can have a unifying philosophy of life. Whether having a unifying philosophy of life that is not based on an organized religion is beneficial for health in the same way intrinsic religious orientation is remains an area for future research.

How to Reduce Prejudice: Optimal Contact

Recall that Gordon Allport first became interested in the difference between intrinsic and extrinsic religious orientation because he noticed that many people who identified as being very religious were also quite prejudiced. Allport, however, was also interested in prejudice more generally, and developing ways to reduce racial prejudice was of the utmost importance to him. Allport (1954) proposed that one of the most important components to reducing prejudice was contact: If members of majority and minority groups interacted more under optimal conditions, there would be less prejudice. This became known as the *contact hypothesis* and the optimal conditions were relatively simple: (1) equal status between the two groups, (2) common goals, (3) cooperation between groups, and (4) support of an authority figure, law, or custom. For example, if African American and European American neighbors got together to form a neighborhood watch group with the common goal of making their neighborhood safer and such a program was endorsed by the mayor or city police department, then this interaction and group effort would be likely to lead to reduced prejudice among residents of the neighborhood.

Although Allport himself conducted some research on the topic of prejudice reduction (Allport, 1954), one of his students, Thomas Pettigrew, has continued the work that Allport began (Pettigrew & Tropp, 2006; Tropp & Pettigrew, 2005). Thomas Pettigrew and Linda Tropp have built a large research program targeted at investigating the conditions under which contact between groups can reduce prejudice. In a complex review of more than 500 studies testing Allport's contact hypothesis, Pettigrew and Tropp found not only that prejudice can be reduced, but also that the four specific criteria originally outlined by Allport are essential to this reduction (Pettigrew & Tropp, 2006). Furthermore, although the concept of optimal contact was originally conceptualized as a way to reduce *racial* prejudice (Allport, 1954), research has found that optimal contact also works to reduce prejudiced attitudes toward the elderly and the mentally ill (Pettigrew & Tropp, 2006).

Some of the studies included in Thomas Pettigrew and Linda Tropp's review (2006) involved relatively simple methods of merely asking people how many friends they have who are of a minority group (a measure of contact) and then having them complete various self-report measures designed to capture the extent to which participants endorse stereotypical views of minority groups. Other studies, however, included in the review involved a more complex methodology whereby participants were randomly assigned to either groups that involved optimal contact with members of a minority group as prescribed by Allport or groups that did not involve the optimal contact prescribed by Allport. Although both types of studies found that optimal contact reduces prejudice, the experiments in which people were randomly assigned to engage in optimal contact or not showed the strongest reduction in prejudice (Pettigrew & Tropp, 2006). Of course, there is no reason such optimal contact must take place in a laboratory, and Pettigrew and Tropp's (2006) findings demonstrate the great potential for community programs to be developed based on Allport's prescription for prejudice reduction. If such programs were implemented, research shows that relations between majority and minority groups would likely be greatly improved.

Overall, Gordon Allport was an immensely insightful personality psychologist whose ideas continue to inspire psychologists today. Although his ideas undoubtedly continue to enrich research in personality psychology, his methods for prejudice reduction have quietly enriched the lives of people who have, perhaps unknowingly, benefited from his deep commitment to reducing prejudice in our society.

Critique of Allport

Allport based his theory of personality more on philosophical speculation and common sense than on scientific investigations. He never intended his theory to be completely new or comprehensive, but rather he was eclectic, carefully borrowing from older theories and recognizing that his detractors could have important things to say. Consistent with this tolerant attitude, Allport (1968) acknowledged that his advisories may have been at least partially right.

To Allport, most people are best thought of as conscious, forward-looking, tension-seeking individuals. To people who believe that deterministic theories have lost sight of the proactive person, Allport's view of humanity is philosophically refreshing. As with any other theory, however, it must be evaluated on a scientific basis.

Allport probably did more than any other psychologist to define personality and to categorize other definitions of the term. But do his writings constitute a *theory* in the sense of stating a set of related assumptions that generate testable hypotheses? On this criterion, Allport's exhortations rate a qualified "Yes." It is a limited theory, offering explanations for a fairly narrow scope of personality, namely, certain kinds of motivation. The functionally autonomous motives of psychologically healthy adults are covered quite adequately by Allport's theory. But what of the motives of children and of mentally disturbed adults? What moves them and why? What about ordinarily healthy adults who uncharacteristically behave in a strange manner? What accounts for these inconsistencies? What explanation did Allport offer for the bizarre dreams, fantasies, and hallucinations of mature individuals? Unfortunately, his account of personality is not broad enough to adequately answer these questions.

Despite its limitations as a useful theory, Allport's approach to personality is both stimulating and enlightening. Anyone interested in building a theory of personality should first become familiar with Allport's writings. Few other psychologists have made as much effort to place personality theory in perspective; few have been as careful in defining terms, in categorizing previous definitions, or in questioning what units should be employed in personality theory. The work of Allport has set a standard for clear thinking and precision that future theorists would do well to emulate.

Has the theory *generated research?* On this criterion, Allport's theory receives a moderate rating. His Religious Orientation Scale, the Study of Values, and his interest in prejudice have led to multiple studies on the scientific study of religion, values, and prejudice.

On the criterion of *falsifiability,* Allport's theory must receive a low rating. The concept of four somewhat independent religious orientations can be verified or falsified, but most of Allport's other insights lie beyond the ability of science to determine whether some other explanation might be equally appropriate.

A useful theory provides an *organization for observations.* Does Allport's theory meet this criterion? Again, only for a narrow range of adult motives does the theory offer a meaningful organization for observations. Much of what is known about human personality cannot be easily integrated into Allport's theory. Specifically, behaviors motivated by unconscious forces as well as those that are stimulated by primary drives were not adequately explained by Allport. He recognized the existence of these kinds of motivations, but seemed content to allow the psychoanalytic and behavioral explanations to stand without further elaboration. This limitation, however, does not invalidate Allport's theory. To accept the validity of other theoretical concepts is a legitimate approach to theory building.

As a *guide for the practitioner*, Allport's theory has moderate usefulness. It certainly serves as a beacon to the teacher and the therapist, illuminating the view of personality that suggests that people should be treated as individuals. The details, unfortunately, are left unspecified.

On the final two criteria of a useful theory, Allport's psychology of the individual is highly rated. His precise language renders the theory both *internally consistent* and *parsimonious.*

Concept of Humanity

Allport had a basically *optimistic* and hopeful view of human nature. He rejected the psychoanalytic and behavioral views of humanity as being too deterministic and too mechanistic. He believed that our fates and our traits are not determined by unconscious motives originating in early childhood but by conscious choices we make in the present. We are not simply automatons blindly reacting to the forces of reward and punishment. Instead, we are able to interact with our environment and make it reactive to us. We not only seek to reduce tensions but to establish new ones. We desire both change and challenge; and we are active, purposive, and flexible.

Because people have the potential to learn a variety of responses in many situations, psychological growth can take place at any age. Personality is not established in early childhood, even though for some people infantile influences remain strong. Early childhood experiences are important only to the extent that they exist in the present. Although early security and love leave lasting marks, children need more than love: They need an opportunity to shape their own existence creatively, to resist conformity, and to be free, self-directed individuals.

Although society has some power to mold personality, Allport believed that it does not hold the answer to the nature of humanity. The factors shaping personality, Allport held, are not as important as personality itself. Heredity, environment, and the nature of the organism are important; but people are essentially proactive and free to follow the prevailing dictates of society or to chart their own life course.

People, however, are not completely free. Allport (1961) adopted a *limited-freedom* approach. He was often critical of those views that allow for absolute freedom, but he also opposed the psychoanalytic and behavioral views, which he regarded as denying free will. Allport's position was somewhere in the middle. Although free will exists, some people are more capable of making choices than are others. A healthy person has more freedom than does a child or a severely disturbed adult. The high-intelligent, reflective person has more capacity for free choice than does the low-intelligent, nonreflective one.

Even though freedom is limited, Allport maintained that it can be expanded. The more self-insight a person develops, the greater that person's freedom of choice. The more objective a person becomes—that is, the more the blindfolds of self-concern and egotism are removed—the greater that person's degree of freedom.

Education and knowledge also expand the amount of freedom we have. The greater our knowledge is of a particular arena, the broader our freedom in that area. To have a broad general education means that, to some extent, one has a wider choice of jobs, recreational activities, reading materials, and friends.

Finally, our freedom can be expanded by our mode of choosing. If we stubbornly adhere to a familiar course of action simply because it is more comfortable, our freedom remains largely restricted. Conversely, if we adopt an open-minded mode of solving problems, then we broaden our perspective and increase our alternatives; that is, we expand our freedom to choose (Allport, 1955).

Allport's view of humanity is more *teleological* than causal. Personality, to some extent, is influenced by past experiences, but the behaviors that make us human are those that are motivated by our expectations of the future. In other words, we are healthy individuals to the extent that we set and seek future purposes and aspirations. Each of us is different from others not so much because we have different basic drives, but because we have different self-erected goals and intentions.

The growth of personality always takes place within a social setting, but Allport placed only moderate emphasis on *social factors*. He recognized the importance of environmental influences in helping to shape personality, but he insisted that personality has some life of its own. Culture can influence our language, morals, values, fashions, and so forth; but how each of us reacts to cultural forces depends on our unique personality and our basic motivation.

In summary, Allport held an optimistic view of humanity, maintaining that people have at least limited freedom. Human beings are goal oriented, proactive, and motivated by a variety of forces, most of which are within their realm of *consciousness*. Early childhood experiences are of relatively minor importance and are significant only to the extent that they exist in the present. Both differences and similarities among people are important, but *individual differences* and *uniqueness* receive far greater emphasis in Allport's psychology.

Key Terms and Concepts

- Allport was *eclectic* in his acceptance of ideas from a variety of sources.
- He defined *personality* as the dynamic organization within the individual of those psychophysical systems that determine a person's behavior and thought.
- *Psychologically healthy people* are motivated largely by conscious processes; have an extended sense of self; relate warmly to others; accept

themselves for who they are; have a realistic perception of the world; and possess insight, humor, and a unifying philosophy of life.
- Allport advocated a *proactive* position, one that emphasized the notion that people have a large measure of *conscious control* over their lives.
- *Common traits* are general characteristics held in common by many people. They may be useful for comparing one group of people with another.
- *Individual traits* (personal dispositions) are peculiar to the individual and have the capacity to render different stimuli functionally equivalent and to initiate and guide behavior.
- Three levels of personal dispositions are (1) *cardinal dispositions,* which only a few people possess and which are so conspicuous that they cannot be hidden; (2) *central dispositions,* the 5 to 10 individual traits that make a person unique; and (3) *secondary dispositions,* which are less distinguishable but far more numerous than central dispositions.
- Personal dispositions that initiate actions are called *motivational traits.*
- Personal dispositions that guide actions are called *stylistic traits.*
- The *proprium* refers to those behaviors and personal dispositions that are warm and central to our lives and that we regard as peculiarly our own.
- *Functional autonomy* refers to motives that are self-sustaining and independent from the motives that were originally responsible for a behavior.
- *Perseverative functional autonomy* refers to those habits and behaviors that are not part of one's proprium.
- *Propriate functional autonomy* includes all those self-sustaining motivations that are related to the proprium.
- Allport used *morphogenic procedures,* such as diaries and letters, which stress patterns of behavior within a single individual.

CHAPTER 14

Eysenck, McCrae, and Costa's Trait and Factor Theories

Eysenck

McCrae

Costa

Chance and fortuity often play a decisive role in people's lives. One such chance event happened to an 18-year-old German youth who had left his native country as a consequence of Nazi tyranny. He eventually settled in England, where he tried to enroll in the University of London. He was an avid reader, interested in both the arts and the sciences, but his first choice of curriculum was physics.

However, a chance event altered the flow of his life and consequently the course of the history of psychology. In order to be accepted into the university, he was required to pass an entrance examination, which he took after a year's study at a commercial college. After passing the exam, he confidently enrolled in the University of London, intending to major in physics. However, he was told that he had taken the wrong subjects in his entrance exam and therefore was not eligible to pursue a physics curriculum. Rather than waiting another year to take the right subjects, he asked if there was some scientific subject that he was qualified to pursue. When told he could always take psychology, he asked, "What on earth is psychology?" He had never heard of psychology, although he had some vague idea about psychoanalysis. Could psychology possibly be a science? However, he had little choice but to pursue a degree in psychology, so he promptly entered the university with a major in a discipline about which he knew almost nothing. Years later the world of psychology would know a great deal about Hans J. Eysenck, probably the most prolific writer in the history of psychology. In his autobiography, Eysenck (1997b) simply noted that by such chance events "is one's fate decided by bureaucratic stupidity" (p. 47).

Throughout his life, Eysenck battled bureaucratic stupidity and any other type of stupidity he came across. In his autobiography, he described himself as "a sanctimonious prig . . . who didn't suffer fools (or even ordinarily bright people) gladly" (Eysenck, 1997b, p. 31).

Overview of Trait and Factor Theories

How can personality best be measured? By standardized tests? Clinical observation? Judgments of friends and acquaintances? Factor theorists have used all these methods and more. A second question is: How many traits or personal dispositions does a single person possess? Two or three? Half a dozen? A couple of hundred? More than a thousand? During the past 25 to 45 years, several individuals (Cattell, 1973, 1983; Eysenck, 1981, 1997a) and several teams of researchers (Costa & McCrae, 1992; McCrae & Costa, 2003; Tupes & Christal, 1961) have taken a factor analytic approach to answering these questions. Presently, most researchers who study personality traits agree that five, and only five, and no fewer than five dominant traits continue to emerge from factor analytic techniques—mathematical procedures capable of sifting personality traits from mountains of test data.

Whereas many contemporary theorists believe that five is the magic number, earlier theorists such as Raymond B. Cattell found many more personality traits, and Hans J. Eysenck insisted that only three major factors can be discerned by a factor analytic approach. In addition, we have seen that Gordon Allport's (see Chapter 13) commonsense approach yielded 5 to 10 traits that are central to each person's life. However, Allport's major contribution to trait theory may have been his identification of nearly 18,000 trait names in an unabridged English language dictionary.

These trait names were the basis for Cattell's original work, and they continue to provide the foundation for recent factor analytic studies.

Eysenck's factor analytic technique yielded three general bipolar factors or types—extraversion/introversion, neuroticism/stability, and psychoticism/superego. The Five-Factor Theory (often called the Big Five) includes neuroticism and extraversion; but it adds openness to experience, agreeableness, and conscientiousness. These terms differ slightly from research team to research team, but the underlying traits are quite similar.

Biography of Hans J. Eysenck

Hans Jurgen Eysenck was born in Berlin on March 4, 1916, the only child of a theatrical family. His mother was Ruth Werner, a starlet at the time of Eysenck's birth. Ruth Werner later became a German silent film star under the stage name of Helga Molander. Eysenck's father, Anton Eduard Eysenck, was a comedian, singer, and actor. Eysenck (1991b) recalled: "[I] saw very little of my parents, who divorced when I was 4, and who had little feeling for me, an emotion I reciprocated" (p. 40).

After his parents' divorce, Eysenck went to live with his maternal grandmother, who had also been in the theater, but whose promising career in opera was cut short by a crippling fall. Eysenck (1991b) described his grandmother as "unselfish, caring, altruistic, and altogether too good for this world" (p. 40). Although his grandmother was a devout Catholic, neither parent was religious, and Eysenck grew up without any formal religious commitment (Gibson, 1981).

He also grew up with little parental discipline and few strict controls over his behavior. Neither parent seemed interested in curtailing his actions, and his grandmother had a quite permissive attitude toward him. This benign neglect is exemplified by two incidents. In the first, his father had bought Hans a bicycle and had promised to teach him to ride. "He took me to the top of a hill, told me that I had to sit on the saddle and pump the pedals and make the wheels go round. He then went off to release some balloons . . . leaving me to learn how to ride all by myself" (Eysenck, 1997b, p. 12). In the second incident, an adolescent Eysenck told his grandmother that he was going to buy some cigarettes, expecting her to forbid it. However, his grandmother simply said: "If you like it, do it by all means" (p. 14). According to Eysenck, environmental experiences such as these two have little to do with personality development. To him, genetic factors have a greater impact on subsequent behavior than do childhood experiences. Thus, his permissive upbringing neither helped nor hindered him in becoming a famous maverick scientist.

Even as a schoolboy, Eysenck was not afraid to take an unpopular stand, often challenging his teachers, especially those with militaristic leanings. He was skeptical of much of what they taught and was not always reluctant to embarrass them with his superior knowledge and intellect.

Eysenck suffered the deprivation of many post–World War I Germans who were faced with astronomical inflation, mass unemployment, and near starvation. Eysenck's future appeared no brighter after Hitler came to power. As a condition of studying physics at the University of Berlin, he was told that he would have to join the Nazi secret police, an idea he found so repugnant that he decided to leave Germany.

This encounter with the fascist right and his later battles with the radical left suggested to him that the trait of tough-mindedness, or authoritarianism, was equally prevalent in both extremes of the political spectrum. He later found some scientific support for this hypothesis in a study that demonstrated that although communists were radical and fascists were conservative on one dimension of personality, on the tough-minded versus tender-minded dimension, both groups were authoritarian, rigid, and intolerant of ambiguity (tough-minded) (Eysenck, 1954; Eysenck & Coulter, 1972).

As a consequence of Nazi tyranny, Eysenck, at age 18, left Germany and eventually settled in England, where he tried to enroll in the University of London. As we saw in the chapter opening vignette, he went into psychology completely by accident. At that time, the psychology department at the University of London was basically pro-Freudian, but it also had a strong emphasis on psychometrics, with Charles Spearman having just left and with Cyril Burt still presiding. Eysenck received a bachelor's degree in 1938, about the same time that he married Margaret Davies, a Canadian with a degree in mathematics. In 1940, he was awarded a PhD from the University of London, but by this time England and most European nations were at war.

As a German national, he was considered an enemy alien and not allowed to enter the Royal Air Force (his first choice) or any other branch of the military. Instead, with no training as a psychiatrist or as a clinical psychologist, he went to work at the Mill Hill Emergency Hospital, treating patients who were suffering from a variety of psychological symptoms, including anxiety, depression, and hysteria. Eysenck, however, was not comfortable with most of the traditional clinical diagnostic categories. Using factor analysis, he found that two major personality factors—neuroticism/emotional stability and extraversion/introversion—could account for all the traditional diagnostic groups. These early theoretical ideas led to the publication of his first book, *Dimensions of Personality* (Eysenck, 1947).

After the war, he became director of the psychology department at Maudsley Hospital and later became a reader in psychology at the University of London. In 1949, he traveled to North America to examine the clinical psychology programs in the United States and Canada with the idea of setting up a clinical psychology profession in Great Britain. He obtained a visiting professorship at the University of Pennsylvania for the year 1949–1950, but he spent much of that year traveling throughout the United States and Canada looking over clinical psychology programs, which he found to be totally inadequate and unscientific (Eysenck, 1980, 1997b).

Eysenck and his wife had been growing steadily apart, and his marriage was not improved when his traveling companion to Philadelphia was Sybil Rostal, a beautiful quantitative psychologist. On returning to England, Eysenck obtained a divorce from his first wife and married Sybil. Hans and Sybil Eysenck coauthored several publications, and their marriage produced three sons and a daughter. Eysenck's son from his first marriage, Michael, is a widely published author of psychology articles and books.

After returning from North America, Eysenck established a clinical psychology department at the University of London and in 1955 became professor of psychology. While in the United States, he had begun *The Structure of Human Personality* (1952b), in which he argued for the efficacy of factor analysis as the best method of representing the known facts of human personality.

Eysenck was perhaps the most prolific writer in the history of psychology, having published some 800 journal articles or book chapters and more than 75 books. Several have titles with popular appeal, such as *Uses and Abuses of Psychology* (1953); *The Psychology of Politics* (1954, 1999); *Sense and Nonsense in Psychology* (1956); *Know Your Own IQ* (1962); *Fact and Fiction in Psychology* (1965); *Psychology Is About People* (1972); *You and Neurosis* (1977b); *Sex, Violence and the Media* (with D. K. B. Nias, 1978); *Smoking, Personality, and Stress* (1991d); *Genius: The Natural History of Creativity* (1995); and *Intelligence: A New Look* (1998a).

Eysenck's range of interests was exceedingly broad, and his willingness to step into almost any controversy was legendary. He was a gadfly to the conscience of psychology since he first entered its ranks. He upset many psychoanalysts and other therapists in the early 1950s with his contention that no evidence existed to suggest that psychotherapy was more effective than spontaneous remission. In other words, those people who receive no therapy were just as likely to get better as were those who underwent expensive, painful, prolonged psychotherapy with expertly trained psychoanalysts and psychologists (Eysenck, 1952a). Eysenck maintained that belief for the remainder of his life. In 1996, he told an interviewer that "psychotherapies are no more effective than . . . placebo treatments" (Feltham, 1996, p. 424).

Eysenck was not afraid to take an unpopular stand, as witnessed by his defense of Arthur Jensen, whose contention was that IQ scores cannot be significantly increased by well-intentioned social programs because they are largely genetically determined. Eysenck's book *The IQ Argument* (1971) was so controversial that elements in the United States "threatened booksellers with arson if they dared to stock the book; well-known 'liberal' newspapers refused to review it; and the outcome was that it was largely impossible in the land of free speech to discover the existence of the book or to buy it" (Eysenck, 1980, p. 175).

In 1983, Eysenck retired as professor of psychology at the Institute of Psychiatry, University of London, and as senior psychiatrist at the Maudsley and Bethlehem Royal hospitals. He then served as professor emeritus at the University of London until his death from cancer on September 4, 1997. Eysenck, who frequently argued that cigarette smoking was not a major risk factor for cancer, had been a heavy smoker until middle age when he gave up cigarettes because he believed that they affected his tennis game.

During his later years, his research continued to reflect a variety of topics, including creativity (Eysenck, 1993, 1995; Frois & Eysenck, 1995), behavioral interventions in cancer and heart disease (Eysenck, 1991d, 1996; Eysenck & Grossarth-Maticek, 1991), and intelligence (Eysenck, 1998a).

Eysenck won many awards, including the 1991 Distinguished Contributions Award of the International Society for the Study of Individual Differences. The American Psychological Association presented him with its Distinguished Scientist Award (1988), the Presidential Citation for Scientific Contribution (1993), the William James Fellow Award (1994), and the Centennial Award for Distinguished Contributions to Clinical Psychology (1996).

The Pioneering Work of Raymond B. Cattell

An important figure in the early years of psychometrics was Raymond B. Cattell (1905–1998), who was born in England but who spent most of his career in the United States. Cattell did not have a direct influence on Eysenck; indeed, the two men had quite different approaches to measuring the structure of personality. Because some familiarity of Cattell's trait theory enhances the understanding of Eysenck's three-factor theory, we briefly discuss Cattell's work and compare and contrast it with that of Eysenck.

First, Cattell used an **inductive method** of gathering data; that is, he began with no preconceived bias concerning the number or name of traits or types. In contrast, Eysenck used a **deductive method** to identify three personality factors. That is, he had some preconceived hypothesis in mind before he began gathering data.

Second, Cattell used three different media of observation to examine people from as many angles as possible. The three sources of data included a person's life record (L data) derived from observations made by other people; self-reports (Q data) obtained from questionnaires and other techniques designed to allow people to make subjective descriptions of themselves; and objective tests (T data), which measure performance such as intelligence, speed of responding, and other such activities designed to challenge people's maximum performance. In contrast, each of Eysenck's three bipolar factors is limited to responses on questioners. These self-reports confine Eysenck's procedures to personality factors.

Third, Cattell divided traits into *common traits* (shared by many) and *unique traits* (peculiar to one individual). He also distinguished *source traits* from trait indicators, or *surface traits*. Cattell further classified traits into *temperament, motivation,* and *ability*. Traits of temperament are concerned with *how* a person behaves, motivation deals with *why* one behaves, and ability refers to *how far* or *how fast* one can perform.

Fourth, Cattell's multifaceted approach yielded 35 primary, or first-order, traits, which measure mostly the temperament dimension of personality. Of these factors, 23 characterize the normal population and 12 measure the pathological dimension. The largest and most frequently studied of the normal traits are the 16 personality factors found on Cattell's (1949) Sixteen Personality Factors Questionnaire (16 PF Scale). By comparison, the Eysenck Personality Questionnaire yields scores on only three personality factors.

Fifth, while Cattell was measuring a large number to traits, Eysenck was concentrating on **types,** or superfactors that make up several interrelated traits. We discuss types and traits in the section titled Hierarchy of Behavior Organization.

Basics of Factor Analysis

A comprehensive knowledge of the mathematical operations involved in **factor analysis** is not essential to an understanding of trait and factor theories of personality, but a general description of this technique should be helpful.

To use factor analysis, one begins by making specific observations of many individuals. These observations are then quantified in some manner; for example, height is measured in inches; weight in pounds; aptitude in test scores; job performance by rating scales; and so on. Assume that we have 1,000 such measures on 5,000 people. Our next step is to determine which of these variables (scores) are related to which other variables and to what extent. To do this, we calculate the **correlation coefficient** between each variable and each of the other 999 scores. (A correlation coefficient is a mathematical procedure for expressing the degree of correspondence between two sets of scores.) To correlate 1,000 variables with the other 999 scores would involve 499,500 individual correlations (1,000 multiplied by 999 divided by 2). Results of these calculations would require a table of intercorrelations, or a *matrix,* with 1,000 rows and 1,000 columns. Some of these correlations would be high and positive, some near zero, and some would be negative. For example, we might observe a high positive correlation between leg length and height, because one is partially a measure of the other. We may also find a positive correlation between a measure of leadership ability and ratings on social poise. This relationship might exist because they are each part of a more basic underlying trait—self-confidence.

With 1,000 separate variables, our table of intercorrelations would be quite cumbersome. At this point, we turn to *factor analysis,* which can account for a large number of variables with a smaller number of more basic dimensions. These more basic dimensions can be called *traits,* that is, factors that represent a cluster of closely related variables. For example, we may find high positive intercorrelations among test scores in algebra, geometry, trigonometry, and calculus. We have now identified a cluster of scores that we might call Factor M, which represents mathematical ability. In similar fashion, we can identify a number of other **factors,** or units of personality derived through factor analysis. The number of factors, of course, will be smaller than the original number of observations.

Our next step is to determine the extent to which each individual score contributes to the various factors. Correlations of scores with factors are called **factor loadings.** For example, if scores for algebra, geometry, trigonometry, and calculus contribute highly to Factor M but not to other factors, they will have high factor loadings on M. Factor loadings give us an indication of the purity of the various factors and enable us to interpret their meanings.

Traits generated through factor analysis may be either unipolar or bipolar. **Unipolar traits** are scaled from zero to some large amount. Height, weight, and intellectual ability are examples of unipolar traits. In contrast, **bipolar traits** extend from one pole to an opposite pole, with zero representing a midpoint. Introversion versus extraversion, liberalism versus conservatism, and social ascendancy versus timidity are examples of bipolar traits.

In order for mathematically derived factors to have psychological meaning, the axes on which the scores are plotted are usually turned or *rotated* into a specific mathematical relationship with each other. This rotation can be either orthogonal or oblique, but Eysenck and advocates of the Five-Factor Theory favor the **orthogonal rotation.** Figure 14.1 shows that orthogonally rotated axes are at right angles to each other. As scores on the *x* variable increase, scores on the *y* axis may have any value; that is, they are completely unrelated to scores on the *x* axis.

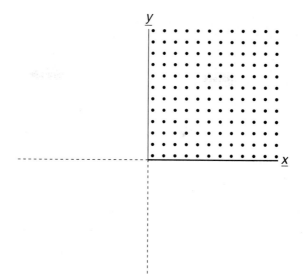

FIGURE 14.1   Orthogonal axes

The **oblique method,** which was advocated by Cattell, assumes some positive or negative correlation and refers to an angle of less than or more than 90°. Figure 14.2 depicts a scattergram of scores in which x and y are positively correlated with one another; that is, as scores on the x variable increase, scores on the y axis have a tendency also to increase. Note that the correlation is not perfect; some people may score high on the x variable but relatively low on y and vice versa. A perfect correlation ($r = 1.00$) would result in x and y occupying the same line. Psychologically, orthogonal rotation usually results in only a few meaningful traits, whereas oblique methods ordinarily produce a larger number.

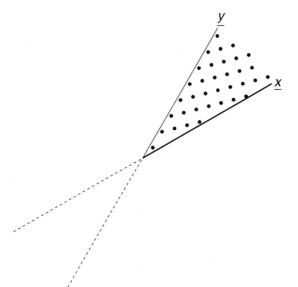

FIGURE 14.2   Oblique axes

Eysenck's Factor Theory

The personality theory of Hans Eysenck has strong psychometric and biological components. However, Eysenck (1977a, 1997a) contended that psychometric sophistication alone is not sufficient to measure the structure of human personality and that personality dimensions arrived at through factor analytic methods are sterile and meaningless unless they have been shown to possess a biological existence.

Criteria for Identifying Factors

With these assumptions in mind, Eysenck listed four criteria for identifying a factor. First, *psychometric evidence* for the factor's existence must be established. A corollary to this criterion is that the factor must be reliable and replicable. Other investigators, from separate laboratories, must also be able to find the factor, and these investigators consistently identify Eysenck's extraversion, neuroticism, and psychoticism.

A second criterion is that the factor must also possess *heritability* and must fit an established genetic model. This criterion eliminates learned characteristics, such as the ability to mimic the voices of well-known people or a religious or political belief.

Third, the factor must *make sense from a theoretical view.* Eysenck employed the *deductive method* of investigation, beginning with a theory and then gathering data that are logically consistent with that theory.

The final criterion for the existence of a factor is that it must *possess social relevance;* that is, it must be demonstrated that mathematically derived factors have a relationship (not necessarily causal) with such socially relevant variables as drug addiction, proneness to unintentional injuries, outstanding performance in sports, psychotic behavior, criminality, and so on.

Hierarchy of Behavior Organization

Eysenck (1947, 1994c) recognized a four-level hierarchy of behavior organization. At the lowest level are *specific acts or cognitions,* individual behaviors or thoughts that may or may not be characteristic of a person. A student finishing a reading assignment would be an example of a specific response. At the second level are the *habitual acts or cognitions,* that is, responses that recur under similar conditions. For example, if a student frequently keeps at an assignment until it is finished, this behavior becomes a habitual response. As opposed to specific responses, habitual responses must be reasonably reliable or consistent.

Several related habitual responses form a *trait*—the third level of behavior. Eysenck (1981) defined traits as "important semi-permanent personality dispositions" (p. 3). For example, students would have the trait of persistence if they habitually complete class assignments and keep working at other endeavors until they are finished. Although traits can be identified intuitively, trait and factor theorists rely on a more systematic approach, namely factor analysis. Trait-level behaviors are extracted through factor analysis of habit-level responses just as habitual responses are mathematically extracted through factor analysis of specific responses. Traits, then,

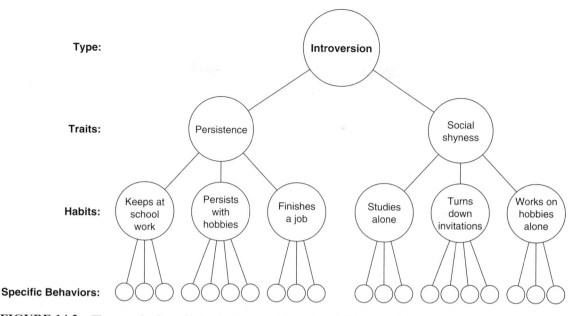

FIGURE 14.3   The organization of behavior into specific actions, habitual responses, traits, and types. Besides persistence and social shyness, other traits such as inferiority, low activity, and serious-mindedness contribute to introversion.

are "defined in terms of significant intercorrelations between different habitual behaviors" (Eysenck, 1990, p. 244). Most of Cattell's 35 normal and abnormal primary source traits are at this third level of organization, which accounts for the fact that he identified far more personality dimensions than either Eysenck or advocates of the Five-Factor Theory.

Eysenck concentrated on the fourth level, that of **types** or superfactors. A type is made up of several interrelated traits. For example, persistence may be related to inferiority, poor emotional adjustment, social shyness, and several other traits, with the entire cluster forming the *introverted type.* Each of the four levels of behavior organization are shown in Figure 14.3.

Dimensions of Personality

We have seen that Eysenck and Cattell arrived at a different number of personality dimensions because they worked at different levels of factoring. Cattell's 35 traits are all at the third level of the hierarchical structure, whereas Eysenck's superfactors are at the fourth level.

How many general superfactors exist? Many current factor theorists insist that ample evidence exists that five—and no more and no fewer—general factors will emerge from nearly all factor analyses of personality traits. Eysenck, however, extracted only three general superfactors. His three personality dimensions are **extraversion (E), neuroticism (N),** and **psychoticism (P),** although he did not rule out "the possibility that further dimensions may be added later" (Eysenck, 1994b, p. 151). Figure 14.4 shows the hierarchical structure of Eysenck's P, E, and N.

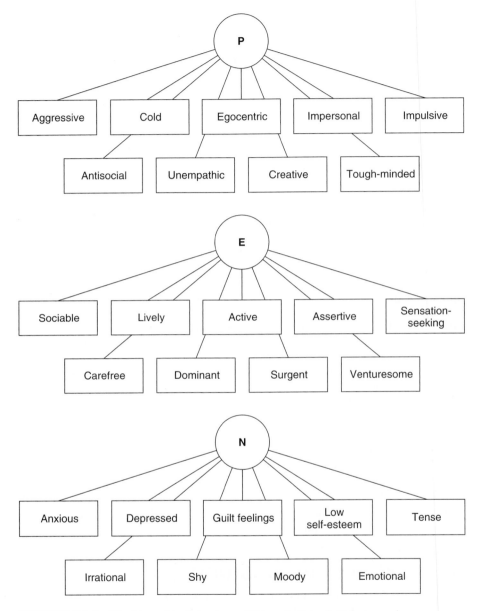

FIGURE 14.4   The hierarchical structure of P (psychoticism), E (extraversion-introversion), and N (neuroticism).

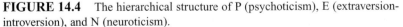

From Biological dimensions of personality by H. J. Eysenck (1990). In L. A. Pervin (Ed.), *Handbook of Personality: Theory and Research* (pp. 224–276). New York: Guilford Press. Reprinted by permission of Guilford Press.

   Neuroticism and psychoticism are not limited to pathological individuals, although disturbed people tend to score higher than normal people on scales measuring these two factors. Eysenck regarded all three factors as part of normal personality structure. All three are bipolar, with extraversion being at one end of Factor E and **introversion** occupying the opposite pole. Similarly, Factor N includes neuroticism at one pole and **stability** at the other, and Factor P has psychoticism at one pole and the **superego function** at the other.

The bipolarity of Eysenck's factors does not imply that most people are at one end or the other of the three main poles. Each factor is unimodally, rather than bimodally, distributed. Extraversion, for example, is fairly normally distributed in much the same fashion as intelligence or height. That is, most people are near the center of a bell-shaped distribution of extraversion. Eysenck contended that each of these factors meets his four criteria for identifying personality dimensions.

First, strong psychometric evidence exists for each, especially Factors E and N. The P factor (psychoticism) emerged later in Eysenck's work but was not taken seriously by other researchers until the mid-1990s (Eysenck, 1997b). Extraversion and neuroticism (or anxiety) are basic factors in nearly all factor analytic studies of human personality, including various versions of the Five-Factor Theory (McCrae & Costa, 1999, 2002; John & Srivastava, 1999).

Second, Eysenck (1994a, 1994b) argued that a strong biological base exists for each of his three superfactors. At the same time, he claimed that traits such as agreeableness and conscientiousness, which are part of the five-factor taxonomy (John, 1990; W. T. Norman, 1963; Tupes & Christal, 1961), do not have an underlying biological foundation.

Third, Eysenck's three personality dimensions make sense theoretically. Carl Jung (see Chapter 4) and others have recognized the powerful effect on behavior of extraversion and introversion (Factor E), and Sigmund Freud (see Chapter 2) emphasized the importance of anxiety (Factor N) on shaping behavior. In addition, psychoticism (Factor P) agrees with theorists, such as Abraham Maslow (see Chapter 10), who propose that psychological health ranges from self-actualization (a low P score) to schizophrenia and psychosis (a high P score).

Fourth, Eysenck repeatedly demonstrated that his three factors relate to such social issues as drug use (Eysenck, 1983), sexual behaviors (Eysenck, 1976), criminality (Eysenck, 1964, 1998b; Eysenck & Gudjonsson, 1989), preventing cancer and heart disease (Eysenck, 1991c, 1991d; Grossarth-Maticek, Eysenck, & Vetter, 1988), and creativity (Eysenck, 1993).

Extraversion

In Chapter 4, we explained that Jung conceptualized two broad personality types, called "extraversion" and "introversion." We also noted some differences between his definitions and the prevailing notion of these two terms. Jung saw extraverted people as having an objective or nonpersonalized view of the world, whereas introverts have essentially a subjective or individualized way of looking at things. Eysenck's concepts of extraversion and introversion are closer to the popular usage. Extraverts are characterized primarily by sociability and impulsiveness but also by jocularity, liveliness, quick-wittedness, optimism, and other traits indicative of people who are rewarded for their association with others (Eysenck & Eysenck, 1969).

Introverts are characterized by traits opposite those of extraverts. They can be described as quiet, passive, unsociable, careful, reserved, thoughtful, pessimistic, peaceful, sober, and controlled. According to Eysenck (1982), however, the principal differences between extraversion and introversion are not behavioral, but rather biological and genetic in nature.

Eysenck (1997a) believed that the primary cause of differences between extraverts and introverts is one of *cortical arousal level,* a physiological condition that is largely inherited rather than learned. Because extraverts have a lower level of cortical arousal than do introverts, they have higher sensory thresholds and thus lesser reactions to sensory stimulation. Introverts, conversely, are characterized by a higher level of arousal, and as a result of a lower sensory threshold, they experience greater reactions to sensory stimulation. To maintain an optimal level of stimulation, introverts, with their congenitally low sensory threshold, avoid situations that will cause too much excitement. Hence, introverts shun such activities as wild social events, downhill skiing, skydiving, competitive sports, leading a fraternity or sorority, or playing practical jokes.

Conversely, because extraverts have a habitually low level of cortical arousal, they need a high level of sensory stimulation to maintain an optimal level of stimulation. Therefore, extraverts participate more often in exciting and stimulating activities. They may enjoy such activities as mountain climbing, gambling, driving fast cars, drinking alcohol, and smoking marijuana. In addition, Eysenck (1976) hypothesized that extraverts, as opposed to introverts, will engage in sexual intercourse earlier, more frequently, with a wider range of partners, in a greater number of positions, with a larger variety of sexual behaviors, and will indulge in longer precoital love play. Because extraverts have a lower level of cortical arousal, however, they become more quickly accustomed to strong stimuli (sexual or otherwise) and respond less and less to the same stimuli, whereas introverts are less likely to become bored and uninterested in routine activities carried on with the same people.

Neuroticism

The second superfactor extracted by Eysenck is neuroticism/stability (N). Like extraversion/introversion, Factor N has a strong hereditary component. Eysenck (1967) reported several studies that have found evidence of a genetic basis for such neurotic traits as anxiety, hysteria, and obsessive-compulsive disorders. In addition, he found a much greater agreement among identical twins than among fraternal twins on a number of antisocial and asocial behaviors such as adult crime, childhood behavior disorders, homosexuality, and alcoholism (Eysenck, 1964).

People who score high on neuroticism often have a tendency to overreact emotionally and to have difficulty returning to a normal state after emotional arousal. They frequently complain of physical symptoms such as headache and backache and of vague psychological problems such as worries and anxieties. Neuroticism, however, does not necessarily suggest a neurosis in the traditional meaning of that term. People can score high on neuroticism and be free of any debilitating psychological symptoms.

Eysenck accepted the **diathesis-stress model** of psychiatric illness, which suggests that some people are vulnerable to illness because they have either a genetic or an acquired weakness that predisposes them to an illness. This predisposition (diathesis) may interact with *stress* to produce a neurotic disorder. Eysenck assumed that people at the healthy end of the N scale have the capacity to resist a neurotic dis-

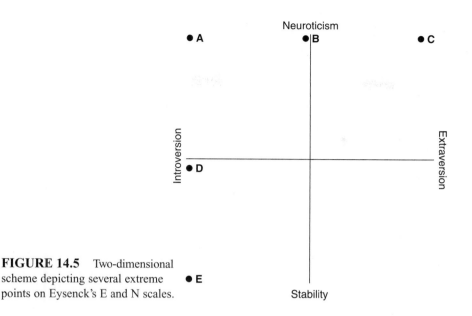

FIGURE 14.5 Two-dimensional scheme depicting several extreme points on Eysenck's E and N scales.

order even in periods of extreme stress. High N scorers, however, may suffer a neurotic reaction as a result of only a minimal level of stress. In other words, the higher the neuroticism score, the lower the level of stress necessary to precipitate a neurotic disorder.

Because neuroticism can be combined with different points on the extraversion scale, no single syndrome can define neurotic behavior. Eysenck's factor analytic technique assumes the independence of factors, which means that the neuroticism scale is at right angles (signifying zero correlation) to the extraversion scale. Thus, several people can all score high on the N scale yet display quite different symptoms, depending on their degree of introversion or extraversion. Figure 14.5 shows the extraversion/introversion pole with zero correlation with the neuroticism/stability pole. Consider persons A, B, and C, all equally high on the neuroticism scale, but representing three distinct points on the extraversion scale. Person A, an introverted neurotic, is characterized by anxiety, depression, phobias, and obsessive-compulsive symptoms; Person B, who is high on neuroticism but only average on extraversion, is likely to be characterized by hysteria (a neurotic disorder associated with emotional instability), suggestibility, and somatic symptoms; Person C, an extraverted neurotic individual, will probably manifest psychopathic qualities such as criminality and delinquent tendencies (Eysenck, 1967, 1997a). Consider, also, Persons A, D, and E, all equally introverted, but with three different levels of emotional stability. Person A is the introverted neurotic individual we just described; Person D is equally introverted but is neither severely neurotic nor emotionally stable; and Person E is both extremely introverted and psychologically stable.

Figure 14.5 shows only five people, all of whom have at least one extreme score. Most people, of course, would score near the mean on both extraversion and introversion. As scores move toward the outer limits of the diagram, they become increasingly less frequent, just as scores on the ends of a bell-shaped curve are less frequent than those near the midpoint.

Psychoticism

Eysenck's original theory of personality was based on only two personality dimensions—extraversion and neuroticism. After several years of alluding to psychoticism (P) as an independent personality factor, Eysenck finally elevated it to a position equal to E and N (Eysenck & Eysenck, 1976). Like extraversion and neuroticism, P is a bipolar factor, with psychoticism on one pole and *superego* on the other. High P scorers are often egocentric, cold, nonconforming, impulsive, hostile, aggressive, suspicious, psychopathic, and antisocial. People low on psychoticism (in the direction of superego function) tend to be altruistic, highly socialized, empathic, caring, cooperative, conforming, and conventional (S. Eysenck, 1997).

Earlier, we saw that Eysenck accepted the diathesis-stress model for people high on the neuroticism scale; that is, stress and high N scores combine to elevate people's vulnerability to psychological disorders. This model also suggests that people who score high on psychoticism and who are also experiencing levels of stress have an increased chance of developing a psychotic disorder. Eysenck (1994a) hypothesized that people high on psychoticism have a high "*predisposition* to succumb to stress and develop a psychotic illness" (p. 20). This diathesis-stress model suggests that high P scorers are genetically more vulnerable to stress than are low P scorers. During periods of little stress, high P scorers may function normally, but when high psychoticism interacts with high levels of stress, people become vulnerable to psychotic disorders. By contrast, people with low P scores are not necessarily vulnerable to stress-related psychoses and will resist a psychotic break even in periods of extreme stress. According to Eysenck (1994a, 1994b), the higher the psychoticism score, the lower the level of stress necessary to precipitate a psychotic reaction.

Psychoticism/superego (P) is independent of both E and N. Figure 14.6 shows each of the three factors at right angles with the other two. (Because three-

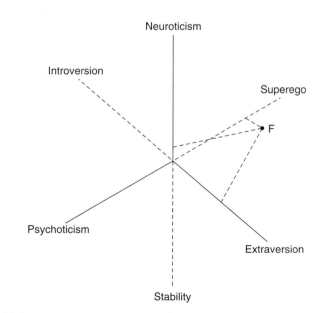

FIGURE 14.6   Three-dimensional scheme depicting one individual's scores on each of Eysenck's major dimensions of personality.

dimensional space cannot be faithfully produced on a two-dimensional plane, the reader is asked to look at Figure 14.6 as if the solid lines represent the corner of a room where two walls meet the floor. Each line can then be seen as perpendicular to the other two.) Eysenck's view of personality, therefore, allows each person to be measured on three independent factors and resultant scores to be plotted in space having three coordinates. Person F in Figure 14.6, for example, is quite high on superego, somewhat high on extraversion, and near the midpoint on the neuroticism/stability scale. In similar fashion, scores of each person can be plotted in three-dimensional space.

Measuring Personality

Eysenck evolved four personality inventories that measure his superfactors. The first, the Maudsley Personality Inventory, or MPI (Eysenck, 1959), assessed only E and N and yielded some correlation between these two factors. For this reason, Eysenck developed another test, the Eysenck Personality Inventory, or EPI. The EPI contains a lie (L) scale to detect faking, but more importantly, it measures extraversion and neuroticism independently, with a near zero correlation between E and N (H. J. Eysenck & B. G. Eysenck, 1964, 1968). The Eysenck Personality Inventory was extended to children 7 to 16 years of age by Sybil B. G. Eysenck (1965), who developed the Junior EPI.

The EPI was still a two-factor inventory, so consequently Hans Eysenck and Sybil Eysenck (1975) published a third personality test, namely the Eysenck Personality Questionnaire (EPQ), which included a psychoticism (P) scale. The EPQ, which has both an adult and a junior version, is a revision of the still-published EPI. Subsequent criticisms of the P scale led to yet another revision, the Eysenck Personality Questionnaire-Revised (H. J. Eysenck & S. B. G. Eysenck, 1993).

Biological Bases of Personality

According to Eysenck, personality factors P, E, and N all have powerful biological determinants. He estimated that about three fourths of the variance of all three personality dimensions can be accounted for by heredity and about one fourth by environmental factors.

Eysenck (1990) cited three threads of evidence for a strong biological component in personality. First, researchers (McCrae & Allik, 2002) have found nearly identical factors among people in various parts of the world, not only in Western Europe and North America but also in Uganda, Nigeria, Japan, China, Russia, and other African and European countries. Second, evidence (McCrae & Costa, 2003) suggests that individuals tend to maintain their position over time on the different dimensions of personality. And third, studies of twins (Eysenck, 1990) show a higher concordance between identical twins than between same-gender fraternal twins reared together, suggesting that genetic factors play a dominant part in determining individual differences in personality.

In Eysenck's theory of personality, psychoticism, extraversion, and neuroticism have both antecedents and consequences. The antecedents are genetic and

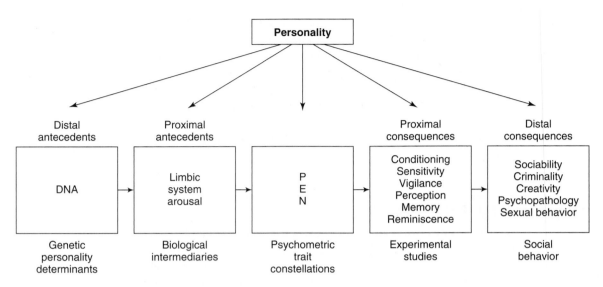

FIGURE 14.7   A model of the major components of Eysenck's theory of personality.

biological, whereas the consequences include such experimental variables as conditioning experiences, sensitivity, and memory as well as social behaviors such as criminality, creativity, psychopathology, and sexual behavior. Figure 14.7 shows that P, E, and N are in the middle of a five-step progression from DNA to social behavior, with biological intermediaries and experimental evidence anchoring the three major personality dimensions. In other words, personality has genetic determinants that indirectly shape biological intermediaries, and these biological intermediaries help mold P, E, and N. In turn, P, E, and N contribute to a wide variety of laboratory learnings as well as social behaviors.

Personality as a Predictor

Eysenck's complex model of personality shown in Figure 14.7 suggests that the psychometric traits of P, E, and N can combine with one another and with genetic determinants, biological intermediates, and experimental studies to predict a variety of social behaviors, including those that contribute to disease.

Personality and Behavior

Do Eysenck's three general personality dimensions predict behavior? According to Eysenck's model shown in Figure 14.7, psychoticism, extraversion, and neuroticism should predict results of experimental studies as well as social behaviors. Recall that Eysenck's theory assumes that extraversion is a product of low cortical arousability. Therefore, introverts, compared with extraverts, should be more sensitive to a variety of stimuli and learning conditions. Eysenck (1997a) argued that an effective theory of personality should predict both proximal and distal consequences (see Figure 14.7), and he and his son Michael (H. J. Eysenck & M. W. Eysenck, 1985) cited studies that demonstrated extraverts' greater demand for change and novelty in both laboratory studies and studies of social behavior.

Eysenck (1997a) further argued that many psychology studies have reached erroneous conclusions because they have ignored personality factors. For example, studies in education comparing the effectiveness of discovery learning and traditional reception learning have often produced either conflicting differences or no differences. Eysenck believed that these studies did not consider that extraverted children prefer and do better with the more active discovery learning, whereas introverted children prefer and do better with the more passive reception learning. In other words, an interaction exists between personality dimensions and learning styles. However, when investigators ignore these personality factors, they may find no differences in the comparative effectiveness of discovery versus reception learning styles.

Eysenck (1995) also hypothesized that psychoticism (P) is related to genius and creativity. Again, the relationship is not simple. Many children have creative ability, are nonconforming, and have unorthodox ideas; but they grow up to be noncreative people. Eysenck found evidence that these people lack the persistence of high P scorers. Children with the same creative potential who are also high in psychoticism (P) are able to resist the criticisms of parents and teachers and to emerge as creative adults.

Similarly, Eysenck and S. B. G. Eysenck (1975) reported that both high P scorers and high E scorers are likely to be troublemakers as children. However, parents and teachers tend to regard the extraverted children as charming rogues and to forgive their misdemeanors, whereas they see high P scorers as more spiteful, disruptive, and unlovable. Thus, the high E scoring troublemakers tend to grow into productive adults, while the high P scoring troublemakers tend to continue to have learning problems, to get into crime, and to have difficulty making friends (S. Eysenck, 1997). Again, Eysenck believed strongly that psychologists can be led astray if they do not consider the various combinations of personality dimensions in conducting their research.

Personality and Disease

Can personality factors predict mortality from cancer and cardiovascular disease (CVD)? Beginning during the early 1960s, Eysenck devoted much attention to this question. He and David Kissen (Kissen & Eysenck, 1962) found that people who scored low on neuroticism (N) on the Maudsley Personality Inventory tended to suppress their emotion and were much more likely than high N scorers to receive a later diagnosis of lung cancer.

Later, Eysenck teamed with Yugoslav physician and psychologist Ronald Grossarth-Maticek (Eysenck & Grossarth-Maticek, 1991; Grossarth-Matick & Eysenck (1989); Grossarth-Maticek, Eysenck, & Vetter, 1988) to investigate not only the relationship between personality and disease, but also the effectiveness of behavior therapy on prolonging the life of cancer and CVD patients. Grossarth-Maticek had used a short questionnaire and a long personal interview to place people into one of four groups or types. Type I included people with a hopeless/helpless nonemotional reaction to stress; Type II people typically reacted to frustration with anger, aggression, and emotional arousal; Type III people were ambivalent, shifting from the typical reaction of Type I people to the typical reaction of Type IIs and then back again; Type IV individuals regarded their own autonomy as an important condition to their personal well-being and happiness. In the original study in Yugoslavia, Type I people were much more likely than others to die of cancer, and Type II people were much more likely to die of heart disease. Type III and Type IV individuals had very low death rates from either cancer or CVD. Grossarth-Maticek, Eysenck, and Vetter replicated this study in Heidelberg, Germany, and found very similar results.

As Eysenck (1996) pointed out, these and other studies on the relationship between personality and disease do not prove that psychological factors *cause* cancer and heart disease. Rather, these diseases are caused by an interaction of many factors. For cardiovascular disease, these factors include family history, age, gender, ethnic background, hypertension, unfavorable ratio of total cholesterol to high-density lipoprotein (HDL), smoking, diet, inactive lifestyle, and several personality factors. For cancer, the risks include smoking, diet, alcohol, sexual practices, family history, ethnic background, and personality factors (Brannon & Feist, 2007). Eysenck (1996) contended that cigarette smoking alone does not cause cancer or CVD, but when it is combined with stress and personality factors, it helps contribute to death from these two diseases. For example, Eysenck and his associates (Marusic, Gudjonsson, Eysenck, & Starc, 1999) developed a complex biopsychosocial model for heart disease that included 11 biological and 7 psychosocial factors. Their research with men in the Republic of Slovenia supported the hypothesis that personality factors interact with a variety of biological factors to contribute to heart disease. One such interaction was for smoking, neuroticism, and emotional reactivity; that is, high P scorers who smoke and who react to stress with anger, hostility, and aggression increase their risk for heart disease.

The Big Five: Taxonomy or Theory?

In Chapter 1, we defined a taxonomy as a classification of things according to their natural relationships. We also suggested that taxonomies are an essential starting point for the advance of science, but that they are not theories. Whereas theories generate research, taxonomies merely supply a classification system.

Eysenck's three-factor approach is a good example of how a scientific theory can use a taxonomy to generate hundreds of hypotheses. In the following discussion of McCrae and Costa's Five-Factor Model (FFM), we will see that their work began as an attempt to identify basic personality traits as revealed by factor analysis. This work soon evolved into a taxonomy and the Five-Factor *Model*. After much additional work, this model became a theory, one that can both *predict* and *explain* behavior.

Biographies of Robert R. McCrae and Paul T. Costa, Jr.

Robert Roger McCrae was born April 28, 1949 in Maryville, Missouri, a town of 13,000 people located about 100 miles north of Kansas City. Maryville is home to Northwest Missouri State, the town's largest employer. McCrae, the youngest of three children born to Andrew McCrae and Eloise Elaine McCrae, grew up with an avid interest in science and mathematics. By the time he entered Michigan State University, he had decided to study philosophy. A National Merit Scholar, he nevertheless was not completely happy with the open-ended and non-empirical nature of philosophy. After completing his undergraduate degree, he entered graduate school at Boston University with a major in psychology. Given his inclination and talent for math and science, McCrae found himself intrigued by the psychometric work of Raymond Cattell. In particular, he became curious about using factor analysis to search for a simple method for identifying the structural traits found in the dictionary. At Boston University, McCrae's major professor was Henry Weinberg, a clinical psychologist with only a peripheral interest in personality traits. Hence, McCrae's interest in traits had to be nourished more internally than externally.

During the 1960s and 1970s, Walter Mischel (see Chapter 17) was questioning the notion that personality traits are consistent, claiming that the situation is more important than any personality trait. Although Mischel has since revised his stance on the consistency of personality, his views were accepted by many psychologists during those years. In a personal communication dated May 4, 1999, McCrae wrote: "I attended graduate school in the years after Mischel's (1968) critique of trait psychology. Many psychologists at the time were prepared to believe that traits were nothing but response sets, stereotypes, or cognitive fictions. That never made any sense to me, and my early research experience showing remarkable stability in longitudinal studies encouraged the belief that traits were real and enduring." Nevertheless, McCrae's work on traits while in graduate school was a relatively lonely enterprise, being conducted quietly and without much fanfare. As it turns out, this quiet approach was well-suited to his own relatively quiet and introverted personality.

In 1975, 4 years into his PhD program, McCrae's destiny was about to change. He was sent by his advisor to work as a research assistant with James Fozard, an adult developmental psychologist at the Normative Aging Study at the Veterans Administration Outpatient Clinic in Boston. It was Fozard who referred McCrae to another Boston-based personality psychologist, Paul T. Costa Jr., who was on the faculty at University of Massachusetts at Boston.

After McCrae completed his PhD in 1976, Costa hired him as project director and co-principal investigator for his Smoking and Personality Grant. McCrae and Costa worked together on this project for 2 years, until they both were hired by the National Institute on Aging's Gerontology Research Center, a division of the National Institutes of Health (NIH) housed in Baltimore. Costa was hired as the chief of the section on stress and coping, whereas McCrae took the position as senior staff fellow. Because the Gerontology Research Center already had large, well-established datasets of adults, it was an ideal place for Costa and McCrae to investigate the question of how personality is structured. During the 1970s, with the shadow of Mischel's influence still hanging heavily over the study of personality and with the concept of traits being nearly a taboo subject, Costa and McCrae conducted work on traits that ensured them a prominent role in the 40-year history of analyzing the structure of personality.

Paul T. Costa, Jr. was born September 16, 1942 in Franklin, New Hampshire, the son of Paul T. Costa, Sr. and Esther Vasil Costa. He earned his undergraduate degree in psychology at Clark University in 1964 and both his master's (1968) and PhD (1970) in human development from the University of Chicago. His longstanding interests in individual differences and the nature of personality increased greatly in the stimulating intellectual environment at the University of Chicago. While at Chicago, he worked with Salvatore R. Maddi, with whom he published a book on humanistic personality theory (Maddi & Costa, 1972). After receiving his PhD, he taught for 2 years at Harvard and then from 1973 to 1978 at University of Massachusetts–Boston. In 1978, he began working at the National Institute of Aging's Gerontology Research Center, becoming the chief for the Section on Stress and Coping and then in 1985 chief for the Laboratory of Personality & Cognition. That same year, 1985, he became president of Division 20 (Adult Development and Aging) of the American Psychological Association. Among his other list of accomplishments are fellow of American Psychological Association in 1977 and president of International Society for the Study of Individual Differences in 1995. Costa and his wife, Karol Sandra Costa, have three children, Nina, Lora, and Nicholas.

The collaboration between Costa and McCrae has been unusually fruitful, with well over 200 co-authored research articles and chapters, and several books, including *Emerging Lives, Enduring Dispositions* (McCrae & Costa, 1984), *Personality in Adulthood: A Five-Factor Theory Perspective,* 2nd ed. (McCrae & Costa, 2003), and Revised NEO Personality Inventory (Costa & McCrae, 1992).

In Search of the Big Five

The study of traits was first begun by Allport and Odbert in the 1930s and continued by Cattell in the 1940s and by Tupes, Christal, and Norman in the 1960s (see John & Srivastava, 1999, for a historical review of the Five-Factor Model, or the Big-Five).

In the late 1970s and early 1980s, Costa and McCrae, like most other factor researchers, were building elaborate taxonomies of personality traits, but they were not using these classifications to generate testable hypotheses. Instead, they were simply using factor analytic techniques to examine the stability and structure of personality. During this time, Costa and McCrae focused initially on the two main dimensions of neuroticism and extraversion.

Almost immediately after they discovered N and E, Costa and McCrae found a third factor, which they called openness to experience. Most of Costa and McCrae's early work remained focused on these three dimensions (see, for example, Costa & McCrae, 1976; Costa, Fozard, McCrae, & Bosse, 1976). Although Lewis Goldberg had first used the term "Big Five" in 1981 to describe the consistent findings of factor analyses of personality traits, Costa and McCrae continued their work on the three factors.

Five Factors Found

As late as 1983, McCrae and Costa were arguing for a three-factor model of personality. Not until 1985 did they begin to report work on the five factors of personality. This work culminated in their new five-factor personality inventory: the NEO-PI (Costa & McCrae, 1985). The NEO-PI was a revision of an earlier unpublished personality inventory that measured only the first three dimensions; N, E, and O. In the 1985 inventory, the last two dimensions—agreeableness and conscientiousness—

were still the least well-developed scales, having no subscales associated with them. Costa and McCrae (1992) did not fully develop the A and C scales until the Revised NEO-PI appeared in 1992.

Throughout the 1980s, McCrae and Costa (1985, 1989) continued their work of factor analyzing most every other major personality inventory, including the *Myers-Briggs Type Indicator* (Myers, 1962) and the *Eysenck Personality Inventory* (H. Eysenck & S. Eysenck, 1975, 1993). For instance, in a direct comparison of their model with Eysenck's, inventory, Costa and McCrae reported that Eysenck's first two factors (N and E) are completely consistent with their first two factors. Eysenck's measure of psychoticism mapped onto the low ends of agreeableness and conscientiousness but did not tap into openness (McCrae & Costa, 1985).

At that time, there were two major and related questions in personality research. First, with the dozens of different personality inventories and hundreds of different scales, how was a common language to emerge? Everyone had his or her own somewhat idiosyncratic set of personality variables, making comparisons between studies and cumulative progress difficult. Indeed, as Eysenck (1991a) wrote:

> Where we have literally hundreds of inventories incorporating thousands of traits, largely overlapping but also containing specific variance, each empirical finding is strictly speaking only relevant to a specific trait. This is not the way to build a unified scientific discipline. (p. 786)

Second, what is the structure of personality? Cattell argued for 16 factors, Eysenck for three, and many others were starting to argue for five. The major accomplishment of the Five-Factor Model (FFM) has been to provide answers to both these questions.

Since the late 1980s and early 1990s, most personality psychologists have opted for the Five-Factor Model (Digman, 1990; John & Srivastava, 1999). The five factors have been found across a variety of cultures, using a plethora of languages (McCrae & Allik, 2002). In addition, the five factors show some permanence with age; that is, adults—in the absence of catastrophic illness such as Alzheimer's—tend to maintain the same personality structure as they grow older (McCrae & Costa, 2003). These findings prompted McCrae and Costa (1996) to write that "the facts about personality are beginning to fall into place" (p. 78). Or as McCrae and Oliver John (1992) insisted, the existence of five factors "is an empirical fact, like the fact that there are seven continents or eight American presidents from Virginia" (p. 194). (Incidentally, it is not an empirical fact that this earth has seven continents: Most geographers count only six.)

Description of the Five Factors

McCrae and Costa agreed with Eysenck that personality traits are bipolar and follow a bell-shaped distribution. That is, most people score near the middle of each trait, with only a few people scoring at the extremes. How can people at the extremes be described?

Neuroticism (N) and extraversion (E) are the two strongest and most ubiquitous personality traits, and Costa and McCrae conceptualize in much the same way as Eysenck defined them. People who score high on *neuroticism* tend to be anxious,

TABLE 14.1

Costa and McCrae's Five-Factor Model of Personality

Extraversion	High Scores	Low Scores
	affectionate	reserved
	joiner	loner
	talkative	quiet
	fun loving	sober
	active	passive
	passionate	unfeeling
Neuroticism	anxious	calm
	temperamental	even-tempered
	self-pitying	self-satisfied
	self-conscious	comfortable
	emotional	unemotional
	vulnerable	hardy
Openness	imaginative	down-to-earth
	creative	uncreative
	original	conventional
	prefers variety	prefers routine
	curious	uncurious
	liberal	conservative
Agreeableness	softhearted	ruthless
	trusting	suspicious
	generous	stingy
	acquiescent	antagonistic
	lenient	critical
	good-natured	irritable
Conscientiousness	conscientious	negligent
	hardworking	lazy
	well-organized	disorganized
	punctual	late
	ambitious	aimless
	persevering	quitting

temperamental, self-pitying, self-conscious, emotional, and vulnerable to stress-related disorders. Those who score low on N are usually calm, even-tempered, self-satisfied, and unemotional.

People who score high on *extraversion* tend to be affectionate, jovial, talkative, joiners, and fun-loving. In contrast, low E scorers are likely to be reserved, quiet, loners, passive, and lacking the ability to express strong emotion (see Table 14.1).

Openness to experience distinguishes people who prefer variety from those who have a need for closure and who gain comfort in their association with familiar people and things. People who consistently seek out different and varied experiences would score high on openness to experience. For example, they enjoy trying new menu items at a restaurant or they like searching for new and exciting restaurants. In contrast, people who are not open to experiences will stick with a familiar item, one they know they will enjoy. People high on openness also tend to question traditional values, whereas those low on openness tend to support traditional values and to preserve a fixed style of living. In summary, people high on openness are generally creative, imaginative, curious, and liberal and have a preference for variety. By contrast, those who score low on openness to experience are typically conventional, down-to-earth, conservative, and lacking in curiosity.

The *Agreeableness Scale* distinguishes soft-hearted people from ruthless ones. People who score in the direction of agreeableness tend to be trusting, generous, yielding, acceptant, and good-natured. Those who score in the other direction are generally suspicious, stingy, unfriendly, irritable, and critical of other people.

The fifth factor—*conscientiousness*—describes people who are ordered, controlled, organized, ambitious, achievement focused, and self-disciplined. In general, people who score high on C are hardworking, conscientious, punctual, and persevering. In contrast, people who score low on conscientiousness tend to be disorganized, negligent, lazy, and aimless and are likely to give up when a project becomes difficult. Together these dimensions make up the personality traits of the five-factor model, often referred to as the "Big Five" (Goldberg, 1981).

Evolution of the Five-Factor Theory

Originally, the five factors constituted noting more than a taxonomy, a classification of basic personality traits. By the late 1980s, Costa and McCrae became confident that they and other researchers had found a stable structure of personality. That is, they had answered the first central question of personality: What is the structure of personality? This advance was an important milestone for personality traits. The field now had a commonly agreed-on language for describing personality, and it was in five dimensions. Describing personality traits, however, is not the same as explaining them. For explanation, scientists need theory, and that was the next project for McCrae and Costa.

McCrae and Costa (1996) objected to earlier theories as relying too heavily on clinical experiences and on armchair speculation. By the 1980s, the rift between classical theories and modern research-based theories had become quite pronounced. It had become clear to them that "the old theories cannot simply be abandoned: They must be replaced by a new generation of theories that grow out of the conceptual insights of the past and the empirical findings of contemporary research" (p. 53). Indeed, this tension between the old and new was one of the driving forces behind Costa and McCrae's development of an alternative theory, one that went beyond the five-factor taxonomy.

What then is the alternative? What could a modern trait theory do that was missing from the classic theories? According to McCrae and Costa, first and foremost, a new theory should be able to incorporate the change and growth of the field that has occurred over the last 25 years as well as be grounded in the current empirical principles that have emerged from research.

For 25 years, Costa and McCrae had been at the forefront of contemporary personality research, developing and elaborating on the Five-Factor Model. According to McCrae and Costa (1999), "neither the model itself nor the body of research findings with which it is associated constitutes a theory of personality. A theory organizes findings to tell a coherent story, to bring into focus those issues and phenomena that can and should be explained" (pp. 139–140). Earlier, McCrae and Costa (1996, p. 78) had stated that "the facts about personality are beginning to fall into place. Now is the time to begin to make sense of them." In other words, it was time to turn the Five-Factor Model (taxonomy) into a Five-Factor Theory (FFT).

Units of the Five-Factor Theory

In the personality theory of McCrae and Costa (1996, 1999, 2003), behavior is predicted by an understanding of three central or core components and three peripheral ones. The three central components include (1) basic tendencies, (2) characteristic adaptations, and (3) self-concept.

Core Components of Personality

In Figure 14.8, the central or core components are represented by rectangles, whereas the peripheral components are represented by ellipses. The arrows represent **dynamic processes** and indicate the direction of causal influence. For example, objective biography (life experiences) is the outcome of characteristic adaptations as well as external influences. Also, biological bases are the sole cause of basic tendencies (personality traits). The personality system can be interpreted either cross-sectionally (how the system operates at any given point in time) or longitudinally (how we develop over the lifetime). Moreover, each causal influence is dynamic, meaning that it changes over time.

Basic Tendencies   As defined by McCrae and Costa (1996), **basic tendencies** are one of the central components of personality, along with characteristic adaptions, self-concept, biological bases, objective biography, and external influences. McCrae and Costa defined basic tendencies as

> the universal raw material of personality capacities and dispositions that are generally inferred rather than observed. Basic tendencies may be inherited, imprinted by early experience or modified by disease or psychological intervention, but at any given period in an individual's life, they define the individual's potential and direction. (pp. 66, 68)

In earlier versions of their theory, McCrae and Costa (1996) made it clear that many different elements make up basic tendencies. In addition to the five stable personal traits, these basic tendencies include cognitive abilities, artistic talent, sexual orientation, and the psychological processes underlying acquisition of language.

In most of their later publications, McCrae and Costa (1999, 2003) focused almost exclusively on the personality traits: more specifically, the five dimensions (N, E, O, A, and C) described in detail above (see Table 14.1). The essence of basic tendencies is their basis in biology and their stability over time and situation.

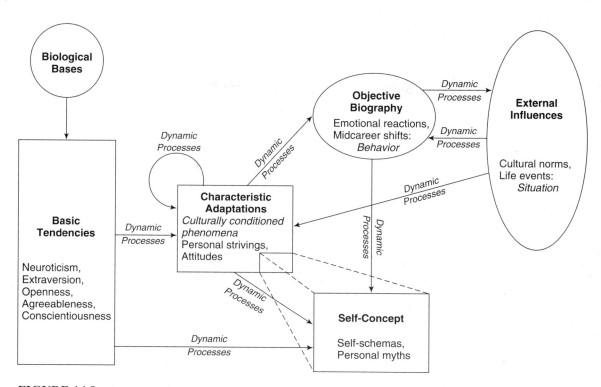

FIGURE 14.8   Operation of the personality system according to FFT. Arrows indicate the direction of causal influences, which operate through dynamic processes. Adapted from McCrae and Costa (1996).

Characteristic Adaptations   Core components of Five-Factor Theory include the **characteristic adaptations,** that is, acquired personality structures that develop as people adapt to their environment. The principal difference between basic tendencies and characteristic adaptations is their flexibility. Whereas basic tendencies are quite stable, characteristic adaptations can be influenced by external influences, such as acquired skills, habits, attitudes, and relationships that result from the interaction of individuals with their environment. McCrae and Costa (2003) explained the relationship between basic tendencies and characteristic adaptations, saying that the heart of their theory "is the distinction between basic tendencies and characteristic adaptations, precisely the distinction that we need to explain the stability of personality" (p. 187).

All acquired and specific skills, such as the English language or statistics, are characteristic adaptations. How quickly we learn (talent, intelligence, aptitude) is a basic tendency; what we learn is a characteristic adaptation. Moreover, our dispositions and tendencies are the direct influence on our characteristic adaptations. Characteristic responses are shaped and molded by basic tendencies. What makes them characteristic is their consistency and uniqueness; hence, they reflect the operation of enduring personality traits. Echoing Allport, they are adaptations because they are shaped as a response to what the environment has to offer us at any given moment. They allow us to fit into or adapt to our environment on an ongoing basis.

Understanding how characteristic adaptations and basic tendencies interact is absolutely central to the FFT. Basic tendencies are stable and enduring whereas characteristic adaptations fluctuate, making them subject to change over a person's lifetime. Characteristic adaptations differ from culture to culture. For instance, the expression of anger in the presence of a superior is much more taboo in Japan than it is in the United States. Distinguishing between stable tendencies and changing adaptations is important because this distinction can explain both the stability of personality and the plasticity of personality. Thus, McCrae and Costa have provided a solution to the problem of stability versus change in personality structure. Basic tendencies are stable, while characteristic adaptations fluctuate.

Self-Concept   McCrae and Costa (2003) explain that **self-concept** is actually a characteristic adaptation (see Figure 14.8), but it gets its own box because it is such an important adaptation. McCrae and Costa (1996) wrote that it "consists of knowledge, views, and evaluations of the self, ranging from miscellaneous facts of personal history to the identity that gives a sense of purpose and coherence to life" (p. 70). The beliefs, attitudes, and feelings one has toward oneself are characteristic adaptations in that they influence how one behaves in a given circumstance. For example, believing that one is an intelligent person makes one more willing to put oneself into situations that are intellectually challenging.

Does self-concept need to be accurate? Learning theorists such as Albert Bandura (Chapter 16) and humanistic theorists such as Carl Rogers (Chapter 11) or Gordon Allport (Chapter 13) believe that the conscious views people have of themselves are relatively accurate, with some distortion perhaps. In contrast, psychodynamic theorists would argue that most of the conscious thoughts and feelings people have of themselves are inherently distorted and the true nature of the self (ego) is largely unconscious. However, McCrae and Costa (2003) include personal myths as part of a person's self-concept.

Peripheral Components

The three peripheral components are (1) biological bases, (2) objective biography, and (3) external influences.

Biological Bases   The Five-Factor Theory rests on a single causal influence on personality traits, namely biology. The principal biological mechanisms that influence basic tendencies are genes, hormones, and brain structures. McCrae and Costa have not yet provided specific details about which genes, hormones, and brain structures play what role in their influence on personality. Advances in behavioral genetics and brain imaging have begun and will continue to fill in the details. This positioning of biological bases eliminates any role that the environment may play in the formation of basic tendencies. This should not suggest that the environment has no part in personality formation—merely that it has no direct influence on basic tendencies (see Figure 14.8). The environment does influence some components of personality. This underscores the need to distinguish the main two components of the model—basic tendencies and characteristic adaptations (McCrae & Costa, 1996, p. 187).

Objective Biography   The second peripheral component is **objective biography,** defined as "everything the person does, thinks, or feels across the whole lifespan" (McCrae & Costa, 2003, p. 187). Objective biography emphasizes what has happened in people's lives (objective) rather than their view or perceptions of their experiences (subjective). Every behavior or response becomes part of the cumulative record. Whereas theorists such as Alfred Adler (style of life) or Dan McAdams (personal narrative) emphasize the subjective interpretations of one's life-story, McCrae and Costa focus on the objective experiences—the events and experiences one has had over one's lifetime.

External Influences   People constantly find themselves in a particular physical or social situation that has some influence on the personality system. The question of how we respond to the opportunities and demands of the context is what **external influences** is all about. According to McCrae and Costa (1999, 2003), these responses are a function of two things: (1) characteristic adaptations and (2) their interaction with external influences (note the two arrows going into the objective biography ellipse in Figure 14.8).

McCrae and Costa assume that behavior is a function of the interaction between characteristic adaptations and external influences. As an example, they cite the case of Joan, who is offered tickets to see the opera *La Traviata* (an external influence). But Joan has a long personal history of detesting opera (a characteristic adaptation) and therefore refuses the offer (an objective biography). To elaborate, Joan may well have a basic tendency toward being closed (rather than open) to new experiences, and she was never around opera as a child or may have simply formed a negative opinion about it based on reputation. Whatever the case, she is more at home with familiar events and with down-to-earth experiences. This background predicts that Joan is likely to respond the way she did to an offer to attend an opera. These decisions to stay away from such experiences reinforce themselves as her distaste for opera grows. This is reflected in the arrow circling back on itself in Figure 14.8.

Basic Postulates

Each of the components of the personality system (except biological bases) has core postulates. Because the components of basic tendencies and characteristic adaptations are most central to the personality system, we will elaborate only on the postulates for these two components.

Postulates for Basic Tendencies

Basic tendencies have four postulates: individuality, origin, development, and structure. The *individuality* postulate stipulates that adults have a unique set of traits and that each person exhibits a unique combination of trait patterns. The precise amount of neuroticism, extraversion, openness, agreeableness, and conscientiousness is unique to all of us, and much of our uniqueness results from variability in our genotype. This postulate is consistent with Allport's idea that uniqueness is the essence of personality.

Second, the *origin* postulate takes a clear if somewhat controversial stance: All personality traits are the result solely of endogenous (internal) forces, such as genetics, hormones, and brain structures. In other words, the family environment plays no role in creating basic tendencies (but again, recall that personality traits are not synonymous with personality as a whole). Figure 14.8 shows but one causal arrow going from biological bases to basic tendencies. Such a claim is based mostly on the robust findings from behavioral genetics that the five dimensions of personality can be almost exclusively explained (about 50% each) by two factors, namely genetics and non-shared environment (Hamer & Copeland, 1998; Loehlin, 1992; Plomin & Caspi, 1999). Genetic influence is demonstrated by what behavioral geneticists refer to as heritability coefficients and comes out of the research on adoption studies and twin studies. Heritability addresses the question of what is the difference in the correlation on a given personality trait between individuals who are genetically identical (identical twins) and those who share only about 50% of their genes (all other siblings). If genes played no role in shaping traits, no differences would be found in correlations between people who vary in their degree of genetic similarity. Identical and fraternal twins would be just as similar or just as different. Evidence indicates that identical twins, even if reared in different environments, show greater similarity in personality than other siblings. And in the case of most personality traits, the degree of similarity suggests that about 50% of the variability in personality is due to heritability or genetics. Most of the remaining 50% is explained by nonshared experiences of siblings of varying ages; that is, siblings usually have different experiences, friends, and teachers. For instance, parents change their own parenting behaviors with time and experience. Thus, a child born three or four years after another is being raised in a somewhat different environment.

Third, the *development* postulate assumes that traits develop and change through childhood, but in adolescence their development slows, and by early to mid-adulthood (roughly age 30), change in personality nearly stops altogether (Costa & McCrae, 1994; Costa, McCrae, & Arenberg, 1980).

McCrae and Costa (2003) speculated that there may be some evolutionary and adaptive reasons for these changes: When people are young and establishing their relationships and careers, high E, O, and even N would be beneficial. As people mature and become settled, these traits are no longer as adaptive as they were earlier. Moreover, increases in agreeableness and conscientiousness might be helpful as people age. In our section on research, we discuss stability of traits during adulthood.

Finally, the *structure* postulate states that traits are organized hierarchically from narrow and specific to broad and general, just as Eysenck (1990) had suggested. This postulate grows out of McCrae and Costa's long-held position that the number of personality dimensions is five and only five. This number is more than the three hypothesized by Eysenck and considerably fewer than 35 found by Cattell. With the structure postulate, McCrae and Costa and other five-factor theorists converge on five as the answer to the long-standing debate among factor theorists.

Postulates for Characteristic Adaptations

The postulate concerning characteristic adaptations states that, over time, people adapt to their environment "by acquiring patterns of thoughts, feelings, and behaviors that are consistent with their personality traits and earlier adaptations" (McCrae & Costa, 2003, p. 190). In other words, traits affect the way we adapt to the changes in our environment. Moreover, our basic tendencies result in our seeking and selecting particular environments that match our dispositions. For instance, an extraverted person may join a dance club, whereas an assertive person may become a lawyer or business executive.

The second characteristic adaptation postulate—maladjustment—suggests that our responses are not always consistent with personal goals or cultural values. For example, when introversion is carried to extreme, it may result in pathological social shyness, which prevents people from going out of the house or holding down a job. Also, aggression carried to an extreme may lead to belligerence and antagonism, which then result in being frequently fired from jobs. These habits, attitudes, and competencies that make up characteristic adaptations sometimes become so rigid or compulsive that they become maladaptive.

The third characteristic adaptation postulate states that basic traits may "change over time in response to biological maturation, changes in the environment, or deliberate interventions" (McCrae & Costa, 2003, p. 190). This is McCrae and Costa's plasticity postulate, one that recognizes that although basic tendencies may be rather stable over the lifetime, characteristic adaptations are not. For example, interventions such as psychotherapy and behavior modification may have a difficult time changing a person's fundamental traits, but they may be potent enough to alter a person's characteristic responses.

Related Research

The trait approach taken by Hans Eysenck, Robert McCrae, and Paul Costa is very popular in the field of personality. Eysenck and Costa and McCrae have developed widely used personality inventories, namely the Eysenck Personality Inventory and its offshoots (Eysenck, 1959; Eysenck & Eysenck, 1964, 1968, 1975, 1993) and the NEO-PI (Costa & McCrae, 1985, 1992).

Traits have been linked to vital outcomes such as physical health (Martin, Friedman, & Schwartz, 2007), well-being (Costa & McCrae, 1980), and academic success (Noftle & Robins, 2007; Zyphur, Islam, & Landis, 2007); but traits have also been linked to more common, everyday outcomes such as mood (McNiel & Fleeson, 2006). As seen below, traits can predict long-term outcomes like GPA (Noftle & Robins, 2007) that are the product of years of work, but traits can also predict more discrete outcomes like how many times you will take a college entrance exam such as the SAT (Zyphur, Islam, & Landis, 2007) and what kind of mood you might be in on any given day (McNiel & Fleeson, 2006).

The Biology of Personality Traits

One of the major thrusts of Eysenck's theory is that personality dimensions are not arbitrary creations of culture but, rather, result from the basic genetic and neurophysiological makeup of the human species. If there were a biological basis to personality, two key assumptions should hold true. First, neurophysiological differences should exist between people high on one end of a dimension (for instance, introversion) and those high on the other end of that dimension (for instance, extraverts). Second, the basic personality dimensions should be universal and not limited to a given culture.

The first domain to test Eysenck's biological model of personality is in neurophysiology. If, as Eysenck proposed, introverts have lower thresholds of arousal than do extraverts, then they should be more reactive (that is, sensitive) to sensory stimulation. One way to test this idea is to present both groups with varying intensities of stimulation and measure their physiological reactivity. If Eysenck's theory is to be supported, then introverts should be more reactive than extraverts.

Over the past 30 years, a substantial amount of research has explored cognitive, behavioral, and physiological measures of reactivity in relation to extraversion-introversion (Beauducel, Brocke, & Leue, 2006; Eysenck, 1990; Stelmack, 1990, 1997). In general, Eysenck's assumption that introverts are more reactive (have lower thresholds) than extraverts has been supported, with the qualification that it is reactivity rather than baseline activity levels that distinguishes introverts from extraverts.

For instance, in a recent study, Beauducel and colleagues (2006) predicted that extraverts would be less cortically aroused and show worse performance on a boring and monotonous task. The researchers selected students who scored either very low or very high on the Eysenck Personality Questionnaire–Extraversion scale. They then presented the participants with a series of tones every 3 seconds for 60 minutes. Participants had to press a button as soon as possible after they heard a target tone. Computers measured both the speed (reaction time) and accuracy of responses. The task was meant to be tedious and boring, and it was. The idea is that extraverts will do worse at the tone task because it is so understimulating. Finally, the participants' cortical activity was measured via EEG throughout the entire tone task. The predictions again were that extraverts would have lower cortical arousal and would do worse on the monotonous task. Beauducel and colleagues found support for both of these hypotheses, which support two of the most basic of Eysenck's assumptions about the biological basis of personality traits.

Similarly, Anthony Gale (1983) summarized the findings from 33 studies examining EEG and extraversion and found that introverts showed greater cortical arousal than did extraverts in 22 of the 33 studies. Later, Robert Stelmack (1997), a major figure in testing Eysenck's neurophysiological hypothesis, reviewed the literature and came to two basic conclusions: First, introverts are more reactive than extraverts on various measures of arousal; and second, extraverts are quicker to respond on simple motor tasks. The faster motoric response rates of extraverts correspond well with their greater spontaneity, social disinhibition, and impulsiveness. In a study by Cynthia Doucet and Stelmack (2000), however, it was only motoric response rate—not cognitive processing speed—that differentiated introverts and extraverts. Extraverts were faster motorically but not cognitively. Extraverts may move faster but they do not think faster than introverts.

Optimal level of arousal is another of Eysenck's hypotheses that has generated some research. Eysenck theorized that introverts should work best in environments of relatively low sensory stimulation, whereas extraverts should perform best under conditions of relatively high sensory stimulation (Dornic & Ekehammer, 1990). In an important study conducted by Russell Geen (1984), introverted and extraverted participants were randomly assigned to either a low noise or high noise condition and then given a relatively simple cognitive task to perform. Results showed that introverts outperformed extraverts under conditions of low noise, whereas extraverts outperformed introverts under conditions of high noise. These findings not only support Eysenck's theory but also suggest that people who prefer to study in public places (like a dorm study area) are more likely to be extraverts.

Introverts, on the other hand, find such noisy environments distracting and therefore tend to avoid them.

In summary, research tends to support Eysenck's notion that personality factors have a biological basis and are not simply dependent on what we have learned. Indeed, consistent with a biological basis of personality, the major traits appear to be consistent in most countries of the world (McCrae, 2002; Poortinga, Van de Vijver, & van Hemert, 2002). How and when personality traits are expressed is clearly influenced by our cultural and social context. But that we all can be described on similar dimensions of personality (e.g., extraversion or neuroticism) is influenced by our biological makeup. Personality, in short, is molded by both nature and nurture.

Traits and Academics

Personality traits are strong predictors of many aspects of life. One area that has received a fair amount of research is the relationship between traits and academic performance, as measured by standardized test scores and GPA. Researchers Erik Noftle and Richard Robins (2007) conducted a large study in which they measured the traits and academic outcomes of more than 10,000 students. To conduct this research, Noftle and Robins gave undergraduates self-report questionnaires to measure their scores on the "Big Five" traits and asked about their SAT scores and high school and college GPAs, which were then checked against university records for accuracy. The most important trait for predicting both high school and college GPA was conscientiousness. Those who are high on the trait of conscientiousness tend to have higher GPAs in both high school and college. Recall that conscientiousness in Costa and McCrae's five-factor model of personality is defined as hardworking, well organized, and punctual. Students high in conscientiousness are those who, day in and day out, tend to make time for studying, know how to study well, and have good attendance in class, all of which contribute to doing well in school.

The relationship between traits and SAT scores followed a different pattern than for traits and GPA. The "Big Five" traits were not strong predictors of scores on the math section of the SAT, but openness was related to scores on the verbal section (Noftle & Robins, 2007). Specifically, those who scored higher on the trait of openness were more likely to do well on the SAT verbal questions. If you think about this, it makes sense. Those who score high on openness are imaginative, creative, and can think broadly, which can be useful approaches to difficult questions on a test.

It may be surprising that in the discussion of predicting SAT scores from traits, conscientiousness was not a strong predictor as it was for GPA. Yet SAT scores and GPA, although both are general measures of academic success, are very different. A person's score on the SAT is more aptitude and based on one single test, whereas GPA is more achievement and the product of years of work. It is more difficult, through studying alone, to change one's SAT score. It is somewhat more akin to an intelligence test score.

Some people take the SAT multiple times, whereas other people take it but once. These different approaches to test taking may reflect differences in the trait of neuroticism. People who score high on neuroticism are anxious and temperamental, whereas people who score low are calm, comfortable, and self-satisfied. Given that those who score high on the trait of neuroticism tend to be more anxious and less self-satisfied, it makes sense that these people may be more likely to take the SAT over and over again.

Michael Zyphur and colleagues (2007) conducted a study to see whether those high on neuroticism were indeed more likely to retake the SAT. To test this prediction, the researchers administered a self-report measure of neuroticism to 207 undergraduate students and then examined the students' transcripts for information on how many times each student took the SAT prior to coming to college and what their scores were. The results supported the researchers' hypothesis in that those who scored high on neuroticism were more likely to take the SAT multiple times. Interestingly, the researchers also found that scores on the SAT tended to increase over time so participants in the study tended to score higher the second time than the first and higher still the third time they took the test. These findings are important: Sometimes high scores on neuroticism are viewed negatively because such people are highly self-conscious, nervous, emotional, and generally worried about everything. But in this study the anxious tendencies of those high in neuroticism were very adaptive because it led them to retake the SAT and score higher when they did.

When it comes to predicting academic performance from traits, the traits that are most important depend on the outcome of interest because there are multiple ways to do well. Conscientiousness is good for GPA but not that important for the SAT. Openness is great for verbal ability but doesn't matter much for mathematical ability. And neuroticism, although generally related to greater feelings of anxiety and self-consciousness, is associated with taking tests over and over again and doing a little better each time.

Traits and Emotion

Personality traits affect more than success at school and other long-term outcomes. Traits can also affect the mood a person experiences on a daily basis. If you look carefully at the descriptors of each trait, particularly extraversion and neuroticism, this is not surprising. To be high on extraversion is to be fun loving and passionate (both positive feelings), whereas to be high on neuroticism is to be anxious and self-conscious (both negative feelings). Therefore, researchers have long considered positive emotion to be the core of extraversion and negative emotion to be the core of neuroticism (Costa & McCrae, 1980). But what has not been clear in most early research on the topic is whether the trait of extraversion or neuroticism causes the experience of positive and negative mood respectively or if it is the experience of the emotions that causes people to behave in ways concordant with the traits. For example, if people are in a good mood it makes sense that they might be more jovial and talkative (i.e., extraverted behavior), but are they in a good mood because they are acting extraverted or are they acting extraverted because they are in a good mood? Similarly, if people are in a bad mood it makes sense that they might act a little self-conscious and experience anxiety (i.e., neurotic behavior), but did the mood cause the behavior or did the behavior cause the mood?

Murray McNiel and William Fleeson (2006) conducted a study to determine the direction of causality for the relationships between extraversion and positive mood and between neuroticism and negative mood. Specifically, they were interested in determining whether acting in an extraverted manner causes people to experience positive feelings and whether acting in a neurotic manner causes people to experience negative feelings. To do this, McNiel and Fleeson had 45 participants come into a psychology laboratory in groups of three and participate in two different group discussions. During the first discussion, one person in the group was instructed to act "bold, spontaneous, assertive, and talkative" (all of which are extraverted behaviors), one person was instructed to act "reserved, inhibited, timid, and quiet" (all of which are introverted behaviors), and the third person received no instructions and instead was a neutral observer of the behavior of the other two group members. After the group discussion, the participants who were instructed to act extraverted or introverted rated their own mood, whereas the neutral observer rated the mood of his or her group members (those who were instructed to act extraverted or introverted). During the second group discussion, the roles of those who were instructed to behave either extraverted or introverted were switched so that whoever acted extraverted in the first discussion acted introverted in the second discussion and vice versa. The neutral observer stayed the same. This type of experimental design allowed the researchers to conclusively determine whether extraverted behavior does indeed cause positive mood.

Just as predicted, participants reported higher positive mood when they were instructed to act extraverted than when they were instructed to act introverted. This finding was also supported by the ratings of the neutral observer and was consistent for people who were high or low on trait extraversion. This suggests that regardless of your natural level of extraversion, just acting in an extraverted manner can make you feel better than if you act introverted.

Recall that although positive mood is thought to be the core of extraversion, negative mood is thought to be the core of neuroticism. McNiel and Fleeson (2006) wanted to extend their findings for extraversion and positive mood, so they conducted another study, but this time investigated the effects for neuroticism and negative mood. The procedure was essentially the same as their previous study, but instead of one person being instructed to act extraverted or introverted, one participant was instructed to act "emotional, subjective, moody, and demanding" (all of which are aspects of high neuroticism) and another participant was instructed to act "unemotional, objective, steady, and undemanding" (all of which are aspects of low neuroticism). The roles of high neuroticism and low neuroticism were switched for the second group discussion. As predicted, participants reported being in a worse mood when they acted neurotic than when they did not. The general conclusion of this research then is that if you are in a bad mood but want to be in a good mood, act extraverted.

So far we've discussed how the trait of neuroticism is generally related to negative emotion and how acting neurotic can cause negative emotion. But there is some recent research that suggests that it is not the case that everybody who scores high on neuroticism experiences more negative emotion (Robinson & Clore, 2007). There are individual differences for the speed with which people process incoming information, and these differences might influence the relationship between neuroticism and negative mood. These differences in speed are measured in milliseconds and are therefore imperceptible both to the individual and to other people, but there are computers that can measure these differences quite accurately. To measure these speed differences, participants sit in front of a computer and complete a Stroop task, which involves identifying whether the color of the font for a word presented on the screen is red or green. This task is more difficult than it sounds because sometimes the word "red" appears in green font, so while the correct response is "green," people will initially want to respond with "red" and have to overcome that tendency.

In the study conducted by Michael Robinson and Gerald Clore (2007), participants first completed this Stroop task while a computer measured how fast they completed the task. After completing the computer task, participants also completed a standard self-report measure of neuroticism. Then participants were asked to record their mood at the end of every day for 2 weeks. According to past research, neuroticism should predict daily negative mood, but Robinson and Clore (2007) predicted that this would be the case only for those who were relatively slow at the categorization task (Stroop task). The reasoning for this prediction is that those who are fast at processing things in their environment do not need to rely on traits such as neuroticism to interpret events and thereby cause negative mood. In other words, fast processors objectively interpret their environment whereas slow processors are more subjective in their evaluations by relying on trait dispositions to interpret events.

Indeed, this is exactly what the researchers found: Neuroticism did predict experiencing more negative mood over the course of the 2-week reporting period but only for those who were slow at the computer task. Those who were high on neuroticism but fast at the computer task did not report any more negative emotion over the course of the 2-week period than their low neuroticism counterparts.

Taken together, the research on traits and emotion shows that although the early research in this area showing that extraversion and neuroticism are related to positive and negative mood respectively is not inaccurate, it does not portray the complete picture of the complex relationship between traits and emotion. The research by McNiel and Fleeson (2006) showed that acting extraverted, even if you are not high on extraversion, can increase positive mood. Furthermore, although neuroticism is related to experiencing more negative mood, Robinson and Clore (2007) demonstrated that this was the case only for those who not only were high on neuroticism but also were relatively slow at categorizing incoming information. Traits are good predictors of grades in school, SAT scores, and even daily mood, but traits are not an immutable destiny. Even if your traits predispose you toward certain types of behavior, your actions can subvert those dispositions.

Critique of Trait and Factor Theories

Trait and factor methods—especially those of Eysenck and advocates of the Big Five model—provide important taxonomies that organize personality into meaningful classifications. As pointed out in Chapter 1, however, taxonomies alone do not explain or predict behavior, two important functions of useful theories.

Do these theories go beyond taxonomies and produce important personality research? The trait and factor theories of Eysenck and Costa and McCrae are examples of a strictly empirical approach to personality investigation. These theories were built by collecting as much data as possible on a large number of people, intercorrelating the scores, factor analyzing correlation matrices, and applying appropriate psychological significance to the resultant factors. A psychometric approach, rather than clinical judgment, is the cornerstone of trait and factor theories. Nevertheless, like other theories, trait and factor theories must be judged by six criteria of a useful theory.

First, do trait and factor theories *generate research*? On this criterion, the theories of Eysenck and Costa and McCrae must be rated very high. Figure 14.7 shows the comprehensiveness of Eysenck's personality theory. The middle square embraces the psychometric properties of his theory; that is, psychoticism, extraversion, and neuroticism. This figure also shows that Eysenck's personality theory is much more than a simple classification. The genetic and biological antecedents of behavior are suggested by the two squares on the left, whereas some of the consequences, or outcomes, of Eysenck's research are found in the two squares on the right. These consequences are a result of experimental studies on conditioning, sensitivity, vigilance, perception, memory, and reminiscence. Areas of research on social behavior are shown in the box on the far right and includes such topics as sociability, criminality, creativity, psychopathology, and sexual behavior. Eysenck and his colleagues have reported significant amounts of research in these and other fields of research.

The trait theory of McCrae and Costa and other advocates of the Big Five personality structure have also generated large amounts of **empirical** research. That research has shown that the traits of extroversion, neuroticism, openness to experience, agreeableness, and conscientiousness are not limited to Western nations, but are found in wide variety of cultures, using myriad translations of the revised NEO-PI. In addition, McCrae and Costa have found that basic personality traits are somewhat flexible up to about age 30, but, after that time, they remain quite stable over the lifespan.

Second, are trait and factor theories *falsifiable?* On this criterion, trait and factor theories receive a moderate to high rating. Much of Eysenck's research results— for example, his investigations of personality and disease—has not been replicated by outside researchers. The work of McCrae and Costa lends itself to falsification, even though some of the research coming from non-Western countries suggests that traits other than the Big Five may be needed to explain personality in Asian countries.

Third, trait and factor theories are rated high on their ability to *organize knowledge.* Anything that is truly known about personality should be reducible to some quantity. Anything that can be quantified can be measured, and anything that can be measured can be factor analyzed. The extracted factors then provide a convenient and accurate description of personality in terms of traits. These traits, in turn, can present a framework for organizing many disparate observations about human personality.

Fourth, a useful theory has the power to *guide the actions of practitioners,* and on this criterion, trait and factor theories receive mixed reviews. Although these theories provide a comprehensive and structured taxonomy, such a classification is less useful to parents, teachers, and counselors than it is to researchers.

Are trait and factor theories *internally consistent?* Again, the rating must be equivocal. The theories of Eysenck and advocates of the Big Five are each a model of consistency, but the two theories taken together are somewhat inconsistent. Eysenck remained convinced that his Giant Three factors were superior to the Big Five model. This inconsistency presents a problem, especially because factor analysis is a precise mathematical procedure and because factor theories are heavily empirical.

The final criterion of a useful theory is *parsimony.* Ideally, trait and factor theories should receive an excellent rating on this standard, because factor analysis is predicated on the idea of the fewest explanatory factors possible. In other words, the very purpose of factor analysis is to reduce a large number of variables to as few as possible. This approach is the essence of parsimony.

Concept of Humanity

How do trait and factor theorists view humanity? Eysenck and the Five-Factor theorists were not concerned with traditional themes such as *determinism versus free choice, optimism versus pessimism,* and *teleological versus causal* influences. In fact, their theories do not lend themselves to speculation of these topics. What, then, can we say concerning their view of humanity?

First, we know that factor analysts see humans as being different from other animals. Only humans have the ability to report data about themselves. From this fact, we can infer that Eysenck believed that humans possess not only *consciousness,* but self-consciousness as well. People are also able to evaluate their performance and to render reasonably reliable reports concerning their attitudes, temperament, needs, interests, and behaviors.

Second, Eysenck, as well as McCrae and Costa, placed heavy emphasis on *genetic factors* of personality. They believe that traits and factors are largely inherited and have strong genetic and biological components. Therefore, we rate trait and factor theories very low on social influences.

On the dimension of *individual differences versus similarities,* trait and factor theories lean toward individual differences. Factor analysis rests on the premise of differences among individuals and thus variability in their scores. Eysenck (1981), for instance, wrote that "people are above all else *individuals*" (p. xi). Thus, trait theories are more concerned with individual differences than with similarities among people.

Key Terms and Concepts

- Trait and factor theories of personality are based on *factor analysis,* a procedure that assumes that human traits can be measured by correlational studies.
- Eysenck used a hypothetico-deductive approach to extract three *bipolar factors*—extraversion/introversion, neuroticism/stability, and psychoticism/superego.
- *Extraverts* are characterized by sociability and impulsiveness; *introverts,* by passivity and thoughtfulness.

- High scores on the *neuroticism* scale may indicate anxiety, hysteria, obsessive-compulsive disorders, or criminality; low scores tend to predict *emotional stability.*
- High scores on *psychoticism* indicate hostility, self-centeredness, suspicion, nonconformity, and antisocial behavior; low scores indicate a strong *superego,* empathy, and cooperation.
- Eysenck insisted that, to be useful, personality must *predict behavior,* and he presented ample evidence to support his three-factor theory.
- McCrae and Costa, like Eysenck, placed heavy emphasis on *biological components of personality.*
- The Five-Factor Theory has been used to assess personality *traits in cultures* throughout the world.
- The NEO-PI-R shows a high level of *stability in personality factors* as people advance from about 30 years old to old age.

PART FIVE

Learning Theories

CHAPTER 15

Skinner: Behavioral Analysis

Skinner

Erik Erikson (see Chapter 9) believed that people go through a series of identity crises, or turning points, that leave them vulnerable to major changes in how they see themselves. One such person was Fred, a man who experienced at least two such crises, and each led to significant turns in his life's course. His first identity crisis occurred during young adulthood, when, armed with an undergraduate degree in English, Fred returned to his parents' home hoping to shape his identity in the world of literature. His father reluctantly agreed to allow Fred 1 year to carve out a niche for himself as a writer. He warned his son of the necessity of finding a job, but he allowed Fred to convert the third-floor attic into a study.

Every morning, Fred climbed the two flights of steps and began his job as a writer. But nothing happened. After only 3 months of trying to become a creative writer, Fred realized that the quality of his work was poor. He blamed his parents, their home town, and literature itself for his failure to produce any worthwhile writing (Elms, 1981). He wasted time with nonproductive activities, sitting in the family library for long periods of time, remaining "absolutely motionless in a kind of catatonic stupor" (Skinner, 1976a, p. 287). Nevertheless, he felt obligated to continue the charade of pursuing a literary career for the one full year he and his father had agreed on. Fred eventually lost hope that he could make any contribution to literature. In later years, he referred to this nonproductive time as his "Dark Year." Erik Erikson would have called it a time of identity confusion—a time for trying to discover who he was, where he was going, and how he was going to get there. The young man experiencing this "Dark Year" was B. F. Skinner, who later became one of the most influential psychologists in the world but not until he experienced a second identity crisis, as we discuss in our biography of Skinner.

Overview of Behavioral Analysis

During the early years of the 20th century while Freud, Jung, and Adler were relying on clinical practice and before Eysenck and Costa and McCrae were using psychometrics to build theories of human personality, an approach called **behaviorism** emerged from laboratory studies of animals and humans. Two of the early pioneers of behaviorism were E. L. Thorndike and John Watson, but the person most often associated with the behaviorist position is B. F. Skinner, whose **behavioral analysis** is a clear departure from the highly speculative psychodynamic theories discussed in Chapters 2 through 9. Skinner minimized speculation and focused almost entirely on observable behavior. However, he did not claim that observable behavior is limited to external events. Such private behaviors as thinking, remembering, and anticipating are all observable—by the person experiencing them. Skinner's strict adherence to observable behavior earned his approach the label **radical behaviorism,** a doctrine that avoids all hypothetical constructs, such as ego, traits, drives, needs, hunger, and so forth.

In addition to being a radical behaviorist, Skinner can rightfully be regarded as a determinist and an environmentalist. As a *determinist,* he rejected the notion of volition or free will. Human behavior does not stem from an act of the will, but like any observable phenomenon, it is lawfully determined and can be studied scientifically.

As an *environmentalist,* Skinner held that psychology must not explain behavior on the basis of the physiological or constitutional components of the organism but rather on the basis of environmental stimuli. He recognized that genetic factors are important, but he insisted that, because they are fixed at conception, they are of no help in the control of behavior. The *history* of the individual, rather than anatomy, provides the most useful data for predicting and controlling behavior.

Watson took radical behaviorism, determinism, and environmental forces beyond Skinner's conception by ignoring genetic factors completely and promising to shape personality by controlling the environment. In a famous lecture, Watson (1926) made this extraordinary promise:

> Give me a dozen healthy infants, well-formed, and my own specified world to bring them up in and I'll guarantee to take any one at random and train him to become any type of specialist I might select—a doctor, lawyer, artist, merchant-chief, and, yes, even into beggar-man and thief, regardless of his talents, penchants, tendencies, abilities, vocations, and race of his ancestors. (p. 10)

Although few radical behaviorists currently accept this extreme position, Watson's promise has led to much discussion and debate.

Biography of B. F. Skinner

Burrhus Frederic Skinner was born on March 20, 1904, in Susquehanna, Pennsylvania, the first child of William Skinner and Grace Mange Burrhus Skinner. His father was a lawyer and an aspiring politician while his mother stayed home to care for their two children. Skinner grew up in a comfortable, happy, upper-middle-class home where his parents practiced the values of temperance, service, honesty, and hard work. The Skinners were Presbyterian, but Fred (he was almost never called Burrhus or B. F.) began to lose his faith during high school and thereafter never practiced any religion.

When Skinner was $2^{1}/_{2}$ years old, a second son, Edward, was born. Fred felt that Ebbie (as he was known) was loved more by both parents, yet he did not feel unloved. He was simply more independent and less emotionally attached to his mother and father. But after Ebbie died suddenly during Skinner's first year at college, the parents became progressively less willing to let their older son go. They wanted him to become "the family boy" and indeed succeeded in keeping him financially obligated even after B. F. Skinner became a well-known name in American psychology (Skinner, 1979; Wiener, 1996).

As a child, Skinner was inclined toward music and literature. From an early age, he was interested in becoming a professional writer, a goal he may have achieved with his publication of *Walden Two* when he was well into his 40s.

At about the time Skinner finished high school, his family moved about 30 miles to Scranton, Pennsylvania. Almost immediately, however, Skinner entered Hamilton College, a liberal arts school in Clinton, New York. After taking his bachelor's degree in English, Skinner set about to realize his ambition of being a creative writer. When he wrote to his father, informing him of his wish to spend a year at home working at nothing except writing, his request was met with lukewarm acceptance. Warning his son of the necessity of making a living, William Skinner reluctantly agreed to support him for 1 year on the condition that he would get a job if his writing career was not successful. This unenthusiastic reply was followed by a more encouraging letter from Robert Frost, who had read some of Skinner's writings.

Skinner returned to his parents' home in Scranton, built a study in the attic, and every morning went to work at writing. But nothing happened. His efforts were unproductive because he had nothing to say and no firm position on any current issue. This "Dark Year" exemplified a powerful identity confusion in Skinner's life, but as we discuss later in this biographical sketch, this was not his last identity crisis.

At the end of this unsuccessful Dark Year (actually 18 months), Skinner was faced with the task of looking for a new career. Psychology beckoned. After reading some of the works of Watson and Pavlov, he became determined to be a behaviorist. He never wavered from that decision and threw himself wholeheartedly behind radical behaviorism. Elms (1981, 1994) contended that such total dedication to an extreme ideology is quite typical of people faced with an identity crisis.

Although Skinner had never taken an undergraduate psychology course, Harvard accepted him as a graduate student in psychology. After he completed his PhD in 1931, Skinner received a fellowship from the National Research Council to continue his laboratory research at Harvard. Now confident of his identity as a behaviorist, he drew up a plan for himself, outlining his goals for the next 30 years. The plan also reminded him to adhere closely to behavioristic methodology and not to "surrender to the physiology of the central nervous system" (Skinner, 1979, p. 115). By 1960, Skinner had reached the most important phases of the plan.

When his fellowship ended in 1933, Skinner was faced for the first time with the chore of hunting for a permanent job. Positions were scarce during this depression year and prospects looked dim. But soon his worries were alleviated. In the spring of 1933, Harvard created the Society of Fellows, a program designed to promote creative thinking among young intellectually gifted men at the university. Skinner was selected as a Junior Fellow and spent the next 3 years doing more laboratory research.

At the end of his 3-year term as a Junior Fellow, he was again in the position of looking for a job. Curiously, he knew almost nothing of traditional academic psychology and was not interested in learning about it. He had a PhD in psychology, $5\frac{1}{2}$ years of additional laboratory research, but he was ill prepared to teach within the mainstream of psychology, having "never even read a text in psychology as a whole" (Skinner, 1979, p. 179).

In 1936, Skinner began a teaching and research position at the University of Minnesota, where he remained for 9 years. Soon after moving to Minneapolis and following a short and erratic courtship, he married Yvonne Blue. The Skinners had two daughters—Julie, born in 1938, and Deborah (Debbie), born in 1944. During his Minnesota years, Skinner published his first book, *The Behavior of Organisms* (1938), but beyond that, he was involved with two of his most interesting ventures—the pigeon-guided missile and the baby-tender built for his second daughter, Debbie. Both projects brought frustration and disappointment, emotions that may have led to a second identity crisis.

Skinner's Project Pigeon was a clever attempt to condition pigeons to make appropriate pecks on keys that would maneuver an explosive missile into an enemy target. Almost 2 years before the United States entered the war, Skinner purchased a flock of pigeons for the purpose of training them to guide missiles. To work full-time on Project Pigeon, Skinner obtained a grant from the University of Minnesota and financial aid from General Mills, the food conglomeration housed in Minneapolis. Unfortunately, he still lacked government support.

In an effort to secure the needed funds, he prepared a film of trained pigeons pecking at the controls of a missile and guiding it toward a moving target. After viewing the film, government officials rekindled their interest and awarded General Mills a substaintal grant to develop the project. Nevertheless, frustrations lay ahead. In 1944, Skinner dramatically demonstrated to government officials the feasibility of the project by producing a live pigeon that unerringly tracked a moving target. Despite this spectacular demonstration, some observers laughed and most remained skeptical. Finally, after 4 years of work, more than 2 of which were full time, Skinner was notified that financial help could no longer be continued, and the project came to a halt.

Shortly after Skinner abandoned Project Pigeon and immediately before the birth of his second daughter, Debbie, he became involved in another venture—the baby-tender. The baby-tender was essentially an enclosed crib with a large window and a continual supply of fresh warm air. It provided a physically and psychologically safe and healthy environment for Debbie, one that also freed the parents from unnecessary tedious labor. The Skinners frequently removed Debbie from her crib for play, but for most of the day, she was alone in her baby-tender. After *Ladies' Home Journal* published an article on the baby-tender, Skinner was both condemned and praised for his invention. Interest from other parents persuaded him to market the device. However, difficulties in securing a patent and his association with an incompetent, unscrupulous business partner led to his abandonment of the commercial venture. When Debbie outgrew the baby-tender at age 2½ years, Skinner unceremoniously fashioned it into a pigeon cage.

 Beyond Biography **How did B. F. Skinner solve his identity crises? For more information on Skinner's identity crises and on his failed Project Pigeon, please go to our website at** *www.mhhe.com/feist7*

At this point in his life, Skinner was 40 years old, still dependent on his father for financial help, struggling unsuccessfully to write a book on verbal behavior, and not completely detached from his Dark Year nearly 20 years earlier. Alan Elms (1981, 1994) believed that the frustrations Skinner experienced over Project Pigeon and the baby-tender led to a second identity crisis, this one at midlife.

Even as Skinner was becoming a successful and well-known behaviorist, he was slow to establish financial independence and in childlike fashion allowed his parents to pay for automobiles, vacations, his children's education in private schools, and a house for his family (Bjork, 1993; Wiener, 1996).

One significant experience occurred while Skinner was still at the University of Minnesota. His father offered to pay him the amount of his summer school salary if he would forego teaching during the summer months and bring his wife and daughter to Scranton. In his autobiography, Skinner (1979, p. 245) questioned his father's motives, saying that the father merely "wanted to see more of his adored granddaughter." Nevertheless, Skinner accepted his father's offer, went to Scranton, set up a table in the basement (as far as possible from the attic that was home base during his Dark Year), and began writing. Once again, Scranton proved to be a sterile environment, and the book he was writing remained unfinished until many years later (Skinner, 1957).

In 1945, Skinner left Minnesota to become chair of the psychology department at Indiana University, a move that added more frustrations. His wife had ambivalent feelings about leaving friends, his administrative duties proved irksome, and he still felt out of the mainstream of scientific psychology. However, his personal crisis was soon to end, and his professional career would take another turn.

In the summer of 1945, while on vacation, Skinner wrote *Walden Two*, a utopian novel that portrayed a society in which problems were solved through behavioral engineering. Although not published until 1948, the book provided its author with immediate therapy in the form of an emotional catharsis. At last Skinner had done what he failed to accomplish during his Dark Year nearly 20 years earlier. Skinner (1967) admitted that the book's two main characters, Farazier and Burris, represented his attempt to reconcile two separate aspects of his own personality. *Walden Two* was also a benchmark in Skinner's professional career. No longer would he be confined to the laboratory study of rats and pigeons, but thereafter he would be involved with the application of behavioral analysis to the technology of shaping human behavior. His concern with the human condition was elaborated in *Science and Human Behavior* (1953) and reached philosophical expression in *Beyond Freedom and Dignity* (1971).

In 1948, Skinner returned to Harvard, where he taught mostly in the College of Education and continued with some small experiments with pigeons. In 1964, at age 60, he retired from teaching but retained faculty status. For the next 10 years, he took two 5-year federal career grants that allowed him to continue to write and to conduct research. He retired as professor of psychology in 1974 but continued as professor emeritus, with few changes in his working conditions. After he retired from teaching in 1964, Skinner wrote several important books on human behavior that helped him attain the status of America's best-known living psychologist. In addition to *Beyond Freedom and Dignity* (1971), he published *About Behaviorism* (1974), *Reflections on Behaviorism and Society* (1978), and *Upon Further Reflection* (1987a). During this period, he also wrote a three-volume autobiography, *Particulars of My Life* (1976a), *The Shaping of a Behaviorist* (1979), and *A Matter of Consequences* (1983).

On August 18, 1990, Skinner died of leukemia. One week before his death, he delivered an emotional address to the American Psychological Association (APA) convention in which he continued his advocacy of radical behaviorism. At this convention, he received an unprecedented Citation for Outstanding Lifetime Contribution to Psychology, the only person to receive such an award in the history of APA. During his career, Skinner received other honors and awards, including serving as William James Lecturer at Harvard, being granted the 1958 APA Distinguished Scientific Award, and winning the President's Medal of Science.

Precursors to Skinner's Scientific Behaviorism

For centuries, observers of human behavior have known that people generally do those things that have pleasurable consequences and avoid doing those things that have punitive consequences. However, the first psychologist to systematically study the consequences of behavior was Edward L. Thorndike, who worked originally with animals (Thorndike, 1898, 1913) and then later with humans (Thorndike, 1931). Thorndike observed that learning takes place mostly because of the effects that follow a response, and he called this observation the **law of effect.** As originally conceived by Thorndike, the law of effect had two parts. The first stated that responses to stimuli that are followed immediately by a *satisfier* tend to be "stamped in"; the second held that responses to stimuli that are followed immediately by an *annoyer* tend to be "stamped out." Thorndike later amended the law of effect by minimizing the importance of annoyers. Whereas rewards (satisfiers) strengthen the connection between a stimulus and a response, punishments (annoyers) do not usually weaken this connection. That is, punishing a behavior merely inhibits that behavior; it does not "stamp it out." Skinner (1954) acknowledged that the law of effect was crucial to the control of behavior and saw his job as making sure that the effects *do* occur and that they occur under conditions optimal for learning. He also agreed with Thorndike that the effects of rewards are more predictable than the effects of punishments in shaping behavior.

A second and more direct influence on Skinner was the work of John B. Watson (J. B. Watson, 1913, 1925; J. B. Watson & Rayner, 1920). Watson had studied both animals and humans and became convinced that the concepts of consciousness and introspection must play no role in the scientific study of human behavior. In *Psychology as the Behaviorist Views It,* Watson (1913) argued that human behavior, like the behavior of animals and machines, can be studied objectively. He attacked not only consciousness and introspection but also the notions of instinct, sensation, perception, motivation, mental states, mind, and imagery. Each of these concepts, he insisted, is beyond the realm of scientific psychology. Watson further argued that the goal of psychology is the prediction and control of behavior and that goal could best be reached by limiting psychology to an objective study of habits formed through stimulus-response connections.

Scientific Behaviorism

Like Thorndike and Watson before him, Skinner insisted that human behavior should be studied scientifically. His scientific behaviorism holds that behavior can best be studied without reference to needs, instincts, or motives. Attributing motivation to human behavior would be like attributing a free will to natural phenomena. The wind does not blow because it wants to turn windmills; rocks do not roll downhill because they possess a sense of gravity; and birds do not migrate because they like the climate better in other regions. Scientists can easily accept the idea that the behavior of the wind, rocks, and even birds can be studied without reference to an internal motive, but most personality theorists assume that people are motivated by internal drives and that an understanding of the drives is essential.

Skinner disagreed. Why postulate a hypothetical internal mental function? People do not eat because they are hungry. Hunger is an inner condition not directly observable. If psychologists wish to increase the probability that a person will eat, then they must first observe the variables related to eating. If deprivation of food increases the likelihood of eating, then they can deprive a person of food in order to better predict and control subsequent eating behavior. Both deprivation and eating are physical events that are clearly observable and therefore within the province of science. Scientists who say that people eat because they are hungry are assuming an unnecessary and unobservable mental condition between the physical fact of deprivation and the physical fact of eating. This assumption clouds the issue and relegates much of psychology to that realm of philosophy known as **cosmology,** or the concern with causation. To be scientific, Skinner (1953, 1987a) insisted, psychology must avoid internal mental factors and confine itself to observable physical events.

Although Skinner believed that internal states are outside the domain of science, he did not deny their existence. Such conditions as hunger, emotions, values, self-confidence, aggressive needs, religious beliefs, and spitefulness exist; but they are not explanations for behavior. To use them as explanations not only is fruitless but also limits the advancement of scientific behaviorism. Other sciences have made greater advances because they have long since abandoned the practice of attributing motives, needs, or willpower to the motion (behavior) of living organisms and inanimate objects. Skinner's scientific behaviorism follows their lead (Skinner, 1945).

Philosophy of Science

Scientific behaviorism allows for an *interpretation* of behavior but not an *explanation* of its causes. Interpretation permits a scientist to generalize from a simple learning condition to a more complex one. For example, Skinner generalized from animal studies to children and then to adults. Any science, including that of human behavior, begins with the simple and eventually evolves generalized principles that permit an interpretation of the more complex. Skinner (1978) used principles derived from laboratory studies to interpret the behavior of human beings but insisted that interpretation should not be confused with an explanation of why people behave the way they do.

Characteristics of Science

According to Skinner (1953), science has three main characteristics: First, science is cumulative; second, it is an attitude that values empirical observation; and third, science is a search for order and lawful relationships.

Science, in contrast to art, philosophy, and literature, advances in a *cumulative* manner. The amount and nature of scientific knowledge that today's high school students have of physics or chemistry is vastly more sophisticated than that of even the most educated Greeks 2,500 years ago. The same cannot be said for the humanities. The wisdom and genius of Plato, Michelangelo, and Shakespeare are clearly not inferior to the wisdom and genius of any modern philosopher, artist, or writer. However, cumulative knowledge is not to be confused with technological progress. Science is unique not because of technology but rather because of its attitude.

The second and most critical characteristic of science is *an attitude* that places value on *empirical observation* above all else. In Skinner's (1953) words: "It is a disposition to deal with facts rather than with what someone has said about them" (p. 12). In particular, there are three components to the scientific attitude: First, it *rejects authority*—even its own authority. Just because some well-respected person, such as Einstein, says something, that in itself does not make the statement true. It must stand the test of empirical observation. Recall from Chapter 1 our discussion of Aristotle's belief that bodies of different masses fall at different rates. That was accepted as fact for roughly 1,000 years simply because Aristotle said it. Galileo, however, tested that idea scientifically and discovered that it was not true. Second, science *demands intellectual honesty,* and it requires scientists to accept facts even when these facts are opposed to their wishes and desires. This attitude does not mean that scientists are inherently more honest than other people. They are not. Scientists have been known to fabricate data and misrepresent their findings. However, as a discipline, science puts a high premium on intellectual honesty simply because the right answer ultimately will be discovered. Scientists have no choice but to report results that go against their hopes and hypotheses, because if they do not, someone else will, and the new results will show that the scientists who misrepresented data were wrong. "Where right and wrong are not so easily or so quickly established, there is no similar pressure" (Skinner, 1953, p. 13): Finally, science *suspends judgment* until clear trends emerge. Nothing is more damaging to a scientist's reputation than to rush into print findings that are insufficiently verified and tested. If a scientist's report of findings does not hold up to replication, then that scientist appears foolish at best and dishonest at worst. A healthy skepticism and willingness to suspend judgment are therefore essential to being a scientist.

A third characteristic of science is *a search for order and lawful relationships.* All science begins with observation of single events and then attempts to infer general principles and laws from those events. In short, the scientific method consists of prediction, control, and description. A scientist makes observations guided by theoretical assumptions, develops hypotheses (makes predictions), tests these hypotheses through controlled experimentation, describes honestly and accurately the results, and finally modifies the theory to match the actual empirical results. This circular relationship between theory and research was discussed in Chapter 1.

Skinner (1953) believed that prediction, control, and description are possible in scientific behaviorism because behavior is both determined and lawful. Human behavior, like that of physical and biological entities, is neither whimsical nor the outcome of free will. It is determined by certain identifiable variables and follows definite lawful principles, which potentially can be known. Behavior that appears to be capricious or individually determined is simply beyond scientists' present capacity to predict or control. But, hypothetically, the conditions under which it occurs can be discovered, thus permitting both prediction and control as well as description. Skinner devoted much of his time to trying to discover these conditions, using a procedure he called operant conditioning.

Conditioning

Skinner (1953) recognized two kinds of conditioning, classical and operant. With classical conditioning (which Skinner called respondent conditioning), a response is drawn out of the organism by a specific, identifiable stimulus. With operant conditioning (also called Skinnerian conditioning), a behavior is made more likely to recur when it is immediately reinforced.

One distinction between classical and operant conditioning is that, in classical conditioning, behavior is *elicited* from the organism, whereas in operant conditioning, behavior is *emitted*. An elicited response is drawn from the organism, whereas an emitted response is one that simply appears. Because responses do not exist inside the organism and thus cannot be drawn out, Skinner preferred the term "emitted." Emitted responses do not previously exist inside the organism; they simply appear because of the organism's individual history of reinforcement or the species' evolutionary history.

Classical Conditioning

In **classical conditioning,** a neutral (conditioned) stimulus is paired with—that is, immediately precedes—an unconditioned stimulus a number of times until it is capable of bringing about a previously unconditioned response, now called the conditioned response. The simplest examples include reflexive behavior. Light shined in the eye stimulates the pupil to contract; food placed on the tongue brings about salivation; and pepper in the nostrils results in the sneezing reflex. With reflexive behavior, responses are unlearned, involuntary, and common not only to the species but across species as well. Classical conditioning, however, is not limited to simple reflexes. It can also be responsible for more complex human learning like phobias, fears, and anxieties.

An early example of classical conditioning with humans was described by John Watson and Rosalie Rayner in 1920 and involved a young boy—Albert B., usually referred to as Little Albert. Albert was a normal, healthy child who, at 9 months of age, showed no fear of such objects as a white rat, a rabbit, a dog, a monkey with masks, and so forth. When Albert was 11 months old, the experimenters presented him with a white rat. Just as Albert was beginning to touch the rat, one of the experimenters struck a bar behind Albert's head. The little boy immediately showed signs of fear, although he did not cry. Then, just as he touched the rat with his other hand, an experimenter struck the bar again. Once more Albert showed fear and began to whimper. A week later, Watson and Rayner repeated the procedure several times and finally presented the white rat without the loud, sudden sound. By this time, Albert had learned to fear the rat by itself and quickly began to crawl away from it. A few days later, the experimenters presented Albert with some blocks. He showed no fear. Next, they showed him the rat by itself. Albert showed fear. Then, they offered him the blocks again. No fear. They followed this part of the experiment by showing Albert a rabbit by itself. Albert immediately began to cry and crawl away from the rabbit. Watson and Rayner then showed Albert the blocks again, then a dog, then blocks again, then a fur coat, and then a package of wool. For all objects except the blocks, Albert showed some fear. Finally, Watson brought in a Santa Claus mask, to which Albert showed signs of fear. This experiment, which was never completed because Albert's mother intervened, demonstrated at least four points. First, infants have few, if any, innate fears of animals; second, they can learn to fear an animal if it is presented in association with an aversive stimulus; third, infants can *discriminate* between a furry white rat and a hard wooden block, so that fear of a rat does not generalize to fear of a block; and fourth, fear of a furry white rat can *generalize* to other animals as well as to other white hairy or furry objects.

The key to this classical conditioning experiment was the pairing of a conditioned stimulus (the white rat) with an unconditioned stimulus (fear of a loud sudden sound) until the presence of the conditioned stimulus (the white rat) was sufficient to elicit the unconditioned stimulus (fear).

Operant Conditioning

Although classical conditioning is responsible for some human learning, Skinner believed that most human behaviors are learned through **operant conditioning.** The key to operant conditioning is the immediate reinforcement of a response. The organism first *does* something and then is reinforced by the environment. Reinforcement, in turn, increases the probability that the same behavior will occur again. This conditioning is called operant conditioning because the organism operates on the environment to produce a specific effect. Operant conditioning changes the frequency of a response or the probability that a response will occur. The reinforcement does not cause the behavior, but it increases the likelihood that it will be repeated.

Shaping

With most cases of operant conditioning, the desired behavior is too complex to be emitted without first being shaped by the environment. **Shaping** is a procedure in which the experimenter or the environment first rewards gross approximations of the behavior, then closer approximations, and finally the desired behavior itself. Through this process of reinforcing **successive approximations,** the experimenter or the environment gradually shapes the final complex set of behaviors (Skinner, 1953).

Shaping can be illustrated by the example of training a severely mentally challenged boy to dress himself. The child's ultimate behavior is putting on all his own clothes. If the parent withheld reinforcement until this target behavior occurred, the child would never successfully complete the chore. To train the boy, the parent must break down the complex behavior of dressing into simple segments. First, the parent gives the child a reward, say, candy, whenever the boy approximates the behavior of positioning his left hand near the inside of the left sleeve of his shirt. Once that behavior is sufficiently reinforced, the parent withholds reward until the child places his hand into the proper sleeve. Then the parent rewards the child only for putting his left arm entirely through the sleeve. Following this, the same procedures are used with the right sleeve, the buttons, trousers, socks, and shoes. After the child learns to dress himself completely, reinforcement need not follow every successful trial. By this time, in fact, the ability to put on all his clothes will probably become a reward in itself. Quite apparently, the child can reach the final target behavior only if the parent breaks up the complex behavior into its component parts and then reinforces successive approximations to each response.

In this example, as in all instances of operant conditioning, three conditions are present: the *antecedent* (A), the *behavior* (B), and the *consequence* (C). The antecedent (A) refers to the environment or setting in which the behavior takes place. In our example, this environment would be the home or any other place the child might be putting on clothes. The second essential condition in this example is the boy's behavior (B) of dressing himself. This response must be within the boy's repertoire and must not be interfered with by competing or antagonistic behaviors,

Even complex behavior, such as learning to work a computer, is acquired through shaping and successive approximation.

such as distractions from siblings or television. The consequence is the reward (C), that is, the candy.

If reinforcement increases the probability that a given response will recur, then how can behavior be shaped from the relatively undifferentiated into the highly complex? In other words, why doesn't the organism simply repeat the old reinforced response? Why does it emit new responses that have never been reinforced but that gradually move it toward the target behavior? The answer is that behavior is not discrete but continuous; that is, the organism usually moves slightly beyond the previously reinforced response. If behavior were discrete, shaping could not occur because the organism would become locked into simply emitting previously reinforced responses. Because behavior is continuous, the organism moves slightly beyond the previously reinforced response, and this slightly exceptional value can then be used as the new minimum standard for reinforcement. (The organism may also move slightly backward or slightly sideways, but only movements toward the desired target are reinforced.) Skinner (1953) compared shaping behavior to a sculptor molding a statue from a large lump of clay. In both cases, the final product seems to be different from the original form, but the history of the transformation reveals continuous behavior and not a set of discrete steps.

Operant behavior always takes place in some environment, and the environment has a selective role in shaping and maintaining behavior. Each of us has a history of being reinforced by reacting to some elements in our environment but not to others. This history of differential reinforcement results in **operant discrimination.** Skinner claimed that discrimination is not an ability that we possess but a consequence of our reinforcement history. We do not come to the dinner table because we discern that the food is ready; we come because our previous experiences of reacting in a similar way have been mostly reinforced. This distinction may seem to be splitting hairs, but Skinner felt that it had important theoretical and practical implications. Advocates of the first explanation see discrimination as a cognitive function, existing within the person, whereas Skinner accounted for this behavior by environmental differences and by the individual's history of reinforcement. The first explanation is beyond the scope of empirical observation; the second can be scientifically studied.

A response to a similar environment in the absence of previous reinforcement is called **stimulus generalization.** An example of stimulus generalization is provided by a college student's purchase of a ticket to a rock concert performed by a group she has neither seen nor heard but one she has been told is similar to her favorite rock group. Technically, people do not generalize from one situation to another, but rather they react to a new situation in the same manner that they reacted to an earlier one because the two situations possess some identical elements; that is, buying a ticket to one rock concert contains elements identical to buying a ticket to a different rock concert. Skinner (1953) put it this way: "The reinforcement of a response increases the probability of all responses containing the same elements" (p. 94).

Reinforcement

According to Skinner (1987a), **reinforcement** has two effects: It *strengthens the behavior* and it *rewards the person.* Reinforcement and reward, therefore, are not synonymous. Not every behavior that is reinforced is rewarding or pleasing to the person. For example, people are reinforced for working, but many find their jobs boring, uninteresting, and unrewarding. Reinforcers exist in the environment and are not something felt by the person. Food is not reinforcing because it tastes good; rather, it tastes good because it is reinforcing (Skinner, 1971).

Any behavior that increases the probability that the species or the individual will survive tends to be strengthened. Food, sex, and parental care are necessary for the survival of the species, and any behavior that produces these conditions is reinforced. Injury, disease, and extremes in climate are detrimental to survival, and any behavior that tends to reduce or avoid these conditions is likewise reinforced. Reinforcement, therefore, can be divided into that which produces a beneficial environmental condition and that which reduces or avoids a detrimental one. The first is called *positive reinforcement;* the second is *negative reinforcement.*

Positive Reinforcement   Any stimulus that, when added to a situation, increases the probability that a given behavior will occur is termed a **positive reinforcer** (Skinner, 1953). Food, water, sex, money, social approval, and physical comfort usually are examples of positive reinforcers. When made contingent on behavior, each has the capacity to increase the frequency of a response. For example, if clear water appears whenever a person turns on the kitchen faucet, then that behavior is strengthened because a beneficial environmental stimulus has been added. Much human and animal behavior is acquired through positive reinforcement. Under controlled conditions, Skinner was able to train animals to perform a multitude of relatively complex tasks.

With humans, however, reinforcement is often haphazard, and therefore learning is inefficient. Another problem with conditioning humans is determining what consequences are reinforcing and which ones are not. Depending on personal history, spankings and scoldings might be reinforcing, and kisses and compliments might be punishing.

Negative Reinforcement The removal of an aversive stimulus from a situation also increases the probability that the preceding behavior will occur. This removal results in **negative reinforcement** (Skinner, 1953). The reduction or avoidance of loud noises, shocks, and hunger pangs would be negatively reinforcing because they strengthen the behavior immediately preceding them. Negative reinforcement differs from positive reinforcement in that it requires the removal of an aversive condition, whereas positive reinforcement involves the presentation of a beneficial stimulus. The effect of negative reinforcement, however, is identical to that of positive reinforcement—both strengthen behavior. Some people eat because they like a particular food; others eat to diminish hunger pangs. For the first group of people, food is a positive reinforcer; for the second group, removal of hunger is a negative reinforcer. In both instances, the behavior of eating is strengthened because the consequences are rewarding.

There is an almost unlimited number of aversive stimuli, the removal of which may be negatively reinforcing. Anxiety, for example, is usually an aversive stimulus, and any behavior that reduces it is reinforcing. These behaviors might include exercising, repressing unpleasant memories, making excuses for inappropriate behavior, smoking cigarettes, drinking alcohol, and a multitude of other behaviors designed intentionally or unintentionally to reduce the unpleasantness of anxiety.

Punishment

Negative reinforcement should not be confused with punishment. Negative reinforcers remove, reduce, or avoid aversive stimuli, whereas **punishment** is the presentation of an aversive stimulus, such as an electric shock, or the removal of a positive one, such as disconnecting an adolescent's telephone. A negative reinforcer strengthens a response; punishment does not. Although punishment does not strengthen a response, neither does it inevitably weaken it. Skinner (1953) agreed with Thorndike that the effects of punishment are less predictable than those of reward.

Effects of Punishment The control of human and animal behavior is better served by positive and negative reinforcement than by punishment. The effects of punishment are not opposite those of reinforcement. When the contingencies of reinforcement are strictly controlled, behavior can be precisely shaped and accurately predicted. With punishment, however, no such accuracy is possible. The reason for this discrepancy is simple. Punishment ordinarily is imposed to prevent people from acting in a particular way. When it is successful, people will stop behaving in that manner, but they still must do something. What they do cannot be accurately predicted because punishment does not tell them what they should do; it merely suppresses the tendency to behave in the undesirable fashion. Consequently, one effect of punishment is to *suppress behavior.* For example, if a boy teases his younger sister, his parents can make him stop by spanking him, but unfortunately this punishment will not improve his disposition toward his sister. It merely suppresses teasing temporarily or while in the presence of his parents.

Another effect of punishment is the *conditioning of a negative feeling* by associating a strong aversive stimulus with the behavior being punished. In the above illustration, if the pain of the spanking is strong enough, it will instigate a response (crying, withdrawal, attack) that is incompatible with the behavior of teasing a younger sibling. In the future, when the boy thinks about mistreating his younger sister, that thought may elicit a classical conditioned response, such as fear, anxiety, guilt, or shame. This negative emotion then serves to prevent the undesirable behavior from recurring. Lamentably, it offers no positive instruction to the child.

A third outcome of punishment is the *spread of its effects.* Any stimulus associated with the punishment may be suppressed or avoided. In our example, the boy may simply learn to avoid his younger sister, stay away from his parents, or develop negative feelings toward the paddle or the place where the paddling occurred. As a result, the boy's behavior toward his family becomes maladaptive. Yet this inappropriate behavior serves the purpose of preventing future punishment. Skinner recognized the classical Freudian *defense mechanisms* as effective means of avoiding pain and its attendant anxiety. The punished person may fantasize, project feelings onto others, rationalize aggressive behaviors, or displace them toward other people or animals.

Punishment and Reinforcement Compared   Punishment has several characteristics in common with reinforcement. Just as there are two kinds of reinforcements (positive and negative), there are two types of punishment. The first requires the presentation of an aversive stimulus; the second involves the removal of a positive reinforcer. An example of the former is pain encountered from falling as the result of walking too fast on an icy sidewalk. An example of the latter is a heavy fine levied against a motorist for driving too fast. This first example (falling) results from a natural condition; the second (being fined) follows from human intervention. These two types of punishment reveal a second characteristic common to punishment and reinforcement: Both can derive either from natural consequences or from human imposition. Finally, both punishment and reinforcement are means of controlling behavior, whether the control is by design or by accident. Skinner obviously favored planned control, and his book *Walden Two* (Skinner, 1948) presented many of his ideas on the control of human behavior.

Conditioned and Generalized Reinforcers

Food is a reinforcement for humans and animals because it removes a condition of deprivation. But how can money, which cannot directly remove a condition of deprivation, be reinforcing? The answer is that money is a **conditioned reinforcer.** Conditioned reinforcers (sometimes called secondary reinforcers) are those environmental stimuli that are not by nature satisfying but become so because they are associated with such unlearned or *primary reinforcers* as food, water, sex, or physical comfort. Money is a conditioned reinforcer because it can be exchanged for a great variety of primary reinforcers. In addition, it is a **generalized reinforcer** because it is associated with more than one primary reinforcer.

Skinner (1953) recognized five important generalized reinforcers that sustain much of human behavior: attention, approval, affection, submission of others, and tokens (money). Each can be used as reinforcers in a variety of situations. Attention, for example, is a conditioned generalized reinforcer because it is associated with such primary reinforcers as food and physical contact. When children are being fed or held, they are also receiving attention. After food and attention are paired a number of times, attention itself becomes reinforcing through the process of respondent (classical) conditioning. Children, and adults too, will work for attention with no expectation of receiving food or physical contact. In much the same way, approval, affection, submission of others, and money acquire generalized reinforcement value. Behavior can be shaped and responses learned with generalized conditioned reinforcers supplying the sole reinforcement.

Schedules of Reinforcement

Any behavior followed immediately by the presentation of a positive reinforcer or the removal of an aversive stimulus tends thereafter to occur more frequently. The frequency of that behavior, however, is subject to the conditions under which training occurred, more specifically, to the various schedules of reinforcement (Ferster & Skinner, 1957).

Reinforcement can follow behavior on either a continuous schedule or an intermittent one. With a **continuous schedule,** the organism is reinforced for every response. This type of schedule increases the frequency of a response but is an inefficient use of the reinforcer. Skinner preferred **intermittent schedules** not only because they make more efficient use of the reinforcer but because they produce responses that are more resistant to extinction. Interestingly, Skinner first began using intermittent schedules because he was running low on food pellets (Wiener, 1996). Intermittent schedules are based either on the behavior of the organism or on elapsed time; they either can be set at a fixed rate or can vary according to a randomized program. Ferster and Skinner (1957) recognized a large number of reinforcement schedules, but the four basic intermittent schedules are *fixed-ratio, variable-ratio, fixed-interval,* and *variable-interval.*

Fixed-Ratio   With a **fixed-ratio schedule,** the organism is reinforced intermittently according to the number of responses it makes. Ratio refers to the ratio of responses to reinforcers. An experimenter may decide to reward a pigeon with a grain pellet for every fifth peck it makes at a disc. The pigeon is then conditioned at a fixed-ratio schedule of 5 to 1, that is, FR 5.

Nearly all reinforcement schedules begin on a continuous basis, but soon the experimenter can move from continuous reward to an intermittent reinforcement. In the same way, extremely high fixed-ratio schedules, like 200 to 1, must begin at a low rate of responses and gradually build to a higher one. A pigeon can be conditioned to work long and rapidly in exchange for one food pellet provided it has been previously reinforced at lower rates.

Technically, almost no pay scale for humans follows a fixed-ratio or any other schedule because workers ordinarily do not begin with a continuous schedule of immediate reinforcement. An approximation of a fixed-ratio schedule would be the pay to bricklayers who receive a fixed amount of money for each brick they lay.

Variable-Ratio   With a fixed-ratio schedule, the organism is reinforced after every nth response. With the **variable-ratio schedule,** it is reinforced after the *n*th response *on the average.* Again, training must start with continuous reinforcement, proceed to

Because slot machines pay off on a variable-ratio schedule, some people become compulsive gamblers.

a low response number, and then increase to a higher rate of response. A pigeon rewarded every third response on the average can build to a VR 6 schedule, then VR 10, and so on; but the mean number of responses must be increased gradually to prevent *extinction*. After a high mean is reached, say, VR 500, responses become extremely resistant to extinction. (More on rate of extinction in the next section.)

For humans, playing slot machines is an example of a variable-ratio schedule. The machine is set to pay off at a certain rate, but the ratio must be flexible, that is, variable, to prevent players from predicting payoffs.

Fixed-Interval   With the **fixed-interval schedule,** the organism is reinforced for the first response following a designated period of time. For example, FI 5 indicates that the organism is rewarded for its first response after every 5-minute interval. Employees working for salary or wages approximate a fixed-interval schedule. They are paid every week, every 2 weeks, or every month; but this pay schedule is not strictly a fixed-interval schedule. Although pigeons typically show a spurt in work toward the end of the time period, most human workers distribute their efforts fairly evenly rather than loafing most of the time and then showing an end-of-the-period spurt. This situation is due in part to such factors as watchful supervisors, threats of dismissal, promises of promotion, or self-generated reinforcers.

Variable-Interval   A **variable-interval schedule** is one in which the organism is reinforced after the lapse of random or varied periods of time. For example, VI 5 means that the organism is reinforced following random-length intervals that average 5 minutes. Such schedules result in more responses per interval than do fixed-interval schedules. For humans, reinforcement results more often from one's effort rather than the passage of time. For this reason, ratio schedules are more common than interval schedules, and the variable-interval schedule is probably the least common of all.

Extinction

Once learned, responses can be lost for at least four reasons. First, they can simply be forgotten during the passage of time. Second, and more likely, they can be lost due to the interference of preceding or subsequent learning. Third, they can disappear due to punishment. A fourth cause of lost learning is **extinction,** defined as the tendency of a previously acquired response to become progressively weakened upon nonreinforcement.

Operant extinction takes place when an experimenter systematically withholds reinforcement of a previously learned response until the probability of that response diminishes to zero. Rate of operant extinction depends largely on the schedule of reinforcement under which learning occurred.

Compared with responses acquired on a continuous schedule, behavior trained on an intermittent schedule is much more resistant to extinction. Skinner (1953) observed as many as 10,000 nonreinforced responses with intermittent schedules. Such behavior appears to be self-perpetuating and is practically indistinguishable from *functionally autonomous* behavior, a concept suggested by Gordon Allport and discussed in Chapter 13. In general, the higher the rate of responses per reinforcement, the slower the rate of extinction; the fewer responses an organism must make or the shorter the time between reinforcers, the more quickly extinction will occur. This finding suggests that praise and other reinforcers should be used sparingly in training children.

Extinction is seldom systematically applied to human behavior outside therapy or behavior modification. Most of us live in relatively unpredictable environments and almost never experience the methodical withholding of reinforcement. Thus, many of our behaviors persist over a long period of time because they are being intermittently reinforced, even though the nature of that reinforcement may be obscure to us.

The Human Organism

Our discussion of Skinnerian theory to this point has dealt primarily with the technology of behavior, a technology based exclusively on the study of animals. But do the principles of behavior gleaned from rats and pigeons apply to the human organism? Skinner's (1974, 1987a) view was that an understanding of the behavior of laboratory animals can generalize to human behavior, just as physics can be used to interpret what is observed in outer space and just as an understanding of basic genetics can help in interpreting complex evolutionary concepts.

Skinner (1953, 1990a) agreed with John Watson (1913) that psychology must be confined to a scientific study of observable phenomena, namely behavior. Science must begin with the simple and move to the more complex. This sequence might proceed from the behavior of animals to that of psychotics, to that of mentally challenged children, then to that of other children, and finally to the complex behavior of adults. Skinner (1974, 1987a), therefore, made no apology for beginning with the study of animals.

According to Skinner (1987a), human behavior (and human personality) is shaped by three forces: (1) natural selection, (2) cultural practices, and (3) the individual's history of reinforcement, which we have just discussed. Ultimately, however, "it is all a matter of natural selection, since operant conditioning is an evolved process, of which cultural practices are special applications" (p. 55).

Natural Selection

Human personality is the product of a long evolutionary history. As individuals, our behavior is determined by genetic composition and especially by our personal histories of reinforcement. As a species, however, we are shaped by the contingencies of survival. Natural selection plays an important part in human personality (Skinner, 1974, 1987a, 1990a).

Individual behavior that is reinforcing tends to be repeated; that which is not tends to drop out. Similarly, those behaviors that, throughout history, were beneficial to the species tended to survive, whereas those that were only idiosyncratically reinforcing tended to drop out. For example, natural selection has favored those individuals whose pupils of their eyes dilated and contracted with changes in lighting. Their superior ability to see during both daylight and nighttime enabled them to avoid life-threatening dangers and to survive to the age of reproduction. Similarly, infants whose heads turned in the direction of a gentle stroke on the cheek were able to suckle, thereby increasing their chances of survival and the likelihood that this rooting characteristic would be passed on to their offspring. These are but two examples of several reflexes that characterize the human infant today. Some, such as the pupillary reflex, continue to have survival value, whereas others, like the rooting reflex, are of diminishing benefit.

The contingencies of reinforcement and the contingencies of survival interact, and some behaviors that are individually reinforcing also contribute to the survival of the species. For example, sexual behavior is generally reinforcing to an individual, but it also has natural selection value because those individuals who were most strongly aroused by sexual stimulation were also the ones most likely to produce offspring capable of similar patterns of behavior.

Not every remnant of natural selection continues to have survival value. In humans' early history, overeating was adaptive because it allowed people to survive during those times when food was less plentiful. Now, in societies where food is continuously available, obesity has become a health problem, and overeating has lost its survival value.

Although natural selection helped shape some human behavior, it is probably responsible for only a small number of people's actions. Skinner (1989a) claimed that the contingencies of reinforcement, especially those that have shaped human culture, account for most of human behavior.

> We can trace a small part of human behavior . . . to natural selection and the evolution of the species, but the greater part of human behavior must be traced to contingencies of reinforcement, especially to the very complex social contingencies we call cultures. Only when we take those histories into account can we explain why people behave as they do. (p. 18)

Cultural Evolution

In his later years, Skinner (1987a, 1989a) elaborated more fully on the importance of culture in shaping human personality. *Selection* is responsible for those cultural practices that have survived, just as selection plays a key role in humans' evolutionary history and also with the contingencies of reinforcement. "People do not observe particular practices in order that the group will be more likely to survive; they observe them because groups that induced their members to do so survived and transmitted them" (Skinner, 1987a, p. 57). In other words, humans do not make a cooperative decision to do what is best for the society, but those societies whose members behaved cooperatively tended to survive.

Cultural practices such as toolmaking and verbal behavior began when an individual was reinforced for using a tool or uttering a distinctive sound. Eventually, a cultural practice evolved that was reinforcing to the group, although not necessarily to the individual. Both toolmaking and verbal behavior have survival value for a group, but few people now make tools and even fewer invent new languages.

The remnants of culture, like those of natural selection, are not all adaptive. For example, the division of labor that evolved from the Industrial Revolution has helped society produce more goods, but it has led to work that is no longer directly reinforcing. Another example is warfare, which in the preindustrialized world benefited certain societies, but which now has evolved as a threat to human existence.

Inner States

Although he rejected explanations of behavior founded on nonobservable hypothetical constructs, Skinner (1989b) did not deny the existence of internal states, such as feelings of love, anxiety, or fear. Internal states can be studied just as any other behavior, but their observation is, of course, limited. In a personal communication of June 13, 1983, Skinner wrote, "I believe it is possible to talk about private events and, in particular, to establish the limits with which we do so accurately. I think this brings so-called 'nonobservables' within reach." What, then, is the role of such inner states as self-awareness, drives, emotions, and purpose?

Self-Awareness

Skinner (1974) believed that humans not only have consciousness but are also aware of their consciousness; they are not only aware of their environment but are also aware of themselves as part of their environment; they not only observe external stimuli but are also aware of themselves observing that stimuli.

Behavior is a function of the environment, and part of that environment is within one's skin. This portion of the universe is peculiarly one's own and is therefore private. Each person is subjectively aware of his or her own thoughts, feelings, recollections, and intentions. Self-awareness and private events can be illustrated by the following example. A worker reports to a friend, "I was so frustrated today that I almost quit my job." What can be made of such a statement? First, the report itself is verbal behavior and, as such, can be studied in the same way as other behaviors. Second, the statement that she was on the verge of quitting her job refers to a nonbehavior. Responses never emitted are not responses and, of course, have no meaning to the scientific analysis of behavior. Third, a private event transpired "within the skin" of the worker. This private event, along with her verbal report to the friend, can be scientifically analyzed. At the time that the worker felt like quitting, she might

Emotions are subjectively real and may have observable concomitants, but they are not directly observable themselves.

have observed the following covert behavior: "I am observing within myself increasing degrees of frustration, which are raising the probability that I will inform my boss that I am quitting." This statement is more accurate than saying "I almost quit my job," and it refers to behavior that, although private, is within the boundaries of scientific analysis.

Drives

From the viewpoint of radical behaviorism, drives are not causes of behavior, but merely explanatory fictions. To Skinner (1953), drives simply refer to the effects of deprivation and satiation and to the corresponding probability that the organism will respond. To deprive a person of food increases the likelihood of eating; to satiate a person decreases that likelihood. However, deprivation and satiation are not the only correlates of eating. Other factors that increase or decrease the probability of eating are internally observed hunger pangs, availability of food, and previous experiences with food reinforcers.

If psychologists knew enough about the three essentials of behavior (antecedent, behavior, and consequences), then they would know why a person behaves, that is, what drives are related to specific behaviors. Only then would drives have a legitimate role in the scientific study of human behavior. For the present, however, explanations based on fictionalized constructs such as drives or needs are merely untestable hypotheses.

Emotions

Skinner (1974) recognized the subjective existence of emotions, of course, but he insisted that behavior must not be attributed to them. He accounted for emotions by the contingencies of survival and the contingencies of reinforcement. Throughout the millennia, individuals who were most strongly disposed toward fear or anger were those who escaped from or triumphed over danger and thus were able to pass on those characteristics to their offspring. On an individual level, behaviors followed by delight, joy, pleasure, and other pleasant emotions tend to be reinforced, thereby increasing the probability that these behaviors would recur in the life of that individual.

Purpose and Intention

Skinner (1974) also recognized the concepts of purpose and intention, but again, he cautioned against attributing behavior to them. Purpose and intention exist within the skin, but they are not subject to direct outside scrutiny. A felt, ongoing purpose may itself be reinforcing. For example, if you believe that your purpose for jogging is to feel better and live longer, then this thought per se acts as a reinforcing stimulus, especially while undergoing the drudgery of jogging or when trying to explain your motivation to a nonrunner.

A person may "intend" to see a movie Friday evening because viewing similar films has been reinforcing. At the time the person intends to go to the movie, she feels a physical condition within the body and labels it an "intention." What are called intentions or purposes, therefore, are physically felt stimuli within the organism and not mentalistic events responsible for behavior. "The consequences of operant behavior are not what the behavior is now for; they are merely similar to the consequences that have shaped and maintained it" (Skinner, 1987a, p. 57).

Complex Behavior

Human behavior can be exceedingly complex, yet Skinner believed that even the most abstract and complex behavior is shaped by natural selection, cultural evolution, or the individual's history of reinforcement. Once again, Skinner did not deny the existence of higher mental processes such as cognition, reason, and recall; nor did he ignore complex human endeavors like creativity, unconscious behavior, dreams, and social behavior.

Higher Mental Processes

Skinner (1974) admitted that human thought is the most difficult of all behaviors to analyze; but potentially, at least, it can be understood as long as one does not resort to a hypothetical fiction such as "mind." Thinking, problem solving, and reminiscing are covert behaviors that take place within the skin but not inside the mind. As behaviors, they are amenable to the same contingencies of reinforcement as overt behaviors. For example, when a woman has misplaced her car keys, she searches for them because similar searching behavior has been previously reinforced. In like manner, when she is unable to recall the name of an acquaintance, she searches for that name covertly because this type of behavior has earlier been reinforced.

However, the acquaintance's name did not exist in her mind any more than did the car keys. Skinner (1974) summed up this procedure, saying that "techniques of recall are not concerned with searching a storehouse of memory but with increasing the probability of responses" (pp. 109–110).

Problem solving also involves covert behavior and often requires the person to covertly manipulate the relevant variables until the correct solution is found. Ultimately these variables are environmental and do not spring magically from the person's mind. A chess player seems to be hopelessly trapped, surveys the board, and suddenly makes a move that allows his marker to escape. What brought about this unexpected burst of "insight"? He did not solve the problem in his mind. He manipulated the various markers (not by touching them but in covert fashion), rejected moves not accompanied by reinforcement, and finally selected the one that was followed by an internal reinforcer. Although the solution may have been facilitated by his previous experiences of reading a book on chess, listening to expert advice, or playing the game, it was initiated by environmental contingencies and not manufactured by mental machinations.

Creativity

How does the radical behaviorist account for creativity? Logically, if behavior were nothing other than a predictable response to a stimulus, creative behavior could not exist because only previously reinforced behavior would be emitted. Skinner (1974) answered this problem by comparing creative behavior with natural selection in evolutionary theory. "As accidental traits, arising from mutations, are selected by their contribution to survival, so accidental variations in behavior are selected by their reinforcing consequences" (p. 114). Just as natural selection explains differentiation among the species without resorting to an omnipotent creative mind, so behaviorism accounts for novel behavior without recourse to a personal creative mind.

The concept of mutation is crucial to both natural selection and creative behavior. In both cases, random or accidental conditions are produced that have some possibility of survival. Creative writers change their environment, thus producing responses that have some chance of being reinforced. When their "creativity dries up," they may move to a different location, travel, read, talk to others, put words on their computer with little expectancy that they will be the finished product, or try out various words, sentences, and ideas covertly. To Skinner, then, creativity is simply the result of *random* or *accidental* behaviors (overt or covert) that happen to be rewarded. The fact that some people are more creative than others is due both to differences in genetic endowment and to experiences that have shaped their creative behavior.

Unconscious Behavior

As a radical behaviorist, Skinner could not accept the notion of a storehouse of unconscious ideas or emotions. He did, however, accept the idea of unconscious *behavior*. In fact, because people rarely observe the relationship between genetic and environmental variables and their own behavior, nearly all our behavior is unconsciously motivated (Skinner, 1987a). In a more limited sense, behavior is labeled unconscious when people no longer think about it because it has been suppressed through punishment. Behavior that has aversive consequences has a tendency to be ignored or not thought about. A child repeatedly and severely punished for sexual play may both *suppress* the sexual behavior and *repress* any thoughts or memories of such activity. Eventually, the child may deny that the sexual activity took place. Such *denial* avoids the aversive aspects connected with thoughts of punishment and is thus a negative reinforcer. In other words, the child is rewarded for *not thinking* about certain sexual behaviors.

An example of not thinking about aversive stimuli is a child who behaves in hateful ways toward her mother. In doing so, she will also exhibit some less antagonistic behaviors. If the loathsome behavior is punished, it will become suppressed and replaced by the more positive behaviors. Eventually the child will be rewarded for gestures of love, which will then increase in frequency. After a time, her behavior becomes more and more positive, and it may even resemble what Freud (1926/1959a) called "reactive love." The child no longer has any thoughts of hatred toward her mother and behaves in an exceedingly loving and subservient manner.

Dreams

Skinner (1953) saw dreams as covert and symbolic forms of behavior that are subject to the same contingencies of reinforcement as other behaviors are. He agreed with Freud that dreams may serve a wish-fulfillment purpose. Dream behavior is reinforcing when repressed sexual or aggressive stimuli are allowed expression. To act out sexual fantasies and to actually inflict damage on an enemy are two behaviors likely to be associated with punishment. Even to covertly think about these behaviors may have punitive effects, but in dreams these behaviors may be expressed symbolically and without any accompanying punishment.

Social Behavior

Groups do not behave; only individuals do. Individuals establish groups because they have been rewarded for doing so. For example, individuals form clans so that they might be protected against animals, natural disasters, or enemy tribes. Individuals also form governments, establish churches, or become part of an unruly crowd because they are reinforced for that behavior.

Membership in a social group is not always reinforcing; yet, for at least three reasons, some people remain a member of a group. First, people may remain in a group that abuses them because some group members are reinforcing them; second, some people, especially children, may not possess the means to leave the group; and third, reinforcement may occur on an intermittent schedule so that the abuse suffered by an individual is intermingled with occasional reward. If the positive reinforcement is strong enough, its effects will be more powerful than those of punishment.

Control of Human Behavior

Ultimately, an individual's behavior is controlled by environmental contingencies. Those contingencies may have been erected by society, by another individual, or by oneself; but the environment, not free will, is responsible for behavior.

Social Control

Individuals act to form social groups because such behavior tends to be reinforcing. Groups, in turn, exercise control over their members by formulating written or unwritten laws, rules, and customs that have physical existence beyond the lives of individuals. The laws of a nation, the rules of an organization, and the customs of a culture transcend any one individual's means of countercontrol and serve as powerful controlling variables in the lives of individual members.

A somewhat humorous example of both unconscious behavior and social control involved Skinner and Erich Fromm, one of Skinner's harshest critics. At a professional meeting attended by both men, Fromm argued that people are not pigeons and cannot be controlled through operant conditioning techniques. While seated across a table from Fromm and while listening to this tirade, Skinner decided to reinforce Fromm's arm-waving behavior. He passed a note to one of his friends that read: " 'Watch Fromm's left hand. I am going to shape a chopping motion' " (Skinner, 1983, p. 151). Whenever Fromm raised his left hand, Skinner would look directly at him. If Fromm's left arm came down in a chopping motion, Skinner would smile and nod approvingly. If Fromm held his arm relatively still, Skinner would look away or appear to be bored with Fromm's talk. After 5 minutes of such selective reinforcement, Fromm unknowingly began to flail his arm so vigorously that his wristwatch kept slipping over his hand.

Like Erich Fromm, each of us is controlled by a variety of social forces and techniques, but all these can be grouped under the following headings: (1) operant conditioning, (2) describing contingencies, (3) deprivation and satiation, and (4) physical restraint (Skinner, 1953).

Society exercises control over its members through the four principal methods of operant conditioning: positive reinforcement, negative reinforcement, and the two techniques of punishment (adding an aversive stimulus and removing a positive one).

A second technique of social control is to describe to a person the contingencies of reinforcement. Describing contingencies involves language, usually verbal, to inform people of the consequences of their not-yet-emitted behavior. Many examples of describing contingencies are available, especially threats and promises. A more subtle means of social control is advertising, designed to manipulate people to purchase certain products. In none of these examples will the attempt at control be perfectly successful, yet each of them increases the likelihood that the desired response will be emitted.

Third, behavior can be controlled either by depriving people or by satiating them with reinforcers. Again, even though deprivation and satiation are internal states, the control originates with the environment. People deprived of food are more likely to eat; those satiated are less likely to eat even when delicious food is available.

Finally, people can be controlled through physical restraints, such as holding children back from a deep ravine or putting lawbreakers in prison. Physical restraint acts to counter the effects of conditioning, and it results in behavior contrary to that which would have been emitted had the person not been restrained.

Some people might say that physical restraint is a means of denying an individual's freedom. However, Skinner (1971) held that behavior has nothing to do with personal freedom but is shaped by the contingencies of survival, the effects of rein-

Physical restraint is one means of social control.

forcement, and the contingencies of the social environment. Therefore, the act of physically restraining a person does no more to negate freedom than does any other technique of control, including self-control.

Self-Control

If personal freedom is a fiction, then how can a person exercise self-control? Skinner would say that, just as people can alter the variables in another person's environment, so they can manipulate the variables within their own environment and thus exercise some measure of self-control. The contingencies of self-control, however, do not reside within the individual and cannot be freely chosen. When people control their own behavior, they do so by manipulating the same variables that they would use in controlling someone else's behavior, and ultimately these variables lie outside themselves.

Skinner and Margaret Vaughan (Skinner & Vaughan, 1983) have discussed several techniques that people can use to exercise self-control without resorting to free choice. First, they can use physical aids such as tools, machines, and financial resources to alter their environment. For example, a person may take extra money when going shopping to give herself the option of impulse buying. Second, people can change their environment, thereby increasing the probability of the desired behavior. For example, a student wanting to concentrate on his studies can turn off a distracting television set. Third, people can arrange their environment so that they can escape from an aversive stimulus only by producing the proper response. For example, a woman can set an alarm clock so that the aversive sound can be stopped only by getting out of bed to shut off the alarm.

Fourth, people can take drugs, especially alcohol, as a means of self-control. For example, a man may ingest tranquilizers to make his behavior more placid. Fifth, people can simply do something else in order to avoid behaving in an undesirable fashion. For example, an obsessive woman may count repetitive patterns in wallpaper to avoid thinking about previous experiences that would create guilt. In these examples, the substitute behaviors are negatively reinforcing because they allow a person to avoid unpleasant behaviors or thoughts.

The Unhealthy Personality

Unfortunately, the techniques of social control and self-control sometimes produce detrimental effects, which result in inappropriate behavior and unhealthy personality development.

Counteracting Strategies

When social control is excessive, people can use three basic strategies for counteracting it—they can escape, revolt, or use passive resistance (Skinner, 1953). With the defensive strategy of *escape,* people withdraw from the controlling agent either physically or psychologically. People who counteract by escape find it difficult to become involved in intimate personal relationships, tend to be mistrustful of people, and prefer to live lonely lives of noninvolvement.

People who *revolt* against society's controls behave more actively, counterattacking the controlling agent. People can rebel through vandalizing public property, tormenting teachers, verbally abusing other people, pilfering equipment from employers, provoking the police, or overthrowing established organizations such as religions or governments.

People who counteract control through *passive resistance* are more subtle than those who rebel and more irritating to the controllers than those who rely on escape. Skinner (1953) believed that passive resistance is most likely to be used where escape and revolt have failed. The conspicuous feature of passive resistance is stubbornness. A child with homework to do finds a dozen excuses why it cannot be finished; an employee slows down progress by undermining the work of others.

Inappropriate Behaviors

Inappropriate behaviors follow from self-defeating techniques of counteracting social control or from unsuccessful attempts at self-control, especially when either of these failures is accompanied by strong emotion. Like most behaviors, inappropriate or unhealthy responses are learned. They are shaped by positive and negative reinforcement and especially by the effects of punishment.

Inappropriate behaviors include excessively vigorous behavior, which makes no sense in terms of the contemporary situation, but might be reasonable in terms of past history; and excessively restrained behavior, which people use as a means of avoiding the aversive stimuli associated with punishment. Another type of inappropriate behavior is blocking out reality by simply paying no attention to aversive stimuli.

A fourth form of undesirable behavior results from defective self-knowledge and is manifested in such self-deluding responses as boasting, rationalizing, or claiming to be the Messiah. This pattern of behavior is negatively reinforcing because the person avoids the aversive stimulation associated with thoughts of inadequacy.

Another inappropriate behavior pattern is self-punishment, exemplified either by people directly punishing themselves or by arranging environmental variables so that they are punished by others.

Psychotherapy

Skinner (1987b) believed that psychotherapy is one of the chief obstacles blocking psychology's attempt to become scientific. Nevertheless, his ideas on shaping behavior not only have had a significant impact on behavior therapy but also extend to a description of how all therapy works.

Regardless of theoretical orientation, a therapist is a controlling agent. Not all controlling agents, however, are harmful, and a patient must learn to discriminate between punitive authority figures (both past and present) and a permissive therapist. Whereas a patient's parents may have been cold and rejecting, the therapist is warm and accepting; whereas the patient's parents were critical and judgmental, the therapist is supportive and empathic.

The shaping of any behavior takes time, and therapeutic behavior is no exception. A therapist molds desirable behavior by reinforcing slightly improved changes in behavior. The nonbehavioral therapist may affect behavior accidentally or unknowingly, whereas the behavioral therapist attends specifically to this technique (Skinner, 1953).

Traditional therapists generally explain behaviors by resorting to a variety of fictional constructs such as defense mechanisms, striving for superiority, collective unconscious, and self-actualization needs. Skinner, however, believed that these and other fictional constructs are behaviors that can be accounted for by learning principles. No therapeutic purpose is served by postulating explanatory fictions and internal causes. Skinner reasoned that if behavior is shaped by inner causes, then some force must be responsible for the inner cause. Traditional theories must ultimately account for this cause, but behavior therapy merely skips it and deals directly with the history of the organism; and it is this history that, in the final analysis, is responsible for any hypothetical internal cause.

Behavior therapists have developed a variety of techniques over the years, most based on operant conditioning (Skinner, 1988), although some are built around the principles of classical (respondent) conditioning. In general, these therapists play an active role in the treatment process, pointing out the positive consequences of certain behaviors and the aversive effects of others and also suggesting behaviors that, over the long haul, will result in positive reinforcement.

Related Research

In its early history, operant conditioning was used mostly in studies with animals, then it was applied to simple human responses; but more recently, Skinner's ideas have been used in a multitude of studies dealing with complex human behaviors.

Some of these studies have been concerned with the relationship between long-term behavior patterns (i.e., personality) and contingencies of reinforcement. These studies are generally of two kinds: They have asked either how conditioning affects personality or how personality affects conditioning.

How Conditioning Affects Personality

In Chapter 1, we said that the key elements of personality are stability of behavior over time and across different situations. By these criteria, personality change occurs when new behaviors become stable over time and/or across different situations. One domain in which personality change may be evidenced is in psychotherapy. In fact, a major goal of therapy is to change behavior, and if the changes are stable over time and situations, then one could talk about changing personality. We say this to make clear that whereas Skinner discussed changing long-term behavior, he never really discussed changing personality.

One basic assumption of Skinnerian conditioning is that reinforcement shapes behavior. Yet, what are the factors that change reinforcement; that is, can certain stimuli become more or less reinforcing for an individual over time? This is an important question in treating people with drug problems, because successful treatment requires that a reinforcer (drug) lose its reinforcing value. For smokers, for example, nicotine gradually becomes a negative reinforcer, as mild states of tension are removed by the effects of this drug.

Some evidence has shown that psychomotor stimulants (such as cocaine or d-amphetamines) increase smoking levels in those who smoke. There are two possible explanations for the effect: First, perhaps the stimulant specifically increases the reinforcing effect of nicotine; second, perhaps psychomotor stimulants simply increase activity levels in general, and smoking is just one of them. In order to test these two competing explanations, Jennifer Tidey, Suzanne O'Neill, and Stephen Higgins (2000) conducted a study with 13 smokers and put them through an elaborate testing procedure (12 separate 5-hour sessions), in which they received either a placebo or the drug d-amphetamine. Ninety minutes later the smokers had to choose between two different reinforcers, money ($0.25) or smoking (two puffs). If they chose money, a running total of the accumulated amount was shown on a computer screen and participants were paid that amount at the end of the testing session. If they chose the cigarette, they were allowed two puffs immediately after doing the desired behavior. If the stimulant simply increases general activity levels, there should be no systematic preference for one reinforcer over the other (compared to baseline preferences). Additionally, after the experimental session ended, they were allowed a period in which they could smoke as much or as little as they wished (free smoking session).

However, results showed that smoking levels in both the experimental choice (compared to money) and in the free smoking sessions increased in proportion to d-amphetamine. The higher the dose of d-amphetamine, the more the participants smoked. Even more importantly, however, smoking was chosen over money in the choice session in direct proportion to the amount of d-amphetamine administered. Therefore, the stimulant must increase the reinforcing value of nicotine specifically and not the other reinforcer (money). In short, the answer to the question of whether reinforcers can change their value over time and in combination with other stimuli is "yes," and in this case nicotine can become even more reinforcing in the presence of psychomotor stimulants.

How Personality Affects Conditioning

If conditioning can affect personality, is the reverse also true? That is, can personality affect conditioning? Several thousand studies with both animals and humans have demonstrated the power that conditioning has to change behavior/personality. With humans in particular, however, it is clear that different people respond differently to the same reinforcers, and personality may provide an important clue about why this may be so.

Returning to research on d-amphetamine and smoking, for example, there appears to be systematic individual differences on the effect; that is, it works for some people but not others. Just as in the previous study, Stacey Sigmon and colleagues (2003) studied the effects that d-amphetamine has on smoking using two different reinforcers: cigarettes and money. In addition to trying to replicate the finding that psychomotor stimulants specifically increase the reinforcing value of nicotine compared to money, they wanted to examine whether there were any individual differences in the effect. If there were, then what might be some possible explanations?

Participants were adult smokers (averaging 20 cigarettes per day) between the ages of 18 and 45, with a mean age of 21; 78% were European American and 61% were female. To be included in the study, participants had to test negative for drugs other than nicotine and report no psychiatric problems, and women had to practice a medically acceptable form of birth control and test negative for pregnancy. Participants were informed that they could receive various drugs, including placebos, stimulants, and sedatives, and that the purpose of the study was to investigate the effects of these drugs on mood, behavior, and physiology. Participants were paid $435 if they completed all nine sessions.

The general procedure included nine sessions, the first of which was a 3.5-hour session to acclimate the participants to the procedures and equipment; no drugs were administered in the first sessions. Sessions 2 through 9 lasted 5 hours each and included breath tests to ensure no prior smoking had occurred. Baseline measures included pre-session questionnaires and physiological measures such as heart rate, skin temperature, and blood pressure. Also, each participant lit a cigarette and smoked at least one puff in order to ensure equal time for all participants since last exposure to nicotine. The experimental drug (or placebo) was then administered followed by baseline mood questions and a light meal in order to prevent nausea. Mood questions included "Do you feel any good effects?" "Do you feel high?" "Do you feel nervous?" and so forth. Using a double-blind procedure, participants received either a placebo or d-amphetamine. The participant then completed a multiple-choice test that pitted money against smoking to assess baseline levels of the monetary value of smoking. For example, the participant was given a series of 45 hypothetical choices between smoking and a progressive amount of money. The point at which the participant stopped choosing smoking and chose money was referred to as the "crossover point" and was considered an index of drug-reinforcement efficacy.

Next, a 3-hour progressive reinforcement (PR) session began. Progressive reinforcement involves increasing the number of responses that are required before reinforcement. In this case, participants had to do a repetitive motor task n-number of times (starting with 160 and going all the way to 8,400 times) to earn either two puffs from a cigarette or $1. Which reinforcer they chose was up to them. The idea behind the progressive nature of the reinforcement procedure was to see how long it took a person to stop responding (give up trying to get a cigarette or money). This breakpoint is considered the strength of the reinforcer. If participants' breakpoint increased more than the drug condition than in baseline, they were considered responders (to the drug); if not, they were considered nonresponders. As in the study by Tidey et al., the last session allowed participants to freely smoke as little or as much as they wished.

The general result was that there was a small effect of d-amphetamine on increasing smoking. However, there were significant individual differences, and when one examined the effects for responders compared to nonresponders, the effect was clear. Smoking breakpoints for the 10 responders became increasingly higher with increased dosages of d-amphetamine, and money breakpoints became increasingly lower. In other words, responders were willing to work harder to get cigarettes under increasing amounts of d-amphetamine. But this pattern of results did not hold for the eight nonresponders; d-amphetamine had no real effect on their cigarette smoking. Possible reasons for this effect were seen in the subjective ratings of the effects of the drug: Responders said they felt high and drowsy and that the drug had good effects. On objective measures (physiological effects), however, there was no difference between the two groups.

Although this study had no direct evidence, other research provides one plausible explanation for the individual differences seen in d-amphetamine: It results in individual differences in sensitivities to the neurotransmitter dopamine, which is associated with most increases in feeling good or having a positive mood. In other words, responders are more likely to be affected by the stimulant, because their sensitivity to dopamine is greater. To the extent that personality has a biological basis (see Chapter 14), it can affect sensitivity to conditioning. Indeed, many researchers consider dopamine to be the "positive reinforcement" system.

Further evidence that temperamental and biological states affect response sensitivity to conditioning comes from the theory of Jeffrey Gray and Alan Pickering and their reinforcement sensitivity theory (RST; Pickering & Gray, 1999). These two researchers have conducted dozens of studies testing their theory, and although results are usually complex, they generally support the RST.

But the association between reinforcement sensitivities and other personality dimensions and their interaction have only recently begun to be explored. Philip Corr (2002), for instance, conducted one of the first studies to examine the differences in anxiety and impulsivity and their association to response sensitivities. Reinforcement sensitivity theory predicts that introverts, like highly anxious individuals, should be more sensitive to punishment due to their strong need to avoid aversive states. Like extraverts, highly impulsive individuals should be more sensitive to reward because of their strong need to experience positive states. Moreover, in the original formulation of the theory, the personality dimensions should operate completely independently, whereas in Corr's reformulation they can operate somewhat jointly and interdependently. To test the reformulated joint influence hypothesis, Corr predicted that impulsivity should interact with anxiety such that anxious but impulsive people should respond less to a startle stimulus when viewing negative images (slides of mutilated bodies) than anxious but nonimpulsive people. By way of contrast, the original formulation of the RST would predict only that anxious people would be more responsive to the startle during a negative mood state and that impulsivity would have no effect.

Results supported the joint subsystem hypothesis and contradicted the separable subsystem hypothesis. That is, participants who were highly anxious but also impulsive showed a lower startle response especially when viewing negative images, compared to participants who were highly anxious but not impulsive. In other words, for highly anxious participants, impulsivity acts as a buffer to being responsive to negative images. The overall point, nevertheless, still holds: People do not respond to reinforcers in the same way, and personality is one of the key mechanisms that moderates their effect.

Reinforcement and the Brain

Recently, researchers have taken reaction sensitivity research a step further by analyzing individual differences in brain activation as a result of being presented with rewarding stimuli such as food (Beaver et al., 2006). Brain activation can be studied in different ways, but researchers in this study used a technology called functional magnetic resonance imaging (fMRI). fMRI is based on the same technology your doctor may use if he or she orders an MRI of your body to diagnose a health problem. Essentially, MRI technology (both fMRI and regular MRI) detects the flow of oxygen within the brain. Oxygen, carried by the blood, is required for all the brain's activities, and the more oxygen there is in one particular area, the more activity there is there. John Beaver and colleagues (2006) used fMRI to examine what parts of the brain were activated when participants looked at various food-related stimuli and if there were individual differences in personality that predicted this brain activation. Food stimuli were ideal for this experiment because some foods are very rewarding (ice cream, cake, etc.), whereas others are not so rewarding (bland rice, potatoes, etc.).

To conduct their experiment, John Beaver and colleagues (2006) first had participants complete the Behavioral Activation Scale (BAS), which is a self-report measure that captures a person's general tendency to actively pursue rewards. To get an idea of what the BAS measures, think about how you would respond to the following item: "I go out of my way to get things I want" (Carver & White, 1994). Someone who has a high tendency to actively pursue rewards would respond very positively to this item. After completing the BAS, participants were put into an MRI scanner that was specially equipped for this experiment. Specifically, the scanner was fitted with a monitor that allowed the researchers to present pictures to each participant while a technician was simultaneously scanning the participant's brain for activation. Several images were presented to participants while in the scanner but, for the purposes of this discussion, you can think of them as falling into two categories: (1) pleasurable (chocolate cake and ice cream sundaes) and (2) bland (uncooked rice and potatoes). The researchers were able to determine which area of the brain was activated during the presentation of pleasurable versus bland pictures and, more importantly, if individual differences in self-reported behavioral activation were related to this activation.

The researchers found that people who scored higher on the personality variable of behavioral activation experienced increased activation to the pictures of cake and ice cream in five specific areas of the brain (right and left ventral striatum, left amygdala, substantia nigra, and left orbitofrontal cortex) than their low behavioral activation counterparts. In other words, the results supported the more general conclusion that personality is related to differences in biological processes of how we respond to reward. At this early stage in brain activation research it is hard to know what increased activation means, but one hypothesis is that the increased activation experienced by some individuals makes it more difficult for those individuals to say no to appealing stimuli. If that hypothesis proves to be correct in future research, it means that personality variables and individual differences in brain activation play an important role in health outcomes such as obesity, and suggests ways that therapists might use rewards to treat such outcomes. More generally, it also means we will be closer to understanding why and what people find rewarding and reinforcing.

Critique of Skinner

The maverick psychologist Hans J. Eysenck (1988) once criticized Skinner for ignoring such concepts as individual differences, intelligence, genetic factors, and the whole realm of personality. These claims are only partly true, because Skinner did recognize genetic factors, and he did offer a somewhat unenthusiastic definition of personality, saying that it is "at best a repertoire of behavior imparted by an organized set of contingencies" (Skinner, 1974, p. 149). Although Eysenck's opinions are interesting, they do not offer a thoughtful critique of Skinner's work. How does Skinner's theory meet the six criteria of a useful theory?

First, because the theory has spawned a great quantity of research, we rate the theory very high on its ability to *generate research.* Second, most of Skinner's ideas can be either falsified or verified, so we rate the theory high on *falsifiability.*

Third, on its ability to *organize all that is known about human personality,* we give the theory only a moderate rating. Skinner's approach was to describe behavior and the environmental contingencies under which it takes place. His purpose was to bring together these descriptive facts and to generalize from them. Many personality traits, such as those of the Five-Factor Model, can be accounted for by the principles of operant conditioning. However, other concepts such as insight, creativity, motivation, inspiration, and self-efficacy do not fit easily into an operant conditioning framework.

Fourth, as a *guide to action,* we rate Skinner's theory very high. The abundance of descriptive research turned out by Skinner and his followers has made operant conditioning an extremely practical procedure. For example, Skinnerian techniques have been used to help phobic patients overcome their fears, to enhance compliance to medical recommendations, to help people overcome tobacco and drug addictions, to improve eating habits, and to increase assertiveness. In fact,

Skinnerian theory can be applied to almost all areas of training, teaching, and psychotherapy.

The fifth criterion of a useful theory is *internal consistency,* and judged by this standard, we rate Skinnerian theory very high. Skinner defined his terms precisely and operationally, a process greatly aided by the avoidance of fictionalized mentalistic concepts.

Is the theory *parsimonious?* On this final criterion, Skinner's theory is difficult to rate. On one hand, the theory is free from cumbersome hypothetical constructs, but on the other, it demands a novel expression of everyday phrases. For example, instead of saying, "I got so mad at my husband, I threw a dish at him, but missed," one would need to say, "The contingencies of reinforcement within my environment were arranged in such a manner that I observed my organism throwing a dish against the kitchen wall."

Concept of Humanity

Without doubt, B. F. Skinner held a *deterministic view* of human nature, and concepts like free will and individual choice had no place in his behavioral analysis. People are not free but are controlled by environmental forces. They may seem to be motivated by inner causes, but in reality those causes can be traced to sources outside the individual. Self-control depends ultimately on environmental variables and not on some inner strength. When people control their own lives, they do so by manipulating their environment, which in turn shapes their behavior. This environmental approach negates hypothetical constructs such as willpower or responsibility. Human behavior is extremely complex, but people behave under many of the same laws as do machines and animals.

The notion that human behavior is completely determined is an extremely problematic one for many people who believe that they observe daily many examples of free choice in both themselves and others. What accounts for this illusion of freedom? Skinner (1971) held that freedom and dignity are reinforcing concepts because people find satisfaction in the belief that they are free to choose and also in their faith in the basic dignity of human beings. Because these fictional concepts are reinforcing in many modern societies, people tend to behave in ways that increase the probability that these constructs will be perpetuated. Once freedom and dignity lose their reinforcement value, people will stop behaving *as if* they existed.

In the days preceding Louis Pasteur, many people believed that maggots spontaneously generated on the bodies of dead animals. Skinner (1974) used this observation to paint an analogy with human behavior, pointing out that the spontaneous generation of behavior is no more of a reality than the spontaneous generation of maggots. Haphazard or random behavior may appear to be freely chosen, but it is actually the product of haphazard or random environmental and genetic conditions. People are not autonomous, but the illusion of autonomy persists due to incomplete understanding of an individual's history. When people fail to understand behavior, they assign it to some internal concept such as free will, beliefs, intentions, values, or motives. Skinner believed that people are capable of reflecting on their own nature and that this reflective behavior can be observed and studied just like any other.

Is Skinner's concept of humanity optimistic or pessimistic? At first thought, it may appear that a deterministic stance is necessarily pessimistic. However, Skinner's view of human nature is highly *optimistic*. Because human behavior is shaped by the principles of reinforcement, the species is quite adaptable. Of all behaviors, the most satisfying ones tend to increase in frequency of occurrence. People, therefore, learn to live quite harmoniously with their environment. The evolution of the species is in the direction of greater control over environmental variables, which results in an increasing repertoire of behaviors beyond those essential for mere survival. However, Skinner (1987a) was also concerned that modern cultural practices have not yet evolved to the point at which nuclear war, overpopulation, and depletion of natural resources can be stopped. In this sense, he was more of a realist than an optimist.

Nevertheless, Skinner provided a blueprint for a utopian society—*Walden Two* (Skinner, 1948, 1976b). If his recommendations were followed, then people could be taught how to arrange the variables in their environments so that the probability of correct or satisfying solutions would be increased.

Is humanity basically good or evil? Skinner hoped for an idealistic society in which people behave in ways that are loving, sensible, democratic, independent, and good, but people are not by nature this way. But neither are they essentially evil. Within limits set by heredity, people are flexible in their adaptation to the environment, but no evaluation of good or evil should be placed on an individual's behavior. If a person typically behaves altruistically for the good of others, it is because this behavior, either in the species' evolutionary history or in the individual's personal history, has been previously reinforced. If one behaves cowardly, it is because the rewards for cowardice outweigh the aversive variables (Skinner, 1978).

On the dimension of causality versus teleology, Skinner's theory of personality is very high on *causality*. Behavior is caused by the person's history of reinforcement as well as by the species' contingencies for survival and by the evolution of cultures. Although people behave covertly (within the skin) when thinking about the future, all those thoughts are determined by past experiences (Skinner, 1990b).

The complex of environmental contingencies responsible for these thoughts, as well as for all other behaviors, is beyond people's awareness. They rarely have knowledge of the relationship between all genetic and environmental variables and their own behavior. For this reason, we rate Skinner very high on the *unconscious dimension of personality*.

Although he believed that genetics plays an important role in personality development, Skinner held that human personality is largely shaped by the environment. Because an important part of that environment is other people, Skinner's concept of humanity inclines more toward social than toward biological determinants of behavior. As a species, humans have developed to their present form because of particular environmental factors that they have encountered. Climate, geography, and physical strength relative to other animals have all helped shape the human species. But *social environment,* including family structure, early experiences with parents, educational systems, governmental organization, and so forth, has played an even more important role in the development of personality,

Skinner hoped that people might be trustworthy, understanding, warm, and empathic—characteristics that his friendly adversary Carl Rogers (see Chapter 11) believed to be at the core of the psychologically healthy personality. In contrast to Rogers, who believed that these positive behaviors are at least partially the result of the human capacity to be self-directed, Skinner held that they are completely under the control of environmental variables. Humans are not by nature good, but they can become so if they are exposed to the proper contingencies of reinforcement. Although his view of the ideal person would be similar to those of Rogers and Abraham H. Maslow (see Chapter 10), Skinner believed that the means of becoming autonomous, loving, and self-actualizing must not be left to chance, but should be specifically designed into the society.

The history of a person determines behavior, and because each human has a singular history of reinforcement contingencies, behavior and personality are relatively unique. Genetic differences also account for *uniqueness among people.* Biological and historical differences mold unique individuals, and Skinner emphasized people's uniqueness more than he did their similarities.

Key Terms and Concepts

- Skinner's theory of personality is based largely on his *behavioral analysis* of rats and pigeons.
- Although *internal states* such as thinking and feeling exist, they cannot be used as explanations of behavior; only overt behavior can be studied by the scientist.
- Human behavior is shaped by three forces: (1) the individual's personal history of *reinforcement,* (2) *natural selection,* and (3) the *evolution of cultural practices.*
- *Operant conditioning* is a process of changing behavior in which reinforcement (or punishment) is contingent on the occurrence of a particular behavior.
- A *positive reinforcer* is any event that, when added to a situation, increases the probability that a given behavior will occur.
- A *negative reinforcer* is any aversive stimulus that, when removed from the environment, increases the probability of a given behavior.
- Skinner also identified two types of *punishment:* The first is the presentation of an aversive stimulus, and the second involves the removal of a positive stimulus.
- Reinforcement can be either *continuous* or *intermittent,* but intermittent schedules are more efficient.
- The four principal intermittent schedules of reinforcement are the *fixed-ratio, variable-ratio, fixed-interval,* and *variable-interval.*

- *Social control* is achieved through (1) operant conditioning, (2) describing the contingencies of reinforcement, (3) depriving or satiating a person, or (4) physically restraining an individual.
- People can also control their own behavior through *self-control,* but all control ultimately rests with the environment and not free will.
- *Unhealthy behaviors* are learned in the same way as all other behaviors, that is, mostly through operant conditioning.
- To change unhealthy behaviors, behavior therapists use a variety of *behavior modification* techniques, all of which are based on the principles of operant conditioning.

CHAPTER 16

Bandura: Social Cognitive Theory

Bandura

People often have their life path permanently altered by unexpected meetings with others or by unplanned happenings. These chance encounters and fortuitous events frequently determine whom people marry, what career they pursue, where they live, and how they will live their lives.

Many years ago, a young graduate student named Al had a chance encounter that altered the course of his life. One Sunday, Al, who was usually a conscientious student, became bored with an uninteresting reading assignment and decided that a round of golf was preferable to tackling schoolwork. Al checked with a friend, and the two young men headed to the golf course. However, they arrived too late to make their tee time and therefore were bumped to a later time slot. By chance, this male twosome found themselves playing behind two slower-playing female golfers. Rather than "playing through," the two men joined the two women and the two twosomes became one foursome. Thus, a boring reading chore and a delayed tee-off time put two people together who otherwise would never have met. By this series of chance events, Albert Bandura and Ginny (Virginia) Varns met in a sand trap on a golf course. The couple eventually married and had two daughters, Mary and Carol, who like most of us, were the products of a chance encounter.

Chance encounters and fortuitous events have been largely ignored by most personality theorists, even though most of us recognize that we have had unplanned experiences that have greatly changed our lives.

Overview of Social Cognitive Theory

Albert Bandura's **social cognitive theory** takes chance encounters and fortuitous events seriously, even while recognizing that these meetings and events do not invariably alter one's life path. How we react to an expected meeting or event is usually more powerful than the event itself.

Social cognitive theory rests on several basic assumptions. First, the outstanding characteristic of humans is *plasticity;* that is, humans have the flexibility to learn a variety of behaviors in diverse situations. Bandura agrees with Skinner (Chapter 15) that people can and do learn through direct experience, but he places much more emphasis on vicarious learning, that is, learning by observing others. Bandura also stresses the idea that reinforcement can be vicarious; people can be reinforced by observing another person receive a reward. This indirect reinforcement accounts for a good bit of human learning.

Second, through a *triadic reciprocal causation model* that includes behavioral, environment, and personal factors, people have the capacity to regulate their lives. Humans can transform transitory events into relatively consistent ways of evaluating and regulating their social and cultural environments. Without this capacity, people would merely react to sensory experiences and would lack the capacity to anticipate events, create new ideas, or use internal standards to evaluate present experiences. Two important environmental forces in the triadic model are *chance encounters* and *fortuitous events.*

Third, social cognitive theory takes an *agentic perspective,* meaning that humans have the capacity to exercise control over the nature and quality of their lives. People are the producers as well as the products of social systems. An important component of the triadic reciprocal causation model is *self-efficacy*. People's performance is generally enhanced when they have high self-efficacy: that is, the confidence that they can perform those behaviors that will produce desired behaviors in a particular situation. In addition to self-efficacy, both proxy agency and collective efficacy can predict performance. With *proxy agency,* people are able to rely on others for goods and services, whereas *collective efficacy* refers to people's shared beliefs that they can bring about change.

Fourth, people regulate their conduct through both external and internal factors. *External factors* include people's physical and social environments, whereas *internal factors* include self-observation, judgmental proess, and self-reaction.

Fifth, when people find themselves in morally ambiguous situations, they typically attempt to regulate their behavior through *moral agency,* which includes redefining the behavior, disregarding or distorting the consequences of their behavior, dehumanizing or blaming the victims of their behavior, and displacing or diffusing responsibility for their actions.

Biography of Albert Bandura

Albert Bandura was born on December 4, 1925, in Mundare, a small town on the plains of northern Alberta. He grew up the only boy in a family of five older sisters. Both parents had emigrated from eastern European countries while still an adolescent—his father from Poland and his mother from the Ukraine. Bandura was encouraged by his sisters to be independent and self-reliant. He also learned self-directiveness in the town's tiny school that had few teachers and little resources. His high school had only two instructors to teach the entire curriculum. In such an environment, learning was left to the initiative of the students, a situation that well suited a brilliant scholar like Bandura. Other students also seemed to flourish in this atmosphere; virtually all of Bandura's classmates went on to attend college, a very unusual accomplishment during the early 1940s.

After graduating from high school, Bandura spent a summer in the Yukon working on the Alaska highway. This experience brought him into contact with a wide variety of fellow workers, many of whom were fleeing creditors, alimony, or their draft board. In addition, several of his coworkers manifested various degrees of psychopathology. Although his observations of these workers kindled in him an interest in clinical psychology, he did not decide to become a psychologist until after he had enrolled in the University of British Columbia in Vancouver.

Bandura told Richard Evans (Evans, 1989) that his decision to become a psychologist was quite accidental; that is, it was the result of a fortuitous event. In college, Bandura commuted to school with premed and engineering students who were early risers. Rather than do nothing during this early hour, Bandura decided to enroll in a psychology class that happened to be offered at that time period. He found the class fascinating and eventually decided to take a psychology major. Bandura later came to consider fortuitous events (such as riding to school with students who were early risers) to be important influences in people's lives.

After graduating from British Columbia in just 3 years, Bandura looked for a graduate program in clinical psychology that had a strong learning theory base. His advisor recommended the University of Iowa, so Bandura left Canada for the United States. He completed a master's degree in 1951 and a PhD in clinical psychology the following year. Then he spent a year in Wichita completing a postdoctoral internship at the Wichita Guidance Center. In 1953, he joined the faculty at Stanford University where, except for 1 year as Fellow at the Center for Advanced Study in the Behavioral Sciences, he has remained.

Most of Bandura's early publications were in clinical psychology, dealing primarily with psychotherapy and the Rorschach test. Then, in 1958, he collaborated with the late Richard H. Walters, his first doctoral student, to publish a paper on aggressive delinquents. The following year, their book, *Adolescent Aggression* (1959), appeared. Since then, Bandura has continued to publish on a wide variety of subjects, often in collaboration with his graduate students. His most influential books are *Social Learning Theory* (1977), *Social Foundations of Thought and Action* (1986), and *Self-Efficacy: The Exercise of Control* (1997).

Bandura has held more than a dozen offices in prestigious scientific societies, including president of the American Psychological Association (APA) in 1974, president of the Western Psychological Association in 1980, and honorary president of the Canadian Psychological Association in 1999. In addition, he has received more than a dozen honorary degrees from prestigious universities throughout the world. Other honors and awards include the Guggenheim Fellowship in 1972, the Distinguished Scientific Contribution Award from Division 12 (Clinical) of APA in the same year, the Award for Distinguished Scientific Contribution from the APA in 1980, and the Distinguished Scientist Award of the Society of Behavior Medicine. He was elected fellow, American Academy of Arts and Sciences, in 1980. In addition, he has won the Distinguished Contribution Award from the International Society for Research on Aggression; the William James Award of the American Psychological Science for outstanding achievements in psychological science; the Robert Thorndike Award for Distinguished Contribution of Psychology to Education, American Psychological Association; and the 2003–2004 James McKeen Cattell Fellow Award from the American Psychological Society. He has also been elected to the American Academy of Arts and Sciences and to the Institute of Medicine of the National Academy of Sciences. Beginning in 2004, the American Psychology Society, in partnership with Psy Chi—The National Honor Society in Psychology—began awarding an outstanding psychology graduate student with the Albert Bandura Graduate Research Award. Bandura currently holds the David Starr Jordan Professorship of Social Science in Psychology at Stanford University.

Learning

One of the earliest and most basic assumptions of Bandura's social cognitive theory is that humans are quite flexible and capable of learning a multitude of attitudes, skills, and behaviors and that a good bit of those learnings are a result of vicarious experiences. Although people can and do learn from direct experience, much of what they learn is acquired through observing others. Bandura (1986) stated that "if knowledge could be acquired only through the effects of one's own actions, the process of cognitive and social development would be greatly retarded, not to mention exceedingly tedious" (p. 47).

Observational Learning

Bandura believes that *observation* allows people to learn without performing any behavior. People observe natural phenomena, plants, animals, waterfalls, the motion of the moon and stars, and so forth; but especially important to social cognitive theory is the assumption that they learn through observing the behavior of other people. In this respect, Bandura differs from Skinner, who held that enactive behavior is the basic datum of psychological science. He also departs from Skinner in his belief that reinforcement is not essential to learning. Although reinforcement facilitates learning, Bandura says that it is not a necessary condition for it. People can learn, for example, by observing models being reinforced.

Bandura (1986, 2003) believes that observational learning is much more efficient than learning through direct experience. By observing other people, humans are spared countless responses that might be followed by punishment or by no reinforcement. Children observe characters on television, for example, and repeat what they hear or see; they need not enact random behaviors, hoping that some of them will be rewarded.

Modeling

The core of observational learning is **modeling.** Learning through modeling involves adding and subtracting from the observed behavior and generalizing from one observation to another. In other words, modeling involves cognitive processes and is not simply mimicry or imitation. It is more than matching the actions of another; it involves symbolically representing information and storing it for use at a future time (Bandura, 1986, 1994).

Several factors determine whether a person will learn from a model in any particular situation. First, the characteristics of the model are important. People are more likely to model high-status people rather than those of low status, competent individuals rather than unskilled or incompetent ones, and powerful people rather than impotent ones.

Second, the characteristics of the observer affect the likelihood of modeling. People who lack status, skill, or power are most likely to model. Children model more than older people, and novices are more likely than experts to model.

Third, the consequences of the behavior being modeled may have an effect on the observer. The greater the value an observer places on a behavior, the more likely the observer will acquire that behavior. Also, learning may be facilitated when the observer views a model receiving severe punishment; for example, seeing another person receive a severe shock from touching an electric wire teaches the observer a valuable lesson.

Processes Governing Observational Learning

Bandura (1986) recognizes four processes that govern observational learning: attention, representation, behavioral production, and motivation.

Attention   Before we can model another person, we must attend to that person. What factors regulate attention? First, because we have more opportunities to observe individuals with whom we frequently associate, we are most likely to attend to these people. Second, attractive models are more likely to be observed than unattractive ones are—popular figures on television, in sports, or in movies are often closely attended. Also, the nature of the behavior being modeled affects our attention—we observe behavior that we think is important or valuable to us.

Representation   In order for observation to lead to new response patterns, those patterns must be symbolically represented in memory. Symbolic representation need not be verbal, because some observations are retained in imagery and can be summoned in the absence of the physical model. This process is especially important in infancy when verbal skills are not yet developed.

Verbal coding, however, greatly speeds the process of observational learning. With language we can verbally evaluate our behaviors and decide which ones we wish to discard and which ones we desire to try. Verbal coding also helps us to rehearse the behavior symbolically: that is, to tell ourselves over and over again how we will perform the behavior once given the chance. Rehearsal can also entail the actual performance of the modeled response, and this rehearsal aids the retention process.

Behavioral Production   After attending to a model and retaining what we have observed, we then produce the behavior. In converting cognitive representations into appropriate actions, we must ask ourselves several questions about the behavior to be modeled. First we ask, "How can I do this?" After symbolically rehearsing the relevant responses, we try out our new behavior. While performing, we monitor ourselves with the question "What am I doing?" Finally, we evaluate our performance by asking, "Am I doing this right?" This last question is not always easy to answer, especially if it pertains to a motor skill, such as ballet dancing or platform diving, in which we cannot actually see ourselves. For this reason, some athletes use video cameras to help them acquire or improve their motor skills.

Motivation   Observational learning is most effective when learners are motivated to perform the modeled behavior. Attention and representation can lead to the acquisition of learning, but performance is facilitated by motivation to enact that particular behavior. Even though observation of others may teach us *how* to do something, we may have no desire to perform the necessary action. One person can watch another use a power saw or run a vacuum cleaner and not be motivated to try either activity. Most sidewalk superintendents have no wish to emulate the observed construction worker.

Enactive Learning

Every response a person makes is followed by some consequence. Some of these consequences are satisfying, some are dissatisfying, and others are simply not cognitively attended and hence have little effect. Bandura believes that complex human behavior can be learned when people think about and evaluate the consequences of their behaviors.

The consequences of a response serve at least three functions. First, response consequences inform us of the effects of our actions. We can retain this information and use it as a guide for future actions. Second, the consequences of our responses motivate our anticipatory behavior; that is, we are capable of symbolically representing future outcomes and acting accordingly. We not only possess insight but also are capable of foresight. We do not have to suffer the discomfort of cold temperatures before deciding to wear a coat when going outside in freezing weather. Instead, we anticipate the effects of cold, wet weather and dress accordingly. Third, the consequences of responses serve to reinforce behavior, a function that has been firmly documented by Skinner (Chapter 15) and other reinforcement theorists. Bandura (1986), however, contends that, although reinforcement may at times be unconscious and automatic, complex behavioral patterns are greatly facilitated by cognitive intervention. He maintained that learning occurs much more efficiently when the learner is cognitively involved in the learning situation and understands what behaviors precede successful responses.

In summary, Bandura believes that new behaviors are acquired through two major kinds of learning: observational learning and enactive learning. The core element of observational learning is modeling, which is facilitated by observing appropriate activities, properly coding these events for representation in memory, actually performing the behavior, and being sufficiently motivated. Enactive learning allows people to acquire new patterns of complex behavior through direct experience by thinking about and evaluating the consequences of their behaviors. The learning process allows people to have some degree of control over the events that shape the course of their lives. Control, however, rests with a three-way reciprocal interaction of person variables, behavior, and environment.

Triadic Reciprocal Causation

In Chapter 15, we saw that Skinner believed that behavior is a function of the environment; that is, behavior ultimately can be traced to forces outside the person. As environmental contingencies change, behavior changes. But what impetus changes the environment? Skinner acknowledged that human behavior can exercise some measure of countercontrol over the environment, but he insisted that, in the final analysis, behavior is environmentally determined. Other theorists, such as Gordon Allport (Chapter 13) and Hans Eysenck (Chapter 14) emphasized the importance of traits or personal disposition in shaping behavior. In general, these theorists held that personal factors interact with environmental conditions to produce behavior.

Albert Bandura (1986, 1999b, 2001, 2002b) adopts quite a different stance. His social cognitive theory explains psychological functioning in terms of *triadic reciprocal causation.* This system assumes that human action is a result of an interaction among three variables—environment, behavior, and person. By "person" Bandura means largely, but not exclusively, such cognitive factors as memory, anticipation, planning, and judging. Because people possess and use these cognitive capacities, they have some capacity to select or to restructure their environment: That is, cognition at least partially determines which environmental events people attend to, what value they place on these events, and how they organize these events for future use. Although cognition can have a strong causal effect on both environment and behavior, it is not an autonomous entity, independent of those two variables. Bandura (1986) criticized those theorists who attribute the cause of human behavior

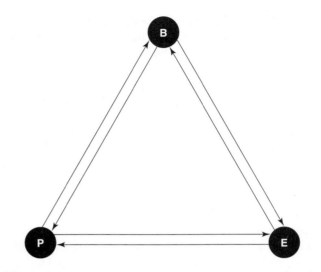

FIGURE 16.1   Bandura's concept of **reciprocal causation.** Human functioning is a product of the interaction of (B) behavior, (P) person variables, and (E) environment.

From Albert Bandura, 1994. Social cognitive theory and mass communication. In J. Bryant & D. Zillmann (Eds.), *Media Effects: Advances in Theory and Research* (p. 62). Hillsdale, NJ: Erlbaum. Reproduced by permission.

to internal forces such as instincts, drives, needs, or intentions. Cognition itself is determined, being formed by both behavior and environment.

Triadic reciprocal causation is represented schematically in Figure 16.1, where B signifies behavior; E is the external environment; and P represents the person, including that person's gender, social position, size, and physical attractiveness, but especially cognitive factors such as thought, memory, judgment, foresight, and so on.

Bandura uses the term "reciprocal" to indicate a triadic interaction of forces, not a similar or opposite counteraction. The three reciprocal factors do not need to be of equal strength or to make equal contributions. The relative potency of the three varies with the individual and with the situation. At times, behavior might be the most powerful, as when a person plays the piano for her own enjoyment. Other times, the environment exerts the greatest influence, as when a boat overturns and every survivor begins thinking and behaving in a very similar fashion. Although behavior and environment can at times be the most powerful contributors to performance, cognition (person) is usually the strongest contributor to performance. Cognition would likely be activated in the examples of the person playing the piano for her own enjoyment and the survivors of an overturned boat. The relative influence of behavior, environment, and person depends on which of the triadic factors is strongest at a particular moment (Bandura, 1997).

An Example of Triadic Reciprocal Causation

Consider this example of triadic reciprocal causation. A child begging her father for a second brownie is, from the father's viewpoint, an environmental event. If the father automatically (without thought) were to give the child a second brownie, then the two would be conditioning each other's behavior in the Skinnerian sense. The behavior of the father would be controlled by the environment; but his behavior, in turn, would have a countercontrolling effect on his environment, namely the child. In Bandura's theory, however, the father is capable of thinking about the consequences of rewarding or ignoring the child's behavior. He may think, "If I give her another brownie, she will stop crying temporarily, but in future cases, she will be more likely to persist until I give in to her now. Therefore, I will not allow her to have another brownie." Hence, the father has an effect on both his environment (the child) and his own behavior (rejecting his daughter's request). The child's subsequent behavior (father's environment) helps shape the cognition and the behavior of the father. If the child stops begging, the father may then have other thoughts. For example, he may evaluate his behavior by thinking, "I'm a good father because I did the right thing." The change in environment also allows the father to pursue different behaviors. Thus, his subsequent behavior is partially determined by the reciprocal interaction of his environment, cognition, and behavior.

This example illustrates the reciprocal interaction of behavioral, environmental, and personal factors from the father's point of view. First, the child's pleas affected the father's behavior ($E \Rightarrow B$); they also partially determined the father's cognition ($E \Rightarrow P$); the father's behavior helped shape the child's behavior, that is, his own environment ($B \Rightarrow E$); his behavior also impinged on his own thoughts ($B \Rightarrow P$); and his cognition partially determined his behavior ($P \Rightarrow B$). To complete the cycle, P (person) must influence E (environment). How can the father's cognition directly shape the environment without first being transformed into behavior? It cannot. However, P does not signify cognition alone; it stands for person. Bandura (1999b) hypothesized that "people evoke different reactions from their social environment by their physical characteristics—such as their age, size, race, sex, and physical attractiveness—even before they say or do anything" (p. 158). The father, then, by virtue of his role and status as a father and perhaps in conjunction with his size and strength, has a decided effect on the child. Thus, the final causal link is completed ($P \Rightarrow E$).

Chance Encounters and Fortuitous Events

Although people can and do exercise a significant amount of control over their lives, they cannot predict or anticipate all possible environmental changes. Bandura is the only personality theorist to seriously consider the possible importance of these *chance encounters and fortuitous events.*

Bandura (1998a) defined a **chance encounter** as "an unintended meeting of persons unfamiliar to each other" (p. 95). A **fortuitous event** is an environmental experience that is unexpected and unintended. The everyday lives of people are affected to a greater or lesser extent by the people they chance to meet and by random events they could not predict. One's marital partner, occupation, and place of residence may largely be the result of a fortuitous meeting that was unplanned and unexpected.

Just as fortuity has influenced the lives of all of us, it has shaped the lives and careers of famous personality theorists. Two such examples are Abraham H. Maslow (Chapter 10) and Hans J. Eysenck (Chapter 14). As a young man, Maslow was exceedingly shy, especially with women. At the same time, he was passionately in love with his cousin Bertha Goodman, but he was too bashful to express his love. One day while he was visiting his cousin's home, Bertha's older sister pushed him toward his beloved cousin, saying: "For the love of Pete, kiss her, will ya!" (Hoffman, 1988, p. 29). Maslow did, and to his surprise, Bertha did not fight back. She kissed him, and from that moment, Maslow's previously aimless life became transformed.

Also, Hans Eysenck, the noted British psychologist, came to psychology completely by chance. He had intended to study physics at the University of London, but first he had to pass an entrance examination. After waiting a year to take the exam, he was told that he had prepared for the wrong test, and that he would have to wait another year to take the right one. Rather than delaying his education further, he asked whether there might be any scientific subject that he could pursue. When told that he could enroll in a psychology program, Eysenck asked, "What on earth is psychology?" (Eysenck, 1982, p. 290). Eysenck, of course, went on to major in psychology and to become one of the world's most famous psychologists.

Fortuity adds a separate dimension in any scheme used to predict human behavior, and it makes accurate predictions practically impossible. However, chance encounters influence people only by entering the triadic reciprocal causation paradigm at point E (environment) and adding to the mutual interaction of person, behavior, and environment. In this sense, chance encounters influence people in the same manner as do planned events. Once a chance encounter occurs, people behave toward their new acquaintance according to their attitudes, belief systems, and interests as well as to the other person's reaction to them. Thus, whereas many chance encounters and unplanned events have little or no influence on people's behavior, "others have more lasting effects, and still others thrust people into new life trajectories" (Bandura, 2001, p. 12).

Chance encounters and fortuitous events are not uncontrollable. Indeed, people can make chance happen. A divorced man looking for an opportunity to remarry will increase his chance of meeting a potential wife by perusing a proactive course of action, for example, by joining a singles club, going to places where he is likely to find single women, or asking a friend to introduce him to an eligible potential mate. If he meets an eligible and desirable woman, he increases his chances for a lasting relationship if he has prepared himself to be attractive or interesting to women. Bandura (2001) quotes Louis Pasteur: "Chance favors only the prepared mind" (p. 12). Conversely, the prepared person is able to escape unpleasant chance encounters and fortuitous events by anticipating their possibility and taking steps to minimize any negative impact they may have on future development.

Human Agency

Social cognitive theory takes an agentic view of personality, meaning that humans have the capacity to exercise control over their own lives (2002b). Indeed, **human agency** is the essence of humanness. Bandura (2001) believes that people are self-regulating, proactive, self-reflective, and self-organizing and that they have the power to influence their own actions to produce desired consequences. Human agency does not mean that people possess a homunculus—that is, an autonomous agent—making decisions that are consistent with their view of self. Neither does it mean that people react automatically to external and internal events. Human agency is not a thing but an active process of exploring, manipulating, and influencing the environment in order to attain desired outcomes.

Core Features of Human Agency

Bandura (2001, 2004) discusses four core features of human agency: intentionality, forethought, self-reactiveness, and self-reflectiveness.

Intentionality refers to acts a person performs intentionally. An intention includes planning, but it also involves actions. "It is not simply an expectation or prediction of future actions but a proactive commitment to bringing them about" (2001, p. 6). Intentionality does not mean that all of a person's plans will be brought to fruition. People continually change their plans as they become aware of the consequences of their actions.

People also possess *forethought* to set goals, to anticipate likely outcomes of their actions, and to select behaviors that will produce desired outcomes and avoid undesirable ones. Forethought enables people to break free from the constraints of their environment. If behavior were completely a function of the environment, then behavior would be more variable and less consistent because we would constantly be reacting to the great diversity of environmental stimuli. "If actions were determined solely by external rewards and punishments, people would behave like weathervanes" (Bandura, 1986, p. 335). But people do not behave like weathervanes, "constantly shifting direction to conform to whatever influence happened to impinge upon them at the moment" (Bandura, 2001, p. 7).

People do more than plan and contemplate future behaviors. They are also capable of *self-reactiveness* in the process of motivating and regulating their own actions. People not only make choices but they monitor their progress toward fulfilling those choices. Bandura (2001) recognizes that setting goals is not sufficient to attaining desired consequences. Goals must be specific, be within a person's ability to achieve, and reflect potential accomplishments that are not too far in the future. (We discuss self-regulation more fully in the section titled Self-Regulation.)

Finally, people have *self-reflectiveness.* They are examiners of their own functioning; they can think about and evaluate their motivations, values, and the meanings of their life goals, and they can think about the adequacy of their own thinking. They can also evaluate the effect that other people's actions have on them. People's most crucial self-reflective mechanism is *self-efficacy:* that is, their beliefs that they are capable of performing actions that will produce a desired effect.

Self-Efficacy

How people act in a particular situation depends on the reciprocity of behavioral, environmental, and cognitive conditions, especially those cognitive factors that relate to their beliefs that they can or cannot execute the behavior necessary to produce desired outcomes in any particular situation. Bandura (1997) calls these expectations **self-efficacy.** According to Bandura (1994), "people's beliefs in their personal efficacy influence what courses of action they choose to pursue, how much effort they will invest in activities, how long they will persevere in the face of obstacles and failure experiences, and their resiliency following setbacks" (p. 65). Although self-efficacy has a powerful causal influence on people's actions, it is not the sole determinant. Rather, self-efficacy combines with environment, prior behavior, and other personal variables, especially outcome expectations, to produce behavior.

In the triadic reciprocal causal model, which postulates that the environment, behavior, and person have an interactive influence on one another, self-efficacy refers to the P (person) factor.

What Is Self-Efficacy?

Bandura (2001) defined self-efficacy as "people's beliefs in their capability to exercise some measure of control over their own functioning and over environmental events" (p. 10). Bandura contends that "efficacy beliefs are the foundation of human agency" (p. 10). People who believe that they can do something that has the potential to alter environmental events are more likely to act and more likely to be successful than those people with low self-efficacy.

Self-efficacy is not the expectation of our action's *outcomes.* Bandura (1986, 1997) distinguished between efficacy expectations and *outcome expectations.* Efficacy refers to people's confidence that they have the ability to perform certain behaviors, whereas an outcome expectancy refers to one's prediction of the likely *consequences* of that behavior. Outcome must not be confused with successful accomplishment of an act; it refers to the consequences of behavior, not the completion of the act itself. For example, a job applicant may have confidence that she will perform well during a job interview, have the ability to answer any possible questions, remain relaxed and controlled, and exhibit an appropriate level of friendly behavior. Therefore, she has high self-efficacy with regard to the employment interview. However, despite these high efficacy expectations, she may have low outcome expectations. A low outcome expectancy would exist if she believes that she has little chance of being offered a position. This judgment might be due to unpromising environmental conditions, such as high unemployment, depressed economy, or superior competition. In addition, other personal factors such as age, gender, height, weight, or physical health may negatively affect outcome expectancies.

Besides being different from outcome expectancies, self-efficacy must be distinguished from several other concepts. First, efficacy does not refer to the ability to execute basic motor skills such as walking, reaching, or grasping. Also, efficacy does not imply that we can perform designated behaviors without anxiety, stress, or fear; it is merely our judgment, accurate or faulty, about whether or not we can execute the required actions. Finally, judgments of efficacy are not the same as levels of aspiration. Heroin addicts, for example, often aspire to be drug free but may have little confidence in their ability to successfully break the habit (Bandura, 1997).

Self-efficacy is not a global or generalized concept, such as self-esteem or self-confidence. People can have high self-efficacy in one situation and low self-efficacy in another. Self-efficacy varies from situation to situation depending on the competencies required for different activities; the presence or absence of other people; the perceived competence of these other people, especially if they are competitors; the person's predisposition to attend to failure of performance rather than to success; and the accompanying physiological states, particularly the presence of fatigue, anxiety, apathy, or despondency.

High and low efficacy combine with responsive and unresponsive environments to produce four possible predictive variables (Bandura, 1997). When efficacy is high and the environment is responsive, outcomes are most likely to be successful. When low efficacy is combined with a responsive environment, people may become depressed when they observe that others are successful at tasks that seem too difficult for them. When people with high efficacy encounter unresponsive environmental situations, they usually intensify their efforts to change the environment. They may use protest, social activism, or even force to instigate change; but if all efforts fail, Bandura hypothesizes, either they will give up that course and take on a new one or they will seek a more responsive environment. Finally, when low self-efficacy combines with an unresponsive environment, people are likely to feel apathy, resignation, and helplessness. For example, a junior executive with low self-efficacy who realizes the difficulties of becoming company president will develop feelings of discouragement, give up, and fail to transfer productive efforts toward a similar but lesser goal.

What Contributes to Self-Efficacy?

Personal efficacy is acquired, enhanced, or decreased through any one or combination of four sources: (1) mastery experiences, (2) social modeling, (3) social persuasion, and (4) physical and emotional states (Bandura, 1997). With each method, information about oneself and the environment is cognitively processed and, together with recollections of previous experiences, alters perceived self-efficacy.

The most influential source of self-efficacy is performance.

Mastery Experiences   The most influential sources of self-efficacy are *mastery experiences,* that is, past performances (Bandura, 1997). In general, successful performance raises efficacy expectancies; failure tends to lower them. This general statement has six corollaries.

First, successful performance raises self-efficacy in proportion to the difficulty of the task. Highly skilled tennis players gain little self-efficacy by defeating clearly inferior opponents, but they gain much by performing well against superior opponents. Second, tasks successfully accomplished by oneself are more efficacious than those completed with the help of others. In sports, team accomplishments do not increase personal efficacy as much as do individual achievements. Third, failure is most likely to decrease efficacy when we know that we put forth our best effort. To fail when only half-trying is not as inefficacious as to fall short in spite of our best efforts. Fourth, failure under conditions of high emotional arousal or distress are not as self-debilitating as failure under maximal conditions. Fifth, failure prior to establishing a sense of mastery is more detrimental to feelings of personal efficacy than later failure. A sixth and related corollary is that occasional failure has little effect on efficacy, especially for people with a generally high expectancy of success.

Social Modeling   A second source of efficacy is social modeling: that is, **vicarious experiences** provided by other people. Our self-efficacy is raised when we observe the accomplishments of another person of equal competence, but is lowered when we see a peer fail. When the other person is dissimilar to us, social modeling will have little effect on our self-efficacy. An old, sedentary coward watching a young, active, brave circus performer successfully walk a high wire will undoubtedly have little enhancement of efficacy expectations for duplicating the feat.

In general, the effects of social modeling are not as strong as those of personal performance in raising levels of efficacy, but they can have powerful effects where inefficacy is concerned. Watching a swimmer of equal ability fail to negotiate a choppy river will likely dissuade the observer from attempting the same task. The effects of this vicarious experience may even last a lifetime.

Social Persuasion   Self-efficacy can also be acquired or weakened through social persuasion (Bandura, 1997). The effects of this source are limited, but under proper conditions, persuasion from others can raise or lower self-efficacy. The first condition is that a person must believe the persuader. Exhortations or criticisms from a credible source have more efficacious power than do those from a noncredible person. Boosting self-efficacy through social persuasion will be effective only if the activity one is being encouraged to try is within one's repertoire of behavior. No amount of verbal persuasion can alter a person's efficacy judgment on the ability to run 100 meters in less than 8 seconds.

Bandura (1986) hypothesizes that the efficacious power of suggestion is directly related to the perceived status and authority of the persuader. Status and authority, of course, are not identical. For example, a psychotherapist's suggestion to phobic patients that they can ride in a crowded elevator is more likely to increase self-efficacy than will encouragement from one's spouse or children. But if that same psychotherapist tells patients that they have the ability to change a faulty light

Verbal persuasion can raise or lower self-efficacy.

switch, these patients will probably not enhance their self-efficacy for this activity. Also, social persuasion is most effective when combined with successful performance. Persuasion may convince someone to attempt an activity, and if performance is successful, both the accomplishment and the subsequent verbal rewards will increase future efficacy.

Physical and Emotional States   The final source of efficacy is people's physiological and emotional states (Bandura, 1997). Strong emotion ordinarily lowers performance; when people experience intense fear, acute anxiety, or high levels of stress, they are likely to have lower efficacy expectancies. An actor in a school play knows his lines during rehearsal but realizes that the fear he feels on opening night may block his recall. Incidentally, for some situations, emotional arousal, if not too intense, is associated with *increased* performance, so that moderate anxiety felt by that actor on opening night may raise his efficacy expectancies. Most people, when not afraid, have the ability to successfully handle poisonous snakes. They merely have to grasp the snake firmly behind the head; but for many people, the fear that accompanies snake handling is debilitating and greatly lowers their performance expectancy.

Psychotherapists have long recognized that a reduction in anxiety or an increase in physical relaxation can facilitate performance. Arousal information is related to several variables. First, of course, is the level of arousal—ordinarily, the higher the arousal, the lower the self-efficacy. The second variable is the perceived realism of the arousal. If one knows that the fear is realistic, as when driving on an icy mountain road, personal efficacy may be raised. However, when one is cognizant of the absurdity of the phobia—for example, fear of the outdoors—then the emotional arousal tends to lower efficacy. Finally, the nature of the task is an added variable. Emotional arousal may facilitate the successful completion of simple tasks, but it is likely to interfere with performance of complex activities.

Although self-efficacy is "the foundation of human agency" (Bandura, 2001, p. 10), it is not the only mode of human agency. People can also exercise control over their lives through proxy and through collective efficacy.

Proxy Agency

Proxy involves indirect control over those social conditions that affect everyday living. Bandura (2001) noted that "no one has the time, energy, and resources to master every realm of everyday life. Successful functioning necessarily involves a blend of reliance on proxy agency in some areas of functioning" (p. 13). In modern American society, people would be nearly helpless if they relied solely on personal accomplishments to regulate their lives. Most people do not have the personal capability to repair an air conditioner, a camera, or an automobile. Through proxy agency, however, they can accomplish their goal by relying on other people to repair these objects. People attempt to change their daily lives by contacting their congressional representative or another potentially influential person; they acquire mentors to help them learn useful skills; they hire a young neighbor to mow their grass; they rely on international news services to learn of recent events; they retain lawyers to solve legal problems; and so on.

Proxy, however, has a downside. By relying too much on the competence and power of others, people may weaken their sense of personal and collective efficacy. One spouse may become dependent on the other to care for the household; late adolescent or early adult-age children may expect parents to take care of them; and citizens may learn to rely on their government to provide for the necessities of life.

Collective Efficacy

The third mode of human agency is *collective efficacy*. Bandura (2000) defined **collective efficacy** as "people's shared beliefs in their collective power to produce desired results" (p. 75). In other words, collective efficacy is the confidence people have that their combined efforts will bring about group accomplishments. Bandura (2000) suggested two techniques for measuring collective efficacy. The first is to combine individual members' evaluations of their personal capabilities to enact behaviors that benefit the group. For example, actors in a play would have high collective efficacy if all had confidence in their personal ability to adequately perform their roles. The second approach proposed by Bandura is to measure the confidence each person has in the group's ability to bring about a desired outcome. For example, baseball players may have little confidence in each of their teammates but possess high confidence that their *team* will perform quite well. These two slightly different approaches to collective efficacy call for separate measuring techniques.

Collective efficacy does not spring from a collective "mind" but rather from the personal efficacy of many individuals working together. A group's collective efficacy, however, depends not only on the knowledge and skills of its individual members but also on their beliefs that they can work together in a coordinated and interactive fashion (Bandura, 2000). People may have high self-efficacy but low collective efficacy. For example, a woman may have high personal efficacy that she can pursue a healthy lifestyle, but she may have low collective efficacy that she can reduce environmental pollution, hazardous working conditions, or the threat of infectious disease.

Bandura (1998b) pointed out that different cultures have different levels of collective efficacy and work more productively under different systems. For example, people in the United States, an individualistic culture, feel greater *self-efficacy* and work best under an individually oriented system, whereas people in China, a collectivist culture, feel greater *collective efficacy* and work best under a group-oriented system.

Bandura (1997, 1998b, 2001) lists several factors that can undermine collective efficacy. First, humans live in a transnational world; what happens in one part of the globe can affect people in other countries, giving them a sense of helplessness. Destruction of the Amazon rain forests, international trade policies, or depletion of the ozone layers, for example, can affect the lives of people everywhere and undermine their confidence to shape a better world for themselves.

Second, recent technology that people neither understand nor believe that they can control may lower their sense of collective efficacy. In past years, many motorists, for example, had confidence in their ability to keep their car in running condition. With the advent of computerized controls in modern automobiles, many moderately skilled mechanics not only have lost personal efficacy for repairing their vehicle but also have low collective efficacy for reversing the trend toward more and more complicated automobiles.

A third condition undermining collective efficacy is the complex social machinery, with layers of bureaucracy that prevent social change. People who attempt to change bureaucratic structures are often discouraged by failure or by the long lapse of time between their actions and any noticeable change. Having become discouraged, many people, "rather than developing the means for shaping their own future, . . . grudgingly relinquish control to technical specialists and to public officials" (Bandura, 1995, p. 37).

Fourth, the tremendous scope and magnitude of human problems can undermine collective efficacy. Wars, famine, overpopulation, crime, and natural disasters are but a few of the global problems that can leave people with a sense of powerlessness. Despite these huge transnational problems, Bandura believes that positive changes are possible if people will persevere with their collective efforts and not become discouraged.

Taking a worldwide view, Bandura (2000) concluded that "as globalization reaches ever deeper into people's lives, a resilient sense of shared efficacy becomes critical to furthering their common interests" (p. 78).

Self-Regulation

When people have high levels of self-efficacy, are confident in their reliance on proxies, and possess solid collective efficacy, they will have considerable capacity to regulate their own behavior. Bandura (1994) believes that people use both reactive and proactive strategies for self-regulation. That is, they *reactively* attempt to reduce the discrepancies between their accomplishments and their goal; but after they close those discrepancies, they *proactively* set newer and higher goals for themselves.

"People motivate and guide their actions through proactive control by setting themselves valued goals that create a state of disequilibrium and then mobilizing their abilities and effort based on anticipatory estimation of what is required to reach the goals" (p. 63). The notion that people seek a state of disequilibrium is similar to Gordon Allport's belief that people are motivated at least as much to create tension as to reduce it (see Chapter 13).

What processes contribute to this self-regulation? First, people possess limited ability to manipulate the external factors that feed into the reciprocal interactive paradigm. Second, people are capable of monitoring their own behavior and evaluating it in terms of both proximate and distant goals. Behavior, then, stems from a reciprocal influence of both external and internal factors.

External Factors in Self-Regulation

External factors affect self-regulation in at least two ways. First, they provide us with a standard for evaluating our own behavior. Standards do not stem solely from internal forces. Environmental factors, interacting with personal influences, shape individual standards for evaluation. By precept, we learn from parents and teachers the value of honest and friendly behavior; by direct experience, we learn to place more value on being warm and dry than on being cold and wet; and through observing others, we evolve a multitude of standards for evaluating self-performance. In each of these examples, personal factors affect which standards we will learn, but environmental forces also play a role.

Second, external factors influence self-regulation by providing the means for reinforcement. Intrinsic rewards are not always sufficient; we also need incentives that emanate from external factors. An artist, for example, may require more reinforcement than self-satisfaction to complete a large mural. Environmental support in the form of a monetary retainer or praise and encouragement from others may also be necessary.

The incentives to complete a lengthy project usually come from the environment and often take the form of small rewards contingent upon the completion of subgoals. The artist may enjoy a cup of coffee after having painted the hand of one of the subjects or break for lunch after finishing another small section of the mural. However, self-reward for inadequate performance is likely to result in environmental sanctions. Friends may criticize or mock the artist's work, patrons may withdraw financial support, or the artist may be self-critical. When performance does not meet self-standards, we tend to withhold rewards from ourselves.

Internal Factors in Self-Regulation

External factors interact with internal or personal factors in self-regulation. Bandura (1986, 1996) recognizes three internal requirements in the ongoing exercise of self-influence: (1) self-observation, (2) judgmental processes, and (3) self-reaction.

Self-Observation

The first internal factor in self-regulation is *self-observation* of performance. We must be able to monitor our own performance, even though the attention we give to it need not be complete or even accurate. We attend selectively to some aspects of our behavior and ignore others altogether. What we observe depends on interests and other preexisting self-conceptions. In achievement situations, such as painting pictures, playing games, or taking examinations, we pay attention to the quality, quantity, speed, or originality of our work. In interpersonal situations, such as meeting new acquaintances or reporting on events, we monitor the sociability or morality of our conduct.

Judgmental Process

Self-observation alone does not provide a sufficient basis for regulating behavior. We must also evaluate our performance. This second process, *judgmental process,* helps us regulate our behavior through the process of cognitive mediation. We are capable not only of reflective self-awareness but also of judging the worth of our actions on the basis of goals we have set for ourselves. More specifically, the judgmental process depends on personal standards, referential performances, valuation of activity, and performance attribution.

Personal standards allow us to evaluate our performances without comparing them to the conduct of others. To a profoundly handicapped 10-year-old child, the act of tying his shoelaces may be highly prized. He need not devalue his accomplishment simply because other children can perform this same act at a younger age.

Personal standards, however, are a limited source of evaluation. For most of our activities, we evaluate our performances by comparing them to a *standard of reference.* Students compare their test scores to those of their classmates, and tennis players judge their personal skills against those of other players. In addition, we use our own previous levels of accomplishment as a reference for evaluating present performance: "Has my singing voice improved over the years?" "Is my teaching ability better now than ever?" Also, we may judge our performance by comparing it to that of a single individual—a brother, sister, parent, or even a hated rival—or we can compare it to a standard norm such as par in golf or a perfect score in bowling.

Besides personal and reference standards, the judgmental process is also dependent on the overall *value* we place on an activity. If we place minor value on our ability to wash dishes or dust furniture, then we will spend little time or effort in trying to improve these abilities. On the other hand, if we place high value on getting ahead in the business world or attaining a professional or graduate degree, then we will expend much effort to achieve success in these areas.

Finally, self-regulation also depends on how we judge the causes of our behavior, that is, *performance attribution.* If we believe that our success is due to our own efforts, we will take pride in our accomplishments and tend to work harder to attain our goals. However, if we attribute our performance to external factors, we will not derive as much self-satisfaction and will probably not put forth strenuous effort to attain our goals. Conversely, if we believe that we are responsible for our own failures or inadequate performance, we will work more readily toward self-regulation than if we are convinced that our shortcomings and our fears are due to factors beyond our control (Bandura, 1986, 1996).

Self-Reaction

The third and final internal factor in self-regulation is *self-reaction.* People respond positively or negatively to their behaviors depending on how these behaviors measure up to their personal standards. That is, people create incentives for their own actions through self-reinforcement or self-punishment. For example, a diligent student who has completed a reading assignment may reward herself by watching her favorite television program.

Self-reinforcement does not rest on the fact that it immediately follows a response: Rather, it relies in large part on the use of our cognitive ability to mediate the consequences of behavior. People set standards for performance that, when met, tend to regulate behavior by such self-produced rewards as pride and self-satisfaction. When people fail to meet their standards, their behavior is followed by self-dissatisfaction or self-criticism.

This concept of self-mediated consequences is a sharp contrast to Skinner's notion that the consequences of behavior are environmentally determined. Bandura hypothesizes that people work to attain rewards and to avoid punishments according to self-erected standards. Even when rewards are tangible, they are often accompanied by self-mediated intangible incentives such as a sense of accomplishment. The Nobel Prize, for example, carries a substantial cash award, but its greater value to most recipients must be the feeling of pride or self-satisfaction in performing the tasks that led to the award.

Self-Regulation Through Moral Agency

People also regulate their actions through moral standards of conduct. Bandura (1999a) sees moral agency as having two aspects: (1) doing no harm to people and (2) proactively helping people. Our self-regulative mechanisms, however, do not affect other people until we act on them. We have no automatic internal controlling agent such as a conscience or superego that invariably directs our behavior toward morally consistent values. Bandura (2002a) insists that moral precepts predict moral behavior only when those precepts are converted to action. In other words, self-regulatory influences are not automatic but operate only if they are activated, a concept Bandura calls **selective activation.**

How can people with strong moral beliefs concerning the worth and dignity of all humankind behave in an inhumane manner to other humans? Bandura's (1994) answer is that "people do not ordinarily engage in reprehensible conduct until they have justified to themselves the morality of their actions" (p. 72). By justifying the morality of their actions, they can separate or disengage themselves from the consequences of their behavior, a concept Bandura calls **disengagement of internal control.**

Disengagement techniques allow people, individually or working in concert with others, to engage in inhumane behaviors while retaining their moral standards (Bandura, 2002a). For example, politicians frequently convince their constituents of the morality of war. Thus, wars are fought against "evil" people, people who deserve to be defeated or even annihilated.

Selective activation and disengagement of internal control allow people with the same moral standards to behave quite differently, just as they permit the same person to behave differently in different situations. Figure 16.2 illustrates the various mechanisms through which self-control is disengaged or selectively activated. First, people can *redefine or reconstruct the nature of the behavior itself* by such techniques

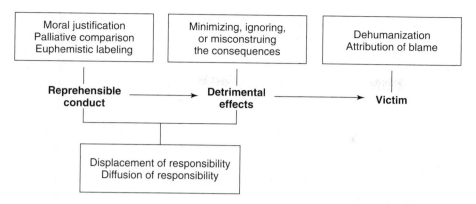

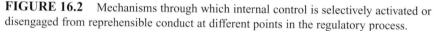

FIGURE 16.2   Mechanisms through which internal control is selectively activated or disengaged from reprehensible conduct at different points in the regulatory process.

as morally justifying it, making advantageous comparisons, or euphemistically labeling their actions. Second, they can *minimize, ignore, or distort the detrimental consequences of their behavior.* Third, they can *blame or dehumanize the victim.* Fourth, they can *displace or diffuse responsibility* for their behavior by obscuring the relationship between their actions and the effects of those actions.

Redefine the Behavior

With *redefinition of behavior,* people justify otherwise reprehensible actions by a cognitive restructuring that allows them to minimize or escape responsibility. They can relieve themselves of responsibility for their behavior by at least three techniques (see upper-left box in Figure 16.2).

The first is *moral justification,* in which otherwise culpable behavior is made to seem defensible or even noble. Bandura (1986) cited the example of World War I hero Sergeant Alvin York who, as a conscientious objector, believed that killing was morally wrong. After his battalion commander quoted from the Bible the conditions under which it was morally justified to kill and after a long prayer vigil, York became convinced that killing enemy soldiers was morally defensible. Following his redefining killing, York proceeded to kill and capture more than 100 German soldiers and, as a result, became one of the greatest war heroes in American history.

A second method of reducing responsibility through redefining wrongful behavior is to make advantageous or *palliative comparisons* between that behavior and the even greater atrocities committed by others. The child who vandalizes a school building uses the excuse that others broke even more windows.

A third technique in redefining behavior is the use of *euphemistic labels.* Politicians who have pledged not to raise taxes speak of "revenue enhancement" rather than taxes; some Nazi leaders called the murder of millions of Jews the "purification of Europe" or "the final solution."

Disregard or Distort the Consequences of Behavior

A second method of avoiding responsibility involves *distorting or obscuring the relationship between the behavior and its detrimental consequences* (see upper-center box of Figure 16.2). Bandura (1986, 1999a) recognized at least three techniques of distorting or obscuring the detrimental consequences of one's actions. First, people can *minimize the consequences of their behavior*. For example, a driver runs a red light and strikes a pedestrian. As the injured party lies bleeding and unconscious on the pavement, the driver says, "She's not really hurt badly. She's going to be okay."

Second, people can *disregard or ignore the consequences of their actions,* as when they do not see firsthand the harmful effects of their behavior. In wartime, heads of state and army generals seldom view the total destruction and death resulting from their decisions.

Finally, people can *distort or misconstrue the consequences of their actions,* as when a parent beats a child badly enough to cause serious bruises but explains that the child needs discipline in order to mature properly.

Dehumanize or Blame the Victims

Third, people can obscure responsibility for their actions by either *dehumanizing their victims or attributing blame to them* (see upper-right box in Figure 16.2). In time of war, people often see the enemy as subhuman, so they need not feel guilty for killing enemy soldiers. At various times in U.S. history, Jews, African Americans, Hispanic Americans, Native Americans, Asian Americans, homosexuals, and street people have become *dehumanized victims.* Otherwise kind, considerate, and gentle people have perpetrated acts of violence, insult, or other forms of mistreatment against these groups in order to avoid responsibility for their own behavior.

When victims are not dehumanized, they are sometimes *blamed* for the perpetrator's culpable conduct. A rapist may blame his victim for his crime, citing her provocative dress or behavior.

Displace or Diffuse Responsibility

The fourth method of dissociating actions from their consequences is to *displace or diffuse responsibility* (see lower box in Figure 16.2). With *displacement,* people minimize the consequences of their actions by placing responsibility on an outside source. Examples include an employee who claims that her boss is responsible for her inefficiency and a college student who blames his professor for low grades.

A related procedure is to *diffuse responsibility*—to spread it so thin that no one person is responsible. A civil servant may diffuse responsibility for her actions throughout the entire bureaucracy with such comments as "That's the way things are done around here" or "That's just policy."

Dysfunctional Behavior

Bandura's concept of triadic reciprocal causation assumes that behavior is learned as a result of a mutual interaction of (1) the person, including cognition and neurophysiological processes; (2) the environment, including interpersonal relations and socioeconomic conditions; and (3) behavioral factors, including previous experiences with reinforcement. Dysfunctional behavior is no exception. Bandura's concept of dysfunctional behavior lends itself most readily to depressive reactions, phobias, and aggressive behaviors.

Depression

High personal standards and goals can lead to achievement and self-satisfaction. However, when people set their goals too high, they are likely to fail. Failure frequently leads to depression, and depressed people often undervalue their own accomplishments. The result is chronic misery, feelings of worthlessness, lack of purposefulness, and pervasive depression. Bandura (1986, 1997) believes that dysfunctional depression can occur in any of the three self-regulatory subfunctions: (1) self-observation, (2) judgmental processes, and (3) self-reactions.

First, during self-observation, people can misjudge their own performance or distort their memory of past accomplishments. Depressed people tend to exaggerate their past mistakes and minimize their prior accomplishments, a tendency that perpetuates their depression.

Second, depressed people are likely to make faulty judgments. They set their standards unrealistically high so that any personal accomplishment will be judged as a failure. Even when they achieve success in the eyes of others, they continue to berate their own performance. Depression is especially likely when people set goals and personal standards much higher than their perceived efficacy to attain them.

Finally, the self-reactions of depressed individuals are quite different from those of nondepressed persons. Depressed people not only judge themselves harshly, but they are also inclined to treat themselves badly for their shortcomings.

Phobias

Phobias are fears that are strong enough and pervasive enough to have severe debilitating effects on one's daily life. For example, snake phobias prevent people from holding a variety of jobs and from enjoying many kinds of recreational activities. Phobias and fears are learned by direct contact, inappropriate generalization, and especially by observational experiences (Bandura, 1986). They are difficult to extinguish because the phobic person simply avoids the threatening object. Unless the fearsome object is somehow encountered, the phobia will endure indefinitely.

Bandura (1986) credits television and other news media for generating many of our fears. Well-publicized rapes, armed robberies, or murders can terrorize a community, causing people to live more confined lives behind locked doors. Most people have never been raped, robbed, or intentionally injured; yet many live in fear of being criminally assaulted. Violent criminal acts that seem random and unpredictable are most likely to instigate phobic reactions.

Once established, phobias are maintained by consequent determinants: that is, the negative reinforcement the phobic person receives for avoiding the fear-producing situation. For example, if people expect to receive aversive experiences (being mugged) while walking through the city park, they will reduce their feeling of threat by not entering the park or even going near it. In this example, dysfunctional (avoidance) behavior is produced and maintained by the mutual interaction of people's expectancies (belief that they will be mugged), the external environment (the city park), and behavioral factors (their prior experiences with fear).

Aggression

Aggressive behaviors, when carried to extremes, can also be dysfunctional. Bandura (1986) contended that aggressive behavior is acquired through observation of others, direct experiences with positive and negative reinforcements, training, or instruction, and bizarre beliefs.

Once established, people continue to aggress for at least five reasons: (1) They enjoy inflicting injury on the victim (positive reinforcement); (2) they avoid or counter the aversive consequences of aggression by others (negative reinforcement); (3) they receive injury or harm for not behaving aggressively (punishment); (4) they live up to their personal standards of conduct by their aggressive behavior (self-reinforcement); and (5) they observe others receiving rewards for aggressive acts or punishment for nonaggressive behavior.

Bandura believes that aggressive actions ordinarily lead to further aggression. This belief is based on the now classic study of Bandura, Dorrie Ross, and Sheila Ross (1963), which found that children who observed others behaving aggressively displayed more aggression than a control group of children who did not view aggressive acts. In this study, the experimenters divided Stanford University nursery school boys and girls into three matched experimental groups and one control group.

Children in the first experimental group observed a live model behaving with both verbal and physical aggression toward a number of toys, including a large inflated Bobo doll; the second experimental group observed a film showing the same model behaving in an identical manner; the third experimental group saw a fantasy film in which a model, dressed as a black cat, behaved equally aggressively against the Bobo doll. Children in the control group were matched with those in the experimental groups on previous ratings of aggression, but they were not subjected to an aggressive model.

After children in the three experimental groups observed a model scolding, kicking, punching, and hitting the Bobo doll with a mallet, they proceeded into another room where they were mildly frustrated. Immediately following this frustration, each child went into the experimental room, which contained some toys (such as a smaller version of the Bobo doll) that could be played with aggressively. In addition, some nonaggressive toys (such as a tea set and coloring materials) were present. Observers watched the children's aggressive or nonaggressive response to the toys through a one-way mirror.

As hypothesized, children exposed to an aggressive model displayed more aggressive responses than those who had not been exposed. But contrary to expectations, the researchers found no differences in the amount of total aggression shown by children in the three experimental groups. Children who had observed the cartoon character were at least as aggressive as those exposed to a live model or to a filmed model. In general, children in each experimental group exhibited about twice as much aggressive behavior as did those in the control group. In addition, the particular kind of aggressive response was remarkably similar to that displayed by the adult models. Children scolded, kicked, punched, and hit the doll with a mallet in close imitation to the behavior that had been modeled.

This study, now more than 40 years old, was conducted at a time when people still debated the effects of television violence on children and adults. Some people argued that viewing aggressive behaviors on television would have a cathartic effect on children: That is, children who experienced aggression vicariously would have little motivation to act in an aggressive manner. The study by Bandura, Ross, and Ross (1963) offered some of the earliest experimental evidence that TV violence does not curb aggression; rather, it produces additional aggressive behaviors.

Therapy

According to Bandura, deviant behaviors are initiated on the basis of social cognitive learning principles, and they are maintained because, in some ways, they continue to serve a purpose. Therapeutic change, therefore, is difficult because it involves eliminating behaviors that are satisfying to the person. Smoking, overeating, and drinking alcoholic beverages, for example, generally have positive effects initially, and their long-range aversive consequences are usually not sufficient to produce avoidance behavior.

The ultimate goal of social cognitive therapy is self-regulation (Bandura, 1986). To achieve this end, the therapist introduces strategies designed to induce specific behavioral changes, to generalize those changes to other situations, and to maintain those changes by preventing relapse.

The first step in successful therapy is to instigate some change in behavior. For example, if a therapist is able to extinguish fear of height in a previously acrophobic person, then change has been induced and that person will have no fear of climbing a 20-foot ladder. A more important level of therapy is to generalize specific changes. For example, the acrophobic person not only will be able to ascend a ladder but also will be able to ride in airplanes or look out windows of tall buildings. Some therapies induce change and facilitate generalization, but in time, the therapeutic effects are lost and the person reacquires the dysfunctional behavior. This relapse is particularly likely when people are extinguishing maladaptive habits such as smoking and overeating. The most effective therapy reaches the third level of accomplishment, which is maintenance of newly acquired functional behaviors.

Bandura (1986) has suggested several basic treatment approaches. The first includes *overt or vicarious modeling*. People who observe live or filmed models performing threatening activities often feel less fear and anxiety and are then able to perform those same activities.

In a second treatment mode, *covert or cognitive modeling,* the therapist trains patients to visualize models performing fearsome behaviors. Overt and covert modeling strategies are most effective, however, when combined with performance-oriented approaches.

A third procedure, called *enactive mastery,* requires patients to perform those behaviors that previously produced incapacitating fears. Enactment, however, is not ordinarily the first step in treatment. Patients typically begin by observing models or by having their emotional arousal lessened through systematic desensitization, which involves the extinction of anxiety or fear through self-induced or therapist-induced relaxation. With systematic desensitization, the therapist and patient work together to place fearsome situations on a hierarchy from least to most threatening (Wolpe, 1973). Patients, while relaxed, enact the least threatening behavior and then gradually move through the hierarchy until they can perform the most threatening activity, all the while remaining at a low state of emotional arousal.

Bandura has demonstrated that each of these strategies can be effective and that they are most powerful when used in combination with one another. Bandura (1989) believes that the reason for their effectiveness can be traced to a common mechanism found in each of these approaches, namely, *cognitive mediation.* When people use cognition to increase self-efficacy—that is, when they become convinced that they can perform difficult tasks—then, in fact, they become able to cope with previously intimidating situations.

Related Research

The social cognitive theory of Albert Bandura continues to produce a great deal of research in several domains of psychology, with the concept of self-efficacy alone generating several hundred studies a year. Self-efficacy has been applied to a wide variety of domains, including academic performance, work production, depression, escaping homelessness, coping with terrorism, and health-related behaviors. Below we have selected just a couple of the many interesting applications of Albert Bandura's concept of self-efficacy: coping with the threat of terrorism and managing Type 2 diabetes.

Self-Efficacy and Terrorism

Terrorism has long been a threat to modern societies, but as anyone who remembers 2001 knows, on September 11 of that year terrorism reached a new level of peril and struck fear in people across the globe. Psychologists, particularly in areas of the world commonly affected by terrorism, have always been interested in both how individuals get drawn into the terrorist culture and how innocent people cope with the constant threat of terrorism (Ben-Zur & Zeidner, 1995; Moghaddam & Marsella, 2004; Zeidner, 2007). But this interest in terrorism increased exponentially after 2001, and it was in the post-9/11 frame of mind that some researchers began considering how self-efficacy might help people cope with terrorism.

In the wake of a terrorist attack, people report experiencing less personal security (Gallup, 2002). Oftentimes, terrorist attacks seem to come out of nowhere, and therefore people feel as if they have no control over preventing or avoiding such attacks. Belief that we can control events is the essence of what Bandura meant by self-efficacy. Therefore, an increased sense of self-efficacy might help to alleviate the negative feelings and sense of insecurity associated with terrorist attacks. Although it may seem unlikely that any given person has a great deal of power to prevent the next big attack, just the sense you can do something to make an attack less likely can be helpful. Maybe this means taking concrete actions like keeping a watchful eye on unattended bags in airports and subway stations, or maybe it means something more abstract like praying or taking some sense of comfort and security in one's religion.

Researchers Peter Fischer and colleagues were interested in investigating the possible link between religion, self-efficacy, and coping with the threat of terrorism (Fischer, Greitemeyer, Kastenmuller, Jonas, & Frey, 2006). To investigate the role of religion, Fischer and colleagues used Gordon Allport's Religious Orientation Scale (ROS; Chapter 13). As you may recall, the ROS measures the degree to which people are intrinsically versus extrinsically religious. Intrinsic religiosity is characterized by truly living your religion, not as a means to an end, but as a striving toward meaning and value. Previous research has found that the use of prayer as a coping mechanism is related to an increased feeling of internal control over events (Ai, Peterson, Rodgers, & Tice, 2005), and so Fischer and colleagues (2006) predicted that intrinsically religious people would experience a greater level of self-efficacy. This enhanced self-efficacy would help them cope with the threat of terrorism as compared to people who are not religious.

To test their prediction, Fischer and colleagues collected data from a German sample in November 2003. During this month the salience of terrorism was very high in Europe because on November 20 suicide bombers attacked two synagogues in Istanbul, Turkey, and 5 days later the British Consulate in Istanbul and the Turkish headquarters of a London-based bank were simultaneously attacked. In total, 38 people lost their lives in these attacks and more than 500 people were injured.

With the threat of more terrorist attacks on the minds of everyone, the researchers recruited participants to complete the ROS, a self-report measure of self-efficacy containing items such as "Thanks to my resourcefulness, I know how to handle unforeseen situations," and a measure of mood. Two months later, as the salience of terrorism waned, the researchers again administered these same measures to a new sample of Germans.

The results mostly supported the researchers' predictions. When the salience of terrorism was high, intrinsically religious people were in a better mood and reported greater self-efficacy than nonreligious people. Furthermore, the researchers found that the better mood experienced by intrinsically religious people was due to their increased feelings of self-efficacy. When the salience of terrorism was low, however, there were no differences on mood or self-efficacy between intrinsically religious and nonreligious people. So, when a person is faced with a threat, self-efficacy is crucial to lessening the detrimental impact of the threat. Religiosity is one, but probably not the only, way to derive a stronger sense of self-efficacy during such threats. The threat of terrorism is not likely to decline anytime soon, but this research from Bandura's personality theory has demonstrated that the more we feel in control and capable of handling unforeseen circumstances, the less the threat of terrorism will negatively affect our well-being.

Self-Efficacy and Diabetes

One of the ways in which Albert Bandura's social cognitive theory has had the greatest impact on the daily lives of many individuals is in the promotion of health and the prevention of disease. Bandura himself has written about the usefulness of his theory for encouraging people to engage in healthy behaviors that can increase overall well-being, health, and longevity (Bandura, 1998b).

Recently, William Sacco and colleagues (2007) studied Bandura's construct of self-efficacy as it relates to Type 2 diabetes. Diabetes is a chronic disease that requires very careful management including a special diet and exercise regime. Diabetes presents people with a variety of physical challenges, but it also is associated with significant mental health challenges. Indeed, the prevalence of depression among those with diabetes is double that of the general population (Anderson, Freedland, Clouse, & Lustman, 2001). One of the hallmark traits of depression is a lack of motivation and, given the strict diet and exercise plan diabetes patients must adhere to, this is particularly problematic for those trying to manage diabetes. The less patients adhere to their disease management plan the greater their diabetes symptoms become, which creates a downward spiral with negative implications for physical and mental health.

Sacco and his colleagues (2007) therefore sought to explore the role of self-efficacy as a variable that could increase adherence to the disease management plan and decrease negative physical and mental health symptoms. Their prediction was that the greater level of self-efficacy patients felt, the more likely people would be to adhere to their disease management plan and therefore the better the patients would feel.

In order to test their prediction, Sacco and colleagues recruited a sample of adults who had been diagnosed with Type 2 diabetes. Participants completed self-report measures of how much they adhered to their diet, exercise, glucose testing, and medication plan, a measure of depression, and a measure of self-efficacy specifically tailored to assess how much self-efficacy they felt with regard to managing their diabetes. Additionally, participants completed a measure of the frequency and severity of their diabetes symptoms, and their body mass index (BMI) was computed based on data from their medical records.

The results of this study clearly demonstrated just how important self-efficacy is to the management of chronic disease. Higher levels of self-efficacy were related to lower levels of depression, increased adherence to doctors' orders, lower BMI, and fewer and decreased severity of diabetes symptoms. Given these compelling results for the importance of self-efficacy, the researchers further examined its role in the management of diabetes. In other analyses, Sacco and his colleagues found that BMI was positively related to depression and that adherence to doctors' orders was negatively related to depression.

But might self-efficacy play a role in these relationships? To answer this question, the researchers conducted more complex analyses and what they found only further highlighted how important it is to feel as though you have a sense of control over your health when it comes to managing a disease like diabetes. Self-efficacy was directly responsible for both the relationship between BMI and depression and the relationship between adherence and depression. Specifically, having a high BMI led people to feel less self-efficacy, which in turn led to increased depression. Conversely, being able to adhere to the disease management plan served to increase self-efficacy, and it was this increase in a sense of control over the disease that was responsible for decreased depression.

There are many aspects of social cognitive theory that have influenced research in psychology, but these studies on coping with terrorism and diabetes management show that self-efficacy is one construct with far-reaching implications. Given this, it is easy to see why Albert Bandura's theory continues to generate the impressive amount of research it does.

Critique of Bandura

Albert Bandura has evolved his social cognitive theory by a careful balance of the two principal components of theory building—innovative speculation and accurate observation. His theoretical speculations have seldom outdistanced his data but have been carefully advanced, only one step in front of observations. This scientifically sound procedure increases the likelihood that his hypotheses will yield positive results and that his theory will generate additional testable hypotheses.

The usefulness of Bandura's personality theory, like that of other theories, rests on its ability to generate research, to offer itself to falsification, and to organize knowledge. In addition, it must serve as a practical guide to action and be internally consistent and parsimonious. How does Bandura's theory rate on these six criteria?

Bandura's theory has generated several thousand research studies and thus receives a very high rating on its capacity to *generate research*. Bandura and his student colleagues have conducted much of the work, but other researchers, too, have been attracted to the theory. Bandura may be the most meticulous writer of all personality theorists. His carefully constructed formulations lend themselves to the formation of numerous testable hypotheses.

On the standard of *falsifiability,* we rate Bandura's theory high. Self-efficacy theory suggests that "people's beliefs in their personal efficacy influence what courses of action they choose to pursue, how much effort they will invest in activities, how long they will persevere in the face of obstacles and failure experiences, and their resiliency following setbacks" (Bandura, 1994, p. 65). This statement suggests several areas of possible research that could lead to falsification of self-efficacy theory.

On its ability to *organize knowledge,* Bandura's theory receives a high rating. Many findings from psychology research can be organized by social cognitive theory. The triadic reciprocal causation model is a comprehensive concept that offers a viable explanation for the acquisition of most observable behaviors. The inclusion of three variables in this paradigm gives Bandura's theory more flexibility to organize and explain behavior than does Skinner's radical behaviorism, which relies heavily on environmental variables.

How *practical* is Bandura's social cognitive theory? To the therapist, teacher, parent, or anyone interested in the acquisition and maintenance of new behaviors, self-efficacy theory provides useful and specific guidelines. In addition to presenting techniques for enhancing personal and collective efficacy and for efficient use of proxies, Bandura's theory suggests ways in which observational learning and modeling can be used to acquire behaviors.

Is the theory *internally consistent?* Because Bandura's social cognitive theory is not highly speculative, it has outstanding internal consistency. Bandura is not afraid to speculate, but he never ventures far beyond the empirical data available to him. The result is a carefully couched, rigorously written, and internally consistent theory.

The final criterion of a useful theory is *parsimony*. Again, Bandura's theory meets high standards. The theory is simple, straightforward, and unencumbered by hypothetical or fanciful explanations.

Concept of Humanity

Bandura sees humans as having the capacity to become many things, and most of these things are learned through modeling. If human learning were dependent on direct experience of trial and error, it would be exceedingly slow, tedious, and dangerous. Fortunately, "humans have evolved an advanced cognitive capacity for observational learning that enables them to shape and structure their lives through the power of modeling" (Bandura 2002a, p. 167).

Bandura believes that people are quite plastic and flexible, and that plasticity and flexibility are the essence of humanity's basic nature. Because humans have evolved neurophysiological mechanisms for symbolizing their experiences, their nature is marked by a large degree of flexibility. People have the capacity to store past experiences and to use this information to chart future actions.

People's capacity to use symbols provides them with a powerful tool for understanding and controlling their environment. It enables them to solve problems without resorting to inefficient trial-and-error behavior, to imagine the consequences of their actions, and to set goals for themselves.

Humans are *goal-directed*, purposive animals who can view the future and bestow it with meaning by being aware of the possible consequences of future behavior. Humans anticipate the future and behave accordingly in the present. The future does not determine behavior, but its cognitive representation can have a powerful effect on present actions. "People set goals for themselves, anticipate the likely consequences of prospective actions, and select and create courses of action likely to produce desired outcomes and avoid detrimental ones" (Bandura, 2001, p. 7).

Although people are basically goal oriented, Bandura believes that they have specific rather than general intentions and purposes. People are not motivated by a single master goal such as striving for superiority or self-actualization but by a multiplicity of goals, some distant and some proximate. These individual intentions, however, are not ordinarily anarchical; they possess some stability and order. Cognition gives people the capacity to evaluate probable consequences and to eliminate behaviors that do not meet their standards of conduct. Personal standards, therefore, tend to give human behavior a degree of consistency, even though that behavior lacks a master motive to guide it.

Bandura's concept of humanity is more *optimistic* than pessimistic, because it holds that people are capable of learning new behaviors throughout their lives. However, dysfunctional behaviors may persist because of low self-efficacy or because they are perceived as being reinforced. Nevertheless, these unhealthy behaviors need not continue, because most people have the capacity to change by imitating the productive behaviors of others and by using their cognitive abilities to solve problems.

Bandura's social cognitive theory, of course, emphasizes *social factors* more than biological ones. However, it recognizes that genetics contributes to the person (P) variable in the triadic reciprocal causation paradigm. But even within this model, cognition ordinarily gains ascendance, so biological factors become less important. Moreover, social factors are clearly more crucial to the other two variables—environment (E) and behavior (B).

We rate Bandura high on *freedom versus determinism* because he believes that people can exercise a large measure of control over their lives. Although people are affected by both their environment and their experiences with reinforcement, they have some power to mold these two external conditions. To some extent, people can manage those environmental conditions that will shape future behavior and can choose to ignore or augment previous experiences. Human agency suggests that people who have high personal and collective efficacy and who make efficient use of proxies have a great amount of influence on their own actions. However, some people have more freedom than others because they are more adept at regulating their own behavior. Bandura (1986) defined freedom as "the number of options available to people and their right to exercise them" (p. 42). Personal freedom, then, is limited; it is restricted by physical constraints such as laws, prejudices, regulations, and the rights of other people. In addition, personal factors such as perceived inefficacy and lack of confidence restrict individual freedom.

On the issue of *causality or teleology,* Bandura's position would be described as moderate. Human functioning is a product of environmental factors interacting with behavior and personal variables, especially cognitive activity. People move with a purpose toward goals that they have set, but motivation exists in neither the past nor the future; it is contemporary. Although future events cannot motivate people, people's conception of the future can and does regulate present behavior.

Social cognitive theory emphasizes *conscious thought* over unconscious determinants of behavior. Self-regulation of actions relies on self-monitoring, judgment, and self-reaction, all of which are ordinarily conscious during the learning situation. "People do not become thoughtless during the learning process. They make conscious judgments about how their actions affect the environment" (Bandura, 1986, p. 116). After learnings are well established, especially motor learnings, they may become unconscious. People do not have to be aware of all their actions while walking, eating, or driving a car.

Bandura (2001) believes that the division of *biological and social factors* is a false dichotomy. Although people are limited by biological forces, they have a remarkable plasticity. Their social environments allow them a wide range of behaviors, including using other people as models. Each person lives in a number of social networks and is thus influenced by a variety of people. Modern technology in the form of the World Wide Web and the media facilitates the spread of social influences.

Because people have a remarkable flexibility and capacity for learning, vast individual differences exist among them. Bandura's emphasis on *uniqueness,* however, is moderated by biological and social influences, both of which contribute to some similarities among people.

Key Terms and Concepts

- *Observational learning* allows people to learn without performing a behavior.
- Observational learning requires (1) *attention* to a model, (2) *organization* and *retention* of observations, (3) *behavioral production,* and (4) *motivation* to perform the modeled behavior.
- *Enactive learning* takes place when our responses produce consequences.
- Human functioning is a product of the mutual interaction of environmental events, behavior, and personal factors, a model called *triadic reciprocal causation.*
- *Chance encounters* and *fortuitous events* are two important environmental factors that influence people's lives in unplanned and unexpected ways.
- *Human agency* means that people can and do exercise a measure of control over their lives.
- *Self-efficacy* refers to people's belief that they are capable of performing those behaviors that can produce desired outcomes in a particular situation.
- *Proxy agency* occurs when people have the capacity to rely on others for goods and services.
- *Collective efficacy* refers to the confidence that groups of people have that their combined efforts will produce social change.
- People have some capacity for *self-regulation,* and they use both external and internal factors to self-regulate.
- *External factors* provide us with standards for evaluating our behavior as well as external reinforcement in the form of rewards received from others.
- *Internal factors* in self-regulation include (1) self-observation, (2) judgmental processes, and (3) self-reaction.
- Through *selective activation* and *disengagement of internal control,* people can separate themselves from the injurious consequences of their actions.
- Four principal techniques of selective activation and disengagement of internal control are (1) *redefining behavior,* (2) *displacing or diffusing responsibility,* (3) *disregarding or distorting the consequences of behavior,* and (4) *dehumanizing or blaming the victims* for their injuries.
- Dysfunctional *behaviors,* such as depression, phobias, and aggression, are acquired through the reciprocal interaction of environment, personal factors, and behavior.
- *Social cognitive therapy* emphasizes cognitive mediation, especially perceived self-efficacy.

CHAPTER 17

Rotter and Mischel: Cognitive Social Learning Theory

Rotter

Mischel

Which pair of items most closely matches your beliefs? Check either a or b.

1. a. Luck is the main reason for people's success.
   b. People make their own luck.
2. a. One way to bring about a thunder storm is to plan a picnic or some other outdoor event.
   b. Weather patterns have nothing to do with people's wishes.
3. a. Students' grades are mostly the result of chance.
   b. Students' grades are mostly the result of hard work.
4. a. People have no control over large industries that pollute the environment.
   b. People can work together to prevent large industries from dumping waste products into the environment.
5. a. Popularity among high school students is due mostly to things beyond their control, for example, good looks.
   b. Popularity among high school students is due mostly to a student's own efforts.
6. a. Injuries from motor vehicle crashes cannot be prevented. When it's your time, it's your time.
   b. Wearing seat belts, having air bags in your automobile, and driving within the speed limit are proven ways of reducing injuries from motor vehicle crashes.

These items are similar to ones Julian Rotter used in developing his Internal-External Control Scale, usually called the locus of control scale. We discuss this widely popular instrument in the section on internal and external control of reinforcement and offer some analysis on the meaning of these items.

Overview of Cognitive Social Learning Theory

The cognitive social learning theories of Julian Rotter and Walter Mischel each rest on the assumption that *cognitive* factors help shape how people will react to environmental forces. Both theorists object to Skinner's explanation that behavior is shaped by immediate reinforcement and instead suggest that one's *expectations* of future events are prime determinants of performance.

Rotter contends that human behavior is best predicted from an understanding of the *interaction* of people with their meaningful environments. As an **interactionist,** he believes that neither the environment itself nor the individual is completely responsible for behavior. Instead, he holds that people's cognitions, past histories, and expectations of the future are keys to predicting behavior. In this respect, he differs from Skinner (Chapter 15), who believed that reinforcement ultimately stems from the environment.

Mischel's cognitive social theory has much in common with Bandura's social cognitive theory and Rotter's social learning theory. Like Bandura and Rotter, Mischel believes that cognitive factors, such as expectancies, subjective perceptions, values, goals, and personal standards, play important roles in shaping personality. His contributions to personality theory have evolved from research on **delay of gratification,** to research regarding the consistency or inconsistency of personality, and presently to work with Yuichi Shoda on the development of a cognitive-affective personality system.

Biography of Julian Rotter

Julian B. Rotter, the author of the locus of control scale, was born in Brooklyn on October 22, 1916, the third and oldest son of Jewish immigrant parents. Rotter (1993) recalled that he fit Adler's description of a highly competitive, "fighting" youngest child. Although his parents observed the Jewish religion and customs, they were not very religious. Rotter (1993) described his family's socioeconomic condition as "comfortably middle class until the Great Depression when my father lost his wholesale stationery business and we became part of the masses of unemployed for two years" (pp. 273–274). The depression sparked in Rotter a lifelong concern for social injustice and taught him the importance of situational conditions affecting human behavior.

As an elementary school and high school student, he was an avid reader and by his junior year had read nearly every book of fiction in the local public library. That being the case, he turned one day to the psychology shelves where he found Adler's (1927) *Understanding Human Nature,* Freud's (1901/1960) *Psychopathology of Everyday Life,* and Karl Menninger's (1920) *The Human Mind.* He was particularly impressed by Adler and Freud and soon returned for more (Rotter, 1982, 1993).

When he entered Brooklyn College, he was already seriously interested in psychology, but he chose to major in chemistry because it seemed to be a more employable degree during the depression of the 1930s. As a junior at Brooklyn College, he learned that Adler was a professor of medical psychology at Long Island College of Medicine. He attended Adler's medical lectures and several of his clinical demonstrations. Eventually, he came to personally know Adler, who invited him to attend meetings of the Society for Individual Psychology (Rotter, 1993).

When Rotter graduated from Brooklyn College in 1937, he had more credits in psychology than in chemistry. He then entered graduate school in psychology at the University of Iowa, from which he received a master's degree in 1938. He completed an internship in clinical psychology at Worcester State Hospital in Massachusetts, where he met his future wife, Clara Barnes. In 1941, Rotter received his PhD in clinical psychology from Indiana University.

That same year Rotter accepted a position as clinical psychologist at Norwich State Hospital in Connecticut, where his duties included training interns and assistants from the University of Connecticut and Wesleyan University. At the advent of World War II, he was drafted into the army and spent more than 3 years as an army psychologist.

After the war, Rotter returned briefly to Norwich, but he soon took a job at Ohio State University, where he attracted a number of outstanding graduate students, including Walter Mischel. For more than a dozen years, Rotter and George Kelly (see Chapter 18) reigned as the two most dominant members of the psychology department at Ohio State. However, Rotter was unhappy with the political effects of McCarthyism in Ohio, and in 1963, he took a position at the University of

Connecticut as director of the Clinical Training Program. He continued in that position until 1987, when he retired as professor emeritus. Rotter and his wife Clara (who died in 1986) had two children, a daughter, Jean, and a son, Richard, who died in 1995.

Among Rotter's most important publications are *Social Learning and Clinical Psychology* (1954); *Clinical Psychology* (1964); *Applications of a Social Learning Theory of Personality,* with J. E. Chance and E. J. Phares (1972); *Personality,* with D. J. Hochreich (1975); *The Development and Application of Social Learning Theory: Selected Papers* (1982); the Rotter Incomplete Sentences Blank (Rotter, 1966); and the Interpersonal Trust Scale (Rotter, 1967).

Rotter served as president of the Eastern Psychological Association and of the divisions of Social and Personality Psychology and Clinical Psychology of the American Psychological Association (APA). He also served two terms on the APA Education and Training Board. In 1988, he received the prestigious APA Distinguished Scientific Contribution Award. The following year, he earned the Distinguished Contribution to Clinical Training Award from the Council of University Directors of Clinical Psychology.

Introduction to Rotter's Social Learning Theory

Social learning theory rests on five basic hypotheses. First, it assumes that *humans interact with their meaningful environments* (Rotter, 1982). People's reaction to environmental stimuli depends on the meaning or importance that they attach to an event. Reinforcements are not dependent on external stimuli alone but are given meaning by the individual's cognitive capacity. Likewise, personal characteristics such as needs or traits cannot, by themselves, cause behavior. Rather, Rotter believes that human behavior stems from the interaction of environmental and personal factors.

A second assumption of Rotter's theory is that *human personality is learned.* Thus, it follows that personality is not set or determined at any particular age of development; instead, it can be changed or modified as long as people are capable of learning. Although our accumulation of earlier experiences gives our personality some stability, we are always responsive to change through new experiences. We learn from past experiences, but those experiences are not absolutely constant; they are colored by intervening experiences that then affect present perceptions.

The third assumption of social learning theory is that *personality has a basic unity,* which means that people's personalities possess relative stability. People learn to evaluate new experiences on the basis of previous reinforcement. This relatively consistent evaluation leads to greater stability and unity of personality.

Rotter's fourth basic hypothesis is that *motivation is goal directed.* He rejects the notion that people are primarily motivated to reduce tension or seek pleasure, insisting that the best explanation for human behavior lies in people's expectations that their behaviors are advancing them toward goals. For example, most college students have a goal of graduation and are willing to endure stress, tension, and hard work in order to reach that goal. Rather than reducing tension, the prospect of several difficult years of college classes promises to increase it.

Other things being equal, people are most strongly reinforced by behaviors that move them in the direction of anticipated goals. This statement refers to Rotter's **empirical law of effect,** which "defines reinforcement as any action, condition, or event which affects the individual's movement toward a goal" (Rotter & Hochreich, 1975, p. 95).

Rotter's fifth assumption is that *people are capable of anticipating events.* Moreover, they use their perceived movement in the direction of the anticipated event as a criterion for evaluating reinforcers. Beginning with these five general assumptions, Rotter built a personality theory that attempts to predict human behavior.

Predicting Specific Behaviors

Because Rotter's primary concern is the prediction of human behavior, he suggested four variables that must be analyzed in order to make accurate predictions in any specific situation. These variables are behavior potential, expectancy, reinforcement value, and the psychological situation. *Behavior potential* refers to the likelihood that a given behavior will occur in a particular situation; *expectancy* is a person's expectation of being reinforced; *reinforcement value* is the person's preference for a particular reinforcement; and the *psychological situation* refers to a complex pattern of cues that a person perceives during a specific time period.

Behavior Potential

Broadly considered, **behavior potential** (*BP*) is the possibility that a particular response will occur at a given time and place. Several behavior potentials of varying strengths exist in any psychological situation. For example, as Megan walks toward a restaurant, she has several behavioral potentials. She might pass by without noticing the restaurant; actively ignore it; stop to eat; think about stopping to eat, but go on; examine the building and contents with a consideration to purchase it; or stop, go inside, and rob the cashier. For Megan, in this situation, the potential for some of these behaviors would approach zero, some would be very likely, and others would be in between these extremes. How can a person predict which behaviors are most or least likely to occur?

The behavior potential in any situation is a function of both expectancy and reinforcement value. If a person wishes to know the likelihood that Megan will rob the cashier rather than purchase the restaurant or stop to eat, for example, we could hold expectancy constant and vary reinforcement value. If each of these behavior potentials carried a 70% expectancy of being reinforced, then a person could make a prediction about their relative probability of occurrence based solely on the reinforcement value of each. If holding up the cashier carries a positive reinforcement value greater than ordering food or buying the restaurant, then that behavior has the greatest occurrence potential.

The second approach to prediction is to hold reinforcement value constant and vary expectancy. If total reinforcements from each possible behavior are of equal value, then the one with the greatest expectation of reinforcement is most likely to occur. More specifically, if reinforcements from robbing the cashier, buying the business, and ordering a dinner are all valued equally, then the response that is most likely to produce a reinforcement has the highest behavior potential.

Rotter employs a broad definition of behavior, which refers to any response, implicit or explicit, that can be observed or measured directly or indirectly. This comprehensive concept allows Rotter to include as behavior such hypothetical constructs as generalizing, problem solving, thinking, analyzing, and so forth.

Expectancy

Expectancy (E) refers to a person's expectation that some specific reinforcement or set of reinforcements will occur in a given situation. The probability is not determined by the individual's history of reinforcements, as Skinner contended, but is subjectively held by the person. History, of course, is a contributing factor, but so too are unrealistic thinking, expectations based on lack of information, and fantasies, so long as the person sincerely believes that a given reinforcement or group of reinforcements are contingent on a particular response.

Expectancies can be general or specific. Generalized expectancies (GEs) are learned through previous experiences with a particular response or similar responses and are based on the belief that certain behaviors will be followed by positive reinforcement. For example, college students whose previous hard work has been reinforced by high grades will have a generalized expectancy of future reward and will work hard in a variety of academic situations.

Specific expectancies are designated as E' (*E prime*). In any situation the expectancy for a particular reinforcement is determined by a combination of a specific expectancy (E') and the generalized expectancy (GE). For example, a student may have general expectancy that a given level of academic work will be rewarded by good grades but may believe that an equal amount of hard work in a French class will go unrewarded.

Total expectancy of success is a function of both one's generalized expectancy and one's specific expectancy. Total expectancy partially determines the amount of effort people will expend in pursuit of their goals. A person with low total expectancy for success in obtaining a prestigious job is not likely to apply for the position, whereas a person with high expectancy for success will exert much effort and persist in the face of setbacks to achieve goals that appear possible.

Reinforcement Value

Another variable in the prediction formula is **reinforcement value** (RV), which is the preference a person attaches to any reinforcement when the probabilities for the occurrence of a number of different reinforcements are all equal.

Reinforcement value can be illustrated by a woman's interactions with a vending machine that contains several possible selections, each costing the same. The woman approaches the machine able and is willing to pay 75 cents in order to receive a snack. The vending machine is in perfect working condition, so there is a 100% probability that the woman's response will be followed by some sort of reinforcement. Her expectancy of reinforcement, therefore, for the candy bar, corn chips, potato chips, popcorn, tortilla chips, and Danish pastry are all equal. Her response—

People do not behave in a vacuum but respond to cues in their perceived environment.

that is, which button she presses—is determined by the reinforcement value of each snack.

When expectancies and situational variables are held constant, behavior is shaped by one's preference for the possible reinforcements, that is, reinforcement value. In most situations, of course, expectancies are seldom equal, and prediction is difficult because both expectancy and reinforcement value can vary.

What determines the reinforcement value for any event, condition, or action? First, the individual's perception contributes to the positive or negative value of an event. Rotter calls this perception **internal reinforcement** and distinguishes it from **external reinforcement,** which refers to events, conditions, or actions on which one's society or culture places a value. Internal and external reinforcements may be either in harmony or at a variance with one another. For example, if you like popular movies—that is, the same ones that most other people like—then your internal and external reinforcements for attending these types of movies are in agreement. However, if your taste in movies runs contrary to that of your friends, then your internal and external reinforcements are discrepant.

Another contributor to reinforcement value is one's needs. Generally, a specific reinforcement tends to increase in value as the need it satisfies becomes stronger. A starving child places a higher value on a bowl of soup than does a moderately hungry one. (This issue is more fully discussed later in this chapter in the section titled Needs.)

Reinforcements are also valued according to their expected consequences for future reinforcements. Rotter believes that people are capable of using cognition to anticipate a sequence of events leading to some future goal and that the ultimate goal contributes to the reinforcement value of each event in the sequence. Reinforcements seldom occur independently of future related reinforcements but are likely to appear in **reinforcement-reinforcement sequences,** which Rotter (1982) refers to as clusters of reinforcement.

Humans are goal oriented; they anticipate achieving a goal if they behave in a particular way. Other things being equal, goals with the highest reinforcement value are most desirable. Desire alone, however, is not sufficient to predict behavior. The potential for any behavior is a function of both expectancy and reinforcement value as well as the psychological situation.

Psychological Situation

The fourth variable in the prediction formula is the **psychological situation** (s), defined as that part of the external and internal world to which a person is responding. It is not synonymous with external stimuli, although physical events are usually important to the psychological situation.

Behavior is the result of neither environmental events nor personal traits; rather, it stems from the *interaction* of a person with his or her meaningful environment. If physical stimuli alone determined behavior, then two individuals would respond in exactly the same way to identical stimuli. If personal traits were solely responsible for behavior, then a person would always respond in a consistent and characteristic fashion, even to different events. Because neither of these conditions is valid, something other than the environment or personal traits must shape behavior. Rotter's social learning theory hypothesizes that the interaction between person and environment is a crucial factor in shaping behavior.

The psychological situation is "a complex set of interacting cues acting upon an individual for any specific time period" (Rotter, 1982, p. 318). People do not behave in a vacuum; instead, they respond to cues within their perceived environment. These cues serve to determine for them certain expectancies for behavior-reinforcement sequences as well as for reinforcement-reinforcement sequences. The time period for the cues may vary from momentary to lengthy; thus, the psychological situation is not limited by time. One's marital situation, for example, may be relatively constant over a long period of time, whereas the psychological situation faced by a driver's spinning out of control on an icy road may be extremely short. The psychological situation must be considered, along with expectancies and reinforcement value, in determining the probability of a given response.

Basic Prediction Formula

As a hypothetical means of predicting specific behaviors, Rotter proposed a basic formula that includes all four variables of prediction. The formula represents an idealistic rather than a practical means of prediction, and no precise values can be plugged into it. Consider the case of La Juan, an academically gifted college student who is listening to a dull and lengthy lecture by one of her professors. To the internal cues of boredom and the external cues of seeing slumbering classmates, what is the likelihood that La Juan will respond by resting her head on the desk in an attempt to sleep? The psychological situation alone is not responsible for her behavior, but it interacts with her expectancy for reinforcement plus the reinforcement value of sleep in that particular situation. La Juan's behavior potential can be estimated by Rotter's (1982, p. 302) basic formula for the prediction of goal-directed behavior:

$$BP_{x_1,s_1,r_a} = f\left(E_{x_1,r_a,s_1} + RV_{a,s_1}\right)$$

This formula is read: The potential for behavior x to occur in situation 1 in relation to reinforcement a is a function of the expectancy that behavior x will be followed by reinforcement a in situation 1 and the value of reinforcement a in situation 1.

Applied to our example, the formula suggests that the likelihood (behavior potential, or *BP*) that La Juan will rest her head on her desk (behavior *x*) in a dull and boring class with other students slumbering (the psychological situation, or s_1) with the goal of sleep (reinforcement, or r_a) is a function of her expectation that such behavior (E_x) will be followed by sleep (r_a) in this particular classroom situation (s_1), plus a measure of how highly she desires to sleep (reinforcement value, or RV_a) in this specific situation (*s*). Because precise measurement of each of these variables may be beyond the scientific study of human behavior, Rotter proposed a strategy for predicting general behaviors.

Predicting General Behaviors

To predict general behaviors, we look at David, who has worked for 18 years in Hoffman's Hardware Store. David has been informed that, because of a business decline, Mr. Hoffman must cut his workforce and that David may lose his job. How can we predict David's subsequent behavior? Will he beg Mr. Hoffman to let him remain with the company? Will he strike out in violence against the store or Mr. Hoffman? Will he displace his anger and act aggressively toward his wife or children? Will he begin drinking heavily and become apathetic toward searching for a new job? Will he immediately and constructively begin looking for another position?

Generalized Expectancies

Because most of David's possible behaviors are new to him, how can we predict what he will do? At this point, the concepts of **generalization** and **generalized expectancy** enter into Rotter's theory. If, in the past, David has generally been rewarded for behaviors that have increased his social status, then only a slight probability exists that he will beg Mr. Hoffman for a job, because such actions are contrary to increased social status. On the other hand, if his previous attempts at responsible and independent behaviors have generally been reinforced and if he has the *freedom of movement*—that is, the opportunity to apply for another job—then, assuming he needs work, a high probability exists that he will apply for another job or otherwise behave independently. This prediction, though not as specific as the one predicting the college student's likelihood of sleeping in a boring classroom, is nevertheless more useful in situations where rigorous control of pertinent variables is not possible. Predicting David's reaction to the probable loss of a job is a matter of knowing how he views the options available to him and also the status of his present *needs*.

Needs

Rotter (1982) defined needs as any behavior or set of behaviors that people see as moving them in the direction of a goal. Needs are not states of deprivation or arousal but indicators of the direction of behavior. The difference between needs and goals is semantic only. When focus is on the environment, Rotter speaks of goals; when it is on the person, he talks of needs.

The concept of needs allows for more generalized predictions than permitted by the four specific variables that comprise the basic prediction formula. Ordinarily, personality theory deals with broad predictions of human behavior. For example, a person with strong needs for dominance will usually try to gain the power position in most interpersonal relationships as well as in a variety of other situations. In specific situations, however, a dominant person may behave in a nondominant or even submissive fashion. The basic prediction formula permits specific predictions, with the assumption, of course, that all relevant information is at hand. It is the more appropriate formula for controlled laboratory experiments but is inadequate in predicting everyday behaviors. For this reason, Rotter introduced the concept of needs and their accompanying *general prediction formula.*

Categories of Needs

Rotter and Hochreich (1975) listed six broad categories of needs, with each category representing a group of functionally related behaviors: that is, behaviors that lead to the same or similar reinforcements. For example, people can meet their recognition needs in a variety of situations and by many different people. Therefore, they can receive reinforcement for a group of functionally related behaviors, all of which satisfy their need for recognition. The following list is not exhaustive, but it represents most of the important human needs.

Recognition-Status   The need to be recognized by others and to achieve status in their eyes is a powerful need for most people. Recognition-status includes the need to excel in those things that a person regards as important: for example, school, sports, occupation, hobbies, and physical appearance. It also includes the need for socioeconomic status and personal prestige. Playing a good game of bridge is an example of the need for recognition-status.

Dominance   The need to control the behavior of others is called dominance. This need includes any set of behaviors directed at gaining power over the lives of friends, family, colleagues, superiors, and subordinates. Talking colleagues into accepting your ideas is a specific example of dominance.

Independence   Independence is the need to be free of the domination of others. It includes those behaviors aimed at gaining the freedom to make decisions, to rely on oneself, and to attain goals without the help of others. Declining help in repairing a bicycle could demonstrate the need for independence.

Protection-Dependency   A set of needs nearly opposite independence are those of protection and dependency. This category includes the needs to be cared for by others, to be protected from frustration and harm, and to satisfy the other need categories. A specific example of protection-dependency is asking your spouse to stay home from work and take care of you when you are ill.

Love and Affection   Most people have strong needs for love and affection: that is, needs for acceptance by others that go beyond recognition and status to include some indications that other people have warm, positive feelings for them. The needs for love and affection include those behaviors aimed toward securing friendly regard, interest, and devotion from others. Doing favors for others in anticipation of receiving verbal expressions of positive regard and gratitude might be an example of this need.

Physical Comfort   Physical comfort is perhaps the most basic need because other needs are learned in relation to it. This need includes those behaviors aimed at securing food, good health, and physical security. Other needs are learned as an outgrowth of needs for pleasure, physical contact, and well-being. Turning on the air conditioner or hugging another person are examples of the need for physical comfort.

Need Components

A need complex has three essential components—*need potential, freedom of movement,* and *need value*—and these components are analogous to the more specific concepts of behavior potential, expectancy, and reinforcement value (Rotter, Chance, & Phares, 1972).

Need Potential   Need potential (*NP*) refers to the possible occurrence of a set of functionally related behaviors directed toward satisfying the same or similar goals. Need potential is analogous to the more specific concept of behavior potential. The difference between the two is that need potential refers to a *group* of functionally related behaviors, whereas behavior potential is the likelihood that a *particular* behavior will occur in a given situation in relation to a specific reinforcement.

Need potential cannot be measured solely through observation of behavior. If different people are seen behaving in apparently the same manner—for example, eating in a fancy restaurant—one should not conclude that they are all satisfying the same need potential. One person may be satisfying the need for physical comfort, that is, food; another may be more interested in love and affection; and the third person may be trying primarily to satisfy the need for recognition-status. Probably any of the six broad needs could be satisfied by eating in this restaurant. Whether or not one's need potential is realized, however, depends not only on the value or preference one has for that reinforcement but also on one's freedom of movement in making responses leading to that reinforcement.

Freedom of Movement   Behavior is partly determined by our expectancies: that is, our best guess that a particular reinforcement will follow a specific response. In the general prediction formula, **freedom of movement** (*FM*) is analogous to expectancy. It is one's overall expectation of being reinforced for performing those behaviors that are directed toward satisfying some general need. To illustrate, a person with a strong need for dominance could behave in a variety of ways to satisfy that need. She might select her husband's clothes, decide what college curriculum her son will pursue, direct actors in a play, organize a professional conference involving dozens of colleagues, or perform any one of a hundred other behaviors aimed at securing reinforcement for her dominance need. The average or mean level of expectancies that these behaviors will lead to the desired satisfaction is a measure of her freedom of movement in the area of dominance.

Freedom of movement can be determined by holding need value constant and observing one's need potential. For example, if a person places exactly the same value on dominance, independence, love and affection, and each of the other needs, then that person will perform those behaviors judged to have the greatest expectancy of being reinforced. If the person performs behaviors leading to physical comfort, for example, then there will be more freedom of movement in that need complex than in any of the other need complexes. Ordinarily, of course, need value is not constant, because most people prefer the satisfaction of one need over others.

Need Value   A person's **need value** (*NV*) is the degree to which she or he prefers one set of reinforcements to another. Rotter, Chance, and Phares (1972) defined need value as the "mean preference value of a set of functionally related reinforcements" (p. 33). In the general prediction formula, need value is the analog of reinforcement value. When freedom of movement is held constant, people will perform those behavior sequences that lead to satisfaction of the most preferred need. If people have equal expectancies of obtaining positive reinforcement for behaviors aimed at the satisfaction of any need, then the value they place on a particular need complex will be the principal determinant of their behavior. If they prefer independence to any other need complex, and if they have an equal expectation of being reinforced in the pursuit of any of the needs, then their behavior will be directed toward achieving independence.

General Prediction Formula

The basic prediction formula is limited to highly controlled situations where expectancies, reinforcement value, and the psychological situation are all relatively simple and discrete. In most situations, however, prediction of behavior is much more complex because behaviors and reinforcements usually occur in functionally related sequences. Consider again the case of La Juan, the gifted student who was having difficulty staying awake in a dull and boring class. The basic prediction formula offers some indication of the likelihood that, in the specific situation of a boring lecture, La Juan will rest her head on her desk. However, a more generalized prediction formula is needed to predict her need potential for gaining the recognition-status that comes from graduating with highest honors. La Juan's likelihood of satisfying this need depends on a complex of behaviors. To make generalized predictions regarding a set of behaviors designed to satisfy needs, Rotter introduced this general prediction formula:

$$NP = f(FM + NV)$$

This equation means that need potential (*NP*) is a function of freedom of movement (*FM*) and need value (*NV*). The formula is analogous to the basic prediction formula, and each factor is parallel to the corresponding factors of that basic formula. To illustrate the general prediction formula, we can look at La Juan's situation with regard to her future academic work. To predict her *need potential* for working toward graduation with highest honors, we must measure her *freedom of movement,* that is, her mean expectancy of being reinforced for a series of behaviors necessary to reach her goal, plus her *need value* of all those reinforcements: that is, the value she places on recognition-status or any other need she associates with receiving academic honors. The value La Juan places on recognition-status (need

Basic prediction formula

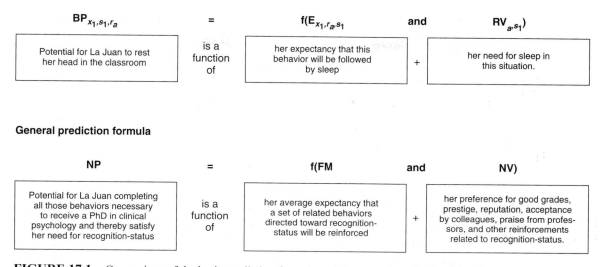

General prediction formula

FIGURE 17.1   Comparison of the basic prediction formula and the general prediction formula.

value), plus her average expectancy of being reinforced for performing the required series of behaviors (freedom of movement), equals her potential for pursuing the set of required behaviors (need potential). A comparison of the basic (specific) prediction formula and the generalized prediction formula is shown in Figure 17.1.

Rotter's general prediction formula allows for people's history of using similar experiences to anticipate present reinforcement. That is, they have a *generalized expectancy* for success. Rotter's two most popular scales for measuring generalized expectancies are the Internal-External Control Scale and the Interpersonal Trust Scale.

Internal and External Control of Reinforcement

At the core of Rotter's social learning theory is the notion that reinforcement does not automatically stamp in behaviors but that people have the ability to see a causal connection between their own behavior and the occurrence of the reinforcer (Rotter, 1954; Rotter & Hochreich, 1975). People strive to reach their goals because they have a *generalized expectancy* that such strivings will be successful.

During the 1950s and early 1960s, Rotter became intrigued by the observation that many people did not increase their feelings of personal control after experiencing success and that others did not lower their expectancies after repeated failure (Rotter, 1990, 1993; Zuroff & Rotter, 1985). In other words, some people tended to explain away successful outcomes as being due to luck or chance, whereas others retained a high sense of personal control even after several nonreinforced behaviors. These tendencies seemed to be especially true in situations that people regarded as ambiguous or novel (Rotter, 1992) or when people were not clear whether the outcome of their behavior was due to their skill or to chance. Rotter (1990) has suggested that both the situation and the person contribute to feelings of personal control. Thus, a person with a generalized expectancy for success in one situation may have low feelings of personal control in another situation.

To assess internal and external control of reinforcement, or **locus of control,** Rotter (1966) developed the Internal-External Control Scale, basing it on the doctoral dissertations of two of his students, E. Jerry Phares (1955) and William H. James (1957). The I-E Scale consists of 29 forced-choice items, 23 pairs of which are scored and 6 of which are filler statements designed to disguise the purpose of the scale. The scale is scored in the direction of external control so that 23 is the highest possible external score and 0 is the highest possible internal score. Table 17.1 shows several sample items from the I-E Scale. People must select either alternative "a" or alternative "b" from each pair of items. Although the internal or external direction of these items may seem obvious, Rotter (1990) reported that scores have only a modest correlation with a social desirability scale.

The I-E Scale attempts to measure the degree to which people perceive a causal relationship between their own efforts and environmental consequences. People who score high on internal control generally believe that the source of control resides within themselves and that they exercise a high level of personal control in most situations. People who score high on external control generally believe that their life is largely controlled by forces outside themselves, such as chance, destiny, or the behavior of other people. At the beginning of this chapter, we asked you to check either "a" or "b" for six items that might assess internal or external locus of control. Marking "b" for all times except Number 2 might indicate internal locus of

TABLE 17.1

Sample Items From Rotter's Internal-External Control Scale

1. a. Many of the unhappy things in people's lives are partly due to bad luck.
   b. People's misfortunes result from the mistakes they make.
2. a. One of the major reasons we have wars is that people don't take enough interest in politics.
   b. There will always be wars, no matter how hard people try to prevent them.
3. a. In the long run, people get the respect they deserve in this world.
   b. Unfortunately, an individual's worth often passes unrecognized no matter how hard he or she tries.
4. a. The average citizen can have an influence in government decisions.
   b. The world is run by the few people in power and there isn't much the little guy can do about it.
5. a. The idea that teachers are unfair to students is nonsense.
   b. Most students don't realize the extent to which their grades are influenced by accidental happenings.
6. a. No matter how hard you try, some people just don't like you.
   b. People who can't get others to like them don't understand how to get along with others.

From J. B. Rotter, 1966. Generalized expectancies for internal versus external control of reinforcement. *Psychological Monographs, 80* (Whole No. 609), p. 11. Reprinted by permission.

control. However, as Rotter (1975, 1990) pointed out, too much internal control is not always socially desirable. For example, Item 2 of the chapter opener taps into a person's generalized expectancy for omnipotence, hardly a socially desirable attitude.

Rotter's Internal-External Control Scale has become one of the most thoroughly investigated topics in psychology as well as in other social sciences, having sparked several thousand publications since its inception. Despite this popularity, the concepts of internal and external control are not always clearly understood. Although Rotter (1975) pointed out several common misconceptions concerning internal and external control of reinforcement (he seldom referred to it as "locus of control"), people continue to misuse and misinterpret the instrument. One misconception is that scores on the scale are determinants of behavior. Rotter insisted that they should not be seen as causes of behavior but as indicators of *generalized expectancies* (*GEs*). As such, they must be considered along with *reinforcement value* (*RV*) when predicting behavior potential.

A second misconception is that locus of control is specific and can predict achievement in a specific situation. Again, the concept refers to *generalized* expectancies of reinforcement and indicates the degree to which people generally believe that they are in control of their lives.

A third common misconception is that the scale divides people into two distinct types—internals and externals. Rotter (1975, 1990) insisted that generalized expectancies imply a *gradient* of generalization and that, in certain specific situations, a person with generally high feelings of internal control may believe that the outcome of his or her behavior is due mostly to fate, chance, or the behavior of powerful others.

Fourth, many people seem to believe that high internal scores signify socially desirable traits and that high external scores indicate socially undesirable characteristics. Actually, extreme scores in either direction would be undesirable. Very high external scores might be related to apathy and despair, with people believing that they have no control over their environments, whereas extremely high internal scores would mean that people accept responsibility for everything that happens to them—business failure, delinquent children, other people's misery, and thunder storms that interfere with planned outdoor activities. Scores somewhere in between these extremes, but inclined in the direction of internal control, would probably be most healthy or desirable.

Interpersonal Trust Scale

Another example of a generalized expectancy (*GE*) that has provoked considerable interest and research is the concept of **interpersonal trust.** Rotter (1980) defined interpersonal trust as "a generalized expectancy held by an individual that the word, promise, oral or written statement of another individual or group can be relied on" (p. 1). Interpersonal trust does not refer to the belief that people are naturally good or that they live in the best of all possible worlds. Neither should it be equated with gullibility. Rotter saw interpersonal trust as a belief in the communications of others when there is no evidence for disbelieving, whereas gullibility is foolishly or naively believing the words of other people.

Pair skating demands a high level of interpersonal trust.

Because many of our rewards and punishments come from other people, we develop generalized expectancies that some type of reinforcement will follow from verbal promises or threats made by others. Sometimes these promises and threats are kept; other times they are broken. In this way, each person learns to trust or distrust the words of others. Because we have differential experiences with the words of others, it follows that individual differences will exist among people with regard to interpersonal trust.

To measure differences in interpersonal trust, Rotter (1967) developed an Interpersonal Trust Scale, which asked people to agree or disagree to 25 items that assessed interpersonal trust and 15 filler items designed to conceal the nature of the instrument. The scale is scored on a 5-point gradation from strongly agree to strongly disagree so that strongly disagree and agree responses would indicate trust on 12 items and strongly disagree and disagree responses would indicate trust on the other 13 items. Table 17.2 reveals several sample items from Rotter's Interpersonal Trust Scale. Scores for each of the 25 items are added so that high scores indicate the presence of interpersonal trust and low scores mean a generalized expectancy of distrust.

Is it more desirable to score high or low on the scale, to be trustful or distrustful? When trust is defined independently of gullibility, as Rotter (1980) contended, then high trust is not only desirable but essential for the survival of civilization. People trust that the food they buy is not poisoned; that the gasoline in their cars will not explode on ignition; that airline pilots know how to fly the plane in which they travel; and even that the postal service will deliver the mail without tampering with it. Societies can function smoothly only when people have at least a moderate amount of trust in each other.

Rotter (1980) summarized results of studies that indicate that people who score high in interpersonal trust, as opposed to those who score low, are (1) less likely to lie; (2) probably less likely to cheat or steal; (3) more likely to give others a second chance; (4) more likely to respect the rights of others; (5) less likely to be

TABLE 17.2

Sample Items From Rotter's Interpersonal Trust Scale

1. In dealing with strangers, one is better off to be cautious until they have provided evidence that they are trustworthy.
2. Parents usually can be relied on to keep their promises.
3. Parents and teachers are likely to say what they believe themselves and not just what they think is good for the child to hear.
4. Most elected public officials are really sincere in their campaign promises.
5. In these competitive times, one has to be alert or someone is likely to take advantage of you.
6. Most people can be counted on to do what they say they will do.
7. Most salesmen are honest in describing their products.

From J. B. Rotter (1967). A new scale for the measurement of interpersonal trust. *Journal of Personality, 35,* p. 654; and M. R. Gurtman, 1992. Trust, distrust, and interpersonal problems: A circumplex analysis. *Journal of Personality and Social Psychology, 62,* p. 997.

unhappy, conflicted, or maladjusted; (6) somewhat more likable and popular; (7) more trustworthy; (8) neither more nor less gullible; and (9) neither more nor less intelligent. In other words, high trusters are not gullible or naive, and rather than being harmed by their trustful attitude, they seem to possess many of the characteristics that other people regard as positive and desirable.

Maladaptive Behavior

Maladaptive behavior in Rotter's social learning theory is any persistent behavior that fails to move a person closer to a desired goal. It frequently, but not inevitably, arises from the combination of high need value and low freedom of movement: that is, from goals that are unrealistically high in relation to one's ability to achieve them (Rotter, 1964).

   For example, the need for love and affection is realistic, but some people unrealistically set a goal to be loved by everyone. Hence, their need value will nearly certainly exceed their freedom of movement, resulting in behavior that is likely to be defensive or maladaptive. When people set their goals too high, they cannot learn productive behaviors because their goals are beyond reach. Instead, they learn how to avoid failure or how to defend themselves against the pain that accompanies failure. For example, a woman whose goal is to be loved by everyone inevitably will be ignored or rejected by someone. To obtain love, she may become socially aggressive (a nonproductive, self-defeating strategy), or she may withdraw from people, which prevents her from being hurt by them but which is also nonproductive.

   Setting goals too high is only one of several possible contributors to maladaptive behavior. Another frequent cause is low freedom of movement. People may have low expectancies of success because they lack information or the ability to perform those behaviors that will be followed by positive reinforcement. A person who values love, for example, may lack the interpersonal skills necessary to obtain it.

People may also have low freedom of movement because they make a faulty evaluation of the present situation. For example, people sometimes underestimate their intellectual abilities because, in the past, they have been told that they were stupid. Even though their need values are not unrealistically high, they have a low expectation of success because they wrongly believe that they are incapable, for example, of performing well in school or competing successfully for a higher level job.

Another possibility is that people have low freedom of movement because they generalize from one situation in which, perhaps, they are realistically inadequate to other situations in which they could have sufficient ability to be successful. For example, a physically weak adolescent who lacks the skills to be an accomplished athlete may erroneously see himself as unable to compete for a role in the school play or to be a leader in a social club. He inappropriately generalizes his inadequacies in sports to lack of ability in unrelated areas.

In summary, maladjusted individuals are characterized by unrealistic goals, inappropriate behaviors, inadequate skills, or unreasonably low expectancies of being able to execute the behaviors necessary for positive reinforcement. Although they have learned inadequate ways of solving problems within a social context, they can unlearn these behaviors and also learn more appropriate ones within the controlled social environment provided by psychotherapy.

Psychotherapy

To Rotter (1964), "the problems of psychotherapy are problems of how to effect changes in behavior through the interaction of one person with another. That is, they are problems in human learning in a social situation" (p. 82). Although Rotter adopts a problem-solving approach to psychotherapy, he does not limit his concern to quick solutions to immediate problems. His interest is more long range, involving a change in the patient's orientation toward life.

In general, the goal of Rotter's therapy is to bring freedom of movement and need value into harmony, thus reducing defensive and avoidance behaviors. The therapist assumes an active role as a teacher and attempts to accomplish the therapeutic goal in two basic ways: (1) changing the importance of goals and (2) eliminating unrealistically low expectancies for success (Rotter, 1964, 1970, 1978; Rotter & Hochreich, 1975).

Changing Goals

Many patients are unable to solve life's problems because they are pursuing skewed or distorted goals. The role of the therapist is to help these patients understand the faulty nature of their goals and to teach them constructive means of striving toward realistic goals. Rotter and Hochreich (1975) listed three sources of problems that follow from inappropriate goals.

First, two or more important goals may be in conflict. For example, adolescents frequently value both independence and protection-dependency. On the one hand, they wish to be free from their parents' domination and control, but on the other, they retain their need for a nurturing person to care for them and protect them from painful experiences. Their ambivalent behaviors are often confusing both to themselves and to their parents. In this situation, the therapist may try to help adolescents see how specific behaviors are related to each of these needs and proceed to work with them in changing the value of one or both needs. By altering need value, patients gradually begin to behave more consistently and to experience greater freedom of movement in obtaining their goals.

A second source of problems is a destructive goal. Some patients persistently pursue self-destructive goals that inevitably result in failure and punishment. The job of the therapist is to point out the detrimental nature of this pursuit and the likelihood that it will be followed by punishment. One possible technique used by a therapist in these cases is to positively reinforce movements away from destructive goals. Rotter, however, is both pragmatic and eclectic and is not bound to a specific set of techniques for each conceivable problem. To him, the appropriate procedure is the one that works with a given patient.

Third, many people find themselves in trouble because they set their goals too high and are continually frustrated when they cannot reach or exceed them. High goals lead to failure and pain, so instead of learning constructive means of obtaining a goal, people learn nonproductive ways of avoiding pain. For example, a person may learn to avoid painful experiences by physically running away or by psychologically repressing the experience. Because these techniques are successful, the person learns to use flight and repression in a variety of situations. Therapy in this case would consist of getting the patient to realistically reevaluate and lower exaggerated goals by reducing the reinforcement value of these goals. Because high reinforcement value is often learned through generalization, the therapist would work toward teaching patients to discriminate between past legitimate values and present spurious ones.

Eliminating Low Expectancies

In addition to changing goals, the therapist tries to eliminate patients' low expectancies of success and its analog, low freedom of movement. People may have low freedom of movement for at least three reasons.

First, they may lack the skills or information needed to successfully strive toward their goals (Rotter, 1970). With such patients, a therapist becomes a teacher, warmly and emphatically instructing them in more effective techniques for solving problems and satisfying needs. If a patient, for example, has difficulties in interpersonal relationships, the therapist has an arsenal of techniques, including extinguishing inappropriate behaviors by simply ignoring them; using the therapist-patient relationship as a model for an effective interpersonal encounter that may then generalize beyond the therapeutic situation; and advising the patient of specific behaviors to try out in the presence of those other people who are most likely to be receptive.

A second source of low freedom of movement is faulty evaluation of the present situation. For example, an adult may lack assertiveness with her colleagues because, during childhood, she was punished for competing with her siblings. This patient must learn to differentiate between past and present as well as between siblings and colleagues. The therapist's task is to help her make these distinctions and to teach her assertiveness techniques in a variety of appropriate situations.

Finally, low freedom of movement can spring from inadequate generalization. Patients often use failure in one situation as proof that they cannot be successful in other areas. Take the example of the physically feeble adolescent who, because he was unsuccessful in sports, generalized his failure to nonathletic areas. His present problems come from faulty generalization, and the therapist must reinforce even small successes in social relationships, academic achievements, and other situations. The patient will eventually learn to discriminate between realistic shortcomings in one area and successful behaviors in other situations.

Although Rotter recognized that therapists should be flexible in their techniques and should utilize different approaches with different patients, he suggested several interesting techniques that he found to be effective. The first is to teach patients to look for alternative courses of action. Patients frequently complain that their spouse, parent, child, or employer does not understand them, treats them unjustly, and is the source of their problems. In this situation, Rotter would simply teach the patient to change the other person's behavior. This change can be accomplished by examining those behaviors of the patient that typically lead to negative reactions by spouse, parent, child, or employer. If the patient can find an alternative method of behaving toward important others, then those others will probably change their behavior toward the patient. Thereafter, the patient will be rewarded for behaving in a more appropriate fashion.

Rotter also suggested a technique to help patients understand other people's motives. Many patients have a suspicious or distrustful attitude toward others, believing that a spouse, teacher, or boss is intentionally and spitefully trying to harm them. Rotter would attempt to teach these patients to look at ways in which they may be contributing to the other person's defensive or negative behavior and to help them realize that the other person is not simply nasty or spiteful but may be frightened or threatened by the patient.

Therapists can also help patients look at the long-range consequences of their behaviors and to understand that many maladaptive behaviors produce secondary gains that outweigh the patients' present frustration. For example, a woman may adopt the role of a helpless child in order to gain control over her husband. She complains to her therapist that she is dissatisfied with her helplessness and would like to become more independent, both for her sake and for the benefit of her husband. What she may not realize, however, is that her current helpless behavior is satisfying her basic need for dominance. The more helpless she acts, the more control she exercises over her husband, who must respond to her helplessness. The positive reinforcement she receives from her husband's recognition is stronger than her accompanying negative feelings. In addition, she may not clearly see the long-range positive consequences of self-confidence and independence. The task of therapists is to train patients to postpone minor contemporary satisfactions for more important future ones.

Another novel technique suggested by Rotter is to have patients enter into a previously painful social situation, but rather than speaking as much as usual, they are asked to remain as quiet as possible and merely observe. By observing other people, the patient has a better chance of learning their motives. Patients can use that information in the future to alter their own behavior, thereby changing the reactions of others and reducing the painful effects of future encounters with those other persons.

In summary, Rotter believes that a therapist should be an active participant in a social interaction with the patient. An effective therapist possesses the characteristics of warmth and acceptance not only because these attitudes encourage the patient to verbalize problems but also because reinforcement from a warm, accepting therapist is more effective than reinforcement from a cold, rejecting one (Rotter, Chance, & Phares, 1972). The therapist attempts to minimize the discrepancy between need value and freedom of movement by helping patients alter their goals or by teaching effective means of obtaining those goals. Even though the therapist is an active problem solver, Rotter (1978) believes that eventually patients must learn to solve their own problems.

Introduction to Mischel's Personality Theory

In general, personality theories are of two types—those who see personality as a dynamic entity motivated by drives, perceptions, needs, goals, and expectancies and those who view personality as a function of relatively stable traits or personal dispositions. The first category includes the theories of Adler (Chapter 3), Maslow (Chapter 10), and Bandura (Chapter 16). This approach emphasizes cognitive and affective dynamics that interact with the environment to produce behavior.

The second category emphasizes the importance of relatively stable traits of personal dispositions. The theories of Allport (Chapter 13), Eysenck (Chapter 14), and McCrae and Costa (Chapter 14) are in this category. This approach sees people as being motivated by a limited number of drives or personal traits that tend to render a person's behavior somewhat consistent. Walter Mischel (1973) originally objected to this trait theory explanation of behavior. Instead, he supported the idea that cognitive activities and specific situations play a major role in determining behavior. However, more recently, Mischel and his colleagues (Mischel & Shoda, 1998, 1999; Mischel, Shoda, & Mendoza-Denton, 2002) have advocated a reconciliation between the processing dynamics approach and the personal dispositions approach. This **cognitive-affective personality theory** holds that behavior stems from relatively stable personal dispositions and cognitive-affective processes interacting with a particular situation.

Biography of Walter Mischel

Walter Mischel, the second son of upper-middle-class parents, was born on February 22, 1930, in Vienna. He and his brother Theodore, who later became a philosopher of science, grew up in a pleasant environment only a short distance from Freud's home. The tranquillity of childhood, however, was shattered when the Nazis invaded Austria in 1938. That same year, the Mischel family fled Austria and moved to the United States. After living in various parts of the country, they eventually settled in Brooklyn, where Walter attended primary and secondary schools. Before he could accept a college scholarship, his father suddenly became ill, and Walter was forced to take a series of odd jobs. Eventually, he was able to attend New York University, where he became passionately interested in art (painting and sculpture) and divided his time among art, psychology, and life in Greenwich Village.

In college, Mischel was appalled by the rat-centered introductory psychology classes that seemed to him far removed from the everyday lives of humans. His humanistic inclinations were solidified by reading Freud, the existential thinkers, and the great poets. After graduation, he entered the MA program in clinical psychology at City College of New York. While working on his degree, he was employed as a social worker in the Lower East Side slums, work that led him to doubt the usefulness of psychoanalytic theory and to see the necessity of using empirical evidence to evaluate all claims of psychology.

Mischel's development as a cognitive social psychologist was further enhanced by his doctoral studies at Ohio State University from 1953 to 1956. At that time, the psychology department at Ohio State was informally divided into the supporters of its two most influential faculty members—Julian Rotter and George Kelly. Unlike most students, who strongly supported one or the other position, Mischel admired both Rotter and Kelly and learned from each of them. As a consequence, Mischel's cognitive social theory shows the influence of Rotter's social learning theory as well as Kelly's cognitively based theory of personal constructs (see Chapter 18). Rotter taught Mischel the importance of research design for improving assessment techniques and for measuring the effectiveness of therapeutic treatment; Kelly taught him that participants in psychology experiments are like the psychologists who study them in that they are thinking, feeling human beings.

From 1956 to 1958, Mischel lived much of the time in the Caribbean, studying religious cults that practiced spirit possession and investigating delay of gratification in a cross-cultural setting. He became determined to learn more about why people prefer future valuable rewards over immediate less valuable ones. Much of his later research has revolved around this issue.

Next, Mischel taught for 2 years at the University of Colorado. He then joined the Department of Social Relations at Harvard, where his interest in personality theory and assessment was further stimulated by discussions with Gordon Allport (see Chapter 13), Henry Murray, David McClelland, and others. In 1962, Mischel moved to Stanford and became a colleague of Albert Bandura (see Chapter 16). After more than 20 years at Stanford, Mischel returned to New York, joining the faculty at Columbia University, where he remains as an active researcher and continues to hone his cognitive social learning theory.

While at Harvard, Mischel met and married Harriet Nerlove, another graduate student in cognitive psychology. Before their divorce, the Mischels collaborated to produce three daughters and several scientific projects (H. N. Mischel & W. Mischel, 1973; W. Mischel & H. N. Mischel, 1976, 1983). Mischel's most important early work was *Personality and Assessment* (1968), an outgrowth of his efforts to identify successful Peace Corps volunteers. His experiences as consultant to the Peace Corps taught him that under the right conditions, people are at least as capable as standardized tests at predicting their own behavior. In *Personality and Assessment,* Mischel argued that traits are weak predictors of performance in a variety of situations and that the situation is more important than traits in influencing behavior. This book upset many clinical psychologists, who argued that the inability of personal dispositions to predict behavior across situations was due to the unreliability and imprecision of the instruments that measure traits. Some believed that Mischel was trying to undo the concept of stable personality traits and even deny the existence of personality. Later, Mischel (1979) answered his critics, saying that he was not opposed to traits as such, but only to generalized traits that negate the individuality and uniqueness of each person.

Much of Mischel's research has been a cooperative effort with a number of his graduate students. In recent years, many of his publications have been collaborations with Yuichi Shoda, who received his PhD from Columbia in 1990 and is presently at the University of Washington. Mischel's most popular book, *Introduction to Personality,* was published originally in 1971 and underwent a 7th revision in 2004, with Yuichi Shoda and Ronald D. Smith as coauthors. Mischel has won several awards, including the Distinguished Scientist award from the clinical division of the American Psychological Association (APA) in 1978 and the APA's award for Distinguished Scientific Contribution in 1982.

Background of the Cognitive-Affective Personality System

Some theorists, such as Hans Eysenck (Chapter 14) and Gordon Allport (Chapter 13), believed that behavior was mostly a product of relatively stable personality traits. However, Walter Mischel objected to this assumption. His early research (Mischel, 1958, 1961a, 1961b) led him to believe that behavior was largely a function of the *situation.*

Consistency Paradox

Mischel saw that both laypersons and professional psychologists seem to intuitively believe that people's behavior is relatively consistent, yet empirical evidence suggests much variability in behavior, a situation Mischel called the **consistency paradox.** To many people, it seems self-evident that such global personal dispositions as aggressiveness, honesty, miserliness, punctuality, and so forth account for much of our behavior. People elect politicians to office because they see them as having honesty, trustworthiness, decisiveness, and integrity; employers and personnel managers select workers who are punctual, loyal, cooperative, hardworking, organized, and sociable. One person is generally friendly and gregarious, whereas another is usually unfriendly and taciturn. Psychologists as well as laypeople have long summarized people's behavior by using such descriptive trait names. Thus, many people assume that global personality traits will be manifested over a period of time and also from one situation to another. Mischel suggested that, at best, these people are only half right. He contended that some basic traits do persist over time, but little evidence exists that they generalize from one situation to another. Mischel strongly objected to attempts to attribute behavior to these global traits. Any attempt to classify individuals as friendly, extraverted, conscientious, and so forth may be one way of defining personality, but it is a sterile taxonomy that fails to explain behavior (Mischel, 1990, 1999, 2004; Mischel et al., 2002; Shoda & Mischel, 1998).

For many years, research has failed to support the consistency of personality traits across situations. Hugh Hartshorne and Mark May, in their classic 1928 study, found that schoolchildren who were honest in one situation were deceitful in another. For example, some children would cheat on tests but not steal party favors; others would break rules in an athletic contest but not cheat on a test. Some psychologists, such as Seymour Epstein (1979, 1980), have argued that studies such as Hartshorne and May's used behaviors that are too specific. Epstein contended that, rather than relying on single behaviors, researchers must aggregate measures of behavior; that is, they must obtain a sum of many behaviors. In other words, Epstein would say that even though people do not *always* display a strong personal trait, for example, conscientiousness, the sum total of their individual behaviors will reflect a generally conscientious core.

However, Mischel (1965) had earlier found that a three-person assessment committee, which used aggregated information from a variety of scores, could not reliably predict performance of Peace Corps teachers. The correlation between the committee's judgment and the performance of the teachers was a nonsignificant 0.20. Moreover, Mischel (1968) contended that correlations of about 0.30 between different measures of the same trait as well as between trait scores and subsequent behaviors represented the outer limits of trait consistency. Thus, these relatively low correlations between traits and behavior are not due to the unreliability of the assessment instrument but to the inconsistencies in behavior. Even with perfectly reliable measures, Mischel argued, specific behaviors will not accurately predict personality traits.

Person-Situation Interaction

In time, however, Mischel (1973, 2004) came to see that people are not empty vessels with no enduring personality traits. He acknowledged that most people have some consistency in their behavior, but he continued to insist that the situation has a powerful effect on behavior. Mischel's objection to the use of traits as predictors of behaviors rested not with their temporal instability but with their inconsistency from one *situation* to another. He saw that many basic dispositions can be stable over a long period of time. For example, a student may have a history of being conscientious with regard to academic work but fail to be conscientious in cleaning his apartment or maintaining his car in working condition. His lack of conscientiousness in cleaning his apartment may be due to disinterest, and his neglect of his car may be the result of insufficient knowledge. Thus, the specific situation interacts with the person's competencies, interests, goals, values, expectancies, and so forth to predict behavior. To Mischel, these views of traits or personal dispositions, though important in predicting human behavior, overlook the significance of the specific situation in which people function.

Personal dispositions influence behavior only under certain conditions and in certain situations. This view suggests that behavior is not caused by global personal traits but by people's perceptions of themselves in a particular situation. For example, a young man who typically is very shy around young women may behave in an outgoing, extraverted manner when he is with men or with older women. Is this young man shy or is he extraverted? Mischel would say that he is both—depending on the conditions affecting the young man during a particular situation.

The conditional view holds that behavior is shaped by personal dispositions *plus* a person's specific cognitive and affective processes. Whereas trait theory would suggest that global dispositions predict behavior, Mischel argues that a person's beliefs, values, goals, cognitions, and feelings interact with those dispositions to shape behavior. For example, traditional trait theory suggests that people with the trait of conscientiousness will usually behave in a conscientious manner. However, Mischel points out that in a variety of situations, a conscientious person may use conscientiousness along with other cognitive-affective processes to accomplish a specific outcome.

In an exploratory study to test this model, Jack Wright and Mischel (1988) interviewed 8- and 12-year-old children as well as adults and asked them to report everything they knew about "target" groups of children. Both adults and children recognized the variability of other people's behavior, but adults were more certain about the conditions under which particular behaviors would occur. Whereas children would hedge their descriptions in such terms as "Carlo sometimes hits other kids," adults would be more specific: for example, "Carlo hits when provoked." These findings suggest that people readily recognize the interrelationship between situations and behavior and that they intuitively follow a conditional view of dispositions.

Neither the situation alone nor stable personality traits alone determine behavior. Rather, behavior is a product of both. Therefore, Mischel and Shoda have proposed a cognitive-affective personality system that attempts to reconcile these two approaches to predicting human behaviors.

Cognitive-Affective Personality System

To solve the classical consistency paradox, Mischel and Shoda (Mischel, 2004; Mischel & Shoda, 1995, 1998, 1999; Shoda & Mischel, 1996, 1998) proposed a **cognitive-affective personality system** (CAPS; also called a cognitive-affective processing system) that accounts for variability across situations as well as stability of behavior within a person. Apparent inconsistencies in a person's behavior are due neither to random error nor solely to the situation. Rather, they are potentially predictable behaviors that reflect stable *patterns of variation* within a person. The cognitive-affective personality system predicts that a person's behavior will change from situation to situation but in a meaningful manner.

Mischel and Shoda (Mischel, 1999, 2004; Mischel & Ayduk, 2002; Shoda, LeeTiernan, & Mischel, 2002) believe that variations in behavior can be conceptualized in this framework: *If A, then X; but if B, then Y.* For example, if Mark is provoked by his wife, then he will react with aggression. However, when the "if" changes, so does the "then." If Mark is provoked by his boss, then he will react with submission. Mark's behavior may seem inconsistent because he apparently reacts differently to the same stimulus. Mischel and Shoda, however, would argue that being provoked by two different people does not constitute the same stimulus. Mark's behavior is not inconsistent and may well reflect a stable lifetime pattern of reacting. Such an interpretation, Mischel and Shoda believe, solves the consistency paradox by taking into account both the long history of observed variability in behavior and the intuitive conviction of both psychologists and laypeople that personality is relatively stable. The frequently observed variability in behavior is simply an essential part of a unifying stability of personality.

This theory does not suggest that behaviors are an outgrowth of stable, global personality traits. If behaviors were a result of global traits, then there would be little individual variation in behavior. In other words, Mark would react in much the same manner to provocation, regardless of the specific situation. However, Mark's long-standing pattern of variability attests to the inadequacy of both the situation theory and the trait theory. His pattern of variability is his **behavioral signature of personality,** that is, his consistent manner of varying his behavior in particular situations (Shoda, LeeTiernan, & Mischel, 2002). His personality has a signature that remains stable across situations even as his behavior changes. Mischel (1999) believes that an adequate theory of personality should "try to predict and explain these signatures of personality, rather than to eliminate or ignore them" (p. 46).

Behavior Prediction

In Chapter 1, we advocated that effective theories should be stated in an *if-then* framework, but Mischel (1999, 2004) is one of only a few personality theorists to do so. His basic theoretical position for predicting and explaining is stated as follows: "If personality is a stable system that processes the information about the situations, external or internal, then it follows that as individuals encounter different situations, their behaviors should vary across the situations" (p. 43). This theoretical position can generate a number of hypotheses about behavior outcomes. It assumes that personality may have temporal stability *and* that behaviors may vary from situation to situation. It also assumes that prediction of behavior rests on a knowledge of how and when various cognitive-affective units are activated. These units include encodings, expectancies, beliefs, competencies, self-regulatory plans and strategies, and affects and goals.

Situation Variables

Mischel believes that the relative influence of situation variables and personal qualities can be determined by observing the uniformity or diversity of people's responses in a given situation. When different people are behaving in a very similar manner—for example, while watching an emotional scene in an engrossing movie—situation variables are more powerful than personal characteristics. On the other hand, events that appear the same may produce widely different reactions because personal qualities override situational ones. For example, several workers may all be laid off from their jobs, but individual differences will lead to diverse behaviors, depending on the workers' perceived need to work, confidence in their level of skill, and perceived ability to find another job.

Early in his career, Mischel conducted studies demonstrating that the interaction between the situation and various personal qualities was an important determinant of behavior. In one study, for example, Mischel and Ervin Staub (1965) looked at conditions that influenced a person's choice of a reward and found that both the situation and an individual's expectancy for success were important. These investigators first asked 8th-grade boys to rate their expectancies for success on verbal reasoning and general information tasks. Later, after the students worked on a series of problems, some were told that they had succeeded on those problems; some were

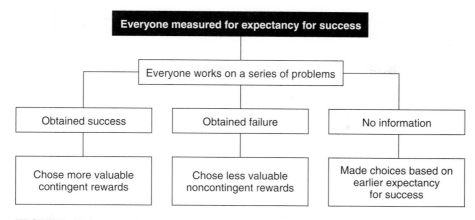

FIGURE 17.2 Model used by Mischel and Staub (1965).

informed that they had failed; and the third group received no information. The boys were then asked to choose between an immediate, less valuable, noncontingent reward and a delayed, more valuable, contingent reward. Consistent with Mischel's interaction theory, students who had been told that they had succeeded on the earlier similar task were more likely to wait for the more valued reward that was contingent on their performance; those who were informed that they had previously failed tended to choose an immediate, less valuable reward; and those who had received no earlier feedback made choices based on their original expectancies for success; that is, students in the no-information group who originally had high expectancies for success made choices similar to those who believed that they were successful, whereas those who originally had low expectancies for success made choices similar to those who believed that they had failed. Figure 17.2 shows how situational feedback interacts with expectancy for success to influence choice of rewards.

Mischel and his associates have also shown that children can use their cognitive processes to change a difficult situation into an easier one. For example, Mischel and Ebbe B. Ebbesen (1970) found that some children were able to use their cognitive ability to change an unpleasant wait for a treat into a more pleasant situation. In this delay-of-gratification study, nursery school children were told that they would receive a small reward after a short period of time, but a larger treat if they could wait longer. Children who thought about the treat had difficulty waiting, whereas children who were able to wait the longest used a variety of self-distractions to avoid thinking about the reward. They looked away from the treat, closed their eyes, or sang songs in order to change the aversive waiting situation into a more pleasant one. These and other research results led Mischel to conclude that both the situation and various cognitive-affective components of personality play a role in determining behavior.

Cognitive-Affective Units

In 1973, Mischel proposed a set of five overlapping, relatively stable person variables that interact with the situation to determine behavior. More than 30 years of research have caused Mischel and his associates to broaden their conception of these variables, which they call *cognitive-affective units* (Mischel, 1999, 2004; Mischel & Ayduk, 2002; Mischel & Shoda, 1995, 1998, 1999). These person variables shifted the emphasis from what a person *has* (i.e., global traits) to what a person *does* in a particular situation. What a person does includes more than actions; it includes cognitive and affective qualities such as thinking, planning, feeling, and evaluating.

Cognitive-affective units include all those psychological, social, and physiological aspects of people that cause them to interact with their environment with a relatively stable pattern of variation. These units include people's (1) encoding strategies, (2) competencies and self-regulatory strategies, (3) expectancies and beliefs, (4) goals and values, and (5) affective responses.

Encoding Strategies

One important cognitive-affective unit that ultimately affects behavior is people's personal constructs and **encoding strategies:** that is, people's ways of categorizing information received from external stimuli. People use cognitive processes to transform these stimuli into personal constructs, including their self-concept, their view of other people, and their way of looking at the world. Different people encode the same events in different ways, which accounts for individual differences in personal constructs. For example, one person may react angrily when insulted, whereas another may choose to ignore the same insult. In addition, the same person may encode the same event differently in different situations. For example, a woman who ordinarily construes a telephone call from her best friend as a pleasant experience may in one situation perceive it as a nuisance.

Stimulus inputs are substantially altered by what people selectively attend, how they interpret their experience, and the way in which they categorize those inputs. Mischel and former PhD student Bert Moore (1973) found that children can transform environmental events by focusing on selected aspects of stimulus inputs. In this delay-of-gratification study, children exposed to pictures of rewards (snacks or pennies) were able to wait longer for the rewards than were children who were encouraged to cognitively construct (imagine) real rewards while viewing the pictures. A previous study (Mischel, Ebbesen, & Zeiss, 1972) had demonstrated that children exposed to real rewards during a wait period had more difficulty waiting than those exposed to no reward. Results of these two studies suggested that, in at least some situations, cognitive transformations of stimuli can have about the same effect as actual stimuli.

Competencies and Self-Regulatory Strategies

How we behave depends in part on the potential behaviors available to us, our beliefs of what we can do, our plans and strategies for enacting behaviors, and our expectancies for success (Mischel, Cantor, & Feldman, 1996). Our beliefs in what we can do relate to our **competencies.** Mischel (1990) used the term "competencies" to refer to that vast array of information we acquire about the world and our relationship to it. By observing our own behaviors and those of others, we learn what we can do in a particular situation as well as what we cannot do. Mischel agreed with Bandura that we do not attend to all stimuli in our environment; rather, we selectively *construct* or generate our own version of the real world. Thus, we acquire a set of beliefs about our performance capabilities, often in the absence of actual performance. For example, an outstanding student may believe that she has the competence to do well on the Graduate Record Exam (GRE) even though she has never taken that test.

Cognitive competencies, such as doing well on the GRE, are generally more stable temporally and cross-situationally than other cognitive-affective units are. That is, people's scores on mental ability tests do not ordinarily show large fluctuations from one time to the next or from one situation to another. In fact, Mischel (1990) has argued that one of the reasons for the apparent consistency of traits is the relative stability of intelligence, a basic trait that underlies many personal dispositions. He contended that cognitive competencies, as measured by traditional mental ability tests, have proven to be some of the best predictors of social and interpersonal adjustment and thus give social and interpersonal traits some appearance of stability. Moreover, Mischel suggested that when intelligence is assessed by nontraditional measures that include a person's potential for seeing alternate solutions to problems, it accounts for even larger portions of the consistency found in other traits.

In Chapter 16, we discussed Bandura's concept of self-regulation, by which people control their own behavior. Similarly, Mischel believes that people use **self-regulatory strategies** to control their own behavior through self-imposed goals and self-produced consequences. People do not require external rewards and punishments to shape their behavior; they can set goals for themselves and then reward or criticize themselves contingent upon whether their behavior moves them in the direction of those goals.

People's self-regulatory system enables them to plan, initiate, and maintain behaviors even when environmental support is weak or nonexistent. People such as Abraham Lincoln and Mohandas Gandhi were able to regulate their own behavior in the face of a nonsupportive and hostile environment, but each of us can persist without environmental encouragement if we have powerful self-produced goals and values. However, inappropriate goals and ineffective strategies increase anxiety and lead to failure. For example, people with inflexible, exaggerated goals may persist in trying to realize those goals, but their lack of competence and environmental support prevent them from achieving those goals.

Expectancies and Beliefs

Any situation presents an enormous number of behavioral potentials, but how people behave depends on their specific *expectancies and beliefs* about the consequences of each of the different behavioral possibilities. Knowledge of people's hypotheses or beliefs concerning the outcome of any situation is a better predictor of behavior than is knowledge of their ability to perform (Mischel et al., 2002).

From previous experience and by observing others, people learn to enact those behaviors that they expect will result in the most subjectively valued outcome. When people have no information about what they can expect from a behavior, they will enact those behaviors that received the greatest reinforcement in past similar situations. For example, a college student who has never taken the GRE nevertheless has had experience preparing for other tests. What that student does in getting ready for the GRE is partially influenced by what previous test preparation behaviors resulted in the most valuable outcome. A student who has previously been rewarded for using self-relaxation techniques to prepare for tests will expect that the same techniques will help in doing well on the GRE. Mischel (1990, 2004) referred to this type of expectancy as a *behavior-outcome expectancy*. People often construe behavior-outcome expectancies in an "if . . . , then . . ." framework. "If I use self-relaxation procedures, then I can expect to do well on the GRE." "If I tell my boss what I really think of her, then I might lose my job."

Mischel also identified a second type of expectancy—*stimulus-outcome expectancies,* which refers to the many stimulus conditions that influence the probable consequences of any behavior pattern. Stimulus-outcome expectancies help us predict what events are likely to occur following certain stimuli. Perhaps the most obvious example is an expectancy of loud, unpleasant thunder following the observance of lightning (the stimulus). Mischel believes that stimulus-outcome expectancies are important units for understanding classical conditioning. For example, a child who has been conditioned to associate pain with nurses in a hospital begins to cry and show fear when she sees a nurse with a hypodermic syringe.

Mischel (1990) believes that one reason for the inconsistency of behavior is our inability to predict other people's behavior. We have little hesitancy in attributing personal traits to others, but when we notice that their behavior is inconsistent with those traits, we become less certain about how to react to them. Our behavior will be cross-situationally consistent to the extent that our expectancies are unchanging. But our expectancies are not constant; they change because we can discriminate and evaluate the multitude of potential reinforcers in any given situation (Mischel & Ayduk, 2002).

Goals and Values

People do not react passively to situations but are active and goal directed. They formulate goals, devise plans for attaining their goals, and in part create their own situations. People's subjective goals, values, and preferences represent a fourth cognitive-affective unit. For example, two college students may have equal academic ability and also equal expectancy for success in graduate school. The first, however, places more value on entering the job market than on going to graduate school, while the second chooses to go to graduate school rather than to pursue an immediate career. The two may have had many similar experiences during college, but because they have different goals, they have made very different decisions.

Values, goals, and interests, along with competencies, are among the most stable cognitive-affective units. One reason for this consistency is the emotion-eliciting properties of these units. For instance, a person may place a negative value on a certain food because he associates it with the nausea he once experienced while eating that food. Without counterconditioning, this aversion is likely to persist due to the strong negative emotion elicited by the food. Similarly, patriotic values may last a lifetime because they are associated with positive emotions such as security, attachment to one's home, and love of one's mother.

Affective Responses

During the early 1970s, Mischel's theory was mostly a cognitive theory. It was based on the assumption that people's thoughts and other cognitive processes interact with a particular situation to determine behavior. Since then, however, Mischel and

One reason for the inconsistency in people's behavior is their inability to predict the behavior of others.

colleagues (Mischel & Ayduk, 2002; Mischel & Shoda, 1998, 1999) have added affective responses to the list of important cognitive-affective units. Affective responses include emotions, feelings, and physiological reactions. Mischel sees affective responses as inseparable from cognitions and regards the interlocking cognitive-affective units as more basic than the other cognitive-affective units.

Affective responses, then, do not exist in isolation. Not only are they inseparable from cognitive processes, but also they influence each of the other cognitive-affective units. For example, the encoding of a person's view of self includes certain positive and negative feelings. "I see myself as a competent psychology student and that pleases me." "I'm not very good at mathematics and I don't like that." Similarly, people's competencies and coping strategies, their beliefs and expectancies, and their goals and values are all colored by their affective responses.

Mischel and Shoda (1995) stated:

> Cognitive-affective representations are not unconnected discrete units that are simply elicited as "responses" in isolation: These cognitive representations and affective states interact dynamically and influence each other reciprocally, and it is the organization of the relationships among them that forms the core of the personality structure and that guides and constrains their impact. (p. 253)

In summary, interrelated cognitive-affective units contribute to behavior as they interact with stable personality traits and a receptive environment. The most important of these variables include (1) *encoding strategies,* or how people construe or categorize an event; (2) *competencies and self-regulating strategies:* that is, what people can do and their strategies and plans to accomplish a desired behavior; (3) behavior-outcome and stimulus-outcome *expectancies and beliefs* regarding a particular situation; (4) subjective *goals, values, and preferences* that partially determine selective attention to events; and (5) *affective responses,* including feelings and emotions as well as the affects that accompany physiological reactions.

Related Research

Rotter's ideas on internal and external control have generated considerable research in psychology with many researchers from across disciplines drawing upon Rotter's concepts for their own research. Mischel's CAPS model, though a relatively new model of personality (it was first proposed in its entirety in the mid-1990s) has generated a strong body of work considering its age with several studies focusing on the if-then framework previously discussed.

Locus of Control and Holocaust Heroes

As you have read throughout this book, personality variables can be used to predict innumerable outcomes. Some outcomes are rather mundane and routine such as whether La Juan will rest her head during a dull lecture, whereas others are extraordinary such as whether La Juan will earn a PhD in psychology. But perhaps no outcome is more extraordinary than the outcome selected by psychologist Elizabeth Midlarsky and her colleagues. Midlarsky sought to use personality variables to predict who was a Holocaust hero and who was a bystander during the tragic years of World War II (Midlarsky, Fagin Jones, & Corley, 2005). The genocide of 6 million Jews by the Nazis was so extreme, so awful, that it is hard to imagine that just one half of 1% of the people in Nazi-occupied territory elected to assist their Jewish neighbors when their neighbors' lives were in such great peril (Oliner & Oliner, 1988). But the danger posed to those who assisted Jews was equal to the danger of being Jewish, so the acts of non-Jewish civilians who put their own lives on the line to assist their persecuted neighbors were truly rare and heroic acts.

To investigate the power of personality to predict such rare, heroic acts, Midlarsky and her colleagues assembled a remarkable sample of people consisting of 80 rescuers of Jews during World War II, 73 bystanders who lived in Europe during World War II but did not assist Jews, and a comparison sample of 43 people who were from Europe but immigrated to North America before the war. The participants were about 72 years of age on average at the time the study was conducted, which means most of them were in their twenties during World War II. Rescuer status was verified by the testimony of Holocaust survivors who were actually rescued by the participants in this study.

The researchers included several personality variables in their effort to predict who was a hero and who was a bystander; one such variable was locus of control. Being oriented more toward an internal sense of control was predicted to relate to being a Holocaust hero because such individuals believe they have control over life events and success is not due to luck or chance (as people with an external sense of control would believe). To use Rotter's language (Rotter, 1966), these internal controls are people who have a generalized expectancy that their acts would be successful in saving the lives of their persecuted neighbors. Other variables Midlarsky and her colleagues examined were autonomy (having a sense of independence), risk taking, social responsibility, authoritarianism (related to holding prejudiced attitudes toward minority groups and is the opposite of tolerance), empathy, and altruistic moral reasoning (high levels of which require abstract reasoning including the use of internalized values). All personality variables were measured using standard self-report measures, and participants completed the measures, during face-to-face interviews with one of the researchers in the participant's home.

The researchers found that possessing an internal sense of control was positively related to all the personality variables measured, which means that those who had a high sense of internal control also were more autonomous, took more risks, had a stronger sense of social responsibility, were more tolerant (less authoritarian), were more empathetic, and exhibited higher levels of altruistic moral reasoning.

To test their primary prediction that personality could predict hero status, the researchers used a statistical procedure that allowed them to pool all the participants (heroes, bystanders, and the comparison sample of pre-war immigrants) and then use each person's scores on the personality variables to predict to which category each participant belonged. In support of the researchers' hypothesis, personality correctly predicted who was a hero and who was not 93% of the time, which is a very high accuracy rate for this type of analysis.

Further analysis revealed that those who put their own life on the line to assist their persecuted neighbors had a higher sense of internal control than those who did not offer assistance. And this makes perfect sense: If a person has an external sense of control, believing that the outcome of events is all chance, then why would that person ever risk his or her own safety to take action to help ensure the safety of others? Having a generalized expectancy that your actions *will* have a positive effect, and that the outcome of events is *not* all chance, is a critical element to being able to help others under extraordinary conditions.

Person-Situation Interaction

Walter Mischel has conducted a great deal of research on the complexities associated with personality, situations, and behavior. His research and theory of cognitive social learning has generated even more research by many scholars in the field. Perhaps the most important of these has been the recent research on the person-situation interaction. The essence of this approach is summed up by the contextual contingency between behavior and context in the statement "If I am in this situation, then I do X; but if I am in that situation, then I do Y." As we discussed in the section on the cognitive-affective personality system, Mischel and Shoda developed conceptual and empirical methods of investigating the person-situation interaction by simply having participants respond to if-then situations.

In a recent study, elegant in its simplicity, one of Mischel's students, Lara Kammrath, and her colleagues demonstrated the "If . . . then . . ." framework very clearly (Kammrath, Mendoza-Denton, & Mischel, 2005). The goal of the study was to show that people understand the if-then framework and use it when making judgments about others. Participants in this study were given just one trait of a fictional female student and then asked to predict how warmly the student would behave in several different situations. The single trait descriptor each participant received was determined randomly from the following list: friendly, a kiss-up, flirtatious, shy, or unfriendly. With just one of these traits in mind, participants then had to predict how the fictional student would behave with peers, with professors, with women, with men, with familiar people, and with unfamiliar people.

What the researchers found perfectly supported the if-then framework of person-situation interactions. For example, when the trait descriptor for the fictional student was kiss-up, participants predicted that she would act very warmly toward professors but not exceptionally warmly toward peers. In other words, *if* the target of the interaction was of a high status (professor), *then* the student was very warm; but *if* the target was not of high status, *then* the student was not warm. Similarly, when the student was described as unfriendly, participants predicted she would be rather warm toward people she knew well but not at all warm toward unfamiliar people. These findings clearly demonstrate the average person understands that people do not behave in the same manner in all situations—depending on their personality, people adjust behavior to match the situation.

In other, but similar, research, Mischel and colleagues have conducted studies on the conditional nature of dispositions in an "I am . . . when . . ." framework (Mendoza-Denton, Ayduk, Mischel, Shoda, & Testa, 2001). For instance, unconditional self-evaluations are statements such as "I am good" or "I am stupid." Conditional self-evaluations, by contrast, are "I am good at tennis" or "I am smart when I am working on math problems." These latter self-evaluations are more complex and situate the person in a particular context. In addition, Mischel and colleagues argue that having such a complex interactionist view of oneself should bode well for one's emotional life; that is, one will become less depressed when things do not go one's way and will not glorify oneself when things do not.

Mischel and colleagues set out to study these assumptions by examining whether having a conditional (interactionist) self-evaluation would mollify negative emotional reactions when confronted with failure (Mendoza-Denton et al., 2001). The researchers asked university students to assess their views that intelligence and personality were fixed and immutable. Then the students went through a procedure that manipulated common failure experiences among students (failing an important exam, giving an oral presentation that flops, and attending a party and having difficulty socializing with anyone). This was done by having participants go into their own cubicle, put on headphones, and listen to an audiotape that described these experiences. Participants were instructed to actively imagine themselves going through each one of these experiences. After listening to each vignette, the students rated their self-evaluation, with half of the sample being given the task of rating themselves unconditionally: "I am a(n) _____"; and the other half conditionally: "I am a(n) _____ when _____." Then, in order to assess what effect these different self-evaluations would have on emotional reactions, students had to imagine what they would have really felt had they been in each situation and rate it on a 1 (very sad) to 10 (very happy) scale. The total emotion score was an average of the three situations.

The unconditional self-evaluations were coded into three distinct categories: traits ("I am a failure"), states ("I am nervous"), and other ("I am going home now"). The conditional "hedge" statements (when _____) were coded into four distinct categories: internally focused conditionals ("when I don't put in the time to write a good paper"), externally focused conditionals ("when the professor grades me unfairly"), situational descriptors ("when there is an oral presentation"), or other.

Results supported the prediction that students would feel more sadness in the unconditional self-evaluation condition than in the conditional one. Moreover, at least when making unconditional self-evaluations, those who made trait-like self-evaluations experienced greater sadness than those who made state-like self-evaluations. Lastly, those who believed intelligence and personality tend to be fixed entities reported greater sadness to the failure experiences than those who believed those traits were more malleable. Overall, it is clear that conditional and interactionist self-evaluations do buffer negative reactions to failure.

Mischel and colleagues concluded that the social-cognitive interactionist conceptualization of the person-situation environment is a more appropriate way of understanding human behavior than the traditional "decontextualized" views of personality in which people behave in a given way regardless of the context.

Critique of Cognitive Social Learning Theory

Cognitive social learning theory is attractive to those who value the rigors of learning theory and the speculative assumption that people are forward-looking, cognitive beings. Rotter and Mischel have both evolved learning theories for thinking, valuing, goal-directed humans rather than for laboratory animals. Like that of other theories, cognitive social learning theory's value rests on how it rates on the six criteria for a useful theory.

First, have the theories of Rotter and Mischel sparked a significant body of *research*? On this criterion, cognitive social learning theories have generated both quantity and quality of research. For example, Rotter's concept of locus of control has been, and continues to be, one of the most widely researched topics in psychological literature. Locus of control, however, is not the core of Rotter's personality theory, and the theory itself has not generated a comparable level of research. In contrast to Rotter's concept of locus of control, Mischel's theory has generated somewhat less research, but that research is more relevant to his core ideas.

Second, are cognitive social learning theories *falsifiable*? The empirical nature of both Rotter's and Mischel's work exposes these theories to possible falsification and verification. However, Rotter's basic prediction formula and general prediction formula are completely hypothetical and cannot be accurately tested.

By comparison, Mischel's theory lends itself somewhat more adequately to falsification. Indeed, research on delay of gratification drove Mischel to place greater emphasis on situation variables and less on the inconsistency of behavior. This de-emphasis on delay of gratification has allowed Mischel to avoid the narrow methodological approaches used in his early research.

On the criterion of *organizing knowledge,* cognitive social theory rates a little above average. Theoretically at least, Rotter's general prediction formula and its components of need potential, freedom of movement, and need value can provide a useful framework for understanding much of human behavior. When behavior is seen as a function of these variables, it takes on a different hue. Mischel's theory now rates above average on this criterion, because he has continued to broaden the scope of his theory to include both personal dispositions and dynamic cognitive-affective units that are able to predict and explain behavior.

Does cognitive social learning theory serve as a useful *guide to action?* On this criterion, we rate the theory only moderately high. Rotter's ideas on psychotherapy are quite explicit and are a helpful guide to the therapist, but his theory of personality is not as practical. The mathematical formulas serve as a useful framework for organizing knowledge, but they do not suggest any specific course of action for the practitioner because the value of each factor within the formula cannot be known with mathematical certainty. Likewise, Mischel's theory is only moderately useful to the therapist, teacher, or parent. It suggests to practitioners that they should expect people to behave differently in different situations and even from one time to another, but it provides them with few specific guidelines for action.

Are the theories of Rotter and Mischel *internally consistent?* Rotter is careful in defining terms so that the same term does not have two or more meanings. In addition, separate components of his theory are logically compatible. The basic prediction formula, with its four specific factors, is logically consistent with the three broader variables of the general prediction formula. Mischel, like Bandura (see Chapter 16), has evolved a theory from solid empirical research, a procedure that greatly facilitates consistency.

Finally, is cognitive social learning theory *parsimonious?* In general, it is relatively simple and does not purport to offer explanations for all human personality. Again, the emphasis on research rather than philosophical speculation has contributed to the parsimony of the cognitive social learning theories of both Rotter and Mischel.

🕺 Concept of Humanity

Rotter and Mischel both see people as cognitive animals whose perceptions of events are more important than the events themselves. People are capable of construing events in a variety of ways, and these cognitive perceptions are generally more influential than the environment in determining the value of the reinforcer. Cognition enables different people to see the same situation differently and to place different values on reinforcement that follows their behavior.

Both Rotter and Mischel see humans as goal-directed animals who do not merely react to their environments but who interact with their psychologically meaningful environments. Hence, cognitive social learning theory is more *teleological,* or future oriented, than it is causal. People place positive value on those events that they perceive as moving them closer to their goals, and they place negative value on those events that prevent them from reaching their goals. Goals, then, serve as criteria for evaluating events. People are motivated less by past experiences with reinforcement than by their expectations of future events.

Cognitive social learning theory holds that people move in the direction of goals they have established for themselves. These goals, however, change as people's expectancies for reinforcement and their preference for one reinforcement over another changes. Because people are continually in the process of setting goals, they have some choice in directing their lives. *Free choice* is not unlimited, however, because past experiences and limits to personal competencies partially determine behavior.

Because both Rotter and Mischel are realistic and pragmatic, they are difficult to rate on the *optimism* versus *pessimism* dimension. They believe that people can be taught constructive strategies for problem solving and that they are capable of learning new behaviors at any point in life. However, these theorists do not hold that people have within themselves an inherent force that moves them inevitably in the direction of psychological growth.

On the issue of *conscious versus unconscious motives,* cognitive social learning theory generally leans in the direction of conscious forces. People can consciously set goals for themselves and consciously strive to solve old and new problems. However, people are not always aware of the underlying motivations for much of their present behavior.

On the issue of personality being shaped by social or biological influences, cognitive social learning theory emphasizes *social factors.* Rotter especially stressed the importance of learning within a social environment. Mischel also highlighted social influences, but he does not overlook the importance of genetic factors. He and Shoda (Mischel & Shoda, 1999) maintained that people have both a genetic and a social predisposition to act in a given manner. The genetic predisposition, of course, flows from their genetic endowment, whereas their social predisposition results from their social history.

As for stressing *uniqueness or similarities,* we place Rotter in a middle position. People have individual histories and unique experiences that allow them to set personalized goals, but there are also enough similarities among people to allow for the construction of mathematical formulas that, if sufficient information were available, would permit reliable and accurate prediction of behavior.

By comparison, Mischel clearly places more emphasis on uniqueness than on similarities. Differences among people are due to each individual's behavioral signature and to unique patterns of variation in each person's behavior. In summary, cognitive social learning theory views people as forward-looking, purposive, unified, cognitive, affective, and social animals who are capable of evaluating present experiences and anticipating future events on the basis of goals they have chosen for themselves.

Key Terms and Concepts

- The *cognitive social learning theories* of both Rotter and Mischel attempt to synthesize the strengths of reinforcement theory with those of cognitive theory.
- According to Rotter, people's behavior in a specific situation is a function of their *expectations of reinforcements* and the strength of the *needs* satisfied by those reinforcements.
- In specific situations, behavior is estimated by the *basic prediction formula* that suggests that the potential for a given behavior to occur is a function of the person's expectancy plus the value of the reinforcement.

- The *general prediction formula* states that need potential is a function of freedom of movement and need value.
- *Need potential* is the possible occurrence of a set of functionally related behaviors directed toward the satisfaction of a goal or a similar set of goals.
- *Freedom of movement* is the average expectancy that a set of related behaviors will be reinforced.
- *Need value* is the degree to which a person prefers one set of reinforcements to another.
- In many situations, people develop *generalized expectancies* for success because a similar set of experiences has been previously reinforced.
- *Locus of control* is a generalized expectancy that refers to people's belief that they can or cannot control their lives.
- *Interpersonal trust* is a generalized expectancy that the word of another is reliable.
- *Maladaptive behavior* refers to those actions that fail to move a person closer to a desired goal.
- Rotter's method of *psychotherapy* aims toward changing goals and eliminating low expectancies.
- Mischel's *cognitive-active personality system* (CAPS) suggests that people's behavior is largely shaped by an interaction of stable personality traits and the situation, which include a number of personal variables.
- *Personal dispositions* have some consistency over time but little consistency from one situation to another.
- Relatively stable personality dispositions interact with *cognitive-affective units* to produce behavior.
- Cognitive-affective units include people's *encoding strategies,* or their way of construing and categorizing information; their *competencies and self-regulatory plans,* or what they can do and their strategies for doing it; their *expectancies and beliefs* about the perceived consequences of their actions; their *goals and values;* and their *affective responses.*

CHAPTER 18

Kelly: Psychology of Personal Constructs

Kelly

Arlene, a 21-year-old college student majoring in engineering, was balancing a heavy academic schedule with a full-time job. Her life suddenly became even more hectic when her 10-year-old car broke down. Now she faces an important decision. As she interprets her world, she sees that she has several choices. She could have her old car repaired; she could borrow money to purchase a nearly new used car; she could walk to and from school and work; she could ask friends for transportation; she could quit school and move back home with her parents; or she could choose among several other options.

The process by which Arlene (or anyone) makes a decision is comparable to those processes followed by scientists when they approach a problem. Like a good scientist, Arlene followed several steps of decision making. First, she observed her environment: ("I see that my car won't run"). Next, she asked questions ("How can I stay in school and keep my job if my car won't run?" "Should I have my old car repaired?" "Should I buy a newer car?" "What other options do I have?"). Third, she anticipated answers ("I can have my old car fixed, buy a newer one, rely on friends for transportation, or quit school"). Fourth, she perceived relationships between events ("Quitting school would mean moving back home, postponing or giving up my goal of becoming an engineer, and losing much of my independence"). Fifth, she hypothesized about possible solutions to her dilemma ("If I have my old car repaired, it might cost more than the car is worth, but if I buy a late-model used one, I'll have to borrow money"). Sixth, she asked more questions ("If I buy a different car, what make, model, and color do I want?"). Next, she predicted potential outcomes ("If I buy a reliable car, I will be able to stay in school and continue my job"). And finally, she attempted to control events ("By purchasing this car, I will be free to drive to work and earn enough money to stay in school"). Later, we return to Arlene's dilemma, but first we look at an overview of personal construct theory as postulated by George Kelly.

Overview of Personal Construct Theory

George Kelly's theory of personal constructs is like no other personality theory. It has been variously called a cognitive theory, a behavioral theory, an existential theory, and a phenomenological theory. Yet it is none of these. Perhaps the most appropriate term is "metatheory," or a theory about theories. According to Kelly, all people (including those who build personality theories) anticipate events by the meanings or interpretations they place on those events (Stevens & Walker, 2002). These meanings or interpretations are called *constructs*. People exist in a real world, but their behavior is shaped by their gradually expanding interpretation or *construction* of that world. They construe the world in their own way, and every construction is open to revision or replacement. People are not victims of circumstances, because alternative constructions are always available. Kelly called this philosophical position *constructive alternativism*.

Constructive alternativism is implied by Kelly's theory of personal constructs, a theory he expressed in one basic postulate and 11 supporting corollaries. The basic postulate assumes that people are constantly active and that their activity is guided by the way they anticipate events.

Biography of George Kelly

Of all the personality theorists discussed in this book, George Kelly had the most unusual variegated experiences—mostly involving education, as either a student or a teacher.

George Alexander Kelly was born April 28, 1905, on a farm near Perth, Kansas, a tiny, almost nonexistent town 35 miles south of Wichita. George was the only child of Elfleda M. Kelly, a former schoolteacher, and Theodore V. Kelly, an ordained Presbyterian minister. By the time Kelly was born, his father had given up the ministry in favor of becoming a Kansas farmer. Both parents were well educated, and both helped in the formal education of their son, a fortunate circumstance because Kelly's schooling was rather erratic.

When Kelly was 4 years old, the family moved to eastern Colorado, where his father staked a claim on some of the last free land in that part of the country. While in Colorado, Kelly attended school only irregularly, seldom for more than a few weeks at a time (Thompson, 1968).

Lack of water drove the family back to Kansas, where Kelly attended four different high schools in 4 years. At first he commuted to high school, but at age 13, he was sent away to school in Wichita. From that time on, he mostly lived away from home. After graduation, he spent 3 years at Friends University in Wichita and 1 year at Park College in Parkville, Missouri. Both schools had religious affiliations, which may explain why many of Kelly's later writings are sprinkled with biblical references.

Kelly was a man of many and diverse interests. His undergraduate degree was in physics and mathematics, but he was also a member of the college debate team and, as such, became intensely concerned with social problems. This interest led him to the University of Kansas, where he received a master's degree with a major in educational sociology and a minor in labor relations and sociology.

During the next few years, Kelly moved several times and held a variety of positions. First, he went to Minneapolis, where he taught soapbox oratory at a special college for labor organizers, conducted classes in speech for the American Bankers Association, and taught government to an Americanization class for prospective citizens (Kelly, 1969a). Then in 1928, he moved to Sheldon, Iowa, where he taught at a junior college and coached drama. While there, he met his future wife, Gladys Thompson, an English teacher at the same school. After a year and a half, he moved back to Minnesota, where he taught a summer session at the University of Minnesota. Next, he returned to Wichita to work for a few months as an aeronautical engineer. From there, he went to the University of Edinburgh in Scotland as an exchange student, receiving an advanced professional degree in education.

At this point in his life, Kelly "had dabbled academically in education, sociology, economics, labor relations, biometrics, speech pathology, and anthropology, and had majored in psychology for a grand total of nine months" (Kelly, 1969a, p. 48). After returning from Edinburgh, however, he began in earnest to pursue a career in psychology. He enrolled at the State University of Iowa and, in 1931, completed a PhD with a dissertation on common factors in speech and reading disabilities.

Once again, Kelly returned to Kansas, beginning his academic career in 1931 at Fort Hays State College in Hays, Kansas, by teaching physiological psychology.

With the dust bowl and the Great Depression, however, he soon became convinced that he should "pursue something more humanitarian than physiological psychology" (Kelly, 1969a, p. 48). Consequently, he decided to become a psychotherapist, counseling college and high school students in the Hays community. True to his psychology of personal constructs, Kelly pointed out that his decision was not dictated by *circumstances* but rather by his *interpretation* of events; that is, his own construction of reality altered his life course.

> Everything around us "calls," if we choose to heed. Moreover, I have never been completely satisfied that becoming a psychologist was even a very good idea in the first place. . . . The only thing that seems clear about my career in psychology is that it was I who got myself into it and I who have pursued it. (p. 49)

Now a psychotherapist, Kelly obtained legislative support for a program of traveling psychological clinics in Kansas. He and his students traveled widely throughout the state, providing psychological services during those hard economic times. During this period, he evolved his own approach to therapy, abandoning the Freudian techniques that he had previously used (Fransella, 1995).

During World War II, Kelly joined the Navy as an aviation psychologist. After the war, he taught at the University of Maryland for a year and then, in 1946, joined the faculty at Ohio State University as a professor and director of their psychological clinic. There he worked with Julian Rotter (see Chapter 17), who succeeded him as director of the clinic. In 1965, he accepted a position at Brandeis University, where, for a brief time, he was a colleague of A. H. Maslow (see Chapter 10).

From his days at Fort Hays State, Kelly began to formulate a theory of personality. Finally, in 1955, he published his most important work, *The Psychology of Personal Constructs.* This two-volume book, reprinted in 1991, contains the whole of Kelly's personality theory and is one of only a few of his works published during his lifetime.

Kelly spent several summers as a visiting professor at such schools as the University of Chicago, the University of Nebraska, the University of Southern California, Northwestern University, Brigham Young University, Stanford University, University of New Hampshire, and City College of New York. During those postwar years, he became a major force in clinical psychology in the United States. He was president of both the Clinical and the Consulting Divisions of the American Psychological Association and was also a charter member and later president of the American Board of Examiners in Professional Psychology.

Kelly died on March 6, 1967, before he could complete revisions of his theory of personal constructs.

Kelly's diverse life experiences, from the wheat fields of Kansas to some of the major universities of the world, from education to labor relations, from drama and debate to psychology, are consistent with his theory of personality, which emphasizes the possibility of interpreting events from many possible angles.

Kelly's Philosophical Position

Is human behavior based on reality or on people's perception of reality? George Kelly would say *both*. He did not accept Skinner's (see Chapter 15) position that behavior is shaped by the environment, that is, reality. On the other hand, he also rejected extreme **phenomenology** (see Combs & Snygg, 1959), which holds that the only reality is what people perceive. Kelly (1955, 1991) believed that the universe is real, but that different people construe it in different ways. Thus, people's **personal constructs,** or ways of interpreting and explaining events, hold the key to predicting their behavior.

Personal construct theory does not try to explain nature. Rather, it is a theory of people's *construction* of events: that is, their personal inquiry into their world. It is "a psychology of the human quest. It does not say what has or will be found, but proposes rather how we might go about looking for it" (Kelly, 1970, p. 1).

Person as Scientist

When you decide what foods to eat for lunch, what television shows to watch, or what occupation to enter, you are acting in much the same manner as a scientist. That is, you ask questions, formulate hypotheses, test them, draw conclusions, and try to predict future events. Like all other people (including scientists), your perception of reality is colored by your *personal constructs*—your way of looking at, explaining, and interpreting events in your world.

In a similar manner, all people, in their quest for meaning, make observations, construe relationships among events, formulate theories, generate hypotheses, test those that are plausible, and reach conclusions from their experiments. A person's conclusions, like those of any scientist, are not fixed or final. They are open to reconsideration and reformulation. Kelly was hopeful that people individually and collectively will find better ways of restructuring their lives through imagination and foresight.

Scientist as Person

If people can be seen as scientists, then scientists can also be seen as people. Therefore, the pronouncements of scientists should be regarded with the same skepticism with which we view any behavior. Every scientific observation can be looked at from a different perspective. Every theory can be slightly tilted and viewed from a new angle. This approach, of course, means that Kelly's theory is not exempt from restructuring. Kelly (1969b) presented his theory as a set of half-truths and recognized the inaccuracy of its constructions. Like Carl Rogers (see Chapter 11), Kelly hoped that his theory would be overthrown and replaced by a better one. Indeed, Kelly, more than any other personality theorist, formulated a theory that encourages its own demise. Just as all of us can use our imagination to see everyday events differently, personality theorists can use their ingenuity to construe better theories.

Constructive Alternativism

Kelly began with the assumption that the universe really exists and that it functions as an integral unit, with all its parts interacting precisely with each other. Moreover, the universe is constantly changing, so something is happening all the time. Added to these basic assumptions is the notion that people's thoughts also really exist and that people strive to make sense out of their continuously changing world. Different people construe reality in different ways, and the same person is capable of changing his or her view of the world.

In other words, people always have alternative ways of looking at things. Kelly (1963) assumed *"that all of our present interpretations of the universe are subject to revision or replacement"* (p. 15). He referred to this assumption as **constructive alternativism** and summed up the notion with these words: "The events we face today are subject to as great a variety of constructions as our wits will enable us to contrive" (Kelly, 1970, p. 1). The philosophy of constructive alternativism assumes that the piece-by-piece accumulation of facts does not add up to truth; rather, it assumes that facts can be looked at from different perspectives. Kelly agreed with Adler (see Chapter 3) that a person's interpretation of events is more important than the events themselves. In contrast to Adler, however, Kelly stressed the notion that interpretations have meaning in the dimension of time, and what is valid at one time becomes false when construed differently at a later time. For example, when Freud (see Chapter 2) originally heard his patients' accounts of childhood seduction, he believed that early sexual experiences were responsible for later hysterical reactions. If Freud had continued to construe his patients' reports in this fashion, the entire history of psychoanalysis would have been quite different. But then, for a variety of reasons, Freud restructured his data and gave up his seduction hypothesis. Shortly thereafter, he tilted the picture a little and saw a very different view. With this new view, he concluded that these seduction reports were merely childhood fantasies. His alternative hypothesis was the Oedipus complex, a concept that permeates current psychoanalytic theory, and one that is 180 degrees removed from his original seduction theory. If we view Freud's observations from yet another angle, such as Erikson's perspective (see Chapter 9), then we might reach a still different conclusion.

Kelly believed that the *person,* not the facts, holds the key to an individual's future. Facts and events do not dictate conclusions; rather, they carry meanings for us to discover. We are all constantly faced with alternatives, which we can explore if we choose, but in any case, we must assume responsibility for how we construe our worlds. We are victims of neither our history nor our present circumstances. That is not to say that we can make of our world whatever we wish. We are "limited by our feeble wits and our timid reliance upon what is familiar" (Kelly, 1970, p. 3). We do not always welcome new ideas. Like scientists in general and personality theorists in particular, we often find restructuring disturbing and thus hold on to ideas that are comfortable and theories that are well established.

Personal Constructs

Kelly's philosophy assumes that people's interpretation of a unified, ever-changing world constitutes their reality. In the chapter opener, we introduced Arlene, the student with the broken-down automobile. Arlene's perception of her transportation problem was not a static one. As she talked to a mechanic, a used-car dealer, a new-car dealer, a banker, her parents, and others, she was constantly changing her interpretation of reality. In similar fashion, all people continually create their own view of the world. Some people are quite inflexible and seldom change their way of seeing things. They cling to their view of reality even as the real world changes. For example, people with anorexia nervosa continue to see themselves as fat while their weight continues to drop to a life-threatening level. Some people construe a world that is substantially different from the world of other people. For example, psychotic patients in mental hospitals may talk to people whom no one else can see. Kelly (1963) would insist that these people, along with everyone else, are looking at their world through "transparent patterns or templates" that they have created in order to cope with the world's realities. Although these patterns or templates do not always fit accurately, they are the means by which people make sense out of the world. Kelly referred to these patterns as *personal constructs:*

> They are ways of construing the world. They are what enables [people], and lower animals too, to chart a course of behavior, explicitly formulated or implicitly acted out, verbally expressed or utterly inarticulate, consistent with other courses of behavior or inconsistent with them, intellectually reasoned or vegetatively sensed. (p. 9)

A personal construct is one's way of seeing how things (or people) are alike and yet different from other things (or people). For example, you may see how Ashly and Brenda are alike and how they are different from Carol. The comparison and the contrast must occur within the same context. For example, to say that Ashly and Brenda are attractive and Carol is religious would not constitute a personal construct, because attractiveness is one dimension and religiosity is another. A construct would be formed if you see that Ashly and Brenda are attractive and Carol is unattractive, or if you view Ashly and Brenda as irreligious and Carol as religious. Both the comparison and the contrast are essential.

Whether they are clearly perceived or dimly felt, personal constructs shape an individual's behavior. As an example, consider Arlene with her broken-down car. After her old car stopped running, her personal constructs shaped her subsequent course of action, but not all her constructs were clearly defined. For instance, she may have decided to buy a late-model automobile because she interpreted the car dealer's friendliness and persuasiveness as meaning that the car was reliable. Arlene's personal constructs may be accurate or inaccurate, but in either case, they are her means of predicting and controlling her environment.

Arlene tried to increase the accuracy of her predictions (that the car would provide reliable, economical, and comfortable transportation) by increasing her store of information. She researched her purchase, asked others' opinions, tested the car, and had it checked by a mechanic. In much the same manner, all people attempt to validate their constructs. They look for better-fitting templates and thus try to improve their personal constructs. However, personal improvement is not inevitable, because the investment people make in their established constructs blocks the path of forward development. The world is constantly changing, so what is accurate at one time may not be accurate at another. The reliable blue bicycle Arlene rode during childhood should not mislead her to construe that all blue vehicles are reliable.

Basic Postulate

Personal construct theory is expressed in one fundamental postulate, or assumption, and elaborated by means of 11 supporting corollaries. The basic postulate assumes that *"a person's processes are psychologically channelized by the ways in which [that person] anticipates events"* (Kelly, 1955, p. 46). In other words, people's behaviors (thoughts and actions) are directed by the way they see the future. This postulate is not intended as an absolute statement of truth but is a tentative assumption open to question and scientific testing.

Kelly (1955, 1970) clarified this fundamental assumption by defining its key terms. First, the phrase *person's processes* refers to a living, changing, moving human being. Kelly was not concerned here with animals, with society, or with any part or function of the person. He did not recognize motives, needs, drives, or instincts as forces underlying motivation. Life itself accounts for one's movement.

Kelly chose the term *channelized* to suggest that people move with a direction through a network of pathways or channels. The network, however, is flexible, both facilitating and restricting people's range of action. In addition, the term avoids the implication that some sort of energy is being transformed into action. People are already in movement; they merely channelize or direct their processes toward some end or purpose.

The next key phrase is *ways of anticipating events,* which suggests that people guide their actions according to their predictions of the future. Neither the past nor the future per se determines our behavior. Rather, our present view of the future shapes our actions. Arlene did not buy a blue car because she had a blue bicycle when she was a child, although that fact may have helped her to construe the present so that she anticipated that her blue late-model car would be a reliable one in the future. Kelly (1955) said that people are tantalized not by their past but by their view of the future. People continuously "reach out to the future through the window of the present" (p. 49).

Supporting Corollaries

To elaborate his theory of personal constructs, Kelly proposed 11 supporting corollaries, all of which can be inferred from his basic postulate.

Similarities Among Events

No two events are exactly alike, yet we construe similar events so that they are perceived as being the same. One sunrise is never identical to another, but our construct *dawn* conveys our recognition of some similarity or some replication of events. Although two dawns are never exactly alike, they may be similar enough for us to construe them as the same event. Kelly (1955, 1970) referred to this similarity among events as the **construction corollary.**

The construction corollary states that *"a person anticipates events by construing their replications"* (Kelly, 1955, p. 50). This corollary again points out that people are forward looking; their behavior is forged by their anticipation of future events. It also emphasizes the notion that people construe or interpret future events according to recurrent themes or replications.

The construction corollary may seem little more than common sense: People see similarities among events and use a single concept to describe the common properties. Kelly, however, felt that it was necessary to include the obvious when building a theory.

Differences Among People

Kelly's second corollary is equally obvious. *"Persons differ from each other in their construction of events"* (Kelly, 1955, p. 55). Kelly called this emphasis on individual differences the **individuality corollary.**

Because people have different reservoirs of experiences, they construe the same event in different ways. Thus, no two people put an experience together in exactly the same way. Both the substance and the form of their constructs are different. For example, a philosopher may subsume the construct *truth* under the rubric of eternal values; a lawyer may view truth as a relative concept, useful for a particular purpose; and a scientist may construe truth as an ever-elusive goal, something to be sought, but never attained. For the philosopher, the lawyer, and the scientist, *truth* has a different substance, a different meaning. Moreover, each person arrived at his or her particular construction in a different manner and thus gives it a different form. Even identical twins living in nearly identical environments do not construe events exactly the same. For example, part of Twin A's environment includes Twin B, an experience not shared by Twin B.

Although Kelly (1955) emphasized individual differences, he pointed out that experiences can be shared and that people can find a common ground for construing experiences. This allows people to communicate both verbally and nonverbally. However, due to individual differences, the communication is never perfect.

Relationships Among Constructs

Kelly's third corollary, the **organization corollary,** emphasizes relationships among constructs and states that people *"characteristically evolve, for [their] convenience in anticipating events, a construction system embracing ordinal relationships between constructs"* (Kelly, 1955, p. 56).

The first two corollaries assume similarities among events and differences among people. The third emphasizes that different people organize similar events in a manner that minimizes incompatibilities and inconsistencies. We arrange our constructions so that we may move from one to another in an orderly fashion, which allows us to anticipate events in ways that transcend contradictions and avoid needless conflicts.

The organization corollary also assumes an ordinal relationship of constructs so that one construct may be subsumed under another. Figure 18.1 illustrates a hierarchy of constructs as they might apply to Arlene, the engineering major. In deciding a course of action after her car broke down, Arlene may have seen her situation in terms of dichotomous superordinate constructs such as good versus bad. At that point in her life, Arlene regarded *independence* (of friends or parents) as good and *dependence* as bad. However, her personal construct system undoubtedly included a variety of constructs subsumed under good and bad. For example, Arlene probably construed intelligence and health as good and stupidity and illness as bad. Furthermore, Arlene's views of independence and dependence (like her constructs of good and bad) would have had a multitude of subordinate constructs. In this situation, Arlene construed staying in school as independence and living with her parents as dependence. In order to remain in school and continue her job, Arlene needed transportation. There were many possible means of transportation, but Arlene considered

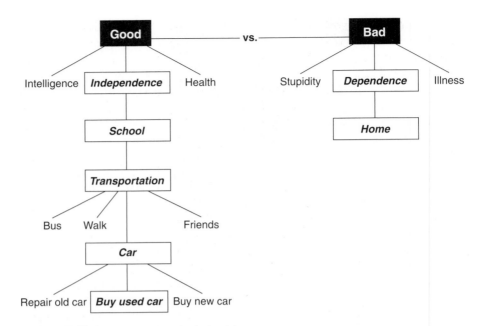

FIGURE 18.1   Complexity of relationships among constructs.

only four: riding a public bus, walking, relying on friends, or driving her own car. Subsumed under the construct of car were three subordinate constructs: repairing her old car, buying a new one, or purchasing a late-model used car. This example suggests that constructs have not only a complex ordinal relationship with each other but a dichotomous relationship as well.

Dichotomy of Constructs

Now we come to a corollary that is not so obvious. The **dichotomy corollary** states that *"a person's construction system is composed of a finite number of dichotomous constructs"* (Kelly, 1955, p. 59).

Kelly insisted that a construct is an either-or proposition—black or white, with no shades of gray. In nature, things may not be either-or, but natural events have no meanings other than those attributed to them by an individual's personal construct system. In nature, the color blue may have no opposite pole (except on a color chart), but people attribute contrasting qualities to blue, such as *light* blue versus *dark* blue or *pretty* versus *ugly.*

In order to form a construct, people must be able to see similarities between events, but they must also contrast those events with their opposite pole. Kelly (1955) stated it this way: "In its minimum context a construct is a way in which at least two elements are similar and contrast with a third" (p. 61). As an example, return to Figure 18.1. How are *intelligence* and *independence* alike? Their common element has no meaning without contrasting it to an opposite. Intelligence and independence have no overlapping element when compared to a hammer or a chocolate bar. By contrasting intelligence with stupidity and independence with dependence, you see how they are alike and how they can be organized under the construct "good" as opposed to "bad."

People choose between alternatives based on their anticipation of future events.

Choice Between Dichotomies

If people construe events in dichotomized fashion, then it follows that they have some choice in following alternative courses of action. This is Kelly's **choice corollary,** paraphrased as follows: *People choose for themselves that alternative in a dichotomized construct through which they anticipate the greater possibility for extension and definition of future constructs.*

This corollary assumes much of what is stated in Kelly's basic postulate and in the preceding corollaries. People make choices on the basis of how they anticipate events, and those choices are between dichotomous alternatives. In addition, the choice corollary assumes that people choose those actions that are most likely to extend their future range of choices.

Arlene's decision to buy a used car was based on a series of previous choices, each of which was between dichotomized alternatives and each of which broadened her range of future choices. First she chose the *independence* of school over the *dependence* of going home to live with her parents. Next, buying a car offered more freedom than relying on friends or on bus schedules or walking (which she perceived as time consuming). Repairing her old car was *financially risky* compared to the greater *safety* of buying a used one. Purchasing a new car was too *expensive* compared to the relatively *inexpensive* used car. Each choice was between alternatives in a dichotomized construct, and with each choice, Arlene anticipated the greater possibility for extending and defining future constructs.

Range of Convenience

Kelly's **range corollary** assumes that personal constructs are finite and not relevant to everything. *"A construct is convenient for the anticipation of a finite range of events only"* (Kelly, 1955, p. 68). In other words, a construct is limited to a particular *range of convenience.*

The construct *independence* was within Arlene's range of convenience when she was deciding to buy a car, but on other occasions independence would be outside those boundaries. Independence carries with it the notion of *dependence.* Arlene's freedom to remain in school, freedom to continue her job, and freedom to move quickly from place to place without relying on others all fall within her independence/dependence range of convenience. However, Arlene's construct of independence excludes all irrelevancies such as up/down, light/dark, or wet/dry; that is, it is convenient only for a finite range of events.

The range corollary allowed Kelly to distinguish between a *concept* and a *construct*. A concept includes all elements having a common property, and it excludes those that do not have that property. The concept *tall* includes all those people and objects having extended height and excludes all other concepts, even those that are outside its range of convenience. Therefore, *fast* or *independent* or *dark* are all excluded from the concept *tall* because they do not have extended height. But such exclusions are both endless and needless. The idea of construct contrasts tall with short, thus limiting its range of convenience. "That which is outside the range of convenience of the construct is not considered part of the contrasting field but simply an area of irrelevancy" (Kelly, 1955, p. 69). Thus, dichotomies limit a construct's range of convenience.

Experience and Learning

Basic to personal construct theory is the anticipation of events. We look to the future and make guesses about what will happen. Then, as events become revealed to us, we either validate our existing constructs or restructure these events to match our experience. The restructuring of events allows us to learn from our experiences.

The **experience corollary** states: *"A person's construction system varies as he [or she] successively construes the replications of events"* (Kelly, 1955, p. 72). Kelly used the word "successively" to point out that we pay attention to only one thing at a time. "The events of one's construing march single file along the path of time" (p. 73).

Experience consists of the successive construing of events. The events themselves do not constitute experience—it is the meaning we attach to them that changes our lives. To illustrate this point, return to Arlene and her personal construct of independence. When her old car (a high school graduation gift from her parents) broke down, Arlene decided to remain in school rather than to return to the security and dependent status of living at home. As Arlene subsequently encountered successive events, she had to make decisions without benefit of parental consultation, a task that forced her to restructure her notion of independence. Earlier, she had construed independence as freedom from outside interference. After deciding to go into debt for a used car, she began to alter her meaning of independence to include responsibility and anxiety. The events themselves did not force a restructuring. Arlene could have become a spectator to the events surrounding her. Instead, her existing constructs were flexible enough to allow her to adapt to experience.

Adaptation to Experience

Arlene's flexibility illustrates Kelly's **modulation corollary.** *"The variation in a person's construction system is limited by the permeability of the constructs within whose range of convenience the variants lie"* (Kelly, 1955, p. 77). This corollary follows from and expands the experience corollary. It assumes that the extent to which people revise their constructs is related to the degree of **permeability** of their existing constructs. A construct is permeable if new elements can be added to it. Impermeable or concrete constructs do not admit new elements. If a man believes that women are inferior to men, then contradictory evidence will not find its way into his range of convenience. Instead, he will attribute the achievements of women to luck or unfair social advantage. A change in events means a change in constructs only if those constructs are permeable.

Arlene's personal construct of *independence versus dependence* was sufficiently permeable to take in new elements. When, without parental consultation, she made the decision to buy a used car, the construct of *maturity versus childishness* penetrated *independence versus dependence* and added a new flavor to it. Previously, the two constructs had been separated, and Arlene's notion of independence was limited to the idea of doing as she chose, whereas dependence was associated with parental domination. Now she construed independence as meaning mature responsibility and dependence as signifying a childish leaning on parents. In such a manner, all people modulate or adjust their personal constructs.

Incompatible Constructs

Although Kelly assumed an overall stability or consistency of a person's construction system, his **fragmentation corollary** allows for the incompatibility of specific elements. *"A person may successively employ a variety of constructive subsystems which are inferentially incompatible with each other"* (Kelly, 1955, p. 83).

At first it may seem as if personal constructs must be compatible, but if we look to our own behavior and thinking, we can easily see some inconsistencies. In Chapter 17, we pointed out that Walter Mischel (a student of Kelly) believed that behavior is usually more inconsistent than trait theorists would have us believe. Children are often patient in one situation yet impatient in another. Similarly, a person may be brave while confronting a vicious dog but cowardly when confronting a boss or teacher. Although our behaviors often seem inconsistent, Kelly saw underlying stability in most of our actions. For example, a man might be protective of his wife, yet encourage her to be more independent. Protection and independence may be incompatible with each other on one level, but on a larger level, both are subsumed under the construct of *love*. Thus, the man's actions to protect his wife and to encourage her to be more independent are consistent with a larger, superordinate construct.

Superordinate systems may also change, but those changes take place within a still larger system. In the previous example of the protective husband, for instance, the man's love for his wife may gradually shift to hatred, but that change remains within a larger construct of *self-interest*. The previous love for his wife and the present hatred are both consistent with his view of *self-interest*. If incompatible constructs could not coexist, people would be locked into a fixed construct, which would make change nearly impossible.

Similarities Among People

Although Kelly's second supporting corollary assumes that people are different from each other, his **commonality corollary** assumes similarities among people. His slightly revised commonality corollary reads: *"To the extent that one person employs a construction of experience which is similar to that employed by another, [that person's] processes are psychologically similar to those of the other person"* (Kelly, 1970, p. 20).

Two people need not experience the same event or even similar events for their processes to be psychologically similar; they must merely *construe* their experiences in a similar fashion. Because people actively construe events by asking questions, forming hypotheses, drawing conclusions, and then asking more questions, different people with widely different experiences may construe events in very similar ways. For example, two people might arrive at similar political views although they come from disparate backgrounds. One may have come from a wealthy family, having lived a life of leisure and contemplation, while the other may have survived a destitute childhood, struggling constantly for survival. Yet both adopt a liberal political view.

Although people of different backgrounds can have similar constructs, people with similar experiences are more likely to construe events along similar lines. Within a given social group, people may employ similar constructions, but it is always the individual, never society, who construes events. This is similar to Albert Bandura's notion of collective efficacy: It is the individual, not society, who has varying levels of high or low collective efficacy (see Chapter 16). Kelly also assumes that no two people ever interpret experiences exactly the same. Americans may have a similar construction of *democracy,* but no two Americans see it in identical terms.

Social Processes

"People belong to the same cultural group, not merely because they behave alike, nor because they expect the same things of others, but especially because they construe their experience in the same way" (Kelly, 1955, p. 94).

The final supporting corollary, the **sociality corollary** can be paraphrased to read as follows: *To the extent that people accurately construe the belief system of others, they may play a role in a social process involving those other people.*

People do not communicate with one another simply on the basis of common experiences or even similar constructions; they communicate because they construe the constructions of one another. In interpersonal relations, they not only observe the behavior of the other person; they also interpret what that behavior means to that

person. When Arlene was negotiating with the used-car dealer, she was aware of not only his words and actions but also their meanings. She realized that to him she was a potential buyer, someone who might provide him with a substantial commission. She construed his words as exaggerations and, at the same time, realized that he construed her indifference as an indication that she construed his motivations differently from her own.

In interpersonal relationships, not only do people observe the behavior of the other person, but they also interpret what that behavior means to that person.

All this seems rather complicated, but Kelly was simply suggesting that people are actively involved in interpersonal relations and realize that they are part of the other person's construction system.

Kelly introduced the notion of **role** with his sociality corollary. A role refers to a pattern of behavior that results from a person's understanding of the constructs of others with whom that person is engaged in a task. For example, when Arlene was negotiating with the used-car dealer, she construed her role as that of a potential buyer because she understood that that was his expectation of her. At other times and with other people, she construes her role as student, employee, daughter, girlfriend, and so on.

Kelly construed roles from a psychological rather than a sociological perspective. One's role does not depend on one's place or position in a social setting but rather on how one interprets that role. Kelly also stressed the point that one's construction of a role need not be accurate in order for the person to play that role.

Arlene's roles as student, employee, and daughter would be considered *peripheral roles*. More central to her existence would be her *core role*. With our **core role,** we define ourselves in terms of who we really are. It gives us a sense of identity and provides us with guidelines for everyday living.

Applications of Personal Construct Theory

Like most personality theorists, Kelly evolved his theoretical formulations from his practice as a psychotherapist. He spent more than 20 years conducting therapy before he published *The Psychology of Personal Constructs* in 1955. In this section, we look at his views of abnormal development, his approach to psychotherapy, and, finally, his Role Construct Repertory (Rep) Test.

Abnormal Development

In Kelly's view, psychologically healthy people validate their personal constructs against their experiences with the real world. They are like competent scientists who test reasonable hypotheses, accept the results without denial or distortion, and then willingly alter their theories to match available data. Healthy individuals not only anticipate events but are also able to make satisfactory adjustments when things do not turn out as they expected.

Unhealthy people, on the other hand, stubbornly cling to outdated personal constructs, fearing validation of any new constructs that would upset their present comfortable view of the world. Such people are similar to incompetent scientists who test unreasonable hypotheses, reject or distort legitimate results, and refuse to amend or abandon old theories that are no longer useful. Kelly (1955) defined a disorder as *"any personal construction which is used repeatedly in spite of consistent invalidation"* (p. 831).

A person's construction system exists in the present—not the past or future. Psychological disorders, therefore, also exist in the present; they are caused neither by childhood experiences nor by future events. Because construction systems are *personal,* Kelly objected to traditional classifications of abnormalities. Using the

Diagnostic and Statistical Manual of Mental Disorders (DSM-IV-TR) of the American Psychiatric Association (2002) to label a person is likely to result in misconstruing that person's unique constructions.

Psychologically unhealthy people, like everyone else, possess a complex construction system. Their personal constructs, however, often fail the test of permeability in one of two ways: They may be too impermeable or they may be too flexible. In the first instance, new experiences do not penetrate the construction system, so the person fails to adjust to the real world. For example, an abused child may construe intimacy with parents as bad and solitude as good. Psychological disorders result when the child's construction system rigidly denies the value of any intimate relationship and clings to the notion that either withdrawal or attack is a preferred mode of solving interpersonal problems. Another example is a man seriously dependent on alcohol who refuses to see himself as addicted to alcohol even as his drinking escalates and his job and marriage disintegrate (Burrell, 2002).

On the other hand, a construction system that is too loose or flexible leads to disorganization, an inconsistent pattern of behavior, and a transient set of values. Such an individual is too easily "shaken by the impact of unexpected minor daily events" (Kelly, 1955, p. 80).

Although Kelly did not use traditional labels in describing psychopathology, he did identify four common elements in most human disturbance: threat, fear, anxiety, and guilt.

Threat

People experience **threat** when they perceive that the stability of their basic constructs is likely to be shaken. Kelly (1955) defined threat as *"the awareness of imminent comprehensive change in one's core structures"* (p. 489). One can be threatened by either people or events, and sometimes the two cannot be separated. For example, during psychotherapy, clients often feel threat from the prospect of change, even change for the better. If they see a therapist as a possible instigator of change, they will view that therapist as a threat. Clients frequently resist change and construe their therapist's behavior in a negative fashion. Such resistance and "negative transference" are means of reducing threat and maintaining existing personal constructs (Stojnov & Butt, 2002).

Fear

By Kelly's definition, threat involves a *comprehensive* change in a person's core structures. **Fear,** on the other hand, is more *specific* and *incidental*. Kelly (1955) illustrated the difference between threat and fear with the following example. A man may drive his car dangerously as the result of anger or exuberance. These impulses become *threatening* when the man realizes that he may run over a child or be arrested for reckless driving and end up as a criminal. In this case, a comprehensive portion of his personal constructs is threatened. However, if he is suddenly confronted with the probability of crashing his car, he will experience *fear*. Threat demands a comprehensive restructuring—fear, an incidental one. Psychological disturbance results when either threat or fear persistently prevents a person from feeling secure.

Anxiety

Kelly (1955) defined **anxiety** as *"the recognition that the events with which one is confronted lie outside the range of convenience of one's construct system"* (p. 495). People are likely to feel anxious when they are experiencing a new event. For example, when Arlene, the engineering student, was bargaining with the used-car dealer, she was not sure what to do or say. She had never before negotiated over such a large amount of money, and therefore this experience was outside the range of her convenience. As a consequence, she felt anxiety, but it was a normal level of anxiety and did not result in incapacitation.

Pathological anxiety exists when a person's incompatible constructs can no longer be tolerated and the person's construction system breaks down. Recall that Kelly's fragmentation corollary assumes that people can evolve construction subsystems that are incompatible with one another. For example, when a person who has erected the rigid construction that all people are trustworthy is blatantly cheated by a colleague, that person may for a time tolerate the ambiguity of the two incompatible subsystems. However, when evidence of the untrustworthiness of others becomes overwhelming, the person's construct system may break down. The result is a relatively permanent and debilitating experience of anxiety.

Guilt

Kelly's sociality corollary assumes that people construe a core role that gives them a sense of identity within a social environment. However, if that core role is weakened or dissolved, a person will develop a feeling of guilt. Kelly (1970) defined **guilt** as *"the sense of having lost one's core role structure"* (p. 27). That is, people feel guilty when they behave in ways that are inconsistent with their sense of who they are.

People who have never developed a core role do not feel guilty. They may be anxious or confused, but without a sense of personal identity, they do not experience guilt. For example, a person with an underdeveloped conscience has little or no integral sense of self and a weak or nonexistent core role structure. Such a person has no stable guidelines to violate and hence will feel little or no guilt even for depraved and shameful behavior (Kelly, 1970).

Psychotherapy

Psychological distress exists whenever people have difficulty validating their personal constructs, anticipating future events, and controlling their present environment. When distress becomes unmanageable, they may seek outside help in the form of psychotherapy.

In Kelly's view, people should be free to choose those courses of action most consistent with their prediction of events. In therapy, this approach means that clients, not the therapist, select the goal. Clients are active participants in the therapeutic process, and the therapist's role is to assist them to alter their construct systems in order to improve efficiency in making predictions.

As a technique for altering the clients' constructs, Kelly used a procedure called *fixed-role therapy.* The purpose of fixed-role therapy is to help clients change their outlook on life (personal constructs) by acting out a predetermined role, first within the relative security of the therapeutic setting and then in the environment be-yond therapy where they enact the role continuously over a period of several weeks. Together with the therapist, clients work out a role, one that includes attitudes and behaviors not currently part of their core role. In writing the fixed-role sketch, the client and therapist are careful to include the construction systems of other people. How will the client's spouse or parents or boss or friends construe and react to this new role? Will their reactions help the client reconstrue events more productively?

This new role is then tried out in everyday life in much the same manner that a scientist tests a hypothesis—cautiously and objectively. In fact, the fixed-role sketch is typically written in the third person, with the actor assuming a new iden-tity. The client is not trying to be another person but is merely playing the part of someone who is worth knowing. The role should not be taken too seriously; it is only an act, something that can be altered as evidence warrants.

Fixed-role therapy is not aimed at solving specific problems or repairing ob-solete constructs. It is a creative process that allows clients to gradually discover pre-viously hidden aspects of themselves. In the early stages, clients are introduced only to peripheral roles; but then, after they have had time to become comfortable with minor changes in personality structure, they try out new core roles that permit more profound personality change (Kelly, 1955).

Prior to developing the fixed-role approach, Kelly (1969a) stumbled on an un-usual procedure that strongly resembles fixed-role therapy. After becoming uncom-fortable with Freudian techniques, he decided to offer his clients "preposterous in-terpretations" for their complaints. Some were far-fetched Freudian interpretations, but nevertheless, most clients accepted these "explanations" and used them as guides to future action. For example, Kelly might tell a client that strict toilet training has caused him to construe his life in a dogmatically rigid fashion but that he need not continue to see things in this way. To Kelly's surprise, many of his clients began to function better! The key to change was the same as with fixed-role therapy—clients must begin to interpret their lives from a different perspective and see themselves in a different role.

The Rep Test

Another procedure used by Kelly, both inside and outside therapy, was the *Role Con-struct Repertory (Rep) test.* The purpose of the Rep test is to discover ways in which people construe significant people in their lives.

With the Rep test, a person is given a Role Title list and asked to designate peo-ple who fit the role titles by writing their names on a card. For example, for "a teacher you liked," the person must supply a particular name. The number of role titles can vary, but Kelly (1955) listed 24 on one version (see Table 18.1). Next, the person is given three names from the list and asked to judge which two people are alike and yet different from the third. Recall that a construct requires both a similar-ity and a contrast, so three is the minimum number for any construct. Say, for ex-ample, that a person construes Number 1 ("A teacher you liked") and Number 6 ("Your mother") as similar and Number 9 ("Your sister nearest your age") as differ-ent. Then the person is asked how mother and favorite teacher are alike and yet dif-ferent from sister. The *reason* a person gives for the similarity and contrast constitutes

TABLE 18.1

Example of a List of Role Titles Used for the Rep Test

 1. A teacher you liked. (Or the teacher of a subject you liked.)
 2. A teacher you disliked. (Or the teacher of a subject you disliked.)
3a. Your wife or present girlfriend.
3b. (for women) Your husband or present boyfriend.
 4. An employer, supervisor, or officer under whom you worked or served and whom you found hard to get along with. (Or someone under whom you worked in a situation you did not like.)
 5. An employer, supervisor, or officer under whom you worked or served and whom you liked. (Or someone under whom you worked in a situation you liked.)
 6. Your mother. (Or the person who has played the part of a mother in your life.)
 7. Your father. (Or the person who has played the part of a father in your life.)
 8. Your brother nearest your age. (Or the person who has been most like a brother.)
 9. Your sister nearest your age. (Or the person who has been most like a sister.)
10. A person with whom you have worked who was easy to get along with.
11. A person with whom you have worked who was hard to understand.
12. A neighbor with whom you get along well.
13. A neighbor whom you find hard to understand.
14. A boy you got along well with when you were in high school. (Or when you were 16.)
15. A girl you got along well with when you were in high school. (Or when you were 16.)
16. A boy you did not like when you were in high school. (Or when you were 16.)
17. A girl you did not like when you were in high school. (Or when you were 16.)
18. A person of your own sex whom you would enjoy having as a companion on a trip.
19. A person of your own sex whom you would dislike having as a companion on a trip.
20. A person with whom you have been closely associated recently who appears to dislike you.
21. The person whom you would most like to be of help to. (Or whom you feel most sorry for.)
22. The most intelligent person whom you know personally.
23. The most successful person whom you know personally.
24. The most interesting person whom you know personally.

From *The psychology of personal constructs* by G. A. Kelly, 1955 (pp. 221–222). New York: Norton. Copyright 1955 by W. W. Norton & Company. Used by permission.

the construct. If the person gives a superficial response such as "They're both old, and my sister is young," the examiner will say, "That's one way they are alike. Can you think of another?" The person might then say, "My mother and my favorite teacher are both unselfish, and my sister is very self-centered." The examiner records the construct and then asks the person to sort three more cards. Not all combinations of sorts are elicited, and the examiner has some latitude in determining which combinations to use.

After a number of sorts are completed, the examiner transfers the information to a repertory grid. Figure 18.2 shows a hypothetical grid in which 19 role titles are listed along the horizontal axis and 22 personal constructs along the vertical axis. On Sort Number 1, the person who filled out this grid construed Persons 17 and 18 alike because they don't believe in God and Person 19 as being different because he or she is very religious. The examinee also checked Persons 7, 10, and 12 because they are construed as similar to the two people in the emergent pole; that is, they too do not believe in God. Similarly, the person checks each row until the entire grid is completed.

There are several versions of the Rep test and the repertory grid, but all are designed to assess personal constructs. For example, a woman can see how her father and boss are alike or different; whether or not she identifies with her mother; how her boyfriend and father are alike; or how she construes men in general. Also, the test can be given early in therapy and then again at the end. Changes in personal constructs reveal the nature and degree of movement made during therapy.

Kelly and his colleagues have used the Rep test in a variety of forms, and no set scoring rules apply. Reliability and validity of the instrument are not very high, and its usefulness depends largely on the skill and experience of the examiner (Fransella & Bannister, 1977).

CONSTRUCTS

1 Self	2 Mother	3 Father	4 Brother	5 Sister	6 Spouse	7 Ex-flame	8 Pal	9 Ex-pal	10 Rejecting Person	11 Pitied Person	12 Threatening Person	13 Attractive Person	14 Accepted Teacher	15 Rejected Teacher	16 Boss	17 Successful Person	18 Happy Person	19 Ethical Person	SORT NO.	EMERGENT POLE	IMPLICIT POLE
					✓		✓		✓							⊗	⊗	○	1	Don't believe in God	Very religious
			✓	✓		✓						⊗	⊗	○	✓				2	Same sort of education	Completely different education
✓		✓	✓	✓	✓			✓	⊗	○	✓	⊗	✓		✓				3	Not athletic	Athletic
	✓			⊗	⊗	○						✓							4	Both girls	A boy
✓	⊗	⊗	○	✓	✓		✓						✓	✓	✓	✓	✓	✓	5	Parents	Ideas different
		⊗	○			✓						⊗	✓			⊗			6	Understand me better	Don't understand at all
	⊗	✓	✓				○					⊗	✓	✓				✓	7	Teach the right thing	Teach the wrong thing
	✓	○	✓										✓	⊗	⊗	✓	✓		8	Achieved a lot	Hasn't achieved a lot
		⊗	✓		✓		○					✓	⊗	✓	✓				9	Higher education	No education
		⊗		✓			⊗					○							10	Don't like other people	Like other people
✓	✓	✓	⊗	✓		✓				○	✓		✓	✓		✓	✓	⊗	11	More religious	Not religious
✓	✓	✓	⊗			✓	✓	○	✓	✓	⊗	✓	✓	✓	✓	✓	✓	✓	12	Believe in higher education	Not believing in too much education
	✓		✓		○					✓	✓	⊗		✓		⊗			13	More sociable	Not sociable
○			⊗	⊗								✓							14	Both girls	Not girls
✓	○		⊗	⊗								✓							15	Both girls	Not girls
✓	✓	✓	✓	✓			⊗	○				⊗	✓	✓		✓	✓	✓	16	Both have high morals	Low morals
⊗		⊗	○	✓		✓		✓			✓	✓	✓	✓			✓	✓	17	Think alike	Think differently
		✓	✓									✓	⊗	⊗		✓	○		18	Same age	Different ages
	⊗	⊗		✓						✓	○		✓	✓	✓	✓	✓	✓	19	Believe the same about me	Believe differently about me
				✓		✓	⊗	⊗	✓	✓	✓	○							20	Both friends	Not friends
						○	✓					⊗	⊗	✓		✓	✓	✓	21	More understanding	Less understanding
⊗		✓			○	✓	⊗					✓		✓		✓		✓	22	Both appreciate music	Don't understand music

FIGURE 18.2 Example of a repertory grid.

From *The psychology of personal constructs*, by G. A. Kelly, 1955, p. 270. New York: Norton. Copyright 1955 by W. W. Norton & Company. Used by permission.

Related Research

Even though George Kelly wrote only one seminal work (1955, 1991), his impact on personality psychology is remarkable. His personal construct theory has generated a sizable number of empirical investigations, including nearly 600 empirical studies on his repertory test, which suggests that his theory has fared quite well in generating research. Because he was among the first psychologists to emphasize cognitive sets, such as schema, Kelly's idea of personal constructs in a very real sense was instrumental in forming the field of social cognition, one of the most influential perspectives in social and personality psychology today. Social cognition examines the cognitive and attitudinal bases of person perception, including schemas, biases, stereotypes, and prejudiced behavior. Social schemas, for instance, are ordered mental representations of the qualities of others and are considered to contain important social information. Although many researchers in the field of social cognition use conventional questionnaires, some have followed Kelly's lead and use phenomenological or idiographic measures such as the Rep test or some modified version of it (Neimeyer & Neimeyer, 1995). More recent applications of the Rep test methodology, for instance, have analyzed the different construct systems of sexually abused and non-abused individuals (Lewis-Harter, Erbes, & Hart, 2004).

In the following three sections, we review some research on gender as a personal construct, smoking and self-concept, and how personal constructs relate to Big Five measures of personality.

Gender as a Personal Construct

Marcel Harper and Wilhelm Schoeman (2003) argued that although gender is perhaps one of the most fundamental and universal schemas in person perception, not all people are equal in the extent to which they organize their beliefs and attitudes about others around gender. In other words, there are individual differences in the degree to which people internalize cultural views of gender. Moreover, Harper and Schoeman hypothesized that those who do use gender to organize their social perceptions will do so in a more stereotypic fashion than those who do not regularly use gender to organize social perceptions. "Gender thus becomes a primary means of resolving social ambiguity" (Harper & Schoeman, 2003, p. 518). Lastly, these authors predicted that the less information someone has about a person, the more likely he or she will use stereotypic gender schemas to evaluate and perceive that person. In other words, with well-known individuals, we should expect more complex and less stereotypic attitudes.

In the Harper and Schoeman study, participants were mostly female students from a university in South Africa. The version of the Rep test used by the researchers required that participants say whether their person portraits were descriptive of women, of men, of neither, or of both women and men. In the first stage of the Rep test procedure, participants wrote down names of people who best represented one of 15 different role titles, such as "liked lecturer/teacher," a person with whom they worked, and "the most successful person known personally." In the second stage of the procedure, people who fit each role title were compared to each other in groups of three, with two role titles being compared to a third. Finally, in the third stage of the procedure, participants rated role titles on whether they were more descriptive of women than of men, men than of women, or neither/both. Gendered ratings were scored 1 and nongendered ratings (either of both or neither) were scored 0, with possible scores ranging from 0 to 20. In addition to the Rep test, participants completed a questionnaire concerning gender stereotyping and whether they applied gender stereotypes to strangers in social situations and a questionnaire on sexist gender attitudes.

Results showed that gender was a basic category for many participants, with no one scoring 0, and the mean was slightly less than 10 out of 20. Additionally, those who used gender most as a way of categorizing people on the Rep also were more likely to apply gender stereotypes to strangers in social situations. Harper and Schoeman (2003) concluded that "participants who frequently engaged in gender stereotyping also organized their person schemas in terms of gender. This suggests that participants who use gender stereotypes in perceiving strangers also tend to circumscribe their perceptions of friends, family members, and acquaintances along gendered lines" (p. 523).

Smoking and Self-Concept

Previous research on self-concept and adolescent smoking has tended to find relatively negative self-concepts of smokers compared with nonsmokers. More specifically, smokers have greater disparity between real and ideal self-concepts as well as lower self-esteem (Burton, Sussman, Hansen, Johnson, & Flay, 1989; Webster, Hunter, & Keats, 1994). Because different smokers smoke for different reasons, however, an idiographic approach such as the Rep test should be better than the conventional methods at measuring these differences.

The idiographic Rep test was used by Peter Weiss, Neill Watson, and Howard Mcguire (2003) in two groups of college students, which included both smokers and nonsmokers. More specifically, these researchers assessed participants' views of smokers' and nonsmokers' personalities using the Rep test. They predicted that smokers would identify with and rate their own personalities more similar to the personality descriptions they had of other smokers than of nonsmokers. They also predicted lower self-concept (e.g., greater real versus ideal self disparity) for smokers than for nonsmokers.

Participants first gave initials of three smokers and three nonsmokers they knew, and the researcher later presented the participants with 18 different triads of two smokers and one nonsmoker and 18 triads of two nonsmokers and one smoker. Participants then used their own words to describe how the two were similar to each other and different from the third. Next, they judged how the two were different from each other and similar to the third. This resulted in 18 smoker personality trait terms and 18 nonsmoker personality trait terms unique to each participant. The 36 personality terms were then used in a self-concept assessment in which participants rated four distinct forms of self-concept using a standard 7-point Likert scale: real self, ideal self, real social self, and ideal social self. The real self-rating was assessed by participants' rating themselves as they really are, whereas the ideal self was the rating as they would ideally be. The social self-ratings were assessed by asking participants to rate themselves as others their age would see them.

As predicted, smokers identified more with their descriptions of smoker personalities, and vice versa for nonsmokers. Among the more frequent traits attributed to smokers were "laid back," "outgoing," "lazy," and "loud," whereas the more frequent traits for nonsmokers were "quiet," "studious," "friendly," and "athletic." Interestingly, however, all participants endorsed and valued nonsmoker traits more highly than smoker traits on all four self-concept measures. That is, both the smokers and nonsmokers identified with and valued more highly the traits of nonsmokers (such as quiet, studious, etc.) than of smokers. The prediction that smokers would have lower self-esteem (greater real versus ideal self disparity) did not hold. Because this self-esteem finding came out of the literature with adolescent smokers, it may not hold with young adult smokers. A main conclusion drawn by Weiss, Watson, and Mcguire is that the Rep test is not only a useful tool for assessing self-concept, but it is perhaps a more valid and more individualized tool than standard questionnaire inventories.

Personal Constructs and the Big Five

Researchers have begun investigating the connections between Kelly's personal constructs and the Big Five traits (Chapter 14). The Big Five traits (neuroticism, extraversion, openness, agreeableness, and conscientiousness) have received a great deal of attention in modern personality research. Kelly's personal constructs have a moderate amount of attention, but not to the same extent as the Big Five model. Not all personality psychologists agree with this disproportionate allocation of research and the value of each approach. James Grice and colleagues, for example, have directly compared Kelly's personal construct theory with the Big Five (Grice, 2004; Grice, Jackson, & McDaniel, 2006).

These two approaches to personality are quite different, and it is worth highlighting the importance of this comparison. The list of the Big Five traits was created by essentially boiling down all the thousands of ways people describe one another into a shorter more manageable list that captured the most common themes. It seeks to describe everyone along the same continuum. Kelly's repertory grid approach, conversely, seeks to capture the uniqueness of individuals. Uniqueness is hard to capture in the Big Five because everybody is described along just five dimensions, but in the repertory grid the rater essentially creates his or her own continuum on which to describe people. For example, as discussed earlier in this chapter, the first continuum described on the sample repertory grid in Figure 18.2 is religiosity, so clearly for the person completing the repertory grid religiosity is an important descriptor, but it is not a descriptor that is directly captured by many measures of the Big Five.

The research by James Grice (Grice, 2004; Grice et al., 2006) essentially sought to determine just how good the repertory grid approach was at capturing uniqueness compared to the Big Five. To do this, Grice (2004) had participants complete a modified version of Kelly's repertory grid and a standard self-report measure of the Big Five. Participants rated both themselves and people they knew using the repertory grid and the Big Five measure. Using complex statistical procedures, the researchers were able to measure the amount of overlap in participants' repertory grid ratings and Big Five scores.

What they found was rather stunning: There was only about 50% overlap (Grice, 2004; Grice et al., 2006). This means that the repertory grid was capturing aspects of people the Big Five was not and that the Big Five was capturing aspects the repertory grid was not. Some of the unique aspects captured by the repertory grid were body type, ethnicity, wealth, smoker status, and political affiliation (Grice et al., 2006). These are important aspects of people to consider, and they can certainly affect how you would interact with a person, yet they do not appear on a typical measure of the Big Five. Despite this, the Big Five is still enormously valuable as a framework for studying personality. In science it is often important, if not imperative, that researchers have common tools and common descriptors for which to compare their targets of study, people in the case of personality psychology. The Big Five framework has provided those common descriptors that have facilitated a great deal of research. But personality psychology is about individual differences and the importance of the individual, and, compared to the Big Five, Kelly's personal construct theory does a very good job at emphasizing the uniqueness of individuals and how individuals define themselves and those around them in their own terms.

Critique of Kelly

Most of Kelly's professional career was spent working with relatively normal, intelligent college students. Understandably, his theory seems most applicable to these people. He made no attempt to elucidate early childhood experiences (as did Freud) or maturity and old age (as did Erikson). To Kelly, people live solely in the present, with one eye always on the future. This view, though somewhat optimistic, fails to account for developmental and cultural influences on personality.

How does Kelly's theory rate on the six criteria of a useful theory? First, personal construct theory receives a moderate to strong rating on the amount of *research* it has generated. The Rep test and the repertory grid have generated a sizable number of studies, especially in Great Britain, although these instruments are used less frequently by psychologists in the United States.

Despite the relative parsimony of Kelly's basic postulate and 11 supporting corollaries, the theory does not lend itself easily to either verification or falsification. Therefore, we rate personal construct theory low on *falsifiability*.

Third, does personal construct theory *organize knowledge* about human behavior? On this criterion, the theory must be rated low. Kelly's notion that our behavior is consistent with our current perceptions helps organize knowledge; but his avoidance of the problems of motivation, developmental influences, and cultural forces limits his theory's ability to give specific meanings to much of what is currently known about the complexity of personality.

We also rate the theory low as a *guide to action*. Kelly's ideas on psychotherapy are rather innovative and suggest to the practitioner some interesting techniques. Playing the role of a fictitious person, someone the client would like to know, is indeed an unusual and practical approach to therapy. Kelly relied heavily on common sense in this therapeutic practice, and what worked for him might not work for someone else. That disparity would be quite acceptable to Kelly, however, because he viewed therapy as a scientific experiment. The therapist is like a scientist, using imagination to test a variety of hypotheses: that is, to try out new techniques and to explore alternate ways of looking at things. Nevertheless, Kelly's theory offers few specific suggestions to parents, therapists, researchers, and others who are trying to understand human behavior.

Fifth, is the theory *internally consistent,* with a set of *operationally defined terms?* On the first part of this question, personal construct theory rates very high. Kelly was exceptionally careful in choosing terms and concepts to explain his fundamental postulate and the 11 corollaries. His language, although frequently difficult, is both elegant and precise. *The Psychology of Personal Constructs* (Kelly, 1955) contains more than 1,200 pages, but the entire theory is pieced together like a finely woven fabric. Kelly seemed to have constantly been aware of what he had already said and what he was going to say.

On the second half of this criterion, personal construct theory falls short, because like most theorists discussed in this book, Kelly did not define his terms operationally. However, he was exemplary in writing comprehensive and exacting definitions of nearly all terms used in the basic postulate and supporting corollaries.

Finally, is the theory *parsimonious?* Despite the length of Kelly's two-volume book, the theory of personal constructs is exceptionally straightforward and economical. The basic theory is stated in one fundamental postulate and then elaborated by means of 11 corollaries. All other concepts and assumptions can be easily related to this relatively simple structure.

Concept of Humanity

Kelly had an essentially *optimistic* view of human nature. He saw people as anticipating the future and living their lives in accordance with those anticipations. People are capable of changing their personal constructs at any time of life, but those changes are seldom easy. Kelly's modulation corollary suggests that constructs are permeable or resilient, meaning that new elements can be admitted. Not all people, however, have equally permeable constructs. Some accept new experiences and restructure their interpretations accordingly, whereas others possess concrete constructs that are very difficult to alter. Nevertheless, Kelly was quite optimistic in his belief that therapeutic experiences can help people live more productive lives.

On the dimension of *determinism versus free choice,* Kelly's theory leans toward free choice. Within our own personal construct system, we are free to make a choice (Kelly, 1980). We choose between alternatives within a construct system that we ourselves have built. We make those choices on the basis of our anticipation of events. But more than that, we choose those alternatives that appear to offer us the greater opportunity for further elaboration of our anticipatory system. Kelly referred to this view as the **elaborative choice;** that is, in making present choices, we look ahead and pick the alternative that will increase our range of future choices.

Kelly adopted a *teleological* as opposed to a causal view of human personality. He repeatedly insisted that childhood events per se do not shape current personality. Our present construction of past experiences may have some influence on present behavior, but the influence of past events is quite limited. Personality is much more likely to be guided by our present anticipation of future events. Kelly's fundamental postulate—the one on which all corollaries and assumptions stand—is that all human activity is directed by the way that we anticipate events (Kelly, 1955). There can be no question, then, that Kelly's theory is essentially teleological.

Kelly emphasized *conscious processes* more than unconscious ones. However, he did not stress conscious *motivation* because motivation plays no part in personal construct theory. Kelly speaks of levels of cognitive awareness. High levels of awareness refer to those psychological processes that are easily symbolized in words and can be accurately expressed to other people. Low-level processes are incompletely symbolized and are difficult or impossible to communicate.

Experiences can be at low levels of awareness for several reasons. First, some constructs are preverbal because they were formed before a person acquired meaningful language, and, hence, they are not capable of being symbolized even to oneself. Second, some experiences are at a low level of awareness because a person sees only similarities and fails to make meaningful contrasts. For example, a person may construe all people as trustworthy. However, the implicit pole of untrustworthiness is denied. Because the person's superordinate construction system is rigid, he or she fails to adopt a realistic construct of trustworthy/untrustworthy and tends to see the actions of others as completely trustworthy. Third, some subordinate constructs may remain at a low level of awareness as superordinate constructs are changing. For instance, even after a person realizes that not everyone is trustworthy, the person may be reluctant to construe one particular individual as being untrustworthy. This hesitation means that a subordinate construct has not yet caught up to a superordinate one. Finally, because some events may lie outside a person's range of convenience, certain experiences do not become part of that person's construct system. For example, such involuntary processes as heartbeat, blood circulation, eye blink, and digestion are ordinarily outside one's range of convenience; and one is usually not aware of them.

On the issue of *biological versus social influences,* Kelly was inclined more toward the social. His sociality corollary assumes that, to some extent, we are influenced by others and in turn have some impact on them. When we accurately construe the constructions of another person, we may play a role in a social process involving that other person. Kelly assumed that our interpretation of the construction systems of important other people (such as parents, spouse, and friends) may have some influence on our future constructions. Recall that, in fixed-role therapy, clients adopt the identity of a fictitious person; and by trying out that role in various social settings, they may experience some change in their personal constructs. However, the actions of others do not mold their behavior; rather, it is their interpretation of events that changes their behavior.

On the final dimension for a conception of humanity—*uniqueness versus similarities*—Kelly emphasized the uniqueness of personality. This emphasis, however, was tempered by his commonality corollary, which assumes that people from the same sociocultural background tend to have had some of the same kinds of experience and therefore construe events similarly. Nevertheless, Kelly held that our individual interpretations of events are crucial and that no two persons ever have precisely the same personal constructs.

Key Terms and Concepts

- Basic to Kelly's theory is the idea of *constructive alternativism,* or the notion that our present interpretations are subject to change.
- Kelly's *basic postulate* assumes that all psychological processes are directed by the ways in which we anticipate events. Eleven corollaries derive from and elaborate this one fundamental postulate.
- The *construction corollary* assumes that people anticipate future events according to their interpretations of recurrent themes.
- The *individuality corollary* states that people have different experiences and therefore construe events in different ways.
- The *organization corollary* holds that people organize their personal constructs in a hierarchical system, with some constructs in superordinate positions and others subordinate to them. This organization allows people to minimize incompatible constructs.
- Kelly's *dichotomy corollary* presumes that all personal constructs are dichotomous; that is, people construe events in an either-or manner.
- His *choice corollary* states that people choose the alternative in a dichotomized construct that they see as extending their range of future choices.
- The *range corollary* assumes that constructs are limited to a particular range of convenience; that is, they are not relevant to all situations.
- The *experience corollary* holds that people continually revise their personal constructs as the result of experience.
- The *modulation corollary* maintains that some new experiences do not lead to a revision of personal constructs because they are too concrete or impermeable.
- The *fragmentation corollary* recognizes that people's behavior is sometimes inconsistent because their construct system can readily admit incompatible elements.
- Kelly's *commonality corollary* states that, to the extent that we have had experiences similar to other people's experiences, our personal constructs tend to be similar to the construction systems of those people.
- The *sociality corollary* states that people are able to communicate with other people because they can construe other people's constructions. Not only do people observe the behavior of another person but they also interpret what that behavior means to that person.
- Kelly's *fixed-role therapy* calls for clients to act out predetermined roles continuously until their peripheral and core roles change as significant others begin reacting differently to them.
- The purpose of Kelly's *Rep test* is to discover ways in which people construe important people in their lives.

References

Adler, A. (1907/1917). *Study of organ inferiority and its psychical compensation*. New York: Nervous and Mental Disease Publishing.

Adler, A. (1925/1968). *The practice and theory of individual psychology*. Totowa, NJ: Littlefield Adams.

Adler, A. (1927). *Understanding human nature*. New York: Greenberg.

Adler, A. (1929/1964). *Problems of neurosis*. New York: Harper Torchbooks.

Adler, A. (1929/1969). *The science of living*. New York: Anchor Books.

Adler, A. (1930). Individual psychology. In C. Murchinson (Ed.), *Psychologies of 1930*. Worcester, MA: Clark University Press.

Adler, A. (1931). *What life should mean to you*. New York: Capricorn Books.

Adler, A. (1956). *The individual psychology of Alfred Adler: A systematic presentation in selections from his writings* (H. L. Ansbacher & R. R. Ansbacher, Eds.). New York: Basic Books.

Adler, A. (1964). *Superiority and social interest: A collection of later writings* (H. L. Ansbacher & R. R. Ansbacher, Eds.). New York: Norton.

Ai, A. L., Peterson, C., Rodgers, W., & Tice, T. N. (2005). Effects of faith and secular factors on locus of control in middle-aged and older cardiac patients. *Aging and Mental Health, 9,* 470–481.

Ainsworth, M., Blehar, M., Waters, E., & Wall, S. (1978). *Patterns of attachment*. Hillsdale, NJ: Erlbaum.

Alexander, I. E. (1990). *Personology: Method and content in personality assessment and psychobiography*. Durham, NC: Duke University Press.

Allport, F. (1974). An autobiography. In G. Lindzey (Ed.), *A history of psychology in autobiography* (Vol. 6, pp. 1–29). Englewood Cliffs, NJ: Prentice-Hall.

Allport, G. W. (1937). *Personality: A psychological interpretation*. New York: Henry Holt.

Allport, G. W. (1950). *The individual and his religion*. New York: Macmillan.

Allport, G. W. (1954). *The nature of prejudice*. Reading, MA: Addison-Wesley.

Allport, G. W. (1955). *Becoming: Basic consideration for a psychology of personality*. New Haven, CT: Yale University Press.

Allport, G. W. (1960). The open system in personality theory. *Journal of Abnormal and Social Psychology, 61,* 301–310.

Allport, G. W. (1961). *Pattern and growth in personality*. New York: Holt, Rinehart and Winston.

Allport, G. W. (1962). The general and the unique in psychological science. *Journal of Personality, 30,* 405–422.

Allport, G. W. (1963). Behavioral science, religion and mental health. *Journal of Religion and Health, 2,* 187–197.

Allport, G. W. (1965). *Letters from Jenny*. San Diego: Harcourt Brace Jovanovich.

Allport, G. W. (1966). Traits revisited. *American Psychologist, 21,* 1–10.

Allport, G. W. (1967). An autobiography. In E. G. Boring & G. Lindzey (Eds.), *A history of psychology in autobiography* (Vol. 5, pp. 1–25). New York: Appleton-Century-Crofts.

Allport, G. W. (1968). *The person in psychology*. Boston: Beacon Press.

Allport, G. W. (1978). *Waiting for the Lord: 33 meditations on God and man*. New York: Macmillan.

Allport, G. W., & Odbert, H. S. (1936). Trait-names: A psycho-lexical study. *Psychological Monographs, 47,* 1–171.

Allport, G. W., & Ross, J. M. (1967). Personal religious orientation and prejudice. *Journal of Personality and Social Psychology, 5,* 432–443.

Allport, G. W., Vernon, P. E., & Lindzey, G. (1960). *A study of values*. Boston: Houghton Mifflin.

American Psychiatric Association. (1994). *Diagnostic and statistical manual of mental disorders* (4th ed.). Washington, DC: American Psychiatric Association.

American Psychiatric Association. (2002). *Diagnostic and statistical manual of mental disorders* (4th ed., Text Revision). Washington, DC: American Psychiatric Association.

American Psychiatric Association. (2002). *DSM-IV-TR: Handbook of differential diagnosis*. Washington, DC: Author.

Anderson, R. J., Freedland, K. E., Clouse, R. E., & Lustman, P. J. (2001). The prevalence of comorbid depression in adults with diabetes: A meta-analysis. *Diabetes Care, 24,* 1069–1078.

Anonymous. (1946). Letters from Jenny. *Journal of Abnormal and Social Psychology, 41,* 315–350, 449–480.

Arndt, J., Schimel, J., & Goldenberg, J. L. (2003). Death can be good for your health: Fitness intentions as a proximal and distal defense against mortality salience. *Journal of Applied Social Psychology, 33,* 1726–1746.

Arnett, J. J. (2000). Emerging adulthood: A theory of development from the late teens through the twenties. *American Psychologist, 55,* 469–480.

Aron, A. R., & Poldrack, R. A. (2005). The cognitive neuroscience of response inhibition: Relevance for genetic research in Attention-Deficit/Hyperactivity Disorder. *Biological Psychiatry, 57,* 1285–1292.

Bachofen, J. J. (1861/1967). *Myth, religion, and Mother Right: Selected writings of Johann Jacob Bachofen* (R. Manheim, Trans.). Princeton, NJ: Princeton University Press.

Bair, D. (2003). *Jung: A biography*. Boston: Little, Brown.

Baldwin, A. F. (1942). Personal structure analysis: A statistical method for investigating the single personality. *Journal of Abnormal and Social Psychology, 37,* 163–183.

Bandura, A. (1977). *Social learning theory*. Englewood Cliffs, NJ: Prentice-Hall.

Bandura, A. (1986). *Social foundations of thought and action: A social cognitive theory*. Englewood Cliffs, NJ: Prentice-Hall

Bandura, A. (1989). Human agency in social cognitive theory. *American Psychologist, 44,* 1175–1184.

Bandura, A. (1994). Social cognitive theory and mass communication. In J. Bryant & D. Zillmann (Eds.), *Media effects: Advances in theory and research* (pp. 61–90). Hillsdale, NJ: Erlbaum.

Bandura, A. (1995). Exercise of personal and collective efficacy in changing societies. In A. Bandura (Ed.), *Self-efficacy in changing societies* (pp. 1–45). Cambridge, England: Cambridge University Press.

Bandura, A. (1996). Ontological and epistemological terrains revisited. *Journal of Behavior Therapy and Experimental Psychiatry, 27,* 323–345.

Bandura, A. (1997). *Self-efficacy: The exercise of control*. New York: Freeman.

Bandura, A. (1998a). Explorations of fortuitous determinants of life paths. *Psychological Inquiry, 9,* 95–99.

Bandura, A. (1998b). Personal and collective efficacy in human adaptation and change. In J. G. Adair, D. Belanger, & K. L. Dion (Eds.), *Advances in psychological science: Vol. 1. Social, personal, and cultural aspects* (pp. 51–71). East Sussex, UK: Psychological Press.

Bandura, A. (1998c). Health promotion from the perspective of social-cognitive theory. *Psychology and Health, 13,* 623–649.

Bandura, A. (1999a). Moral disengagement in the perpetration of inhumanities. *Personality and Social Psychology Review, 3,* 193–209.

Bandura, A. (1999b). Social cognitive theory of personality. In L. A. Pervin & O. P. John (Eds.), *Handbook of personality: Theory and research* (pp. 154–196). New York: Guilford Press.

Bandura, A. (2000). Exercise of human agency through collective efficacy. *Current Directions in Psychological Science, 9,* 75–78.

Bandura, A. (2001). Social cognitive theory: An agentic perspective. *Annual Review of Psychology, 52,* 1–26.

Bandura, A. (2002a). Selective moral disengagement in the exercise of moral agency. *Journal of Moral Education, 31,* 101–119.

Bandura, A. (2002b). Social cognitive theory in cultural context. *Applied Psychology: An International Review, 51,* 269–290.

Bandura, A. (2003). On the psychosocial impact and mechanisms of spiritual modeling. *International Journal for the Psychology of Religion, 13,* 167–174.

Bandura, A. (2004). Swimming against the mainstream: The early years from chilly tributary to transformative mainstream. *Behavior Research and Theory, 42,* 613–630.

Bandura, A., Ross, D., & Ross, S. A. (1963). Imitation of film-mediated aggressive models. *Journal of Abnormal and Social Psychology, 66,* 3–11.

Bandura, A., & Walters, R. H. (1959). *Adolescent aggression*. New York: Ronald Press.

Barenbaum, N. B. (1997). The case(s) of Gordon Allport. *Journal of Personality, 65,* 743–755.

Bargh, J. A., & Chartrand, T. L. (1999). The unbearable automaticity of being. *American Psychologist, 54,* 461–479.

Bauer, J. J., & McAdams, D. P. (2004a). Growth goals, maturity, and well-being. *Developmental Psychology, 40,* 114–127.

Bauer, J. J., & McAdams, D. P. (2004b). Personal growth in adults' stories of life transitions. *Journal of Personality, 72,* 573–602.

Beauducel, A., Brocke, B., & Leue, A. (2006). Energetical bases of extraversion: Effort, arousal, EEG, and performance. *International Journal of Psychophysiology, 62,* 212–223.

Beaver, J. D., Lawrence, A. D., van Ditzhuijzen, J., Davis, M. H., Woods, A., & Calder, A. J. (2006). Individual differences in reward drive predict neural responses to images of food. *Journal of Neuroscience, 26,* 5160–5166.

Belangee, S. E. (2006). Individual psychology and eating disorders: A theoretical application. *Journal of Individual Psychology, 62,* 3–17.

Belangee, S. E. (2007). Couples and eating disorders: An individual psychology approach. *Journal of Individual Psychology, 63,* 294–305.

Bell, M. D., Billington, R., & Becker, B. (1986). A scale for the assessment of object relationships. Reliability, validity, and factorial invariance. *Journal of Clinical Psychology, 42,* 733–741.

Ben-Zur, H., & Zeidner, M. (1995). Coping patterns and affective reactions under community crisis and daily routine conditions. *Anxiety, Stress & Coping: An International Journal, 8,* 185–201.

Bernard, M. M., Gebauer, J. E., & Maio, G. R. (2006). Cultural estrangement: The role of personal and societal value discrepancies. *Personality and Social Psychology Bulletin, 32,* 78–92.

Bettelheim, B. (1982, March 1). Freud and the soul. *The New Yorker,* pp. 52–93.

Bettelheim, B. (1983). *Freud and man's soul.* New York: Knopf.

Bilmes, M. (1978). Rollo May. In R. S. Valle & M. King (Eds.), *Existential-phenomenological alternatives for psychology* (pp. 290–294). New York: Oxford University Press.

Bjork, D. W. (1993). *B. F. Skinner: A life.* New York: Basic Books.

Block, J. H., & Block, J. (1980). The role of ego-control and ego-resiliency in the organization of behavior. In W. A. Collins (Ed.), *Minnesota symposium on child psychology* (Vol. 13, pp. 39–101). Hillsdale, NJ: Erlbaum.

Block, J., & Block, J. H. (2006). Nursery school personality and political orientation two decades later. *Journal of Research in Personality, 40,* 734–749.

Blum, D. (2002). *Love at Goon Park: Harry Harlow and the science of affection.* Cambridge, MA: Cambridge Center.

Boag, S. (2006). Freudian dream theory, dream bizarreness, and the disguise-censor controversy. *Neuro-Psychoanalysis, 8*(1), 5–16.

Borkovec, T. D., & Sharpless, B. (2004). Generalized anxiety disorder: Bringing cognitive-behavioral therapy into the valued present. In S. C. Hayes, V. M. Follette, & M. M. Linehan (Eds.), *Mindfulness and acceptance: Expanding the cognitive-behavioral tradition* (pp. 209–242). New York: Guilford Press.

Bottome, P. (1939). *Alfred Adler: Apostle of freedom.* London: Faber & Faber.

Bottome, P. (1957). *Alfred Adler: A portrait from life.* New York: Vanguard.

Bowlby, J. (1969/1982). *Attachment and loss: Vol. 1. Attachment* (2nd ed.). New York: Basic Books.

Bowlby, J. (1973). *Attachment and loss: Vol. 2. Separation: Anxiety and anger.* New York: Basic Books.

Bowlby, J. (1980). *Attachment and loss: Vol. 3. Loss: Sadness and depression.* New York: Basic Books.

Bowlby, J. (1988). *A secure base: Parent-child attachment and healthy human development.* New York: Basic Books.

Bradley, C. L., & Marcia, J. E. (1998). Generativity vs. stagnation: A five-category model. *Journal of Personality, 66,* 39–64.

Brannon, L. (2005). *Gender: Psychological perspectives* (4th ed.). Boston: Allyn and Bacon.

Brannon, L., & Feist, J. (2007). *Health psychology: An introduction to behavior and health* (6th ed.). Belmont, CA: Wadsworth.

Breger L. (2000). *Freud: Darkness in the midst of vision.* New York: Wiley.

Breuer, J., & Freud, S. (1895/1955). *Studies on hysteria.* In J. Strachey (Ed. and Trans.), *The standard edition of the complete psychological works of Sigmund Freud* (Vol. 2). London: Hogarth Press.

Brome, V. (1978). *Jung.* New York: Atheneum.

Burrell, M. (2002). Deconstructing and reconstructing: Substance use and "addiction": Constructivist perspectives. In R. A. Neimeyer & G. J. Neimeyer (Eds.), *Advances in personal construct psychology: New directions and perspectives* (pp. 203–232). Westport, CT: Praeger.

Burton, C. M., & King, L. A. (2004). The health benefits of writing about intensely positive experiences. *Journal of Research in Personality, 38,* 150–163.

Burton, J., Sussman, S., Hansen, W., Johnson, C., & Flay, B. R. (1989). Image attributions and smoking: Intentions among seventh grade students. *Journal of Applied Social Psychology, 19,* 656–666.

Carver, C. S., & White, T. L. (1994). Behavioral inhibition, behavioral activation, and affective responses to impending reward and punishment: The BIS/BAS scales. *Journal of Personality and Social Psychology, 67,* 319–333.

Cattell, R. B. (1949). *Manual for Forms A and B: Sixteen Personality Factors Questionnaire.* Champaign, IL: IPAT.

Cattell, R. B. (1973). A check on the 29-factor Clinical Analysis Questionnaire structure on normal and pathological subjects. *Journal of Multivariate Experimental Personality and Clinical Psychology, 1,* 3–12.

Cattell, R. B. (1983). *Structured personality—learning theory: A wholistic multivariate research approach.* New York: Praeger.

Chapman, A. H. (1976). *Harry Stack Sullivan: His life and his work.* New York: Putnam.

Chodorow, N. J. (1989). *Feminism and psychoanalytic theory.* New Haven, CT: Yale University Press.

Chodorow, N. J. (1991). Freud on women. In J. Neu (Ed.), *The Cambridge companion to Freud: Cambridge companions to philosophy* (pp. 224–248). New York: Cambridge University Press.

Chodorow, N. J. (1994). *Femininities, masculinities, sexualities: Freud and beyond.* Lexington: University of Kentucky Press.

Chow, T. W., & Cummings, J. L. (1999). Frontal-subcortical circuits. In B. L. Miller and J. L. Cummings (Eds.), *The human frontal lobes: Functions and disorders* (pp. 3–26). New York: Guilford Press.

Clark, R. W. (1980). *Freud: The man and the cause.* New York: Random House.

Clark, A. J. (2002). *Early recollections: Theory and practice in counseling and psychotherapy.* New York: Brunner-Routledge.

Clements, L. B., York, R. O., & Rohrer, G. E. (1995). The interaction of parental alcoholism and alcoholism as a predictor of drinking-related locus of control. *Alcoholism Treatment Quarterly, 12,* 97–110.

Combs, A. W., & Snygg, D. (1959). *Individual behavior: A perceptual approach to behavior.* New York: Harper & Row.

Compton, W. C., Smith, M. L., Cornish, K. A., & Qualls, D. L. (1996). Factor structure of mental health measures. *Journal of Personality and Social Psychology, 71,* 406–413.

Corr, P. J. (2002). J. A. Gray's reinforcement sensitivity theory: Tests of the joint subsystems hypothesis of anxiety and impulsivity. *Personality and Individual Differences, 33,* 511–532.

Costa, P. T., Fozard, J. L., McCrae, R. R., & Bosse, R. (1976). Relations of age and personality dimensions to cognitive ability factors. *Journal of Gerontology, 31,* 663–669.

Costa, P. T., & McCrae, R. R. (1976). Age differences in personality structure: A cluster analytic approach. *Journal of Gerontology, 31,* 564–570.

Costa, P. T., & McCrae, R. R. (1980). Influence of extraversion and neuroticism on subjective well-being: Happy and unhappy people. *Journal of Personality and Social Psychology, 38,* 668–678.

Costa, P. T., & McCrae R. R. (1985). *Manual for the NEO Personality Inventory.* Odessa, FL: Psychological Assessment Resources.

Costa, P. T., & McCrae R. R. (1992). *NEO-PI-R Professional manual.* Odessa, FL: Psychological Assessment Resources.

Costa, P. T., & McCrae R. R. (1994). Set like plaster? Evidence for the stability of adult personality. In T. Heatherton & J. Weinberger (Eds.), *Can personality change?* (pp. 21–40). Washington, DC: American Psychological Association.

Costa, P. T., McCrae R. R., & Arenberg, D. (1980). Enduring dispositions in adult males. *Journal of Personality and Social Psychology, 38,* 793–800.

Costa, P. T., & McCrae, R. R. (2002). Looking backward: Changes in the mean levels of personality traits from 80 to 12. In D. Cervone & W. Mischel (Eds.), *Advances in personality science.* (pp. 219–237). New York: Guilford Press.

Cox, C. R., Goldenberg, J. L., Arndt, J., & Pyszczynski, T. (2007). Mother's milk: An existential perspective on negative reactions to breast-feeding. *Personality and Social Psychology Bulletin, 33,* 110–122.

Cox, C. R., Goldenberg, J. L., Pyszczynski, T., & Weise, D. (2007). Disgust, creatureliness and the accessibility of death-related thoughts. *European Journal of Social Psychology, 37,* 494–507.

Cramer, D. (1994). Self-esteem and Rogers' core conditions in close friends: A latent variable path analysis of panel data. *Counseling Psychology Quarterly, 7,* 327–337.

Cramer, D. (2002). Linking conflict management behaviours and relational satisfaction: The intervening role of conflict outcome satisfaction.

Journal of Social and Personal Relationships, 19, 425–432.

Cramer, D. (2003). Acceptance and need for approval as moderators of self-esteem and satisfaction with a romantic relationship or a closest friendship. *Journal of Psychology, 137,* 495–505.

Cramer, P. (2007). Longitudinal study of defense mechanisms: Late childhood to late adolescence. *Journal of Personality, 75,* 1–23.

Crandall, J. E. (1975). A scale for social interest. *Individual Psychology, 31,* 187–195.

Crandall, J. E. (1981). *Theory and measurement of social interest: Empirical tests of Alfred Adler's concept.* New York: Columbia University Press.

Crews, F. (1995). *The memory wars: Freud's legacy in dispute.* New York: The New York Review of Books.

Crews, F. (1996). The verdict on Freud. *Psychological Science, 7,* 63–68.

Csíkszentmihályi, M. (1990). *Flow: The psychology of optimal experience.* New York: Harper and Row.

Davidovitz, R., Mikulincer, M., Shaver, P. R., Izsak, R., & Popper, M. (2007). Leaders as attachment figures: Leaders' attachment orientations predict leadership-related mental representations and followers' performance and mental health. *Journal of Personality and Social Psychology, 93,* 632–650.

de Zavala, A. G., & Van Bergh, A. (2007). Need for cognitive closure and conservative political beliefs: Differential mediation by personal worldviews. *Political Psychology, 28,* 587–608.

Digman, J. M. (1990). Personality structure: Emergence of the five-factor model. *Annual Review of Psychology, 41,* 417–440.

Dornic, S., & Ekehammer, B. (1990). Extraversion, neuroticism, and noise sensitivity. *Personality and Individual Differences, 11,* 989–992

Doucet, C., & Stelmack, R. M. (2000). An event-related potential analysis of extraversion and individual differences in cognitive processing speed and response execution. *Journal of Personality and Social Psychology, 78,* 956–964.

Dunne, C. (2000). *Carl Jung: Wounded healer of the soul. An illustrated biography.* New York: Parabola Books.

Ellenberger, H. F. (1970). *The discovery of the unconscious.* New York: Basic Books.

Elliot, A. J., & Thrash, T. M. (2002). Approach-avoidance motivation in personality: Approach and avoidance temperaments and goals. *Journal of Personality and Social Psychology, 82,* 804–818.

Elms, A. C. (1981). Skinner's dark year and *Walden Two. American Psychologist, 36,* 470–479.

Elms, A. C. (1994). *Uncovering lives: The uneasy alliance of biography and psychology.* New York: Oxford University Press.

Epstein, S. (1979). The stability of behavior: I. On predicting most of the people most of the time. *Journal of Personality and Social Psychology, 37,* 1097–1126.

Epstein, S. (1980). The stability of behavior: II. Implications for psychological research. *American Psychologist, 35,* 790–806.

Erikson, E. H. (1950). *Childhood and society.* New York: Norton.

Erikson, E. H. (1958). *Young man Luther: A study in psychoanalysis and history.* New York: Norton.

Erikson, E. H. (1963). *Childhood and society* (2nd ed.). New York: Norton.

Erikson, E. H. (1968). *Identity: Youth and crisis.* New York: Norton.

Erikson, E. H. (1969). *Gandhi's truth: On the origins of militant nonviolence.* New York: Norton.

Erikson, E. H. (1974). *Dimensions of a new identity: The 1973 Jefferson Lectures in the Humanities.* New York: Norton.

Erikson, E. H. (1975). *Life history and the historical moment.* New York: Norton.

Erikson, E. H. (1977). *Toys and reasons: Stages in the ritualization of experience.* New York: Norton.

Erikson, E. H. (1980). *Identity and the life cycle.* New York: Norton.

Erikson, E. H. (1982). *The life cycle completed: A review.* New York: Norton.

Erikson, E. H. (1985). *Childhood and society* (3rd ed.). New York: Norton.

Erikson, E. H. (1987). *A way of looking at things: Selected papers of Erik Erikson.* (S. Schlein, Ed.). New York: Norton.

Erikson, E. H. (1989). Elements of a psychoanalytic theory of psychosocial development. In S. I. Greenspan & G. H. Pollock (Eds.), *The course of life, Vol. 1: Infancy* (pp. 15–83). Madison, CT: International Universities Press, Inc.

Erikson, E. H., Erikson, J. M., & Kivnick, H. Q. (1986). *Vital involvement in old age.* New York: Norton.

Evans, R. I. (1966). *Dialogue with Erich Fromm.* New York: Harper & Row.

Evans, R. I. (1967). *Dialogue with Erik Erikson.* New York: Harper & Row.

Evans, R. I. (1989). *Albert Bandura: The man and his ideas—A dialogue.* New York: Praeger.

Eysenck, H. J. (1947). *Dimensions of personality.* London: Routledge & Kegan Paul.

Eysenck, H. J. (1952a). The effects of psychotherapy: An evaluation. *Journal of Consulting Psychology, 16,* 319–324.

Eysenck, H. J. (1952b). *The structure of human personality.* London: Methuen.

Eysenck, H. J. (1953). *Uses and abuses of psychology.* Baltimore: Penguin.

Eysenck, H. J. (1954). *The psychology of politics.* London: Routledge & Kegan Paul.

Eysenck, H. J. (1956). *Sense and nonsense in psychology.* London: Penguin.

Eysenck, H. J. (1959). *Manual for the Maudsley Personality Inventory.* London: University of London Press.

Eysenck, H. J. (1962). *Know your own IQ.* London: Penguin.

Eysenck, H. J. (1964). *Crime and personality.* Boston: Houghton Mifflin.

Eysenck, H. J. (1965). *Fact and fiction in psychology.* London: Penguin.

Eysenck, H. J. (1967). *The biological basis of personality.* Springfield, IL: Charles C Thomas.

Eysenck, H. J. (1971). *The IQ argument.* New York: Library Press. (British edition: *Race, intelligence, and education.* London: Maurice Temple Smith, 1971.)

Eysenck, H. J. (1972). *Psychology is about people.* London: Allen Lane.

Eysenck, H. J. (1976). *Sex and personality.* Austin: University of Texas Press.

Eysenck, H. J. (1977a). Personality and factor analysis: A reply to Guilford. *Psychological Bulletin, 84,* 405–411.

Eysenck, H. J. (1977b). *You and neurosis.* London: Temple Smith.

Eysenck, H. J. (1980). An autobiography. In G. Lindzey (Ed.), *A history of psychology in autobiography* (Vol. 7, pp. 153–187). San Francisco: Freeman.

Eysenck, H. J. (Ed.). (1981). *A model for personality.* New York: Springer.

Eysenck, H. J. (1982). *Personality, genetics and behavior: Selected papers.* New York: Praeger.

Eysenck, H. J. (1983). Psychopharmacology and personality. In W. Janke (Ed.), *Response variability to psychotropic drugs* (pp. 127–154). Oxford, England: Pergamon Press.

Eysenck, H. J. (1988). Skinner, Skinnerism, and the Skinnerian in psychology. Special Issue: Stress counseling. *Counseling Psychology Quarterly, 1,* 299–301.

Eysenck, H. J. (1990). Biological dimensions of personality. In L. A. Pervin (Ed.), *Handbook of personality: Theory and research* (pp. 244–276). New York: Guilford Press.

Eysenck, H. J. (1991a). Dimensions of personality: 16, 5, or 3? Criteria for a taxonomic paradigm. *Personality and Individual Differences, 12,* 773–790.

Eysenck, H. J. (1991b). Hans J. Eysenck: Maverick psychologist. In C. E. Walker (Ed.), *The history of clinical psychology in autobiography* (Vol. 2, pp. 39–86). Pacific Grove, CA: Brooks/Cole.

Eysenck, H. J. (1991c). Personality as a risk factor in coronary heart disease. *European Journal of Personality, 5,* 81–92.

Eysenck, H. J. (1991d). *Smoking, personality and stress: Psychosocial factors in the prevention of cancer and coronary heart disease.* New York: Springer-Verlag.

Eysenck, H. J. (1993). Creativity and personality: Suggestions for a theory. *Psychological Inquiry, 4,* 147–179.

Eysenck, H. J. (1994b). Normality-abnormality and the three-factor model. In S. Strack & M. Lorr (Eds.), *Differentiating normal and abnormal personality* (pp. 3–25). New York: Springer.

Eysenck, H. J. (1994c). Personality: Biological foundations. In P. A. Vernon (Ed.), *The neuropsychology of individual differences* (pp. 151–207). San Diego, CA: Academic Press.

Eysenck, H. J. (1995). *Genius: The natural history of creativity.* Cambridge, England: Cambridge University Press.

Eysenck, H. J. (1996). Personality and cancer. In C. L. Cooper (Ed.), *Handbook of stress, medicine, and health* (pp. 193–215). Boca Raton, FL: CRC Press.

Eysenck, H. J. (1997a). Personality and experimental psychology: The unification of psychology and the possibility of a paradigm. *Journal of Personality and Social Psychology, 73,* 1224–1237.

Eysenck, H. J. (1997b). *Rebel with a cause: The autobiography of H. J. Eysenck* (Rev. ed.). New Brunswick: Truncation Publishers.

Eysenck, H. J. (1998a). *Intelligence: A new look.* New Brunswick: Transaction Publishers.

Eysenck, H. J. (1998b). Personality and crime. In T. Millon, E. Simonsen, M. Birket-Smith, & R. D. Davis (Eds.), *Psychopathy: Antisocial, criminal, and violent behavior* (pp. 40–49). New York: Guilford Press.

Eysenck, H. J. (1999). *The psychology of politics* (Rev. ed.). New Brunswick: Transaction Publishers.

Eysenck, H. J., & Coulter, T. (1972). The personality and attitudes of working class British Communists and Fascists. *Journal of Social Psychology, 87,* 59–73.

Eysenck, H. J., & Eysenck, M. W. (1985). *Personality and individual differences: A natural science approach.* New York: Plenum Press.

Eysenck, H. J., & Eysenck, S. B. G. (1964). *Manual of the Eysenck Personality Inventory.* London: University of London Press.

Eysenck, H. J., & Eysenck, S. B. G. (1968). *Manual for the Eysenck Personality Inventory.* San Diego, CA: Educational and Industrial Testing Service.

Eysenck, H. J., & Eysenck, S. B. G. (1969). *Personality structure and measurement.* San Diego, CA: R. R. Knapp.

Eysenck, H. J., & Eysenck, S. B. G. (1975). *Manual of the Eysenck Personality Questionnaire (Junior and Adult).* London: Hodder & Stoughton.

Eysenck, H. J., & Eysenck, S. B. G. (1976). *Psychoticism as a dimension of personality.* London: Hodder & Stoughton.

Eysenck, H. J., & Eysenck, S. B. G. (1993). *The Eysenck Personality Questionnaire-Revised.* London: Hodder & Stoughton.

Eysenck, H. J., & Grossarth-Maticek, R. (1991). Creative novation behaviour therapy as a prophylactic treatment for cancer and coronary heart disease: Part II. Effects of treatment. *Behaviour Research Therapy, 29,* 17–31.

Eysenck, H. J., & Gudjonsson, G. (1989). *The causes and cures of criminality.* New York: Plenum Press.

Eysenck, H. J., & Nias, D. K. B. (1978). *Sex, violence and the media.* New York: Harper & Row.

Eysenck, S. (1965). *Manual for the Junior Eysenck Personality Inventory.* San Diego, CA: Educational and Industrial Testing Service.

Eysenck, S. (1997). Psychoticism as a dimension of personality. In H. Nyborg (Ed.), *The scientific study of human nature: Tribute to Hans J. Eysenck at eighty* (pp. 109–121). Oxford, England: Pergamon Press.

Federn, E. (1988). Psychoanalysis: The fate of a science in exile. In E. Timms & N. Segal (Eds.), *Freud in exile: Psychoanalysis and its vicissitudes* (pp. 156–162). New Haven, CT: Yale University Press.

Feist, G. J. (1993). A structural model of scientific eminence. *Psychological Science, 4,* 366–371.

Feist, G. J. (1994). Personality and working style predictors of integrative complexity: A study of scientists' thinking about research and teaching. *Journal of Personality and Social Psychology, 67,* 474–484.

Feist, G. J., & Gorman, M. E. (1998). Psychology of science: Review and integration of a nascent discipline. *Review of General Psychology, 2,* 3–47.

Feltham, C. (1996). Psychotherapy's staunchest critic: An interview with Hans Eysenck. *British Journal of Guidance and Counseling, 24,* 423–435.

Fern, T. L. (1991). Identifying the gifted child humorists. *Roeper Review, 14,* 30–34.

Ferris, P. (1997). *Dr. Freud: A life.* Washington, DC: Counterpoint.

Ferster, C. B., & Skinner, B. F. (1957). *Schedules of reinforcement.* New York: Appleton-Century-Crofts.

Fiebert, M. S. (1997). In and out of Freud's shadow: A chronology of Adler's relationship with Freud. *Journal of Individual Psychology, 53,* 241–269.

Filbeck, G., Hatfield, P., & Horvath, P. (2005). Risk aversion and personality type. *Journal of Behavioral Finance, 6,* 170–180.

Fischer, P., Greitemeyer, T., Kastenmuller, A., Jonas, E., & Frey, D. (2006). Coping with terrorism: The impact of increased salience of terrorism on mood and self-efficacy of intrinsically religious and nonreligious people. *Personality and Social Psychology Bulletin, 32,* 365–377.

Fransella, F. (1995). *George Kelly.* London: Sage.

Fransella, F., & Bannister, D. (1977). *A manual for repertory grid technique.* London: Academic Press.

Freud, A. (1946). *The ego and the mechanisms of defense.* New York: International Universities Press.

Freud, S. (1900/1953). *The interpretation of dreams.* In *Standard edition* (Vols. 4 & 5).

Freud, S. (1901/1953). On dreams. In *Standard edition* (Vol. 5).

Freud, S. (1901/1960). *Psychopathology of everyday life.* In *Standard edition* (Vol. 6).

Freud, S. (1905/1953a). Fragment of an analysis of a case of hysteria. In *Standard edition* (Vol. 7).

Freud, S. (1905/1953b). Three essays on the theory of sexuality. In *Standard edition* (Vol. 7).

Freud, S. (1905/1960). *Jokes and their relation to the unconscious.* In *Standard edition* (Vol. 8).

Freud, S. (1905/2002). *The joke and its relation to the unconscious.* Translated by Joyce Crick. London: Penguin Classics.

Freud, S. (1910/1957). Leonardo da Vinci and a memory of his childhood. In *Standard edition* (Vol. 11).

Freud, S. (1911/1958). Formulations on the two principles of mental functioning. In *Standard edition* (Vol. 12).

Freud, S. (1913/1953). *Totem and taboo.* In *Standard edition* (Vol. 13).

Freud, S. (1914/1953). The Moses of Michelangelo. In *Standard edition* (Vol. 13).

Freud, S. (1914/1957). On narcissism: An introduction. In *Standard edition* (Vol. 14).

Freud, S. (1915/1957a). Instincts and their vicissitudes. In *Standard edition* (Vol. 14).

Freud, S. (1915/1957b). The unconscious. In *Standard edition* (Vol. 14).

Freud, S. (1917/1955a). A difficulty in the path of psycho-analysis. In *Standard edition* (Vol. 17).

Freud, S. (1917/1955b). On transformations of instinct as exemplified in anal erotism. In *Standard edition* (Vol. 17).

Freud, S. (1917/1963). *Introductory lectures on psychoanalysis*. In *Standard edition* (Vols. 15 &16).

Freud, S. (1920/1955a). *Beyond the pleasure principle.* In *Standard edition* (Vol. 18).

Freud, S. (1920/1955b). The psychogenesis of a case of homosexuality in a woman. In *Standard edition* (Vol. 18).

Freud, S. (1922/1955). Some neurotic mechanisms in jealousy, paranoia and homosexuality. In *Standard edition* (Vol. 18).

Freud, S. (1923/1961a). *The ego and the id.* In *Standard edition* (Vol. 19).

Freud, S. (1923/1961b). The infantile genital organization: An interpolation into the theory of sexuality. In *Standard edition* (Vol. 19).

Freud, S. (1924/1961). The dissolution of the Oedipus complex. In *Standard edition* (Vol. 19).

Freud, S. (1925/1959). *An autobiographical study.* In *Standard edition* (Vol. 20).

Freud, S. (1925/1961). Some psychical consequences of the anatomical distinction between the sexes. In *Standard edition* (Vol. 19).

Freud, S. (1926/1959a). *Inhibitions, symptoms and anxiety.* In *Standard edition* (Vol. 20).

Freud, S. (1926/1959b). *The question of lay analysis.* In *Standard edition* (Vol. 20).

Freud, S. (1931/1961). Female sexuality. In *Standard edition* (Vol. 21).

Freud, S. (1933/1964). *New introductory lectures on psychoanalysis*. In *Standard edition* (Vol. 22).

Freud, S. (1960). *Letters of Sigmund Freud* (E. L. Freud, Ed.; T. Stern & J. Stern, Trans.). New York: Basic Books.

Freud, S. (1985). *The complete letters of Sigmund Freud to Wilhelm Fliess, 1887–1904* (J. M. Masson, Ed. and Trans.). Cambridge, MA: Harvard University Press.

Freud, S., & Bullitt, W. C. (1967). *Thomas Woodrow Wilson: A psychological study*. Boston: Houghton Mifflin.

Frick, W. B. (1982). Conceptual foundations of self-actualization: A contribution to motivation theory. *Journal of Humanistic Psychology, 22,* 33–52.

Friedman, L. J. (1999). *Identity's architect: A biography of Erik H. Erikson.* New York: Scribner.

Frois, J. P., & Eysenck, H. J. (1995). The Visual Aesthetic Sensitivity Test applied to Portuguese children and fine arts students. *Creativity Research Journal, 8,* 277–284.

Fromm, E. (1941). *Escape from freedom.* New York: Holt, Rinehart and Winston.

Fromm, E. (1947). *Man for himself: An inquiry into the psychology of ethics.* New York: Holt, Rinehart and Winston.

Fromm, E. (1950). *Psychoanalysis and religion.* New Haven, CT: Yale University Press.

Fromm, E. (1951). *The forgotten language: An introduction to the understanding of dreams, fairy tales and myths.* New York: Rinehart.

Fromm, E. (1955). *The sane society.* New York: Holt, Rinehart and Winston.

Fromm, E. (1956). *The art of loving.* New York: Harper & Brothers.

Fromm, E. (1959). *Sigmund Freud's mission.* New York: Harper & Brothers.

Fromm, E. (1961). *Marx's concept of man.* New York: Ungar.

Fromm, E. (1962). *Beyond the chains of illusion.* New York: Simon and Schuster.

Fromm, E. (1963). *The dogma of Christ and other essays on religion, psychology, and culture.* New York: Holt, Rinehart and Winston.

Fromm, E. (1964). *The heart of man.* New York: Harper & Row.

Fromm, E. (1973). *The anatomy of human destructiveness.* New York: Holt, Rinehart and Winston.

Fromm, E. (1976). *To have or be.* New York: Harper & Row.

Fromm, E. (1981). *On disobedience and other essays.* New York: Seabury Press.

Fromm, E. (1986). *For the love of life* (H. J. Schultz, Ed.; Robert Kimber & Rita Kimber, Trans.). New York: Free Press. (Original work published 1972, 1974, 1975, 1983)

Fromm, E. (1992). *The revision of psychoanalysis.* Boulder, CO: Westview Press.

Fromm, E. (1994). *On being human.* New York: Continuum.

Fromm, E. (1997). *Love, sexuality, and matriarchy: About gender.* New York: Fromm International.

Fromm, E., & Maccoby, M. (1970). *Social character in a Mexican village*. Englewood Cliffs, NJ: Prentice-Hall.

Gale, A. (1983). Electroencephalographic studies of extraversion-introversion: A case study in the psychophysiology of individual differences. *Personality and Individual Differences, 4,* 371–380.

Gallup, G., Jr. (2002). *The 2001 Gallup poll: Public opinion*. Washington, DC: Gallup.

Gay, P. (1988). *Freud: A life for our time*. New York: Norton.

Geen, R. G. (1984). Preferred stimulation levels in introverts and extraverts: Effects on arousal and performance. *Journal of Personality and Social Psychology, 46,* 1303–1312.

Gendlin, E. T. (1988). Carl Rogers (1902–1987). *American Psychologist, 43,* 127–128.

Gholson, B., Shadish, W. R., Neimeyer, R. A., & Houts, A. C. (Eds.) (1989). *The psychology of science: Contributions to metascience*. Cambridge, England: Cambridge University Press.

Gibson, H. B. (1981). *Hans Eysenck: The man and his work*. London: Peter Owen.

Gleason, T. R. (2002). Social provisions of real and imaginary relationship in early childhood. *Developmental Psychology, 39,* 979–992.

Gleason, T. R., & Hohmann, L. M. (2006). Concepts of real and imaginary friendships in early childhood. *Social Development, 15,* 128–144.

Goble, F. G. (1970). *The third force: The psychology of Abraham Maslow*. New York: Grossman.

Gold, J. M., & Rogers, J. D. (1995). Intimacy and isolation: A validation study of Erikson's theory. *Journal of Humanistic Psychology, 35*(1), 78–86.

Goldberg, L. R. (1981). Language and individual differences: The search for universals in personality lexicons. In L. Wheeler (Ed.), *Review of personality and social psychology* (Vol. 2, pp. 141–165). Beverly Hills, CA: Sage.

Goldenberg, J. L., Pyszczynski, T., Greenberg, J., Solomon, S., Kluck, B., & Cornwell, R. (2001). I am not an animal: Mortality salience, disgust, and the denial of human creatureliness. *Journal of Experimental Psychology: General, 130,* 427–435.

Goldwert, M. (1992). *The wounded healers: Creative illness in the pioneers of depth psychology*. Lanham, MD: University Press of America.

Govorun, O., Fuegen, K., & Payne, B. K. (2006). Stereotypes focus defensive projection. *Personality and Social Psychology Bulletin, 32,* 781–793.

Greever, K. B., Tseng, M. S., & Friedland, B. U. (1973). Development of the social interest index. *Journal of Consulting and Clinical Psychology, 41,* 454–458.

Grey, L. (1998). *Alfred Adler, the forgotten prophet: A vision for the 21st century*. Westport, CT: Praeger.

Grice, J. W. (2004). Bridging the idiographic-nomothetic divide in ratings of self and others on the Big Five. *Journal of Personality, 72,* 203–241.

Grice, J. W., Jackson, B. J., & McDaniel, B. L. (2006). Bridging the idiographic-nomothetic divide: A follow-up study. *Journal of Personality, 74,* 1191–1218.

Grossarth-Maticek, R., & Eysenck, H. J. (1989). Length of survival and lymphocyte percentage in women with mammary cancer as a function of psychotherapy. *Psychological Reports, 65,* 315–321.

Grossarth-Maticek, R., Eysenck, H. J., & Vetter, H. (1988). Personality type, smoking habit and their interaction as predictors of cancer and coronary heart disease. *Personality and Individual Differences, 9,* 479–495.

Grosskurth, P. (1986). *Melanie Klein: Her world and her work*. New York: Knopf.

Grosskurth, P. (1998). Psychoanalysis: A dysfunctional family? *The Journal of Analytical Psychology, 43,* 87–95.

Gurtman, M. R. (1992). Trust, distrust, and interpersonal problems: A circumplex analysis. *Journal of Personality and Social Psychology, 62,* 989–1002.

Haidt, J., McCauley, C. R., & Rozin, P. (1994). Individual differences in sensitivity to disgust: A scale sampling seven domains of disgust solicitors. *Personality and Individual Differences, 16,* 701–713.

Hall, E. (1983, June). A conversation with Erik Erikson. *Psychology Today, 17,* 22–30.

Hall, M. H. (1967, September). An interview with "Mr. Humanist": Rollo May. *Psychology Today, 1,* 25–29, 72–73.

Hall, M. H. (1968, July). A conversation with Abraham Maslow. *Psychology Today, 22,* 35–37, 54–57.

Hamer, D., & Copeland, P. (1998). *Living with our genes*. New York: Doubleday.

Handlbauer, B. (1998). *The Freud-Adler controversy*. Oxford, England: Oneworld.

Harper, M., & Schoeman, W. J. (2003). Influences of gender as a basic-level category in person perception on the gender belief system. *Sex Roles, 49,* 517–526.

Harris, T. G. (1969, August). The devil and Rollo May. *Psychology Today, 3,* 13–16.

Hart, J. J. (1982). Psychology of the scientist: XLVI. Correlation between theoretical orientation in psychology and personality type. *Psychological Reports, 50,* 795–801.

Hartshorne, H., & May, M. A. (1928). *Studies in the nature of character: Vol. 1. Studies in deceit.* New York: Macmillan.

Hausdorff, D. (1972). *Erich Fromm.* New York: Twayne.

Havens, L. (1987). *Approaches to the mind: Movement of psychiatric schools from sects toward science.* Cambridge, MA: Harvard University Press.

Hayman, R. (2001). *A life of Jung.* New York: Norton.

Hazan, C., & Shaver, P. R. (1987). Romantic love conceptualized as an attachment process. *Journal of Personality and Social Psychology, 52,* 511–524.

Higgins, E. T. (1987). Self-discrepancy: A theory relating self and affect. *Psychological Review, 94,* 319–340.

Hillman, J. (1985). *Anima: An anatomy of a personified notion.* Dallas, TX: Spring.

Hobson, A. A. (2004, May). Freud returns? Like a bad dream. *Scientific American, 290,* 89.

Hoffman, E. (1988). *The right to be human: A biography of Abraham Maslow.* Los Angeles: Tarcher.

Hoffman, E. (1994). *The drive for self: Alfred Adler and the founding of individual psychology.* Reading, MA: Addison-Wesley.

Holder, A. (1988). Reservations about the *Standard Edition.* In E. Timms & N. Segal (Eds.), *Freud in exile: Psychoanalysis and its vicissitudes* (pp. 210–214). New Haven, CT: Yale University Press.

Holland, J. (1973). *Making vocational choices: A theory of careers.* Englewood Cliffs, NJ: Prentice-Hall.

Horney, K. (1917/1968). The technique of psychoanalytic therapy. *American Journal of Psychoanalysis, 28,* 3–12.

Horney, K. (1937). *The neurotic personality of our time.* New York: Norton.

Horney, K. (1939). *New ways in psychoanalysis.* New York: Norton.

Horney, K. (1942). *Self-analysis.* New York: Norton.

Horney, K. (1945). *Our inner conflicts: A constructive theory of neurosis.* New York: Norton.

Horney, K. (1950). *Neurosis and human growth: The struggle toward self-realization.* New York: Norton.

Horney, K. (1967). The flight from womanhood: The masculinity-complex in women as viewed by men and women. In H. Kelman (Ed.), *Feminine psychology* (pp. 54–70). New York: Norton.

Horney, K. (1987). *Final lectures* (D. H. Ingram, Ed.). New York: Norton.

Horney, K. (1994). Woman's fear of action. In B. J. Paris, *Karen Horney: A psychoanalyst's search for self-understanding* (pp. 233–238). New Haven, CT: Yale University Press.

Hornstein, G. A. (2000). *To redeem one person is to redeem the world: The life of Frieda Fromm-Reichmann.* New York: Free Press.

Hughes, J. M. (1989). *Reshaping the psychoanalytic domain: The work of Melanie Klein, W. R. D. Fairbairn, and D. W. Winnicott.* Berkeley: University of California Press.

Irigaray, L (1986). This sex which is not one. In H. Cixous & C. Clement (Eds.), *The newly born woman.* Minneapolis: University of Minnesota Press.

Isbister, J. N. (1985). *Freud: An introduction to his life and work.* Cambridge, England: Polity Press.

James, W. H. (1957). *Internal versus external control of reinforcement as a basic variable in learning theory.* Unpublished doctoral dissertation. Ohio State University.

John, O. P. (1990). The "Big Five" factor taxonomy: Dimensions of personality in the natural language and in questionnaires. In L. A. Pervin (Ed.), *Handbook of personality: Theory and research* (pp. 66–100). New York: Guilford Press.

John, O. P., & Srivastava, S. (1999). The Big Five taxonomy: History, measurement, and theoretical perspectives. In L. A. Pervin & O. P. John (Eds.), *Handbook of personality: Theory and research* (pp. 102–138). New York: Guilford Press.

Johnson, J. A., Germer, C. K., Efran, J. S., & Overton, W. F. (1988). Personality as the basis for theoretical predilections. *Journal of Personality and Social Psychology, 55,* 824–835.

Jones, A., & Crandall, R. (1986). Validation of a Short Index of Self-actualization. *Personality and Social Psychology Bulletin, 12,* 63–73.

Jones, E. (1953, 1955, 1957). *The life and work of Sigmund Freud* (Vols. 1–3). New York: Basic Books.

Jost, J. T., Glaser, J., Kruglanski, A. W., & Sulloway, F. J. (2003). Political conservatism as motivated social cognition. *Psychological Bulletin, 129,* 339–375.

Jung, C. G. (1916/1960). General aspects of dream psychology. In H. Read, M. Fordham, & G. Adler (Eds.) and R. F. C. Hull (Trans.), *The collected works of C. G. Jung* (Vol. 8). New York. Pantheon Books.

Jung, C. G. (1921/1971). Psychological types. In *Collected works* (Vol. 6).

Jung, C. G. (1928/1960). On psychic energy. In *Collected works* (Vol. 8).

Jung, C. G. (1931/1954a). The aims of psychotherapy. In *Collected works* (Vol. 16).

Jung, C. G. (1931/1954b). Problems of modern psychotherapy. In *Collected works* (Vol. 16).

Jung, C. G. (1931/1960a). The stages of life. In *Collected works* (Vol. 8).

Jung, C. G. (1931/1960b). *The structure of the psyche.* In *Collected works* (Vol. 8).

Jung, C. G. (1934/1954a). The development of personality. In *Collected works* (Vol. 17).

Jung, C. G. (1934/1959). Archetypes of the collective unconscious. In *Collected works* (Vol. 9, Pt. 1).

Jung, C. G. (1934/1960). The soul and death. In *Collected works* (Vol. 8).

Jung, C. G. (1935/1968). The Tavistock lectures. In *Collected works* (Vol. 18).

Jung, C. G. (1937/1959). The concept of the collective unconscious. In *Collected works* (Vol. 9, Pt. 1).

Jung, C. G. (1939/1959). Conscious, unconscious, and individuation. In *Collected works* (Vol. 9, Pt. 1).

Jung, C. G. (1943/1953). *The psychology of the unconscious.* In *Collected works* (Vol. 7).

Jung, C. G. (1945/1953). *The relations between ego and the unconscious.* In *Collected works* (Vol. 7).

Jung, C. G. (1948/1960a). Instinct and the unconscious. In *Collected works* (Vol. 8).

Jung, C. G. (1948/1960b). On the nature of dreams. In *Collected works* (Vol. 8).

Jung, C. G. (1950/1959). Concerning rebirth. In *Collected works* (Vol. 9, Pt. 1).

Jung, C. G. (1951/1959a). *Aion: Researches into the phenomenology of the self.* In *Collected works* (Vol. 9, Pt. 2).

Jung, C. G. (1951/1959b). The psychology of the child archetype. In *Collected works* (Vol. 9, Pt. 1).

Jung, C. G. (1952/1956). *Symbols of transformation.* In *Collected works* (Vol. 5).

Jung, C. G. (1952/1968). *Psychology and alchemy* (2nd ed.). In *Collected works* (Vol. 12).

Jung, C. G. (1954/1959a). *Archetypes and the collective unconscious.* In *Collected works* (Vol. 9, Pt. 1).

Jung, C. G. (1954/1959b). Concerning the archetypes, with special reference to the anima concept. In *Collected works* (Vol. 9, Pt. 1).

Jung, C. G. (1954/1959c). Psychological aspects of the mother archetype. In *Collected works* (Vol. 9, Pt. 1).

Jung, C. G. (1961). *Memories, dreams, reflections* (A. Jaffé, Ed.). New York: Random House.

Jung, C. G. (1964). *Man and his symbols.* Garden City, NY: Doubleday.

Jung, C. G. (1975). *Letters*: II. 1951–1961 (G. Adler & A. Jaffé, Eds.) (R. F. C. Hull, Trans.). Princeton, NJ: Princeton University Press.

Jung, C. G. (1979). *Word and image* (A. Jaffé, Ed.). Princeton, NJ: Princeton University Press.

Jung, C. G., & Riklin, F. (1904/1973). The associations of normal subjects. In *Collected works* (Vol. 2).

Kammrath, L. K., Mendoza-Denton, R., Mischel, W. (2005). Incorporating if . . . then . . . personality signatures in person perceptions: Beyond the person-situation dichotomy. *Journal of Personality and Social Psychology, 88,* 605–618.

Kandel, E. R. (1999). Biology and the future of psychoanalysis: A new intellectual framework for psychiatry revisited. *American Journal of Psychiatry, 156,* 505–534.

Kasler, J., & Nevo, O. (2005). Early recollections as predictors of study area choice. *Journal of Individual Psychology, 61,* 217–232.

Kelly, G. A. (1955). *The psychology of personal constructs* (Vols. 1 and 2). New York: Norton.

Kelly, G. A. (1963). *A theory of personality: The psychology of personal constructs.* New York: Norton.

Kelly, G. A. (1969a). The autobiography of a theory. In B. Maher (Ed.), *Clinical psychology and personality: The selected papers of George Kelly* (pp. 46–65). New York: Wiley.

Kelly, G. A. (1969b). Man's construction of his alternatives. In B. Maher (Ed.), *Clinical psychology and personality: The selected papers of George Kelly* (pp. 66–93). New York: Wiley.

Kelly, G. A. (1970). A brief introduction to personal construct theory. In D. Bannister (Ed.), *Perspectives in personal construct theory.* London: Academic Press. Also in J. C. Mancuso (Ed.), *Readings for a cognitive theory of personality.* New York: Holt, Rinehart and Winston.

Kelly, G. A. (1980). A psychology of the optimal man. In A. W. Landfield & L. M. Leitner (Eds.), *Personal construct psychology: Psychotherapy and personality.* New York: Wiley.

Kelly, G. A. (1991). *The psychology of personal constructs* (Vols. 1 and 2). London: Routledge. (Original work published 1955)

Keys, A., Brozek, J., Henschel, A., Mickelsen, O., & Taylor, H. L. (1950). *The biology of human starvation* (Vols. 1 and 2). Minneapolis: University of Minnesota Press.

King, P., & Steiner, R. (Eds.). (1991). *The Freud-Klein controversies 1941–1945.* London: Tavistock/Routledge.

Kissen, D. M., & Eysenck, H. J. (1962). Personality in male lung cancer patients. *Journal of Psychosomatic Research, 6,* 123–137.

Klein, M. (1930/1964). The importance of symbol-formation in the development of the ego. In M. Klein, *Contributions to psycho-analysis, 1921–1945* (pp. 236–250). New York: McGraw-Hill.

Klein, M. (1932). *The psycho-analysis of children.* London: Hogarth Press.

Klein, M. (1933/1964). The early development of conscience in the child. In M. Klein, *Contributions to psycho-analysis, 1921–1945* (pp. 267–277). New York: McGraw-Hill.

Klein, M. (1935/1980). A contribution to the psychogenesis of manic-depressive states. In J. Mitchell (Ed.), *The selected Melanie Klein* (pp. 145–166). New York: Free Press.

Klein, M. (1943/1991). Memorandum on her technique by Melanie Klein. In P. King & R. Steiner (Eds.), *The Freud-Klein controversies 1941–45* (pp. 635–638). London: Tavistock/Routledge.

Klein, M. (1945/1984). The Oedipus complex in the light of early anxieties. In M. Klein, *Love, guilt, and reparation and other works, 1921–1945* (pp. 370–419). New York: Macmillan.

Klein, M. (1946/1975). Notes on some schizoid mechanism. In M. Klein, *Envy and gratitude and other works, 1946–1963* (pp. 1–24). New York: Delta Books.

Klein, M. (1948). *Contributions to psycho-analysis, 1921–45.* London: Hogarth.

Klein, M. (1952). *Envy and gratitude.* London: Tavistock.

Klein, M. (1955/1980). The psycho-analytic play technique: Its history and significance. In J. Mitchell (Ed.), *The selected Melanie Klein* (pp. 35–54). New York: Free Press.

Klein, M. (1959/1984). Our adult world and its roots in infancy. In M. Klein, *Envy and gratitude and other works, 1946–1963* (pp. 247–263). New York: Macmillan.

Klein, M. (1991). The emotional life and ego-development of the infant with special reference to the depressive position. In P. King & R. Steiner (Eds.), *The Freud-Klein controversies 1941–45* (pp. 752–797). London: Tavistock/Routledge.

Knapp, G. P. (1989). *The art of living: Erich Fromm's life and works.* New York: Peter Lang.

Kohut, H. (1971). *The analysis of the self: A systematic approach to the treatment of narcissistic personality disorders.* New York: International Universities Press.

Kohut, H. (1977). *The restoration of the self.* New York: International Universities Press.

Kohut, H. (1987). *The Kohut Seminars on self psychology and psychotherapy with adolescents and young adults* (M. Elson, Ed.). New York: Norton.

Krausz, E. O. (1994). Freud's devaluation of women. *Individual Psychology: Journal of Adlerian Theory, Research and Practice, 50,* 298–313.

Kurzweil, E. (1989). *The Freudians: A comparative perspective.* New Haven, CT: Yale University Press.

Laird, T. G., & Shelton, A. J., (2006). From an Adlerian perspective: Birth order, dependency, and binge drinking on a historically black university campus. *Journal of Individual Psychology, 62,* 18–35.

Landis, B., & Tauber, E. S. (1971). Erich Fromm: Some biographical notes. In B. Landis & E. S. Tauber (Eds.), *In the name of life: Essays in honor of Erich Fromm.* New York: Holt, Rinehart and Winston.

Lewis-Harter, S., Erbes, C. R., & Hart, C. C. (2004). Content analysis of the personal constructs of female sexual abuse survivors elicited through repertory grid technique. *Journal of Constructivist Psychology, 17,* 27–43.

Liao, F., & Fan, P. (2003). Discrepancy of self-concepts and mental health of college students. *Chinese Mental Health Journal, 17,* 117.

Loehlin, J. C. (1992). *Genes and environment in personality development.* Newbury Park, CA: Sage.

Lowes, I., & Tiggeman, M. (2003). Body dissatisfaction, dieting awareness and the impact of parental influence in young children. *British Journal of Health Psychology, 8,* 135–147.

Lowry, R. J. (1973). *A. H. Maslow: An intellectual portrait.* Monterey, CA: Brooks/Cole.

Lyubomirsky, S., King, L., & Diener, E. (2005). The benefits of frequent positive affect: Does happiness lead to success? *Psychological Bulletin, 131,* 803–855.

Lyubomirsky, S., Sousa, L., & Dickerhoof, R. (2006). The costs and benefits of writing, talking, and thinking about life's triumphs and defeats. *Journal of Personality and Social Psychology, 90,* 692–708.

Maddi, S. R., & Costa, P. T., Jr. (1972). *Humanism in personality: Allport, Maslow and Murray.* Chicago: Aldine.

Mahler, M. S. (1952). On child psychosis and schizophrenia: Autistic and symbiotic infantile psychoses. *Psychoanalytic Study of the Child, 7,* 286–305.

Mahler, M. S. (1967). On human symbiosis and the vicissitudes of individuation. *Journal of the American Psychoanalytic Association, 15,* 740–762.

Mahler, M. S. (1972). On the first three subphases of the separation-individuation process. *International Journal of Psycho-Analysis, 53,* 333–338.

Mahler, M. S., Pine, F., & Bergman, A. (1975). *The psychological birth of the human infant.* New York: Basic Books.

Martin, L. R., Friedman, H. S., & Schwartz, J. E. (2007). Personality and mortality risk across the life span: The importance of conscientiousness as a biopsychosocial attribute. *Health Psychology, 26,* 428–436.

Marusic, A., Gudjonsson, G. H., Eysenck, H. J., & Starc, R. (1999). Biological and psychosocial risk factors in ischaemic heart disease: Empirical findings and a biopsychosocial model. *Personality and Individual Differences, 26,* 286–304.

Maslow, A. H. (1943). A theory of human motivation. *Psychological Review, 50,* 370–396.

Maslow, A. H. (1950). Self-actualizing people: A study of psychological health. *Personality Symposia. Symposium #1 on Values* (pp. 11–34). New York: Grune & Stratton.

Maslow, A. H. (1962). Was Adler a disciple of Freud? A note. *Journal of Individual Psychology, 18,* 125.

Maslow, A. H. (1964). *Religions, values, and peak-experiences.* Columbus: Ohio State University Press.

Maslow, A. H. (1966). *The psychology of science.* New York: Harper & Row.

Maslow, A. H. (1967). A theory of metamotivation: The biological rooting of the value-life. *Journal of Humanistic Psychology, 7*(2), 93–127.

Maslow, A. H. (1968a). Self-actualization [Film]. Santa Ana, CA: Psychological Films.

Maslow, A. H. (1968b). *Toward a psychology of being* (2nd ed.). New York: Van Nostrand.

Maslow, A. H. (1970). *Motivation and personality* (2nd ed.). New York: Harper & Row.

Maslow, A. H. (1971). *The farther reaches of human nature.* New York: Viking.

Maslow, A. H. (1979). *The journals of A. H. Maslow* (Vols. 1–2). (R. J. Lowry, Ed.). Monterey, CA: Brooks/Cole.

Maslow, A. H. (1996). Higher motivation and the new psychology. In E. Hoffman (Ed.), *Future visions: The unpublished papers of Abraham Maslow.* Thousand Oaks, CA: Sage.

Masters, K. S., Lensegrav-Benson, T. L., Kircher, J. C., & Hill, R. D. (2005). Effects of religious orientation and gender on cardiovascular reactivity among older adults. *Research on Aging, 27,* 221–240.

May, R. (1950). *The meaning of anxiety.* New York: Ronald Press.

May, R. (1953). *Man's search for himself.* New York: Norton.

May, R. (1958a). Contributions of existential psychotherapy. In R. May, E. Angel, & H. F. Ellenberger (Eds.), *Existence: A new dimension in psychiatry and psychology* (pp. 37–91). New York: Basic Books.

May, R. (1962). Dangers in the relation of existentialism to psychotherapy. In H. M. Ruitenbeek (Ed.), *Psychoanalysis and existential philosophy.* New York: Dutton.

May, R. (1967). *Psychology and the human dilemma.* Princeton, NJ: Van Nostrand.

May, R. (1969a). The emergence of existential psychology. In R. May (Ed.), *Existential psychology* (2nd ed., pp. 1–48). New York: Random House.

May, R. (1969b). *Love and will.* New York: Norton.

May, R. (1972). *Power and innocence: A search for the sources of violence.* New York: Norton.

May, R. (1981). *Freedom and destiny.* New York: Norton.

May, R. (1982). The problem of evil: An open letter to Carl Rogers. *Journal of Humanistic Psychology, 22*(3), 10–21.

May, R. (1990a). The meaning of the Oedipus myth. *Review of Existential Psychology and Psychiatry: 1986–87. [Special Issue], 20,* 169–177.

May, R. (1990b). On the phenomenological bases of therapy. In K. Hoeller (Ed.), *Readings in existential psychology & psychiatry* (pp. 49–61). Seattle, WA: Review of Existential Psychology & Psychiatry.

May, R. (1991). *The cry for myth.* New York: Norton.

May, R., Angel, E., & Ellenberger, H. F. (Eds.). (1958). *Existence: A new dimension in psychiatry and psychology.* New York: Basic Books.

May, R., & Yalom, I. (1989). Existential psychotherapy. In R. J. Corsini & D. Wedding (Eds.), *Current psychotherapies* (pp. 354–391). Itasca, IL: Peacock.

McAdams, D. P. (1999). Personal narratives and the life story. In L. A. Pervin & O. P. John (Eds.), *Handbook of personality: Theory and research* (pp. 478–500). New York: Guilford Press.

McAdams, D. P., & de St. Aubin, E. (1992). A theory of generativity and its assessment through self-report, behavioral acts, and narrative themes in autobiography. *Journal of Personality and Social Psychology, 62,* 1003–1015.

McCrae, R. R. (2002). NEO-PI-R data from 36 cultures: Further intercultural comparisons. In R. R. McCrae & J. Allik (Eds.), *The Five-Factor Model of personality across cultures* (pp. 105–125). New York: Kluwer Academic/Plenum Publishers.

McCrae, R. R., & Allik, J. (Eds.). (2002). *The Five-Factor model of personality across cultures.* New York: Kluwer Academic/Plenum Publishers.

McCrae, R. R., & Costa, P. T., Jr. (1984). *Emerging lives, enduring dispositions: Personality in adulthood.* Boston: Little, Brown.

McCrae, R. R., & Costa P. T. (1985). Comparison of EPI and psychoticism scales with measures of the Five-Factor model of personality. *Personality and Individual Differences, 6,* 587–597.

McCrae, R. R., & Costa, P. T. (1989). Reinterpreting the Myers-Briggs Type Indicator from the perspective of the Five-Factor model of personality. *Journal of Personality, 57,* 17–40.

McCrae, R. R., & Costa, P. T. (1996). Toward a new generation of personality theories: Theoretical contexts for the Five-Factor model. In J. S. Wiggins (Ed.), *The Five-Factor model of personality: Theoretical perspectives* (pp. 51–87). New York: Guilford Press.

McCrae, R. R., & Costa, P. T. (1999). A Five-Factor theory of personality. In L. A. Pervin & O. P. John (Eds.), *Personality theory and research* (pp. 139–153). New York: Guilford Press.

McCrae, R. R., & Costa, P. T. (2003). *Personality in adulthood: A five-factor theory perspective* (2nd ed.). New York: Guilford Press.

McCrae, R. R., & John, O. P. (1992). An introduction to the five-factor model and its applications. *Journal of Personality, 60,* 175–215.

McGuire, W. (Ed.). (1974). *The Freud/Jung letters: The correspondence between Sigmund Freud and C. G. Jung* (R. Manheim & R. F. C. Hull, Trans.). Princeton, NJ: Princeton University Press.

McGuire, W., & McGlashan, A. (Eds.). (1994). *The Freud/Jung letters: The correspondence between Sigmund Freud and C. G. Jung* (abridged ed.) (R. Manheim & R. F. C. Hull, Trans.). Princeton, NJ: Princeton University Press.

McLynn, F. (1996). *Carl Gustav Jung.* New York: St. Martin's Press.

McNiel, J. M., & Fleeson, W. (2006). The causal effects of extraversion on positive affect and neuroticism on negative affect: Manipulating state extraversion and state neuroticism in an experimental approach. *Journal of Research in Personality, 40,* 529–550.

Mendoza-Denton, R., Ayduk, O., Mischel, W., Shoda, Y., & Testa, A. (2001). Person-situation interactionism in self-encoding (I am . . . when . . .): Implications for affect regulation and social information processing. *Journal of Personality and Social Psychology, 80,* 533–544.

Menninger, K. A. (1920). *The human mind.* New York: Knopf.

Midlarsky, E., Fagin Jones, S., & Corley, R. P. (2005). Personality correlates of heroic rescue during the Holocaust. *Journal of Personality, 63,* 907–934.

Milton, J. (2002). *The road to malpsychia: Humanistic psychology and our discontents.* San Francisco: Encounter Books.

Mischel, H. N., & Mischel, W. (Eds.). (1973). *Readings in personality.* New York: Holt, Rinehart and Winston.

Mischel, W. (1958). Preference for delayed reinforcement: An experimental study of cultural observation. *Journal of Abnormal and Social Psychology, 56,* 57–61.

Mischel, W. (1961a). Delay of gratification, need for achievement, and acquiesce in another culture. *Journal of Abnormal and Social Psychology, 62,* 543–552.

Mischel, W. (1961b). Preference for delayed reinforcement and social responsibility. *Journal of Abnormal and Social Psychology, 62,* 1–7.

Mischel, W. (1965). Predicting success of Peace Corps volunteers in Nigeria. *Journal of Personality and Social Psychology, 1,* 510–517.

Mischel, W. (1968). *Personality and assessment.* New York: Wiley.

Mischel, W. (1971). *Introduction to personality.* New York: Holt, Rinehart and Winston.

Mischel, W. (1973). Toward a cognitive social learning reconceptualization of personality. *Psychological Review, 80,* 252–283.

Mischel, W. (1976). *Introduction to personality* (2nd ed.). New York: Holt, Rinehart and Winston.

Mischel, W. (1979). On the interface of cognition and personality: Beyond the person-situation debate. *American Psychologist, 34,* 740–754.

Mischel, W. (1990). Personality dispositions revisited and revised: A view after three decades. In L. A. Pervin (Ed.), *Handbook of personality: Theory and research* (pp. 111–134). New York: Guilford Press.

Mischel, W. (1999). Personality coherence and dispositions in a cognitive-affective personality system (CAPS) approach. In D. Cervone & Y. Shoda (Eds.), *The coherence of personality: Social-cognitive bases of consistency, variability, and organization* (pp. 37–66). New York: Guilford Press.

Mischel, W. (2004). Toward an integrative science of the person. *Annual Review of Psychology, 55,* 1–22.

Mischel, W., & Ayduk, O. (2002). Self-regulation in a cognitive-affective personality system: Attentional control in the service of the self. *Self and Identity, 1,* 213–220.

Mischel, W., Cantor, N., & Feldman, S. (1996). Principles of self-regulation: The nature of willpower and self-control. In E. T. Higgins & A. W. Kruglanski (Eds.), S*ocial psychology: Handbook of basic principles* (pp. 329–360). New York: Guilford Press.

Mischel, W., & Ebbesen, E. B. (1970). Attention in delay of gratification. *Journal of Personality and Social Psychology, 16,* 329–337.

Mischel, W., Ebbesen, E. B., & Zeiss, A. R. (1972). Cognitive and attentional mechanisms in delay of gratification. *Journal of Personality and Social Psychology, 21,* 204–218.

Mischel, W., & Mischel, H. N. (1976). A cognitive social learning approach to morality and self-regulation. In T. Lickona (Ed.), *Moral development and behavior: Theory, research, and social issues.* New York: Holt, Rinehart and Winston.

Mischel, W., & Mischel, H. N. (1983). Development of children's knowledge of self-control strategies. *Child Development, 54,* 603–619.

Mischel, W., & Moore, B. (1973). Effects of attention to symbolically presented rewards upon self-control. *Journal of Personality and Social Psychology, 28,* 172–179.

Mischel, W., & Shoda, Y. (1994). Personality psychology has two goals: Must it be two fields? *Psychological Inquiry, 5,* 156–158.

Mischel, W., & Shoda, Y. (1995). A cognitive-affective system theory of personality: Reconceptualizing situations, dispositions, dynamics, and invariance in personality structure. *Psychological Review, 102,* 246–268.

Mischel, W., & Shoda, Y. (1998). Reconciling processing dynamics and personality dispositions. *Annual Review of Psychology, 49,* 229–258.

Mischel, W., & Shoda, Y. (1999). Integrating dispositions and processing dynamics within a unified theory of personality: The cognitive-affective personality system. In L. A. Pervin & O. P. John (Eds.), *Handbook of personality: Theory and research* (pp. 197–218). New York: Guilford Press.

Mischel, W., Shoda, Y., & Mendoza-Denton, R. (2002). Situation-behavior profiles and a locus of consistency in personality. *Current Directions in Psychological Science, 11,* 50–54.

Mischel, W., & Staub, E. (1965). Effects of expectancy on working and waiting for larger rewards. *Journal of Personality and Social Psychology, 2,* 625–633.

Mitchell, S. A., & Black, M. J. (1995). *Freud and beyond: A history of modern psychoanalytic thought.* New York: Basic Books.

Moghaddam, F. M., & Marsella, A. J., (Eds.). (2004). *Understanding terrorism: Psychosocial roots, consequences, and interventions.* Washington, DC: American Psychological Association.

Mosak, H., & Maniacci, M. (1999). *A primer of Adlerian psychology: The analytic-behavioral-cognitive psychology of Alfred Adler.* Philadelphia: Brunner/Mazel.

Murray, H. A. (1938). *Explorations in personality.* New York: Oxford University Press.

Myers, I. B. (1962). *Myers-Briggs Type Indicator Manual.* Princeton, NJ: Educational Testing Service.

Neimeyer, R. A., & Neimeyer, G. J. (Eds.). (1995). *Advances in Personal Construct Psychology* (Vol. 3). Greenwich, CT: JAI Press.

Newton, P. M. (1995). *Freud: From youthful dream to mid-life crisis.* New York: Guilford Press.

Noftle, E. E., & Robins, R. W. (2007). Personality predictors of academic outcomes: Big Five correlates of GPA and SAT scores. *Journal of Personality and Social Psychology, 93,* 116–130.

Noland, R. W. (1999). *Sigmund Freud revisited.* New York: Twayne.

Noll, R. (1994). T*he Jung cult: Origins of a charismatic movement.* Princeton, NJ: Princeton University Press.

Norman, W. T. (1963). Toward an adequate taxonomy of personality attributes. Replicated factor structure in peer nomination personality ratings. *Journal of Abnormal and Social Psychology, 66,* 574–583.

Oesterreich, D. (2005). Flight into security: A new approach and measure of the authoritarian personality. *Political Psychology, 26,* 275–297.

Ogden, T. H. (1990). *The matrix of the mind: Object relations and the psychoanalytic dialogue.* Northvale, NJ: Aronson.

O'Hara, M. (1995). Carl Rogers: Scientist and mystic. *Journal of Humanistic Psychology, 35,* 40–53.

Oliner, S. P., & Oliner, P. M. (1988). *The altruistic personality: Rescuers of Jews in Nazi Europe.* New York: Free Press.

Paris, B. J. (1994). *Karen Horney: A psychoanalyst's search for self-understanding.* New Haven, CT: Yale University Press.

Perry, H. S. (1982). *Psychiatrist of America: The life of Harry Stack Sullivan.* Cambridge, MA: Belknap Press.

Pervin, L. A. (1999). Epilogue: Constancy and change in personality theory and research. In L. A. Pervin & O. P. John (Eds.), *Handbook of personality: Theory and research* (pp. 609–704). New York: Guilford Press.

Peterson, B. E. (2006). Generativity and successful parenting: An analysis of young adult outcomes. *Journal of Personality, 74,* 847–869.

Petot, J-M. (1990). *Melanie Klein. Vol. 1. First discoveries and first system: 1919–1932* (C. Trollop, Trans.). Madison, CT: International Universities Press. (Original work published 1979)

Pettigrew, T. F., & Tropp, L. R. (2006). A meta-analytic test of intergroup contact theory. *Journal of Personality and Social Psychology, 90,* 751–783.

Phares, E. J. (1955). *Changes in expectancy in skill and chance situations.* Unpublished doctoral dissertation. Ohio State University.

Phillips, A. G., & Silvia, P. J. (2005). Self-awareness and the emotional consequences of self-discrepancies. *Personality and Social Psychology Bulletin, 31,* 703–713.

Pickering, A. D., & Gray, J. A. (1999). The neuroscience of personality. In L. A. Pervin & O. P. John (Eds.), *Handbook of personality theory and research* (pp. 277–299). New York: Guilford Press.

Pincus, J. H. (2001). *Base instincts: What makes killers kill?* New York: W.W. Norton.

Plomin, R., & Caspi, A. (1999). Behavioral genetics and personality. In L. A. Pervin & O. P. John (Eds.), *Handbook of personality theory and research* (pp. 251–276). New York: Guilford Press.

Poortinga, Y., Van de Vijver, F. J. R., & van Hemert, D. A. (2002). Cross-cultural equivalence of the Big Five. In R. R. McCrae & J. Allik (Eds.), *The Five-Factor Model of personality across cultures* (pp. 281–302). New York: Kluwer Academic/Plenum Publishers.

Popper, M., & Mayseless, O. (2003). Back to basics: Applying a parenting perspective to transformational leadership. *Leadership Quarterly, 14,* 41–65.

Powell, L. H., Shahabi, L., & Thoresen, C. E. (2003). Religion and spirituality: Linkages to physical health. *American Psychologist, 58,* 36–52.

Praamstra, P., & Seiss, E. (2005). The neurophysiology of response competition: Motor cortex activation and inhibition following subliminal response priming. *Journal of Cognitive Neuroscience, 17,* 483–493.

Pratt, M. W., Norris, J. E., Arnold, M. L., & Filyer, R. (1999). Generativity and moral development as predictors of value-socialization narratives for young persons across the adult life span: From lessons learned to stories shared. *Psychology and Aging, 14,* 414–426.

Quinn, S. (1987). *A mind of her own: The life of Karen Horney.* New York: Summit Books.

Rabinowitz, F. E., Good, G., & Cozad, L. (1989). Rollo May: A man of meaning and myth. *Journal of Counseling and Development, 67,* 436–441.

Raine, A., Buchsbaum, M., & LaCasse, L. (1997). Brain abnormalities in murderers indicated by positron emission tomography. *Biological Psychiatry, 42,* 495–508.

Rattner, J. (1983). *Alfred Adler* (H. Zohn, Trans.). New York: Frederick Ungar.

Reiss, S., & Havercamp, S. M. (2005). Motivation in developmental context: A new method for studying self-actualization. *Journal of Humanistic Psychology, 45,* 41–53.

Rholes, W. S., Simpson, J. A., Tran, S., Martin III, A M., & Friedman, M. (2007). Attachment and information seeking in romantic relationships. *Personality and Social Psychology Bulletin, 33,* 422–438.

Roazen, P. (1993). *Meeting Freud's family.* Amherst: University of Massachusetts Press.

Roazen, P. (1995). *How Freud worked: First-hand accounts of patients.* Lanham, MD: Jason Aronson.

Roazen, P. (1996). Erich Fromm's courage. In M. Cortina & M. Maccoby (Eds.), *A prophetic analyst: Erich Fromm's contribution to psychoanalysis* (pp. 427–453). Northvale, NJ: Aronson.

Robinson, M. D., & Clore, G. L. (2007). Traits, states, and encoding speed: Support for a top-down view of neuroticism/state relations. *Journal of Personality, 75,* 95–120.

Robinson, M. D., Ode, S., Wilkowski, B. M., & Amodio, D. M. (2007). Neurotic contentment: A self-regulation view of neuroticism linked distress. *Emotion, 7,* 579–591.

Rogers, C. R. (1939). *The clinical treatment of the problem child.* Boston: Houghton Mifflin.

Rogers, C. R. (1942). *Counseling and psychotherapy: Newer concepts in practice.* Boston: Houghton Mifflin.

Rogers, C. R. (1947). Some observations on the organization of personality. *American Psychologist, 2,* 358–368.

Rogers, C. R. (1951). *Client-centered therapy: Its current practice, implications, and theory.* Boston: Houghton Mifflin.

Rogers, C. R. (1953). *A concept of the fully functioning person.* Unpublished manuscript, University of Chicago Counseling Center, Chicago.

Rogers, C. R. (1954). Introduction. In C. R. Rogers & R. F. Dymond (Eds.), *Psychotherapy and personality change: Co-ordinated research studies in the client-centered approach* (pp. 3–11). Chicago: University of Chicago Press.

Rogers, C. R. (1957). The necessary and sufficient conditions of therapeutic personality change. *Journal of Consulting Psychology, 21,* 95–103.

Rogers, C. R. (1959). A theory of therapy, personality, and interpersonal relationships, as developed in the client-centered framework. In S. Koch (Ed.), *Psychology: A study of a science* (Vol. 3). New York: McGraw-Hill.

Rogers, C. R. (1961). *On becoming a person: A therapist's view of psychotherapy.* Boston: Houghton Mifflin.

Rogers, C. R. (1962). Toward becoming a fully functioning person. In A. W. Combs (Ed.), *Perceiving, behaving, becoming: Yearbook* (pp. 21–33). Washington, DC: Association for Supervision and Curriculum Development.

Rogers, C. R. (1963). The concept of the fully functioning person. *Psychotherapy: Theory, Research, and Practice, 1*(1), 17–26.

Rogers, C. R. (1968). Some thoughts regarding the current presuppositions of the behavioral sciences. In W. R. Coulson & C. R. Rogers (Eds.), *Man and the science of man.* Columbus, OH: Merrill.

Rogers, C. R. (1973). My philosophy of interpersonal relationships and how it grew. *Journal of Humanistic Psychology, 13,* 3–15.

Rogers, C. R. (1978). The formative tendency. *Journal of Humanistic Psychology, 18*(1), 23–26.

Rogers, C. R. (1980). *A way of being.* Boston: Houghton Mifflin.

Rogers, C. R. (1982). Notes on Rollo May. *Journal of Humanistic Psychology, 22*(3), 8–9.

Rogers, C. R. (1983). *Freedom to learn for the 80's.* Columbus, OH: Merrill.

Rogers, C. R. (1986). Carl Rogers on the development of the person-centered approach. *Person-Centered Review, 1,* 257–259.

Rogers, C. R. (1995). What understanding and acceptance mean to me. *Journal of Humanistic Psychology, 35,* 7–22.

Rogers, C. R., & Dymond, R. F. (Eds.). (1954). *Psychotherapy and personality change: Co-ordinated research studies in the client-centered approach.* Chicago: University of Chicago Press.

Rogers, C. R., Gendlin, E., Kiesler, D., & Truax, C. (Eds.). (1967). *The therapeutic relationship and its impact: A study of psychotherapy with schizophrenics.* Madison: University of Wisconsin Press.

Rogers, C. R., & Skinner, B. F. (1956). Some issues concerning the control of human behavior. *Science, 124,* 1057–1066.

Rose, A. J. (2002). Co-rumination in the friendships of girls and boys. *Child Development, 73,* 1830–1843.

Rose, A. J., Carlson, W., & Waller, E. M. (2007). Prospective associations of co-rumination with friendship and emotional adjustment: Considering the socioemotional trade-offs of co-rumination. *Developmental Psychology, 43,* 1019–1031.

Rose, A. J., & Rudolph, K. D. (2006). A review of sex differences in peer relationship processes: Potential trade-offs for the emotional and behavioral development of girls and boys. *Psychological Bulletin, 132,* 98–131.

Rotter, J. B. (1954). *Social learning and clinical psychology.* Englewood Cliffs, NJ: Prentice-Hall.

Rotter, J. B. (1964). *Clinical psychology.* Englewood Cliffs, NJ: Prentice-Hall.

Rotter, J. B. (1966). Generalized expectancies for internal versus external control of reinforcement. *Psychological Monographs, 80* (Whole No. 609).

Rotter, J. B. (1967). A new scale for the measurement of interpersonal trust. *Journal of Personality, 35,* 651–665.

Rotter, J. B. (1970). Some implications of a social learning theory for the practice of psychotherapy. In D. J. Levis (Ed.), *Learning approaches to therapeutic behavior change.* Chicago: Aldine.

Rotter, J. B. (1975). Some problems and misconceptions related to the construct of internal vs. external control of reinforcement. *Journal of Consulting and Clinical Psychology, 43,* 56–67.

Rotter, J. B. (1978). Generalized expectancies for problem solving and psychotherapy. *Cognitive Therapy and Research, 2,* 1–10.

Rotter, J. B. (1980). Interpersonal trust, trustworthiness, and gullibility. *American Psychologist, 35,* 1–7.

Rotter, J. B. (1982). *The development and applications of social learning theory: Selected papers.* New York: Praeger.

Rotter, J. B. (1990). Internal versus external control of reinforcement: A case history of a variable. *American Psychologist, 45,* 489–493.

Rotter, J. B. (1992). Cognates of personal control: Locus of control, self-efficacy, and explanatory style: Comment. *Applied and Preventive Psychology, 1,* 127–129.

Rotter, J. B. (1993). Expectancies. In C. E. Walker (Ed.), *The history of clinical psychology in autobiography*

(Vol. 2, pp. 273–284). Pacific Grove, CA: Brooks/Cole.

Rotter, J. B., Chance, J. E., & Phares, E. J. (1972). *Applications of a social learning theory of personality.* New York: Holt, Rinehart and Winston.

Rotter, J. B., & Hochreich, D. J. (1975). *Personality.* Glenview, IL: Scott, Foresman.

Rowan, D. G., Compton, W. C., & Rust, J. O. (1995). Self-actualization and empathy as predictors of marital satisfaction. *Psychological Reports, 77,* 1011–1016.

Rudikoff, E. C. (1954). A comparative study of the changes in the concepts of the self, the ordinary person, and the ideal in eight cases. In C. R. Rogers & R. F. Dymond (Eds.), *Psychotherapy and personality change: Co-ordinated research studies in the client-centered approach* (pp. 85–98). Chicago: University of Chicago Press.

Runco, M. A., Ebersole, P., & Mraz, W. (1991). Creativity and self-actualization. *Journal of Social Behavior and Personality, 6,* 161–167.

Sacco, W. P., Wells, K. J., Friedman, A., Matthew, R., Perez, S., & Vaughan, C. A. (2007). Adherence, body mass index, and depression in adults with type 2 diabetes: The mediational role of diabetes symptoms and self-efficacy. *Health Psychology, 26,* 693–700.

Sartre, J. P. (1957). *Existentialism and human emotions.* New York: Wisdom Library.

Savill, G. E., & Eckstein, D. G. (1987). Changes in early recollections as a function of mental status. *Individual Psychology, 43,* 3–17.

Sayers, J. (1991). *Mothers of psychoanalysis: Helene Deutsch, Karen Horney, Anna Freud, Melanie Klein.* New York: Norton.

Schacter, D. L. (1987). Implicit memory: History and current status. *Journal of Experimental Psychology: Learning, Memory, and Cognition, 13,* 501–518.

Schneider, B. (1987). The people make the place. *Personnel Psychology, 40,* 437–453.

Schur, M. (1972). *Freud: Living and dying.* New York: International Universities Press.

Schwartz, S. J., & Waterman, A. S. (2006). Changing interests: A longitudinal study of intrinsic motivation for personality salient activities. *Journal of Research in Personality, 40,* 1119–1136.

Segal, H. (1979). *Melanie Klein.* New York: Viking Press.

Segal, J. (1992). *Melanie Klein.* London: Sage.

Seligman, M., & Csikszentmihalyi, M. (2000). Positive psychology: An introduction. *American Psychologist, 55,* 5–14.

Sheldon, K. M., Arndt, J., & Houser-Marko, L. (2003). In search of the organismic valuing process: The human tendency to move towards beneficial goal choices. *Journal of Personality, 71,* 835–869.

Shevrin, H., Ghannam, J. H., & Libet, B. (2002). A neural correlate of consciousness related to repression. *Consciousness & Cognition, 11,* 334–341.

Shoda, Y., LeeTiernan, S., & Mischel, W. (2002). Personality as a dynamic system: Emergence of stability and distinctiveness from intra- and interpersonal interactions. *Personality and Social Psychology Review, 6,* 316–326.

Shoda, Y., & Mischel, W. (1996). Toward a unified intra-individual dynamic conception of personality. *Journal of Research in Personality, 30,* 414–428.

Shoda, Y., & Mischel, W. (1998). Personality as a stable cognitive-affective activation network: Characteristic patterns of behavior variation emerge from a stable personality structure. In S. J. Read & L. C. Miller (Eds.), *Connectionist models of social reasoning and social behavior* (pp. 175–208). Mahwah, NJ: Erlbaum.

Shostrom, E. L. (1963). *Personal Orientation Inventory.* San Diego, CA: Educational and Industrial Testing Service.

Shostrom, E. L. (1974). *Manual for the Personal Orientation Inventory.* San Diego, CA: Educational and Industrial Testing Service.

Sigmon, S. C., Tidey, J. W., Badger, G. J., & Higgins, S. T. (2002). Acute effects of D-amphetamine on progressive-ratio performance maintained by cigarette smoking and money. *Psychopharmacology, 167,* 393–402.

Silverstein, B. (2003). *What was Freud thinking? A short historical introduction to Freud's theories and therapies.* Dubuque, IA: Kendall/Hunt.

Simonton, D. K. (2000). Methodological and theoretical orientation and the long-term disciplinary impact of 54 eminent psychologists. *Review of General Psychology, 4,* 13–24.

Singer, J. (1994). *Boundaries of the soul: The practice of Jung's psychology* (2nd ed.). New York: Doubleday.

Skinner, B. F. (1938). *The behavior of organisms: An experimental analysis.* Englewood Cliffs, NJ: Prentice-Hall.

Skinner, B. F. (1945). The operational analysis of psychological terms. *Psychological Review, 52,* 270–277, 291–294.

Skinner, B. F. (1948). *Walden two.* New York: Macmillan.

Skinner, B. F. (1953). *Science and human behavior.* New York: Macmillan.

Skinner, B. F. (1954). The science of learning and the art of teaching. *Harvard Educational Review, 24,* 86–97.

Skinner, B. F. (1957). *Verbal behavior.* New York: Appleton-Century-Crofts.

Skinner, B. F. (1967). An autobiography. In E. G. Boring & G. Lindzey (Eds.), *A history of psychology in autobiography* (Vol. 5, pp. 385–413). New York: Appleton-Century-Crofts.

Skinner, B. F. (1971). *Beyond freedom and dignity.* New York: Knopf.

Skinner, B. F. (1974). *About behaviorism.* New York: Knopf.

Skinner, B. F. (1976a). *Particulars of my life.* New York: Knopf.

Skinner, B. F. (1976b). *Walden Two revisited.* In *Walden Two.* New York: Macmillan.

Skinner, B. F. (1978). *Reflections on behaviorism and society.* Englewood Cliffs, NJ: Prentice-Hall.

Skinner, B. F. (1979). *The shaping of a behaviorist.* New York: Knopf.

Skinner, B. F. (1983). *A matter of consequences.* New York: Knopf.

Skinner, B. F. (1987a). *Upon further reflection.* Englewood Cliffs, NJ: Prentice-Hall.

Skinner, B. F. (1987b). Whatever happened to psychology as the science of behavior? *American Psychologist, 42,* 780–786.

Skinner, B. F. (1988). The operant side of behavior therapy. *Journal of Behavior Therapy and Experimental Psychiatry, 19,* 171–179.

Skinner, B. F. (1989a). The origins of cognitive thought. *American Psychologist, 44,* 13–18.

Skinner, B. F. (1989b). *Recent issues in the analysis of behavior.* Columbus, OH: Merrill.

Skinner, B. F. (1990a). Can psychology be a science of the mind? *American Psychologist, 45,* 1206–1210.

Skinner, B. F. (1990b). To know the future. *Behavior Analyst, 13,* 103–106.

Skinner, B. F., & Vaughan, M. E. (1983). *Enjoy old age: A program for self-management.* New York: Norton.

Smith, T. B., McCullough, M. E., & Poll, J. (2003). Religiousness and depression: Evidence for a main effect and the moderating influence of stressful life events. *Psychological Bulletin, 129,* 614–636.

Smolak, L., & Levine, M. P. (1993). Separation-individuation difficulties and the distinction between bulimia nervosa and anorexia nervosa in college women. *International Journal of Eating Disorders, 14,* 33–41.

Sobel, D. (1980, March 19). Erich Fromm. *The New York Times,* p. B11.

Solms, M. (2000). Dreaming and REM sleep are controlled by different brain mechanisms. *Behavioral and Brain Sciences, 23,* 845–850.

Solms, M. (2004, May). Freud returns. *Scientific American, 290,* 87–88.

Solms, M., & Turnbull, O. (2002). *The brain and the inner world: An introduction to the neuroscience of subjective experience.* New York: Other Press.

Solomon, S., Greenberg, J., & Pyszczynski, T. (1991). A terror-management theory of social behavior: The psychological functions of self-esteem and cultural worldviews. In M. P. Zanna (Ed.), *Advances in experimental social psychology* (pp. 91–159). San Diego, CA: Academic Press.

Statton, J. E., & Wilborn, B. (1991). Adlerian counseling and the early recollections of children. *Individual Psychology, 47,* 338–347.

Steiner, R. (1985). Some thoughts about tradition and change arising from an examination of the British Psycho-Analytical Society's controversial discussions (1943–1944). *International Review of Psycho-Analysis, 12,* 27–71.

Stelmack, R. M. (1990). Biological bases of extraversion: Psychophysiological evidence. *Journal of Personality, 58,* 293–311.

Stelmack, R. M. (1997). The psychophysics and psychophysiology of extraversion and arousal. In H. Nyborg (Ed.), *The scientific study of human nature: A tribute to Hans Eysenck at eighty* (pp. 388–403). Oxford, England: Pergamon Press.

Stephenson, W. (1953). *The study of behavior: Q-technique and its methodology.* Chicago: University of Chicago Press.

Stevens, C. D., & Walker, B. M. (2002). Insight: Transcending the obvious. In R. A. Neimeyer & G. J. Neimeyer (Eds.), *Advances in personal construct psychology: New directions and perspectives* (pp. 39–79). Westport, CT: Praeger.

Stojnov, D., & Butt, T. (2002). The relational basis of personal construct psychology. In R. A. Neimeyer & G. J. Neimeyer (Eds.), *Advances in personal construct psychology: New directions and perspectives* (pp. 81–110). Westport, CT: Praeger.

Strozier, C. B. (2001). *Heinz Kohut: The making of a psychoanalyst.* New York: Farrar, Straus, and Giroux.

Sulliman, J. R. (1973). The development of a scale for the measurement of social interest. *Dissertation Abstracts International, 34*(6-B), 2914.

Sullivan, H. S. (1953a). *Conceptions of modern psychiatry.* New York: Norton.

Sullivan, H. S. (1953b). *The interpersonal theory of psychiatry*. New York: Norton.

Sullivan, H. S. (1954). *The psychiatric interview*. New York: Norton.

Sullivan, H. S. (1956). *Clinical studies in psychiatry*. New York: Norton.

Sullivan, H. S. (1962). *Schizophrenia as a human process*. New York: Norton.

Sullivan, H. S. (1964). *The fusion of psychiatry and social science*. New York: Norton.

Sulloway, F. J. (1992). *Freud, biologist of the mind: Beyond the psychoanalytical legend* (Rev. ed.). Cambridge, MA: Harvard University Press.

Sumerlin, J. R., & Bundrick, C. M. (1996). Brief Index of Self-Actualization: A measure of Maslow's model. *Journal of Social Behavior and Personality, 11*, 253–271.

Sumerlin, J. R., & Bundrick, C. M. (1998). Revision of the Brief Index of Self-Actualization. *Perceptual and Motor Skills, 87*, 115–125.

Thomas, A., Benne, M. R., Marr, M. J., Thomas, E. W., & Hume, R. M. (2000). The MBTI predicts attraction and attrition in an engineering program. *Journal of Psychological Type, 55,* 35–42.

Thompson, G. G. (1968). George A. Kelly (1905–1967). *Journal of General Psychology, 79,* 19–24.

Thorndike, E. L. (1898). Animal intelligence: An experimental study of the associative processes in animals. *Psychological Monographs, 2* (Whole No. 8).

Thorndike, E. L. (1913). *The psychology of learning*. New York: Teachers College.

Thorndike, E. L. (1931). *Human learning*. New York: Appleton-Century.

Tidey, J. W., O'Neill, S. C., & Higgins, S. T. (2000). D-amphetamine increases choice of cigarette smoking over monetary reinforcement. *Psychopharmacology, 153,* 85–92.

Tropp, L. R., & Pettigrew, T. F. (2005). Differential relationships between intergroup contact and affective and cognitive dimensions of prejudice. *Psychological Science, 16,* 951–957.

Tupes, E. C., & Christal, R. E. (1961). *Recurrent personality factors based on trait ratings* (Technical Report No. ASD-TR-61-97). Lackland, TX: U.S. Air Force.

Vaihinger, H. (1911/1925). *The philosophy of "as if."* New York: Harcourt, Brace.

Van Heil, A., Mervielde, I., & De Fruyt, P. (2006). Stagnation and generativity: Structure, validity, and differential relationships with adaptive and maladaptive personality. *Journal of Personality, 74,* 543–869.

van Dijken, S. (1998). *John Bowlby: His early life*. London: Free Association Books.

Veale, D., Kinderman, P., Riley, S., & Lambrou, C. (2003). Self-discrepancy in body dysmorphic disorder. *British Journal of Clinical Psychology, 42,* 157–169.

Vitz, P. C. (1988). *Sigmund Freud's Christian unconscious*. New York: Guilford Press.

Watson, J. B. (1913). Psychology as the behaviorist views it. *Psychological Review, 20,* 158–177.

Watson, J. B. (1925). *Behaviorism*. New York: Norton.

Watson, J. B. (1926). What the nursery has to say about instincts. In C. Murchison (Ed.), *Psychologies of 1925* (pp. 1–35). Worcester, MA: Clark University Press.

Watson, J. B., & Rayner, R. (1920). Conditioned emotional reactions. *Journal of Experimental Psychology, 3,* 1–14.

Webster, R. (1995). *Why Freud was wrong: Sin, science, and psychoanalysis*. New York: Basic Books.

Webster, R. A., Hunter, M., & Keats, J. A. (1994). Personality and sociodemographic influences on adolescents' substance use: A path analysis. *International Journal of the Addictions, 29,* 941–956.

Wegner, D. M., Wenzlaff, R. M., & Kozak, M. (2004). Dream rebound: The return of suppressed thoughts in dreams. *Psychological Science, 15,* 232–236.

Weiss, A. S. (1991). The measurement of self-actualization: The quest for the test may be as challenging as the search for the self. *Journal of Social Behavior and Personality, 6,* 265–290.

Weiss, P. A., Watson, N., & McGuire, H. (2003). Smoking and self-concept in young adults: An idiographic method of measurement. *Journal of Constructivist Psychology, 16,* 323–334.

Whitbourne, S. K., Zuschlag, M. Z., Elliot, L. B., & Waterman, A. S. (1992). Psychosocial development in adulthood: A 22-year sequential study. *Journal of Personality and Social Psychology, 63,* 260–271.

Whitson, E. R., & Olczak, P. V. (1991). The use of the POI in clinical situations: An evaluation. *Journal of Social Behavior and Personality, 6,* 291–310.

Wiener, D. N. (1996). *B. F. Skinner: Benign anarchist*. Boston: Allyn and Bacon.

Willing, D. C., Guest, K., & Morford, J. (2001). Who is entering the teaching profession? MBTI profiles of 525 master in teaching students. *Journal of Psychological Type, 59,* 36–44.

Winter, D. G. (1993). Gordon Allport and "Letters from Jenny." In K. H. Craik, R. Hogan, & R. N. Wolfe (Eds.), *Fifty years of personality psychology* (pp. 147–163). New York: Plenum Press.

Wolfe, W. L., & Maisto, S. A. (2000). The effect of self-discrepancy and discrepancy salience on alcohol consumption. *Addictive Behaviors, 25*, 283–288.

Wolpe, J. (1973). *The practice of behavior therapy.* New York: Pergamon Press.

Wortis, J. (1954). *Fragments of an analysis with Freud.* New York: McGraw-Hill.

Wright, J. C., & Mischel, W. (1988). Conditional hedges and the intuitive psychology of traits. *Journal of Personality and Social Psychology, 55,* 454–469.

Zachar, P., & Leong, F. T. L. (1992). A problem of personality: Scientist and practitioner differences in psychology. *Journal of Personality, 60,* 665–677.

Zeidner, M. (2007). Anxiety and coping with community disasters: The Israeli experience. *Journal of Research in Personality, 41,* 213–220.

Zuroff, D. C., & Rotter, J. B. (1985). A history of the expectancy construct in psychology. In J. B. Dusek (Ed.), *Teacher expectancies* (pp. 7–36). Hillsdale, NJ: Erlbaum.

Zyphur, M. J., Islam, G., & Landis, R. (2007). Testing 1, 2, 3 . . . 4? The personality of repeat SAT test takers and their testing outcomes. *Journal of Research in Personality, 41,* 715–722.

Glossary

A

accusation Adlerian safeguarding tendency whereby one protects magnified feelings of self-esteem by blaming others for one's own failures.

active imagination Technique used by Jung to uncover collective unconscious material. Patients are asked to concentrate on an image until a series of fantasies are produced.

actualizing tendency (Rogers) Tendency within all people to move toward completion or fulfillment of potentials.

adolescence (Erikson) An important psychosocial stage when ego identity should be formed. Adolescence is characterized by puberty and the crisis of identity versus identity confusion.

adulthood (Erikson) The stage from about ages 31 to 60 that is characterized by the psychosexual mode of procreativity and the crisis of generativity versus stagnation.

aesthetic needs (Maslow) Needs for art, music, beauty, and the like. Although they may be related to the basic conative needs, aesthetic needs are a separate dimension.

agape Altruistic love.

aggression (Adler) Safeguarding tendencies that may include depreciation or accusation of others as well as self-accusation, all designed to protect exaggerated feelings of personal superiority by striking out against other people.

aggression (Freud) One of two primary instincts or drives that motivate people. Aggression is the outward manifestation of the death instinct.

anal character Freudian term for a person who is characterized by compulsive neatness, stubbornness, and miserliness.

anal phase (Freud) Sometimes called the anal-sadistic phase, this second stage of the infantile period is characterized by a child's attempts to gain pleasure from the excretory function and by such related behaviors as destroying or losing objects, stubbornness, neatness, and miserliness. Corresponds roughly to the second year of life.

anal triad (Freud) The three traits of compulsive neatness, stubbornness, and miserliness that characterize the anal character.

anal-urethral-muscular Erikson's term for the young child's psychosexual mode of adapting.

analytical psychology Theory of personality and approach to psychotherapy founded by Carl Jung.

anima Jungian archetype that represents the feminine component in the personality of males and originates from men's inherited experiences with women.

animus Jungian archetype that represents the masculine component in the personality of females and originates from women's inherited experiences with men.

anxiety A felt, affective, unpleasant state accompanied by the physical sensation of uneasiness.

anxiety (Kelly) The recognition that the events with which one is confronted lie outside the range of convenience of one's construct system.

anxiety (May) The experience of the threat of imminent nonbeing.

anxiety (Rogers) Feelings of uneasiness or tension with an unknown cause.

anxiety (Sullivan) Any tension that interferes with satisfaction of needs.

apathy (Sullivan) Dynamism that reduces tensions of needs through the adoption of an indifferent attitude.

archetypes Jung's concept that refers to the contents of the collective unconscious. Archetypes, also called primordial images or collective symbols, represent psychic patterns of inherited behavior and are thus distinguished from instincts, which are physical impulses toward action. Typical archetypes are the anima, animus, and shadow.

attitude (Jung) A predisposition to act or react in a characteristic manner, that is, in either an introverted or an extraverted direction.

authoritarianism (Fromm) The tendency to give up one's independence and to unite with another person or persons in order to gain strength. Takes the form of masochism or sadism.

autistic language (Sullivan)   Private or parataxic language that makes little or no sense to other people.

B

basic anxiety (Fromm)   The feeling of being alone and isolated, separated from the natural world.

basic anxiety (Horney)   Feelings of isolation and helplessness in a potentially hostile world.

basic anxiety (Maslow)   Anxiety arising from inability to satisfy physiological and safety needs.

basic conflict (Horney)   The incompatible tendency to move toward, against, and away from people.

basic hostility (Horney)   Repressed feelings of rage that originate during childhood when children fear that their parents will not satisfy their needs for safety and satisfaction.

basic strength   The ego quality that emerges from the conflict between antithetical elements in Erikson's stages of development.

basic tendencies   McCrae and Costa's term for the universal raw material of personality.

behavior potential (Rotter)   The possibility of a particular response occurring at a given time and place as calculated in relation to the reinforcement of that response.

behavioral analysis   Skinner's approach to studying behavior that assumes that human conduct is shaped primarily by the individual's personal history of reinforcement and secondarily by natural selection and cultural practices.

behavioral signature of personality (Mischel)   An individual's unique and stable pattern of behaving differently in different situations.

behaviorism   A "school" of psychology that limits its subject matter to observable behavior. John B. Watson is usually credited with being the founder of behaviorism, with B. F. Skinner its most notable proponent.

being-in-the-world   (*See Dasein*)

biophilia   Love of life.

bipolar traits   Traits with two poles: that is, those traits scaled from a minus point to a positive point, with zero representing the midpoint.

B-love (Maslow)   Love between self-actualizing people and characterized by the love for the *being* of the other.

B-values (Maslow)   The values of self-actualizing people, including beauty, truth, goodness, justice, wholeness, and the like.

C

cardinal disposition (Allport)   Personal disposition so dominating that it cannot be hidden. Most people do not have a cardinal disposition.

care (Erikson)   A commitment to take care of the people and things that one has learned to care for.

castration anxiety (Freud)   (See **castration complex**)

castration complex (Freud)   Condition that accompanies the Oedipus complex, but takes different forms in the two sexes. In boys, it takes the form of *castration anxiety,* or fear of having one's penis removed, and is responsible for shattering the Oedipus complex. In girls, it takes the form of *penis envy,* or the desire to have a penis, and it precedes and instigates the Oedipus complex.

catharsis   The process of removing or lessening psychological disorders by talking about one's problems.

causality   An explanation of behavior in terms of past experiences.

central dispositions (Allport)   The 5 to 10 personal traits around which a person's life focuses.

chance encounter (Bandura)   An unintended meeting of persons unfamiliar to each other.

character (Fromm)   Relatively permanent acquired qualities through which people relate themselves to others and to the world.

character orientation (Fromm)   Productive or nonproductive patterns of reacting to the world of things and the world of people.

characteristic   Unique qualities of an individual that include such attributes as temperament, physique, intelligence, and other aptitudes.

characteristic adaptations (McCrae and Costa)   Acquired personality structures that develop as people adapt to their environment.

choice corollary   Kelly's assumption that people choose the alternative in a dichotomized construct that they perceive will extend their range of future choices.

classical conditioning   Learning by which a neutral stimulus becomes associated with a meaningful stimulus and acquires the capacity to elicit a similar response.

client-centered therapy   Approach to psychotherapy originated by Rogers, which is based on respect for the person's capacity to grow within a nurturing climate.

cognitive-affective personality theory   Mischel's theory that views people as active, goal-directed individuals capable of exerting influence on both their situation and themselves.

cognitive needs (Maslow)   Needs for knowledge and understanding; related to basic or conative needs, yet operating on a different dimension.

collective efficacy (Bandura)   The confidence people have that their combined efforts will produce social change.

collective unconscious   Jung's idea of an inherited unconscious, which is responsible for many of our behaviors, ideas, and dream images. The collective unconscious lies beyond our personal experiences and originates with repeated experiences of our ancestors.

common traits (Allport)   (*See* **trait, common**)

commonality corollary   Kelly's theory that personal constructs of people with similar experiences tend to be similar.

competencies (Mischel)   People's cognitive and behavioral construction of what they can and cannot do, based on their observations of the world, themselves, and others.

complex (Jung)   An emotionally toned conglomeration of ideas that comprise the contents of the personal unconscious. Jung originally used the word association test to uncover complexes.

conative needs   Needs that pertain to willful and purposive striving, for example Maslow's hierarchy of needs.

conditioned reinforcer (Skinner)   Environmental event that is not by nature satisfying but becomes so because it is associated with unlearned or unconditioned reinforcers such as food, sex, and the like.

conditions of worth (Rogers)   Restrictions or qualifications attached to one person's regard for another.

conformity (Fromm)   Means of escaping from isolation and aloneness by giving up one's self and becoming whatever others desire.

congruence (Rogers)   The matching of organismic experiences with awareness and with the ability to express those experiences. One of three "necessary and sufficient" therapeutic conditions.

conscience (Freud)   The part of the superego that results from experience with punishment and that, therefore, tells a person what is wrong or improper conduct.

conscious (Freud)   Those mental elements in awareness at any given time.

conscious (Jung)   Mental images that are sensed by the ego and that play a relatively minor role in Jungian theory.

consistency paradox   Mischel's term for the observation that clinical intuition and the perceptions of laypeople suggest that behavior is consistent, whereas research finds that it is not.

constructing obstacles (Adler)   Safeguarding tendency in which people create a barrier to their own success, thus allowing them to protect their self-esteem by either using the barrier as an excuse for failure or by overcoming it.

construction corollary   Kelly's assumption that people anticipate events according to their interpretations of recurrent themes.

constructive alternativism   Kelly's view that events can be looked at (construed) from a different (alternative) perspective.

continuous schedule (Skinner)   The reinforcement of an organism for every correct trial; opposed to the intermittent schedule in which only certain selected responses are reinforced.

core pathology (Erikson)   A psychosocial disorder at any of the eight stages of development that results from too little basic strength.

core role (Kelly)   People's construction of who they really are; their sense of identity that provides a guide for living.

correlation coefficient   A mathematical index used to measure the direction and magnitude of the relationship between two variables.

cosmology   The realm of philosophy dealing with the nature of causation.

countertransference   Strong, undeserved feelings that the therapist develops toward the patient during the course of treatment. These feelings can be either positive or negative and are considered by most writers to be a hindrance to successful psychotherapy.

creative power   Adler's term for what he believed to be an inner freedom that empowers each of us to create our own style of life.

D

Dasein   An existential term meaning a sense of self as a free and responsible person whose existence is embedded in the world of things, of people, and of self-awareness.

deductive method   Approach to factor analytical theories of personality that gathers data on the basis of previously determined hypotheses or theories, reasoning from the general to the particular.

defense mechanisms (Freud)   Techniques such as repression, reaction formation, sublimation, and the like, whereby the ego defends itself against the pain of anxiety.

defensiveness (Rogers)   Protection of the self-concept against anxiety and threat by denial and distortion of experiences that are inconsistent with it.

delay of gratification   A reference to the observation that some people some of the time will prefer more valued delayed rewards over lesser valued immediate ones.

denial (Rogers)   The blocking of an experience or some aspect of an experience from awareness because it is inconsistent with the self-concept.

depreciation   Adlerian safeguarding tendency whereby another's achievements are undervalued and one's own are overvalued.

depressive position (Klein)   Feelings of anxiety over losing a loved object coupled with a sense of guilt for wanting to destroy that object.

desacralization (Maslow)   The process of removing respect, joy, awe, and rapture from an experience, which then purifies or objectifies that experience.

destructiveness (Fromm)   Method of escaping from freedom by eliminating people or objects, thus restoring feelings of power.

diathesis-stress model   Eysenck accepted this model of psychiatric illness, which suggests that some people are vulnerable to illness because they have both genetic and an acquired weakness that predisposes them to an illness.

dichotomy corollary   Kelly's assumption that people construe events in an either/or (dichotomous) manner.

disengagement of internal control (Bandura)   The displacement or diffusion of responsibility for the injurious effects of one's actions.

displacement   A Freudian defense mechanism in which unwanted urges are redirected onto other objects or people in order to disguise the original impulse.

disposition, cardinal (Allport)   Personal traits so dominating in an individual's life that they cannot be hidden. Most people do not have a cardinal disposition.

disposition, central (Allport)   The 5 to 10 personal traits around which a person's life focuses.

disposition, secondary (Allport)   The least characteristic and reliable personal traits that still appear with some regularity in an individual's life.

dissociation (Sullivan)   The process of separating unwanted impulses, desires, and needs from the self-system.

distortion (Rogers)   Misinterpretation of an experience so that it is seen as fitting into some aspect of the self-concept.

D-love (Maslow)   Deficiency love or affection (attachment) based on the lover's specific deficiency and the loved one's ability to satisfy that deficit.

dream analysis (Freud)   The therapeutic procedure designed to uncover unconscious material by having a patient free associate to dream images. (*See also* **free association**)

dynamisms (Sullivan)   Relatively consistent patterns of action that characterize the person throughout a lifetime. Similar to traits or habit patterns.

dystonic   Erikson's term for the negative element in each pair of opposites that characterizes the eight stages of development.

dynamic processes   McCrae and Costa's term for the interconnectedness of central and peripheral components of personality.

E

early childhood (Erikson)   The second stage of psychosocial development, characterized by the anal-urethral-muscular psychosexual mode and by the crisis of autonomy versus shame and doubt.

early recollections   Technique proposed by Adler to understand the pattern or theme that runs throughout a person's style of life.

eclectic   Approach that allows selection of usable elements from different theories or approaches and combines them in a consistent and unified manner.

ego (Freud)   The province of the mind that refers to the "I" or those experiences that are owned (not necessarily consciously) by the person. As the only region of the mind in contact with the real world, the ego is said to serve the reality principle.

ego (Jung)   The center of consciousness. In Jungian psychology, the ego is of lesser importance than the more inclusive self and is limited to consciousness.

ego-ideal (Freud)   The part of the superego that results from experiences with reward and that, therefore, teaches a person what is right or proper conduct.

eidetic personifications (Sullivan)   Imaginary traits attributed to real or imaginary people in order to protect one's self-esteem.

Eigenwelt   An existentialist term meaning the world of one's relationship to self. One of three simultaneous modes of being-in-the-world.

elaborative choice (Kelly)   Making choices that will increase a person's range of future choices.

empathic listening (Rogers)   The accurate sensing of the feelings of another and the communication of these perceptions. One of three "necessary and sufficient" therapeutic conditions.

empathy (Sullivan)   An indefinite process through which anxiety is transferred from one person to another, for example, from mother to infant.

empirical   Based on experience, systematic observation, and experiment rather than on logical reasoning or philosophical speculation.

empirical law of effect (Rotter)   The assumption that behaviors that move people in the direction of their goals are more likely to be reinforced.

encoding strategies (Mischel)   People's ways of transforming stimulus inputs into information about themselves, other people, and the world.

energy transformations (Sullivan)   Overt or covert actions designed to satisfy needs or reduce anxiety.

enhancement needs (Rogers)   The need to develop, to grow, and to achieve.

epigenetic principle   Erikson's term meaning that one component grows out of another in its proper time and sequence.

epistemology   The branch of philosophy that deals with the nature of knowledge.

erogenous zones   Organs of the body that are especially sensitive to the reception of pleasure. In Freudian theory, the three principal erogenous zones are the mouth, anus, and genitals.

eros   The desire for an enduring union with a loved one.

essential freedom (May)   The freedom of being or the freedom of the conscious mind. Essential freedom cannot be limited by chains or bars.

esteem needs   The fourth level on Maslow's hierarchy of needs; they include self-respect, competence, and the perceived esteem of others.

ethology   The scientific study of the characteristic behavior patterns of animals.

euphoria (Sullivan)   A complete lack of tension.

exclusivity (Erikson)   The core pathology of young adulthood marked by a person's exclusion of certain people, activities, and ideas.

excuses   Adlerian safeguarding tendencies whereby the person, through the use of reasonable sounding justifications, becomes convinced of the reality of self-erected obstacles.

existential freedom (May)   The freedom of doing one's will. Existential freedom can be limited by chains or bars.

existential living   Rogers's term indicating a tendency to live in the moment.

existential needs (Fromm)   Peculiarly human needs aimed at moving people toward a reunification with the natural world. Fromm listed relatedness, transcendence, rootedness, a sense of identity, and a frame of orientation as existential, or human, needs.

expectancy   The subjective probability held by a person that any specific reinforcement or set of reinforcements will occur in a given situation.

experience corollary   Kelly's view that people continually revise their personal constructs as the result of experience.

exploitative characters (Fromm)   People who take from others, by either force or cunning.

external evaluations (Rogers)   People's perception of other people's view of them.

external influences (McCrae and Costa)   Knowledge, views, and evaluations of the self.

external reinforcement (Rotter)   The positive or negative value of any reinforcing event as seen from the view of societal or cultural values.

extinction   The tendency of a previously acquired response to become progressively weakened upon nonreinforcement.

extraversion (E) (Eysenck)   One of three types of superfactors identified by Eysenck and consisting of two opposite poles—extraversion and introversion. *Extraverts* are characterized behaviorally by sociability and impulsiveness and physiologically by a low level of cortical arousal. *Introverts,* by contrast, are characterized by unsociability and caution and by a high level of cortical arousal.

extraversion (Jung)   An attitude or type marked by the turning outward of psychic energy so that a person is oriented toward the objective world.

F

factor   A unit of personality derived through factor analysis. However, the term is sometimes used more generally to include any underlying aspect of personality.

factor analysis   A mathematical procedure for reducing a large number of variables to a few; used by Eysenck and others to identify personality traits and factors.

factor loadings   The amount of correlation that a score contributes to a given factor.

falsifiable   An attribute of a theory that allows research to either support or fail to support that theory's major tenets. A falsifiable theory is accountable to experimental results.

fear (Kelly)   A specific threat to one's personal constructs.

feeling (Jung)   A rational function that tells us the value of something. The feeling function can be either extraverted (directed toward the objective world) or introverted (directed toward the subjective world).

fiction (Adler)   A belief or expectation of the future that serves to motivate present behavior. The truthfulness of a fictional idea is immaterial, because the person acts as if the idea were true.

fixation   A defense mechanism that arises when psychic energy is blocked at one stage of development, thus making change or psychological growth difficult.

fixation (Fromm)   The nonproductive form of rootedness marked by a reluctance to grow beyond the security provided by one's mother.

fixed-interval (Skinner)   Intermittent reinforcement schedule whereby the organism is reinforced for its first response following a designated period of time (e.g., FI 10 means that the animal is reinforced for its initial response after 10 minutes have elapsed since its previous reinforcement).

fixed-ratio (Skinner)   Reinforcement schedule in which the organism is reinforced intermittently according to a specified number of responses it makes (e.g., FR 7 means that the organism is reinforced for every seventh response).

formative tendency (Rogers)   Tendency in all matter to evolve from simpler to more complex forms.

fortuitous events (Bandura)   Environmental events that are unexpected and unintended.

fragmentation corollary   Kelly's assumption that behavior is sometimes inconsistent because one's construct systems can admit incompatible elements.

frame of orientation (Fromm)   The need for humans to develop a unifying philosophy or consistent way of looking at things.

free association   Technique used in Freudian psychotherapy in which the therapist instructs the patient to verbalize every thought that comes to mind, no matter how irrelevant or repugnant it may appear.

freedom of movement (Rotter)   The mean expectancy of being reinforced for performing all those behaviors that are directed toward the satisfaction of some general need.

Freudian slips   Slips of the tongue or pen, misreading, incorrect hearing, temporary forgetting of names and intentions, and the misplacing of objects, all of which are caused by unconscious wishes. Also called parapraxes.

fully functioning person (Rogers)   (*See* **person of tomorrow**)

functional autonomy (Allport)   The tendency for some motives to become independent from the original motive responsible for the behavior.

G

Gemeinschaftsgefühl   (*See* **social interest**)

generalization   The transfer of the effects of one learning situation to another.

generalized expectancy (Rotter)   Expectation based on similar past experiences that a given behavior will be reinforced.

generalized reinforcer (Skinner)   A conditioned reinforcer that has been associated with several primary reinforcers. Money, for example, is a generalized reinforcer because it is associated with food, shelter, and other primary reinforcers.

genitality (Erikson)   Period of life beginning with puberty and continuing through adulthood and marked by full sexual identity.

genital-locomotor   Erikson's term for the preschool child's psychosexual mode of adapting.

genital stage (Freud)   Period of life beginning with puberty and continuing through adulthood and marked by full sexual identity.

genital stage (Klein)   Comparable to Freud's phallic stage: that is, the time around ages 3 to 5 when the Oedipus complex reaches its culmination.

great mother   Jungian archetype of the opposing forces of fertility and destruction.

guilt (Kelly)   The sense of having lost one's core role structure.

guilt (May)   An ontological characteristic of human existence arising from our separation from the natural world (*Umwelt*), from other people (*Mitwelt*), or from oneself (*Eigenwelt*).

H

hero   A Jungian archetype representing the myth of the godlike man who conquers or vanquishes evil, usually in the form of a monster, dragon, or serpent.

hesitating (Adler)   Safeguarding tendency characterized by vacillation or procrastination designed to provide a person with the excuse "It's too late now."

hierarchy of needs   Maslow's concept that needs are ordered in such a manner that those on a lower level must be satisfied before higher level needs become activated.

hoarding characters (Fromm)   People who seek to save and not let go of material possessions, feelings, or ideas.

holistic-dynamic   Maslow's theory of personality, which stresses both the unity of the organism and the motivational aspects of personality.

human agency (Bandura)   The ability of people to use cognitive abilities to control their lives.

human dilemma (Fromm)   The present condition of humans who have the ability to reason but who lack powerful instincts needed to adapt to a changing world.

humanistic psychoanalysis   Fromm's personality theory that combines the basics of both psychoanalysis and humanistic psychology.

hypochondriasis   Obsessive attention to one's health; typically characterized by imaginary symptoms.

hypothesis An assumption or educated guess that can be scientifically tested.

hysteria (Freud) A mental disorder marked by the conversion of repressed psychical elements into somatic symptoms such as impotency, paralysis, or blindness, when no physiological bases for these symptoms exist.

I

id (Freud) The region of personality that is alien to the ego because it includes experiences that have never been owned by the person. The id is the home base for all the instincts, and its sole function is to seek pleasure regardless of consequences.

ideal self (Rogers) One's view of self as one would like to be.

idealistic principle (Freud) A reference to the ego-ideal, a subsystem of the superego that tells people what they should do.

idealized self-image (Horney) An attempt to solve basic conflicts by adopting a belief in one's godlike qualities.

identity crisis Erickson's term for a crucial period or turning point in the life cycle that may result in either more or less ego strength. Identity crises can be found in those Eriksonian stages that follow the development of identity, ordinarily during adolescence.

idiographic Approach to the study of personality based on the single case.

incestuous symbiosis (Fromm) Extreme dependence on a mother or mother substitute.

incongruence (Rogers) The perception of discrepancies between organismic self, self-concept, and ideal self.

individual psychology Theory of personality and approach to psychotherapy founded by Alfred Adler.

individuality corollary Kelly's assumption that people have different experiences and therefore construe events in different ways.

individuation Jung's term for the process of becoming a whole person, that is, an individual with a high level of psychic development.

inductive method A form of reasoning based on observation and measurement without preconceived hypotheses.

infancy (Erikson) The first stage of psychosocial development—one marked by the oral-sensory mode and by the crisis of basic trust versus basic mistrust.

infantile stage (Freud) First four or five years of life characterized by autoerotic or pleasure-seeking behavior and consisting of the oral, anal, and phallic substages.

inferiority complex (Adler) Exaggerated or abnormally strong feelings of inferiority, which usually interfere with socially useful solutions to life's problems.

instinct (Freud) From the German *Trieb*, meaning drive or impulse; refers to an internal stimulus that impels action or thought. The two primary instincts are sex and aggression.

instinct (Jung) An unconscious physical impulse toward action. Instincts are the physical counterpart of archetypes.

instinctoid needs (Maslow) Needs that are innately determined but that can be modified through learning. The frustration of instinctoid needs leads to various types of pathology.

intentionality (May) The underlying structure that gives meaning to our experience.

interactionist One who believes that behavior results from an interaction of environmental variables and person variables, including cognition.

intermittent schedule (Skinner) The reinforcement of an organism on only certain selected occurrences of a response; opposed to a continuous schedule in which the organism is reinforced for every correct trial. The four most common intermittent schedules are fixed-ratio, variable-ratio, fixed-interval, and variable-interval.

internal reinforcement (Rotter) The individual's perception of the positive or negative value of any reinforcing event.

internalization (object relations theory) A process in which the person takes in (introjects) aspects of the external world and then organizes those introjections in a psychologically meaningful way.

interpersonal theory Sullivan's personality theory that emphasizes the importance of interpersonal relationships during each stage of development from infancy to adulthood.

interpersonal trust (Rotter) A generalized expectancy held by a person that other people can be relied on to keep their word. The Interpersonal Trust Scale attempts to measure degree of interpersonal trust.

intimacy (Erikson) The ability to fuse one's identity with that of another person without fear of losing it. The syntonic element of young adulthood.

intimacy (Sullivan) Conjunctive dynamism marked by a close personal relationship with another person who is more or less of equal status.

introjection (Freud) A defense mechanism whereby people incorporate positive qualities of another person into their ego.

introjection (Klein) Fantasizing taking external objects, such as the mother's breast, into one's own body.

introversion (Eysenck) (*See* **extraversion, Eysenck**)

introversion (Jung)   An attitude or type characterized by the turning inward of psychic energy with an orientation toward the subjective.

intuition (Jung)   An irrational function that involves perception of elementary data that are beyond our awareness. Intuitive people "know" something without understanding how they know.

isolation (Erikson)   The inability to share true intimacy or to take chances with one's identity. The dystonic element of young adulthood.

J

Jonah complex   The fear of being or doing one's best.

L

latency (Erikson)   The psychosexual mode of the school-age child. A period of little sexual development.

latency stage (Freud)   The time between infancy and puberty when psychosexual growth is at a standstill.

latent dream content (Freud)   The underlying, unconscious meaning of a dream. Freud held that the latent content, which can be revealed only through dream interpretation, was more important than the surface or manifest content.

law of effect   Thorndike's principle that responses to stimuli followed immediately by a satisfier tend to strengthen the connection between those responses and stimuli; that is, they tend to be learned.

libido (Freud)   Psychic energy of the life instinct; sexual drive or energy.

life instinct (Freud)   One of two primary drives or impulses; the life instinct is also called Eros or sex.

locus of control (Rotter)   The belief people have that their attempts to reach a goal are within their control (internal locus of control) or are primarily due to powerful events such as fate, chance, or other people (external locus of control). Locus of control is measured by the Internal-External Control Scale.

love (Erikson)   The basic strength of young adulthood that emerges from the crisis of intimacy versus isolation.

love (Fromm)   A union with another person in which a person retains separateness and integrity of self.

love (May)   To delight in the presence of the other person and to affirm that person's value and development as much as one's own.

love and belongingness needs   The third level on Maslow's hierarchy of needs; they include both the need to give love and the need to receive love.

lust (Sullivan)   Isolating dynamism in which one person has an impersonal sexual interest in another.

M

maintenance needs (Rogers)   Those basic needs that protect the status quo. They may be either physiological (e.g., food) or interpersonal (e.g., the need to maintain the current self-concept).

malevolence   Sullivan's term for those destructive behavior patterns dominated by the attitude that people are evil and harmful and that the world is a bad place to live.

malignant aggression (Fromm)   The destruction of life for reasons other than survival.

mandala (Jung)   Symbol representing the striving for unity and completion. It is often seen as a circle within a square or a square within a circle.

manifest dream content (Freud)   The surface or conscious level of a dream. Freud believed that the manifest level of a dream has no deep psychological significance and that the unconscious or latent level holds the key to the dream's true meaning.

marketing characters (Fromm)   People who see themselves as commodities, with their personal value dependent on their ability to sell themselves.

masculine protest   Adler's term for the neurotic and erroneous belief held by some men and women that men are superior to women.

masochism   A condition characterized by the reception of sexual pleasure from suffering pain and humiliation inflicted either by self or by others.

maturity (Freud)   The final psychosexual stage following infancy, latency, and the genital period. Hypothetically, maturity would be characterized by a strong ego in control of the id and the superego and by an ever-expanding realm of consciousness.

metamotivation (Maslow)   The motives of self-actualizing people, including especially the B-values.

metapathology (Maslow)   Illness, characterized by absence of values, lack of fulfillment, and loss of meaning, that results from deprivation of self-actualization needs.

Mitwelt   An existentialist term meaning the world of one's relationship to other people. One of three simultaneous modes of being-in-the-world.

modeling (Bandura)   One of two basic sources of learning; involves the observation of others and thus learning from their actions. More than simple imitation, modeling entails the addition and subtraction of specific acts and the observation of consequences of others' behavior.

modulation corollary (Kelly)   Theory that states that personal constructs are permeable (resilient), that they are subject to change through experience.

moral anxiety (Freud)   Anxiety that results from the ego's conflict with the superego.

moral hypochondriasis (Fromm)   Preoccupation with guilt about things one has done wrong.

moralistic principle (Freud)   Reference to the conscience, a subsystem of the supergo that tells people what they should not do.

morphogenic science   Allport's concept of science, which deals with various methods of gathering data on patterns of behavior within a single individual.

moving against people   One of Horney's neurotic trends in which neurotics protect themselves against the hostility of others by adopting an aggressive strategy.

moving away from people   One of Horney's neurotic trends in which neurotics protect themselves against feelings of isolation by adopting a detached attitude.

moving backward (Adler)   Safeguarding inflated feelings of superiority by reverting to a more secure period of life.

moving toward people   One of Horney's neurotic trends in which neurotics develop a need for others as a protection against feelings of helplessness.

myth (May)   Belief system that provides explanations for personal and social problems.

N

narcissism   Love of self or the attainment of erotic pleasure from viewing one's own body.

necrophilia   Love of death.

need potential (Rotter)   A reference to the possible occurrence of a set of functionally related behaviors directed toward the satisfaction of the same goal or a similar set of goals.

need value (Rotter)   The degree to which a person prefers one set of reinforcements to another.

negative reinforcer   Any aversive stimulus that, when removed from a situation, increases the probability that the immediately preceding behavior will occur.

negative transference   Strong, hostile, and undeserved feelings that the patient develops toward the analyst during the course of treatment.

neurosis   Somewhat dated term signifying mild personality disorders as opposed to the more severe psychotic reactions. Neuroses are generally characterized by one or more of the following: anxiety, hysteria, phobias, obsessive-compulsive reactions, depression, chronic fatigue, and hypochondriacal reactions.

neurotic anxiety (Freud)   An apprehension about an unknown danger facing the ego but originating from id impulses.

neurotic anxiety (May)   A reaction that is disproportionate to the threat and that leads to repression and defensive behaviors.

neurotic claims (Horney)   Unrealistic demands and expectations of neurotics to be entitled to special privilege.

neurotic needs (Horney)   Original 10 defenses against basic anxiety.

neurotic needs (Maslow)   Nonproductive needs that are opposed to the basic needs and that block psychological health whether or not they are satisfied.

neurotic pride (Horney)   A false pride based on one's idealized image of self.

neurotic search for glory   Horney's concept for the comprehensive drive toward actualizing the ideal self.

neurotic trends   Horney's term for the three basic attitudes toward self and others—moving toward people, moving against people, and moving away from people; a revision of her original list of 10 neurotic needs.

neuroticism (N) (Eysenck)   One of three types or superfactors identified by Eysenck. Neuroticism is a bipolar factor consisting of neuroticism at one pole and stability at the other. High scores on N may indicate anxiety, hysteria, obsessive-compulsive disorders, or criminality. Low scores indicate emotional stability.

nomothetic   An approach to the study of personality that is based on general laws or principles.

nonbeing   The awareness of the possibility of one's not being, through death or loss of awareness.

normal anxiety (May)   The experience of threat that accompanies growth or change in one's values.

normal autism (Mahler)   The stage in an infant's development when all his or her needs are satisfied automatically, that is, without the infant having to deal with the external world.

normal symbiosis (Mahler)   The second developmental stage marked by a dual unity of infant and mother.

nothingness   (*See* **nonbeing**)

O

object   Psychoanalytic term referring to the person or part of a person that can satisfy an instinct or drive.

object relations theory   A reference to the work of Melanie Klein and others who have extended Freudian psychoanalysis with their emphasis on early relations to parents (objects) that influence later interpersonal relationships.

objective biography (McCrae and Costa)   All experiences of a person across the lifespan.

oblique method   A method of rotating the axes in factor analysis that assumes some intercorrelation among primary factors.

obsession   A persistent or recurrent idea, usually involving an urge toward some action.

Oedipus complex   Term used by Freud to indicate the situation in which the child of either sex develops feelings of love and/or hostility for the parent. In the simple male Oedipus complex, the boy has incestuous feelings of love for the mother and hostility toward the father. The simple female Oedipus complex exists when the girl feels hostility for the mother and sexual love for the father.

old age (Erikson)   The eighth and final stage of the life cycle, marked by the psychosocial crisis of integrity versus despair and the basic strength of wisdom.

operant conditioning (Skinner)   A type of learning in which reinforcement, which is contingent upon the occurrence of a particular response, increases the probability that the same response will occur again.

operant discrimination   Skinner's observation that an organism, as a consequence of its reinforcement history, learns to respond to some elements in the environment but not to others. Operant discrimination does not exist within the organism but is a function of environmental variables and the organism's previous history of reinforcement.

operant extinction (Skinner)   The loss of an operantly conditioned response due to the systematic withholding of reinforcement.

operational definition   A definition of a concept in terms of observable events or behaviors that can be measured.

oral phase (Freud)   The earliest stage of the infantile period characterized by attempts to gain pleasure through the activity of the mouth, especially sucking, eating, and biting; corresponds roughly to the first 12 to 18 months of life.

oral-sensory   Erikson's term for the infant's first psychosexual mode of adapting.

organ dialect (Adler)   The expression of a person's underlying intentions or style of life through a diseased or dysfunctional bodily organ.

organismic self (Rogers)   A more general term than self-concept; refers to the entire person, including those aspects of existence beyond awareness.

organismic valuing process (OVP)   Process by which experiences are valued according to optimal enhancement of organism and self.

organization corollary   Kelly's notion that people arrange their personal constructs in a hierarchical system.

orthogonal rotation   A method of rotating the axes in factor analysis that assumes the independence of primary factors.

P

paranoia   Mental disorder characterized by unrealistic feelings of persecution, grandiosity, and a suspicious attitude toward others.

paranoid-schizoid position (Klein)   A tendency of the infant to see the world as having the same destructive and omnipotent qualities that it possesses.

parapraxes   Freudian slips such as slips of the tongue or pen, misreading, incorrect hearing, temporary forgetting of names and intentions, and the misplacing of objects, all of which are caused by unconscious wishes.

parataxic (Sullivan)   Mode of cognition characterized by attribution of cause and effect when none is present; private language not consensually validated (i.e., not able to be accurately communicated to others).

parataxic distortion (Sullivan)   The process of seeing a cause-and-effect relationship between two events in close proximity when there is no such relationship.

parsimony   Criterion of a useful theory that states that when two theories are equal on other criteria, the simpler one is preferred.

peak experience (Maslow)   An intense mystical experience, often characteristic of self-actualizing people but not limited to them.

penis envy (Freud)   (*See* **castration complex**)

perceptual conscious (Freud)   The system that perceives external stimuli through sight, sound, taste, and the like and that communicates them to the conscious system.

permeability (Kelly)   A quality of personal constructs that allows new information to revise our way of viewing things.

perseverative functional autonomy (Allport) Functionally independent motives that are not part of the proprium; includes addictions, the tendency to finish uncompleted tasks, and other acquired motives.

person of tomorrow (Rogers)   The psychologically healthy individual in the process of evolving into all that he or she can become.

persona   Jungian archetype that represents the side of personality that one shows to the rest of the world. Also, the mask worn by ancient Roman actors in the Greek theater and thus the root of the word "personality."

personal constructs (Kelly)   A person's way of interpreting, explaining, and predicting events.

personal disposition (Allport)   A relatively permanent neuropsychic structure peculiar to the individual, which has the capacity to render different stimuli functionally equivalent and to initiate and guide personalized forms of behavior.

Personal Orientation Inventory (POI)　Test designed by E. L. Shostrom to measure Maslow's concept of self-actualizing tendencies in people.

personal unconscious　Jung's term for those repressed experiences that pertain exclusively to one particular individual; opposed to the collective unconscious, which pertains to unconscious experiences that originate with repeated experiences of our ancestors.

personality　A global concept referring to a relatively permanent pattern of traits, dispositions, or characteristics that give some degree of consistency to a person's behavior.

person-centered　The theory of personality founded by Carl Rogers as an outgrowth of his client-centered psychotherapy.

personifications (Sullivan)　Images a person has of self or others, such as "good-mother," "bad-mother," "good-me," and "bad-me."

phallic phase (Freud)　The third and last stage of the infantile period, the phallic phase is characterized by the Oedipus complex. Although anatomical differences between the sexes are responsible for important differences in the male and female Oedipal periods, Freud used the term "phallic phase" to signify both male and female development.

phenomenology　A philosophical position emphasizing that behavior is caused by one's perceptions rather than by external reality.

physiological needs　The most basic level on Maslow's hierarchy of needs; they include food, water, air, etc.

philia　Brotherly or sisterly love; friendship.

phylogenetic endowment　Unconscious inherited images that have been passed down to us through many generations of repetition. A concept used by both Freud and Klein.

placebo effect　Changes in behavior or functioning brought about by one's beliefs or expectations.

play age (Erikson)　The third stage of psychosocial development, encompassing the time from about ages 3 to 5 and characterized by the genital-locomotor psychosexual mode and the crisis of initiative versus guilt.

pleasure principle (Freud)　A reference to the motivation of the id to seek immediate reduction of tension through the gratification of instinctual drives.

positions (Klein)　Ways in which an infant organizes its experience in order to deal with its basic conflict of love and hate. The two positions are the paranoid-schizoid position and the depressive position.

positive freedom (Fromm)　Spontaneous activity of the whole, integrated personality; signals a reunification with others and with the world.

positive psychology　A relatively new field of psychology that combines an emphasis on hope, optimism, and well-being with an emphasis on research and assessment.

positive regard (Rogers)　The need to be loved, liked, or accepted by another.

positive reinforcer　Any stimulus that, when added to a situation, increases the probability that a given behavior will occur.

positive self-regard (Rogers)　The experience of valuing one's self.

post-Freudian theory　Erikson's theory of personality that extended Freud's developmental stages into old age. At each age, a specific psychosocial struggle contributes to the formation of personality.

posttraumatic stress disorder　A psychological disorder resulting from extremely stressful experiences; it includes nightmares and flashbacks of the traumatic experience.

preconscious (Freud)　Mental elements that are currently not in awareness, but that can become conscious with varying degrees of difficulty.

primary narcissism (Freud)　An infant's investment of libido in its own ego; self-love or autoerotic behavior of the infant (*See* **narcissism**)

primary process (Freud)　A reference to the id, which houses the primary motivators of behavior, called instincts.

proactive (Allport)　Concept that presupposes that people are capable of consciously acting upon their environment in new and innovative ways, which then feed new elements into the system and stimulate psychological growth.

procreativity (Erikson)　The drive to have children and to care for them.

progression (Jung)　The forward flow of psychic energy; involves the extraverted attitude and movement toward adaptation to the external world.

projection　A defense mechanism whereby the ego reduces anxiety by attributing an unwanted impulse to another person.

projective identification (Klein)　A psychic defense mechanism in which infants split off unacceptable parts of themselves, project them onto another object, and then introject them in a distorted form.

propriate functional autonomy (Allport)　Allport's concept of a master system of motivation that confers unity on personality by relating self-sustaining motives to the proprium.

propriate strivings (Allport)   Motivation toward goals that are consistent with an established proprium and that are uniquely one's own.

proprium (Allport)   All those characteristics that people see as peculiarly their own and that are regarded as warm, central, and important.

prototaxic (Sullivan)   Primitive, presymbolic, undifferentiated mode of experience that cannot be communicated to others.

proxy (Bandura)   One of three modes of human agency, proxy involves self-regulation through other people.

pseudospecies (Erikson)   The illusion held by a particular society that it is somehow chosen to be more important than other societies.

psychoanalysis   Theory of personality, approach to psychotherapy, and method of investigation founded by Freud.

psychoanalytic social theory   Horney's theory of personality that emphasizes cultural influence in shaping both normal and neurotic development.

psychodynamic   Loosely defined term usually referring to those psychological theories that heavily emphasize unconscious motivation. The theories of Freud, Jung, Adler, Sullivan, Horney, Klein, Erikson, and perhaps Fromm are usually considered to be psychodynamic.

psychohistory   A field of study that combines psychoanalytic concepts with historical methods.

psychological situation (Rotter)   That part of the external and internal world to which an individual is responding.

psychology of science   A subdiscipline of psychology that studies both science and the behavior of scientists.

psychoses   Severe personality disorders, as opposed to the more mild neurotic reactions. Psychoses interfere seriously with the usual functions of life and include both organic brain disorders and functional (learned) conditions.

psychoticism (P) (Eysenck)   One of three superfactors or types identified by Eysenck. Psychoticism is a bipolar factor consisting of psychoticism at one pole and superego function at the other. High P scores indicate hostility, self-centeredness, suspicion, and nonconformity.

punishment   The presentation of an aversive stimulus or the removal of a positive one. Punishment sometimes, but not always, weakens a response.

Q

Q sort   Inventory technique originated by William Stephenson in which the subject is asked to sort a series of self-referent statements into several piles, the size of which approximates a normal curve.

R

radical behaviorism   Skinner's view that psychology as a science can advance only when psychologists stop attributing behavior to hypothetical constructs and begin writing and talking strictly in terms of observable behavior.

range corollary   Kelly's assumption that personal constructs are limited to a finite range of convenience.

reaction formation   A defense mechanism in which a person represses one impulse and adopts the exact opposite form of behavior, which ordinarily is exaggerated and ostentatious.

reactive (Allport)   Term for those theories that view people as being motivated by tension reduction and by the desire to return to a state of equilibrium.

realistic anxiety (Freud)   An unpleasant, nonspecific feeling resulting from the ego's relationship with the external world.

reality principle (Freud)   A reference to the ego, which must realistically arbitrate the conflicting demands of the id, the superego, and the external world.

receptive characters (Fromm)   People who relate to the world through receiving love, knowledge, and material possessions.

reciprocal causation (Bandura)   Scheme that includes environment, behavior, and person as mutually interacting to determine personal conduct.

regression (Freud)   A defense mechanism whereby a person returns to an earlier stage in order to protect the ego against anxiety.

regression (Jung)   The backward flow of psychic energy; regression involves the introverted attitude and movement toward adaptation to the internal world.

reinforcement (Skinner)   Any condition within the environment that strengthens a behavior (*See* also **negative reinforcer** and **positive reinforcer**)

reinforcement-reinforcement sequences   Rotter's term indicating that the value of an event is a function of one's expectation that a reinforcement will lead to future reinforcements.

reinforcement value (Rotter)   The preference a person attaches to any reinforcement when the probabilities are equal for the occurrence of a number of different reinforcements.

relatedness (Fromm)   The need for union with another person or persons. Expressed through submission, power, or love.

reliability   The extent to which a test or other measuring instrument yields consistent results.

repetition compulsion (Freud)   The tendency of an instinct, especially the death instinct, to repeat or recreate an earlier condition, particularly one that was frightening or anxiety arousing.

repression (Freud)   The forcing of unwanted, anxiety-laden experiences into the unconscious as a defense against the pain of that anxiety.

resacralization (Maslow)   The process of returning respect, joy, awe, and rapture to an experience in order to make that experience more subjective and personal.

resistance   A variety of unconscious responses by patients, designed to block therapeutic progress.

role (Kelly)   A pattern of behavior that results from people's understanding of the constructs of others with whom they are engaged in some task.

role repudiation (Erikson)   The inability to synthesize different self-images and values into a workable identity.

rootedness (Fromm)   The human need to establish roots, that is, to find a home again in the world.

S

sadism   A condition in which a person receives sexual pleasure by inflicting pain or humiliation on another person.

safeguarding tendencies (Adler)   Protective mechanisms such as aggression, withdrawal, and the like that maintain exaggerated feelings of superiority.

safety needs   The second level on Maslow's hierarchy of needs; they include physical security, protection, and freedom from danger.

school age (Erikson)   The fourth stage of psychosocial development; covers the period from about ages 6 to 12 or 13 and is characterized by psychosexual latency and the psychosocial crisis of industry versus inferiority.

science   A branch of study concerned with observation and classification of data and with the verification of general laws through the testing of hypotheses.

secondary narcissism (Freud)   Self-love or autoerotic behavior in an adolescent (*See* **narcissism**)

secondary process (Freud)   A reference to the ego, which chronologically is the second region of the mind (after the id or primary process). Secondary process thinking is in contact with reality.

secondary dispositions (Allport)   The least characteristic and reliable personal dispositions that appear with some regularity in a person's life.

security operations (Sullivan)   Behaviors aimed at reducing interpersonal tension.

selective activation   Bandura's belief that self-regulatory influences are not automatic but rather operate only if they are activated.

selective inattention (Sullivan)   The control of focal awareness, which involves a refusal to see those things that one does not wish to see.

self (Jung)   The most comprehensive of all archetypes, the self includes the whole of personality, although it is mostly unconscious. The self is often symbolized by the mandala motif.

self-accusation   Adlerian safeguarding tendency whereby a person aggresses indirectly against others through self-torture and guilt.

self-actualization needs (Maslow)   The highest level of human motivation; they include the need to fully develop all of one's psychological capacities.

self-actualization (Rogers)   A subsystem of the actualizing tendency; the tendency to actualize the self as perceived.

self-concept (McCrae and Costa)   The knowledge, views, and evaluations of the self.

self-concept (Rogers)   Aspects of one's being and experiences that an individual is consciously aware of.

self-efficacy (Bandura)   People's expectation that they are capable of performing those behaviors that will produce desired outcomes in any particular situation.

self-hatred (Horney)   The powerful tendency for neurotics to despise their real self.

selfobjects (Kohut)   Parents or other significant adults in a child's life who eventually become incorporated into the child's sense of self.

self-realization (Jung)   The highest possible level of psychic maturation; necessitates a balance between conscious and unconscious, ego and self, masculine and feminine, and introversion and extraversion. All four functions (thinking, feeling, sensing, and intuiting) would be fully developed by self-realized people.

self-regulatory strategies (Mischel)   Techniques used to control one's own behavior through self-imposed goals and self-produced consequences.

self-system (Sullivan)   Complex of dynamisms that protect a person from anxiety and maintain interpersonal security.

sensation (Jung)   An irrational function that receives physical stimuli and transmits them to perceptual consciousness. People may rely on either extraverted sensing (outside perceptions) or on introverted sensing (internal perceptions).

sense of identity (Fromm)   The distinctively human need to develop a feeling of "I."

separation anxiety   Reactions of infants upon losing sight of their primary caregiver; at first infants protest, then despair, and finally become emotionally detached.

separation-individuation (Mahler)   The third major stage of development, marked by the child's becoming an individual, separate from its mother; spans the period from ages 4 or 5 months to about 30 to 36 months.

shadow   Jungian archetype representing the inferior or dark side of personality.

shaping   Conditioning a response by first rewarding gross approximations of the behavior, then closer approximations, and finally the desired behavior itself.

social cognitive theory   Bandura's assumption that personality is molded by an interaction of behavior, personal factors, and one's environment.

social interest (Adler)   Translation of the German *Gemeinschaftsgefühl,* meaning a community feeling or a sense of feeling at one with all human beings.

sociality corollary   Kelly's notion that people can communicate with others because they are able to construe others' constructions.

somnolent detachment (Sullivan)   Dynamism that protects a person from increasingly strong and painful effects of severe anxiety.

splitting (object relations theory)   A psychic defense mechanism in which the child subjectively separates incompatible aspects of an object.

stability (Eysenck)   (*See* **neuroticism**)

standing still (Adler)   Safeguarding tendency characterized by lack of action as a means of avoiding failure.

stimulus generalization   (*See* **generalization**)

style of life (Adler)   A person's individuality that expresses itself in any circumstance or environment; the "flavor" of a person's life.

sublimation   A defense mechanism that involves the repression of the genital aim of Eros and its substitution by a cultural or social aim.

successive approximations   Procedure used to shape an organism's actions by rewarding behaviors as they become closer and closer to the target behavior.

superego (Freud)   The moral or ethical processes of personality. The superego has two subsystems—the conscience, which tells us what is wrong, and the ego-ideal, which tells us what is right.

superego function (Eysenck)   (*See* **psychoticism**)

suppression   The blocking or inhibiting of an activity either by a conscious act of the will or by an outside agent such as parents or other authority figures. It differs from repression, which is the unconscious blocking of anxiety-producing experiences.

syntaxic (Sullivan)   Consensually validated experiences that represent the highest level of cognition and that can be accurately communicated to others, usually through language.

syntonic   Erikson's term for the positive element in each pair of opposites that characterize his eight stages of development.

T

Taoistic attitude (Maslow)   Noninterfering, passive, receptive attitude that includes awe and wonder toward that which is observed.

taxonomy   A system of classification of data according to their natural relationships.

teleology   An explanation of behavior in terms of future goals or purposes.

tenderness (Sullivan)   Tension within the mothering one that is aroused by the manifest needs of the infant. The child feels tenderness as the need to receive care.

tension (Sullivan)   The potentiality for action, which may or may not be experienced in awareness.

theory   A set of related assumptions that permit scientists to use logical deductive reasoning to formulate testable hypotheses.

thinking (Jung)   A rational function that tells us the meaning of an image that originates either from the external world (extraverted) or from the internal world (introverted).

third force   Somewhat vague term referring to those approaches to psychology that have reacted against the older psychodynamic and behavioristic theories. The third force is usually thought to include humanistic, existential, and phenomenological theories.

threat (Kelly)   The anticipation of danger to the stability of one's personal constructs.

threat (Rogers)   Feeling that results from the perception of an experience that is inconsistent with one's organismic self.

trait   A relatively permanent disposition of an individual, which is inferred from behavior.

traits, bipolar   (See **bipolar traits**)

traits, unipolar   (See **unipolar traits**)

transcendence (Fromm)   The need for humans to rise above their passive animal existence through either creating or destroying life.

transference   Strong, undeserved feelings that the patient develops toward the analyst during the course of treatment. These feelings may be either sexual or hostile, but they stem from the patient's earlier experiences with parents.

transformation   Psychotherapeutic approach used by Jung in which the therapist is transformed into a healthy individual who can aid the patient in establishing a philosophy of life.

types (factor theorists)   A cluster of primary traits. Eysenck recognized three general types—extraversion (E), neuroticism (N), and psychoticism (P).

types (Jung)   Classification of people based on the two-dimensional scheme of attitudes and functions. The two attitudes of extraversion and introversion and the four functions of thinking, feeling, sensing, and intuiting combine to produce eight possible types.

tyranny of the should (Horney)   A key element in the neurotic search for glory; includes an unconscious and unrelenting drive for perfection.

U

Umwelt   An existentialist term meaning the world of things or objects. One of three simultaneous modes of being-in-the-world.

unconditional positive regard (Rogers)   The need to be accepted and prized by another without any restrictions or qualifications; one of three "necessary and sufficient" therapeutic conditions.

unconscious (Freud)   All those mental elements of which a person is unaware. Two levels of the unconscious are the unconscious proper and the preconscious. Unconscious ideas can become conscious only through great resistance and difficulty.

unipolar traits   Traits with only one pole: that is, those traits scaled from zero to some large amount, as opposed to bipolar traits that are scaled from a minus point, through zero, to a positive point.

V

validity   The extent to which a test or other measuring instrument measures what it is supposed to measure; accuracy.

variable-interval (Skinner)   Intermittent reinforcement schedule in which the organism is reinforced after a lapse of random and varied periods of time (e.g., VI 10 means that the animal is reinforced for its first response following random-length intervals that average 10 minutes).

variable-ratio (Skinner)   Intermittent reinforcement schedule in which the organism is reinforced for every *n*th response on the average (e.g., VR 50 means that the animal is reinforced on the average of one time for every 50 responses.

vicarious experience   Learning by observing the consequences of others' behavior.

vulnerable (Rogers)   A condition that exists when people are unaware of the discrepancy between their organismic self and their significant experiences. Vulnerable people often behave in ways incomprehensible to themselves and to others.

W

will (May)   A conscious commitment to action.

wise old man   Jungian archetype of wisdom and meaning.

withdrawal (Adler)   Safeguarding one's exaggerated sense of superiority by establishing a distance between oneself and one's problems.

Y

young adulthood (Erikson)   The stage from about ages 18 to 30 during which a person gains mature genitality and experiences the crisis of intimacy versus isolation.

Photo Credits

Name Index

Subject Index

D

d-amphetamine, 468, 469, 470
death, 349, 365–366
   dreams of, 51
   instinct of Klein, 141
decay, syndrome of, 205–206
deductive reasoning, 405
defense mechanisms, 55–56
   of Freud, 34–38
   neurotic, 171*f*
   normal, 171*f*
   psychic, of Klein, 143–145
   safeguarding tendencies
      compared to, 84*t*
defensiveness, 319
defiance, 259
dehumanized victims, 498
delay of gratification, 511
democratic character structure, 294
denial, 319
depreciation, 82
depression, 499
depressive position, of
      development, 142–143
desacralization, 297
despair, 153
   integrity v., 262–263
destiny, 358–359
   freedom and, 357–359
destructiveness, 197
determinism v. free choice, 11
   Adler's individual psychology
      on, 96
   Bandura's social cognitive
      theory, 507
   of Erikson's psychosocial
      development stages, 271
   Freud's psychoanalysis on,
      61–62
   of Fromm's humanistic
      psychoanalysis, 210
   of Horney's psychoanalytic
      social theory, 183–184
   Jung's analytic psychology, 132
   Kelly's personal construct
      theory, 571
   psychology of the individual, of
      Allport, 398
   reciprocal, 484*f*
   Rotter and Mischel's cognitive
      social learning theory, 544

Skinner's behavioral analysis, 473
trait and factor theories, of
      Eysenck, Costa, &
      McCrae on, 436
*The Development and Application
   of Social Learning
   Theory: Selected Papers*
   (Rotter), 512
development stages, of Freud, 38–47
   genital period, 46
   infantile period, 38–45
   latency, 45–46
   maturity, 46–47
development stages, of Jung,
      120–123, 121*f*
   childhood, 121
   middle life, 122
   old age, 122–123
   youth, 121
*Diagnostic and Statistical Manual
   of Mental Disorders,
   Fourth Edition (DSM-IV)*,
   320, 562
diathesis-stress model, 412
dichotomy corollary, 556
   choice between, 557
differences, among people, 555
Dimensions of a New Identity
   (Erikson), 246
dimensions of personality, 409–415,
   414*f*, 416*f*
Dimensions of Personality
   (Eysenck), 403
discrimination
   between means and ends,
      294–295
   operant, 451
disease, personality and, 417–418
disorganization, 320
displacement, 36, 50
dispositional theories
   Allport's psychology of
      individual, 374–399
   Eysenck, Costa, & McCrae trait
      and factor theories,
      400–437
dissociation, 221
distortion, 319
D-love, 296
dominance, 518
doubt, 253

dramatizations, 228
dreams, 463
   in Adler's individual psychology,
      88–89
   archetypes and, 106
   big, 104, 125
   earliest, 125
   Freud's analysis of, 48–52
   of Jung, 101, 124–126
   research on, 56–57
drives, 31–33
   compulsive, 169–174
   inner states, 460
   of Skinner, 460
*DSM-IV. See Diagnostic and
      Statistical Manual of
      Mental Disorders, Fourth
      Edition*
dynamic organization, 378
dynamics of personality, of Jung's
      analytic psychology,
      114–115
dynamisms, 219–222, 225*t*
   intimacy, 220
   lust, 220–221
   malevolence, 219–220
   self-system, 221–222
dysfunctional behavior, 498–501
   aggression, 500–501
   depression, 499
   phobias, 499–500
dystonic, 249

E

earliest dreams, 125
early adolescence, 230–232, 233*t*
early childhood, 252–254
early recollections (ERs), 86–88
   career choice and, 90, 92
   counseling outcomes and,
      92–93
eating disorders, 155–156
eclectic, 375
ego, 27, 28*f*, 29, 30*f*
   of Erikson's post-Freudian
      theory, 246–249
   -ideal, 30
   inhibition and, 54–55
   internalizations of Klein, 145–146
   of Jung's analytic psychology,
      103–104